T3-BSJ-485

COMPLETE PROSE WORKS

OF

John Milton

This publication is made possible
through grants of the Bollingen
and Littauer Foundations

Complete Prose Works

OF

John Milton

VOLUME IV

1650-1655

PART I

NEW HAVEN AND LONDON: YALE UNIVERSITY PRESS

MCMLXVI

Set in Old Style No. 7 type and
printed in the United States of America by
Vail-Ballou Press, Inc., Binghamton, New York.

Library of Congress catalog card number: 52-5371

EDITOR OF VOLUME IV

DON M. WOLFE

PREFACE

The present volume sets forth in chronological sequence Milton's prose works of the years 1650–1655, with appropriate analysis of the historical background and suitable attention to the Phillips' *Response*, in the writing or revision of which Milton participated. The gifted editors of *A Defence, Second Defence, Defence of Himself,* and the *Response,* William J. Grace, Donald A. Roberts, Kester Svendsen, and Robert W. Ayers, have had the collaboration of distinguished translators in Donald Mackenzie, Helen North, Paul Blackford, and James Armstrong. The prose of Milton's opponents has also received full attention; for the first time, through the imaginative scholarship of Kathryn McEuen and Paul Blackford, typed copies of full English texts have been made available of Salmasius' *Defensio Regia,* Du Moulin's *Regii Sanguinis Clamor ad Coelum,* and More's *Fides Publica.* Large selections of these three indispensable sources appear in Appendices C, D, and E.

The textual principles governing this edition have been set forth in Volume I, pp. ix and 1040. The Latin texts used in the three *Defences* of this volume are described in textual notes by Robert W. Ayers, pp. 295, 546, 695. Analysis of the variants in the London editions of *A Defence* appear on pp. 1129–40. Authorized editions of the three *Defences* are described on pp. 1140–46. Corrections of the Columbia text of *A Defence,* also by Robert W. Ayers, may be found on pp. 1146–49.

This volume of the *Prose Works* is indebted more than any other thus far to the unstinted help of the members of the Board, without whose timely correction and revision of proof (and resolution of technical and interpretive dilemmas) the volume could not have been completed with the distinction and accuracy hoped for in a cooperative venture, a task in which the pooling of specialized resources is an indispensable asset. No scholar can attain mastery of all phases of Miltonic genius; nor can any two masters of Milton's prose agree on all interpretations, even after years of close study of the texts. The Board, despite the loss by death of three of its most resourceful members, J. Milton French, Alexander Witherspoon, and A. S. P. Woodhouse, has labored successfully to establish all key policies of style and acceptance or rejection of correlative materials in Volume IV.

The volume owes much also to various foundations which have made possible periods of leisure in which to concentrate on the work at hand. Among these are the Institute for Advanced Study, the American Philosophical Society, and the American Council of Learned Societies. The project also is indebted to the continuing imaginative support of the edition by the officers of the Bollingen Foundation, Mr. John D. Barrett and Mr. Ernest Brooks, Jr., and to Mr. Harry Starr, President of the Littauer Foundation, for his active participation in many meetings of the Board. The warm encouragement of Dr. Alvin Johnson, President Emeritus of the New School, has also been especially valuable. Among the dozens of scholars in universities and libraries who have assisted in the project, the following have given help much beyond the call of duty: Professor James Holly Hanford, Western Reserve University; Professors Robert Cawley and Blanchard Bates, Princeton University; Mr. Howard Nixon, Mr. Arthur Commins, Mr. Albert White, Mr. Peter Meade, Mr. Ronald Pick, Mr. Richard Bancroft, and Dr. Cyril Wright, of the Library of the British Museum. The project owes special thanks for the untiring assistance of Mrs. Sue M. Foster and her successor, Mr. Richard Pachella, curators of the McAlpin Collection at the Union Theological Seminary Library.

ALEXANDER M. WITHERSPOON

1894–1964

Born in Bowling Green, Kentucky, in 1894, Alexander Witherspoon was graduated from Ogden College in 1916 and received his B.A. degree from Yale University in 1918. In 1918–19 he served as corporal of artillery in the American Expeditionary Force in France. Returning to Yale a year or two later, he received his M.A. degree in 1921 and the Ph.D. in 1923. From 1923 until his retirement in 1963 Mr. Witherspoon served in the Department of English, first as instructor, then as assistant professor, and finally as associate professor. As a teacher and colleague Professor Witherspoon was one of the most inspiring and beloved men of his generation. No one gave more time to his students, or was more proficient than he in raising their standards of writing and deepening their insight into great works of literature. From 1949 until his death in 1964, Mr. Witherspoon served on the Board of Editors of the Milton *Prose*. He was invariably faithful in meeting his obligations to the Board, traveling at times long distances for a single meeting, and participating in all crucial decisions with steadfast courtesy and rare scholarly discernment. His loss, not only to Volume IV, of which he was to have been coeditor, but also to the project as a whole, is irreparable. The members of the Board who served with him have been enriched in hundreds of ways by his moderation, his long intellectual background, his rich, deep understanding of Milton's prose and poetry. In all those who knew him, Alexander Witherspoon lives on as scholar, teacher, and friend: He inspired all around him with his love of great books and noble aspirations.

LIBRARY ABBREVIATIONS

AVM	Albert and Victoria Museum
BML	Library of the British Museum
BNL	Bibliothèque Nationale
BNV	Biblioteca Nazionale Marciana in Venezia
BOD	Bodleian Library, Oxford
BPL	Boston Public Library
CLL	Columbia University Law Library
CUL	Columbia University Library
EMU	Emory University Library
ENC	New College Library, Edinburgh University
EUL	Edinburgh University Library
FSL	Folger Shakespeare Library
HCL	Harvard College Library
HDSL	Harvard Divinity School Library
HHL	Huntington Library
HLH	Houghton Library of Harvard
IUL	Indiana University Library
JRL	John Rylands Library
LC	Library of Congress
MUL	University of Michigan Library
NEW	Newberry Library, Chicago
NUL	Northwestern University Library
NYPL	New York Public Library
PML	Pierpont Morgan Library, New York
PUL	Princeton University Library
RUL	Rutgers University Library
SOR	Library of the Sorbonne, University of Paris
UCA	University of California, Clark Library
UCL	University of Chicago Library
UIL	University of Illinois Library
UML	University of Minnesota Library
UPL	University of Pennsylvania Library
UTSL	Union Theological Seminary Library
WCL	Williams College Library
YUL	Yale University Library

ABBREVIATONS OF PUBLICATIONS

Bohn	Milton, *Prose Works* (1848–1853)
Columbia	Milton, *Works* (1931–1938)
Complete Prose	*Complete Prose Works of John Milton*
CSPD	*Calendar of State Papers, Domestic*
CS	*Camden Society Publications*
DNB	*Dictionary of National Biography*
ELH	*Journal of English Literary History*
ERE	*Encyclopaedia of Religion and Ethics*
HLQ	*Huntington Library Quarterly*
JEGP	*Journal of English and Germanic Philology*
McAlpin	*McAlpin Catalogue*
MLN	*Modern Language Notes*
NED, OED	*New English Dictionary*
N&Q	*Notes and Queries*
PMLA	*Publications of the Modern Language Association*
RES	*Review of English Studies*
SP	*Studies in Philology*
TLS	*London Times Literary Supplement*
Thomason	*Catalogue of the Thomason Tracts*

MILTON AND HIS ANTAGONISTS: 1649–1660

Salmasius, *Defensio Regia* [1]	May 11, 1649
Milton, *Pro Populo Anglicano Defensio* [2]	February 24, 1651
Rowland, *Pro Rege et Populo . . . Apologia* [3]	1651
Phillips, *Responsio* [4]	December, 1651
Du Moulin, *Regii Sanguinis Clamor* [5]	August, 1652
Rowland, *Polemica* [6]	1653
Milton, *Defensio Secunda* [7]	May 30, 1654
More, *Fides Publica* [8]	October, 1654
More, *Supplementum* [9]	April (?), 1655
Milton, *Pro Se Defensio* [10]	August 8, 1655
Salmasius, *Opus Posthumum* [11]	December, 1660

[1] French, II, 246; Masson, IV, 162–75.

[2] French, II, 350; Masson, IV, 251, 312.

[3] Reply to Milton's *A Defence,* French, II, 340–41; Masson, IV, 347.

[4] Reply to Rowland, French, IV, 44; Masson, IV, 470–74.

[5] Reply to *A Defence,* French, III, 234; Masson, IV, 453–58; V, 216–25.

[6] Reply to Phillips' *Response,* French, III, 304; Masson, IV, 536.

[7] French, III, 376; Masson, IV, 580–616.

[8] Reply to Milton's accusations of More in *Second Defence,* French, III, 424; Masson, V, 216–25.

[9] Further reply to Milton's charges against More, French, IV, 22; Masson, V, 192–93.

[10] French, IV, 44; Masson, V, 198–212.

[11] Posthumous reply to Milton's *A Defence,* French, IV, 346 ff.; Masson, VI, 203–11.

CONTENTS

INTRODUCTION

By Don M. Wolfe

COMPLETE PROSE WORKS

OF

John Milton

CHAPTER I

MILTON IN JANUARY, 1650

IN January, 1650, when Milton was forty-one years old, he was more deeply than ever before committed to the service of the new Commonwealth rather than to the service of poetry and his dream of an immortality of fame. Eight years before, in *The Reason of Church-Government*, he had written, "It were sad for me if I should draw back." One may ask, "Draw back from what?" "Draw back toward what?" The context of Milton's own statements [1] makes it clear he thought it would be sad for him if he should draw back toward the life of the poet, taking refuge not in action but in contemplation; not in obligations of the citizen but in the delights of intellectual exploration exemplified in his leisurely years at Horton. If he was not a soldier, he would still fight, like Dante, with weapons of his mind for those patterns in an enlightened commonwealth he had visualized in his reading of great minds "in the order of time." Unlike most of his fellow-poets, Milton could not separate the function of the poet from the duties of the citizen; he thought of himself as a complete man in the tradition of David, Sophocles, Dante, and Spenser. Thus, on March 15, 1649, Milton had accepted from the new Commonwealth an offer to serve as Secretary for Foreign Tongues, a position that was soon to involve him in the justification of English regicide before the horrified nations of Europe. That decision, taken now more than nine months ago, had drawn him further than ever away from the tranquillity indispensable to the creative flow of images and ideas. We may be certain that he could not have taken the decision of 1649, when the sight in his left eye had been gradually fading for several years, without new wrestlings with his conscience about the further postponement of his great dream: to be as great a poet for England as David had been for Israel, Homer for Greece, and Virgil for Rome. Once more, as in 1640, the vision of a New Jerusalem on English soil emerged triumphant in Milton's mind as of more pressing moment than the central life task that had possessed him since his youth.

Milton had committed his capacious mind and energies to the new Commonwealth with no thought that his sense of social forces was unbalanced or inadequate. In the analysis of secular tides and trends he

[1] *Complete Prose Works of John Milton* (8 vols., New Haven: Yale University Press, 1953), I, 805, 821, 822. Hereafter cited as *Complete Prose*.

was not a disciplined political thinker like Harrington or Hobbes or even Henry Vane. Though Milton possessed strong historical reasons for his attacks on kingship, lords, and bishops, he did not foresee the constitutional difficulties of an England whose dissenting members of the Commons were denied their places by the sword. An army commanded by a righteous Cromwell could tear down the old constitutional structure; it could not establish a new one. The Levellers had anticipated this critical dilemma in insisting that an *Agreement of the People* be promulgated before the Army had marched on London or purged members of Parliament antagonistic to its purposes. Such a proposal, if put into effect, would in time undoubtedly have restored kingship in preference to a Cromwellian dictatorship: a prospect no leader of the Independent minority could have sanctioned, least of all Milton, who had no confidence in a vote of the masses, or of electors he afterward called "the hucksters of the state from city taverns."[2] Yet the Levellers at least had a program for returning the government to the people; Milton and the Independents had none. Moreover, unlike Walwyn and Winstanley, Milton gave scarcely a thought to the economic salvation of England's masses or to the political rights of the disenfranchised. What difference between Commonwealth and monarchy, asked Winstanley, if the plain man ate scantily under both and under each felt the heel of perpetual inequalities as old as the Normans? No more than a name and a shadow. Whereas Winstanley coveted earth's substance for all as the fruit of reformation, and Lilburne a bill of rights, Milton wanted the superior moral and intellectual tone of the Commonwealth as an end to the degrading subservience of monarchical custom. He stood for the dominance of nature's talented aristocrats over both the insolent assumption of hereditary privilege and the incoherent political gropings of the confused multitude. But how to achieve such a consummation? By what means and what groups, in an England accustomed for centuries to the forms of kingship, whatever the emerging realities of democratic strivings and Puritan economic gains? Had Milton possessed any inkling of the hazards the new Commonwealth faced in establishing a constitutional structure alone, it is inconceivable that he could have committed his energies so confidently to the new republic. But here was he, a private citizen, asked suddenly to sit daily with the leaders of the Commonwealth to help create a New Jerusalem on English soil. "The Council of State . . ." he wrote afterward, "summoned me . . . and desired to employ my services, especially in . . . foreign affairs."[3] Such an opportunity he could reject no more than Dante or Plato could renounce similar assignments in other ages. He did not know how many years of brooding over the great poems

[2] *Second Defence,* below, p. 682. [3] *Second Defence,* below, p. 628.

he hoped to write, how many flights of fancy in early morning, when the sunlight first touched his pillow, went glimmering with his fateful choice.

At first Milton did not commit himself, it is true, to a full-time allegiance: He accepted the post of Secretary for Foreign Tongues. Inducted into office on March 20, 1649, Milton had translated only one letter when he was asked (March 28) to add to his duties a task more arduous than composing a hundred state letters: writing a reply to *The Second Part of Englands New-Chaines Discovered.*[4] Though there is no record that Milton refused or accepted this assignment, he did not reply to the Leveller tract; he was certainly present in the Council chambers on March 28 when Cromwell pounded his fist on the table and demanded the incarceration of the four Leveller leaders.[5] On that day Milton was ordered to "make some observations upon the Complicacion of interest" [6] represented in *Articles of Peace with the Irish Rebels,* a document the Commons had ordered to be printed. Meanwhile Milton had been asked to make a reply to *Eikon Basilike;* writing *Eikonoklastes* had cost him months of labor in 1649. It was natural that the Council of State should turn to Milton as one of the few literary men of England who had written against kingship as an institution; but there is no evidence that to write tracts in defense of the new Commonwealth had been an explicitly stated part of his duties. Already, however, the Council was coming to think of Milton as a kind of propaganda minister and censorship minister combined. When a pamphleteering opponent of the new state was arrested, Milton was usually the one chosen to examine his papers. Thus Milton was chosen on May 30 to examine the papers of John Lee; on June 23, he was ordered to examine copies of Marchamont Needham's *Mercurius Pragmaticus.*[7] On May 22, the Commons had discharged Gilbert Mabbott as official licenser of the press, a man who had so taken *Areopagitica* to heart he could no longer serve, saying, "Licens-

[4] The assignment reads as follows (J. Milton French, *Life Records of John Milton* [4 vols., New Brunswick: Rutgers University Press, 1949–58; hereafter referred to as French, or French, *Life Records*], II, 239–40): "That Mr. Milton be appointed to make some observations upon a paper lately printed called old & new Chaines." It is usually assumed that the Council referred to Lilburne's *New-Chaines Discovered,* which had appeared February 26. It is much more likely, however, that the Council was concerned with *The Second Part of Englands New-Chaines Discovered,* which had appeared on March 24, a much more fiery and provocative pamphlet than the original. It is likely that the Commons was already aroused by *The Second Part,* against which they made a declaration on March 27. See *Life Records,* II, 240. For the text of *The Second Part,* see my *Milton in the Puritan Revolution* (New York: Thomas Nelson, 1941), pp. 399–415.

[5] For Lilburne's story of this action, see my *Leveller Manifestoes* (New York: Thomas Nelson, 1944), pp. 100–101.

[6] French, II, 240.

[7] Masson, IV, 92; French, II, 256–57.

ing is as great a monopoly as ever was in this nation, in that all men's judgment and reasoning are to be bound up in the Licenser's." [8] Like all his comrades in the Council, however, Milton found that as a government official he could hold to his theories of freedom, if at all, only in adulterated form. He took upon himself the duties of censorship no doubt as the one best qualified among his colleagues to know when to censor; for once in England's history a man with no inferior mind held the power Milton had so dreaded in *Areopagitica.* "He was scarce well warm in his secretaryship," wrote Edward Phillips, "before other work flowed in upon him." [9] The censorship work alone was a full-time job. That Milton coped with his multifarious tasks without draining all his energy each day is not to be imagined.

In January, 1650, Milton was living with his family in lodgings formerly occupied by Sir John Hippesley in the Scotland Yard end of Whitehall, lodgings assigned to him by the Council of State. His wife Mary Powell, now twenty-five years old, had returned to Milton in July or August, 1645. If Edward Phillips' story of the occasion can be trusted, the manner and origin of the reconciliation had not augured for a happy union. The Powell family, according to Phillips, wished a reconciliation for family reasons, it being royalist and the king's cause declining. Friends of the two families arranged a meeting at the house of one Blackborough, a mutual friend, who lived in the lane of St. Martin's-le-Grand. When Milton entered the house on one of his usual visits, Mary Powell hid in another room. "On a sudden," writes Phillips, "he was surprised to see one whom he thought to have never seen more, making Submission and begging Pardon on her Knees before him." [10] Though he was at first reluctant, Milton's chivalrous impulse overcame his doubts and "soon brought him to an Act of Oblivion, and a firm League of Peace for the future." [11] About a year later, on July 29, 1646, Milton's first child, Anne, was born. A second daughter, Mary, was born on October 25, 1648. From time to time John Phillips may have been a part of the Whitehall household; but Edward Phillips had entered Magdalen Hall, Oxford, in March, 1649. Such was Milton's household in January, 1650, in lodgings where the Council might find him quickly; where such friends or former students as Dury, Hartlib, Marvell, and Skinner might chance by to chat with him. As his custom was, Milton rose before sunrise. The Council of State met at seven o'clock.

Milton's first work for the Council of State in January, 1650, was

[8] Masson, IV, 94.

[9] James H. Hanford, *A Milton Handbook* (New York: F. S. Crofts, 1946), p. 47.

[10] French, *Life Records*, II, 119. [11] *Ibid.*

composing a letter to the Senate at Hamburg, explaining the necessity of the *Engagement,* an oath of allegiance taken by all officials of the commonwealth (and required of all citizens after January 2, 1650), reading as follows: "I Do declare and promise, That I will be true and faithful to the Commonwealth of *England,* as it is now Established, without a King or House of Lords." [12] Why the *Engagement* was such an explosive issue appears from the text of the oath itself and from a showering of pamphlets on the topic: The forcing of conscience, at least in political matters, was not to be limited to the Presbyterians and the Anglicans. The new republic required that its citizens abroad as well as at home take the new oath. This requirement the Hamburgers had resisted, preventing the English merchants of their city from obeying the command of their new government.

From his first state papers to Hamburg we are aware of a refreshingly new Miltonic personality; his diplomatic Latin is infinitely more persuasive than his polemic; he shows immense imagination in appealing to the psychology of national pride. Would not the Hamburgers think it a hostile action, he asks, if the Commonwealth were to forbid their residents in England to swear fealty to their great city? This issue is not to be compared to interference with the business of private British citizens about which he has written earlier. In this matter of an oath of allegiance, that national honor is at stake which the Hamburgers would be the last to dispute. Must not each country be the judge of its own terms and forms of allegiance? Thus Milton's diplomatic reasoning. The great city of Hamburg will surely not suffer any one among them to violate such a vital principle.[13]

On January 8 the Council of State assigned Milton the task of answering the great Salmasius, whose *Defensio Regia* had appeared in England May 11, 1649. The new republic had in vain attempted to prevent the importation of Salmasius' treatise from the continent. "Out comes in Publick," wrote Milton's nephew of the event, "the great Kill-cow of *Christendom,* with his *Defensio Regis contra Populum Anglicanum;* a Man so Famous and cryed up for his *Plinian Exercitations,* and other Pieces of reputed Learning, that there could no where have been found a Champion that durst lift up the Pen against so formidable an Adversary, had not our little *English David* had the Courage." [14] It is doubtful if

[12] *Collection of the Several Acts of Parliament* (3 vols., 1648–54; UTSL), I, 658. Hereafter referred to as *Acts of Parliament* (1648–54); *Acts and Ordinances of the Interregnum,* ed. R. S. Raib and Sir Charles H. Firth (3 vols., London, 1911), II, 325.

[13] *The Works of John Milton* (18 vols., New York: Columbia University Press, 1931–38; hereafter cited as Columbia), XIII, 12.

[14] French, II, 248.

anyone on the Council of State understood the magnitude of the task they were assigning their half-blind Latin Secretary. Even the way the order was phrased tended to minimize the work Milton knew would be involved: "That Mr Milton does prepare something in answer to the Booke of Salmatius, and when hee hath done itt bring itt to the Councell." [15] It is evident from his own later words that Milton did not for a moment count the cost of this assignment. Rather, he felt honored that "the greatest men of our state" had asked him in his presence to undertake the task. Though to arms of combat belonged the chief glory for the triumph of the new Commonwealth, Milton would "as the next highest deed, defend by another kind of arms against envy and calumny, forces against which the steel and the equipment of war are powerless." [16] In *Defensio Secunda* Milton returned to the theme of his great pride in the Council's choice, though exaggerating the extent of national support it represented: "It was I and no other who was deemed equal to a foe of such repute and to the task of speaking on so great a theme, and who received from the liberators of my country this role . . . the task of publicly defending . . . the cause of the English people." [17] He had now lost the sight of his left eye and felt the imminent danger of total blindness. This fateful moment of conscious choice, like the later one of writing *The Readie & Easie Way* a few weeks before the triumphant return of Charles II, shows the depth of Milton's dedication to the cause of a New Jerusalem on English soil.

Chapter II

CONTEMPORARIES AT WORK

January, 1650

1. BUNYAN: "DOWN FELL I"

IN January, 1650, John Bunyan, twenty-two years old, was following his tinker's trade at Elstow and Bedford, gradually transforming his life under the influence of his young wife, his Bible, and his associations with the Bedford congregation. Struggling with Biblical language, Bunyan found he could follow the narrative portions with ease and profit; but the subtleties of doctrine, as in St. Paul, eluded his mind's grasp. In this period of self search a single incandescent moment revealed to him the limitations of his spiritual ascent. In Bedford one

[15] *Ibid.*, II, 286. [16] French, II, 287.
[17] *Second Defence*, below, p. 549.

day he chanced to overhear several poor women talking together "about a new birth, the work of God on their hearts," and the assaults of Satan upon their spirits. Yet they spoke with a joy, a light in their faces, such as Bunyan had never known. The spiritual growth inherent in this casual conversation among people as humble as himself was a revelation to Bunyan of explosive might. What he sought was a new birth, a spirit that might gain a high pinnacle while the growth of his mind lagged and faltered. "I began to look into the Bible with new eyes." In rare moments a conviction possessed him that a loving Saviour held him tight. At other moments despair overwhelmed him, and "down fell I, as a bird that is shot from the top of a tree." To no mind of his time was the terror of God's impending rejection so shattering as to Bunyan's: "My soul did hang as in a pair of scales again, sometime up and sometime down, now in peace and anon again in terror." Perhaps no writer in all England was more remote and alien in embodiment of genius than Bunyan from Milton. In Bunyan's life no watchful father, graced with memories of music and great books, gave him leisure, great teachers, the high reach of Cambridge moments with England's most gifted youth. His ancestry, wrote Bunyan (perhaps by way of encouraging the lowliest of birth), was "of a low and inconsiderable generation; my father's house being of that rank that is meanest and most despised of all the families in the land." An untrained mind, a primitive: The Bible alone was his Eton, his Trinity College, his Sistine Chapel, his Aristotle and Plato, his Luther and Calvin.[1]

2. LOVELACE: "WENT IN RAGGED CLOATHS"

In 1650 Richard Lovelace, thirty-two years old, was obsessed with poverty and melancholy. Aubrey described him as "an extraordinary handsome man, but prowd."[2] In the Dulwich College portrait the artist portrays Lovelace as having a long, narrow face, lips tightened at the corners, a wisp of black moustache, and long black hair. A red scarf is draped across his armor. Taken prisoner by the Commonwealth forces in 1648, he had been confined at Peterhouse, where he made ready *Lucasta* for the printer. Though freed at last from prison (December 10, 1649), his book of poems published, one of the most admired and chivalrous

[1] *Grace Abounding to the Chief of Sinners* (Everyman edition, 1963), pp. 16, 19, 44, 7, 65. Still the best account of Bunyan's spiritual conflict is found in John Brown's *John Bunyan* (Boston and New York, 1885), pp. 53–68. The several poor women Bunyan heard talking introduced him (Brown, p. 69) to their minister, "holy Mr. Gifford," the royalist veteran who became pastor (Brown, pp. 80–82) of the Free Church at Bedford in 1650.

[2] John Aubrey, *Brief Lives,* ed. Andrew Clark (2 vols., Oxford, 1898), II, 37.

men of his age, Lovelace fell into a mood of despair from which he could not recover. In the words of Wood, "After the murther of king Charles I. Lovelace was set at liberty, and having by that time consumed all his estate, grew very melancholy, (which brought him at length into a consumption) became very poor in body and purse, was the object of charity, went in ragged cloaths (whereas when he was in his glory he wore cloth of gold and silver) and mostly lodged in obscure and dirty places, more befitting the worst of beggars, and poorest of servants." [3]

3. MARVELL AT NUN APPLETON

In 1650 Andrew Marvell was twenty-nine years old, a man of middle height, brown-haired, red-cheeked, with piercing hazel eyes; he looks out from the Hannemann portrait of a later decade with a glance more skeptical than trustful. In midsummer, 1650, when Fairfax laid down his commission, Marvell accompanied him to Nun Appleton House in Yorkshire, to serve as the tutor of Fairfax' daughter Mary. Nun Appleton, built during the war, possessed an aristocratic grace and grandeur at a remote pole from Puritan values; remote from Bunyan's humble cottage at Elstow, from the rustic charm of the cottage at Chalfont St. Giles, where Milton was to live some months in 1665–1666. The great hall at Nun Appleton, fifty yards long, stretched between two wings, above which towered clusters of chimneys. On the walls of the great hall hung thirty wooden shields painted with the family arms. Marble of rich and varied colors decorated the fireplaces of the great rooms. To the north lay a park wherein grazed some three hundred deer; to the south a flower garden planted with beds of tulips, pinks, and roses.[4] This garden was the delight of Fairfax and his protégé Lambert. Now it became the delight of Andrew Marvell, too, who wrote of it:

> Bind me, ye *Woodbines,* in your 'twines,
> Curle me about, ye gadding *Vines,*
> And oh so close your Circles lace,
> That I may never leave this Place.

And in "The Garden":

> No white nor green was ever seen
> So am'rous as this lovely green.[5]

[3] Anthony à Wood, *Anthenae Oxonienses,* ed. Philip Bliss (4 vols., London, 1813–20), III, 462.

[4] Clements R. Markham, *Life of the Great Lord Fairfax* (London and New York, 1870), pp. 365–66.

[5] *Poems & Letters of Andrew Marvell,* ed. H. M. Margoliouth (2 vols., Oxford: Oxford University Press, 1952), I, 78, 48.

As these lines show, Marvell at twenty-nine still made rhymed couplets a central resource, though at times relieved by personification and less often by images of color or touch. Marvell was at once less of an experimenter and less of a traditionalist than Milton. Milton had already given up rhyme as "a trivial thing, of no true musical delight." Even his earliest rhymes seem almost accidental when compared with Marvell's habitual elevation of rhyme as a primary ingredient of poetic fire.

"A Horatian Ode upon Cromwel's Return from Ireland," written probably in the summer of 1650, reveals a Marvell divided within himself between sympathy for Charles I and admiration for Cromwell. Since the poem was not published until 1681, it is impossible to unravel part by part the chronology of the poem's conception or composition. The ode opens and closes with lines of admiration for Cromwell. The opening lines praise him for his restless energy in war and peace; the last lines strike a similar strain, but with a note of stronger approval: "March indefatigably on . . . Still keep the sword erect." The ending of the poem anticipates with implicit approval the necessity of a strong military leader in the maintenance of the new Commonwealth. But side by side with such approbation of military might Marvell inserted fervent praise of Charles I and condemnation of his execution:

That thence the *Royal Actor* borne
The *Tragick Scaffold* might adorn,
While round the armed Bands,
Did clap their bloody hands:
He nothing common did or mean,
Upon that memorable Scene,
But with his keener Eye
The Axes edge did try:
Nor call'd the gods with vulgar spight
To vindicate his helpless Right,
But bow'd his comely Head
Down as upon a bed.[6]

If Marvell showed his poem to Fairfax and his lady in the summer of 1650, it is impossible to imagine that this passage about Charles was omitted. If Marvell, on the other hand, showed it to Milton, could he have included this fervent admiration of Charles I? Yet even Milton, whose brother Christopher was a royalist, was accustomed to shades of ambivalent allegiance. In him, as in every man of his age, personal ties often transcended ideological ones. In letting "A Horatian Ode" stand in its present form, Marvell evidently wished to bequeath to posterity an image of himself in 1650 as divided between personal admiration for

[6] *Ibid.*, pp. 88–89.

Charles' mien and carriage at his execution and admiration for Cromwell's talents as a military leader reshaping his country's institutions.[7]

4. BROWNE: "NO GENIUS FOR DISPUTES"

In January, 1650, Sir Thomas Browne, forty-four years old, was practicing medicine in Norwich. A contemporary artist, possibly Joan Carlile, pictured Browne as a black-haired man with a symmetrical oval face, a small pointed beard, and large luminous eyes. "I could never divide my selfe from any man upon the difference of an opinion," he had written in *Religio Medici*, "or be angry with his judgement for not agreeing with mee in that, from which perhaps within a few dayes I should dissent my selfe. I have no Genius to disputes in religion."[8] A curious blend of mystic and rationalist, despite his attacks on popular superstitions, Sir Thomas retained his beliefs in witchcraft, astrology, and Ptolemaic astronomy. In 1650 Sir Hamon L'Estrange, explorer of Ceylon and the Northwest Passage, read *Vulgar Errors* and became a patient and friend of Sir Thomas. Browne had also ministered to Joseph Hall, that noble but incorrigible enemy of the Commonwealth, then living in a small house at Heigham, his great cathedral services in eclipse, his revenues impounded, the glories of Elizabethan church and monarch still incandescent in his mind. At times Browne preferred philosophy and the authority of Aristotle to Baconian observation. In less degree than Boyle and Bacon and Harvey, could Browne depend on the authority of his own unaided eye; he could not separate as unerringly as Bacon the judgment of tradition from a fresh sensory inspection of the problem, as if he were the first man to look at the evidence. Sir Thomas would say, like Bacon, "we have not made experiment." When asked to speak at the witches' trial, he did not judge the guilt or innocence of the woman accused; but he acknowledged his belief in witchcraft and the devil, a belief shared even by Bacon, Boyle, and Harvey. On the other hand, in *Vulgar Errors* Browne had tested hundreds of common myths. He had weighed a live chicken on the scales, strangled it, and weighed it again, discovering no immediate difference in the weight before death and after. At times he eyed life almost as impartially as the camera of a

[7] The most compelling analysis of Marvell's ambivalent thought in "A Horatian Ode" is found in Lawrence W. Hyman, "Politics and Poetry in Andrew Marvell," *PMLA*, LXXIII (December, 1958), 475–79. For a more balanced analysis of Marvell's poetic gifts than is possible here, see, for example, Douglas Bush, *English Literature in the Earlier Seventeenth Century* (Oxford: Clarendon Press, 1945), pp. 158–64; and Lawrence W. Hyman, *Andrew Marvell* (New York: Twayne Publishers, 1964).

[8] *Religio Medici*, ed. Jean-Jacques Denonain (Cambridge: Cambridge University Press, 1955), p. 9.

later era. He had examined a spermaceti whale, sixty feet long, cast up on the coast of Norfolk near Wells. "Out of the head of this Whale," wrote Browne, "having been dead divers days, and under putrifaction, flowed streams of oyl and Sperma-Ceti . . . lying in folds and courses, in the bigness of goose eggs, encompassed with large flaxie substances, as large as a man's head, in form of hony-combs." Some vulgar errors Sir Thomas rejected out of hand, such as that held by James Howell and many others that Jews stink; still, asserted Sir Thomas, "every Man may have a proper and peculiar savour," as Plutarch and Theophrastus had reported of Alexander the Great.[9]

5. FAITHORNE: "SYMMETRY OF PARTS"

In 1650 William Faithorne, thirty-four years old, engraver and portrait painter, a veteran of the Cavalier forces, received permission to return from France to London, where he married Mary, the sister of the famous Captain Grand, and settled in a house near Temple Bar. Faithorne had been a pupil of Robert Peake, Senior, painter to Charles I, and of John Payne, the engraver. Made prisoner of war at the surrender of Basing House on October 18, 1645, Faithorne had refused to take the oath of loyalty to Parliament; he had been confined in Aldersgate, where he had engraved the heads of a number of noblemen, including the famous one of the Duke of Buckingham. Released upon condition that he leave England, Faithorne lived some years in Paris, where he brought his art "to perfection" and studied the French masters of etching, Callot and Bosse.[10] In 1649 he had engraved the frontispiece of *Lucasta,* picturing six child angels in flight, three of them carrying lighted tapers. Perfection in his art Faithorne called "the result of Ayre, the Symetrie of parts, the exact harmony of Proportions, of lights and Shadows." When Faithorne's textbook on engraving was published in 1662, his friend Flatman spoke of him as *"That hand, whose curious Art protracts the date/ Of frail Mortalitie, and baffles Fate/ With Brass and Steel."* [11]

[9] *Works of Sir Thomas Browne,* ed. Sir Geoffrey Keynes (6 vols., London, 1928–1931), III, 34; II, 288; III, 42–43. For a critical commentary, see the still timely edition of Simon Wilkin (4 vols., 1835–36); for judicious bibliographical selection, see Douglas Bush, *English Literature in the Earlier Seventeenth Century* (Oxford: Clarendon Press, 1962), pp. 499–501. The vast range of Browne's reading is brilliantly analyzed in Robert R. Cawley, "Sir Thomas Browne and His Reading," *PMLA,* XLVIII (June, 1933), 426–70.

[10] Louis Fagan, *A Descriptive Catalogue of the Engraved Works of William Faithorne* (London, 1888), pp. ix–xii, 70. Fagan lists around 157 of Faithorne's portraits (excluding royalty), among them Fairfax, Joseph Hall, Robert Boyle, Land, Sir Henry Vane, John Wallis, Milton (the 1670 portrait).

[11] Faithorne, *The Art of Graveing and Etching* (1662; PUL), sigs. A2, A2v, A3.

6. WILLIAMS: "NO FROSTS OR SNOWS"

In January, 1650, Edward Williams sent forth his *Virgo Triumphans,* describing the immense natural resources of England's Virginia colony: an Elizabethan rather than a Puritan justification of the fruits of empire, but tuned to the titles and forms of the new republic. Williams compared the Parliament to the senates of Rome; it has *"made the Land tremble under the terrour of their Armies."* [12] Such a Parliament should follow the example of Rome in securing the benefits of colonization. Thousands of the poor, the parish charges, the orphans, the ruffians on the highway, the "hereditary beggars," the discontented, will find in Virginia a useful outlet for their energies and talents, an "ample theater to make their merits and abilities emergent." [13] Such Englishmen as are now only lowly shrubs in their native land will find in America a wide field in which to make their talents count. The greatest lack in Virginia is willing and eager workers, whereas in England thousands of humble people, especially disbanded soldiers, are restless, discontented, and often without jobs. Beyond useful employment Williams visualized many other advantages: the increase in ships, "the brazen wall of this Nation," with which to transport materials to England in which Virginia abounds, grains, furs, timber, potashes, soap ashes, iron, cotton, rice, sugar. With the aid of this colony's superior fish, England can compete with Holland for the sale of this staple to Europe. The streams and bays of Virginia abound in fish, its woods in venison, elk, and squirrels, its skies with birds. "The ayre it selfe is often clouded with flights of Pigeons, Partridges, Blackbirds, Thrushes . . . . infinites of wilde Turkeyes" (that usually weigh at least forty pounds). In Virginia no frosts or snows hinder the growth of crops. The land is so fertile that the sowing of seed wheat will often yield thirty times its weight.[14] As for market values, Williams gives many examples: Beaver skins sell for seven shillings, honey two shillings a gallon, soap ashes six to eight shillings a hundred weight, grass to be used for cordage, six pence the pound. Thus Williams' emphasis on colonization is pragmatic and realistic; he is eager to convince the new republic that it should shape a colonial policy in Virginia in keeping with England's historic role in world affairs.

[12] *Virgo Triumphans* (January 10, 1650), E589(11), sig. B1, pamphlet listed in *Catalogue of the Pamphlets, Books, Newspapers, and Manuscripts Relating to the Civil War, the Commonwealth, and Restoration, Collected by George Thomason, 1640–1661.* (2 vols., London: British Museum, 1908), I, 783. Hereafter referred to as Thomason.

[13] *Ibid.,* sig. B2. [14] *Ibid.,* p. 2.

Chapter III

THE NEW COMMONWEALTH: PERILS AND CONTRADICTIONS

January, 1650

In January, 1650, the new English commonwealth was one year old, a government without roots or precedents in British annals, upheld by the might of Independent swords and the uneasy guidance of a purged House of Commons. In Sir Henry Vane's view the republic had failed to win a single convert, despite its victories on the battlefield. To the average Englishman the annihilation of the Lords as a political body mattered little. But the banishment of a king's person and a king's office was another matter: The Independents had broken the continuity of a hundred customs deriving from his office, threads of social fabric which no nation, least of all England, could cut without peril and confusion. But beyond these shattered customs lay a deeper reality: The property each Englishman possessed in the king's figure had passed away. Aristocrat, commoner, servant, or vagrant, each Englishman had a precious possession in his image of the king, an image that made him kin to all other subjects in time of crisis or despair. Never had this vision of kingship been more persuasive than that of Charles at prayer before the block of execution. The poorer, the more ignorant the subject, the deeper his subjection to his image of his king. For centuries the illiterate laborer had knelt to the king in far-off London and claimed him for his own. This image, that Milton rejected scornfully as superstitious idolatry, was a force that no manifesto, no law, no victorious army, no execution, could banish from the land.

1. INDEPENDENCY: MOTHER OF HERESIES

On February 26, 1649, Parliament had passed an act requiring all Papists and delinquents residing in London to depart from the city by March 20. Thereafter they were to notify the parish authorities of their dwelling places, from which they could not travel in any direction more than five miles. In the final week before March 20, reported *A Perfect Diurnall,* "there is gone from the Cities of *London* and *Westminster* . . . about 30 or 40000 people above 1000 Coaches have been met upon the severall Roads; Search also hath been made in divers places of *London* to apprehend some that were suspected to stay contrary to the articles."[1] This harsh separation was only one of a number of measures taken by the Independents to protect the new republic against subversion. However necessary to the republic's survival, it opened thousands of old wounds in those who, treated magnanimously, might have reconciled themselves to the new order. The new republic could not hope for reconciliation from the vanquished who had forfeited two-thirds of their estates by remaining loyal to King Charles; but the Commonwealth gave little thought to winning the allegiance of those millions, literate and illiterate, who had only tenuous loyalties to the king and his traditions.

The Independents were a small minority of Englishmen, their supporters numbering no more than 150,000 or 200,000 out of a population of four millions.[2] From no group of citizens, political or religious, could they command coherent mass approval. The Independents had lost the support of the Levellers, who drew most of their active adherents from tradesmen, shopkeepers, apprentices, skilled workers, and common soldiers, who numbered as classes about five per cent of the population. At their most persuasive moments in 1647 and 1648 the Levellers may have commanded the support of 500,000 people.[3] But now the Levellers, to such an extent as they were vocal under the leadership of John Lilburne, were hostile to the new republic. Nor could Cromwell and his colleagues command allegiance from the great body of farmers, freeholders, lawyers, clergymen, merchants, and naval officers, who numbered, with their retainers, perhaps forty per cent of the population. Over twenty per cent of the farmers and freeholders were traditionally loyal to the king. As for esquires and gentlemen, about two per cent of the population, they were in the main royalists, either Anglican or Presbyterian, although many of the Independent leaders, including Cromwell himself, were of the gentleman class. The aristocracy as a whole, which may have numbered, with their adherents, six-tenths of one per cent of the people, were inveterately hostile to the new regime.[4] For none of these groups did the rule of the Independents hold out any promise either of economic improvement or of political stability. As for the two millions of workers at

[1] E534(21), p. 143 (mispaged as 119), March 18–25, 1649.

[2] Godwin (*History of the Commonwealth* [4 vols., London, 1824–28], III, 116), estimated the support of the Independents to be one Englishman in three. But this is obviously an exaggeration.

[3] Though they drew from a much larger body of citizens than did the Independents, the Levellers were not strongly organized outside of London and its suburbs. Nevertheless *The Remonstrance of Many Thousands of the Free People of England* (September 21, 1649, E574[15]) claimed it had signatures of 98,000 people.

[4] See Gregory King, *Natural and Political Observations . . . Condition in England, 1696* (London, 1810), British Museum 1137k27, pp. 48–49.

the bottom of the social scale, comprising servants, laborers, common seamen, cottagers, paupers, and vagrants, the Independents could win their support least of all. The new government could not add even a penny more a day to their twelve-pence wage. Despite the many manifestoes for the relief of the poor, the Commonwealth gave little thought to the economic betterment of the inarticulate mass.

The very dynamics of Independency, especially as practiced in Cromwell's army and among self-appointed prophets of utopia in the offing, bore fruit in scores of strange beliefs the new republic could not ignore. On January 4, 1650, the ranter Abiezer Coppe sent forth two pamphlets: *A Flying Fiery Roll: A Word from the Lord to the Great Ones* and *A Second Fiery Flying Roule: To All the Inhabitants of the Earth.*[5] Coppe's pamphlets contained a compound of errors and heresies of Fifth Monarchy persuasion: A new world loomed in the offing, in which all institutions would yield miraculously to the visions of God's justice, past and present, visions of prophets old and new. God is not a personality but the spirit of universal love, the greatest of all Levellers: "High Mountaines! lofty Cedars! it's high time for you to enter into the Rocks, and to hide you in the dust."[6] The new government, asserts Coppe, is no more willing to level all than King Charles I himself. Coppe is a pacifist (whoring and drinking are no more sinful to him than fighting). He would relieve the poor ploughman of the "hellish burden" of tithes and free quarter. But it is plain he does not believe in the efficacy of laws or constitutional precedents. Only the sudden vision of justice in each man's soul (a miracle now imminent in England), will level the high mountains and mighty cedars. To bring his strange notions into the ken of the average reader, Coppe describes a bout with his own conscience. On Sabbath day, September 30, 1649, having ridden about eight miles without food, he met in the open fields "a most strange deformed man, clad with patcht clouts."[7] He wanted to give the man help, but even as he spoke the harlot part of his conscience battled with that love of man which was a part of God in his soul. The harlot said, "Give him two-pence." Coppe finally offered the man a sixpence if he would change a shilling. When the man said, "I have never a penny," Coppe was tempted to ride away. Still

[5] E587(13), January 4, 1650. Coppe was a ranter of unique and unpredictable behavior. The *Weekly Intelligencer* of October 1–8, 1650, E614(5), reported the following (p. 16): "I had almost forgot to acquaint you with the arrogant and wild deportment of Mr. *Copp* the great Ranter, who made the *Fiery Roll,* who being lately brought before the Committee of Examinations, refused to be uncovered, and disguised himself into a madnesse, flinging Apples and Pears about the roome, whereupon the Committee returned him to Newgate from whence he came."

[6] E587(13), p. 2.

[7] *A Second Fiery Flying Roule* (January 4, 1650), E587(14), p. 4.

the beggar's face haunted him, a visage "more marr'd then any mans that ever I saw." Moreover, "The rust of my silver rose up in judgement against me, and consumed my flesh as with fire." [8] Finally he gave the man all his money and rode on. Such a struggle with conscience, however tinged with sentimental self-praise, was a deep reality to the many-heresied zealots whom Cromwell welcomed as his supporters. Coppe is at a remote pole from those Presbyterians who justified the amassing of wealth by the Biblical saying that he who provides not for his own family "is worse than an infidel." Unrealistic in coming to terms with constitutional and social precedents, many of the Fifth Monarchists found themselves in conflict with the new republic, thrust into prison for conscience sake, or their pamphlets, like Coppe's, ordered by the Rump to be burned by the common hangman.

2. INNOCENT FREEDOMS AND SINS OF THE FLESH

April–August, 1650

In the spring and summer of 1650 the new republic further intensified divisions among its citizens by censorship of belief and action utterly hostile to the beliefs of their Secretary of Foreign Tongues, at least as set forth in *Areopagitica*. On April 19th, for example, it passed *An Act for the Better Observation of the Lords-Day, Days of Thanksgiving and Humiliation.*[1] By this law no traveler, drayman, or butcher was permitted to engage lodging at an inn after 12 o'clock on Saturday night. By the same law the conduct of guests on the Sabbath day in inns and ale houses was severely restricted. On that day no one was to sing in a profane manner; no one was to dance, drink, or tipple. Moreover no one was to grind corn or grain in any mill on the Sabbath, except in an emergency certified by a justice of the peace. Nor could any man labor for hire on the Sabbath day. No one was permitted to hire a boat, a sedan, or a horse and coach. The act provided, moreover, that on the first Sabbath in each March the new law on observation of the Sabbath was to be read from every pulpit in the land. Such a law was as obnoxious to the consciences of liberal Puritans like Milton, Henry Parker, and Roger Williams as it was to the beliefs and habits of the royalists themselves. The act invaded the free choice of daily habits unmolested by generations of kings and bishops, creating immense and widespread resentments against the new republic in every parish of the land.

An even sterner and more absurd act than the one upholding the purity

[8] *Ibid.*, pp. 4, 5, 6.

[1] *Acts and Ordinances of the Interregnum* (1911), II, 383–87.

of the Sabbath was that of May 10, 1650, *An Act for Suppressing the Detestable Sins of Incest, Adultery and Fornication.*[2] The penalty for incest and adultery was to be death "without benefit of clergy," with the exception of women whose husbands had been continually out of the country for three years or "by common fame be reputed to be dead." The first offense of fornication was to be punished by three months' imprisonment without bail. Even the first conviction for adultery was henceforth to require the sentence of death. A woman convicted of being a prostitute or keeping a brothel was to be first whipped and pilloried and then branded by a hot iron in the forehead with the letter *B* for *bawd.* But this was not all. Any person so convicted and branded was afterward to be sent to prison or reformatory to labor for three years without bail. The lawmakers mercifully modified this severity in a provision which required indictments within twelve months after the offense of adultery was committed. The law also provided that persons indicted would be permitted to produce witnesses in proof of their innocence. Finally no confession on the part of the indicted one was to be used in court against any other person than the one making the confession. How far such an extreme attempt to regulate the sins of the flesh deviated from the beliefs of the average Puritan, Independent or Presbyterian, we can only guess. Certainly among the Puritan pamphleteers, whatever the color of their creed, none came forth to praise the new government for its campaign against adultery and fornication. But almost weekly a royalist satirist held up in a glee the example of Marten's wanderings from the paths of virtue. *"Harry Martyn,"* wrote *The Royall Diurnall* on April 14th, "is a Saint of another kidney, and discharges his Conscience at the *Crosse-guns* in *Covent-garden* twice or thrice a week against the *Butts of Venus* . . . *Levells* point blanck at the *mark;* but if she recoyl through much fowlnesse, the next day you may know what *exercise* he hath been at, by his wide stradling."[3] No triumph of Cromwell on the battle field could banish from English minds the contradictions inherent in such raillery.

The new republic made itself further unpopular by proscribing beliefs that were atheistical or blasphemous. On August 9, 1650, Parliament passed an act defining unrighteous action in speech as well as in deed.[4] The act defined blasphemy as a denial of the righteousness of God. Anybody who cursed God or swore profanely by using God's name became a criminal. Indeed anyone who lied became a criminal, as well as those who stole, cheated, or defrauded. Anyone who spoke in a filthy or lascivious way was breaking the civil law. Moreover, anyone who insisted that fornication or drunkenness or filthy speaking was not sinful and detest-

[2] *Ibid.,* II, 387–90.
[3] E598(16), sig. G2v.
[4] *Acts and Ordinances* (1911), II, 409–12.

able was subject to the penalties prescribed by the act. Not only, then, was every Englishman to desist from fornication, drunkenness, and swearing; he was also prohibited from stating an opinion that any of these acts was not wicked. No one was to maintain that whoring and drunkenness "may be committed without sin." For the first offense against such law, offenders were to be punished by six months' imprisonment; for the second offense they were to be banished from the land. Thus did the new Commonwealth assume the right to define blasphemy, maintaining its judgment over the conscientious definitions of its most devout supporters. Not only the state but its army officers assumed prerogative over the consciences of its members. On July 23 *True Intelligences for the Head-Quarters* reported that "A Souldier in Colonel *Okeys* Regiment was yesterday sentenced by a Court Martial, to be boared through the tongue with a hot Iron, for blasphemous words." [5]

3. ROYALIST SATIRE IN FULL CRY

Meanwhile the royalist underground found many voices in satirical outbursts of the day, in pamphlets printed overnight, often composed, set up in type, and run off in a single room. Among the satirists the author of *The Man in the Moon* dealt the most telling blows at the Commonwealth, appealing to the apprentices in its championship of John Lilburne, finding the new tyranny more biting than that of kingship. In the issue of December 26–January 2 *The Man in the Moon* protested the nullification by the Commonwealth of the December election of John Lilburne to the London Common Council, claiming that many citizens had been imprisoned and fined for supporting Lilburne. Indeed, writes the satirist, "Master *Chetwin* a Mercer in Cheapside, [has been] committed close Prisoner to Warwick-Castle, where he is to remaine during the pleasure of the Rebellious House at Westminster, and a Crackfart Act to disable him from ever being a Free-man of the Citie of NOD-NOL, or enjoy any liberty therefrom." [1] The satirist stingingly compares the Puritanical actions of the new Commonwealth with the government of kings and bishops. Of Chetwin's imprisonment *The Man in the Moon* exclaims: "This is *Libertie* indeed; did ever the King or the Bishops exercise the like Tyranny? Ha, ha, ha; I pitty not my Cozens, they have fought faire, faire, and bought themselves very good peniworths of *Libertie,* to be flung into prisons for their free choice of an honest man into an Office of their Citie, this is a high crime indeed, and not to be indured; from Free men to become Bond-men, and to our owne Natives too: for shame my Cozens, put out your hornes, else I feare LONDON

[5] E608(17), p. 14.

[1] E587(10), p. 289.

will be in a far worse case then *Athens* whose thirty Tyrants hanged up all the chiefe *Citizens* that were honestest, or richest; brought that famous *Citie* unto sudden confusion." [2] The long tenure of the Rump Parliament called forth the satirists' ire: "What hath this everlasting Parliament done these eight yeares, but oppresse, rack, and raven on the people?" [3] Thus *The Man in the Moon* appealed to the London apprentices, the Leveller sympathizers, whose hopes for political freedoms dimmed with each passing month.

The satirist appeals especially to low-income Londoners by his frequent attacks on the excise tax, which the Levellers had protested in their petition of January 11, 1650, entitled *To the Commons of England.* With the triumph of the Rump, wrote the Levellers, everyone hoped that the excise would come to an end. But now the Levellers find it "more oppressive then all the Pattents, Projects, and Shipmoney put together." [4] A clever and witty appeal to poor consumers appeared on January 4 in *The Good Womens Cryes against the Excise.* Though signed by "Mary Stiff, Chair-woman," this pamphlet also shows the hand of Richard Overton. A typical passage runs as follows: "Excise on Sugar browne and white, Excise on Candles that wee light, but when King *Charles* comes, then wee'l fight, *and quit scores.* Excise on *Spirits* they doe lay, but from such *Spirits* Lord we pray, deliver us and chase away, *these vermin."* [5] While children "starve for want of meat," parents must pay excise on pots and pans, paper, tobacco, soap, pewter, tin, brass, cheese, butter, pepper, currants, figs, capons, candy, ribbons, gloves, children's tops.[6] As in *The Man in the Moon,* the author of *The Good Womens Cryes* uses images of fornication and excretion to take captive more readers of his mass audience. The sophistication of the satire reflects the mind of no common analyst of political trends.

Another satirical weekly, *Mercurius Pragmaticus,* on January 22 attacked the new republic with sharp thrusts similar to those of *The Man in the Moon:* "They pretend to bee servants to the Kingdome, but make themselves Lords and Masters over the subjects." England has become a stench in the air of all Europe: "Most Nations are Enemies to the English, and scorne a complyance with so degenerate a People; Forraign Enmitie being arived at that height, that Trading is denied to the English Merchants, which was the stay of this Kingdom, and the glory of our Nation." *Mercurius Pragmaticus* ridicules the setting up of courts for administration of justice, particularly for cases of marriage and divorce. Then the satirist makes a thrust at Milton himself: "When such a Court is erected these *Regicides* will choose Mr. *Mylton* (who houlds

[2] *Ibid.* [3] E589(8), p. 294. [4] E621(12), p. 2.
[5] E589(1), p. 2. [6] *Ibid.*, p. 3.

forth the Doctrine of *Divorce,* and, like a State Champion, sham'd himselfe with handling his penne to oppose those Divine *Meditations* of our late King of happy memory) to bee Judge and then bee sure the *Junctoes* Wills must bee obeyed." [7]

A common strain in both *Pragmaticus* and *The Man in the Moon* is the use of scurrilous slander of Cromwell and other leaders of state. *The Man in the Moon* for January 2 to January 9 reported that Cromwell was with Mistress Simmes; "Mistris *Simmes* it may be goes to Bull." [8] Cromwell is often attacked as the "town bull of Ely." The satirists sent forth dozens of images of Cromwell's nose: "his *flaming* Nose," "*Rubinose,*" "his *Noseship,*" "*Salamander* Nose," "*Nose almighty.*" [9] As may have been expected, Henry Marten was attacked in the royalist press for his evening searches: "*Harry Martin* . . . would venture about with the *Seamstresse* in *Westminsterhall* for a new breed, and if shee fail'd, hee had choyce in other places." [10] *The Man in the Moon* for February 6 to February 14 reported that Marten read to his comrades "a Lecture of Chastity in Hell," [11] whereas Fairfax lectured on allegiance and Cromwell on mercy.

Chapter IV

ON CLOUDS WITHOUT RAIN: GERRARD WINSTANLEY

January, 1650

In January, 1650, a group of visionaries and malcontents called Diggers lived on in makeshift huts on the common land of St. George's Hill, near Cobham, in Surrey. Their occupation of St. George's Hill had occurred on April 1, 1649, when a few of them had dug up the common land and planted parsnips, carrots, and peas.[1] Within five days their numbers had increased to more than twenty; within six months, despite persecutions, their numbers at times had mounted to fifty. On April 19, upon complaint of Henry Sanders of Walton-upon-Thames, Parliament had asked General Fairfax to disperse the Diggers. When, only a few days later, Gerrard Winstanley and his fellow-Digger

[7] E590(6), pp. [2], [8], [5]. [8] E589(8), p. 296.
[9] E590(6), pp. [4], [2]; E593(4), p. 330; E590(6), p. [4].
[10] E590(6), p. [2] [11] E593(4), p. 330.
[1] *Clarke Papers,* ed. Sir Charles Firth (4 vols., *CS,* 1891–1901), II, 209; *New-Yeers Gift* (January 1, 1650), E587(6), pp. 4, 6, 8.

Everard appeared before Fairfax, they stoutly defended their course of action, declaring that they would disturb no man's property, but would "meddle with what was common and untilled." [2] When asked why they refused to take off their hats in the general's presence, they had said, "Because he was but their fellow-creature." Having heard them with respectful bearing, Fairfax visited the Diggers at their work some five weeks later; he did not disperse them, but according to Winstanley he permitted some of his soldiers to accompany the sheriff when the tenants of two lords of the manor pulled down one of the Diggers' houses. Nevertheless the soldiers were "moderate and rationall men," in no way responsible for the actions of the lords.

Meanwhile the Diggers' unprecedented action had aroused the community to a pitch of mob excitement. Twice mobs had overrun the Digger camp, one of which carried a number of zealots to the Walton church and there beat them. Their houses meanwhile had been pulled down and burned, their spades and hoes cut to pieces, their corn dug up. Five of them had been kept in prison for five weeks.[3] On April 28, 1649, *A Modest Narrative of Intelligence* had erroneously reported the Diggers' "new Creation utterly destroyed." [4] The Diggers had held on, though few in number, through spring, summer, and autumn. "And now," wrote Winstanley, on January 1, 1650, "those Diggers that remain, have made little Hutches to lie in like Calf-cribs, and are cheerful; taking the spoyling of their Goods patiently." [5] Accused meanwhile with his followers of owning women in common, Winstanley had been moved to write, in February, 1649, an attack on licentiousness in general and community of women in particular.[6]

Behind the feeble experiment of St. George's Hill lay the growth of a mind which the dynamics of Protestantism forced to a more extreme position than any recorded in the Puritan Revolution. The habit of mind Charles I embodied in extending royalist patterns to their logical extreme, Gerrard Winstanley assumed with a fanaticism equally intense in his justification of economic revolution. A Londoner by birth and upbringing, Winstanley had been "beaten out both of estate and trade, and forced to accept of the good will of friends crediting of me, to live a Countrey-life." [7] There he began to write, evolving his blueprint of

[2] Bulstrode Whitelocke, *Memorials* (4 vols., Oxford, 1853), III, 18.

[3] *New-Yeers Gift,* pp. 44–46. [4] E552(7), p. 32.

[5] *New-Yeers Gift,* p. 46.

[6] *A Vindication of those . . . called Diggers* (1649), E1365(1). See also Winstanley's denial of the report in *New-Yeers Gift,* p. 16.

[7] *A Watch-Word to the City of London and the Armie* (1649), E573(1), prefatory address.

economic reformation from the Bible only; his first pamphlet appeared in 1648, his last in 1652. No historian hoping to understand the deepest impacts of the Puritan Revolution, or the interweaving of intellectual positions from royalist to communist poles, can ignore Winstanley's social criticism, many strands of it unique in the annals of the era. To understand Winstanley, as to understand Charles I, is to give new lights and shadings to the historian's portraits of Prynne, Cromwell, Milton, Lilburne, and Fox.

In 1650 each radical and revolutionary group of Milton's England was still seeking those privileges that the old order had failed to provide for its members. The Presbyterians, though abhorring the sentence and execution of Charles I, sought an end to divine right and a constitutional monarchy in which ecclesiastically Presbyterian church government would replace the Anglican hierarchy. More revolutionary than the Calvinists in secular and religious outlook, the Independents ultimately sought a state free from domination of king and lords, in which a large freedom of conscience would prevail. The Levellers, representing substantial sections of the lower middle class, especially Londoners, apprentices, artisans, and soldiers who had risen from the ranks, demanded all this and more: they sought a drastic extension of the franchise and a constitutional guarantee of those personal liberties which, roughly speaking, now appear in the American Bill of Rights. These groups of Englishmen were for the most part literate and sufficiently prosperous in varying degrees not to pose economic reform as their main aim. In the manifestoes of the Presbyterians, the Independents, and the Levellers, we find pleas for economic reform only among the Levellers, and those few; there are few demands for jobs, few complaints of landlords robbing the poor or of masters mistreating their apprentices. Possessed, then, of varying degrees of economic security, the three main parties actively engaged in reform sought those spiritual, intellectual, and political privileges denied to them under Charles and James. Their leaders were renowned and powerful: Baillie, Prynne, Cromwell, Bradshaw, Milton, Vane, Ludlow, Lilburne, Harrison, Peters.

For at least half of England's four million inhabitants, however, for the most part illiterate, the quest of food and raiment for daily needs was of pre-eminent concern.[8] In April, 1649, the *Moderate* had complained that 16,000 families in Westmoreland County "have not bread to put in their Mouths."[9] Another contemporary account (March 12, 1650) ran as follows: "We are in Wellinborrow in one Parish 1169 persons that re-

[8] James E. Thorold Rogers, *Six Centuries of Work and Wages* (2 vols., London, 1884), I, 431.

[9] Issue of April 17–24, E551(20), p. 425.

ceive Alms . . . but as yet we see nothing is done, nor any man that goeth about it; we have spent all we have . . . our wives and children cry for bread, our lives are a burden to us, divers of us having 5.6.7.8.9. in Family, and we cannot get bread for one of them by our labor; rich mens hearts are hardened."[10] One of Winstanley's own complaints ran as follows: "At this very day poor people are forced to work in some places at 4, 5, and 6 pence a day; in other places for 8, 10, and 12 pence a day."[11] Such were the wages while mutton, beef, and pork sold for three pence a pound, butter six pence, cheese two pence halfpenny, hens a shilling each, eggs four to five pence a dozen, salt eight and nine pence a pound. A day's labor, then, figured at twelve pence, could buy two pounds of butter, a little more than two dozen eggs, or three pounds of beef or mutton. The average laborer at ten, twelve, or fifteen pence a day could not have earned more than fifteen or sixteen pounds a year, whereas his bare expenses amounted to eighteen or nineteen pounds.[12] At best, then, the laborer was unable to gain with his toil an assured daily hold on the necessities of life. Freedom of speech or freedom of conscience were terms to him of uncertain meaning and distant application. Thousands of such laborers fought loyally for the king without questioning the inevitability of their economic lot; thousands more fought for Cromwell without any vision of higher wages to follow the abolition of kingship. The mass of England's illiterate were inarticulate, submissive, content perforce with the hardships bequeathed them by centuries of economic custom.[13]

Whereas the Presbyterians, Independents, and Levellers were rich in talented, resourceful leaders, only one personality of stature emerged from the Civil War years as the champion of economic betterment for England's mass of poor citizens. Gerrard Winstanley was an unlearned man, of little popularity or notice in the newspapers of the day, possessed of no oratorical or military talent such as that of Lilburne or Harrison. Winstanley was of such obscurity that in 1652 Cromwell thought his petition and suggested utopia too inconsequential even to acknowledge. To the Digger dreamers political and theological reforms as compared with economic betterment were as chaff whirled by the wind. Lilburne's *Agreement of the People* to these men represented a shallow notion of freedom, "too . . . shallow to free us at all." The heart of the matter was economic relief: "What stock . . . is provided [by the *Agreement of the People*] for the *poor, fatherless, widows, and impoverished people?*

[10] *A Declaration of . . . the Poor Inhabitants of . . . Wellinborrow* (March 12, 1650), 669f15(21).

[11] *New-Yeers Gift*, p. 40. [12] See below, pp. 187–88.

[13] For analysis of incomes of other classes and occupations, see below, pp. 188–89.

And what advancement of encouragement for the *laboring and industrious,* as to take off burthens, is there?"[14] In like terms Winstanley's associates declared: *"England* is not a Free People, till the Poor that have no Land, have a free allowance to dig and labour the Commons."[15] Like many other fanatic idealists, Winstanley could not visualize the gulf of time and custom over which such words must cross before they could take root in even a few minds among his countrymen. Nor could he evaluate realistically the perennial assumptions of practical men about the inherent differences in human beings that brought in their wake inevitable inequalities in comforts and possessions.

Like Milton and Lilburne, Winstanley hated kingship; his reasons throw into sharp focus the difference between his aims and theirs. Whereas Milton hated kingship mainly for its assumption of hereditary privilege and superiority unrelated to merit or achievement, Winstanley visualized in the king the vested economic interests secured to the rich from generation to generation since William the Conqueror. It is plain that Winstanley had read Lilburne's pamphlets, which reflect the general theory of Norman oppression, though always with an emphasis on the political and legal freedoms that in his view it attempted to suppress. The Norman William, runs Winstanley's theory, turned the English out of their lands, gave them to his favorites, granted control of the common land to his nobles (thus requiring the poor to pay for the use of it), had the law written in French, and required the English to pay fees to lawyers; thus the Conqueror perpetuated the whole harassing system of landholding.[16] When a Digger exclaimed, "Oh why are you so mad as to cry up a King?"[17] he was thinking of the king as a symbol of the economic oppression of centuries. To destroy the king without destroying these vested interests was only a mockery of true reformation and of the name *commonwealth* under which in theory the English nation now lived. To free the land of one kind of kingly power only to entangle in another kind of kingly power was a fraud and a delusion.

In their bitter criticism of the clergy, the Diggers protest again and again their blindness to the needs of poor people. The clergy in general preferred "a wicked man in place of a God, as they did Charls Stuart."[18] When one of the ministers actively opposed the efforts of the Diggers to take possession of the common land, Winstanley wrote: "He forgets his Master Christ, that is persecuted in naked, hungry, and houseless mem-

[14] *More Light Shining in Buckingham-shire* (1649), E548(33), p. 15.
[15] *The True Levellers Standard Advanced* (1650), E552(5), p. 15.
[16] *An Appeal to the House of Commons* (1649), E564(5), pp. 15–16.
[17] *Light Shining in Buckingham-shire* (1649), E475(11), p. 6.
[18] *More Light Shining in Buckingham-shire* (1649), p. 16.

bers." [19] Living comfortably on their hundred pounds a year, meanwhile blinding the people with the glories of Heaven, the clergy so befuddle their parishioners that they do not demand an economic realization of Christ's teachings. "This," concludes Winstanley, "is the filthy Dreamer, and the Cloud without rain." [20] But what if a poor man, not daring to steal, says to the minister, "We that work most have least comfort in the earth, and they that work not at all, enjoy all; contrary to the Scripture which saith, *The poor and meek shall inherit the earth*"? [21] Then, exclaims Winstanley, the priest stops his mouth with the lie that by this saying is meant the inward satisfactions that the poor are to have in heaven. Thus he berates the clergy, scoffing at their hypocrisy, taunting them with possessing a Heaven both here and hereafter. Why may not the poor, as well as the priests, have Heaven on earth in the form of a decent subsistence, and Heaven hereafter, too, since God is no respecter of persons? [22] Such strange interpretation of Christian duty finds no echoes in the pamphlets of the Presbyterians, the Independents, or the Levellers. In the Putney debates with Cromwell, even the Leveller Rainsborough made the poor man's right to vote his most extreme demand. Rainsborough pointed out indeed that private property had Biblical support in the commandment, "Thou shalt not steal." Though Lilburne was not indifferent to the plight of the poor, he made no attempt to apply Christian duty to economic reform. He took pains, moreover, to separate his movement from the feeble communist experiment of the Diggers at St. George's Hill, saying, "The Community amongst the primitive Christians, was *Voluntary*, not *Coactive*. . . . We profess that we never had it in our thoughts to Level men's estates." [23] Thus men found in the Bible strangely various blueprints of the New Jerusalem on English soil: Milton his commonwealth of men in plain clothes, Williams his liberty of conscience, Lilburne his widened suffrage, Winstanley his utopia of a livelihood in the earth for every citizen.

From the Scriptures alone, declared Winstanley, he derived his fundamental economic principle (and here he parts completely from Milton, Lilburne, and Cromwell) that the earth should be made a *"common Treasury of livelihood to whole mankind, without respect of persons."* [24] In the beginning God intended his creation to be enjoyed by all; but certain teachers and rulers hedged in much of the land, took it for them-

[19] *New-Yeers Gift*, p. 17.
[20] *Law of Freedom in a Platform* (1652), E655(8), p. 62.
[21] *New-Yeers Gift*, pp. 40–41.
[22] *An Appeale to All Englishmen* (March 26, 1650), 669f15(23).
[23] *A Manifestation from . . . Lilburn*, etc. (April 14, 1649), E550(25), pp. 4–5.
[24] *A Watch-Word* (1649), E573(1), preface.

selves, and thus made other people their servants and slaves. Subsequently, through more buying and selling and expropriation, the will of God has been further frustrated. To own the land in common again is to realize, therefore, the Creator's dream for man's happiness:

> If ever the Creation be Restored, this is the way which lies in this two fold power:
>
> First *Community of Mankind,* which is comprised in the unity of spirit of Love, which is called Christ in you, or the Law writen in the heart, leading mankind into all truth, and to be of one heart and one mind.
>
> The Second is *Community of the Earth,* for the quiet livelihood in food and raiment without using force, or restraining one another: These two Communities, or rather one in two branches, is the true Levelling which Christ will work at his more glorious appearance; for Jesus Christ the Saviour of all men, in the greatest, first, and truest Leveller that ever was spoke of in the world.
>
> Therefore you rulers of *England,* be not ashamed not afraid of Levellers, hate them not, Christ comes to you riding upon these clouds.[25]

Time after time Winstanley returns to his conception of Jesus as an exponent of economic freedom, pointing out that the early Christians were communists, and claiming that the Scriptural promise of the poor inheriting the earth is "really and materially to be fulfilled." To give the land to the poor "is the work of the true Saviour to doe, who is the true and faithful Leveller even the Spirit and power of universall love."[26] Laugh and jeer as you like at the word *Leveller,* cries Winstanley, "I tell you Jesus Christ . . . is the head *Leveller.*"[27] Could it possibly be, he asks bitterly, that God delights in inequalities, deeming one person more deserving of possessions and comforts than another? Man has a body, God's gift, but "better not to have had a body, than not to have food and rayment for it." On many occasions Winstanley identifies the right of survival with the right to gain a livelihood from the land: "Take away land from any people, and those people are in a way of continuall death and misery."[28]

The high tide of the Digger movement was March, 1650, when Winstanley sent forth his *An Appeale to all Englishmen,* a tract more triumphant in tone than any of its predecessors: "Behold, behold, all *Englishmen,* The Land of *England* is now your free inheritance: all *Kingly* and Lordly entanglements are declared against . . . The *Norman* power is beaten in the field, and his head is cut off."[29] In *An Appeale* Winstanley extended greetings to two other Digger colonies, one in Wellingborough, Northamptonshire, and one in Cox Hall, Kent; he was confident that

[25] *New-Yeers Gift,* pp. 37–38. [26] *Ibid.,* p. 42.
[27] *Ibid.,* p. 43. [28] *Ibid.,* p. 21. [29] 669f15(23).

though Parliament, London, and the army had ignored the Digger pleas, the poor would emancipate themselves by appropriating the common land. His mind afire with his vision, Winstanley dreamed and worked in an historical vacuum, unaware of the tentacles of economic custom reaching back over the centuries. Within weeks after his triumphant *Appeale* the Digger colonies collapsed and expired; henceforth the members were too discouraged to effect even sporadic organization.

Despite repeated rebuffs, Winstanley continued to struggle for the realization of economic reformation until the spring of 1652. Like Milton, when no help was forthcoming from one authority, he appealed to another, this time to Cromwell himself. By the summer of 1650 he had drawn up detailed blueprints of his ideal commonwealth, called *The Law of Freedom in a Platform;* and in February, 1652, he presented his utopia to Cromwell (see below, pp. 154–68).

Although Winstanley's ideas diverged drastically from those of such reformers as Milton and Lilburne, each was at heart deeply religious. Each of the three found himself a rebel in theology before he struck out against the economic or political conventions of the time. All three strenuously opposed the established church. An Independent by 1644, Milton veered more and more toward an extreme individualism difficult to classify but sufficiently revolutionary for him to leave his *Christian Doctrine* unpublished at his death. Milton was one with Winstanley in his antipathy toward a professional ministry; he, too, urged that one who preached should labor on week days at a trade or a profession. Long before he adopted Leveller views, Lilburne was a hater not only of Episcopalian but also of Presbyterian doctrine. Thomas Edwards recorded in horrified accents that a certain Mr. Knowles had prayed for Lilburne's release from prison.[30] Each of the three reformers hated tithes, each hated kingship and nobility, and each wanted England to establish a republic.

The ideological separation of the three reformers was more striking, however, than the views they held in common. Understanding more fully than either Winstanley or Milton the evolution of English law and the tenacity of English legal traditions, Lilburne sought precedents and justification of commoners' rights in the law of the land; moreover, he favored the adoption of a new constitution by vote of the people. To Milton, however, laws were in the main only "norman gibbrish," and to Winstanley they were weighted with so much economic tyranny that they were not worth preservation. Had the three men sat down together over a cup of ale, they could not have agreed, moreover, on war as a

[30] *Gangraena,* Part I (February 26, 1646), E323(2), p. 40.

Christian duty. Like most Puritans, Lilburne and Milton thought that war for a just cause had Biblical justification;[31] Winstanley, however, leaned to pacifism: "Jesus Christ was Gods anointed not because he conquered with a Sword of iron, but because he conquered by love."[32] Then, too, whereas Milton and Lilburne were strongly nationalistic, Winstanley, like Dury in his ideas of peace and Comenius in his hope for education, thought in world-wide terms: "Not only this Common . . . should be taken in and Manured by the People, but all the Commons and waste Grounds in *England,* and in the whole World."[33]

Finally, in their philosophy of economic reform, Milton and Lilburne were as sharply hostile to the views of Winstanley as they were to the political views of the royalists. Of the three men only Winstanley had known actual want or been forced by privation into intimate observation of the laborer's economic plight. Lilburne's family was fairly prosperous, and Leveller followers as a whole were sufficiently removed from dire want to make political agitation their main concern. When the Levellers were accused of communistic tenets, Lilburne replied in *A Manifestation* that his party had never advocated equalization of property.[34] A provision against leveling estates was incorporated into the *Agreement* of May 1, 1649, and the *Agreement* of July 23, 1649.[35] The only economic reform advocated by the Levellers was a provision in one of the *Agreements* that interest above six per cent be prohibited. Lilburne, however, always speaks of the Diggers sympathetically; his attitude toward them is suggested by the words *"all the erronious tenents of the poor Diggers at George hill."*[36] But his rejection of socialism was decisive and complete.

On the need for economic reform, Milton and Winstanley stand at remote poles in the ideological annals of their era. No pacifist and no internationalist, Milton did not conceive of the revolution as a means of aiding the poor or redistributing the national income in even the smallest degree. As a youth, it is true, he had written the following:

> If every just man that now pines with want
> Had but a moderate and beseeming share
> Of that which lewdly-pampered Luxury
> Now heaps upon som few with vast excess,

[31] *Cf. Souldiers Catechism,* British Museum 8122.b.15, p. 1:

Q. Is it lawfull for Christians to be soldiers?
A. Yea doubtless: we have arguments enough to warrant it.

[32] *A Watch-Word* (1649), p. 11.

[33] *True Levellers Standard Advanced* (1650), p. 16.

[34] *A Manifestation* (1649), pp. 4–5.

[35] Wolfe, *Leveller Manifestoes,* p. 409; *An Agreement of the People of England* (July 23, 1649), 669f14(59).

[36] *Legall Fundamentall Liberties* (June 8, 1649), E560(14), p. 75.

> Nature's full blessings would be well dispenc't
> In unsuperfluous eevn proportion.[37]

This sentiment, however, did not grow into a belief grafted firmly to the structure of Milton's political thought. The only later reference to the scattering of fortunes is the decisively hostile one in *The Readie & Easie Way*. His own plan, he writes, "requires no perilous, no injurious alteration or circumscription of mens lands and proprieties [as Harrington's model would]." [38] If, Milton adds, the temporal and spiritual lords in accordance with his proposal are extirpated, "no man or number of men can attain to such wealth or vast possession, as will need the hedge of an agrarian law." From this statement, and from his old outbursts against the ostentatious wealth of the prelates, we know that Milton was no believer in great wealth settled in a few families. As for himself, he cared little for money except as a means to that leisure that a poet and thinker, living a life of "spare temperance," requires. He was unwilling, however, to disturb the fundamental practices of the economic order, even to that measure advocated by Harrington.

To the extent that one's ideas spring in part from his circumstances, it is easy to understand why Milton and Winstanley stood at remote poles in their ideas of economic reformation. Unlike Winstanley, who accepted the charitable hospitality of his friends in the country after being impoverished by the "cheating sons" of London, Milton was never forced into an examination of the laborer's struggle for bread. From birth to death Milton was surrounded by economic plenty. So well had his father provided for his needs that he enjoyed not only seven years of uninterrupted study at Cambridge, but also some years of detached study at Horton. Not requiring employment during his middle years to sustain his family, Milton earned a salary for the first time in March, 1649, when he was appointed Secretary for Foreign Tongues. Though Milton suffered heavy losses in 1660, he spent even the fourteen remaining years of his life in comparative comfort. He still had 1500 pounds variously invested, yielding him about two hundred pounds annually.[39] When one compares this with the ten, fifteen, or twenty pounds' annual income of the agricultural laborer, he is instantly aware of the gulf in living standards that separated such men as Milton, Cromwell, and Vane from Winstanley and the two million least prosperous members of the new republic.

[37] *Comus*, ll. 768–73. [38] *Readie & Easie Way* (second ed., 1660), pp. 65–66.
[39] Masson, VI, 718.

Chapter V

THE ADVENT OF THOMAS HOBBES

February–May, 1650

THE advent of Thomas Hobbes on the English political scene in 1650[1] was in striking contrast, as were his beliefs, to the advent of Milton in 1641. Almost half a century before, Hobbes had entered Magdalen Hall as a boy of fifteen; there a rough and disorderly Puritanism had whirled round him without effectual grip on his growing, darting mind. Hobbes' subsequent young manhood, however, had stamped him with ideas of man and society at the opposite pole from those of men such as Harrington, Milton, Williams, and Vane. At the age of twenty Hobbes had become page of William Cavendish, son of the first Earl of Devonshire. For the next two decades Hobbes was an honored member of the Cavendish household, serving as tutor and friend, gracing the dinner table with his delightful wit and learned sallies, entertaining, among the choice spirits of the day, Hyde, Bacon, Chillingworth, Hammond, and Hales. He had twice toured Europe, visiting Galileo in Florence in 1636. He had fallen "in love with geometry" and translated Thucydides.[2] Even after he had gained fame both at home and abroad as one of England's great intellectuals, Hobbes continued to write and study under the patronage of the Cavendish family, committed both by friendship and conviction to the cause of Charles I. In November, 1640, when it became evident that the Long Parliament might fall not only upon Strafford, but also upon all leading apologists for the royal cause, Hobbes exiled himself from England. "Doubting," he wrote later, "how they would use him, [he] went over into France, the first of all that fled, and there continued eleven years, to his damage some thousands of pounds deep."[3] In 1650 Hobbes was sixty-two years old, a man of strange notions, as unpopular among Anglicans and Roman Catholics as among Presbyterians, fearing somewhat to remain in France and reluctant to return to England.

[1] *De Cive* was published in Paris in 1642 and republished in Amsterdam in 1647. It was little known in England, however, until Hobbes published his own translation of the tract in London, 1651.

[2] John Laird, *Hobbes* (1934), pp. 5–6 ff.

[3] *English Works of Thomas Hobbes, ed.* Sir William Molesworth (11 vols., London, 1839), IV, 414.

Appearing in February and May, 1650, though written long before, *Humane Nature* and *De Corpore Politico* set forth Hobbes' central ideas now crystallized in *Leviathan,* published in Paris in 1651. From these ideas Hobbes never advanced or retreated; they represented a profound and original mind set at every point of the intellectual compass against what Hobbes considered the most dangerous conception of his time: the right of the individual to judge the truth from his reading of the Bible. There is evidence in *De Corpore* that Hobbes hoped his own philosophical and political system would become a counterforce to the liberal Puritan doctrine and the addiction to popular government inculcated in the universities. "There is no doubt," he wrote, "if the true doctrine concerning the law of nature, and the properties of a body politic, and the nature of law in general, were perspicuously set down and taught in the Universities, but that young men, who come hither void of prejudice, and whose minds are as white paper, capable of any instruction, would more easily receive the same, and afterward teach it to the people, both in books and otherwise, than now they do to the contrary."[4] In this sentence Hobbes can be thinking only of his own concept of the law of nature described in earlier chapters of *De Corpore;* a concept fundamentally hostile to the usual Ciceronian notion that the law of nature is a body of ideas tracing the elements of ideal justice in each man's mind.

According to Hobbes, all men are free and equal in a state of nature. In this condition each man acknowledges every other as his equal; one man's blood is as good as that of any other. Each is free to take what he needs from nature or from another man, to protect himself from danger. Therefore, concludes Hobbes, the "estate of man in this natural liberty, is the estate of war," a condition that no civilized man wishes to maintain. What, then, is his alternative?

The leading principle of Hobbes' law of nature is that man escape his warlike condition by divesting himself of the rights he possesses in a state of nature. To maintain a secure peace,[5] he gives over these rights to one leader for "fear of not otherwise preserving himself."[6] All men must thus acknowledge the sovereignty of a single person, "including the wills of many in the will of one man," for the sake of peace and concord. A sovereign thus yielded to is absolute in his power. To Hobbes sovereignty

[4] *Works,* IV, 219; *De Cive,* ed. Sterling P. Lamprecht (New York: Appleton-Century-Crofts, 1949), p. 29.

[5] *De Cive,* p. 32.

[6] *Works,* IV, 123. In *Leviathan,* which appeared under the Commonwealth (1651), Hobbes makes it clear that he could accept absolute sovereignty of a body of men as well as of a single person. See *Leviathan,* ed. Michael Oakeshott (Oxford: Basil Blackwell, 1960), p. 112. In *Behemoth,* which appeared under Charles II (1679), Hobbes' emphasis is on single-person sovereignty.

is indivisible, whether reposed in one man or a single body of men. The sovereign rules by terror; he possesses "absolute use of the sword in peace and war." [7] He has the right to compel any man to fight for the kingdom. If and when the sovereign fails to enforce safety and peace, society falls again into a state of nature and each man again trusts to his own sword to preserve his life.

In *Behemoth* Hobbes stoutly defends Charles I, whom he calls "the best king perhaps that ever was." Blameless in his quarrels with the Parliament, Charles had been persecuted by a seditious faction. The king Hobbes looked upon as God's lieutenant, vested with absolute rule, empowered not only to decide all civil disputes, but also to mold all religious teaching with his interpretation of religious and moral truth. "The King owes his crown to God only, and to no man, ecclesiastic or other." [8] The duty a subject owes to his monarch "is a science, and built upon sure and clear principles, and to be learned by deep and careful study." [9] The king's subjects may not resist or punish him, though he may put a subject to death without being called to account by anyone.[10] On such absolute rule Hobbes was unswervingly insistent from first to last; it was the first necessity in maintaining civil order and defense against enemies.

Notwithstanding his consistent absolutism, Hobbes interpreted with brilliant astuteness the ideological patterns by which the Puritans, Milton among them, justified their antagonism to the old social order. The universities, insisted Hobbes, had planted in men's minds the seeds of sedition, feeding their fancies with the ideal of mixed monarchy and the virtues of the ancient commonwealths. They were the Trojan horse of the great rebellion. In the classics of Greece and Rome, wrote Hobbes, "the popular government was extolled by that glorious name of liberty, and monarchy disgraced by the name of tyranny." [11] Had not the leaders of the House of Commons learned sedition at Oxford and Cambridge? "For who can be a good subject in a monarchy," demanded Hobbes, "whose principles are taken from the enemies of monarchy, such as were Cicero, Seneca, Cato, and other politicians of Rome, and Aristotle of Athens, who seldom spake of kings but as of wolves and other ravenous beasts?" [12] Even men like the Earl of Essex, complains Hobbes, though not tainted with Presbyterianism, were carried away by the broad stream of seditious thought "to think that England was not an absolute, but a mixed monarchy." [13] To see how accurate Hobbes was in these assumptions, one has only to turn to the pages of Milton, Harrington, Algernon Sydney, Vane, or the speeches of Hampden and Pym.

[7] *Works,* IV, 132; *De Cive,* p. 74. [8] *Works,* VI, 236. [9] *Ibid.,* VI, 362.
[10] *Leviathan,* ed. A. D. Lindsay (New York: E. P. Dutton, 1914), pp. 92, 114.
[11] *Behemoth,* in *Works,* VI, 168. [12] *Ibid.,* VI, 362. [13] *Ibid.,* VI, 303.

To Hobbes the rise of Presbyterianism loomed as an even more destructive intellectual explosive than the reading of the classics. Educated at Cambridge and Oxford, the Presbyterian leaders had drunk deep of the classics while deducing from the Scripture principles inimical to their monarch. Even though the Presbyterian merchants of the cities made the poorer people "sell their labour to them at their own prices," says Hobbes, their ministers persuaded the common sort to unite with them against the king. The main cause of Parliament's resistance to Charles and his followers was "the envy of the Presbyterians, that incensed the people against them, and against episcopacy itself."[14] In Hobbes' opinion the common people, by whom he apparently means the less prosperous members of the middle class, chiefly city dwellers, understood little of the real issues, and might easily have been persuaded to obey the king with loyal alacrity. "To the contrary," writes Hobbes, "our rebels were publicly taught rebellion in the pulpits; and that there was no sin, but the doing of what the preachers forbade, or the omission of what they advised."[15] The Presbyterians were determined "to set up a democracy and depose the King, or to let him have the title only so long as he should act for their purposes."[16] In this drastic statement, Hobbes was, of course, mistaken; the Presbyterians from beginning to end had no intention of deposing the king; in 1660 they were to rejoice in the return of Charles II. What they did strive for consistently was a strict subordination of the king's power to that of Parliament.

Still another disruptive revolutionary activity, according to Hobbes' analysis, was the private individualistic interpretation of the Scriptures, "exposed to every man's scanning in his mother-tongue."[17] After the translation of the Bible, complained Hobbes, every man began to have an exalted notion of his own wisdom: "Every boy and wench," he wrote, "that could read English, thought they spoke with God Almighty, and understood what he said, when by a certain number of chapters a day they had read the Scriptures once or twice over."[18] From the Scriptures men drew their justification of rebellion, denying that the will of the king was superior to their interpretation of obedience to God. Widespread reading of the Bible, nourished by the Presbyterians themselves, inevitably brought further divergencies of opinion, consequently factious disputation, quarreling, resistance to authority, and finally open rebellion. Sects and factions sprang up denouncing and dividing each other, "out-doing the Reformation, as they pretended, both of Luther and Calvin." Among these factions Hobbes names the Brownists, Anabaptists, Independents, Fifth-Monarchy men, and Quakers, all so fanatical that they became bitter enemies of the Presbyterians, though the very

[14] *Ibid.*, VI, 275. [15] *Ibid.*, VI, 343. [16] *Ibid.*, VI, 275.
[17] *Ibid.*, VI, 167. [18] *Ibid.*, VI, 190.

"brood of their own hatching."[19] No force, thought Hobbes, was more dynamically destructive to the peace of the kingdom than the endless sectarian disputes arising from private interpretation of the Bible. On the Presbyterians, said Hobbes, especially upon the agitation of the Presbyterian ministers, lay the blame for the Civil War. "Had it not been much better that those seditious ministers, which were not perhaps 1000, had been all killed before they had preached? It had been, I confess, a great massacre; but the killing of 100,000 [in the Civil War] is a greater."[20] In Hobbes' opinion England might have escaped all this confusion if men had only placed their reliance in the king as head of the church and final authority on the interpretation of Scriptural meaning.

In his emphasis on the disruptive and revolutionary implications of the Protestant intellectual method, Hobbes was on solid ground. While attempting to rally their congregations to enthusiastic support of Calvinist dogma, the Presbyterian ministers had urged the efficacy of daily study of the Bible. This persistent reading of the Gospels cracked and shattered the theological molds of Calvinism itself, loosing them gradually from thousands of minds, snapping them abruptly from others; and the sayings of the Bible marked no two minds alike. The cobbler, the apprentice, and the common soldier, when they could read at all, found in the Bible ideas of society disturbingly strange to those of the prayer book and the Sunday sermon. In the Scriptures Milton found justification, if not the origins, of his essential social ideas. The sharp transitions inherent in the Protestant intellectual method stirred no mind more profoundly than his own. Not only did his interpretation of the Scriptures provide the central impetus for his rejection of Anglicanism and Presbyterianism; it also inspired in good part the utopian reforming zeal of the divorce tracts and *Areopagitica*. Idealists like Roger Williams, Overton and Winstanley, Lilburne and Walwyn seized eagerly upon the dynamite of revolution which they claimed to find in the Scriptures. Around the campfires of Cromwell's victorious army soldiers quoted the Bible feverishly, arguing for strange notions with a political curiosity unparalleled in military annals. In the army debates so vividly recorded in the *Clarke Papers*, the soldier Rainsborough attacked traditional property rights with scriptural dialectic; time after time Milton contrasted the meekness of Jesus with the ceremonial pomp of bishops and kings; Richard Overton appealed for toleration of the hated Papists; Gerrard Winstanley wove his utopian pattern from the Scriptures only.[21]

In the dynamics of Protestant searching it was inevitable that the insurgents should disagree among themselves; each reformer hastened in

[19] *Ibid.*, VI, 333. [20] *Ibid.*, VI, 282.

[21] See Overton's *The Araignement of Mr. Persecution* (1645), pp. 11–12; and Winstanley's *A New-Yeers Gift* (1650), pp. 37–38.

vain to erect restrictive outposts to the spreading movement of theological and political heterodoxy. As the Independents scoffed at the Presbyterians for refusing to punish the king after warring against him, so the Levellers derided the Independents for their hostility to a popular constitution, and the Diggers chided the Levellers for demanding only votes, not food and clothing, for England's poor. Hobbes was accurate, then, in denominating private interpretation of religious truth as a disruptive, disintegrating power. In 1658–60 the work of Cromwell broke to pieces in the clash of parties and factions. The end was an England confused and chaotic, torn by civil strife, returning gladly in 1660 to the relative security of the traditional kingship. As a prophet of England's immediate destiny, Hobbes was therefore a more searching, realistic analyst than Milton.

Aware of the extreme applications of Protestant ideology, Hobbes set his face against popular reform, distrusting as well the curious dreams of the Renaissance utopians. "France of the absolute monarchy, rather than Puritan England," writes Gooch, "was his spiritual home." [22] Not a commonwealth that might be, or ought to be, but a state that had proved its stability: king, lords, and bishops, every man uncomplainingly in his place, doing the will of the monarch—this was Hobbes' answer to the Puritan pamphleteers. From 1640 to 1676 he shifted but little ground, made no advances, no retreats. Of this answer and this man Milton said: "[He] did not like him [Hobbes] at all, but would acknowledge him to be a man of great parts, and a learned man." [23]

Hobbes turned upon the liberal writers of the day, Milton among them, the very ideological machinery (the law of nature, the social contract), by which they had justified rebellion against kings. Yes, asserts Hobbes, we were created equal, equal in hope of personal gain, in quest for peace and the world's approbation. By Hobbes' definition man is selfish, competitive, egotistic; in the social contract having voluntarily relinquished his natural freedom, he is now forbidden even to speak rebellious thoughts, pledged with his fellow-men to perpetual obedience to his sovereign. In the state of nature, before having made their contract, men were free. But when the state of nature drifted inevitably to anarchy, they preferred security to freedom, servitude to war.

To Hobbes the dread of war was an irrefutable objection to civil re-

[22] George P. Gooch, "Hobbes," *Proceedings of the British Academy,* XXV (1939), 86.

[23] John Aubrey, *Brief Lives,* ed. Andrew Clark (2 vols., London, 1898), II, 72. Hobbes mentions Milton only once in *Behemoth,* calling him "an English Independent." Of Salmasius' *Defensio Regia* and Milton's *Defence,* Hobbes wrote (*English Works,* VI, 368): "I have seen them both. They are very good Latin both, and hardly to be judged which is better; and both very ill reasoning, hardly to be judged which is worse. . . . So like is a Presbyterian to an Independent."

forms visualized by such idealists as Thomas More, Henry Vane, Milton, and Locke. War was the supreme evil among man's demoniac inventions. In time of war, he wrote, there is

> no culture of the Earth, no Navigation . . . no commodious Building . . . no Knowledge of the face of the Earth; no account of Time; no Arts; no Letters; no Society; and which is worst of all, continuall feare, and danger of violent death; And the life of man, solitary, poore, nasty, brutish, and short.[24]

Absolutism in Hobbes' opinion was the only effective preventive of these horrors; any conditions upon which peace could be preserved were justified. Why then reach for the moon, stirring civil strife in a quest fruitless and ironic? Appoint a sovereign to keep the peace; forget injustice, forego utopias. This is the law of nature.

Milton, on the contrary, embodied in the law of nature and the social contract a revolutionary explosiveness. The law of nature he conceived as a code of absolute justice derived both from man's natural reason and his reflections upon Christian principles, as visualization of perfection inherent in Plato's doctrine of recollection and God's revelations. To him it was "the only law of laws truly and properly to all mankinde fundamental."[25] It assumed to Milton (even in the pamphlets of 1660) the presence of reason in man and his capacity for rising socially and politically "by degrees to perfection."[26] Milton invoked the law of nature to justify divorce, his ideal of the ruler, popular self-rule, denunciations of kingships, violent overthrow of tyrants. The Levellers and many other Puritans shared with Milton this ideal, which Richard Hooker had so systematically expounded, and Locke was to extend so drastically. Was there anything in the law of nature, asked Rainsborough in the army debates with Ireton and Cromwell, to forbid the suffrage to the poorest man in England?[27] Typical of Puritan liberalism, Milton's ideal of the law of nature reflects his impulsive and poetic nature. A romantic, impatient reformer, he was not a realistic critic of the changes in custom and habits of thought by which permanent changes may be effected; he demanded a sudden jump from reality to the New Jerusalem, content with no intermediate stations.

In the beginning, asserts Milton in *The Tenure,* men were "born free, being the image and resemblance of God himself."[28] This was the first

[24] *Leviathan,* p. 65. [25] *The Readie & Easie Way,* second ed. (1660), p. 9.
[26] *Ibid.,* p. 62. [27] *Clarke Papers,* I, 304.
[28] *The Tenure,* in *Complete Prose,* III, 198–99. In *Doctrine and Discipline of Divorce* (*Complete Prose,* II, 297), Milton speaks of "the law of nature and of equity imprinted in us."

state of nature. But falling into dispute through Adam's sin, men made compacts with each other to keep the peace, appointing rulers to restrain and punish any who might violate the social contract. In this action, insists Milton, the people did not forfeit their natural freedom; they had not appointed kings and magistrates to be their masters, but rather their "Deputies and Commissioners, to execute . . . that justice, which else every man . . . must have executed for himself." [29] When kings thus appointed began to use their power despotically, the people framed laws to limit royal authority, that not a person but law and reason might be their ruler. Further to limit the king's power, they established Parliaments and exacted a coronation oath, their right to govern themselves and depose a king, "though no tyrant," remaining all the while unalterable.

To Hobbes the *summum bonum* in a commonwealth was peace and tranquillity; to Milton it was progress and justice. Hobbes therefore preferred a static society at peace to a dynamic social order constantly in the state of internal dispute, which to him was merely another form of warfare. Hobbes would have established a strict censorship; he points out in both *Leviathan* and *Behemoth* the danger of permitting liberty of discussion against absolute rule, agitation carried on mainly by the very dregs of the people, stirred up by pernicious doctrines. Milton, on the contrary (at least as late as *Areopagitica*), believed that in a society aspiring to the just treatment of all its members, the dynamic internal warfare of ideas was indispensable. In *Areopagitica* he had called for the open and imaginative consideration of new ideas, however strange or utopian. Such liberty to Hobbes was the seedground of rebellion and social chaos.

Chapter VI

CROMWELL'S ASCENDANT STAR

March–September, 1650

In 1650 events in England moved rapidly toward the ascendancy of Cromwell's will in civil affairs. The execution of the king had broken from the constitutional structure a link of such ancient forging and prolonged acceptance as to be irreplaceable, forcing the new rulers into improvisations irreconcilable with the central political customs of the realm. The *Engagement* was an ominous symbol of the rent in the con-

[29] *Complete Prose*, III, 199.

stitutional fabric. Pride's Purge had destroyed in one blow the validity of the Commons as a body elected according to constitutional custom; the High Court of Justice that convicted Charles had been set up without pretext of legal precedent, at least on the part of Cromwell. In March, 1650, the Commons set up a new High Court of Justice as far removed from traditional legal precedents as the Star Chamber itself.[1] For the study of precedents, such as Lilburne claimed justified ancient freedoms as well as abuses, Cromwell and his officers substituted a daily interpretation of the will of God. A long night of prayer had preceded their momentous decision to bring Charles to justice. Had not their prayers for victory been repeatedly answered by the Lord of Hosts? Legal precedents to Cromwell and Harrison, and certainly to John Milton, were as chaff whirled by the wind when weighed with God's continuing approval of Independent aims on the field of battle. Month after month in 1650 brought fresh proof to realists among the Independents that their government could claim no popular support; their tenure was upheld by the power of the sword alone, a condition that made their dependence on Cromwell increasingly acute. According to one report, Richard Bradshaw had admitted in early May, 1650, that "not any one cavalier was heartyly converted to them." [2] About the same time Vane was reported fearful not only of resentment at large for the new republic, but of the intentions as well of Cromwell and his army: Neither could be trusted.[3]

In this state of constitutional uncertainty, Cromwell's successes on the battlefields of 1650, particularly his spectacular victory at Dunbar, made him with each passing month a more dominant figure in English national decisions. If the Rump's constitutional position was a shaky one in a legal sense, the army's power that upheld it was a reality inseparable from the dominance of Cromwell's will and talents. With every victory the magic of his name wrote itself anew in the consciousness of all citizens, whether peasant, lord, tradesman, or shipowner. Not until November, 1652, over two years away, would Cromwell say to Whitelocke, "What if a man should take upon him to be king?" [4] When this idea was born in Cromwell's mind is still a mystery. But he could not have been less oblivious in 1650 than Presbyterian observers to the constitutional vacuum which the execution of Charles had imposed upon the nation.

[1] Gardiner, *Commonweath and Protectorate,* I, 256.

[2] *Letters and Papers . . . Charles II and Scotland in 1650,* ed. Samuel R. Gardiner (Edinburgh, 1894), p. 100. In *Commonwealth and Protectorate,* I, 248, Gardiner attributes this remark to John Bradshaw.

[3] Gardiner, *Commonwealth and Protectorate,* I, 277.

[4] Whitelocke, *Memorials* (4 vols., London, 1853), III, 471.

1. THE CONQUEST OF IRELAND

Since July, 1649, Cromwell had been occupied with the conquest of Ireland. On September 11, after breaching the defenses of Drogheda, Cromwell in the heat of rage had ordered first the defenders of Mill Mount and then "any that were in arms in the town" to be put to the sword. It was the bloodiest massacre in the annals of English warfare, an action Cromwell would not have taken against any but Irish Papists. His conscience ill at ease, he had sought to identify the defenders of Drogheda with those Irishmen who had murdered English citizens in the Rebellion of 1641. "I am persuaded," he had written to Lenthall, "that this is a righteous judgment of God upon these barbarous wretches, who have imbrued their hands in so much innocent blood." He had recorded with satisfaction the murder of all the friars in the town. Was it not clear, he had asked Lenthall, that this great work, indeed all great work, was wrought, "not by power or might, but by the Spirit of God"? [5] Cromwell knew his House of Commons. There were few who would not take satisfaction, as he had, in any slaughter of the Irish. In this even the Presbyterians were one with him, and the future author of *Paradise Lost*.

Town after town had fallen. Under the fierce impetus of Cromwell's will and the religious ardor of its soldiers, the English army had been irresistible, despite the incredible bravery of the defenders. In February, 1650, Cromwell had sent a letter to Lenthall from Castletown, reporting on further victories and exhorting the Commons to supply them faithfully with arms and money, so that the enemy might be soon conquered and the soldiers relieved of "the trade of war."

By April 2, when he wrote again to the Parliament, a new note appeared in Cromwell's letters. His ugly work for the Lord was almost finished. It is evident that he was not a little uneasy about Parliament's delay in commanding his return to England. He had received various "intimations of your pleasure to have me come in person to wait upon you in England." [6] He has received copies of votes of Parliament for his return; yet thus far he has received no orders.[7] His desire is only to know explicitly the will of Parliament; their orders, be they what they may, he will obey with loyal alacrity. But beneath the flow of Cromwellian fervor

[5] *The Writings and Speeches of Oliver Cromwell,* ed. Wilbur C. Abbott (4 vols., Cambridge: Harvard University Press, 1937–47), II, 126, 127. Hereafter cited as Abbott, or Abbott, *Cromwell.*

[6] *Ibid.,* II, 234.

[7] This delay, as Gardiner points out (*Commonwealth and Protectorate,* I, 216), was due to the Commons' conviction that danger from the union of the Scots' army with Charles II was not imminent, as they had supposed.

and humility, one senses a distrust of the Parliament's motives. The Commons at once pressed him to return to England at the moment of his choice. Leaving the completion of the conquest in Ireton's hands, Cromwell set sail for Bristol on May 26. On May 31, the Commons granted him lands sufficient to bring him an annual income of 2500 pounds. On June 1 he was received on Hounslow Heath as a conquering hero by Fairfax, officers of the army, members of Parliament and the Council of State. On June 4 he received the thanks of the Commons. On June 11 he made a report on Ireland, with recommendations which the House at once approved.[8] *Mercurius Politicus* reported that Cromwell's victories in Ireland, together with his previous victories in England, "have crowned him in the opinion of all the world for one of the wisest and most accomplished leaders."[9] That Cromwell was already thought of as a single person who could stabilize England in an era of constitutional upheaval was evident from the proposals of some that he be entrusted with large power for the defense of the nation, with the title of Protector.[10] Thus far, however, Cromwell gave no sign that he thought of himself in such a role, though he was acutely aware of Ludlow's distrust of his motives. At the same time, the House was already under the suspicion that it had designs to perpetuate itself.[11]

Ludlow's account of his conversation with Cromwell about this time throws some light on both Cromwell's ideas of reformation and his skill in winning men, even those who had doubted his honesty, to the ends he visualized. He acknowledged to Ludlow his mistake in attempting to come to agreement with the king in 1647, defending his execution of the Leveller soldier at Ware, however, as necessary to "keep things from falling into confusion." But now, he assured Ludlow, he had no other thought than to settle the government in "a free and equal Commonwealth, acknowledging that there was no other probable means to keep out the old family and government from returning upon us." According to Ludlow, Cromwell then spent an hour expounding the applications of the 110th Psalm, saying that he wished most of all to "make a thorow reformation of the Clergy and [the] Law," but that opposition to these measures is as yet too strong, saying "we design to destroy propriety." In Cromwell's view the law, as then written and administered in England, served "only to maintain the lawyers, and to encourage the rich to oppress the poor." He asserted that John Cook, then Justice in Ireland, "de-

[8] I am here following Gardiner, *Commonwealth and Protectorate,* I, 286–87.

[9] *Memoirs of Edmund Ludlow,* ed. Sir Charles Firth (2 vols., Oxford, 1894), I, 242 n.

[10] Gardiner, *Commonwealth and Protectorate,* I, 287.

[11] Ludlow, *Memoirs,* I, 246, 241.

termined more causes in a week, than Westminster-Hall in a year."[12] With England's assistance in framing new laws, Ireland would become a model for the inexpensive preservation of property. Cromwell then urged upon Ludlow the need for a deputy in Ireland to carry out reforms and assist Ireton in the military government. On June 27 Cromwell proposed Ludlow's name for this post to the Council of State. On July 2, after protests and misgivings, Ludlow accepted the post in Ireland. Though some of Ludlow's friends believed that Cromwell wanted him out of his path to power, Ludlow did not believe he was of such importance in state affairs as to call forth such fears. Whatever Cromwell's private thoughts about Ludlow as an obstacle to his ascendant star, he had voiced precisely the sentiments to appeal to Ludlow's patriotism and reassure him on the score of his republican principles. In his selection of times and means to impose his will upon other men, Cromwell's judgment was seldom wanting. In this instance he also judged correctly that Ludlow had the political stature needed for the task; Ludlow possessed, moreover, the full confidence of the Commons.

2. FAIRFAX: DILEMMA AND RESOLUTION

At this crisis in English affairs, when a Scots army was gathered at the borders for war against the Commonwealth, an army soon to carry in its bosom the magic presence of Charles II, Fairfax refused to serve as the commanding general, thus further enhancing Cromwell's power in the state. Though most people in England already thought of Cromwell as a more inspired military leader than Fairfax, Fairfax was still the supreme commander until his resignation on June 26, this despite his refusal to take the Engagement. Already he had broken with Cromwell on the crucial issue of Charles' execution, the warrant for which he had refused to sign. Though he was willing for Charles to be tried for his crimes, and had even sat one day on the High Court of Justice, he did not expect the punishment to be the extreme penalty. Pride's Purge had been carried out without his knowledge or consent.[13] Fairfax could not now bring himself to make war on his Presbyterian brethren of Scotland; his wife and many of his friends were of Presbyterian persuasion, standing for the limitation, not the abolition, of kingly power. In this position Fairfax was consistent from the dramatic moment on Heworth Moor, June 3, 1642, when he had placed a petition on the saddle bow of Charles I, to the crucial weeks before the Restoration of 1660, when he organized an armed force to expedite the return of Charles II, demanding assurance, however, that the new king would accept constitutional restrictions of

[12] *Ibid.*, I, 246. [13] Masson, III, 698; Gardiner, *Great Civil War*, IV, 272.

his power. Unlike Milton and Cromwell, Harrison and Ludlow, Fairfax was never a republican at heart. His emotional roots extended too deep into the tradition of chivalry, of which his family had been a continuing part for generations; such a tradition without a king at the pinnacle of the social structure was unthinkable. Though he might resist the king's power on political grounds, he would hasten to kiss his hand. He would follow the king's example as a patron of arts and letters.[14] This attachment to the king as the symbol of social unity and coherence was too strong in Fairfax's life to be dissolved by the Civil War or the persuasiveness of place and power. Unlike Cromwell and Milton, Fairfax could separate the figure of Charles II as a symbol of chivalric England from the image of Charles as a profligate, irresponsible youth willing to sign away his conscience to the Presbyterian Scots for a chance to ascend the throne of his father.

The June 25 conversation with Fairfax recorded by Whitelocke, in which Cromwell, Lambert, St. John, Whitelocke, and Harrison endeavored to persuade Fairfax not to lay down his commission, shows as no other document the crisis in the Commonwealth, as well as in the lives of Cromwell and Fairfax. Aside from his services as a general, the new republic needed Fairfax as a link with Presbyterian waverers who might in time support the government. For Cromwell, and for those who feared the enhancement of his power, the impending withdrawal of Fairfax was a crucial shifting of forces in favor of Cromwell's ascendancy. For Fairfax, the conversation crystallized his decision to retire from the affairs of the new government and await the return of the monarchy.

As one reads the document,[15] one has a sense of a ritual record of a decision already made on the part of Fairfax and anticipated by the committee. No one doubted that Fairfax's scruple of conscience was an honest one; with the Scots, he asserted, "we are joined in the national league and covenant." To this Cromwell replied that since the signing of the Covenant the Scots had invaded England once and now they intend "another invasion, joining with their king with whom they have made a full agreement." Would not Fairfax rather have war in Scotland than in England? Though Fairfax agreed that war was likely, his scruple lay in taking the offensive: "What warrant have we to fall upon them unless we can be assured of their purpose to fall upon us?" In reply to this question Harrison pointed out that the Scots were levying men and money and concentrating soldiers along the borders. Could there be any greater assurance of human probability than these actions? To this Fair-

[14] Mildred A. Gibb, *The Lord General* (London: Lindsay Drummond, 1938), p. 231.

[15] Whitelocke, *Memorials,* II, 207–11.

fax replied that "human probabilities are not sufficient grounds to make war upon a neighbor nation." When St. John interposed to point out that the Covenant was first broken by the Scots, and Cromwell suggested that England was no longer bound by a Covenant that the Scots had already violated, Fairfax took refuge in an unassailable objection: "I am to answer only for my own conscience; and what that yields unto as just and lawful, I shall follow." Fairfax then acknowledged that what the committee said carried "much weight and reason with it," also that no group could have more influence with him than this particular committee. Even when Lambert appealed to him not to relinquish the "most glorious cause that ever men were engaged in," not to leave his trusted officers in a situation in which "mischiefs . . . might ensue," Fairfax stood by his scruple of conscience. The committee did not ask him whether his wife and her Presbyterian friends had influenced his decision. Nor did they ask him whether he scrupled to fight against the young king of Scotland as well as the signers of the Covenant. In view of Fairfax's subsequent actions,[16] and of Whitelocke's suggestion to Cromwell in November, 1652,[17] it is possible that this scruple was an unspoken factor in Fairfax's decision.

3. CROMWELL AT DUNBAR

Cromwell's spectacular victory at Dunbar on September 2 made his ascendant star shine with a luster thus far unmatched even by the brilliant career of Fairfax. When he saw that Leslie's army of 22,000 was drawn up for offensive action, Cromwell in a flash of insight resolved to attack. Though his own army could count on only 12,000 foot and horse, they were seasoned veterans still afire with religious fervor for the Good Old Cause. Throughout the battle, as before the battle of Naseby, Cromwell was so filled with the ecstasy of impending or actual combat that he laughed "as if he had been drunk." [18] The battle lasted only three hours;

[16] At the Restoration Fairfax was willing to act for the king only if the Presbyterian members excluded by Pride's Purge in 1648 were restored to their places; or, if a free and full Parliament were elected. When Monk could not give him this assurance, Fairfax disbanded the old soldiers and officers he had called together. See Clarendon, *History of the Rebellion,* XVI, 117, ed. W. Dunn MacCray (6 vols., Oxford, 1958), VI, 165. Though his wife was an ardent Presbyterian, it is plain that Fairfax was more concerned with constitutional scruples than with religious ones.

[17] That Cromwell place Charles II on the throne, with stated limitations of his power, and Cromwell to be appointed commander of the nation's armed forces. See *Memorials,* III, 474.

[18] Abbott, *Cromwell,* II, 319.

the best of the enemy's horse and foot had broken within an hour. Cromwell wrote to Lenthall that the Lord had made the enemy "as stubble to their swords."[19] Soldiers of the Covenant, inspired by Scots ministers, would never again challenge the might of English arms.

In his report to Parliament about Dunbar, Cromwell was more emphatic than ever before about reforms in civil affairs, his language colored as always with praise of the Lord of Hosts:

> We pray you own His people more and more, for they are the chariots and horsemen of Israel. Disown yourselves, but own your authority, and improve it to curb the proud and the insolent, such as would disturb the tranquillity of England, though under what specious pretences soever; relieve the oppressed, hear the groans of poor prisoners in England; be pleased to reform the abuses of all professions; and if there be any one that makes many poor to make a few rich, that suits not a Commonwealth.[20]

As this passage shows, Cromwell could be fiercely pious about a course of action difficult to unravel in concrete terms. Here he urges action in such exhortative generalities that no specific program emerges. Who are the proud and the insolent? Who are the oppressed? The "groans of poor prisoners" is more specific, but what prisoners would Cromwell except from a more humane treatment? We cannot imagine that he would not except the Irish sold into slavery in Barbadoes or the Scots of Dunbar sold into penal servitude in New England.[21] Though he had seen horrors enough on field, wall, and battlement, it is not recorded that Cromwell visited prisoners to observe conditions at first hand, even in the years of the Protectorate. Nothing in Cromwell's record thus far suggests that he wanted an economic reform that would reduce large incomes and augment small ones. The more one studies this passage, the more it appears to be an appeal to the groups of London, Levellers among them, who were thus far disappointed in the reforms achieved by the Rump. At the same time, the passage served notice to the Commons that its commanding general would not remain aloof from crucial issues of civil reform. In this letter Cromwell spoke about more topics of civil affairs and with more emphatic confidence than in any previous report to the Commons.

With what high hopes Milton regarded the rise of Cromwell's star we may judge from subsequent events. As between the Rump Commons and Cromwell, Milton preferred to trust the military leader to impose order in civil affairs. Sitting almost daily in the Council of State, he had some

[19] *Ibid.,* II, 324. [20] *Ibid.,* II, 325.

[21] Cotton wrote to Cromwell (Gardiner, I, 296 n.) that the prisoners were sold as slaves "for 6 or 7 or 8 years," required to work three days a week for their owners, and permitted to work four days a week for themselves.

idea of the cross currents of political forces. As Hobbes had pointed out, power in the executive could not long remain divisible. In the constitutional vacuum in which the Independents found themselves, the Council could not take the place of a single ruler; nor could the Commons act with the authority of a duly elected body. Though they desired to dissolve to make way for such a body, they feared, especially in the emergency of the war with Scotland, to give up their own power. One emergency after another was to postpone their dissolution. Comparing Moses to the Commonwealth, Marten asserted that they themselves "were the true mother to this fair child," and therefore the "fittest nurses."[22] As Marchamont Needham pointed out in *The Case of the Common-Wealth* (May 8), power alone was now the basis of the new republic.[23] Like Needham, Milton justified the use of force for righteous ends, and in this he was not alone. Even the Levellers of 1647–49 had visualized in Cromwell the agency by which their ideals of constitutional settlement might be realized. Milton's deliberate choice between Cromwell and his friends of the Rump in April, 1653, was nearly three years in the future; we have no suggestion that his admiration for Cromwell was tainted in 1650 by the doubts of a Ludlow or a Vane.

Though Milton was weak in anticipating constitutional dilemmas, he had foreseen that the conquest of England's enemies could not be achieved alone on the field of battle. To Fairfax he had written:

O yet a nobler task awaits thy hand;
For what can war but endless war still breed,
Till truth and right from violence be freed,
And public faith cleared from the shameful brand
Of public fraud? In vain doth valor bleed
While avarice and rapine share the land.

These lines had been written about the time of the siege of Colchester, in September, 1648, when Milton himself had been denied fair treatment by a Parliamentary committee in the compounding of the Powell property. The lines show that Milton hoped for a leadership in civil affairs from Fairfax, renowned for his personal virtue, comparable to his success on the battlefield. By 1650, when Fairfax had withdrawn from the public scene, Milton's hopes became centered on Cromwell. In May, 1652, he would write:

Cromwell, our chief of men, who through a cloud
Not of war only, but detractions rude,
Guided by faith and matchless fortitude
To peace and truth thy glorious way hast ploughed,

[22] Gardiner, *Commonwealth and Protectorate,* I, 243.
[23] E600(7), pp. 19–23. See below, p. 51.

And on the neck of crownèd Fortune proud
Hast reared God's trophies and his work pursued,
While Darwen stream, with blood of Scots imbrued,
And Dunbar field resounds thy praises loud,
And Worcester's laureate wreath; yet much remains
To conquer still: peace hath her victories
No less renowned than war; new foes arise
Threat'ning to bind our souls with secular chains.
Help us to save free conscience from the paw
Of hireling wolves whose gospel is their maw.[24]

To Milton freedom of conscience in religion was far more crucial than freedom of conscience in political expression, despite the coalescence of these two principles in *Areopagitica;* whereas now Milton himself justified the repression of William Prynne's secular ideas, for example, he considered toleration of sectarian belief a central issue. The constitutional implications of placing a dictator in power were of no moment at all to him compared to the use of such force for the principle of religious toleration. It was well known throughout England that Cromwell's fierce defense of his soldiers' rights to private religious opinions was consistent and habitual; Milton now trusted to Cromwell for the same action in civil affairs. In the field of constitutional theory Milton was not a disciplined thinker like Bulstrode Whitelocke, Henry Parker, or even John Lilburne; in 1650 he saw only the immediate gains or losses to particular reforms, not the erosion of those processes by which the English nation had resolved, however painfully, internal differences in past centuries.

The two greatest decisions of Cromwell's career were first, to bring the king to justice; and second, to make himself the dictator of England. In the decision to bring the king to justice, Cromwell and his officers were influenced by the agitation of the Levellers, who as early as 1646 and early 1647, in *The Remonstrance of Many Thousand Citizens* and *Regall Tyrannie Discovered,* had emphasized the monarch's accountability to the people. In the face of the formidable psychology of reverence for kingship built up over the centuries, such a decision, even after prolonged failure to deal with Charles, could not have been made except in the heat of victory believed to carry the seal of God's favor. In this loss of traditional reverence for the king's person and station, as the Leveller leaders preceded the army chiefs, so men like Rainsborough and Harrison preceded Cromwell and Ireton, both of whom were more aware than the Levellers of the constitutional dilemmas involved in the dethroning of

[24] Text of sonnets both to Fairfax and Cromwell are taken from *Complete Poetical Works of John Milton,* ed. Douglas Bush (Boston: Houghton Mifflin Company, 1965), pp. 188, 190–91.

the king.[25] But gradually, among the Independent leaders, the reverence for kingship faded before the image of a man likely by the magic of his name and station to frustrate all their victories on the battlefield. After two victorious wars against his forces, when commissioners from Parliament were sent to Charles at the Isle of Wight in August, 1648, the king was, according to Thomas May, "attended with a prince-like retinue; and was allowed what servants he would choose, to make up the Splendor of a Court."[26] Though Marvell called May "a most servile wit and mercenary pen," May's history of this phenomenon is amply supported by other sources.[27] The magic of the king's name forced his conquerors to treat for peace in his name on their knees before him. Against such an irony the Leveller and the Independent leaders rebelled, first Overton and Lilburne, then Rainsborough and Harrison, finally Cromwell and Ireton. Milton had taken the step intellectually as far back as his entries in the *Commonplace Book* (*ca.* 1639–41), but openly and defiantly in his *Tenure of Kings and Magistrates*.[28] Once having taken a decisive step, Cromwell never looked back to doubt or bewail; and in this step to bring Charles to justice, Milton was with him heart and soul. Meanwhile, however, Fairfax himself, most Presbyterian leaders, and the literate popu-

[25] For the sequence of change of heart in individual leaders, see Wolfe, *Milton in the Puritan Revolution*, pp. 183–86.

[26] Thomas May, *A Breviary of the History of the Parliament of England* (licensed June 10, 1650), pp. 211–12. Born in 1595, May had attended Sidney Sussex College, Cambridge, and Gray's Inn. His translation of Lucan (1630) had been praised by Ben Jonson. When Jonson died in 1637, May did not succeed to the poet laureatship, as he had hoped. At the opening of the Civil War, he sided with the Parliament and was eventually engaged as one of the secretaries to the House of Commons. In 1647 appeared his *History of the Long Parliament*. May died November 13, 1650.

A Breviary ends with the events of November, 1648. According to May, the petitions for bringing the king to justice, especially the one of September 11, 1648, represented a decisive transformation of public opinion. Actually, however, the petitions he cites were the work of the Levellers, whether from the Londoners or the army. Whether May knew this but preferred to represent the movement as a generally popular one remains a mystery. Elsewhere, however (pp. 186, 162), he calls the apprentices "scum of the people" and the petitioners of July 26, 1646, "a dissolute multitude."

[27] See Sir Thomas Herbert's narrative, *Memoirs of the Last Two Years of the Reign of . . . King Charles I*, in *Charles I in Captivity*, ed. Gertrude S. Stevenson (New York, 1927), p. 117. The king was permitted a large retinue of servants and nobility for the occasion of discussions with Parliament's Commissioners. But in his imprisonment at Carisbrooke Castle his attendants had been severely curtailed.

[28] See *The Tenure*, in *Complete Prose*, III, 203–15; and the *Commonplace Book*, in *Complete Prose*, I, 430 ff.

lace at large remained uneasily in the intellectual postures of their ancestors, their reverence for kingship imbedded centuries deep in the tenacious memory of social custom.

4. DUNBAR AFTERMATH: THE FACE OF WAR

October, 1650

The demoralization of the Scots after the battle of Dunbar was intensified by the loss of some nine thousand fighting men taken prisoners by Cromwell. The prisoners were an encumbrance and embarrassment to the victors, the main problems being, as Cromwell wrote Haselrig, "the not losing them and the not starving them." [1] The Council of State sent Sir Arthur Haselrig north to take charge of the prisoners, who numbered about five thousand after Cromwell had set free the wounded and disabled. The five thousand were marched from Dunbar to Newcastle by Major Hobson. But at Morpeth on the way, the prisoners were guided into a large walled garden, where, having eaten little for eight days, they devoured quantities of raw cabbage, roots, and leaves. Marching thence to Newcastle, wrote Sir Arthur afterward, some men died along the way. Placed in a large church at Newcastle, many men were deathly ill, three died during the night, and some one hundred forty prisoners were not able to march the next morning. On the march from Newcastle to Durham, many more prisoners died along the road. Congregated in the great cathedral church at Durham, the prisoners now numbered only 3500. The sick were removed by Sir Arthur's orders from the cathedral church to the bishop's castle. "When I sent them first to *Durham,*" wrote Sir Arthur, "I writ to the Major, and desired him to take care, that they wanted not any thing that was fit for Prisoners, and what he should disburse for them, I would repay it. I also sent them a daily supply of bread from *Newcastle,* and an allowance equal to what had been given to former Prisoners: But their Bodies being infected, the Flux increased amongst them." Haselrig directed the officers to provide for each man daily a full quart of soup made from beef and cabbage. He ordered cooks to be employed, straw to be brought for makeshift beds, and coal for fires; as many as a hundred fires burned night and day. Moreover, a physician was employed to let blood and give medicine to the sick. "There was never the like care taken," wrote Sir Arthur, "for any such Number of prisoners that ever were in *England.*" Nevertheless many prisoners died of the flux, despite the purchase of milk from towns round about, which when boiled the physicians considered an excellent rem-

[1] Abbott, *Cromwell,* II, 331.

edy. Of the five thousand who had begun the march from Dunbar, Sir Arthur estimated that 1600 had died. "They still dye daily," added Sir Arthur. Moreover some that "are seemingly healthy, and have not at all been sick, suddenly dye, and we cannot give any reason of it, onely we apprehend they are all infected, and that the strength of some holds it out till it seize upon their very hearts." [2] The prisoners were often barbarous to each other, robbing and even killing their fellow-soldiers. Thus did Haselrig trace one of the manifold faces of war: the sword turned fiercely against a comrade, the solitary youth alone with his final antagonist, in his last hours turning his gaze to the wall, away from lives already forfeit like his own.

Chapter VII

MILTON AND MARCHAMONT NEEDHAM

May, 1650–April, 1651

On May 8, 1650, appeared a brilliant if in part cynical vindication of the new republic, *The Case of the Common-Wealth of England Stated,* by Marchamont Needham. Now thirty years old and a clerk at Gray's Inn, Needham had taken his B.A. at Oxford in 1637. Recognized early as a youth of "pregnant parts," in Wood's phrase, he had entered All Souls at fourteen.[1] Behind the writing of *The Case* worked a bright blade of a mind that had explored most of the sources by which Milton and a few other intellectuals constructed the rationale of the Commonwealth. In 1643 Needham had helped to start a weekly newspaper named *Mercurius Britannicus,* a propaganda medium for the Parliamentary cause. According to Wood, he began to take sides with "the rout, and scum of the people." [2] In 1645 he was accused of writing *Hue and Cry after a Wilful King,* for which action he and his fellow-editor Audley had been confined in the Gatehouse. It is likely that this early commitment to the Parliamentary faction represented a core of intellectual conscience not entirely erased by Needham's subsequent deviations. According to Wood, Needham in 1647 procured an introduction to Charles I at Hampton Court, kissed his hand, and vowed to support his cause.[3] In his new royalist organ, *Mercurius Pragmaticus,* Need-

[2] *A Letter from Sir Arthur Hesilrige* (October 31, 1650), E615(18), pp. 4, 5, 7.

[1] Wood, *Athenae Oxonienses,* III, col. 1180.

[2] *Ibid.,* col. 1181. [3] *Ibid.*

ham ridiculed Cromwell, calling him "Copper-face," "Nose Almighty," "The Town-Bull."[4] Arrested on June 18, 1649, Needham had been committed to Newgate.[5] On June 23, Milton was ordered by the Council of State to examine *Mercurius Pragmaticus*.[6] On August 14 the Council of State issued another order for his arrest, identifying Needham as "now escaped" from Newgate.[7] On November 14, 1649, however, Needham was discharged from custody upon taking the Engagement.[8] Wood reports that Bradshaw and Lenthall secured his pardon and saved his life.[9] The appearance of *The Case* six months later was the first sign of Needham's conversion. "Perhaps thou art of an Opinion contrary to what is here written," says the author, in his preface to the reader. "I confesse, that for a Time I my Self was so too, till some Causes made me reflect with an impartial eie upon the Affairs of this new Government. . . . Putting them in order, and comparing them all together, They soon made a Conquest over mee and my Opinion."[10] Most citizens, asserts Needham, are led more by convenience than by conscience; he makes clear his intention to appeal to the necessities of expediency no less than to reason and justice.

In keeping with his analysis of the Englishman's dominant concern, Needham devotes the opening pages of his pamphlet to an appeal now to the reader's fears, now to his need for order and tranquillity. As Aristotle has taught, no government is static; if it is an aristocracy, it gives way gradually to a democracy, then to tyranny, a transition of "fatall necessity" from one form of government to another. In every kind of government, moreover, the power of the sword is the foundation stone, as it was before the Norman Conquest in England, and has continued ever since. The rule of the Independents is based upon a reality none can deny: By the test of victory in battle Charles has lost his kingdom. Needham cites Grotius frequently to prove it lawful and just to submit to superior

[4] Masson, IV, 39. [5] *Ibid.*, IV, 89. [6] *Ibid.*
[7] *Ibid.*, IV, 146. [8] *Ibid.*, IV, 149–50. [9] Wood, III, col. 1181.
[10] To support his thesis that power confers title, Needham was not averse to citing the greatest European enemy of the Commonwealth, Salmasius himself. In the second edition of *The Case* (first noted by J. Milton French in "Milton, Needham, and *Mercurius Politicus*," *Studies in Philology*, XXXIII [1936], 236–52) Needham inserted an appendix (pp. 103–11) in which he translates and analyzes passages from Salmasius' *Regia* and Hobbes' *De Corpore Politico*. "Not," wrote Needham, "that I esteem their Authorities any whit more Authentick than those which I have already alledged; but only in regard of the great reputation allowed unto those Books by the two Parties, *Presbyterian* and *Royall*." The second edition of *The Case* appeared after June 11, when *A Plea for Non-Scribers* (E603 [1], Thomason, I, 800) was published, a tract to which Needham refers. For *The Case,* second edition, see McAlpin, II, 708.

powers, whatever they may be. How can one kind of government among all others be selected in time of war? A democratic choice of government or leaders is not possible. The issue can only be resolved by force of arms, and Grotius affirms that conquest by the sword places the title of possession in the hands of the victor. Unlike Cromwell and Milton, Needham does not labor the claim that victory is evidence of God's favor; it is simply a reality men must learn to live with. Though there are burdens under the Independent government, think of the new burdens that might have to be borne under a king; if now you have whips, under Charles II you might have scorpions. Is it not better, asks Needham, to have some justice now than none at all under a king?

Moreover, insists Needham, it is a delusion to think that the king can muster power sufficient to reclaim his throne, this despite the magic aura of his name in the minds of the royal party. The kings of Europe, though sympathetic to the young prince, are too involved in their own pressing problems to come to his assistance. The Scots will help him only on condition that he "lay his Scepter at the Foot-stoole of the *Kirke*," a prospect pregnant with catastrophe for all Englishmen who do not wish to be ridden by the "furious *Jockies*."[11] If Charles invades England with the help of the Scots, he will not be able to raise an army even of loyal Englishmen that can stand up against the disciplined and victorious New Model. Nor can Charles expect aid from Ireland, where every month brings word of brilliant new triumphs of commonwealth arms.

Like Milton in *The Tenure* but especially in *The Readie & Easie Way*, Needham shows great contempt for the superstitious reverence for kingship ingrained by social custom: The royalists' "eyes are dazled with that *Sun* which seems to rise upon their Party; supposing the *golden Age* must needs return again with him, and that he will climb up to the *Meridian*, in spight of all opposition."[12] Needham recognizes the pervasiveness ("education and Custome from the *Cradle*, even upon . . . reasonable Souls"[13]) but not the tenacity of the psychology he describes, a state of mind before which all visions of commonwealth ideals, inculcated mainly by classical republicans like Milton and Needham, would a few years later collapse and expire. Needham marshals many bitter arguments against kingship as an institution, citing the Athenian commonwealths and the sayings of Sallust, Demosthenes, Aratus, Guicciardini, Machiavelli, Dante on the weaknesses of hereditary monarchy. The hereditary Roman emperors proved themselves for the most part "no better than savage Beasts."[14] Needham scoffs at the notion that

[11] *The Case of the Common-Wealth* (1650), E600(7), p. 47.
[12] *Ibid.*, pp. 34, 35. [13] *Ibid.*, p. 80. [14] *Ibid.*, p. 87.

virtue is transmitted "from Father to Sonne, as the Sap of a Tree is from the Root to the Branches." [15] People of the north countries generally, being more vigorous and freedom-loving than the Asiatics, have been hostile to kingship: Witness the Hollanders, the Swiss, and the Britons themselves before the coming of the Romans. Education under a monarchy debases the spirit of man. A regal tyranny offers "little Security for the bravest Spirits," [16] which have appeared in free commonwealths of Greece and Rome in greater numbers than in any other countries.

Needham's most caustic satire in *The Case* was reserved for the Presbyterians, in hatred of whom he was strikingly consistent in the windings and retreats of his turbulent career. In 1646 he had attacked the Presbyterians in *Independencie No Schisme,* stoutly defending such forward thinkers as John Goodwin, John Saltmarsh, and Philip Nye, and the author of *Londons Last Warning* (Richard Overton), against the barbs of John Vicars. Like Milton, Needham drives home the argument that the Presbyterians fought against the king both in Parliament and on the field of battle. "Though They laid him not downe upon the Block," wrote Needham, "yet They brought him to the *Scaffold.*" [17] Though no group is more hostile than the Presbyterians to regal dignity, and though they want a king in name only, "a Scar-crow of *Royalty,*" yet they would now return him to the throne.[18] At the same time the Presbyterians want to set up in the land a parochial tyranny over conscience, punishing those who do not agree with them with suspensions and excommunications as rigorous as those of the papists their predecessors. Like Milton, Needham never tires of returning to the theme that *"New Presbyter* is but *Old Priest* writ large." In their present agitation for the restoration of monarchy, every *"Prayer* is a strategem, most *Sermons* meer *plots"* against the state and their audiences as well.

Needham places the genius of a free state as far from the Leveller licentiousness as from royalist arrogance and Presbyterian stratagems. He develops more complete and persuasive arguments against the Levellers than Milton or any other Independent apologist. The word *Leveller,* according to Needham, takes its origin from the central idea of the *Agreement of the People,* namely, that all ranks of men over twenty-one possess the right to vote and stand for office. Such an absurd provision is certain to lead, argues Needham, as Cromwell had claimed more tentatively in the army debates with the Levellers, to an equality of estates. Needham ridicules the Leveller idea that the rude multitude have minds capable of reason; they can absorb no political truth more complicated than mending "their own out of other men's Fortunes." [19] To Needham, as to

[15] *Ibid.,* p. 85. [16] *Ibid.,* pp. 88–89. [17] *Ibid.,* p. 65.
[18] *Ibid.,* p. 66. [19] *Ibid.,* p. 71.

the numerous writers he cites from Greek and Roman history, the masses are dissolute, licentious, and void of reason, "trampling down all respects of things Sacred and Civill, to make way for their *Liberty*." [20] Thus does Needham, like most intellectuals of his day, identify virtue in the Roman sense with social class; the multitude, by the nature of its impulsiveness and instability, is the greatest enemy of liberty. Tumults and mob action are certain to break out; buying and selling of elections will be inevitable. Needham is particularly suspicious of the *Agreement* provisions that Parliaments are to be elected annually and that no member is to serve two years in succession. Furthermore, the Levellers demand the elimination of the Council of State, which Needham compares as a stabilizing force to the Senate of Rome and the Areopagus of Athens. Needham cites the dire catastrophes that struck Greece and Rome when the Athenian and the Roman Levellers were elevated to power. Does not Livy record that the Tribunes of Rome asked the Senators, *"how they durst possesse more than fifty Acres apeece, yet find fault with a division made of two apeece to the People"?* [21] And now in England, behold still another Levelling faction! The Diggers show the high pitch of madness to which Levelling ideas ascend, claiming that all land must be owned in common. For all these reasons a Leveller tyranny is more to be feared by sensible men even than one imposed by a single tyrant.

On May 24, 1650, only two weeks after the appearance of *The Case of the Common-Wealth,* Needham was rewarded by the Council with a gift of fifty pounds. Also on that date the Council agreed to pay Needham one hundred pounds annually for "services of the commonwealth," the first year to be probationary.[22] What services the Commonwealth expected became apparent with the appearance of *Mercurius Politicus* on June 13, 1650. A royalist satirist wrote as follows: "Now appeared in Print as the weekly champion of the new Commonwealth and to bespatter the King [Charles II] with the basest of scurrilous raillery, one *Marchamount Needham* under the name of *Politicus;* a *Jack of all sides,* transcendently gifted in approbrious and treasonable Droll." [23] Another satirist wrote: "And indeed, this *Mercurius Politicus* is his third Mercury Pill, by which he has cast himselfe into this high and last salivation: That as at first he spet his Venome against the King, and next bespatter'd the Independent, so now he may flux himself upon the Presbyterian. . . . But who, since the Act against Bawdy-houses, hath allow'd him this publique Brothell in his Mouth?" [24] Wood does not exaggerate the long-term influence of Needham's pen and the persistent impact of *Mercurius Politicus,* which,

[20] *Ibid.* [21] *Ibid.*, p. 79. [22] Masson, IV, 226.

[23] Heath, *Chronicle* (1676), p. 267.

[24] *The Character of Mercurius Politicus,* August 14, 1650, E609(12), pp. 2–3.

he writes, "flew every week to all parts of the nation for more than 10 years." By comparison with the talent of lesser men, says Wood, Needham's style was "like a weaver's beam."[25]

The first number of *Mercurius Politicus* traced in part the pattern of Needham's editorial method for the decade of issues to follow: a lead article grappling seriously or satirically with a crucial grievance against the Commonwealth; news stories of various days of the week, properly colored to propaganda needs; foreign news from the Commonwealth's intelligencers rewritten by Needham. In *Politicus* No. 1 the vein of *Pragmaticus* was very strong. "Why Should not the *Common-wealth,*" asked Needham, "have a *Fool,* as well as the *King* had?"[26] Needham then sets forth a part of his creed, an unwavering alloy of which was hostility to the Scots:

> Is not this a ticklish time then to write Intelligence? But whatever happens, you shall have it to the purpose; for, I fear no *Colours,* neither *Black-coat,* nor *Blew-cap,* nor that *Raw head and bloody-bones* in the Royall Banner of *Scotland;* which was the only *Legacy* (beside the *Favour* of the *Kirk*) that *Montross* left his *Master.* And much good may it do him among his *gude Subjects;* long may the *Scotch* Royall-Progeny and *Priesthood* be *all fellows at Foot ball.*[27]

Needham's apparent contempt for kingship breaks out again and again in his denunciation of the Scots' overtures to Charles II. The following week, in *Mercurius Politicus* for June 13–20, he wrote that the Scots adorn Charles "with *Sacred* and *Majestick* Titles, crouch to him below the posture of a *Spaniel.*" No debasement before his majesty was too much for their taste. Even the ministers were taught "to pant, and howl, and *tune their noses* after him, every day in the *Pulpit.*"[28]

Another strain in *Politicus* No. 1 is Needham's attempt to minimize such issues as the widespread hostility to the *Engagement* and Fairfax's impending withdrawal as military leader. "From *Leverpoole* in *Lancashire,* and divers other places," writes Needham, ". . . the *Engagement* goes down merrily, for all the Barking and Bleating of the bold *Pharisees,* of that and *Cheshire,* the adjoyning County, who have listed themselves in Print under the notion of *Non-scribers.*" It is plain that Needham attributes resistance to the *Engagement* as coming mainly from the Presbyterian ministers. "The eyes of men are opened," he wrote, "and begin to see how they are *Priest ridden* in every County."[29] Such coloring of domestic facts to diminish the republic's weaknesses was insistent and inevitable. In describing Cromwell's reception in London on June 6, Needham tried to portray a unity of national purpose between Fairfax

[25] Wood, III, 1182. [26] June 6–13, 1650, E603(6), p. 1.
[27] *Ibid.,* p. 2. [28] E603(13), p. 24. [29] E603(6), p. 4.

and Cromwell that did not exist: "Upon *Hounslow-heath* he was met by his Excellency the Lord *General,* with a great Train of the Members of *Parliament,* and *Councel of State,* divers Companies and Troops of Foot and Horse, and many thousands of the *Wel-affected;* so that the waies were thronged down to *Westminster.* Upon the *Monday* following, the *Lord Lieutenant* visited the *Lord General* at his house in *Queen-street,* where there passed many remarkable expressions of mutuall love and courtesie, sufficient to check the false Tongues and wishes of the enemies of the Nation." [30] Here the factual information was correct and valuable to readers of all persuasions; but the implication of harmony on all issues between the two leaders was in essence false.

No pamphleteer was more skillful than Needham in crystallizing and refuting the main arguments against the new republic. In Number 19, for example, October 10, 1650, Needham opened his weekly sheet as follows: "Wee have shewen how the *supreme Power,* resides in the *Peoples Representatives,* without, and against both *King,* and *House of Lords:* The main *Quere* further is, *Whether this present Assembly of Parliament be a complete House, and have a just Title to the Legislative, and supreme Power?* This may be made apparent by viewing the present constitution of the House, and by clearing of mistakes which are entertained concerning the *Breach of Priviledge,* and the Force which is conceived to have been used against the *House.*" [31] This passage shows how acutely Needham was aware of the accusation that the House of Commons under the Commonwealth was lacking in constitutional authority, having been purged of recalcitrant members by Colonel Pride. His reply to the question of constitutional justification is that under the old House of Commons, forty members were usually considered to "make a full House." However, asserts Needham, in the present House more than one hundred and sixty members were now meeting, all of whom have taken the *Engagement.* In 1642–45, asserts Needham, when crucial problems of the kingdom were resolved, only fifty to sixty members usually sat in the House, deciding issues often against not only the will of the king but also that of the Lords. Here Needham warily confuses the issue, which is that of representation of all political parties and not the mere number of members sitting in the House. Still he was more willing than any of his pamphleteering contemporaries to state the full implications of his opponent's reasoning. As for breach of privilege, was not the arrest of William Waller, one of its own members, made without action by the Commons? Yet the House afterward gave this action its full approval. As for the excluded members, asserts Needham, "whatever may be the cause of the absence of such as appeare not, it can derogate nothing from

[30] *Ibid.,* p. 3. [31] E614(12), p. 309.

the Right of those that are present."[32] Among the intellectual waverers in the population, such an argument was bound to be persuasive. There was no constitutional deviation in the new regime for which Needham could not find a parallel in the old. Moreover, he was as resourceful as Milton in justifying the new order by precedents in Greek and Roman history.

Despite the success of *Mercurius Politicus,* the Council decided to place it under the supervision of a more predictable servant that Needham. By January, 1651, *Mercurius Politicus* was issued under Milton's supervision; and on March 17 Milton through the new printer, Thomas Newcomb, submitted six issues of *Politicus* to the licensers of the Stationers Company.[33] Henceforth Milton acted as censor of his friend Needham's journal. Needham's close touch with Milton is shown by a number of references in *Politicus* to Milton and Salmasius in the early months of 1651, such as "A very victorious Reply to *Salmasius* is now in motion at the Presse,"[34] and, "I am thankfully glad of the promise *Politicus* gives us of *Salmasius* Answer, which we greedily expect."[35] Through these months, when he was in weekly if not daily communication with Milton, it was natural that Needham should absorb Milton's viewpoint; from time to time it would have been natural for him to ask Milton (or for Milton to volunteer) to write the vital leading article. Yet there is no solid evidence that Milton actually did write for *Mercurius.*

Beginning with the issue of September 19–26, 1650, the title page article in *Mercurius Politicus* took on a more searching and philosophical tone than in the previous three months. French has shown that many of these introductory essays had already appeared in Needham's book, *Case of the Common-Wealth,* which had appeared May 8. For eleven straight weeks, from No. 16, September 19–26 onward to No. 26, November 28–December 5, Needham quoted the body of each of his lead articles from the *Case.* Many of these lead articles have a tone and quality suggestive of *Tenure of Kings and Magistrates.* On October 24–31, justifying the overthrow of kingship by consent of the people, Needham wrote:

> If by *Consent* be meant the *expresse Consent* of the Body of the People, or of the major-part of their *Representatives,* this may hold requisite in a State not turmoiled by *Civill warre,* but at peace and unity within it selfe; For, then it were most consonant to Reason, that in case there were occasion to elect a *supreame Magistrate* or *Magistrates,* the election should be carryed by the Peoples *Vote,* in such manner as *Votes* are usually given in that State. But now in a *Civill warr* the case is altered, when the Contro-

[32] *Ibid.,* p. 310.
[33] Masson, IV, 325; French, *Life Records,* III, 9.
[34] No. 33, January 16–23, 1651, E622(8), p. 546.
[35] No. 39, February 13–20, 1651, E625(1), p. 604.

> versie touching Government is decided by the *Sword:* For, *ipso facto* the *Sword* creates a Title for Him, or Them, that beare it, and installs Them with a new Majestie of Empire, abolishing the old.[36]

To those who would reply that such an assumption might hold good in a war between nations, but not in a civil war, Needham replies:

> Where a Nation is engaged in a *Civill* warr, and divided into *Parties,* the eye of the *Law of Nations* looks not on Them as one Nation, but as two, according to that of a late learned *Royallist,* by name *Grotius,* who affirms; That *in a divided State, one Nation, during the time of it's Nationall Divisions, is esteemed as two Nations.*[37]

These passages, though lacking in the high seriousness of Milton's *Tenure,* are superior to it in sophistication of political reasoning on the point of popular consent by vote to the rule of the new order. Needham's talents were more than journalistic; he possessed the capacity to rise to heights of original style and passionate utterance of compelling tone, whether or not inspired by his friend Milton's dedication to Commonwealth ideals.

Though both Masson and Gardiner have suggested that the Ishbosheth article of *Politicus* No. 43 (March 27–April 3), was written by Milton himself, French has shown that Needham had lifted this also from his own *Case of the Common-Wealth:*

> I Am often in contemplation of a memorable example, recorded in the second Book of *Sam.* chap. 4; and that is of *Ishbosheth* the son of King *Saul,* who laying Claim to the Kingdome after his Father, by prerogative of succession, made warr against *David,* who was placed in the Government according to Gods appointment: But to shew that *hereditary succession* is no Plea to justifie a warr against the powers ordained by him, he placed marks of displeasure against all that took part with *Ishbosheth;* so that he being heir of the Curses of his Familie, his fortune declining, and all his designes proving succesless, and himself a burden to his Party, he in the end had his head strook off by some of his own Commanders, and brought to *David.*
>
> Now, when God hath opened the eyes of the *Scots* so farr as to consider; that they have an *Ishbosheth* among them, Heir of a Family of the very same Complexion and Condition, against whom destruction hath been written in broad Characters by the speciall hand of Providence. . . . When they observe and remember what an attempt he made to run away to the *Royallists* in the north of *Scotland;* how he rejoyced at the defeat at *Dunbarr,* and took occasion thereby to over-top all his Tutors both of *Kirk* and *State;* the principall whereof he hath outed from Command, and either discontented or debarred them from his Councels, to make room for Cavaliers and Malignants of all sorts and sizes, who now are the only Courtiers.[38]

[36] *Mercurius Politicus,* No. 21 (October 24–31, 1650), E651(10), pp. 341–42.
[37] *Ibid.,* p. 342.
[38] E626(17), pp. 685–86.

Such a passage is somewhat Miltonic both in gravity of style and appeal to God's justice by trial of battle, as in *The Tenure*. Since we are now certain that Needham, not Milton, wrote this passage, we have further proof of Needham's uncanny ability as a propagandist to use, consciously or not, not only the elevated seriousness of Milton's style but also the Biblical applications Milton would have deemed most appropriate. In this passage, curiously enough, as pointed out by Masson and Gardiner, appear two distinctly Miltonic words, *strook* and *outed*. The latter Milton had used in his memorable phrase, "Church-outed by the Prelats." [39] The fact that Needham uses these two words is further proof of his capacity to adapt his style, not only to Commonwealth ideas, but also to the high seriousness exemplified in the pamphlets against kingship by his distinguished colleague.

Chapter VIII

CLASH OF IDEOLOGY: PARKER, LILBURNE, AND JONES

June–November, 1650

Though Leveller and Independent could unite in their hatred of kingship as an institution, the events of passing months sharpened their differences about England's constitutional future. Whereas the Levellers still agitated for a mass signing of *An Agreement of the People,* the Independents ruled with a Parliament purged by the Army of its Presbyterian dissenters. Each party was a minority. If the Levellers numbered half a million persons and sympathizers in a population of four millions, the Independents could scarcely have mustered more than two hundred thousand supporters. Had the Levellers been able to force a signing of the *Agreement,* they could not have won the signatures of even an eighth of the adult population; but this was a hard reality they refused to face. The Independents, on the other hand, made little pretense of setting up a representative Commonwealth; Milton himself claimed for them only the support of an heroic and godly minority. Later, when Salmasius asked, "Was it the people that cut off part of the House of Commons, forcing some away," Milton replied, "I say it was the people; for why should I not say that the act of the better,

[39] *Prose Works,* I, 822.

the sound part of the Parliament, in which resides the real power of the people, was the act of the people?"[1] The Independents had tried Charles without a jury; this to Lilburne was a violation of the most fundamental element of the British constitution, reaffirmed in the Petition of Right within the memory of living men. "The way of tryall by 12 sworn men of the Neighborhood is infringed," wrote Lilburne, "all liberty of exception against the tryers, is over-ruled by a Court consisting of persons pickt and chosen in an un-usual way; the practice whereof we cannot allow of, though against open and notorious enemies."[2] In an interview with Hugh Peters, which according to Lilburne took place on May 25, 1649, Lilburne declared that he would "rather desire to live in Turkie under the great Turk, then in *England* under your religious Masters at White-hall and Westminster."[3] Predicting the return of the monarchy, Lilburne declared that he would choose to live under a limited kingship rather than under a tyranny.

1. PARKER ON THE BREED OF KINGS

Appalled at the unflickering magic of the king's image in the minds of the populace at large, Henry Parker came forth on August 7 with *True Portraiture of the Kings of England*. Parker could touch on no subject of his time without flashes of unique illumination. Four years older than Milton, ten years older than Lilburne, he had taken his M.A. at St. Edmund's Hall, Oxford; in 1637 he had been called to the bar at Lincoln's Inn. Veering from Presbyterian to Independent doctrines, Parker had become Lilburne's teacher with the appearance of *Observations upon Some of His Majesties Late Answers and Expresses* (1642), from which Lilburne had drawn long passages about the law of nature and the original of power in the people. "All men," runs Parker's first principle, "are equally born free."[4] The democratic radicalism of the Leveller position Parker had supported with more brilliant persuasiveness than any barrister of his day. In 1645 he had served as one of the secretaries of the House of Commons; in 1649 he had become secretary to Cromwell's

[1] *A Defence*, below, p. 457.

[2] *Englands New Chains in England Discovered* (February 26, 1649), E545(27), no pagination. Later Lilburne granted the power of the House of Commons to set up a court of justice, provided none of the members of the Commons took places on the Court. In this analysis Lilburne was following his usual insistence on separation of powers: Parliament had a right to make the laws, not to execute them. See *Picture of the Councell of State*, second edition (April 27, 1649), p. 8.

[3] *A Discourse Betwixt . . . Lilburne . . . & Mr. Hugh Peter* (May 25, 1649), E556(26), p. 8.

[4] *True Portraiture*, E609(2), p. 4.

army in Ireland. *True Portraiture* begins by restating his basic premise: "Choice and election [by the people] is the foundation of just authority & . . . none can rule over them but whom they appoint."[5] But this assumption, runs Parker's reasoning, is antithetical to the very concept of hereditary succession, which England now has a chance to slough off forever. To Parker it was inconceivable that England, after five or six centuries of bitter experiences with the uneven and capricious descendants of William the Conqueror, should still believe that "Kings have such a *vis formativa* in their loyns, as to beget Kings in the likeness of their Office."[6] Indeed God himself could not bestow upon any line of men talents suitable to the responsibilities of kingship. Parker traces with some care the history of British kingship, emphasizing the capriciousness of fate that makes children and women and weak men masters of the nation's destiny, usurping meanwhile the right of the people to govern themselves: "Though the people be compared to the Sea, yet as the Sea, they have no turbulent motion of their own, but what is occasioned by violent and uncertain winds; but the great change hath been by the temper, and actings of Princes, and commonly the next successor hath been the omen and fate of the times."[7] Was not the Norman line, moreover, established by conquest, when the flower of English youth were sent to Normandy as hostages, and is not the right to rule England really the right of possession by conquest? Would anyone call such a monarchy justified by law? Parker, like Milton, had depended much on Speed; he quotes Speed's question: "What right had *Will* the Conqueror, the Father of all our glorious Tyrants?" To which Parker adds, "What right had all the rest?" Let Charles the son stay with the Scots, concludes Parker, "and seeing we have conquered the Conqueror, and got the possession of the true English title, by justice, and gallantry; Let us not lose it again, by any pretence of a particular, and debauched person."[8]

In *The Portraiture* Parker was addressing himself not to the Levellers, advocates of a utopian democracy, but to the mass of English citizens in whose minds the image of the king had been stamped afresh and indelibly with the martyrdom of Charles. The Independents opposed in vain the justice of reason to centuries of social custom by which the poorest man in the land felt he had a property in the king's person. To the mass of workmen, servants, and tenant farmers, comprising perhaps half the population, the king's person, whatever his deficiencies, was a symbol, like the images and candles of the Anglican ritual, against which

[5] *True Portraiture*, E609(2), p. 3. [6] *Ibid.*, pp. 5–6. [7] *Ibid.*, p. 9.
[8] *Ibid.*, p. 42.

no rational appeal obtained. The eye and ear held, and the heart accepted, what the reason could not unravel. In this mystery lay the failure of the Puritan appeal to rationality. Only in minds liberated by education, persecution, sense of new economic power or military prowess, or brooding perception of Biblical principles could Parker's appeal gain a foothold. The Presbyterians, it is true, combined their Bible reading with an inexplicable devotion to the king, not as a symbol of identification, but as a symbol of continuity in political institutions. In each Puritan mind the potential of revolutionary thought and action wavered from left to right, and no explanation of this wavering can be complete. But the Independents in the trial of the king had violated traditional freedoms in the most dramatic way possible. Hence *The Portraiture,* like Milton's *Tenure* and *Eikonoklastes,* brought no traceable converts to the Commonwealth from any segment of the population.

2. PARKER'S ATTACK ON LILBURNE

Nowhere was the ideological gulf between Independent and Leveller more clearly set forth than in Parker's analysis of Lilburne's trial in *A Letter of Due Censure . . . to Lieut. Coll: John Lilburne* (June 21). *Due Censure* is a searching exposition of Independent outlook, portraying dilemmas newly confronted but centuries old in social custom. Ancient distinctions imposed their own barriers between the gentleman barrister and the man Parker thought of as an apprentice agitator.

Though *Due Censure* opens with a plea for the brotherly right to admonish Lilburne, the tone of the pamphlet soon changes to one of acute resentment of Lilburne's contempt for his judges, who had treated him with great courtesy and consideration: "Your Judges were by you treated as the most abject captives in the world, and, as it were, dragd up and down before the vulgar only to grace your chariot wheels." [9] Indeed Lilburne throughout the trial had reversed the ranks of men to whom respect was due, preferring the approval of the ignorant vulgar to that of learned men. "You had the breeding of an Apprentice . . . ," exclaims Parker, "and want Latin and French to inable you for Law, or for the true understanding of its terms: yet you neverthelesse must interpret Law to the Judges, and by your interpretation make them meer Ciphers; and this is your birth-right due to you, as an Englishman." [10] Because the judges understand the law, and "are commonly gentlemen by birth," Lilburne has only contempt for them, whereas the jurors, who are generally illiterate workmen, he would elevate as judges of the law. Moreover, even when Lilburne admits that a law is contrary to his con-

[9] *A Letter of Due Censure* (June 21, 1649), E603(14), p. 6. [10] *Ibid.,* p. 22.

clusion, he slashes through it "as great flies use to do through cobwebs: tis sufficient for you to say 'twas part of the *Norman* yoke, or an irrationall innovation . . . You a prisoner judge, and condemne your Judges for going against the Law." [11] The verbatim record of Lilburne's trial shows that his judges had treated him with remarkable forbearance (allowing him almost unlimited freedom of speech), as compared, for example, to the treatment of Charles I by the High Court of Justice. Moreover, Lilburne's was a jury trial, whereas that of Charles made no such obeisance to English custom, even granting, as Charles rightly claimed, that there were no peers to judge his case. On the other hand, Parker does not mention the fact that Lilburne was tried for treason by a special Commission of Oyer and Terminer, which Lilburne (and many Leveller petitions) claimed was contrary to the Petition of Right. Nor does Parker attempt to relate the most important consideration of all to Lilburne's tactics and attitude: the charge of treason for assuming the freedom of publishing a book against the Commonwealth.

3. JOHN JONES DISSENTS

Not all Independents, however, even Independent gentlemen, were of one mind about Lilburne's trial or Parker's rough identification of superior knowledge of the law with scholarly pursuits and gentle ancestry. On August 2 John Jones, 1650, gentleman and Leveller sympathizer, sent forth a sharp and bitter reply to Parker in *Jurors Judges of Law and Fact*. Jones' approach to law is like that of Lilburne: Those laws made contrary to such charters as Magna Charta and Petition of Right are null and void. On June 18 he had issued *The New Returna Brevium, or the Law Returned from Westminster,* in which he had reprinted the Petition of Right "for cheapness to the Generalitie to inform themselvs what is their Rights." [12] On May 6 Jones had issued *Judges Judged* to show that justice is always safer in the hands of juries (which are more ancient than justices of the peace) than in the interposition of learned judges. In *Judges Judged* Jones reprints passages from *Magna Charta,* among them the following: "No Free-man shall be taken, or imprisoned, or be disfeifed of his Freehold . . . but by lawfull judgement of his Peers, or by the Law of the Land." [13] Extending this principle with the aid of Coke's commentary, Jones asks: "Are not Debtors disfeifed of their Livelihood, Libertie, and Freedom which belonged unto them as their Freehold by Birth right, when they are imprisoned . . . by Arrests, and Actions for Debt . . . without any judgement, or ver-

[11] *Ibid.* [12] E1414(2); E1411(2); title page. [13] E1414(1), pp. 31–32.

dict of their equals, and without Due course, or Proces of Law?"[14] When he wrote, "That Law which is called, and ought to be common, they have made it proper to themselves only," he was at a remote pole from Parker's intellectual positions in *Due Censure.* As in every revolution, it was easier for the Independents to pull down the old constitutional structure than to agree on the patterns and customs to be preserved or obliterated.

In *Jurors Judges* Jones reveals marked social antagonisms of his own in replying to Parker's attacks on juries of mechanics and other unlearned persons. He catches up Parker's taunt that Lilburne knows no French or Latin: "As if there were no learning but in Pedlers French and Law-Latin, the very disguises of the Law . . . as a foul face of a Mask." The law would be represented "more gloriously, more learnedly in plain English, then in that Canting . . . which would but cheat us of necessaries to sustain their lives." Can there be no justice from a jury of plowmen? Are they not "the best kinde of free men in *England*"? Lilburne's jury was a jury of mechanics, "whose persons or Estates I know not, but their carriage and Resolution in that matter declare them knowing and understanding Men." Jones is resentful of Parker's disparagement, not only of Lilburne's jurors, but also of "the generalitie of all the constant Inhabitants of all Cities and Corporations in *England* and *Wales,* of whom not one in a Million, ever knew Mr. *Lilburn,* or heard of his Cause, all Mechanicks."[15] When a merchant uses his own hands in weighing commodities, is he ashamed? Does not a lawyer himself learn to write before he learns to debate? Is not writing itself a handicraft? Nowhere is Jones' resentment of traditional class distinctions more acerbic than in his question about marriage: "May not a Judg bestow his daughter upon a Citizen, and a Citizen his upon a Judg, or an Earl, (as we have seen usuall)?" To Parker such question implied an irrelevant and irrational extension of the Puritan Revolution; to a Cromwellian soldier who had proved his mettle and the favor of his God on the field of battle, the ancient distinctions of clothes and mansions, family and learning, could not quite recover their pristine assurance. Though Parker had reminded Lilburne that "even amongst the Angels there are different thrones and Preeminences,"[16] the divisions of men into orders and degrees was a reality in England of diminishing acceptance. And on the shores of the New World, for thirty years past, a community of Englishmen had lived by a code strange and remote from the assumptions of fixed human nature they had left behind.

Beneath the agitation, then, for juries and against juries, Independent

[14] *Ibid.*, p. 34. [15] August 2, 1650, E1414(2), pp. 76, 76–77, 93, 58, 59–60.
[16] *Ibid.*, p. 80; *Due Censure*, p. 23.

and Leveller minds of all shadings were probing more fundamental dilemmas. On November 14, anticipating the impending reformation of legal procedures, Henry Robinson came forth with *Certaine Considerations,* aiming at "a more *speedy, cheap,* and *equall* distribution of Justice throughout the Nation." The central point in Robinson's plan was the abolition of juries in favor of more efficient court decisions by well-trained judges appointed by Parliament. Among Robinson's seven objections to juries appeared assumptions unacceptable to men like John Jones, Henry Marten, Rainsborough, Lilburne and Walwyn, Milton himself. Robinson contended that there was a lack of *"understanding and fit men to be had in the lesser Divisions of a County, for tryall of all Causes."* Do not many jurors vote with the majority, not from conviction but from fatigue? And do not *"most commonly one or two active & nimble-pated men over-sway all the rest, of the Jury, and too often for the worst"?* [17] Even Henry Parker, who published his *Reformation of Courts* on the same day, did not recommend such a drastic departure from ancient custom, whatever his reservations about juries of workmen and apprentices.[18]

On December 2 William Walwyn broke his long silence as a pamphleteer and replied to Robinson with his *Juries Justified.* "Though a silence had seiz'd me," began Walwyn, "equal to his that was born and continued dumb . . . I could not hold my peace; but must tell Mr *Robinson,* he deals most injuriously with his Country." There is not the smallest division in England, not even a parish, that does not afford "a double competency of understanding and fit men." Juries are the most ancient of English rights; even the Conqueror, asserts Walwyn, did not attempt to take them away. Does Mr. Robinson want the present Parliament "to deal worse with us then the Conquerour did with our Predecessors?" The present Parliament has vowed "to maintain inviolable, those fundamentals, in all things touching life, liberty, and estate." How can Robinson's proposal be of service to the Parliament that has granted Robinson so many favors and "profitable places"? To take away juries will make the present Parliament "more odious to the people." Trial by jury is the principal law guaranteed by the Petition of Right. As for understanding, asserts Walwyn, "there is not so great want therof in *England,* as there is of Conscience . . . . feeding the Hungry, clothing the Naked, visiting the Sick and the imprisoned." [19]

One fundamental difference, then, between Leveller and Independent, was that the Independents often appealed to God or Scripture for revela-

[17] *Certaine Considerations* (November 14, 1649), E616(2), title page, p. 2.
[18] E616(5). [19] E618(9), pp. 1, 2, 5, 3–4.

tion of civil justice, whereas the Levellers appealed to documents and precedents in law which they considered charters of freedom. To the Leveller mind the new regime was all too willing to set up high courts of justice in which the right of trial by jury was abrogated in favor of the judgment of highly educated judges. That Charles I himself had been sentenced by a court in which the jury principle was violated was a fact that the Levellers returned to again and again. Hostile as they were to the assumptions of kingship, the rejection of a trial jury was a much more profound and far-reaching violation of constitutional rights than Charles himself had been guilty of. The documents of court procedure and the constitutional rights of the prisoner as interpreted by Edward Coke were a resource by which Lilburne mustered limitless resistance to procedure even in a jury trial. Though the Independents opposed the king and brought him to trial, they knew that they dare not grant him the immunities and rights to which their ancestors had been accustomed even under the worst of kings. Even highly arbitrary monarchs, James and Elizabeth, had not sought to bring their enemies to trial except by the procedures acceptable to the legal community at large. Not so Cromwell and his Independents: They had by their own example broken down the tradition of constitutional privilege, first by Pride's Purge, and second by the trial and execution of Charles. Moreover, to the Independents the appeal of trial by battle, in which their troops had been victorious, was in itself a proof of the justice of their cause. The Levellers, on the other hand, did not attempt to interpret events as an extension of God's will. Hence their appeals to law, to precedents, to charters such as Magna Charta and the Petition of Right.

Chapter IX

PURITAN FANATICS: EXCESS AND SYMBOL

September–October, 1650

The right of each believer, however untrained, to erect his private architecture of belief upon the authority of Scripture extended itself afresh under the impetus of Cromwell's victories and the establishment of the Commonwealth. In vain did the new establishment, whether in bivouac or London streets, attempt to restrain the excesses to which its own leaders had given rise. Even among highly trained theologians, the reading of the Bible was full of quarrels, pitfalls, vagaries of interpretation that no Protestant, even John Dury, could reconcile. Among untrained minds unpredictable heresies grew apace. Search of Scripture by either theologian or humble apprentice was indeed an intellectual method quite opposite to the inspection of nature verifiable by eye, ear, and fingertips as proposed by Bacon, Comenius, Boyle, and Winstanley. But such an approach to truth lacked the passionate prayer, the companionship of God, the search for brotherhood with Christ which lifted the humble believer to great heights with effortless leaps.

1. FRANCIS FREEMAN: PURITAN CAPTAIN IN DISGRACE

October, 1650

On October 29, 1650, appeared *Light Vanquishing Darknesse,* by Captain Francis Freeman, veteran of five years of fighting with Colonel Okey's regiment of horse. Freeman's story of his clashes with Colonel Okey, of his visions and disputes, of his intransigence toward his superior officers, illuminates as few other documents the mingling of explosive forces in the victorious Puritan army. According to his own account, Freeman had the almost unanimous confidence of his troop, all of whom wished to accompany him to Ireland and signed a petition to Fairfax on behalf of his continuance as their leader. Despite Cromwell's injunction that no soldier should suffer for his religious opinions, Freeman's ideas were so extreme, and his temperament so fiery, that challenges of his beliefs by both superiors and subordinates were inevitable. Freeman's main heresy was his belief that the Scripture God had planted in his own mind was superior to the instruction of the Bible. Two of Freeman's own men, Captain Lieutenant Leigh and Cornet Friend, first reported Freeman's strange talk to Colonel Okey, who accosted and questioned him in the presence of other officers. Freeman had a naive confidence that he could make his ideas clear and evident even to hostile minds. "I had certain evidences," he said, "and demonstrations of the spirit of God working in my spirit . . . I saw a glorious change in me . . . I had bin a Papist, Protestant, Presbyterian, Antinomian, Independant, Anabaptist, Seeker &c. But I gave God thanks, I had past through them all; and that Scripture was fulfilled in me, which was a promise made by Christ, that he would *put his laws in our minds, he would writ them in our hearts.*" The law thus revealed, asserted Freeman, "is far above any law without me." [1] After this and other such inflammatory statements, Okey and

[1] *Light Vanquishing Darknesse* (October 29, 1650), E615(7), pp. 5, 6. This tract was first noticed, I believe, by Sir Charles Firth, *Cromwell's Army* (London, 1902), pp. 307–11.

several of his officers darted at him like so many bees. Okey reminded Freeman that years ago, at Taunton, he had declared himself to be Christ; at that time Freeman would have been cashiered for his dangerous tenets had it not been for the intercession of Okey himself. In his earliest long conversation with Okey, Freeman was supported by Mr. Close, a chaplain, and by a Captain Neale. Together the three men urged Okey in vain that he allow them to be tried for their alleged heresy by a Council of War.

From this time forth, according to Freeman, Okey was determined to remove him from his command. Convinced at last that the colonel would disband the whole troop of seventy men in order to be rid of him, Freeman finally agreed to lay down his commission, an engagement which Okey eagerly accepted. But lacking all sense of the need for organizational unity, Freeman brooded over the injustice of his lot and wrote a summary of his case in these words:

The accusation, indictment, araignment, conviction, and sentence, against Captain Francis Freeman without a Court.

Captain *Freeman,* thou art accused and indicted by the name of Captain *Francis Freeman,* for that thou hast felloniously denyed the *Scriptures,* and made God the *Author of sin.* Thou hast said thou art *Christ,* and thou hast countenanced *blasphemy;* all which is against our *Soveraign Lords* the *people,* if we could but prove it. Therefore what canst thou say for thy self? art thou guilty; or not guilty? not guilty, by whom wilt thou be tried? *I'le be tried by a generall Counsell at Warre;* no; thou canst not, thou must be tryed by Colonel *Okey,* how? *must I be tryed by Col. Okey?* why, *he hath condemned me already;* what though he hath? thou canst not be admitted to any other Tryall, Therefore stand up and heare thy Sentence.

Thy Troop shall be disbanded for thy sake, for that thou holdest dangerous Tenets; how? shall my Troop be disbanded for my sake? *shall seventy men suffer for one?* if I have either said or done any thing worthy of punishment; *then let me suffer according to my demerits.* Well, tis the Generals pleasure to disband thy whole Troop, to disband thee: nay, rather then let my whole troop suffer I will lay down my commission. If thou wilt engage to lay down thy commission; I will speak to the Generall to save thy Troop. And thus I have stated my case truly, by way of Indictment.[2]

When Freeman told his troop about his impending resignation, they sent a petition to Fairfax for his continuance as their captain. Granting the petition, Fairfax released Freeman from his engagement to resign and ordered him to continue his command, whereupon Okey raged at him more passionately than ever, declaring to Freeman that he would rather

[2] *Ibid.*, pp. 12–13.

"have a drunkard or a whore-master in his regiment" than such a man as he.[3]

Meanwhile Okey had addressed Freeman's troop in a vain attempt, asserts Freeman, to turn the troop against him, assuring the soldiers that Freeman was "a dangerous fellow, and he would place an honest man in my room." But the troop replied that "they desired no other Captain; they had long time had experience of me, & that I had alwaies proved an honest man to them." Undeterred by this rebuff, Okey called all the commissioned officers of the regiment before Freeman's troop and made a speech to them, declaring that Freeman "held dangerous tenets and [was] not fit to be in the Army." Moreover, asserted Okey, it was Freeman and others like him who "were the occasion of these warres." [4] Okey then attempted to deprive Freeman of his command by ordering his major to give him no more orders, relaying them to the lieutenant instead. Whereupon Freeman said to Okey that he would not accept a discharge in such a manner; he had his commission from the same general as Okey himself: "I told him, that we had fought against arbitrarinesse to good purpose, if mens wils must be laws." Continuing the vendetta with Okey, Freeman ordered his troop to march to a certain place where he could speak to them privately, asked them if they had grievances against him to speak up, and if they wished to have another captain he would gladly withdraw. Whereupon, according to Freeman, they cried out unanimously, *"No other Captain, no other Captain."* [5]

One of Okey's complaints against Freeman was that he had sung bawdy songs on the march. This accusation was reinforced by an incident in which Freeman sang songs in quarters occupied by one of his friends in the troop, Roger Daniel. Daniel had invited him to supper in his quarters. As soon as supper was over, Daniel rose from the table and took from a cupboard a fife, recorder, and cithern, which instruments he handed to two other guests, father and son, who played half a dozen pieces of music for them. At this point two other soldiers of Freeman's troop came into the room, one of them singing a tune. In the conversation that followed Freeman offered to teach the three soldiers some songs (Daniel having made a special request for instruction), whereupon he directed them in some part singing. After this Freeman sang a number of songs alone, among them "Joan of Kent" and "There Dwells a Pretty Maid, Her Name Is Sis." "And these are the two songs," continues Freeman, "that goe under the notion of baudy songs; which *I* shall appeal to all those that know what they are, and what the Musick is. And truly for my part, I sung but mearly for the musick sake, not thinking any hurt at all. Neither had I indeed any evil thoughts in my heart in singing any of

[3] *Ibid.*, p. 14. [4] *Ibid.*, p. 16. [5] *Ibid.*, pp. 16, 17.

those songs; which my conscience can beare me witnesse."[6] However, the woman of the house dropped a chance remark to her brother at Darby Market about a merry fellow by the name of Freeman; the brother in turn spoke of the mirthful soldier to a Colonel Barton, who had heard from Colonel Okey of Freeman's reputation. Colonel Barton immediately sent for the lady, gathered the relevant facts, and drew up a formal charge against Freeman.

In recounting this story, Freeman compares his singing of harmless songs with Okey's treatment of a poor drunken man whom he had forced to walk a board placed in the middle of a room, to see if the poor fellow could make it to the other end; then he made sport of him for half an hour afterward. Colonel Okey can engage with impunity in such cruel horseplay, verifying the old proverb, *"One man may better steale a horse, then another man may look over the hedge."* Okey also engages in absurd pillow fights with his brother officers. Sometimes he is very merry; at other times he is in such a state of mind that his officers do not dare to speak to him. "And truly for my part," concludes Freeman, "I have not had a good word from him, in eight moneths together."[7]

At Alnwick, in the campaign against Scotland, Freeman was finally forced out of his command. At Lancaster he had written a letter to Okey (a letter which he reprints in the pamphlet), hoping to assuage his hostility. But Okey did not answer the letter; and reaching Alnwick before Freeman, according to Freeman's account, he had prevailed upon Cromwell to approve his dismissal of Freeman without an appeal to the Council of War. Hastening to headquarters, Freeman spoke with secretary William Clarke, who assured him his letter to Okey had been received and that a hearing before a Council of War was likely. But at that moment Okey appeared and began to berate him for a "base and scurrilous" letter. Freeman asked for a reading of the letter. When Clarke began to read the letter aloud, Okey interrupted with more threats against Freeman, but finally allowed Clarke to finish his reading. Admitted shortly to Cromwell's presence, Freeman was presenting his case when Okey and other officers came into the room, Okey again attacking him during Cromwell's questioning, and one officer saying, "Oh was there ever any officer in the Army, that ever gave such language to their Colonel?" Cromwell asked Freeman if he had engaged to lay down his commission; he also asked if Freeman had sung bawdy songs. He concluded that for the present he thought it best to part Okey and Freeman; but by the end of the conversation, during which another colonel had interrupted to admonish Freeman for his disrespectful language to Okey, Freeman knew that Cromwell's decision was to remove him from his command

[6] *Ibid.*, p. 19. [7] *Ibid.*, p. 20.

without an immediate Council of War. "I saw their resolutions, and that it was but a folly for me to presse him any farther," wrote Freeman. "I told him, though *I* were subject to many aspersions, and that I should ly under a cloud for a time . . . I should submit to his pleasure, and so took my leave of the Generall." [8] Freeman's account of this scene, whatever the exaggerations of his wrongs, carries a general authenticity not to be denied: the harassed general in the midst of a campaign, in desperate need of harmony among his officers, the colonel's recommendation already made and approved, the uneasy captain in the midst of colonels, Cromwell reluctant to do injustice but in an emergency deferring to the men he knew best—all this rings true between the lines of Freeman's narrative.

Though Freeman still hoped for a trial by Council of War, as he understood Cromwell's statement to promise, there is no record that he was given such a hearing or ever re-entered the Puritan army. His next action was to expose Okey in print, which action the colonel had anticipated in his accusations before Cromwell. The closing pages of the pamphlet reveal in startling outline Freeman's historical outlook, owing much to Lilburne's pamphlets, with an emphasis on economic wrongs almost as extreme as those of Winstanley. Freeman addresses himself to rulers; the "Lord sometimes stirres up poor weak and despised instruments," he wrote, "to give councel and advice to Princes and great wise men of the World." [9] With striking variations, Freeman's analysis of early English history follows the simplifications set forth by Parker, Lilburne, Jones, and Milton. The English have been held in bondage ever since the Norman Conquest, when William the Norman changed the course of English history by distributing the land among his favorites and making them lords of the manors. The poor people, asserts Freeman, became their tenants, required to pay "a small rent at first: to bring them under the yoak . . . and hence came in that which we call propriety, as derived from the *Norman* Conquest." [10] But this action was only the beginning of centralized economic power. The wealthy lords gave their sons and daughters in marriage to each other, joining "house to house, and land to land, and so became greater Lords then ever . . . And so the poor people comes to be meer slaves to their Lords and Masters (their rents being continually raised and set upon the rack . . .) not able to maintain themselves and families." These evils, after hundreds of years of tyranny, are still living realities. The distribution of income, asserts Freeman, is appallingly unequal; many great lords "have ten, fifteen, twenty thousand pounds *per annum,* which is more then two hundred thousand

[8] *Ibid.,* pp. 23, 24. [9] *Ibid.,* p. 31. [10] *Ibid.,* p. 55.

families have: and yet they can spend all in rioteousnesse, and wantonnesse, and in superfluity of dainties." Freeman was appalled at the sight of the disinherited poor he had seen in the North, "bare-footed and bare-legged, and scarce a ragge of clothes, to cover their nakednesse, or having any bread . . . to put into their bellies." Ask these poor people where they lived, on whose land, "they would tell us, that it was either the Earl of *Northumberland,* or the Lord *Gray."* [11] Thus the laws upholding the Norman conquest are as biting and oppressive as they were centuries ago. Abolish these laws, admonishes Freeman; make new and equitable ones. Erect hundred courts again; determine all causes by twelve sworn men of the neighborhood; and take away the intolerable tithes.

The apology of Captain Freeman throws into bold relief the contradictory assumptions that agitated the minds of Cromwell's army. The Protestant method of individualistic Bible reading, nowhere more violent than in this agitated island of fierce warriors, drove men from one extreme position to another, as shown in the sharp transitions of Freeman's own religious experience. Moreover, what was heresy to Okey the Independent was the foundation of faith to Freeman the Seeker, who possibly could have found no other Seeker with views precisely like his own. As Okey ridiculed Freeman, so Freeman ridiculed his subordinates for their strange beliefs. If all men are the same to you, Cornet Friend asked Freeman, why do you wear your sword?

"To maintain our just rights and priviledges . . ." answered Freeman, *"& to relieve the oppressed,* & not intentively to kill any man." Why did Friend keep his sword?

"To kill the Caveliers," answered Friend.

"Then . . . *you are a man of blood, you kill all the day long,* and I had as live keep a drunkard company, as keep you company," answered Freeman.[12]

The strong sense of reverence Freeman felt for his own beliefs and the worth of a personality tested on the battlefield was constantly violated by the urgent necessities of military discipline, in which every officer must perforce in exigent moments play the part of an absolute monarch. The traditions of feudal gradation in former centuries had imposed their patterns in the chain of army command; but now, for the first time in the annals of English warfare, rank was roughly proportionate to leadership and fighting skill: Harrison was the son of a butcher; Okey had been a drayman, stoker in a brew house, and chandler before entering the Parliamentary army. But the lowly born, once elevated to officer status,

[11] *Ibid.,* pp. 55, 56. [12] *Ibid.,* p. 8.

took easily to the perquisites of rank. Freeman himself cashiered men for drunkenness, reproved his troopers for their vices, and most revealingly of all, called Roger Daniel his *Buckingham.*

In a mind such as Freeman's may be traced that explosive power generated in thousands of minds by Biblical principles justified by victorious arms. He experienced the rage of men who feel their cause is just but whose language and rhetoric are crude and inarticulate. He wrote bitterly of his suppression by Okey: "To have my spirits bound up, and tyed fast to the wils of men, and to be in bondage and slavery, through the beggerly rudiments of the world, by the doctrines and traditions of men, and all by an arbitrary power exercised over us . . . I shall rather chuse to traile a pike under the great Turke, then to have any command under Colonel *Okey.*" [13] Relieved of his command, Freeman wrote his pamphlet and vanished without further apologies. But in the wavering between authority and self-expansion described in his pages, between orderly gradation imposed by society and the chaos of a rank justified by arms and Biblical promise, we may trace one of the most relentless dilemmas of the Puritan Revolution.

2. AN AGE OF WONDERS

September, 1650

On September 20 appeared *A Most Faithful Relation of Two Wonderful Passages,* asserting that "since the deplorable Fall of our first Parents . . . the ill spirit was never so busie, he never made such a harvest . . . as he hath had lately in this Island." The author then relates the story of a minister, Dr. Pordich of Bradfield,[1] who began to preach as usual on Sunday, September 8, but after speaking fifteen minutes fell down in a trance. The minister then rose up and ran out of the church, "bellowing like a Bull, saying that he was called, and must be gon." Arriving at his house, the minister found his wife as distracted as himself, dressed in white lawn and holding a white rod in her hand. Shortly afterward, a Mrs. Chevill rushed in, fell on her knees before Mrs. Pordich, and addressed her as a prophetess. When another neighbor woman appeared, similarly demented, the women "fell all to dancing the Hays." [2]

[13] *Ibid.,* p. 29.

[1] E613(3), p. 1. Christopher Hill has pointed out that Dr. Pordich is evidently John Pordage (1607–1681), associate of Theaurau John, John Robins, and William Everard. See *DNB* and Christopher Hill's *Puritanism and Revolution* (London: Secker and Warburg, 1958), pp. 316–17.

[2] *Ibid.,* p. 2.

A calm spectator of this hysteria, continues the pamphleteer, was Mr. William Foster, son of Sir Humphrey Foster; but William Foster could elicit from neither the minister nor the women any rational explanation for their strange behavior. Dr. Pordich said they were rejoicing because they had overpowered Satan. But only the previous Sunday, September 1, an event had occurred in church that presaged strange happenings in the congregation. A boy of thirteen, son of a potash maker named Snelling, had fallen "into a very strange Fit, foaming at the mouth for the space of two hours." When the youth finally spoke, he said he was to go to London with his father to find an old man known to be possessed by devils and to have in him the "Root of Corruption." The Snellings went to London and found the old man, who upon seeing them emerged from his trance and directed them to Hampshire, near Beacon Hill, where they would find a crooked stick; this stick boy and father found with miraculous quickness. The boy found that he could now write for the first time in his life. Father and son heard strange voices in the air. They "saw the King with his head off, and then again . . . with his head on, and a Crown upon it." All the large Snelling family, insists the narrator, were "in a very strange frantick condition."[3] When the father's fits were over, he was as rational as any man, asserting he would give anything to be rid of his strange delusions.

On May 27 had appeared *Pseudochristus,* a tract revealing the manias to which unfettered reading of the Bible under the new Commonwealth, especially among the poorer believers, gave rise and sanction. William Franklin, a London ropemaker by trade, diligent and steady in his duties, was about forty years old when he first began to have delusions about his identity with Christ. He was married and the father of three children. Testimony gathered by the pamphleteer agreed that he had been "an eminent Saint . . . a choyce Professor of godliness," though his physcian testified that as early as 1646 he had been distracted by the conviction that God had deserted him; the physician had bled him for his distemper.[4] In this distemper Franklin for the first time announced his identity with Christ, pretending to have visions and revelations. About the same time he began to abuse his wife and keep company with other women, for which latter deviation he was finally excluded from the congregation. Among the women known to Franklin was Mary Gadbury, thirty years of age, separated from her husband, a woman who made her living by selling laces, pins, and bandstrings to gentlewomen; of honest repute but accused by some of "vicious, lewd, light behaviour," even to the extent of keeping a "naughty house."[5] Like Franklin she also had

[3] *Ibid.,* pp. 4, 5. [4] *Pseudochristus* (May 27, 1650), E602(12), p. 6.
[5] *Ibid.,* p. 8.

visions; according to her own confession, after meeting Franklin for the first time, she woke from her first sleep "full of joy and singing," later having convulsions that "would set her whole body in a trembling." A voice said to her, *"It is the Lord."* After some exchange of greetings with the strange visitor, the voice said, *"I will send my Son in person of a man, who shall rule over the Nations."* When Mary Gadbury told Franklin of her vision, he said, *"I am the man."* Franklin acknowledged to Mary that he had a wife and children, but asserted that he had now a new body; his original body, "conceived in sin and brought forth in iniquity, the Lord had destroyed." Further, God had commanded him to separate from his wife, with whom he had had no marital congress for three years. The foolish Mary, continues the pamphleteer, believed his story; she also believed his assertion that she was "set apart for him." [6]

After it was known that Mary had allowed Franklin to stay in her house, she was finally brought before the Lord Mayor, to whom she declared that she "had no husband but the Lord of Hosts," but she was nevertheless committed to the Counter until she could be released on bail. She went over the countryside with Franklin, asserting that he was Christ, she his spouse; the couple attached to themselves fifteen or twenty followers in Southamptonshire. The rumors spread: Was this man really the Christ? Who could be certain he was not? Mary declared that the second coming was at hand, used many words of self-praise, says the narrator, "as if she were the Bride, the Lambs wife, yea, and did take it no robbery to be equall to God . . . the greatest Authorities . . . was her owne visions and revelations." [7] Finally, in January, 1650, the justices of Southampton county acted to bring the distemper under control. Warrants were issued for William Franklin, Mary Gadbury, and a number of their followers. Witnesses made affidavits against the holy couple. When Franklin was persuaded to sign a recantation of his blasphemies, Mary Gadbury for the first time expressed disillusionment in him (*"Hast thou done this? is this thy hand?"*), that she would have "layd down her life for the truth of what she had declared concerning him." Edward Spradbury, one of the faithful, lifted his fist as though to strike Franklin, exclaiming, *"Thou Villain, how hast thou deceived us by thy lyes?"* [8] Franklin and Gadbury were both committed to Bridewell, where many people came to see them. Some of Franklin's followers were also arrested and jailed, but released with Mary, upon providing security for their good behavior. But Franklin, unable to provide security, still lay in prison in May, 1650, when *Pseudochristus* appeared. The pamphleteer could not close his work without the usual warning

[6] *Ibid.*, pp. 9, 10, 11, 12. [7] *Ibid.*, p. 19. [8] *Ibid.*, p. 43.

against heresy and blasphemy delivered in *"Scripture-phrase, language, and expression.* The *Devil* thus transforming *himself into an Angel of light,* thereby the better to deceive them."[9]

In this spectrum of Protestant aberrations of Milton's time, those of William Franklin and Francis Freeman stand at remote poles from each other. It is plain that Franklin was first seduced by his own persuasiveness and then by sexual need of an adoring disciple. Freeman, on the other hand, represents a logical extension of the Protestant intellectual method, the free roaming mind imbued with the heresy that each searcher's conclusion may be as valid as that of any other. For the authority of the church the Protestant substituted the authority of the Bible. To the Presbyterian the authority of the minister in interpreting the Bible was one above which he dared not place his own. Not so the Independent: He felt free to differ from his minister in interpreting the Bible by the authority of his own unaided reason. The next step in the dynamics of Protestant search inevitably followed: to substitute the authority of one's own conscience, as the Quakers were now doing in their appeal to the inner light, for the authority of Scripture. In the sharp transition from one extreme position to another, Freeman had now assumed a dependence on his own God-endowed reason that superseded the authority of the Bible itself.

Had Milton known the workings of Freeman's mind, he would have been contemptuous of his intellectual premises, especially of his recurring rejections of Biblical authority. Unlike the Quakers and the Seekers, Milton recognized no persistent inner voice; he quoted Scripture for all his fundamental intellectual positions, including two of the most heretical of his day, a belief in unitarianism and a belief in polygamy. In *Areopagitica* he had spoken for a national open mind to all new ideas, whether derived from Scripture or supported like his own by a vast secular knowledge. Milton had never known in himself or his friends the untutored religious search of such humble aspirants as Freeman. However delusionary in its effects, this kind of reasoning enlarged the average man's sense of his own worth, both as a thinker and a participant in the tumultuous agitation of his time. In the army to which Freeman belonged, the psychology of such groping and striving was intensified and extended many times by the triumphant march of the Commonwealth's armies and the electric thrust and rhetoric of campfire dialectic.

[9] *Ibid.,* p. 56.

CHAPTER X

MILTON AMONG HIS CONTEMPORARIES

January, 1651

IN January, 1651, Milton was living in Whitehall in the end nearest Scotland Yard, with his wife and two daughters; Mary was pregnant with John, whose birth was two months away. Milton rose each day at dawn. On free mornings one of his friends or former students came in to read to him. At seven he often made his way, no doubt with the aid of a friend or one of his daughters, to the chambers of the Council of State, a few minutes' walk away. After meeting with the Council of State, and doing the work assigned him, Milton often had to spend precious hours in business affairs, nagging problems at this time of the Powell estate. Meanwhile, enveloping darkness descended. Month by month his sight had been growing dimmer. Blindness in his left eye was now complete. But for a tiny shaft of light that occasionally pierced his right eye, as through a chink, he had to grope his way with his hands from chair to chair and door to door. Light dimmed; darkness loomed. At no time in his life had Milton felt a deeper need to serve his country than in 1650 and 1651, years of diminishing light. Finally, by February, 1652, his darkness would be complete. Meanwhile, what of the fresh hours for his art, for the fulfillment of his lofty architecture of aspiration, to write a great play like those of Sophocles, a dialogue like the book of Job, an epic like that of Homer? The leisure, the calm of expectant concentration, in which great poetry is born, he had foregone for service to the new republic. Though his political passions pierced him deep, he had not forsaken his vision of an immortality of fame. The new republic, the utopia of his dreams, might soon emerge. Time then for that noble work, "something so written to aftertimes, as they should not willingly let it die."

Meanwhile, what was happening to Milton's gifted contemporaries at home and abroad? His great antagonist Joseph Hall, seventy-seven years old, in retirement at Norwich, was bewailing the calamities befallen his England: "*Wo is me, too too long banished from the Christian world, with such animosity, as if it* [*peace*] *were the worst of enemies. . . . How is the earth every where drenched with humane bloud? poured out, not by the hands of cruell Infidels, but of brethren. . . . Who sees not what Spirits of Errour are gone forth into the world, for the seducing of simple, and ungrounded souls . . . . one despises the dead letter of the Scriptures, another distorts it to his own erroneous sense."* [1] But John Bunyan, twenty-two years old, was writing his autobiography, *Grace Abounding to the Chief of Sinners,* preparing to enter the church of "holy Mr. Gifford" at Bedford. At a remote pole, this Bunyan, from Hall's Elizabethan world of fixed order and gradation, each man in his place: the lord, the bishop, the knight, the solicitor, the apprentice, the tinker, the chimney sweep. In 1651 the worth of a man, alas, was no longer fixed and measurable; and Hall was ending his days in a warring world of brother against brother, friend against trusted friend, knight against knight. Of all his contemporaries, Hall was perhaps least able to measure the explosion of religious energy in a mind like that of Bunyan. As Scriptural fervor expanded hope and courage and sense of worth in minds like those of Harrison and Cromwell, so it released in Bunyan a flow of eloquent imagery such as Milton himself would have been proud to create. But the interior world of John Bunyan would have been almost as strange to Milton as to Joseph Hall. The roots of the intellectual Milton, like those of Hall, reached simultaneously to Athens and Jerusalem. Bunyan's preoccupation with a sense of sin, with assurance, now of his soul lost, and now of Christ's arms again around him, was foreign to Milton's temperament. To Bunyan, Christ was the embodiment of surpassing love; to Milton Christ represented in greater degree the rationality of righteousness than the forgiving grace of a compassionate redeemer.

1. JOHN DONNE: BEAMS OF ONE SUN

On February 9, 1651, appeared *Letters to Severall Persons of Honour,* by John Donne, dead now these twenty years. In these letters alone one may trace the gap between the soul in reverent suspension over the theological and political dilemmas of his day, and the soul committed, like Milton, to violent revolution in both religion and politics. "I never fettered nor imprisoned the word Religion," wrote Donne, ". . . nor immuring it in a *Rome,* or a *Wittenberg,* or a *Geneva;* they are all virtuall beams of one Sun, and wheresoever they finde clay hearts, they harden them, and moulder them into dust . . . They are not so contrary as the North and South Poles; and . . . they are connaturall pieces of one

[1] "Epistle," *The Great Mysterie of Godliness* (November 14, 1651), E1277, sigs. *3v–*4, [*12v].

circle."[1] By Milton's time men's souls were fettered each to his sect; and this sect had a political concomitant and economic vision of life as well. Long ago, certainly before writing "Lycidas," Milton had repudiated the beauty of the Anglican service as well as its theology. His hatred of the bishops was more persuasive than his youthful love for the poetry of the Anglican ritual. Driven from Anglicanism to Presbyterianism and finally to Independency by the dynamic clash and comparison of ideas, he had rejected kingship for republicanism, a transition impossible in the relatively stable times of Elizabeth and James I. One cannot imagine a Cromwell or a Milton in Elizabeth's day, setting his foot on the neck of a king; or a Winstanley thrust up from the boiling cauldron of agitation for reform. Nor is it possible to imagine a John Donne, a Walter Raleigh, or a Shakespeare giving over two decades of his life, as would Milton, to a violent revolution. To place Donne and Milton together is to visualize the stability of a Catholic or Anglican society, based upon the traditional and accepted security of gradation, and the instability of a society in which the whole literate population was engaged in interpreting, for the first time since the Reformation, the application of Biblical truths to political and economic dilemmas.

2. NEW AND EXPERIMENTAL PHILOSOPHY

In 1651 the weekly meetings of scholars from which the Royal Society was to grow had persisted in London and Oxford for six years. They had begun about 1645, wrote Wallis afterward, at the suggestion of Theodore Haak (friend of Hartlib and Comenius), for the purpose of discussing "new and experimental philosophy," excluding from the first political and theological topics. Among the original group were Dr. John Wilkins, Dr. Wallis; the physicians Dr. Jonathan Goddard, Dr. George Ent, Dr. Francis Glisson, Dr. Christopher Merret; Mr. Samuel Foster, professor of astronomy at Gresham College; "and many others." At times the meetings were held at Dr. Goddard's house on Wood Street; at other times at Gresham College or nearby. Among other topics they discussed circulation of the blood, valves in the veins, the nature of comets, spots on the sun, the improvement of telescopes, the weight of air, acceleration in the fall of heavy bodies.[1] In his letters of 1646 and 1647, when Boyle

[1] *Letters to Severall Persons of Honour* (February 9, 1651), E622(17), p. 29. See, however, instances of Donne's Anglican intolerance as cited from his sermons by Douglas Bush in *Literature of the Earlier Seventeenth Century* (1962), pp. 324–25.

[1] "Dr. Wallis's Account of Some Passages of His Own Life," in Thomas Hearne, *Works* (4 vols., London, 1810), III, clxi–clxiv. For Haak's part in these early meetings, see Pamela R. Barnett, *Theodore Haak, F.R.S.* (Mouton & Co., The Hague, 1962), pp. 76–77.

(then only nineteen) mentions "our *Invisible College*" and "the Philosophical College," he may have referred to the meetings of this small group.[2] In 1648–51, three leading members were called to Oxford, Wilkins as warden of Wadham College, and Wallis as Savilian professor of geometry, and Goddard as warden of Merton College. The meetings at London continued as before, the Oxford members joining them when possible. At Oxford, however, the members had separate meetings of their own and "brought those Studies into fashion there," joined by Dr. Ralph Bathurst and Dr. William Petty. Upon Petty's appointment to Ireland in September, 1652, the group met at Dr. Wilkins' quarters at Wadham College, until his removal to Trinity College, Cambridge, in 1659. After 1659 the group met at the home of Robert Boyle, who had returned from Ireland to Oxford in June, 1654.[3] Meanwhile, however, the group in London continued their Wednesday meetings, usually at Gresham College, with Boyle and Christopher Wren often in attendance.

3. HARVEY AND THE ESSENCE OF PROOF

In January, 1651, Dr. William Harvey, seventy-three years old, was living again in London. In 1642 Harvey had withdrawn with Charles I to Oxford and had been present at the battle of Edgehill. Harvey had lectured on circulation of the blood as early as 1616.[1] His master work, *Exercitatio Anatomica de Motu Cordis et Sanguinis,* had been published in Frankfurt in 1628.[2] Harvey reported his findings in a style intensely visual and figurative: "In the hearts of all creatures," he wrote, "being dissected whilst they are yet alive, opening the breast, and cutting up the capsule, which immediately environeth the heart, you may observe that the heart moves sometimes, sometimes rests. . . . The heart being grasp'd in one's hand whilst it is in motion, feels harder . . . like as if

[2] Thomas Birch, "Life of the Honourable Robert Boyle," in Boyle, *Works,* ed. Birch (5 vols., London, 1744), I, 17 ff. Birch quotes at some length from Boyle's correspondence with Hartlib (pp. 22, 24, 27, 28), who was his "intimate friend"; he also quotes a letter from Boyle to John Dury (p. 23). See also Louis T. More, *Life and Works of the Honorable Robert Boyle* (London: Oxford University Press, 1944). On the debate about the "Invisible College" and the Comenian group, see Douglas Bush, *English Literature of the Earlier Seventeenth Century* (1962), p. 510.

[3] "Dr. Wallis's Account"; Thomas Birch, *The History of the Royal Society of London* (4 vols., London, 1756), I, 2–3.

[1] See Harvey's lecture notes in his own hand, *De Anatomica,* preserved in a bound manuscript of ninety-seven small leaves in the British Museum, Sloan Ms. SL230.

[2] British Museum C.54.b.8(1). *De Motu* next appeared in Rotterdam in 1648. See British Museum 234.a.52(1).

one taking hold of the tendons of one's arm by the Elbow whilst they are moving the fingers, shall feel them bent and more resisting." [3] In 1649 Harvey had replied to Riolanus in *Exercitatio Anatomica de Circulatione Sanguinis ad Joannem Riolanum filium Parisiensem.*[4] In December, 1650, Dr. George Ent visited Harvey and brought away the manuscript of another seminal work, *Exercitationes de Generatione Animalium,* published in London and Amsterdam in 1651.[5] To a greater degree than Sir Thomas Browne (and most physicians of his day), Harvey possessed a genius for distinguishing between proof of the senses and proof from tradition and authority. In 1634 he had supervised the examination of four Lancashire women accused of witchcraft. Ten midwives and seven surgeons assisting Harvey examined the women and reported "nothing unnatural in their bodies." [6] Harvey expected to learn from every man, whatever his station in the world's eyes. "He did delight to be in the darke," wrote Aubrey, "and told me he could then best contemplate." [7]

Within twenty or thirty years, as Hobbes points out in *De Corpore,* Harvey's theory of circulation of the blood was accepted in all the great universities of Europe.[8] Yet the average man without learning, says Aubrey, would not trust Harvey the physician after his strange theory became part of the talk of the town; people considered him *crack-brained.* In his investigations Harvey had fulfilled the Baconian ideal of trusting only to prolonged verification of truth by the senses only, holding in suspense all predilections of intellectual custom. He had a rare genius for taking hints from his great predecessors in the field of anatomy without becoming a slave to either their discipline or their conclusions. In his psychology of research he looked at man with the fresh eyes of a Greek rather than with the Christian training of his age. His reliance on sensory proof only in the pursuit of true knowledge was revolutionary. The tempestuous whirlwind of the Reformation touched him not. No man of the seventeenth century was more remote from Milton's outlook than William Harvey. One cannot imagine Harvey passing by Bacon's great work, *Novum Organum,* when it appeared in 1620. But there is no hint in all of Milton's work, much as he admired Bacon, that he read *Novum Organum.* Had he absorbed even the aphorisms of Part II, his capacious mind could not have remained unaware of the explosive power loosed into the world by Bacon's scientific creed. Milton trusted con-

[3] *De Motu Cordis,* in *The Anatomical Exercises of Dr. William Harvey,* ed. Geoffrey Keynes, reprinted from first English edition of 1653 (London, 1928), pp. 19–20.

[4] British Museum C.31.C.46. [5] London edition, British Museum 461.c1

[6] *DNB.*

[7] Aubrey, *Brief Lives,* ed. Clark (2 vols., Oxford, 1898), I, 298.

[8] *Ibid.,* I, 300–301.

sistently in moral, religious, aesthetic, and political values: not scientific ones.

4. REMBRANDT: MYSTERY IN LIGHT AND SHADOW

In 1651 Rembrandt, forty-three years old, was living in Jode-Breestraat, Amsterdam. Saskia had died June 5, 1642. Titus was now eight years old, a handsome lad, fair hair curling round an oval face, brown eyes wide with innocence.[1] Hendrickje Stoffels was Rembrandt's housekeeper, model, mistress, and stepmother to Titus. No deep joy or profound sadness could stay the hand of the painter. A creative frenzy possessed him almost daily, sick or well, debt-ridden or prosperous, meditative or joyous. He painted the people he knew best, people who could sit for him daily: Hendrickje, Titus, his brother, himself. In the portrait of himself with a cap over a red net, he looks out with quizzical, sad eyes, brown and tired. The emblems of finery he has donned, a dark doublet with green sleeves, a yellow neckcloth, a gold-embroidered shirt, only accentuate the wrinkled forehead, slanting line on his right cheek, the drooping of his lip corners under the mustache. From the left a shaft of light falls on the forehead, the strong, jutting nose, the embroidered shirt. But the deepest meaning, as always with Rembrandt, lurks in the shadows, veiled in the mystery the viewer must unravel for himself.[2]

In 1651 Milton's poetic genius had not yet flowered, whereas the artistry of his great contemporary already represented the most original resources of his vision. Rembrandt wanted his art to pierce the onlooker's psyche with one electric flash. Milton wanted his reader's mind to absorb bit by bit the philosophical architecture of his great epic, meanwhile opening his eye and ear to its manifold poetic riches. Rembrandt's greatness lay in painting mysteries he could not himself give voice to; he painted with intentions that eluded the speech of theory, perhaps even the speech of thought. But Milton's art, deep as it pierced, and whatever unfinished thoughts rose up here and there in his verse, was always articulate and clear to those who unravelled the whole with years of patience and meditation. Milton trusts repeatedly to images of light and dark, with few images of color. In this he is more like Rembrandt than Shakespeare or Homer or Keats.

Like Rembrandt, Milton was fascinated from early youth by Biblical subjects. As Milton drew a portrait of Jesus in *Paradise Lost* and *Paradise Regained,* so Rembrandt executed dozens of paintings and drawings

[1] *The Paintings of Rembrandt,* ed. Abraham Bredius (London, 1937), No. 119.

[2] See *The Complete Work of Rembrandt,* ed. Wilhelm Bode and C. Hofstede de Groot (8 vols., Paris, 1897–1906), V, 346; Bredius, No. 39.

picturing Jesus. Their characterizations, however, are utterly dissimilar. In *Paradise Regained* Jesus is the embodiment of rationality and justice, not compassion.[3] But in the main Rembrandt's paintings and drawings of Jesus embody attitudes of love and forgiveness for erring man, as in "The Hundred Guilder Print," "La Petite Tombe," and "The Woman Taken in Adultery," even "The Raising of the Cross." But in his various portraits of Jesus alone (seven from one model) Rembrandt was never able to suggest the depth of characterization he achieved in visualization of attitudes among groups of figures. Of these seven portraits of the same model, the large canvas in the Metropolitan (Bredius, 626) and the smaller canvas in the Kaiser Friedrich Museum (Bredius, 622) are the most expressive of what one might call the Christ image that repeats itself in Rembrandt's characterizations.[4] Yet even this one we feel did not satisfy Rembrandt; the range and intensity of sorrow seen in faces of older Jews Rembrandt painted is somehow not fully visualized in the young Christ. In the Metropolitan painting the head of the young Christ is slightly inclined to the left, facing the light. Thick black hair, parted in the middle, curls back from a low forehead and falls over his shoulders. The smooth freshness of his upper cheeks is framed by a beard; a mustache and chin tuft circle his mouth. The subdued illumination in the large gray eyes suggests at once an incandescent intelligence and a comprehension of all depths of evil and suffering into which he follows man. The eyelids droop in weariness, not despair; even the lips express acceptance of utmost dark and brightest light in erring man. Even though this portrait may not have satisfied Rembrandt's vision of the Christ, one feels that it expressed the torment of the artist's awareness of tragedy in the life about him as well as the life of the crucified Jew. Every man's portrait of another man is his own portrait too, even as Milton painted himself in his characterization of Jesus in *Paradise Regained*. Resistance

[3] Milton's characterization of Christ in his early poems and in *Paradise Lost* stresses compassion and forgiveness. But this is not Milton's emphasis in his portrayal of Christ in *Paradise Regained,* the only portrayal dealing with the Son's life on earth. For important studies of *Paradise Regained* see E. M. Pope, *Paradise Regained: The Tradition and the Poem* (Baltimore: Johns Hopkins University Press, 1947); Arnold Stein, *Heroic Knowledge* (Minneapolis: University of Minnesota Press, 1957). Of the shorter studies, see especially A. S. P. Woodhouse, "Theme and Pattern in *Paradise Regained,*" *University of Toronto Quarterly,* XXV, 1956, pp. 167–82; Wolfe, "Milton's Christ in *Paradise Regained,*" *Sewanee Review,* Vol. LI, No. 4 (autumn, 1943), pp. 466–75. Other important studies are listed in Douglas Bush, *English Literature of the Earlier Seventeenth Century* (1962), p. 620.

[4] Bredius, Nos. 626 and 622. A striking exception (Bredius No. 532) in Rembrandt's portrayal is the scene in which Christ drives the money changers out of the temple. The face is harsh, cruel, biting; there is no trace of righteousness or even dignity in the countenance.

to temptation, however, and the essence of rationality in judging others, as in Milton's portrait, had no place in Rembrandt's conception of Jesus; nor did it have a place in his own life. No two great artists could have had more diverse conception of the man Jesus than Rembrandt and Milton.

In 1650 and 1651 Rembrandt painted portraits of a number of elderly Jews. The words "Portrait of a Jew" and "Portrait of a Rabbi" appear more frequently in Rembrandt's works than in those of any other artist. Why Rembrandt chose so many such men as models no one has explained. Amsterdam had a much larger Jewish community than London or any other capital in Europe. Rembrandt lived in a neighborhood in which dwelled many Jews, descendants of refugees from Spain and Portugal. Preoccupied as he was with Biblical subjects, did Rembrandt consciously choose as models men and women of Hebraic ancestry? Or did he choose Jews because in their faces he found a deeper quintessence of sorrow and despair than in any other countenances of his age? Only in his portraits of younger Jews are the faces unlined with sorrow and the eyes without deeps of sadness. In one portrait of a younger Jew (Bredius, 246), the eyes are shadowed under a velvet hat, the black beard neat and trimmed, the lips tranquil.[5] In 1650 Rembrandt painted a portrait (Bredius, No. 258) of an elderly Jew in a gray cap, the light falling full on his wrinkled forehead, his right cheek, his black beard spotted with white patches. The brown eyes have the look of a life rooted in centuries of sorrow; a sturdy man, still wanting to live, sustained by the great sayings of his tradition, but a man without laughter: The world is too sad.[6]

Chapter XI

1651: THE MARCH OF EVENTS

In the year 1651 the armies of the Commonwealth completed their conquest of Ireland and Scotland and shattered the enemy at Worcester, where more than half the Scottish nobility were killed, wounded, or taken prisoner. Charles II escaped and fled to France, not to return until the Restoration. But in early 1651 Charles' hopes had soared high. On January 1 he had been crowned king at Scone. Within six months after landing in Scotland on June 23, 1650, he had succeeded in uniting behind him a large proportion of both royalists and Presbyterians. Even the crushing defeat at Dunbar on September 3 did not destroy Scottish resistance. The English enemy the Scots still held in the south of Scotland. Leslie was a skillful and formidable general, un-

[5] Bredius, No. 246.

[6] *Ibid.,* No. 258.

beatable in his mountain fastnesses. A new invasion of England, as in 1648, in which royalists there would flock to the king's banner, was Charles' great hope and a dire threat to the new republic.

Cromwell realized that the Scottish resistance must be totally annihilated before the Commonwealth would be safe and he be free to turn his mind to civil reforms. In the spring of 1651 sickness and death among his troops, and Cromwell's own illness of intermittent fever, delayed a new offensive against the Scots. Now fifty-two years old, Cromwell had spent much of the past nine years in camp or field. The flow of his energies, supported by his religious zeal, had been phenomenal. But the day after Dunbar he had written to his wife, "I have been in my inward man marvellously supported; though I assure thee, I grow an old man, and feel infirmities of age marvellously stealing upon me."[1] The Council of State, in alarm, sent him two doctors; gradually he recovered and was able to take the field again. At Dunbar he had defeated an enemy of twenty-two thousand with eleven thousand men; he needed and received reinforcements. Even so, he was not sure he could defeat Leslie decisively in Scotland. In a change of strategy (described below, page 146), Cromwell allowed the Scots to march into England, confident that the English would not now rally in great numbers to Charles' banner. The result was overwhelmingly successful. Charles and his armies were annihilated at Worcester on September 3 (see below, pp. 150–51). The enemy was now broken, the Commonwealth triumphant. The tasks of peace awaited Cromwell and his officers, less disposed now than at Pride's Purge to brook further delay in those civil reforms to which their victories on the field had entitled them. But the Long Parliament was determined as never before to cling to its power. Not until November 18, two months after Worcester, did the Rump vote to dissolve itself in favor of a new representative; even then indeed it set a time for its dissolution three years hence, November 3, 1654.[2] To Cromwell and his men such an action seemed an affront to the republic, a repudiation of the civil hopes for which they had risked their lives on the battlefield.

Meanwhile the House of Commons (denominated "the Parliament" since the abolition of the Lords on March 19, 1649) had vigorously pushed forth legislation in support of the new republic and its armies in the field. On February 13 it had approved an act setting up a new Council of State, to serve until December 1 of the current year. Any nine of the forty members appointed might sit as the official body, which as in preceding Councils had very broad powers indeed: to suppress plots for the restoration of kingship; to direct and arm the militia; to reduce any

[1] *Letters and Speeches,* ed. Sophie C. Lomas, 3 vols. (London, 1904), II, 114.
[2] Gardiner, *Commonwealth and Protectorate,* II, 72.

parts of the Commonwealth not submissive to its dominion; to build ships; to carry on correspondence with foreign countries; to send out messengers and spies; to prohibit dangerous meetings and imprison men without due process; to charge the public revenue with sums of money necessary for carrying on foreign affairs; to prevent abuses of free quarter by recruits on the march for service in Ireland and Scotland.[3] In the Council were concentrated, then, broader powers than the king had possessed in foreign and domestic affairs, both military and civil. On February 13 the Parliament extended for another year their establishment of the powers of the Lord Admiral of England and the Lord Warden of the Cinque Ports in the Council of State.[4] Thus the Commons had delegated to its Council a massive burden of daily responsibility. The Council members who also sat in Parliament were often called upon to give forth a double toll of time and energy. Work in the Commons was more spasmodic and leisurely than that of the Council, where daily decisions required unremitting vigilance.

In the midst of war and internal danger to the new republic, the work of reform marched but slowly. The need for new revenue for the armed forces overshadowed all other considerations, yielding only now and then to a deep concern for the plight of the hungry and imprisoned that Cromwell had written about after Dunbar. "Relieve the oppressed," he had written Lenthall, "hear the groans of poor prisoners in England; be pleased to reform the abuses of all professions; and if there be any one that makes many poor to make a few rich, that suits not a Commonwealth." [5] But the plight of the poor was only a whisper, the needs of war a daily bugle call. On March 28 the House laid a new impost on coal, the revenue to go to the building of ships to guard the seas, a portion of it (from October 12 to April 1) to be reserved for relief of the poor.[6] Such an impost bore more heavily upon the poorer consumers of coal, despite the aid to the destitute incorporated in the measure. On April 15, to maintain the armed forces, the House continued the assessment of 120,000 pounds monthly for the six months to come.[7] On April 18 a new law was passed for the conscription of soldiers, empowering the militia commissioners of the various counties to impress men for service in Ireland.[8] Meanwhile, on April 9, the House yielded to long agitation for legal reform, passing a law requiring all laws be translated into English.[9] The maw of war, however, never long closed, forced Parliament to dire new measures. On July 16 it passed an act "for the sale of several Lands

[3] *Acts and Ordinances of the Interregnum,* II, 500–504.
[4] *Ibid.,* II, 504.
[5] *Letters and Speeches,* ed. Lomas, II, 108.
[6] *Acts and Ordinances,* II, 505–509.
[7] *Ibid.,* II, 511–13.
[8] *Ibid.,* II, 513–14.
[9] *Ibid.,* II, 510–11.

and Estates forfeited to the Commonwealth for Treason." [10] On the next day, July 17, the Parliament passed a similar act for the sale of goods belonging to Charles I, Henrietta, and Prince Charles. The act specified paintings, statues, jewels, silver plate, hangings, furs. In the sale of libraries the act excepted St. James, now under the direction of John Dury, not only its books, but also its medals, globes, mathematical instruments.[11] The vast collections of the paintings owned by Charles I had already been dispersed.[12] In the midst of such actions to increase the flow of revenue, Parliament passed an act on August 8 prohibiting any person from accepting more than six per cent interest on money loaned.[13]

In the late months of 1651, the great issue facing the nation was the calling of a new Parliament. Cromwell and his officers stood for dissolution. In the wave of patriotism following the victory at Worcester, might not the country return a new representative favorable to the actions and philosophy of the new republic? The Parliament stood firm against such a trial. Whatever constitutional legality the new republic could claim, whatever links with the past, rested in that body of determined men. They, not the army, were the trustees of the constitutional tradition. Some of them no doubt feared dissolution because they were profiting from royalist spoils. Some feared they would not be re-elected. For the first time since Pride's Purge there was now another dread danger of military intervention in civil rule. The officers could rightfully claim indeed that the House purged by Colonel Pride was no Parliament at all. The action by the Rump to dissolve itself on November 3, 1654, was a compromise that neither the Rump nor the officers heartily believed in.

[10] *Ibid.*, II, 520–45. [11] *Ibid.*, II, 546–48.

[12] Gardiner, *Commonwealth and Protectorate,* II, 22. No adequate history of the dispersal of Charles' magnificent collection of paintings has yet been written. Among the 1,760 paintings (estimate of Hewlett) were fifty-four Titians, fifteen Tintorettos, eighteen Corregios, eight del Sartos, thirty-one Van Dycks, twenty-three Holbeins. Charles' unerring taste is revealed in a remarkably informative article by Henry G. Hewlett, "Charles I as a Picture Collector," *The Nineteenth Century,* August, 1890, pp. 201–217; and in such an analysis as Claude Phillips, *The Picture Gallery of Charles I* (London, 1896). In its disposal of Charles' art treasures during the Civil War, Parliament had acted with a capricious haste and hostility to art difficult to ascribe to leaders such as Vane, Whitelocke, and Cromwell. On July 23, 1645, when Sir Robert Harle's report on the paintings in York House was presented by the appropriate committee to the Commons, it was voted (*Commons Journals,* IV, 216) that all paintings found there that visualized the Virgin Mary, the Holy Ghost, Christ, or God himself should be burned! All others were to be sold to support the armies of the Parliament. Cromwell's direct intervention prevented the sale of a number of paintings at Hampton Court. For a brief but valuable account of the dispersal, see Francis H. Taylor, *The Taste of Angels* (Boston: Little Brown and Company, 1948), pp. 235–41.

[13] *Acts and Ordinances,* II, 548–50.

To the officers the day of dissolution seemed ages away; to the Rump it meant the end of an enlightened civil authority. They knew from their talk with Cromwell and his officers (see below, pp. 152–54) that the officers would resist any monarchy at all, even if Cromwell were named king; yet to legal minds monarchy was the only means whereby a constitutional government could again become a reality in England.

UNCERTAINTY AND THE LAW'S DELAY

January, 1651

In January, 1651, Captain Samuel Chappel, merchant and veteran of Cromwell's army, had been in prison for twelve weeks for failure to pay a debt: the cost of a suit. The amount owed was thirty-four shillings, two pence. Chappel had sold to an apothecary a debenture for 135 crowns, three shillings, four pence, for money owed him by the state. When the apothecary refused to pay, Chappel had brought a suit and lost. Unable to pay the costs of the suit, he had been thrust into prison. On November 11, 1650, he had joined with others imprisoned for debt to appeal through Colonel Pride to the Commons. The petitioners had been living in London, going into debt for bread and drink, waiting in vain for arrears to be paid. Now they have been thrust into prison, the prey of unscrupulous jailers, who charge them for food and drink much more than prisoners pay in foreign countries. Cannot the government force merchants to accept its own debentures? Can it not pass the act long promised to set free men imprisoned for debt? To suffer for not being paid is "much to the dishonour of God, and our Profession and Liberty." [1] Chappel exhorts the Commons to appoint a committee of Godly men to examine the prisons and "make good orders for the prisoners for debt, that we starve not for our good service, as some have, and others lye starving at present." [2] Does the Commonwealth not realize that its faithful veterans, "in these wavering times," may turn against Parliament for "not being paid?"

On January 30 Marchamont Needham, writing in *Mercurius Politicus*, warned the New Commonwealth that it must be vigilant to suppress the family that lost the war, which family, "if ever they return again, will own no other Interest, but that of *Tyranny* and *revenge*, against those that did expell them." [3] For this reason the new state must select men who have unequivocally accepted the Engagement and proved their irreconcilable opposition to the royal party. In the issue of February 6 Needham continued in this vein, calling for the suppression of the king's

[1] January 4, 1651, *A Diamond or Rich Jewel*, E621(6), p. 20.
[2] *Ibid.*, p. 20.
[3] E623(5), p. 567.

family and "admitting none into Places of Trust and Power, or to have a share in government, but such onely as were the prime *Ingagers*."[4] Needham is never without parallels in recent or ancient history. Remember, he warns his readers, what means Henry VIII used to wrest the church from the Pope. Did he not impose on his subjects his oath of supremacy and adjuration of the Pope's power? When the Dutch overthrew the Spaniard, did they not take an oath to renounce forever the power of King Philip and his family? So, suggests Needham, our Engagement is justified. The nation must support it with vigor and resolution. The Commonwealth can depend fully only on the men who take and support it without equivocation.

On February 4, 1651, a petition on the reform of laws was circulated in London, entitled *To the Supreme Authority, the Parliament of the Common-wealth of England.* First the petitioners congratulate the Commons on voting that the law and all its proceedings be in English. The Commons has taken cognizance of the many "tedious, chargeable, and corrupt practices in Law, as one of the greatest Grievances of the Nation." But, insist the petitioners, the burdens and grievances have increased, not diminished. Members of the Supreme Authority itself, trained as lawyers, occupy great places in the Commonwealth, receiving as much as £3000 a year; others require unreasonable fees "in every court." Men who suffer from the injustices of lawyers' fees and wish to give information are threatened. Lawyers, assert the petitioners, are "a generation of men yet remaining amongst us, that turn judgement into Gall, and the fruit of Righteousness into Hemlock, that oppress the Widdow and Fatherless, and turn aside the Stranger from his Right, that feed upon afflicted Prisoners, and nourish the cruelty of Goalers." To accelerate the great work of reforming the law and curbing the power of lawyers, the petitioners appeal for specific measures. No lawyer should be a member of the Commons or be permitted to sit on the committee forming the courts of justice. No man receiving an income from the law should sit on any court of justice. If any man wishes to plead his own case, or to ask friends or lawyers to do so, he should have that right in any court of law. The petitioners plead that trials go forward more speedily, without all *"those many Lab'rinths that have been devised by Lawyers."*[5] Moreover, trials of all kinds should be limited in time; no trial should be permitted to last more than six months. The petitioners request, too, that all persons interested in law reform be admitted to the meetings of the Honourable Committee for Regulation. In the midst of agitation for reform of the law courts, this petition was a timely and pertinent document. But neither the petitioners nor Cromwell himself,

[4] E623(14), p. 575. [5] 669f15(78).

who was eager to expedite reform of legal procedure, had any conception of the depth and complexity of the problem they faced or the centuries of entrenched property in legalistic ritual and fees alone.

CHAPTER XII

DILEMMAS OF PRINCIPLE: RECURRING AND UNRESOLVED

January–February, 1651

IN the Puritan Revolution each main sect spoke, in a sense, for the future of England as well as for its past. Thus the Presbyterians spoke for monarchy, but disavowed the absolutism of James I; they wanted a monarchy newly limited by rising men of substance not of the aristocracy. With this view many Anglicans and aristocrats concurred; they had not forgotten, men like Falkland and Hyde, the limitations on the monarch's power inherent in Magna Charta and the Petition of Right. The Independents in the main did not wish to disturb the economic structure the benefits of which they had inherited; nor did they wish at first to overthrow the monarchy. Only when faced on the one hand with a monarch's unperturbed fixation on the absolutism of the past, and on the other with a resolute army in which many elements of the future had crystallized with triumphant suddenness, did they choose to destroy kingship and establish a commonwealth. The Levellers looked to Coke's interpretation of the past for basic freedoms; but in the construction of a new England, they wanted an extension of these basic freedoms, especially in widening of the suffrage. In the boiling cauldron of ideas, no searcher of the Bible could remain untouched by the fire of reformation, whether a reshaping of himself, his village, or the customs of his country. Of all the parties and sects, only Winstanley and his Diggers proposed a clean break with the past on all fronts: economic, political, theological. Only Winstanley among the partisans of the day repudiated the essence of the past for a utopia remote from England's realities in ancient customs, whether of church, village, commerce, or private property. But even Winstanley would allow the old England and its adherents to live side by side with the pioneers of the new Commonwealth. Of all his contemporaries, only Winstanley would have believed that the outcome of such a test would have been a victory for that head Leveller, Jesus, and his company of true disciples, the Diggers.

Meanwhile each village, indeed each citizen, found himself living a part of each day in the past and a part in the future of an England strange and unpredictable.

1. HENRY PARKER AND THE GALL OF THE SCOTS

On January 17, in the midst of Cromwell's advance on Edinburgh, appeared Henry Parker's defense of the Commonwealth, *Scotlands Holy War*. Parker was a paid writer for the Council of State; but no party could buy his convictions, which were as sturdy as those of Harrison or Cromwell, or his flow of rhetoric, which was far more persuasive and skillful than that of Milton or Needham. Parker's polemic method was the most enlightened of his day, a method that refrained from epithets like those of Milton or fiery maledictions like those of Prynne. No one more persuasively than Parker traces the inconsistencies of the Scots' actions toward the king or the necessities of the Commonwealth's main decisions. Parker's method is to present at each step the Scots' interpretation of events before he presents his own. "Who is responsible?" asks Parker. "Whether the *English*, or *Scots*, whether the *Presbyterians*, or *Independents* are most blameable before God, and Men, for the scandall which has been given by occasion of this *Solemn League, and Covenant*." [1] Parker traces again the history of the Covenant, saying that if Henderson had lived, the bitterness between the two nations might have been prevented. As for the Covenant, "the couching of it was obscure, and left liable to so many false glosses," [2] but the Scots in 1646 began to resolve its meaning in favor of the king. Parker reminds the Scots that when the king had first separated himself from the Parliament, "half the Clergie at least fell away from this cause." When, by 1647, the army had triumphed over the king's forces, then the Scots strangely began to hold back from any further action against him, "and that halting had as strange an operation upon the King." This hesitation of the Scots prolonged the war. The Scots' position was to defeat him in battle, to imprison him, but not to make him suffer further. "In summe, the King must again be more humbly sought to then ever." [3] Then Parker sets forth a weak proof of his point (by trial of battle) to which he seldom descends: Had not an army inspired by God resolved the issue by victorious arms? Parker ringingly justifies Pride's Purge; there was no alternative but to "lay a hand of force upon the affirmative Voters in Parliament, and to bring the King to a tryall, which were done accordingly, and so both they prevail'd and we were preserved as to this day." [4] Now the Scots, much

[1] *Scotlands Holy War* (January 17, 1651), E621(16), p. 9. [2] *Ibid.*, p. 34.
[3] *Ibid.*, pp. 33, 20, 21. [4] *Ibid.*, p. 24.

to their sorrow, have their king at last. The king wishes he had never come to their throne, and they wish he had never come to Scotland.

Parker's long pamphlet is more an appeal to the Presbyterians of England than to the irreconcilable Scots. Will the English Presbyterians, having made war on the tyrant father, uphold the Scots in taking the son to their bosom? Moreover, do the Presbyterians of England really prefer to be ruled by the kirk? By the agreement at Breda the Scots "have since conspired with our open Enemy against us, making their cause his, and his theirs." [5] Is it possible that any Parliament set up in England should be thought worse by Englishmen than servitude to the kirk? The Commonwealth cannot survive unless the Scottish armies and their new king are annihilated. Meanwhile, Parker appeals to the reason of both Scots and Englishmen. Though he cannot avoid some inflammatory sentences, his appeal on the whole is more moderate and persuasive than that of any champion of the new republic.

In *One Blow More at Babylon,* which appeared on February 15, another Independent attempted the persuasive and reasonable approach toward the recalcitrant Presbyterians. "*Though we are not of the same mind in all things,*" says the writer, "*yet so far as we have attained let us joyn together, and help on the Work of the Lord.*" When Presbyterians and Independents cannot agree, continues the author, let us not separate or speak evil of each other. The writer praises the talents of the Commonwealth's Presbyterian enemies: "*You have many of you very excellent gifts and parts, both of nature and grace.*" [6] The Presbyterian ministers have preached many excellent sermons and published to the world. Why should all these gifts be lost now in the morass of strife and recrimination? In the dialogue that follows, one traveler says to the other, "What is that doth so much stomach the *Ministers* against the *Parliament* and *Independents?*" [7] The fellow-traveler replies that he cannot fathom the attitude of the Presbyterians, but he agrees that they bear a deep grudge against the Independents, a grudge expressed both in their preaching and in their praying. It was the taking away of the king that most offended them. But, replied his comrade, did the Presbyterians themselves not war against the king and applaud the Parliament for its resistance of kingship? The comrade concludes that the Presbyterians are intransigent only against the instrument, not the program, by which God has achieved his purpose. Though the Independents have justification from the Bible for their actions, the Presbyterians condemned them as sectaries and schismatics. The traveler from the East attempts to summarize the objections that the Presbyterians have toward the new government as follows: First, they permit "*Toleration of . . . blasphemous* Opinions" ; second,

[5] *Ibid.,* p. 64. [6] E623(16), Preface. [7] *Ibid.,* p. 1.

the Independents have no means for upholding truth against corruption; third, "they gather *Churches* out of *Churches*," fourth, "They *seldome stay* at Independency, but from thence run into all manner of *corrupt* opinions and practices." Whether these attacks are true or not, says the traveler from the East, they "are often in the mouths of many *honest* men, both *Ministers* and others."[8] Furthermore, it is well known that the Independents of the army have always opposed these particular sins in their private lives and teaching. But, says West, have not the Independents punished those sectaries who deny the divinity of Christ? Have they not passed laws against Sabbath-breaking, whoredom, incest, fornication, swearing—measures which all Presbyterians should approve?

2. WILLIAM PRYNNE: INDEPENDENCY UNMASKED

February, 1651

Fearless and incorrigible as always, William Prynne on February 27 sent forth a new edition of his *Independency Examined, Unmasked, Refuted,*[1] a tract now seven years old but as apt and explosive as ever. No writer more accurately than Prynne traced the fragmentation of sects and heresies inherent in the Puritan and Protestant reliance on individualistic interpretation of the Bible. As the new republic was soon to realize, in dealing with nine thousand parish ministers, it, too, must set bounds to the fragmentation of sects to which Independency had given rise. By the theory of Independency, Prynne had written, "every minister hath a divine right and liberty, to gather to himself an Independent Church, not of Pagans, Infidels converted by himself alone, but of all the eminentest Christians formerly converted." Moreover, according to Independent theory, "every Christian hath a free liberty, by the Law of God, to unite himself to what Independent Congregation he pleaseth; the husband to one Congregation, the wife to another, the children to a third, the servants to a fourth." This licentiousness, says Prynne contemptuously, he cannot designate as freedom of conscience. If a man can have that freedom of conscience asserted by the Independents, Prynne asks, then why should he not have the same right to set up what secular government he pleases? Does he not have a right to set up a "new Independent Republike, Corporation, Kingdom, Magistracy . . . and to cast off all former civill Governours, Governments, Laws at pleasure, as well as Ecclesias-

[8] *Ibid.*, p. 33.

[1] The new tract, February 27, 1651, E625(7), is identical in wording with the original tract of September 26, 1644, E257(3).

ticall"?[2] For his audience, the pious and bitter Presbyterians, Prynne in 1651 does not need to add a gloss to this dire prediction of 1644. In the rise of the Leveller movement; the trial and execution of Charles; the abolition of the House of Lords; the establishment of the new commonwealth; in such wild heretics as Biddle the unitarian and Winstanley of the socialist effusion, the warnings of Prynne possessed a validity in Presbyterian eyes no prophet among them would have denied. Prynne represented, moreover, a far greater body of public opinion than such men as Milton, Cromwell, and Vane. The country was ready for Prynne's partial revolution, a shift of power from the monarch to the Commons; it was not ready to execute its king, however tyrannical, and establish a new republic, a new republic brought to birth by that fiery agitation Milton had welcomed in *Areopagitica*.

3. TITHE ECONOMY UNDER GLASS: *MINISTERS HUE AND CRY*
February, 1651

In his total opposition to tithes Milton was unaware, to a greater extent than even Henry Vane, of the vast complexities and confusion their removal would have engendered in England's agricultural life. But there was scarcely a member of the Commons who did not almost weekly encounter a parish minister or a parishioner whose livelihood was diminished or enhanced by the payment of tithes. Early recognizing the need for stabilizing economic expectations and duties as far as possible, the Commons had on June 8, 1649, passed *An Act for Maintenance of Preaching Ministers*.[1] On April 5, 1650, the Commons had transferred the payment of tithes from the parish minister to agents of its own in every county; but even a year later this act in many parishes was still not effective.[2] Agitation in some communities, however, justified such a resistance to tithes altogether that the income of some ministers was precarious indeed, despite the help given them by the Commons' Committee for Plundered Ministers, which had been active as early as August, 1647. Of nine thousand parish ministers, no more than one thousand, in Hobbes' opinion, had suffered from the contagion of Puritanism in extreme degree; and of these one thousand, no more than a few hundred could have been ardent supporters of the new Commonwealth in 1651, though all who continued had been required to take an Engagement in January, 1650. Those refusing were gradually forced out of their livings in favor of loyal supporters of the Independent regime. The ministers

[2] E625(7), pp. 7, 8, 9.

[1] *Acts and Ordinances*, II, 142–51, April 5, 1650. [2] *Ibid.*, II, 369, 372–73.

loyal to the Rump in many instances imposed Puritanical measures utterly hostile to parish tradition and psychology; these actions, including the prohibition of Sunday games, "innocent freedoms," as Milton later called them, contributed heavily to the wave of sturdy resentment that beset the Commonwealth from its earliest years. An unpopular minister bringing legal action (or the Commonwealth's committee for him) to collect the tithes due the parish compounded the resentments against both the minister and the new government.

The most enlightening analysis in depth of the economic problems involved in tithe disputes appeared in Richard Culmer's *Ministers Hue and Cry,* February 27, 1651. *Hue and Cry* is written in the form of conversation involving four men: Paul Shepherd, the parish minister; Barnaby Sheaf, an impropriator, or lay parson; Robin Rob-Minister, a former Leveller, "one that robs and defrauds the Minister of his Maintenance"; and Tom Tytheshort, one who tries in one way or another to return to the minister in money or goods less than by custom is due. When Tom and Robin meet in a field at the beginning of the discussion, Tom says, "I hear the Priests and Impropriators shall have no more Tythes," to which Robin replies, "Then I'le sing, *Hey down go they,* I mean those called Able, Orthodox Divines and Ministers; I hope they will be stubb'd up root and branch; for we have no more need of them, then of a fift wheel to a waggon." But Tom is more realistic than Robin; he wants to reduce the tythes by stealth and fraud, not abolish them: "I am not of your minde, for there is a Parliament Declaration, that they shall have liberall and settled maintenance: and then if Tythes go down, our Landlords will raise up our rent, and we must maintain a Minister [by voluntary offerings], and what get we by that?" Both Robin and Tom are pictured as victims of extremist propaganda, hating all ministers; they differ only on how to defraud them. "Of all men," asserts Robin, "I hate a Minister most . . . if it were in my power, I would sheathe my sword in the bowels of all the Ministers in *England:* I call them *Baals*-Priests, I wonte come neer their Steeple-house." The old ministers were jovial and relaxed; the sour new one appointed by Parliament "begins already to play the Roundhead"; he discards the service book, denies communion to whom he will, refuses to give comforting words over the bodies of the dead. Moreover, continues Tom, "we can't so much as swear on Oath, or be merry, but the Pulpit rings on't." Under such provocation Robin and Tom have no hesitation in devising one scheme or another to defraud the minister of his tithe. Formerly Tom had bound his corn in sheaves, leaving one in ten for the minister of his tither to carry away; but often now he does not bind his corn into sheaves at all, but leaves only a heap of corn here and there, on the pretext that he is leaving a tenth. When the tither is present, he leaves all the corn on the ground and goes about other business until the tither is gone. "But when his back is turned then we load lustily: and if he wait all day, we never carry till dark night." Tom has still another trick: he keeps trash in the barn to substitute at night for good heaps in the tither's part of the field: "I have called my sonne up many a night to do these righteous things." The ways of cheating the priests are many and various. Robin says: "I heap thirteen or fourteen sheaves in all my nine shocks, and but ten sheaves in all the Tythe-heaps." Each tythe heap of corn is marked by the bough of a tree. When the gleaners come, Robin winks and nods when they take corn from the tither's heap, knowing that the more they glean from the tither's corn, the less they will glean from his. How can the priest keep them from cheating him? He would have to keep watchers in the field day and night. Moreover, should he go to law to obtain his tythe, the farmer is entitled to a trial by jury and therefore likely to win his case; for now the will of all juries is law, and jurymen now are "all Kings." In a recent case at Sandwich, the jury decided against the priest, even though his case was fully proved and the judge's direction in his favor.[3]

When the minister Paul Shepherd comes upon the scene, Robin breaks out in bitter railing: "You are one of *Baals* Priests, and rob us of our goods, and of our labours, to maintain you, and trullirugs your wife, and gillflurt your daughter." The minister, dignified and courteous, nevertheless replies in sharp reproof: "You call me robber, but you are the robber in name and deed. You rob me of my good name by slanderous words and Articles: and you rob and defraud me of my maintenance." In a long speech the minister laments the capricious moods of some members of his congregation: "Some people are . . . like hounds, that when one yalps, presently all open, though they sent not the game."[4] Shepherd then reviews the types of slander against ministers appointed by Parliament, passed from one member to another: the pastor was turned out of another parish; he never preached of regeneration; he denied a certain member the sacrament. In response to a challenge by Tom, Shepherd admits that Christ and his disciples took only voluntary offerings for their labours. But do the parishioners themselves follow in Christ's steps when they persecute their ministers? Is not their free benevolence rather a wolfish hatred? When Robin breaks out, "You should work for your living as *Paul* did: but we work for you, and you live on our labours," Shepherd replies with great patience. Paul worked for a living, it is true; but the other apostles lived from the gifts of the faithful. Moreover, in those days there were no lands set aside to support the church and its ministers. When you rented your farm, continues Shepherd, "You were to pay two Rents for it, Tythe-rent . . . as well as Landlords Rent." When Tom protests that "Your Tyther is still at our heels, and watcheth us," Shep-

[3] E625(8), pp. 1, 2, 4.

[4] *Ibid.*, pp. 7, 8.

herd replies, "If you devour my Tythes when my man watcheth you, what will you do if he were gone?" To this Robin replies that the minister came to the parish against the wishes of its members; if they had chosen their own minister, they "would have paid him to a farthing." [5]

Shepherd's biting altercation with the two radicals is interrupted by the appearance of Barnaby Sheaf, a parson who is attached to the parish only by his purchase of a tithe income. Sheaf's aim, like Shepherd's, is to justify the institution of tithes. He freely admits that tithes have formerly in England been put to superstitious uses: the support of abbeys, bishoprics, deans, and chapters. But now tithes no longer support the bishops, but rather are put to many good uses; moreover, they are in a sense a property like any other, not subject to religious considerations: "They are our Propriety, our Estate, our Inheritance, our Livelihood, to us, our families and heirs: and if you . . . take them from us, without just satisfaction, we are wronged." To this argument, speaking in a tone of moderation, as throughout the dialogue, Shepherd adds other lines of reasoning: Are ministers and all the tithe receivers not forced to pay taxes, fifth parts and tenths? Are they not required out of their income to "finde Arms, Quarter Souldiers, repair Houses . . . according to the utmost full value . . . of our revenues in Tythes?" Shepherd claims that ministers often pay out more than they receive in tithes: "We pay a certainty out of an uncertainty. . . . Our livings are our dyings. . . . Men laugh at us in their sleeves, and are hereby induced to beleeve the Kingdom of Christ to be a Kingdom of fools." [6] Are ministers covetous when, like other men, they wish to lay up money for their children? The solution of the problem, continues Shepherd, is not to require a money payment for tithes; such a payment is more difficult to collect than goods. In a final speech Shepherd expresses his hope that ministers will have an income from the state, not from the people of the parish, so that they will "not be a cheating stock and derision, through oppression, poverty and contempt." To Shepherd's farewell, Robin replies: "Farewell and be hang'd . . . *Tom,* hear none of them all, come not near their Steeple-house: If the Parliament settle any certain Maintenance for the Ministers, I am as much against that as against Tythes." [7]

4. NATHANIEL BACON: WHOSE POWER IS THE MILITIA?

February, 1651

On February 17 appeared Nathaniel Bacon's *The Continuation of an Historical Discourse, of the Government of England,* in which the thorny question of power over the militia was again crystallized. Long a friend

[5] *Ibid.,* pp. 9, 10, 11, 12, 13. [6] *Ibid.,* pp. 18, 19. [7] *Ibid.,* p. 21.

of Cromwell from the days when the Eastern Association helped to muster arms and men for the Parliament, Bacon had sent forth in 1647 *An Historical Discourse of the Uniformity of the Government of England.* The *Discourse* was a detailed and many-sided study of constitutional dilemmas before the time of Edward III. The *Continuation* traced Bacon's interpretation of events to the end of the reign of Elizabeth. At basis the key problem was this: In a conflict between the Commons and the king, who controls the militia? When the king had withdrawn to Windsor in January, 1642, the militia of Puritan counties had joined the Parliamentary forces. Did the militia men who marched with the Parliament violate the constitutional rights of the monarch? Bacon does not answer this question directly; the events themselves are beyond the scope of his history, and Bacon is a historian who never underestimates the complexity of his task. Nevertheless his bias runs persistently toward the defense of Parliamentary rights as opposed to regal. "Because some mens Pens of late have ranged into a denyall of the Commons ancient right in the Legislative power;" wrote Bacon, "and others, even to adnull the right, both of Lords and Commons therein, resolving all such power into that one principle of a King . . . so making the breach much wider then at the beginning; I shall intend my course against both." [1] What does one mean, asks Bacon, by the word *militia?* His answer runs as follows:

> . . . raising, arming, ordering, and paying of the Souldiery. The Title of the Supreme Power in all this work hath been of late put to the question, and brought us to this sad condition of triall by Battail. . . . In war he is the Peoples General by his place; yet if any impediment do befall . . . to render the person incapable of the managing of the Service, there is no question but the People may order the matter as they please.[2]

When the Parliament is not sitting, the monarch may initiate military action with the advice of his council; but when the Parliament is in session, "no History or Record do mention that ever he moved but by their concurrent advice and direction." [3] The levying of money is a main part of making war; the militia, asserts Bacon, "must be allowed to such as beare the purse." Even in Norman times, the king could not raise extra sums except by authority of the Grand Council: "the laws were setled that no Tax should be made or taken, but such as were due in the Confessors time." It is true that all knights in Norman times held their estates under contract to be "ready with their Armes to assist the King for the defence of the Realme: So as they were not bound by their tenure to ayd

[1] *The Continuation of an Historical Discourse* (February 17, 1651), E624(1), sigs. A2–A2v.

[2] *Ibid.*, p. 290.

[3] *Ibid.*, p. 291.

him in any other cases."[4] At each point in his history Bacon reaches deep into particulars and bounds his main conclusions with dispassionate qualifications.[5] No royalist historian of the day wrote a treatise of equal depth and insight on constitutional dilemmas. In 1665, when Bacon's treatise was republished in England, the government promptly forbade its circulation.

Bacon does not analyze the constitutional dilemma of the militia as crystallized in his own time. When Charles withdrew from London on January 10, 1642, the burning question was this: Would the militia of the various counties support him or support the Parliament? In the months that followed, as Gardiner points out, each side was appealing to the country for support of its constitutional position. By the Ordinance of March 5, 1642, the Lords and Commons asserted their right to control the militia and designated officers to command it. Charles indignantly refused: "By God, not for an hour!"[6] In *Eikon Basilike* Charles (or Gauden for him) declared that the control of the militia was his "undoubted Right no lesse than the Crowne" itself.[7] The Parliamentary position Milton exemplified in the fiery language of *Eikonoklastes*. "It hath bin oft anough told him," wrote Milton, "that he hath no more authority over the sword then over the Law; over the Law he hath none, either to establish or to abrogate, to interpret, or to execute, but onely by his Courts and in his Courts, wherof the Parlament is highest, no more therfore hath he power of the *Militia* which is the Sword, either to use or to dispose; but with consent of Parlament; give him but that, and as good give him in a lump all our Laws and Liberties."[8] Thus far, neither the

[4] *An Historical Discourse* (1647), B.M. 1129.a1, p. 153.

[5] "What shall the People do . . ." asks Bacon (*The Continuation*, p. 246), "if dayes come like those of *Henry* the sixth, wherein the Subjects should be between two millstones, of one King in Title and another King in possession, for whom must they take up Armes, if for *Edward* the fourth, then are they Traitors to *Henry* the sixth; if for *Henry* the sixth, then are they traitors to *Edward* the fourth, and so now if for *Henry* the seventh then they may be Traitors to the Duke of *Yorke,* if for the Duke of *Yorke,* then are they Traitors to *Henry* the seventh."

[6] Gardiner, *History of England* (10 vols., London, 1883–84), X, 172. The great historians of constitutional law have not dealt in depth with Charles' claim. The best brief account is found in Sir David Keir, *Constitutional History* (7th ed., London: Adam and Charles Black, 1964), p. 217. Hallam, *Constitutional History* (3 vols., London, 1884), has several illuminating pages (see particularly II, 127–28, n. *f*). In Holdsworth, *History of English Law* (4th ed., 16 vols., London, 1936–64) only one page (VI, 140) deals with the militia dispute of the 1640's. Holdsworth declares that the militia was given to Charles "by the law of the constitution." See below, pp. 196–97.

[7] *Eikon Basilike* (February 9, 1649), B.M. C59.a.24, p. 69.

[8] *Complete Prose,* III, 454. For the positions of Whitelocke and Clarendon, see below, pp. 196–97.

king nor the Parliament had come to actual trial by battle; but the issue of the militia dramatized as no other the division between royal and Parliamentary authority.

Even now neither the king nor the Parliamentarians had broken the long tradition of constitutional ties that Bacon called "the Uniformity of the Government of England." When Charles left Whitehall on January 10, 1642, and refused to return to London, each side was keenly aware of the dangers of an irretrievable severance of the monarch's person from the functions of the Parliament. Charles wished to possess the actual power that the symbols of divine right had bestowed on him from centuries of ritual. In the England of expanding and confident Puritan classes, the actualities of such power were no longer possible. Still there was no sharp break in the fabric of constitutional custom until Colonel Pride, on December 6, 1648, acting for a joint committee of officers and civilians, purged the House of over ninety Presbyterian members and arrested over forty others. Until this time a return to an uneasy compromise between Charles and the Parliament had remained a possibility. From 1642 until 1648 Parliament controlled the militia; but from the day of Pride's Purge until the Restoration, neither king nor Parliament controlled the militia. Pride's Purge prepared the way for further pressures from the army, the setting up of the High Court of Justice (an entirely unconstitutional action), and the execution of Charles. Had Bacon written another continuation of his constitutional history, it is impossible to imagine that he would have justified Pride's Purge and the trial of the king; he was at heart an historian, not a polemicist. Yet he served the new Commonwealth as an admiralty judge, the Protectorate as a Master of Requests to Cromwell; he was a member of two Parliaments under the Protectorate, of Richard Cromwell's Parliament, and even of the revived Long Parliament of 1660.

It is generally said that at the beginning of the seventeenth century the militia by common consent was subject to the king's authority only, not that of the Commons. By the end of the seventeenth century the control of the militia had shifted from the crown to the Parliament. But such a description of so profound a constitutional change in the control of the militia is too absolute to be acceptable. Bacon's *Continuation* alone shows that authority over the militia could not be separated at any time from the means necessary to arm and support it. Nevertheless, assuming the large accuracy of the generalization, what were the specific steps by which Parliament gradually removed from the crown the control of the militia? These gradual steps have yet to be traced in minute enough detail to form an intelligible and compelling pattern of constitutional change. The Militia Act of 1662 declared solemnly that the power over the militia was the monarch's only. Yet in fact the magnates of each shire controlled the militia; and it was the militia that forced out James II and carried through the Revolution of 1688.[9]

Any investigation of the fundamental dilemmas of principle in 1651 reveals a baffling complexity of intellectual positions the effects of which are difficult to unravel. But Prynne, rigid and intransigent as he was, understood the effects of the king's magic on the population as a whole more clearly than Parker or Milton. Himself a fearless radical in his resistance against the bishops, teacher of Lilburne in the search for seminal libertarian documents in England's past, he came to a point, as did every reformer of the period (except Winstanley), at which he resisted changes toward which his own positions had been signposts and signals. But better than Parker or Milton, Prynne knew the terms and the timing by which reform in England had to come. As a lawyer he comprehended the complexities of tenure and ownership and payment of tithes reaching back over the centuries; but of these complexities Milton had no knowledge whatever. To Milton the tithe support of "blind guides" was reason enough to tilt against the windmills of injustice. Neither he nor idealists like Feake, Vane, and Williams visualized the conditions described in *The Ministers Hue and Cry*. The failure of the Barebones Parliament, as contrasted to the relative success of the Rump Parliament, may be traced in part to the lack of realism inherent in speculations of religious minds.

In the last analysis the principle most destructive to a lasting settlement in church and state was the Protestant assumption that every man had both the right and the talent to find ultimate truth by perusing the Scripture. This principle such a man as Jeremy Taylor claimed for all Christians in *A Discourse of the Liberty of Prophesying* (1647).[10] Prynne claimed this principle for the Presbyterians but denied it to the Independents and their followers. The principle was destructive in the sense that it was perpetually revolutionary and unpredictable. Yet the same spectrum of Protestant believers who differed so sharply among themselves would not permit the Catholics freedom to search the Scriptures or interpret Christianity in their own way. On this all Protestant sects, whatever the divisions among themselves, were agreed. In the Catholic church, it is true, believers were not permitted to set up sects

[9] Tanner, *English Constitutional Conflicts* (Cambridge University Press, 1962), pp. 223–24.

[10] Taylor wrote (*Liberty of Prophesying*, 1647, p. 41): "Every man beleeving Scriptures, and seriously laboring to deduce a *probable* sense out of them, is sufficiently provided for in order to his salvation."

interpreting the Bible each by his own light. The Catholic trusted to his church to interpret the Bible with final authority, to interpret justly also his relations to his God, his magistrate, his national government. Such a religious viewpoint made for an orderly society of secure and predictable gradations. Had England remained Catholic, there could have been no Puritan Revolution. As Philip Scot wrote in his *Treatise of the Schism of England,* "Catholick tenents must by a great necessity be always constant: because they depend not upon our daily changable reasons, or ratiocination, but upon the unvariable word of God, revealed and delivered by the Church." [11] Such a belief made for stability and gradual reform, not revolution. However much they differed among themselves, all Protestant sects were agreed on the prohibition of Catholic conscience, though Hooker had written, "We willingly acknowledge Papists to be of the family of Christ." The main dilemma of principle, in 1651, then, was still this: To deny toleration of conscience to any sect was a violation of the most fundamental Protestant principle. To accept the principle meant a constant turmoil of jarring beliefs, spineless without action, as the Quakers and the Diggers and Prynne himself knew to their sorrow, but destructive to stability and order in church and state.

CHAPTER XIII

DEFENSIO REGIA OF SALMASIUS

November, 1649

SALMASIUS' *Defensio Regia pro Carolo I* was in print in Europe as early as November, 1649. In essence the *Regia* was a clarion call to the kings of Europe to unite against the new English republic and place on the throne the rightful successor, Prince Charles, then a refugee at The Hague. On the title page appears the phrase *Sumptibus Re-*

[11] December 5, 1650, E1395, p. 143. Scot thinks of the great schism of England as the departure from the Catholic faith. In Scot's view (p. 161) Henry VIII initiated the schism "out of a fained and adulterate conscience." Not for religious reasons, but for reasons of state, Queen Elizabeth "perverted the Schism into Heresie." Those who have agitated for extreme toleration, declares Scot, have been unwilling to extend this freedom to Catholic citizens. "Many indeed," he wrote (pp. 82–83), "have for some years cryed out for immunitie, in order to tender consciences: and yet they themselves, who were the heads of those Tenderlings, did not endure to have Recusants accounted such."

giis. It is not yet proved that Charles paid a hundred pounds for the writing and printing of the *Regia*. But so great a celebrity was Salmasius that he could represent the royal cause more successfully before the crowned heads of Europe than any other writer. Moreover, to represent Prince Charles' claims effectively to his English adherents, Salmasius had the advantage of being a Protestant.

The *Regia* as a whole has a much more scholarly and detached tone than Milton's reply. No scathing personal epithets mar its style, though accents of horror at the deeds of the regicides echo often through its pages. But unlike Milton, Salmasius did not place his name on the title page of his work. It was to Charles' advantage that the renowned intellect of Salmasius should champion his cause; but the failure of Salmasius to attach his name to the *Regia* suggests a reluctance to cast his new work in the scales of his great reputation. From the preface of the work alone, it is evident that Salmasius had not taken pains to acquire the thorough knowledge he needed of English history or of the immediate events that led to the execution of Charles on January 30, 1649. Whatever the *Regia's* weaknesses, however, the great name of Salmasius required an answer from the men who now dominated the daily policies of the new republic; and Milton had been selected for the task. All through the year 1650, his left eye already sightless, his right eye failing month by month, Milton toiled on his answer to Salmasius, *A Defence of the People of England*, which appeared on the streets of London about February 24, 1651.[1]

The preface of the *Regia* reveals the violent condemnations, the lack of precise information about English constitutional history, which was to plague Salmasius throughout his long tract. Exclamations of horror pervade even Salmasius' first pages. In his first sentence Salmasius calls the execution of the king a parricide, an act "committed by a nefarious conspiracy of impious men."[2] So great was the crime that civilized men recoiled at the news with a state of shock, their bodies rigid, their hair on end, their voices mute. It was as incredible as if they had heard that rivers are now flowing backward, statues are breaking out in perspiration, rain has turned to blood. The English rebels have declared war on humanity itself. They grasp not only at the thrones of kings but at all authority, all magistrates, all laws. Instead of one king they now have appointed forty tyrants.[3] If the English heretics had abolished the king only, they could

[1] See William J. Grace, preface to *A Defence*, below, p. 285. On new evidence which leaves unproved the alleged payment to Salmasius, see W. McNeill, "Milton and Salmasius, 1649," *English Historical Review*, LXXX, No. 313 (January, 1965), 107–108.

[2] *Defensio Regia* (1649), p. 1, ll. 3–5: "De parricidio apud Anglos in persona Regis sacrilegorum hominum nefaria conspiratione admisso." [All English quotations from *Regia* are from the distinguished translation by Kathryn McEuen.]

[3] Salmasius always refers to the Council of State as "quadraginta tyrannos."

have had democracy consisting of bishops, the nobility, and the "representatives of the cities." [4] But they were not content with that. They had abolished representation of the bishops, the nobility, and the people, concentrating all power in forty tyrants (by which term Salmasius always means the Council of State). Abolish bishops! What a horror! Why, even at the time of reformation the English still kept their bishops. Indeed, as long as bishops lasted "1000 baleful sects and heresies did not sprout in England." [5] Of these heresies, the worst are the Independents, the Brownists. The Independents! They are the ones who took from Charles I his kingdom and life. "Is it a democracy," exclaims Salmasius, "which consists of the wickedest rabble, the nobles being excluded?" [6] The Independents are the "dregs of the people." With the victory of such a rabble, every king is now in danger: "Why therefore do kings delay, if they wish to be secure and safe [they must] run together and . . . assemble in one place, so that their forces and strength being joined, they may prepare arms for exterminating those pests of kingdoms and states." [7] The blood of Charles calls for revenge by all who sit upon thrones. Wage war, then, exhorts Salmasius, against the English heretics: "Persecute this hated root and wicked sect." Salmasius lauds and upholds the divine right of kings: By law the king of England "has supreme power over his subjects, which is answerable to no other power except divine." [8] But now, if God hear the prayers of these fanatics, no king would stay alive. They prophesy no king in the world will stay on his throne more than ten years longer. Moreover, no friendship, no ordinary conversation, is possible with these devils. We must, concludes Salmasius, defend the English king, whose destiny is one with that of all other kings of Europe.

At one point in his preface Salmasius does come to grips with an issue of inherent intellectual quality. The Independents, he insists, had no precedent and no law which could justify either the trial of the king or his execution. Here Salmasius was on firm ground. The trial and execution of the king, he continues, were a tyrannical action "advanced beyond kingly power." [9] Had Salmasius studied the record of the trial more carefully and stressed the most telling defense Charles made of himself, namely that he had no peers by whom he could be tried according to the law of the land, his attack on the Independents would have held greater validity in the minds of European intellectuals. No provision existed in

[4] *Defensio Regia* (1649), p. 4, ll. 26–27.

[5] *Ibid.*, p. 4, ll. 35–37: "Quod quandiu fuit Episcopatus mille pestiferae sectae & haereses in Anglia non pullularunt."

[6] *Ibid.*, p. 5, ll. 3–4: "An Democratia est quae ex vilissima tantum plebe conflata est, exclusis Optimatibus?"

[7] *Ibid.*, p. 11, ll. 8–11.

[8] *Ibid.*, p. 11, ll. 38–39; p. 12, ll. 28–30.

[9] *Ibid.*, p. 6, l. 10.

English law for the erection of a high court of justice for the trial of a monarch. Moreover, asserts Salmasius, "if the king had seen to it, that any senator at all from the upper or lower house of that august council had been visited with such punishment, not rightly and without the order of law, he would not have escaped the name of tyrant." [10]

In chapter II of *Defensio Regia* Salmasius traces the long tradition of absolute monarchy in the ancient world, among the Romans, the Persians, the Greeks, the Assyrians, the Jews. The Israelites, weary of the rule of judges, pleaded with God, "Appoint over us a king." Kingship, though sometimes a failure, was at times a government of remarkable stability. Solomon was the wisest of all kings and dear to God's heart, as was David. Clement declared that kings are created by God, and said: "You will fear the king, knowing his choice to be of the Lord." [11] In the Hebrew nation absolutism in kings was the rule rather than the exception. Moreover, God directed the king's decisions. Does not David say in Psalm 17, "Let my sentence come forth from thy presence"? God forgave his kings more freely than he forgave other men. After sending Uriah to his death and committing adultery with the dead man's wife, did not David say to the Lord, "Against thee only have I sinned"? [12] When God gave the Israelites a king, in response to their pleas, the gift was not a punishment, but a benefit, even a blessing. In such terms does Salmasius attempt to prove that absolute kingship has an ancient and honorable place in the history of great nations. Moreover, continues Salmasius, some of the greatest rulers were kings in fact if not in name. Was not Moses, though called a prophet, an absolute monarch in actuality? [13] Thus does Salmasius show that divine right in a king was an actuality among the Hebrews. Why, then, should kingship by the English be condemned now, as a wicked government, and a pious and honorable king be executed as a common ruffian?

When one king overthrows another, argues Salmasius, the people are driven to acceptance of the new king in return for which he grants them the right of life itself.[14] For the right to life the people also owe their king faithful service. Salmasius accepts with equanimity a revolution in which one king drives out another, as the Saxons drove out the Romans, and the Danes drove out the Saxons; then England fell to William the Conqueror. In these violent overturns, one king replaced another: The form

[10] *Ibid.*, p. 6, ll. 12–15: "Si rex quemlibet ex superiore vel inferiore domo augusti illius Consilii sui Senatorem, tali supplicio non rite, ac sine juris ordine curasset afficiendum, tyranni notam non effugisset."

[11] *Ibid.*, p. 39, ll. 35–37.

[12] *Ibid.*, p. 40, ll. 23, 24, 30.

[13] *Ibid.*, pp. 44–45.

[14] *Ibid.*, p. 149, ll. 23–25: "Hoc igitur debent beneficium victori pro data vita ut fideliter illi serviant & subjecti sint."

of government remained unchanged. But the overthrow of Charles I, insists Salmasius, is a revolution of a sinister new kind. No new monarch has driven out another, claiming for himself a kingdom by right of conquest. The English have set up a totally new kind of government; they have not, as in former centuries, given allegiance to a new conqueror. Are the new rulers conquerors from a foreign strand, Danes, Angles, or Saxons?[15] Do they have a right to destroy a six-hundred-year succession of Norman rulers? Kingdoms are sacred, even when one replaces another. But when subjects rise against a king born, a king confirmed by heredity and succession, place him in prison, force him to plead for his life, sentence him, afflict him with shameful punishment, this is horrible and unthinkable. Such a degradation of kingship deserves the condemnation and hostility of all men: "This was not the crime of subjects, but of traitors; not of men, but of monsters; not of criminals of the common brand, but of worse than parricides."[16] Thus Salmasius: A new danger to that order of government accepted for ages has been let loose upon the world. Beware of such men as these English revolutionists!

At the end of chapter III Salmasius pauses to synthesize his arguments from the Bible and the church fathers against the English revolutionists. However unjust they may be, asserts Salmasius, kings are appointed by God himself; not even the pope can release Christians from their duties to their king. Whatever their grievances against their monarch, no group of subjects can free themselves from their oath of allegiance; nor can a people lawfully make war on their king, bring him to judgment, accuse and condemn him, or deprive him of his life or his possessions. To Salmasius a kingdom is as much a possession as a house or a carriage. If a king could be the subject of a people, the world would be in a state of revolution against the customs of centuries and the teachings of the Christian tradition. Kings are above laws, above the will of their subjects. To assert that kings can be judged by their subjects, that a king can rightfully be made subordinate to a people, is untrue to the teachings of centuries, both secular and religious. Salmasius summarizes thus:

> Maneat ergo indubitatum & certum id quod hoc capite demonstravimus ex doctrina patrum, primorum quatuor saeculorum, quae sola Evangelica & Christiana censeri debet, reges etiam malos & injustos à Deo constitui, & proinde Deum solum habere judicem, supra leges esse, nullam esse legem scriptam, non scriptam, naturalem neq; divinam, qua rei possint fieri à subditis suis, neque apud subditos suos. Quia si hi possent judices sedere contra reges suos, rerum vices inversae viderentur, & populus pro rege imperaret, rex vero populo subjectus haberetur. Ita nulla uspiam foret regia dominatio, nulla optimatum, sed ubique populus rex esset, resque publicas gubernaret.[17]

[15] *Ibid.*, p. 151, ll. 6–7. [16] *Ibid.*, p. 152, ll. 26–28.
[17] *Regia* (1649), p. 73, ll. 26–36.

Such a synthesis, assuming that it represents Salmasius' honest judgment, shows the distance between royalist French and royalist English assumptions about the rights of kings. As Milton says, even the most ardent English royalist did not make the claims for kingship that Salmasius set forth so easily. Even Hobbes could not have supported Salmasius in this extreme statement. Certainly no supporter of Charles, such as Jeremy Taylor, Clarendon, or even the Earl of Strafford, would have agreed with Salmasius that "reges etiam malos & injustos à Deo constitui, & proinde Deum solum habere judicem, supra leges esse." Indeed no such claim for the rights of Charles appears either in *Eikon Basilike* or in the court record of his trial. For English minds, whatever their sympathies, Salmasius' most extreme views may have represented a royalist France of the seventeenth century, but not a royalist England.

Salmasius' most compelling arguments for the rights of kings appear in his chapter IX, in which he lays by for the moment airy claims of divine right and trusts to records of English constitutional history. Is it not true, asks Salmasius, that the convocation of Parliament has always been the king's prerogative, not the Parliament's? Could Parliament sit at all except by the king's command? The king, it is true, could not make laws except by consent of both Houses; but on the other hand Parliament could not make a law except with the king's affirmative voice. Moreover, did not the king rule during that time when the Parliament was not sitting? One of Salmasius' most compelling arguments for the king's power is that in time of reformation the king became the head of the church and still retains this ecclesiastical supremacy.[18] The kings of England had huge incomes quite apart from those approved by Parliament. Indeed King James boasted that no ruler in Europe had so many estates attached to the crown as he. Moreover, the king had private incomes from customs and a huge income from the church property appropriated by Henry VIII; James had yields from such estates, claims Salmasius, totaling 1,500,752 pounds. Thus the king has many unusual subsidies apart from those granted by Parliament. The king, moreover, holds supreme command over the armed forces; only he can raise the standard and call men to arms.[19] All knights of the realm at such a call are bound to rally to his banner and fight his cause, as decreed by a statute in the seventh year of the reign of King Edward I. In addition to his key power over the militia and the ecclesiastical rule and property, the king has direct power over the House of Lords. Only he can create a peer. Moreover, why is the highest court in the land called the King's Bench? The judges of this court sat at the king's pleasure. It was the king's vehicle for defining justice to all the inferior courts of the land. Thus, concludes Salmasius, the king

[18] *Ibid.*, p. 231.

[19] *Ibid.*, pp. 237–38.

was the acknowledged ruler of the church, the army, the highest court of justice. Of these rights, the key to the king's power is the army: Without this power the people will be king, not he.[20]

In such a constitutional approach to the rights of kingship, Salmasius touched on one of the essential contradictions inherent in the Puritan Revolution. The education of Charles I in the rights and privileges of kingship had a deep validity in historical precedents in the reigns of Elizabeth and James and the centuries preceding. Bacon had been a spokesman for the rights of kingship as opposed to the rights of Parliament. Side by side with this emphasis, however, came a searching of records century by century that justified a limitation of the king's power as crystallized in the *Institutes* of Sir Edward Coke. With each passing decade and growth of wealth among the untitled classes, their spokesmen, men like John Pym, Henry Parker, and John Lilburne, sought in the records those laws and precedents that justified the reduction of the king's power and the enhancement of Parliament's prerogative. Each of these opposing interpretations of constitutional privileges could be justified. The forms and customs of earlier centuries, when the king's divine right had gone unchallenged, were maintained even in the midst of Parliament's growing prerogatives, prerogatives demanded in part by the expansion of Puritan wealth and power. When Charles withdrew to Oxford, Parliament continued to act in the name of the king. Its armies fought the king in the name of the king; they did not wish to break the forms of custom even though the custom itself no longer obtained.

Chapter XIV

MILTON'S REPLY TO THE GREAT SALMASIUS

February, 1651

In February, 1651, Milton was forty-two years old, living at Whitehall with his wife and daughters. At seven o'clock on many mornings he attended the meeting of the Council of State. Now completely blind in his left eye, he was not able even to see a "vague iridescent halo that there used to be round objects on that side."[1] On September 28, 1654, in describing his symptoms to the Athenian physician, Leonard Philaras, Milton wrote about his oncoming blindness in 1651 as follows:

[20] *Ibid.*, pp. 234, 238, 239.

[1] Masson, IV, 251.

> I observed, some months before my sight was wholly gone, that objects I looked at without myself moving seemed all to swim, now to the right, now to the left. Inveterate mists now seemed to have settled in my forehead and temples, which weigh me down and depress me with a kind of sleepy heaviness, especially from meal-time to evening. . . . But I should not forget to mention that, while yet a little sight remained, when first I lay down in bed, and turned myself to either side, there used to shine out a copious glittering light from my shut eyes; then that, as my sight grew less from day to day, colours proportionally duller would burst from them, as with a kind of force and audible shot from within.[2]

In January and February, 1651, the right eye was failing fast, though after February 24, when the *Defensio* appeared, he was able to sign his name in a number of presentation copies. For a full year, despite warnings from his physician, Milton had deliberately sacrificed his remaining eyesight to write his apology for the new republic.

On December 23, 1650, the manuscript now ready, Milton had been ordered to print the *Defensio*. On December 31 it had been entered in the Stationers' Registry by William Dugard, now won over from his imprisonment in Newgate (no doubt against his conscience) to labor for the Commonwealth.[3] On January 16 *Mercurius Politicus* reported obliquely that *Defensio* was in the press. By January 30 the *Defence* was almost ready for publication. It appeared on or near February 24.[4]

In opening *A Defence,* Milton justifies his theme as one "deserving eternal remembrance," the noblest he could choose for enlightenment of the ages to come. The majesty of the English people shone more brightly than that of any monarch when they shook off the old superstition of divine right, toppled Charles from his throne, and set his head upon the block. Did not God himself speak at that moment through the voice of the English patriots? A king overthrown who thought himself immune to human laws, superior indeed to the human condition, justified by divine approval: This overthrow of tyranny was the action of a great and noble people. What man can muster genius of style enough to tell the story of this great action to future generations? Only now and then, in similar moments of past ages, has a man emerged who thought himself equal to the task of assessing the great actions of heroes and nations. A signal honor, then, that England has chosen him, Milton, before all others, to refute Salmasius, even as her generals had scattered her foes upon the battlefield. Nor is he, Milton shows, without preparation for the noble task. From his youth he has studied great deeds, perhaps, he suggests, in the hope of touching greatness himself; but if not, at least to praise his heroes. Had he not refuted and thrown into confusion the king himself,

[2] *Ibid.*, pp. 640–41. Total blindness did not come until about February 28, 1652. See French, *Life Records,* III, 197.

[3] *Ibid.*, II, 335.

[4] *Ibid.*, II, 350.

who sending forth a book after his execution, had in effect risen from the grave to plead his cause? Beyond this preparation for the defense of his native country, he has the assurance of God's own help. Thus in *A Defence,* as in *Paradise Lost,* Milton crystallizes the essence of his great task in the opening sentences. He shows why its theme is of far-reaching worth in the perspective of history, why it requires a man of great talent, and why he is the one chosen to act in this national crisis. As in all of *A Defence,* his attacks on Salmasius have a bitter, personal quality unworthy of the theme he exalts and the man chosen to defend the Independents to the European world.

How Salmasius, the greatest of European scholars, could seriously accept the principle of divine right is incomprehensible to Milton. And here indeed to the modern reader Salmasius seems curiously unaware of the teachings of the Greek and Roman republicans, so familiar to Milton's contemporaries from their reading at Oxford and Cambridge. Even Hobbes knew these republicans, much as he hated them. "Kings," writes Salmasius, "are coeval with the sun's creation." [5] A king is a father to his people. Not so, says Milton. "You are wholly in the dark in failing to distinguish the rights of a father from those of a king." [6] The distinction is this: "Our fathers begot us, but our kings did not, and it is we rather who created the king. It is nature which gave the people fathers, and the people who gave themselves a king; the people therefore do not exist for the king, but the king for the people." [7] Even so, consider a father a king for a moment. What if he be a tyrant? What if he murder his son? Then by law we hang him, do we not? Why, then, should not a king by law have the same penalty we mete out to a father who murders his son? Milton gibes at Salmasius for his ignorance of English political affairs, especially his ignorance of Charles I and his actions. Had he not been an enemy to his own people for a full ten years? Many kings have suffered death by violence. But you deplore our trying him in a court of law, requiring him to plead for his life, bringing him to sentence and then execution. Would you have preferred that we "slaughter him like a beast without trial in the hour of his capture?" Would he himself not have preferred a trial? Had we murdered him privately, all ages of the future would have lost the benefit of our example. They would have thought that we avoided the light and took his life in the dark. No, Salmasius: "If the deed was fair and noble, those who performed it deserve the greater praise in acting for the right alone, unmastered by passion . . . moving not by blind impulse but on careful deliberation" [8] In such passages Milton is at

[5] *A Defence,* below, p. 326.

[6] *Ibid.,* p. 326. All English quotations are from the distinguished new translation of *A Defence* by Donald Mackenzie, below, pp. 326–27.

[7] *Ibid.,* p. 327.

[8] *Ibid.,* p. 329.

his best in logic and rhetoric, though at no time does he mention the names of eminent patriots like Fairfax and Algernon Sidney, who withdrew from the High Court of Justice when they saw that Cromwell and his officers had no intention of allowing Charles a trial in which he would have the slightest chance of escaping execution.

Milton's main polemic tactic is to follow his antagonist argument by argument, source by source, definition by definition. When Salmasius cites Biblical examples, Milton deals him stinging blows from the same sources; when Salmasius cites the histories of Greece and Rome, Milton replies with a deeper lore than Salmasius can muster. When Salmasius defines a king in terms of divine right, as one "responsible to none but God, one who may do as he will and is not subject to the laws," he gives an advantage Milton uses with uttermost effect.[9] It is true indeed that no more than a fanatical fraction of Charles I's party would have subscribed to such a definition. As Milton says, "Those among us most favorable towards the king have ever been guiltless of a belief so base."[10] Even Salmasius himself, insists Milton, did not hold this opinion "before he was bribed" by Charles II. And now, asks Milton, is there any person in the world, except Salmasius himself, who can really believe in such a principle? No precedent for such a statement exists in the best writers of the Hebrews, the Greeks, or the Romans. It is true that eastern peoples were prone to slavery "while Jews and Syrians were born for it." But the best Hebrew writers disavow despotism in the strongest terms. Josephus wrote: "Aristocracy is the best form of government . . . If however you are so bent on having a king, let him rely more on God and on the law than on his own wisdom, and let him be prevented from aiming at greater power than suits your best interests."[11] Philo Judaeus is even more emphatic: "King and tyrant are contraries . . . A king not only compels but complies."[12] In making his claim that kings must be subordinate to the law, Milton misses the opportunity used so effectively by Lilburne in earlier years, namely, that English kings have always promised at their coronations to obey the laws. "May kings," exclaims Milton, ". . . steal, kill, and commit adultery with impunity?" When a king "is witless, wicked, and passionate," shall the nobility of the nation be silent?[13] Shall the magistrates and the masses of the people be acquiescent? Suppose a king massacres his people or burns their cities, what then? In such passages Milton's arguments against Salmasius have an

[9] *Cf. Defensio Regia* (1649), p. 73, ll. 28–31: "Reges etiam malos & injustos à Deo constitui, & proinde Deum folum habere judicem, supra leges esse, nullam esse legem scriptam, non scriptam."

[10] *A Defence,* below, p. 341.

[11] *A Defence,* below, pp. 343, 344.

[12] *Ibid.,* p. 345.

[13] *Ibid.,* pp. 352, 347.

irrefutable quality they would have lacked had Salmasius stood for constitutional kingship as opposed to divine right. In the Britain of 1651, even in the Britain of 1660, there were few voices raised, even in private, for the absolutism exemplified by James I's theory of divine right.

When Salmasius defends monarchy from New Testament sources, Milton's deeper energies begin to flow, and he summons up some of the most telling arguments of *A Defence*. Christ the healer of souls and Christ the champion of political freedom, asserts Milton, are inseparably entwined. Without civic freedom the prophecy spoken to Mary, "He hath put down the mighty from their seats, and exalted them of low degree," would be meaningless chatter.[14] Though Christ took the form of a slave, he was a true liberator of men in a political as well as a psychological sense. Milton dwells at some length on the story of the tribute coin, and Jesus' conclusion: "Render therefore unto Caesar the things which are Caesar's; and unto God the things that are God's." Did Christ mean that freedom belonged to Caesar, or only one denarius? To surrender our freedom to any Caesar "would be an act of shame most unworthy of man's origin."[15] From whom are we descended? Look into a man's face, says Milton confidently and naively, and it is easy to see there the image of God himself. We are God's image, God's property, God's children; nor can we without maligning our creator surrender ourselves slaves to Caesar or any other tyrant. Yes, God gave the Israelites a king despite his unwillingness and his anger at them. But Christ went further: "It shall not be so among you," meaning that the haughtiness of kings cannot be reconciled with humility and reverence for the face of man. Whoever is first among men, Christ taught, must be the servant of men, not their master: "Amongst Christians, then, there will either be no king at all, or else one who is the servant of all; for clearly one cannot wish to dominate and remain a Christian."[16] To Milton the very nature of kingship, in its assumption of social superiority alone, made it irreconcilable with Christianity. Nowhere more fully expanded than in *A Defence,* this extreme hostility to kingship was in Milton a bone-deep conviction.

To Salmasius' claim, repeated in many forms, that kings are appointed by God, that they are bound by no laws, that therefore whoso kills a king is worse than a parricide, Milton replies with thrusts of fierce rhetoric: "If it was God alone who gave Charles his kingdom, it was he who took it away and gave it to the nobles and people." When Salmasius says, "Even wicked kings are appointed by God," Milton grants that "in a sense every evil is appointed by God." But this does not mean that kings should not be punished: "Reason, justice, and morality command

[14] *Ibid.,* p. 374. [15] *Ibid.,* p. 376. [16] *Ibid.,* p. 379.

the punishment of all sinners without distinction."[17] Salmasius' view of kingly responsibility, asserts Milton, makes even a slayer above the law. In his *Dissertatio de Episcopis ac Presbyteris* Salmasius had justified the deposing of a bishop dealing tyrannically only with acts of belief or doctrine; now he rejects the toppling of a tyrant who has power over men's lives and goods. In *De Primatu Papae* Salmasius had called the greatest heretic one who sits in Christ's place. The heretic would be infallible in spirituals and omnipotent in temporals. But, cries Milton, are kings infallible? "Why then should they be omnipotent?"[18] Why should we allow them to bring ruin to the state any more than you would permit the pope to bring disaster to the church? Does God care only for the church and not at all for secular affairs?

A Defence, chapter by chapter, does not fulfill the promise of Milton's preface and other eloquent passages. The book for the writing of which he lost his remaining sight is at a remote pole from the originality of thought and diction one finds in *Areopagitica,* parts of *Church-Government,* and *Apology against Smectymnuus.* Milton is chained to the earth by his opponent's limitations; chained also by his own method of a hammering, almost mechanical rebuttal; weakened by his invective, his epithets, his failure to analyze at eloquent length the cause for which his colleagues have ventured their lives and fortunes—the good old cause for which he turned aside from poetry at the age of thirty-two; and now at the age of forty-three still a revolutionist, his approaching blindness a daily cloud, reminder of the total darkness to come and his life's central hope of three great poems unfulfilled. In *A Defence* there is scarcely an autobiographical note. The tone is dominantly severe, caustic, unrelieved even by humor or lightness or originality.

In chapter VI of *Defensio Regia* Salmasius deals some telling blows against Milton in his analysis of the forces that toppled Charles from his throne. It was not the people, however defined, charges Salmasius, nor the aristocracy, who sent the king to the block. It was not the people who ejected the nobles from Parliament; who dragged Charles from one prison to another; who set up a tribunal for his condemnation; not the people who forced him to plead his cause; who turned him over to the executioner. Nor was it the people who purged the lower house: "The army with their leaders did this."[19] Salmasius asks a number of rhetorical questions which show a greater knowledge of events in England than we expect from the quality of his earlier chapters:

> Who now rules the people of England with more than kingly power? Who levies taxes on them? and indeed far heavier taxes than any king ever imposed? Who disarmed the citizens of London? Who bore away

[17] *A Defence,* below, pp. 394, 397. [18] *Ibid.,* p. 398.
[19] *Regia,* below, p. 989.

> and concealed in a tower the chains by which the streets of the city were defended? Who filled the city with armed men? Who seized the public treasury? Was it the people? All these are acts of the army which perpetrated them by order of its own leaders.[20]

England is now governed, continues Salmasius, not by its people but by a military tyranny such as set up Claudius as emperor in ancient Rome. When Rome acted thus, "not only did liberty depart far into the future, but also [Rome] lost absolutely the right of making a ruler, which from that time forth began to be with the soldiery." [21] Salmasius attributes the abolition of the House of Lords also to the action of military leaders. What, Mr. Milton! do you still hold that the people have carried through this revolution and this parricide that has so shocked civilized men of all Europe?

Milton's replies to Salmasius' analysis of actions of the military leaders, and his definition of the word *people,* throw into sharp relief a central weakness of Milton's intellectual position. The purging of the House by Colonel Pride, the trial and execution of the king, were actions representing a relatively small segment of the English population. When Salmasius asks, "Did the people do violence to the commoners of the lower house, putting some to flight?" Milton replies, "I say it was the people; for why should I not say that the act of the better, the sound part of the Parliament, in which resides the real power of the people, was the act of the people?" [22] Realizing the absurdity of this argument, Milton later qualifies his insistence that the English revolution had broad mass support. When Salmasius later returns to the attack, saying, "You must explain what you mean by the word people," Milton replies, "By *people* we mean all citizens of every degree." [23] You, Salmasius, do not understand the structure of our society. Just because we have abolished the House of Lords, we have not abolished our aristocracy. We include them, too, when we use the word *people,* and they are represented in the House of Commons. If Salmasius were not such an ignorant man, he would not assume that by the word *people* the English would mean the word *populace,* excluding the middle classes as well as the aristocracy. When Salmasius attacks the populace as "blind and brutish, without skill in ruling, and most fickle of men, the emptiest, and unsteadiest, and most inconstant," Milton replies, "It may be true of the dregs of the populace, but hardly of the middle class, which produces the greatest number of men of good sense and knowledge of affairs." [24] Thus in the last

[20] Below, p. 989; from the translation by Kathryn McEuen; *cf.* Salmasius, *Regia* (1649), p. 133, ll. 23–29.

[21] *Regia,* p. 134, ll. 27–29.

[22] *A Defence,* below, p. 457.

[23] *Ibid.,* p. 471.

[24] *Ibid.,* p. 471.

analysis Milton defines the word *people* as a qualitative concept: that minority, neither debased by ignorance and sloth nor ennobled by titles, that has acted in a timely fashion to free the nation from a tyrannous kingship.

In later passages of *A Defence* Milton tacitly grants that the Independents, however righteous and intrepid, were a small group of the English nation. When Salmasius writes, "Not one hundred thousandth part of the people agreed to this condemnation," Milton merely replies, "What of the rest, then, who let such a crime take place against their will? Were they trunks of trees?"[25] The king had been conquered. Should the English now bend the knee again to the tyrant they had deposed and face anew an endless slavery? The Presbyterians indeed had made a new alliance with the king; they preferred a new slavery under Charles to a government of equals. In this emergency only the Independents were true champions of English freedom:

> Only those called Independents knew how to be true to themselves until the end and how to use their victory. They did not wish the enemy who had been king to change again from enemy to king, and in my opinion they were wise. It was not that they opposed peace, but that, with good reason, they feared a new war or endless slavery concealed under the name of peace.[26]

In this dilemma, what course should the Independents have followed? "On our side, was an army famous for its loyalty, moderation, and courage. With the help of the army, it was possible for us to keep our freedom and save the state; do you believe we should have betrayed everything through cowardice and folly?"[27] Milton admits that a "great part of the people" deserted the Independents in the emergency of pulling down the kingship and setting up a republic. By gradual steps, then, Milton accepts Salmasius' claim that the revolution was against the will of the majority. In so doing he clarifies the issues and exalts the choices of Cromwell and the Rump Parliament, glorifying the patriotism of the middle class Puritans from which they sprang.

No rhetorical device in *A Defence* is more destructive to Milton's persuasiveness than his persistent use of epithets, the variety and dullness of which is astonishing in a mind so capacious. Not only is Salmasius a ***knave,*** a ***brute beast,*** a ***blockhead,*** a ***dull brute;*** his hectoring wife is a ***barking bitch,*** and Salmasius as "a talkative ass sat upon by a woman," "a eunuch priest, your wife for a husband." In the art of dishonesty, no writer is superior to Salmasius: he is a "prince of liars," a "wretched false prophet," a "lying hired slanderer," an "agent of royal roguery," the

[25] *A Defence,* below, pp. 508–509.

[26] *Ibid.,* below, pp. 511–12.

[27] *Ibid.,* p. 511.

"Arbiter-in-Chief of the Royal Lies," "mouthpiece of . . . infamy."[28] Milton plays persistently upon the idea that Salmasius is a writer hired and purchased to oppose the freedom of the new republic: "hireling pimp of slavery," "concealer of slavery's blemishes," *monstrous scoundrel.*[29] Descending still further into his resources, Milton denominates his antagonist as a *gallic cock,* a *dung-hill Frenchman,* a *French vagrant,* a "cheap French mountebank."[30] As for Salmasius' books, "no one has heaped up more dung than you . . . I promise to stuff you with chicken feed if by pecking through this whole dunghill of yours you can find me a single gem." Salmasius is moreover so "foul a procurer . . . that even the lowest slaves on any auction block should hate and despise you."[31] Thus does Milton lash his antagonist in chapter after chapter, with a whole rhetoric of epithets unrelieved by flashes of originality or sardonic playfulness such as one finds in the caustic pages of *Animadversions.*

Milton's arguments against Salmasius have most searching persuasiveness when they deal with the nature of kingship and the responsibility of the king to the laws of the land. They have least validity when they define the word *people* and attempt to justify the actual events of Charles' trial and execution. Thus *A Defence* is the least consistent in rational argument of any Miltonic tract. As the chapters of *A Defence* march in furious attack on Salmasius, one feels Milton tiring of his self-imposed method of grappling with a mind inferior to his own, exploding his opponent's statements one by one. Even *Eikonoklastes* presents a more persuasive if not less bitter justification of regicide than *A Defence;* and page by page it contains in its diction more Miltonic glow and flame than its successor. Despite its weaknesses, *A Defence* was considered a brilliantly successful refutation of Salmasius by European intellectuals. In what intrinsic sense did Milton grapple most realistically with the reasoning of his renowned opponent?

One reason for Milton's republican fervor was that he had experienced a fire of reforming agitation denied to Salmasius. This agitation left no mind of England unchanged, least of all one of Milton's intense and fearless imagination; it was a mind so dedicated to action as to forego these ten years past his great hope of leaving "something so written to aftertimes, as they should not willingly let it die."[32] In this agitation Milton's extreme religious views had finally clashed with the very essence of kingship: Its assumption not only of divine right but also of social superiority

[28] *Ibid.,* pp. 339, 365, 380, 397, 404, 468, 469, 476, 534.
[29] *Ibid.,* pp. 461, 529. [30] *Ibid.,* pp. 428, 508, 527.
[31] *Ibid.,* pp. 428, 461. [32] *Complete Prose,* I, 810.

as an hereditary gift.[33] The contrast between the poverty and lowly station of Christ and the worldly finery of kingship left an indelible mark on Milton's thought. One can imagine Henry Vane or Thomas Fairfax kissing the king's hand before fighting him next day on the battlefield; not so Milton or Cromwell or Harrison. On the Protestant Salmasius, however, such a contrast had made no impact whatever: Neither the divine right of kings nor their elevation in worldly grace seemed to him an irony or a riddle. Roger Williams had pictured Jesus as a "turner of the world upside down," as a prophet *"who disdained not to enter this World in a Stable . . . Who past through this World with the esteeme of a Madman, a Deceiver, a Conjurer, a Traytor against Caesar, and destitute of an house wherein to rest his head: Who made choice of his first and greatest Embassadours out of Fisher-men, Tent-makers, &c. and at last chose to depart on the stage of a painfull shamefull Gibbet."* [34] Such a picture of Christ, as *Paradise Regained* was to show, was not an obsession to Milton as it was to Williams; but it held a place in his imagination, whereas it was totally foreign to the thought of Salmasius.

Another strain in Milton's arguments on kingship is his deep knowledge of the Greek and Roman classics. Hobbes' assertion in *Behemoth* that education at Oxford and Cambridge undermined faith in kingship and prepared the way for the Puritan republic finds no more striking justification than in Milton's own experience. His fundamental principle is that "there is by nature no right of succession, and no king but the one who surpasses all others in wisdom and courage." He refers to the words of Aristotle: "The perversion of kingship is tyranny . . . a king is not a king unless he is self-sufficient and superior to his subjects in all that is good." [35] Milton quotes Plato, Aeschylus, Sophocles, Euripides, Cicero,

[33] *Cf. Eikonoklastes,* in *Complete Prose,* III, 486–87: "Indeed if the race of Kings were eminently the best of men, as the breed at *Tutburie* is of Horses, it would in some reason then be their part onely to command, ours always to obey. But Kings by generation no way excelling others, and most commonly not being the wisest or the worthiest by far of whom they claime to have the governing, that we should yeild them subjection to our own ruin, or hold of them the right of our common safety, and our natural freedom by meer gift, as when the Conduit pisses Wine at Coronations, from the superfluity of thir royal grace and beneficience, we may be sure was never the intent of God, whose ways are just and equal; never the intent of Nature, whose works are also regular; never of any People not wholly barbarous, whom prudence, or no more but human sense would have better guided when they first created Kings, then so to nullifie and tread to durt the rest of mankind, by exalting one person and his Linage without other merit lookt after, but the meer contingencie of a begetting, into an absolute and unaccountable dominion over them and their posterity."

[34] *Mr. Cottons Letter . . . Examined* (February 5, 1644), E31(16), Preface.

[35] *Ethics,* VIII, xii, tr. James E. C. Welldon (London, 1902), pp. 266–67.

Tacitus, Livy, to prove the accountability of the rulers to the people of Greece and Rome. Outstanding Romans killed their tyrants; the Greeks gave religious honors to tyrannicides. By comparison with the Greeks and Romans, have not the English treated their tyrant with gentle consideration? It is plain that Milton regards the Independents as creating a republic in the tradition of Greece and Rome, not a democracy, but an association of middle-class equals: "Where there are many equals, and in most states there are very many, I hold that they should rule alike and in turn." [36] From these and many other passages, it is plain that Milton found in Greek and Roman republics, like the American revolutionists of a later era, principles that justified his rejection of kingship as an institution.

In *A Defence,* then, Milton's break with kingship was more complete than ever before, a break cut deep by two chief forces: a secular preoccupation with the examples of Greek and Roman republics, and an extreme Puritan zeal for unification of vision and deed, the actuality of a New Jerusalem on English soil. In *A Defence* Milton's break with kingship becomes irrevocable. As he points out, even after the execution of Charles, he had attacked tyranny rather than kingship itself. Even in *A Defence* he repeats this statement. But gradually he reveals that now he will have no kingship at all, however benign. Addressing his countrymen near the end of *A Defence,* he writes:

> If you long for wealth, freedom, peace, and power, would it not be much better, much more in accord with your own deserts, to strive resolutely for those ends through your own virtue, industry, prudence and courage than to hope for them in vain under a king's control? Surely those who suppose that these ends cannot be attained without a king and master must think of themselves as unspeakably abject and ignoble.[37]

From this extreme position Milton was never to retreat. When the new republic was in its last throes in April, 1660, the blind champion neither quailed nor tried to flee. Rather he wrote a new plea to his countrymen to preserve the republic, knowing they would scorn his words: "What I have spoken, is the language of what is not call'd amiss *the good Old Cause* . . . Thus much I should perhaps have said though I were sure I should have spoken only to trees and stones; and had none to cry to, but with the Prophet, *O earth, earth, earth!* to tell the very soil it self, what her perverse inhabitants are deaf to." [38] Whatever the intellectual blindness Milton suffered, along with his fellow-Independents, it was for this cause he gave his remaining sight in writing *A Defence* and risked his life in 1660.

[36] *A Defence,* below, pp. 366–67. [37] *Ibid.*, below, p. 532.
[38] *The Readie & Easie Way* (2nd ed., 1660), pp. 106–107.

CHAPTER XV

FOR THE KING: RESISTANCE AND DEATH ON THE SCAFFOLD

March–June, 1651

THE new Commonwealth, now two years old, maintained its existence by the power of its arms and a fanatical minority, not by the support of public opinion. Although, as Parker had pointed out to the Presbyterians, the new republic had forbidden blasphemy, swearing, scandalous sects, and adultery,[1] and though the theatres had been closed, such a series of suppressive acts dear to the Puritan heart did not assuage the Presbyterian anger. The image of the king at his prayers upon the block was more persuasive to the average Presbyterian mind than legal abolition of sins of the flesh. Pictures of the late king were still displayed in London streets.[2] A satirical account of young Charles' coronation at Scone on January 1, 1651, appeared on the streets of London about February 27. To pious Presbyterians the romantic picture of the young king on horseback and the oath he took "to maintain the true Kirke of God" was more significant than the author's sneers at Charles' swarthy complexion, his expressionless countenance as he scattered coins to the vulgar, his allegiance to his Catholic mother, his obsessive passion for young maidens.[3] Much as individual Presbyterians deplored Charles' excesses as a man (he was indeed the antithesis in every way of the Puritan ideal), he symbolized that vision of kingship in which the average Englishman felt he had a property. Many Presbyterians, even ministers, were ready to risk their lives to bring young Charles to the throne of England. The Council of State employed spies to uncover plots against the government. Upon evidence of one such plot by Eusebius Andrews and others, the new high court of justice had sentenced Andrews to execution, which had taken place August 22, 1650; another such execution had taken place October 7. Many Presbyterian ministers had refused to observe the day of thanksgiving for Cromwell's victory at Dunbar. Through a spy named George Bishop, who had in his pay a number of royalist agents, the Council learned in January that an uprising for Charles was

[1] *Scotlands Holy War* (January 17, 1651), E621(16), p. 32.

[2] Gardiner, *Commonwealth and Protectorate,* II, 8.

[3] *The True Manner of the Crowning of Charles the Second King of Scotland,* 669f15(81).

imminent, with officers appointed in every English county. To meet this danger, Parliament ordered the re-arrest of dangerous persons who had been imprisoned and then released. For fear of cloaked uprisings, it also prohibited sports gatherings such as horse races, football, hunting, and hawking matches. It further directed that a substantial body of cavalry be ordered to advance toward the Scottish border.[4] Such counter measures against internal resistance, which in themselves proclaimed the restlessness of the country at large, were to become an increasingly familiar pattern in the years to come.

1. HYDE: UNDAUNTEDNESS OF SPIRIT

A different kind of resistance, that of royalist idealism, was reflected in the execution of Sir Henry Hyde, which took place at the Old Exchange in London on March 4. According to the accusation, Hyde had served Charles as ambassador to the emperor of Turkey and had attempted to discharge the Commonwealth's representative, Sir Thomas Bendish. For two years past he had obstructed commerce between English merchants and the Turks. The English merchants, having discovered his design, intercepted him on his way from Constantinople to Smyrna, and had him shipped to England. "When he came upon the Scaffold," ran a contemporary account, "he put off his hat to the spectators, deporting himself with great cheerfulnesse, and undantednesse [*sic*] of spirit: then turning himself about, he desired to see his Coffin, which was accordingly shewed him, a black mourning cloth being also prepared to cover the same."[5] Assured freedom of speech by the sheriff, who was standing nearby, Hyde spoke to the multitude, asserting his undying loyalty to Charles but denying that he had in any way obstructed commerce between the Turks and the English. He was not an ambassador, only a messenger from one monarch to another. "My Master," said Hyde, "hath suffered bitterly in *England;* and if there be any failing in his Service, the fault is onely mine." At the end of his speech Hyde asked for the executioner, gave him four pounds, kissed the block, and later the axe itself. Returning the axe to the executioner, Hyde said to him: "I will onely say, *Lord Jesus receive my Soul;* and when I lift up my Righthand, do your work."[6] He lay down again, and after a pause lifted up his right hand, whereupon the executioner struck off his head in one blow. The ritual thus followed reflected the psychology of a mind untouched by

[4] Gardiner, *Commonwealth and Protectorate,* II, 7.

[5] *The Speech . . . of Sir Henry Hide* (March 5, 1651), E625(13), p. 2.

[6] *A True Copy of Sir Henry Hide's Speech* (March 7, 1651), E625(16), pp. 12, 15.

the fierce tracings of Puritan dynamics, simple and secure in the old faith in which his memories held nothing to the contrary. "I thank God I am otherwise bred."[7] Hyde's language, for which he apologized on the scaffold, was broken and halting; unafraid of death, he was appalled and dismayed at the strange forms of the new order, the unwitting victim of a new world he did not comprehend.

2. CHRISTOPHER LOVE: "PRECIOUS IN GOD'S ACCOUNT"

In July and August the trial and execution of Christopher Love brought into focus the kind of stiff-backed resistance to the new republic the Independents could overcome by neither threat nor persuasion. Love was a leading Presbyterian minister of London, a brilliant expositor of his creed, highly esteemed by the most distinguished of his clerical contemporaries. From his own "A Brief and Full Narrative," written just before his execution, it is evident that Love was friendly toward Charles' cause, willing to contribute small amounts of money, willing to have sympathizers of Charles meet at his house.[8] To the Independents this was treason enough; but to many observers it was a dubious definition. Love was arrested on May 14, 1651, and charged with high treason. On June 20 he was brought from the Tower to the High Court of Justice in Westminster Hall and charged with corresponding with Charles II, sending and receiving letters from the Scots, conspiring with the Commonwealth's enemies to raise money for Charles' subversion of the Commonwealth. His trial took place on June 20, 21, 25, 27, and July 5. He was condemned to be executed on July 16.[9] On July 9 Love petitioned Parliament, saying that he "goeth not about to plead Excuse . . . acknowledging he hath offended against the Acts of this Commonwealth." On July 11 he wrote another petition, asserting that he knew of "no Plot or Design against the present Government," a new plea on July 15, "humbly acknowledging he hath incurred your high Displeasure," and still another on August 14, "humbly acknowledgeth he hath so highly violated the Laws of the Commonwealth, as that thereby he hath rendered himself guilty of the Sentence of death, justly passed on him by the High Court of Justice."[10] These petitions waver between abasement and justification. Love addressed Parliament, not the high court, which court nevertheless had treated him with great respect. Attorney General Prideaux indeed had asserted that "it was far from the intentions or desires of that honorable court to thirst after bloud, but rather desired a confession & contrition of heart."[11]

[7] *Ibid.*, p. 13. [8] In *Mr. Love's Case* (August 22, 1651), E641(10), pp. 5–14.
[9] *DNB.* [10] *Mr. Love's Case,* pp. 1, 2, 3, 5.
[11] *The Tryall of Mr. Love* (June 22, 1651), E632(16), p. 3.

Love was executed on Tower Hill on August 22. His speech on the scaffold throws into clear focus not only his position but also that of his most brilliant and resourceful colleagues among the Presbyterians. *"As for the person of the late King,"* said Love, *"I never thirsted after his blood, but according to the Covenant desired nothing more then his restauration to Honour and Freedom. Secondly, I never engaged against the person of the King, but only against his followers, endeavouring the true settlement of a firm and lasting peace."* [12] Illogical as this seemed to such men as Cromwell, Milton, and Ludlow, to restore to his place a king whom they had negotiated with in vain and whom their armies had defeated on the battlefield, Love's view represented not only the Presbyterians but also the Anglicans in his loyalty to the king. It spoke as well the views of such men as Richard Baxter and Thomas Lord Fairfax. On the scaffold Love declared he had written no letter to Charles, to the Queen Mother, or to any Scot; nor had he received any letters from them; nor had he collected any money to be paid to the king. He had been condemned, Love asserted, for giving money to Massey and for being present when letters were read from Massey and others. This to his mind was not treason. Love exclaimed, *"Did I ever invite the Scots to invade* England? . . . *Did I ever encourage our English army to invade* Scotland?" [13] When later he uttered a dire prophecy, saying, *"Those who have gotten Power into their hands by Policy and use it by Cruelty, they will lose it with Ignominy,"* the sheriff interrupted him, saying, "Sir, be modest: I am not able to endure this, indeed I am not." To which Love replied, *"Sir, I shall look God in the face with what I say."* Then Love gave a definition of treason inherent in his defense from the beginning, a definition that had left the Independents no alternative: The Scots were not malignant to him when they defended their nation and the title to their king. Such a position was not malignancy *"but an honest and a justifiable Cause."* [14] On the scaffold, then, Love asserted both his guilt by the definition of the high court of justice and his innocence by his own. Edmund Calamy (of the Smectymnuans) attended him on the scaffold. Following the ritual of the day, Love turned to the executioner and said, "Friend, are all things in readinesse?" Whereupon he took off his doublet, gave it to a friend, and handed the executioner a red scarf to spread upon the block. He then placed his head upon the block, rose up again, and said to the executioner, "When I lift up my left hand do thy Office." [15] After the fatal stroke the head and body of the dead man were placed in the black coffin and carried away.

Love's execution crystallized one of the main dilemmas of the Com-

[12] *Two Speeches Delivered* (August 22, 1651), E640(16), p. 3.
[13] *Mr. Love's Case,* p. 19. [14] *Ibid.,* pp. 20, 21.
[15] *Two Speeches Delivered,* pp. 5, 6.

monwealth in incandescent clarity: How were the Presbyterians and the Independents to be reconciled? Without such a reconciliation the Commonwealth could not hope to prosper. Their leaders saluted each other on the street, attended conferences together; yet now Love, "a man precious in God's account," [16] had suffered for his loyalty to those principles which a minority in power had rejected. In *Love's Advocate,* which had appeared a week before the execution, the writer compared the prisoner Love, condemned to execution, to cavaliers taken on the battlefield, men who had shed the blood of Puritan patriots, but now, when they laid down their arms, given mercy by their captors upon their pledge not to take arms any more against the Parliament. Does not Love deserve as much mercy as a Cavalier thus forgiven on the battlefield? The author excuses Love as a man as ignorant in civil affairs as he is knowledgeable in theological ones. Certainly Love was not responsible for the initiation of the war against the Scots. They were in arms against the Commonwealth before the king came to their country, long before Love had any part in it. Let us try to understand each other, exhorts the writer. Certain Independents and Presbyterians meet each other weekly "to seek God for a happy reconciliation of the difference between them." These men hope to close that dangerous breach between the two parties. The fault is not all on the side of the Presbyterians. The policies of the Independents, asserts the writer, have "stumbled many honest godly Christians." [17]

3. NEEDHAM AND MILTON: GOD'S ESPECIAL CARE

Scorning such a plea for reconciliation, John Hall, in *A Gagg to Loves Advocate* (August 29) asserted that the Commonwealth had no choice but to bring Love to justice. Was it more just to sentence Love to death than to allow a plot against the state to grow and flourish? By day the average Presbyterian appears to conform to the laws; but by night he addresses Charles Stuart as his king, whom Parliament denounces as a traitor. The writer calls up the old enemies of the state whom the Presbyterians are still willing to serve: a banished king, courtiers, "people of Criminal and luxurious lives," a papist queen mother, the Scottish kirk. Was Love not the chief architect of the plot against the Commonwealth? Moreover, the Council of State had dealt with him humanely and magnanimously, but in vain; no answers from him forthcoming, the Council at last had turned him over to the high court. The evidence had been full

[16] *Love's Advocate* (August 15, 1651), E640(11), p. 4.

[17] *Ibid.,* pp. 6, 7. *Cf.* p. 7: "Ingenious spirits are wrought more upon by cords of love, then by thousand stripes."

and conclusive; the judges had treated him with respect and generosity. Yet he "would neither confess, what had been clearly proved against him, nor yet acknowledg the Autoritie against which hee had so highly offended." [18] Not one judge dissented from the conviction. Finally, just before his execution, Love had written a full narrative of the whole proceeding, in which he explicitly admitted those actions which in court he had expressly denied.

As spokesman for the Commonwealth in the emergency of Love's trial and execution, Marchamont Needham was vehement and emphatic for drastic repression of the resistance. "It is high time now," wrote Needham (without naming Love) in *Mercurius Politicus* for June 19, "to assert the honor and integrity of the Parliament, against the Passions and Proceedings of our male-contents of the ministry." [19] Never content with settling one score against the Presbyterians, Needham holds up in derision their sins of the past. No sooner had Parliament humbled the bishops, insists Needham, than the Presbyterian faction began to intermeddle in secular affairs, demanding that the Parliament set up a state Presbyterian church as *jure divino*. Frustrated in their attempts to subdue England to their discipline, the Presbyterians fastened their hopes first upon Charles and then upon his son, "to hedg in him and his Interest with their own, in hope of a Revenge, and a Recovery." By this policy the Presbyterian ministers brought about two wars between England and Scotland. Even now, after the establishment of the Commonwealth, they "fill their pulpits with alarms and Invectives, preach disobedience and treason with open mouth, keep privat Fasts for the destruction of the Parliament, dam them and all their Friends for Hereticks and Schismaticks; and in their licentious way, excommunicate the State out of all possibilities of heaven . . . and out of the very hearts of the people." [20] Now these same ministers are preparing new insurrections. In the next issue of *Politicus,* June 26, Needham accuses the Presbyterians by name, opening his tirade with, "*Treason* never walks so secure as under the cloak of *Religion.*" Now the Presbyterians are trying openly to overturn the peace and freedom of England, "as it hath appeared clearly to the world, upon the Trial of Mr. *Love,* before the High *Court of Justice.*" [21] They have used wiles and subtleties such as circulating letters without signatures, leaving sums of money inclosed in paper on a table so that the donors may swear in court they never gave money to any person. They have been carefully coached how to respond in court if arrested and accused. Though the conspirators met in Love's own house,

[18] *A Gagg to Love's Advocate* (August 29, 1651), E640(28), pp. 2, 5–6.
[19] June 12–19, 1651, E632(15), p. 863. [20] *Ibid.*, pp. 864, 865.
[21] June 19–26, 1651, E632(20), pp. 879, 880.

he claimed that he took no money and did not know who received money in his house. No Jesuit understands better the art of defense by mental reservation than this pious Presbyterian minister. Meanwhile in his own defence he cites his own sufferings, asperses the testimony of witnesses, misapplies the Scriptures to his own ends, cites the precious Covenant.[22]

Some weeks later, in his issue of August 14, Needham was in an ideal position to justify his indictment of the Presbyterian faction. The Scots armies were on the march into northern England. Needham attributes the march of the Scots to the machinations of Mr. Love: "See now the fruits of Mr. *Love's* godly Ministry! for he hath lived to see the day, and receiv tydings of his *yong Masters* being mounted, and upon a march in *England*." [23] All of which the nation owes, insists Needham, to Love and his fellow-conspirators:

> It is the *old Cavalier* interest that comes in now, clad with a new cloak of the *Covenant*, after the *Scotish* fashion . . . Let the *Presbyterians* remember, that though they laid not the old *Tyrant* down upon the Block, yet the *young One* knowes, they were the men that brought him to the *Scaffold*, and that they are the *old Enemies* of his *Family*.[24]

Did not young Charles take great joy in the Scots' defeat at Dunbar? After Dunbar he banished all the more conscientious Presbyterians from his presence, choosing tried and true Cavaliers to stand nearest him in his court. Needham exhorts the Scots not to attempt an invasion "for the sake of a *Toy* called King." He then lists the invasions of England by the Scots over the centuries and the utter frustration and defeat that attended their efforts. The present invasion can have no other end than the bitter defeat of their armies, and the triumph of the commonwealth.

How fully Milton believed at this moment in the duty of the state to execute Love may be judged only by implication. At no time does he mention Love by name. When Needham's words about Love appeared in *Politicus* of March and April, *A Defence* had just appeared, too late for even a side glance in defense of Love's trial and execution. In serious polemic passages Milton's style resembles that of Needham more closely than that of any other writer. From the history of Milton's attitude toward the Presbyterian ministers, however, it is virtually certain that he would have justified the execution of Love as a necessity to the protection of the Commonwealth. Milton's words in *Second Defence* reflect the intensity of his antagonism:

> But when, at length, some Presbyterian ministers, who had formerly been the most bitter enemies to Charles, became jealous of the growth of the independents, and of their ascendency in the parliament, most tumult-

[22] *Ibid.*, p. 881. [23] August 7–14, E640(9), p. 981. [24] *Ibid.*, p. 982.

> uously clamoured against the sentence, and did all in their power to prevent the execution . . . I thought it became me to oppose such a glaring falsehood.[25]

Milton's hostility against the ministers he expressed in both the opening and the closing pages of *The Tenure,* on ground that Needham was to trace over again in 1651. At the beginning of *The Tenure,* Milton wrote that after the Presbyterians had "born arms against thir King, devested him, disannointed him, nay curs'd him all over in thir Pulpits and thir Pamphlets . . . not only [did they] turne revolters from those principles, which only could at first move them, but lay the staine of disloyaltie . . . on those proceedings, which are the necessary consequences of their own former actions."[26] Like Needham after him, Milton again and again vilifies the Presbyterian ministers, recalling their repeated attacks on kingship. Some "who have been fiercest against thir Prince, under the notion of a Tyrant, and no mean incendiaries of the Warr against him, when God out of his providence and high disposal hath deliver'd him into the hand of thir brethren, on a suddain and in a new garbe of Allegiance . . . they plead for him, pity him, extoll him, protest against those that talk of bringing him to the tryal of Justice, which is the Sword of God, superior to all mortal things, in whose hand soever by apparent signes his testified will is to put it."[27] At the end of *The Tenure* Milton again returns to the contradictions inherent in the Presbyterian horror of tyrannicide, deriding them for their stand that "the deposing and punishing of a King or Tyrant, *is against the constant Judgement of all Protestant Divines.*" In view of these attacks on the Presbyterian ministers of London, we may conclude that Milton was one with Needham in justifying the trial and execution of Christopher Love.

The following week, in his *Politicus* of July 3, Needham dealt still sharper blows against Presbyterian resistance to Love's trial. No Independent knew better than Needham the thoughts and feelings of the Commonwealth's opponents. Now he couples the fate of Love with the fate of Charles I. He reminds the Presbyterians that the time is past when "this Nation was wedded to the vanity of admiring *Kings,* placing Them in a lofty seat of *Impunity,* like *Gods,* that were not bound to give men any accompt of their Actions."[28] In those years the might of kingship was elevated far above the privileges of Parliaments. No longer now can kingly traitors escape. But any of the same people who did not hesitate to support the execution of Charles are loath to deal the same justice to "a very godly and painfull *Preacher.*" But by law a priestly traitor must not escape either. However pious the man, he cannot justly

[25] See *Milton in the Puritan Revolution,* p. 211. [26] *Complete Prose,* III, 191.
[27] *Ibid.,* III, 193. [28] June 26–July 3, 1651, E633(6), p. 885.

escape trial and punishment for treason. To exempt any particular persons, however godly, from punishment for their crimes is "to pervert Justice, and lose the end of Government." [29] If Love is guilty of treason, he is responsible in part for the blood shed at Dunbar and many other battles. If guilty, he would be willing to see members of Parliament murdered, the Council of State, indeed all the well affected. He is in part responsible for the hardships of the soldiers, the cold marches, the long nights; he is even responsible for the high taxes people must pay to sustain their armies. "Behold M. *Love* in all these Respects," concludes Needham, "and then what think you of his being a *Godly minister*." [30]

Needham never tired of equating the victories of the English armies with the approval of the Lord for the actions of the Commonwealth. In his issue of September 4–11 he paused to review God's mercies, beginning with the victory at the battle of Naseby; the destruction of Hamilton's army in Lancashire; the bringing of the king to justice; the victories in Ireland and Scotland, particularly the miraculous triumph at Dunbar and a year later at Worcester. Does it not seem that God's finger was pointing "out to all the world his Resolutions for *England*"? [31] In his issue of September 11 Needham continued in this vein, asserting that God had shown his disapproval first of the bishops and now of the Presbyterian clergy. On August 22 young Charles had raised his standard at Nottingham, doomed by God's will to defeat at Worcester. As Charles I had proclaimed himself a martyr, so had Christopher Love. On August 22 Christopher Love had lost his head on Tower Hill, "a just Judgement of God for his implacable Apostacie and enmity." Furthermore, asserts Needham, what reception did the young king have when he marched south into England? He was in England twenty-eight days. In that time did the English rush to his banners? Did the Presbyterians, themselves assured in vain of a great uprising for the king, hasten to his side? All these events show the favor of God upon the Commonwealth: "The Result of all which may serve as an undeniable evidence of Gods especial care, and good will, for the conservation of this Government; and to instruct all the world, how fatall it is for men to fight against his Decrees." [32] Love had helped to destroy the old malignancy; then, turning apostate, he set up a new malignancy of his own and justly suffered execution for his treason. Thus Needham interpreted the will of God, as indeed did Cromwell after every victory, and Milton himself in praising him. Looking back, few observers will doubt that such verification of God's justice made a deep impress on the average citizen. Needham knew

[29] *Ibid.*, p. 886. [30] *Ibid.*, p. 887.

[31] *Mercurius Politicus*, E641(12), p. 1046.

[32] September 11–18, 1651, E641(20), p. 1063.

his audience well, however much or little he disbelieved his own proof of God's mercies.

CHAPTER XVI

NOAH BIGGS: CHEMISTRY AND THE TOPOGRAPHY OF IGNORANCE

March, 1651

On March 10, 1651, appeared Noah Biggs' *The Vanity of the Craft of Physick,* a long tract in the Baconian tradition, filled with scathing attacks on the medical practices of the day and pleading for reformation in the teaching of medicine. Not in religious and civic life alone, insists Biggs, but in science as well must Parliament combat the tyranny of error: *"The Reformation of the body of a whole Art . . . has layn long eclips'd and deformed."* [1] The health of the body is hardly less crucial than the health of the soul. Biggs believed that chemistry was the foundation of the physician's art; yet what was known about chemistry was as yet only a small promontory in a vast *terra incognita.* Instead of leading bold explorations into this vast unknown, the universities are slaves to traditional paths of knowledge. But even traditional knowledge is upheld by a blind faith rather than the constant and doubting scrutiny of the laboratory. Nor is there any bold new science on the march. *"Where,"* asked Biggs, *"is there an examination and consecution of Experiments? encouragements to a new world of Knowledge, promoting, compleating, and actuating some new Inventions? . . . Where a Review of the old Experiments and Traditions, and casting out the rubbish that has pestered the Temple of Knowledge?"* [2] Parliament cannot be insensible to the failures of the medical profession, which derive inevitably from errors in science perpetuated by the universities. In a time of reformation cannot Parliament call into being a great conclave of intellectuals to make a new beginning in the teaching of science, a great Academy of Philosophical Freedom? Though Biggs does not mention Bacon, his tract carries many an echo of *Novum Organum.* As he addresses Parliament, his vision glows with prophecy and dims with doubt. Will the Commons understand the terrible urgency of his proposal for reformation, which will affect the health of every citizen of the land? If no one acts now, his countrymen *"may sit hereafter and bemoan*

[1] E625(17), sig. a2v.   [2] *Ibid.,* sig. b.

themselves, to have neglected through faintness the onely remedy of their heavy sufferings." [3] There is no hope for the reformation of medicine by action of the physicians themselves: They are for the most part opposed to the Commonwealth. Moreover, they occupy such superior positions in community life that they are lulled into perpetuating their errors by a feeling of security and grandeur.

1. TOWARD REFORMATION IN SCIENCE

Despite his resolution to proceed against all odds, Biggs anticipates the failure of his appeal for reformation; he gauges the obstacles as almost insuperable. The reform of medicine in both theory and practice must be initiated against the wills of the physicians; yet it cannot be carried through without their cooperation, though most of them dislike "this present government." Perhaps, muses the chemist, it is better to silence oneself, leaving the reform he seeks to time, "the Mid-wife rather then the mother of truth." Yet the reform itself is inevitable; he cannot imagine that an enlightened Commonwealth England will reject his ideas for those of reformers to follow; his work will "do more then whisper to the next Ages," not only to Britain but to all Europe as well.[4] But even as his hopes soar, his vision of the obstacles pulls at their wings. When a layman criticizes the medical profession, their subservience, for example, to Galen and Paracelsus, he wars against a tenacious reverence for antiquity, an intellectual custom so prejudicial to science "that till it be rejected, it is impossible any *new* learning can be acquired." The physicians have no conception of the depths of their ignorance. Whereas other arts by small discoveries advance almost daily toward the remote pinnacle of full illumination, medicine lags behind in the dark bogs of antiquity: "To what end tends the Anatomy of these two thousand years, with those tedious lectures, if the Sanation of diseases, be not more happier at this day, then of old? What meanes that tearing and Cadaverous dissection of bodies, with that curious inspection and inquisition into the capillary veines, if we may not learn by the Errors of the *Ancients,* and if we may not make an emendation of those things that are past?" Is it possible that the best minds of the English people are fit only to be "the Hinch-boys of *Aristotle* . . . as if we had no brick to make, without raking the straw, and stubble of *Galen, Hyppocrates, Mesine* and other huddle of tongue Physitians"? [5] Another obstacle to reform is the scorn felt by physicians for laboratory tools and procedures. Such practitioners are as remote from true knowledge as a ship pilot who knows the sea

[3] *Ibid.,* sig. b4. [4] *Ibid.,* pp. 3, 4. [5] *Ibid.,* pp. 8, 9, 9–10.

only from books or a painter who understands the theory of art but deigns not to use the brush.

Biggs exposes with vehement satire the common treatments of the day; the theory of which he finds shaky with superstition. He has many long passages on the harm done by blood letting, the chief effect of which is to reduce the patient's strength and deprive him of vital juices when he needs them most. The use of induced ulcers Biggs considers brutal and harmful treatment. He condemns the theory of not allowing water to patients in a fever: "A *beast* never dyed, because he satisfied his thirst." [6] It is presumptuous ignorance to feed the feverish sick; in acute fevers the patient should have only liquids. Biggs is also contemptuous of the use of laxatives and sugared compounds, which the physicians scorn to mix themselves but farm out to still more ignorant apothecaries. Honey is a benign sweet, sugar a dangerous one. Biggs is opposed to the use of compounds generally, without citing experiments to justify his position. Falling into the psychology he condemns, he cites Paracelsus and God as his authorities for the use of simples only: "Hence *Paracelsus* writeth to the *Chirurgians;* to what purpose do you *superadde vinegar* to the root of *Comfrey,* or *bole* . . . while God hath compos'd this *simple* sufficient to cure the fracture of the bones?" [7] In a later passage Biggs qualifies his condemnation of compounds to say that in some cases additional elements may be added when experiment justifies their use.

The range and variety of quackery practiced on the public in the name of medicine Biggs pictures with acid scorn in a cross-section analysis of physicians and imitators. Some men without even university education claim to have an hereditary faculty for healing the sick, but treat only their friends or humble people in need; old soldiers turn to medicine, parading their wounds as proof of their knowledge; unsuccessful ministers, or ministers silenced by the government, who believe that the cloth of their profession gives them insight into the art of healing; still others who stress the healing quality of herbs; men learned in mathematics, or men who can quote Aristotle or Galen in a compelling manner; still others who are sons of physicians, assuming that closeness to doctor and patients has bestowed upon them knowledge; unsuccessful apprentices in the art of chemistry, fit only to make poisons, but bragging "of select and precious things"; "*baptiz'd Jewes* (more wicked then the not baptiz'd) who have learn'd from the *Kabala* how to mortifie *mercury* divers wayes"; still other charlatans who dispense cosmetics, ointments, oils, and perfumes, claiming the power to preserve womanly beauty, "or repair it if ruin'd." [8] Finally there are those slothful and rule-bound phy-

[6] *Ibid.,* p. 203. [7] *Ibid.,* p. 34. [8] *Ibid.,* p. 26.

sicians who sometimes administer "a *miscellany* of a thousand simples, that if one would not helpe, another should." [9] Thus, concludes Biggs, the citizens of England are in a sad condition indeed when illness besets them, victims not only of "internall calamities" but also "expos'd to so many external outrages and violences of such ignorant pretenders." [10]

The theories of medicine taught in the schools are riddled with fallacies and unsupported by any program of experimentation. In the teaching of theories much stress is laid on contraries and the clashing of forces within the body, as if elements of chemistry had wills and opinions of their own. "The schools reduce all *sanation* to the means of *Contrariation* in their vain and ridiculous Comments of *heat* and *Cold*." But it is mere superstition to assume that heat and cold in the same body are necessarily contrary in their effects; each may have its function and "*unity* is not contrary to *Duality*." Instead of giving attention to specific remedies, the schools continue ignorant of both causes and treatments, and "wavering twixt negligence and uncertainty suspend all farther inquiry." [11] It is a sad thing for England that the superstitions of the physicians, and their trifling with the lives of men and women, have their justification in the great colleges of the land.

2. MEDICAL PRACTICE: HAZARDS AND SUPERSTITIONS

The popular medical treatises of the day illuminate as no other evidence the layers of ignorance passed on from one generation to another by learned practitioners. On April 12, 1651, Nicholas Culpeper sent forth his *Directory for Midwives,* deploring the acceptance of tradition in preference to dependence on one's own eyes: "I weigh not a Rush the nice definition of *Aristotle,* and the *Peripatetics,* nor of all the fools that dance after their Pipes." Yet Culpeper unhesitatingly declares that mutilated or deformed children result from "the act of Copulation . . . at that time when the woman had her Menstruis upon her." [1] On May 11 was republished *The Surgions Directory for Young Practitioners,* by Thomas Vicary, who had been surgeon to Henry VIII, Edward VI, Queen Mary, and Queen Elizabeth. To break a plague sore, wrote Vicary, "Take blacke Snayles and leavened Bread, stampe them very well together, make a Plaister thereof and apply it to the Sore, and it will breake sodainly by Gods helpe." [2] For swelling or pain in the genital organs, Vicary recommended a poultice made of white wine and cow dung; after application of the poultice, one should add oil of roses. On May 15 came forth still another medical treatise titled *Physical Rarities,* by Ralph

[9] *Ibid.,* pp. 30–31. [10] *Ibid.,* p. 28. [11] *Ibid.,* pp. 215, 216, 229.
[1] E1340(1), p. 59, pp. 140–41. [2] E1265, p. 331.

Williams, "Practitioner in Physick and Chyrurgerie." To remove an infected tooth, Williams advocates the root of a mulberry tree soaked in vinegar several days, then dried in the sun, made into a powder, and rubbed on the offending tooth, whereupon "it will fall out"![3] On December 2 Leo Sowerby sent forth his *Ladies Dispensatory,* recommending "Sheeps dung layd to with vinegar" for warts on the genitals; for pain in urination, "Wood-lice drunk in wine"; to alleviate headache, "flowers of privet laid to with vinegar."[4] Several unsigned treatises of the day, such as *A Book of Fruits and Flowers,* passed on remedies scarcely more superstitious than those by reputable practitioners. For a breast canker, wrote the author, "Take *Goose*-dung, and *Celedonie,* stamp them well together, and lay it plaister-wise to the soare, it will cleanse the *Canker,* kill the wormes, and heale the soare."[5] In his *Treatise of the Nature and Qualities of Simples,* Robert Pemell advocated lettuce for a "hot stomack," the application of saffron, mixed with egg yolk and oil of roses, to ease the pain of the gout.[6] In a subsequent tract, *De Facultatibus Simplicium,* Pemell recommended onions (mixed with rue and honey) to ease stomach pains, accelerate the flow of urine, reduce the danger from the bite of a mad dog, destroy worms in children, and increase sperm.[7] In his *De Morbis Puerorum* Pemell deals with diseases of children, among which he cites lice breeding, scab and itch, and "Of Pissing in Bed." "If persons of years do live nastily and not change often," writes Pemell, "they soon become lousey. But tis very familiar for Children to breed Lice." Lice "arise from a hot and moist matter which putrifieth in the skin, or pores of the body."[8] For treatment of itch and scab, Pemell proposes an ointment composed of oil of roses, "quick Brimstone" in powder form, and lemon juice. For the treatment of stone in the bladders of children, Pemell advocates a mild diet of little meat and bathing the child with a liquid in which are mingled mallows, marshmallows, pellitory of the wall, parsley, dill, linseed, and fenegreek. Finally, the places around the bladder should be bathed with an ointment of marshmallows, oil of white lilies, and oil of scorpions, one part of each mixed together.[9]

These analyses of diseases and treatments are not extreme cases but typical of the medical recommendations of Milton's time. Only rarely does one read of an experiment based entirely on step-by-step observation performed in the laboratory, such as Nathaniel Highmore's *History of Generation* (1651), which traces day by day the development of the chick in the embryo.[10] As in later centuries Latin was the language of the

[3] E1302, p. 33. [4] E1258, pp. 144, 133, 3. [5] April 2, 1653, E690(13), p. 18.
[6] April 27, 1652, E660(8), chaps. 117, 21.
[7] November 29, 1653, E721(2), chap. 28. [8] November 29, 1653, E721(3), p. 3.
[9] *Ibid.,* pp. 5, 54. [10] October 28, 1651, E1369(4).

physicians in making prescriptions, and the layman was reluctant to challenge the doctor's diagnosis, even when the life of one of his own children was at stake. At no point in seventeenth-century life did ignorance cost so much agony and frustration as in medical practice.

Chapter XVII

COMENIUS AND PETERS: PATTERNS OF STATE REFORM

June, 1651

Of all his contemporaries, no intellectual pursued a single embracing reform more tenaciously than Comenius. To him the secret of all progress was the vast expansion of mental powers possible in each boy and girl, however lowly born, under the watchful direction of the gifted teacher. Comenius devoted his whole working life to the elaboration of this central passion. Hugh Peters, on the other hand, set forth no hierarchy of principles, no single revolutionary idea from which a New Jerusalem might rise. Like Milton and Cromwell, he was not a systematic thinker in meeting the active needs of a society in ferment. He could dramatize the distance between a London "swarming with poor" and a New England without beggars: "I have lived in a Countrey, where seven years I never saw beggar, nor heard an oath, nor looked upon a drunkard; why should there be beggars in your *Israel* where there is so much work to do?" [1] For the moment Peters meant the word *beggar* to take precedence over the word *oath* and the word *drunkard*. But over a lifetime of thought, which word was most crucial? However gifted as an observer, he never selected, in his own analysis of revolution, the one wheel that moved all others toward the New Jerusalem.

1. HUGH PETERS: REFORMER AT LARGE

Like Vane and Williams, Peters had drunk of the fiery wine of the future in both Holland and New England. A Cambridge man, Peters had entered Trinity at fourteen and earned an M.A. at the age of twenty-two. He had attended Cromwell as chaplain in Scotland and Ireland, supporting him invariably in his most extreme measures against the king and now for civil reforms. In the spring of 1651 Peters was at the height of

[1] *Gods Doings and Mans Duty* (April 2, 1645), p. 41.

his influence, established as one of the preachers at Whitehall, lodging there and receiving a salary of £200 a year.[2]

On June 17 appeared Peters' *Good Work for a Good Magistrate*, a utopia comprehensive in its range though very uneven in style and quality of ideas. "None can bee free of great injustice," wrote Peters, "who by persecution for Religion take awaie libertie of conscience from anie." [3] In recommending this sweeping freedom, Peters does not name either the Jews or the Roman Catholics, though elsewhere he writes, "Let no difference bee made between Jews, or Gentiles, bond or free, stranger or Natives, in either *Criminal,* or *Civil* things." [4] In his most extreme pleas for toleration, Peters, unlike Williams, omits particular applications to the hated Papists. In a curious postscript, evidently added as an afterthought, Peters favors a full machinery of censorship: *"All Popish and offensive Books, Libels, and loos Pamphlets may bee suppressed."* [5] All books are to be licensed; none is to be printed without the approval of judicious censors appointed by the state. Peters does not face the contradiction inherent in his support of extreme toleration and his proposal of a close censorship of the press. Around the campfire each soldier might argue as freely as he liked, supported by Cromwell and his chaplain; but now that the war was won, neither Hugh Peters nor John Milton could claim for him the complete freedom of conscience expressed in the printed word.

Peters touches on many reforms, none of which he expands into a full, unique pattern. On educational matters he does not speak like Comenius before him, for every child in a state school, or like Milton of a decade later, for state schools in every county, "not in grammar only, but in all liberal arts and exercises." [6] Peters confines himself to recommendations for Oxford and Cambridge, the colleges of which he thinks should be removed to various cities. He is far more concerned about increasing the preparation of ministers at Oxford and Cambridge than about extending the traditions of classical learning. Let half the colleges at Cambridge confine themselves to preparing young men for the ministry, men often chosen, as by the Jesuits, from humble families, "in anie place, or condition where wee finde them at plough or trade, which are godlie and tractable." [7] Peters' views on Oxford and Cambridge reflect a curious blind-

[2] In this section on Peters I am indebted to the thorough and painstaking study of Raymond P. Stearns, *The Strenuous Puritan* (Urbana: University of Illinois, 1954); see especially pp. 371–82, which give a much more complete summary of Peters' utopia than is possible here.

[3] *Good Work for a Good Magistrate* (June 17, 1651), E1364(2), p. 34.

[4] *Ibid.,* p. 53.

[5] *Ibid.,* Postscript, no pagination.

[6] *Readie & Easie Way* (second ed., 1660), pp. 97–98.

[7] E1364(2), p. 6.

ness in the Puritan spectrum of reform. At no time did Cromwell or his close associates realize, as Milton was to do in 1660, that the new state needed desperately to buttress its strength by a widespread plan of public education in which the main ideas and principles of the Commonwealth could be inculcated. Nor did Peters or any other reformer consider the possibility of a new Oxford at York or a new Cambridge at Bristol, in which the genius of the two great universities would take new root, where communal living in one house would be enriched and electrified by association with students and fellows from many other colleges of the university.[8]

On legal and economic reforms Peters anticipates many of the recurring demands of the future. Let England give freedom and protection to foreigners; let them freely dwell and trade among us. He proposes a number of measures to succor the poorer citizens. Let us establish banks for poor people in distress, charging a low rate of interest—three, three and a half, four per cent—as in Holland. Let us have a court to "advance the estates of fatherless Children." Let us see to it that poor men are not cooped up in prison for small debts, "and thereby they and their families undon in a short time, becaus hee is not able to put in Bail." Peters dwells at some length on the injustices of prison life: "Great cruelties are committed in Prisons, by great charges for fees, chambers, and dear victuals, and by stinking and unwholsom rooms." The worst of men, "even an Armie of Caterpillers," are now employed as bailiffs. Let written summonses be served to men at their own houses. Peters inveighs also against the impressment of soldiers into the army or navy, urging the state to pay their service men higher wages: "Pay well, you shall never want men."[9] Let no man be barred from following the trade of his choice. Let a trade school for orphans be created in every town. Peters recommends tax relief for those single men earning less than ten pounds a year; married men who earn £40 should still pay no taxes.

Peters also agitates for a drastic change in the laws of inheritance. Let the Commonwealth abolish entails once and for all. A father must have the liberty to bestow his property upon his children as he wishes, the daughters to have equal portions with the sons, the eldest son to receive a double portion. "What mischiefs have com'n upon families by greatning the eldest, and abasing the rest," writes Peters, "let *Englishmen* judg." One of the destructive effects of debasing the younger sons was their enforced employment in buying and selling. "It is an unpleasing spectacle to see in the Cities so manie men," wrote Peters, "fit for nobler

[8] But see Christopher Hill, *Century of Revolution,* p. 181; and below, p. 138, n. 5.

[9] *Ibid.,* pp. 21, 22, 23, 25, 26, 91.

things, to sell those wares, which were properly the imploiment of women, and their daughters . . . that men should not blush to bee sitting in shops, yea, the choice Gentrie of the Nation, I much wonder."[10]

Like Milton after him in *Readie & Easie Way,* Peters was reluctant to extend the suffrage even to men of small property. "If a thousand meet to choos [a member of Parliament]," wrote Peters, "let these choos an hundred out of that number to choos for them, and the rest depart; the one hundred then out of themselvs choos twentie, to choos one for that service."[11] This passage is a curious revelation of Peters' reluctance to trust the direct suffrage of property owners. Whether or not he derived the idea from Peters, Milton presented a somewhat similar proposal for limiting the franchise nine years later in *Readie & Easie Way.* Milton's suggestion is more complicated than that of Peters. The rightly qualified citizens, says Milton, may nominate as many candidates as they wish.[12] Then a smaller number of citizens "of a better breeding" than the original large number, should choose from the first group a second group of candidates. Following a third or a fourth repetition of this process, the exact number would remain to fill up the seats of his proposed national senate. Milton does not specify how he would choose the second, third, or fourth groups of voters. He simply says that the second group should be "others of a better breeding." Of the two proposals, Peters' is far more practical and workable than Milton's. He trusts to each group to choose the superior men among them, whereas Milton makes no such concession to popular judgment. The two plans show that each Puritan distrusted popular judgment as opposed to the choices of the discriminating few. But Milton's distrust, heightened as it was by the outcries of all classes for the impending Restoration, is much more profound than that of Peters.

In Peters' utopia his ideas about rebuilding London are among the most original and arresting of the pamphlet. He would tear down (the Great Fire was fifteen years in the future) all the wooden houses; and all new houses should be built with brick and stone. Thames Street should be broadened and paved with "flat four-square stones, as in *Holland.*" The street and all new streets should be high in the middle, with a paved gutter on each side, and brick pavements between the street and the houses. As fast as the London streets are newly paved, the stones taken up should be used to pave the highways leading out of London, each highway rounded in the middle so that they will stay clean during all the seasons of the year. Peters also proposed a rebuilding of the riverside facilities for unloading of ships: a large quay, a mile long and forty or fifty feet broad, to be built out into the river, where as many as two

[10] *Ibid.,* pp. 31, 32. [11] *Ibid.,* pp. 30–31.

[12] I am here following *Milton in the Puritan Revolution,* p. 301.

thousand ships might lie safely at anchor in any weather; a place where merchants could come and look at goods on display and make their purchases.[13] Not once in his utopian pattern does Peters recommend the beautification of London, as opposed to utilitarian spaciousness. He does not propose the appointment of artists and architects. There is no evidence that Peters even knew such a man as Christopher Wren. Like Cromwell, despite years at Cambridge in presence of exquisite towers and fan-vaulted reaches, he possessed only a weak sense of aesthetics. There is no record that Peters or Cromwell or Milton protested against the dispersal of the great painting collections of Charles I or the neglect of England's great cathedrals.

Peters was not a turner of the world upside down, like Winstanley, or a searcher like Lilburne of precedents that justify extreme democratic reforms. He was an impatient revolutionist ready to erase legal precedents rather than amend and apply them anew. Victories on the battlefield had justified the good cause of the Independents; Peters wished to act with equal directness and speed in achieving civil liberties for his cause. Let a body of new laws be created. Then, said Peters, "burn all the old Records; yea, even those in the Tower, the Monuments of tyrannie."[14] But were all these old laws evil in themselves? Men as diverse in outlook as Parker, Prynne, and Lilburne had gleaned many precedents and charters of freedom from the old law books. Among the shocked readers of Peters' proposals was Richard Vaughan, who defined the common laws as those "laudable and righteous Customs, iterated and multiplyed in their common use among the people of this Land time out of minde."[15] Surely ministers like Peters, without knowledge of the foundations of the law, should not "meddle beyond their *own* calling." The abolition of entail, as proposed by Peters, would precipitate the "unsettlement of most estates in this Nation." Vaughan is shocked that Peters should want to bar lawyers from some cases at law. If lawyers are continued in such cases, says Peters, let them be paid by the state and speak for the sake of justice, not for their fees. Peters complains that fees are "bottomless."[16] But this is no argument against lawyers, replies Vaughan, that some of the profession make their fees too high. Let such fees be regulated by the state, not abolished. "What! Do you wish to make the profession itself unlawful?" asks Vaughan, in effect. Peters is too rash, too precipitate. Let him not pluck up the wheat with the tares. Though Vaughan would not object to an orderly and detached inquiry into any profession

[13] E1364(2), pp. 106, 102, 107, 101.

[14] *Ibid.*, p. 33.

[15] *A Plea for the Common-Laws of England* (July 3, 1651), E1379(4), sig. A2v–A3.

[16] *Ibid.*, pp. 19, 6, 9.

by a member of another, he declares that "*the* Harmony *of the World lies in the* diversity *of Professions, bounded with their* particular limits: *and in the* gradual *subordination of the one unto the other.*" [17]

2. COMENIUS: DIVINE MAGIC OF EYE AND EAR

On June 19, 1651, appeared Comenius' scientific treatise, *Naturall Philosophie Reformed by Divine Light.* As a pupil of Bacon, Comenius regretted that although the great Verulam had presented the world with a true key to scientific inquiry, he had not himself brought to light the "secrets of Nature, onely shewing us by a few examples, how they were to be opened." Comenius absorbed and applied Bacon's emphasis on the sensory fact for the first time to an irresistible learning process. *"Fetch all things,"* wrote Comenius, *"from sense, reason* and *Scripture."* Sense is the foundation of all knowledge. Everything valuable in reason and revelation has its origin in sensory accuracy. Does not the Scripture itself direct us to "hear, see, taste, consider"? Faith itself comes from listening and hearing. Campanella, whom Comenius read "with incredible joy," concluded that the certain progression to true knowledge was from sense to reason to Scripture. Any one of these means to truth without the other was to Comenius "a most ready precipice into errors." When, for example, a man sees an oar under water it may look broken, but reason corrects his sensory illusion. One must observe before he reasons; then one must understand before he can believe. To Comenius, as to Winstanley, the great book of nature was the best and truest revelation of life. "Why do we not . . . turn over the living book of the world," he asked, "instead of dead papers?" [1] What happens when a man uses reason to pursue the truth, without sensory verification? Such a man is likely to be carried away by "meer phantasmes, and create himself a new world." Similarly, when a man concentrates on the Scriptures, blotting out verification of the reason and the senses, he is carried away by the sublimity and magnitude of his ideas, which, unchecked by rationality, lead him to absurd superstitions, such as, adds Comenius, the papist belief in transubstantiation. Begin with these senses, then, and ascend by slow degrees into knowledge verified by reason and Scripture. The highest knowledge comes from the surest, slowest steps, and the average man is more capable of high ascents than he dreams of. "Every man is able to get up to the top of an high Tower," Comenius had written, ". . . if there be steps for him." [2] Moreover, God "hath . . . conferred means upon man to contemplate his won-

[17] *Ibid.*, sig. [A7v].

[1] E1335, Preface (signatures confused), pp. [8], [9], [7], [10], [14], [24], [12].

[2] *Complete Prose,* I, 162.

drous things." [3] Everybody can be trained to observe, to read the great book of nature. Then he will not be carried away by too hasty use of his reasoning faculties or too hasty ascent into the empyrean of sublime religious concepts.

On November 25 appeared a new edition of Jeremy Collier's translation of Comenius' *A Patterne of Universall Knowledge,* which he had sent forth first in 1643. Collier dedicated his translation to Samuel Hartlib, whom he praised for acquainting the public with the works of Comenius. Hartlib is also praised by Comenius in *A Patterne* as having a "fervent, and extraordinary desire of promoting the publick good," [4] drawing not only Comenius but many others into kindred efforts. Collier reminds his readers that Comenius had been invited to England "by certaine Honourable and active Patrons of Learning in this present Parliament." The ideas of Comenius deserve respectful attention in a time of reformation. The causes of Puritan blindness to the need for pervasive educational reform in the midst of religious and political agitation are one of the unsolved mysteries of Milton's time.[5] Milton himself recognized the need in the *Readie & Easie Way,* but not until the Restoration was already knocking at the doors of the old Long Parliament reassembled at Westminster.

Comenius' grand plan for state schools in which every child would be won to the pursuit of knowledge in large or small degree was as far away in 1651 as it had been in 1643. Comenius' main educational resource, once such schools would be established, for rich and poor, boys and girls, alike, was a great textbook or series of textbooks presenting the organized knowledge of the various disciplines in a progression of ascending difficulty. *A Patterne* is not such a textbook itself, nor even the prospectus of such a book. It is rather a series of aphorisms setting forth educational principles after the manner of Bacon in *Novum Organum.* The first part of *A Patterne,* called "Ichnography of the Temple of Wisdome," contains seventy-two aphorisms. The second part, "An Orthographical Delinea-

[3] E1335, Preface, p. [18]. [4] E1304(1), p. 172.

[5] For a balanced perspective of Puritan educational achievement, see Christopher Hill, *Century of Revolution,* especially p. 181. Hill cites W. K. Jordan, *Philanthropy in England,* to show that in the ten counties studied by Jordan for the period 1480–1660, few boys by 1660 lived more than twelve miles from an endowed free grammar school. Jordan does not show how many of these schools were endowed by Puritan private philanthropy of this period. A state system of elementary education was started in Wales during the Commonwealth for the first time in British history. Fifty-nine schools were established there in 1651 to 1653. As W. A. L. Vincent shows, however, in his *State and School Education 1640–1660,* p. 135, all of these schools except the one at Cardigan apparently disappeared at the Restoration.

tion," in which Comenius intended to give illustrations of his principles, contains eighty-six sections, almost all of which deal also with ideas rather than concrete illustrations.

Comenius intended Pansophia to be an encyclopedia for children as well as for adults, an encyclopedia of ideas as well as facts, progressing from the sensory to the logical, philosophical, and metaphysical learning. It would show, as Bacon had in *The Advancement of Learning,* what investigations were needed by man, and what his hopes were for the future as well as his accomplishments of the past. The most complete definition of Pansophia in *A Patterne* runs as follows:

> A Booke should be compiled, for the containing of all things which are necessary to be knowne and done, believed and hoped for by man . . . in that order, that the mindes of men by *medium's* may be (as it were by a kind of an artificiall Ladder) advanced from the first to the last, the lowest to the highest.[6]

By the use of Pansophia, progressing in easy stages, child or man would gain confidence in his intellectual powers, acquiring not only knowledge but sure ways of using his mind. He would be trained to see, to hear, to touch, to reason, to converse, to have faith.

How Comenius meant to construct Pansophia we can only surmise from his textbooks. In *Orbis Sensualium Pictus,* the world's first illustrated textbook, he presented 150 short lessons in Latin, each with a picture. In the first lesson the master says to the pupil, "Come, Boy, learn to be wise." The boy replies, "What doth this mean, to be wise?" The master replies, "To understand rightly." [7] Though the book begins, then, with an abstraction, it soon concentrates on the world of the senses: the sounds of animals, children, insects; fire, air, water, clouds; fruits, metals, stones, trees; flowers, herbs, corn, shrubs; birds, water fowl, cattle, camels; wild beasts, creatures that live on the land and in the water; kinds of fish. Then, after many pages of valuable information likely to arouse the child's curiosity, he comes to a philosophical topic, "The Seven Ages of Man," then "The Outward Parts of a Man," then "The Head and the Hand," then "The Flesh and the Bowels," and finally "The Outward and Inward Senses." [8] This progression in itself is one of increasing abstraction, difficulty, and significance, while the author appeals on every page to the child's eye, ear, and finger tips. Yet this is a textbook for learning Latin, not an all-embracing encyclopedic textbook such as Comenius intends. The progression from stones to flowers to animals to men, to the parts of man's body, to the seven ages of man, shows Comenius' genius for applying his own principle of progression in

[6] *Ibid.,* p. 4. [7] *Orbis Sensualium Pictus* (1664), tr. Charles Hoole, p. 2.
[8] *Ibid.,* pp. 2–86.

images the child cannot resist. As Hezekiah Woodward pointed out, *"Pictures are the most intelligible Books, that Children can look upon. They come closest to Nature."* [9] Only when the child's senses give electric response, in Comenius' view, do his reason and understanding reach the pitch and acuteness he is capable of.

In constructing *Orbis Sensualium Pictus,* Comenius used the same method and even somewhat the progression of topics that he had used in his famous *Janua Linguarum Reserata,* the sixth edition of which had appeared in London in 1643, translated by John Robotham. The *Janua* of 1643 had ninety-nine chapters and one thousand numbered sentences. Opposite each Latin sentence, on the same page, appears its English equivalent. The first eight chapters after the first, which begins, "God save you, friendly Reader," deal with such topics as "Of the Worlds originall and Creation," "Of the Elements," "Of the Firmament," "Of Fire." With Chapter 9, however, Comenius begins his progression of concrete topics, on stones, metals, trees and fruits, shrubs, insects. Toward the end of the book he turns again to a few abstract topics such as No. 95, "Of a Scholar's Course of Life," and No. 99, "Angels." [10] Within each chapter, the ideas and vocabulary progress in difficulty in keeping with the central educational concept of small steps of fascinating knowledge as the certain prelude to substantial intellectual achievement. The astounding success of the *Janua,* first published in 1631, translated into twelve European languages, and in Arabic, Turkish, and Persian tongues as well, was continuing reassurance to Comenius that his central principles were even more sound and fruitful than he had believed possible.

Like his master Bacon, Comenius believed that the greatest fruit of the mind comes from the contemplation of things, not from wrestling with unprovable abstractions. Only in sensory search do men lay aside their prejudices and preconceptions: *Things are the same to all,* because all have the same senses, however divergent may be their opinions and conceptions. Men in sensory search find it easy to reconcile their conclusions, the inspection of material objects and their conclusions, the inspection of material objects and phenomena being open and plain before the eyes and under the finger tips. In the schoolroom or university, insists Comenius, "Let no man be compell'd to swear to his Masters words, but let the things themselves constrain the intellect: Nor let a Master have any more credit given him, then hee can demonstrate in very deed." [11] Let the searcher seek truth first through his senses, then through his reason, and finally from the study of Scripture. But "if a man contemplate on abstract

[9] *Ibid.,* sig. [A8v].

[10] *Janua* (1643), British Museum 12935aa14, chaps. 1–8, 9, 95, 99.

[11] *Naturall Philosophie Reformed by Divine Light* (June 19, 1651), E1335, Preface, p. [33].

things and consult onely with reason without the testimony of sense, he will be rapt away with meer phantasmes, and create himself a new world." [12] All three ways to truth have overwhelming validity, but only when man has trained his mind to approach truth in the sequence intended by nature and practiced by the greatest minds.

Time after time Comenius returns to his central principle, the "artifice of gradation." A person unused to high places, asserts Comenius, if suddenly taken up to the top of a high tower, may feel a sudden giddiness and fear to look toward the earth. Any unaccustomed sight may "vehemently amaze and trouble the senses," and "sets their mindes atrembling." [13] But let a person take a few steps and then look down before he ascends further, and he feels secure in his high place. Let the steps be small toward any ascent in learning; let them also be many. If there are enough steps, and small enough steps, any boy or girl, man or woman, can reach the top of a high tower. By the use of the principle of gradation, moreover, people may be securely grounded in one principle before going on to another. By means of small steps, particulars can act on the mind with overwhelming force and precision. Comenius compares his artifice of gradation to the growth of a tree, the stock rising from the root, the boughs from the stock, the twigs from the boughs; then from the buds leaves, blossoms, and finally fruits. Comenius is convinced that the mind of child or man is capable of an almost unlimited elasticity. From infinite small steps, then, to great heights: This is to Comenius the key secret in the pursuit of truth.

In Milton's day the minds of humble Englishmen expanded more violently and unpredictably than in any preceding era: in new visions of their powers in push of pike and cavalry charge; in the lofty flights of extempore prayer; in dialogue about men's rights and nature's intention in the councils of Cromwell's army. Every prayer was a search of one's powers as well as an appeal to God's infinite beneficence. In Bunyan's prayers a further reach: the gold of language instinct with unique rhythms and unforgettable metaphor. But to Comenius all such expansion of men's minds was of minute importance compared with the daily unfolding of sensory phenomena under the watchful eye of an expectant teacher aware, as he was, of vast untilled reaches of the most unpromising mind. To Comenius no genetic fences and boundaries could restrain the explosive brain afire with curiosity. The only genetic gold he cherished was infinite teachability, a virtue he probably gauged too optimistically. To Milton, as to every classicist of his day, nature bequeathed to every

[12] *Ibid.*, p. [12].
[13] *A Patterne of Universall Knowledge* (November 25, 1651), E1304(1), p. 110.

child an unchangeable supply of innate intelligence. An iron father, in Plato's figure, would sometimes have a golden son, or a golden father an iron son; but "the species will generally be preserved in the children." Thus Plato: Nature bestowed the gold of greatness, not the slow steps up a high tower under a great teacher. To the theory of genetic determinism most leaders subscribed, whether Puritan or royalist. The Puritan upheaval changed this prevailing belief about human nature not one iota. The intellectual explosions claimed by Comenius as possible in every child came not to trial, even in a single classroom sponsored by the Commonwealth.

Milton himself realized belatedly, it is true, the failure of the Commonwealth to set up free schools in every community. In such schools, thought Milton, some students might even combine the practice of a trade with humanistic studies. In *The Likeliest Means* (1659) Milton proposed that funds be used "to erect in greater number all over the land schooles and competent libraries to those schools, where languages and arts may be taught free together."[14] Though intended mainly to train young ministers sympathetic to Commonwealth ideas, such a proposal for free schools supported by the state was revolutionary. In *The Readie & Easie Way* (1660) Milton stressed again free public academies in every county: "They should have here also schools and academies of their own choice, wherein their children may be bred up in their own sight to all learned and noble education; not in grammar only but in all liberal arts and exercises."[15] These two suggestions show the gap in Milton's mind between his educational outlook in 1644, which was traditional and aristocratic, and his view in the shadow of Commonwealth defeat, which at least would have extended state subsidies for education to boys and girls of all ranks. There is no evidence that behind these suggestions lay any steady growth of fundamental theory about the potential of humble people such as animated Comenius. Nor was Cromwell or Vane or Overton or any of Milton's colleagues animated by any great dream to build schools as revolutionary as their victories on the battlefield or their overturning of old laws and customs in the House of Commons.

[14] *The Likeliest Means* (1659), E2110(2), p. 96. On tradesmen attending such schools, Milton writes (p. 98): "the hours of teaching so ordered, as thir studie may be no hindrance to thir labor or other calling."

[15] *Readie & Easie Way* (2nd ed., 1660), pp. 97–98.

CHAPTER XVIII

MILTON AND THE COUNCIL OF STATE

February–October, 1651

MILTON's attendance at the Council of State, which met every morning except Sunday at seven o'clock, reveals a multiplicity of tasks and interests engaged in at the very seat of national authority. The Council met at Whitehall, where Milton had lodgings. Some morning late in the year 1651, or early in 1652, he needed for the first humiliating time a guiding hand to lead him from his apartment to the meeting of the Council five or ten minutes away. Once at the meeting, he would have needed assistance that morning in reaching a chair. Then the daily work of the Council began, this year with Sir Henry Vane as its presiding officer. In tenuous theory he held more power than Cromwell himself. The Council issued orders to its commanders in the field; it directed the raising of the militia against the new threat from Scottish armies and the young Prince Charles; it dealt on behalf of the government with foreign powers and dignitaries; it directed the putting down of potential plots and uprisings, of scurrilous pamphlets, of royalist agitators; it employed men to edit newspapers for the government and write special pamphlets on behalf of the republic. Its key members were also members of the House of Commons. Its relations with Milton alone show the extent and variety of its tasks.

On its first meeting of the year, February 19, the Council voted that "Mr. John Milton be Secretary for the Foreign Languages for the time of the Council."[1] The record shows that despite his impending total blindness, Milton was still counted on for manifold duties beyond his skill in translating foreign tongues and casting letters of state into suitable Latin. But just now his skill in languages was an effective tool of Commonwealth propaganda abroad. *A Defence* appeared on February 24. On March 5 the Council ordered the "Committee on Examinations to view over Mr. Milton's book, and give order for reprinting of it as they think fit; and that they also examine the complaint by him made about Peter Cole his printing a copy concerning the Rickets, which Mr. Dugard allegeth to be his."[2] The reference to "Mr. Milton's book" is not to

[1] Masson, IV, 313; *Calendar of State Papers, Domestic,* 1651, p. 53 (SP 25/65, p. 11). Hereafter referred to as *CSPD.*

[2] Masson, IV, 313; *CSPD,* 1651, p. 70 (SP 25/65, p. 63). The book on rickets referred to is E1267, March 7, 1651.

Eikonoklastes, as Masson points out, but to *A Defence.* Masson concludes that since Dugard was the printer of *A Defence* and meeting frequently with Milton while *A Defence* was going through the press, Milton had interceded with the Council for him against a rival printer, Peter Cole, whose publication, *A Treatise of the Rickets,* reached Thomason on March 7. On March 27 the Council ordered that "the letters that are to be sent to the Ambassador of Spain shall be sent unto him by Mr. Milton." [3] Masson believed that one of these letters mentioned is "Council of State to the Spanish Ambassador," protesting against cruelties committed against British subjects at Malaga.[4] Milton at this time was representing the Council in negotiations with both the Spanish ambassador Cardeñas and the Portuguese representative Guimaraes. On March 28 Milton was ordered to "translate the *Intercursus Magnus* which he is to have from Sir Henry Vane." [5] On April 4 the Council still further suggested an expansion of Milton's duties by ordering that "such dispatches as come to this Council from foreign parts in any foreign tongue are to be translated for the use of the Council." [6] On May 16 it was ordered that "Mr. Milton do repair to the Public Minister of Portugal and desire of him from the Council a list of the names of such persons as he desires to carry with him as his retinue, that the same may be affixed to his pass." [7] On May 20 another sign of the Council's concern for propaganda abroad in which Milton could help: John Dury was ordered to proceed with a French translation of *Eikonoklastes.*[8] These orders show that Milton was counted on as a prompt, resourceful coworker in the immense variety of duties imposed upon the Council by the daily issues faced by the new republic.

The Council's actions to keep Milton in his lodgings at Whitehall show their high esteem for his services and talents. On April 10 the Council gave a sharp reproof to Mr. George Vaux, housekeeper at Whitehall, by ordering him "to forbear the removing of Mr. Milton out of his lodgings in Whitehall, until Sir H. Mildmay and Sir Gilbert Pickering shall have spoken with that Committee concerning that business." [9] In directing Milton to move, Vaux was only following the directions of a special Parliamentary committee appointed on February 14 to regulate Whitehall

[3] Masson, IV, 314; *CSPD,* 1651, p. 114 (SP 25/65, p. 175).

[4] Masson refers to John Thurloe, *Collection of State Papers,* ed. Thomas Birch, 7 vols. (London, 1742), I, 175–76. Hereafter cited as Thurloe.

[5] Masson, IV, 314; *CSPD,* 1651, p. 116 (SP 25/65, p. 180).

[6] Masson, IV, 314; *CSPD,* 1651, p. 130 (SP 25/65, p. 216).

[7] Masson, IV, 315; *CSPD,* 1651, p. 203 (SP 25/65, p. 138).

[8] Masson, IV, 315; *CSPD,* 1651, p. 208 (SP 25/65, p. 146).

[9] Masson, IV, 314; *CSPD,* 1651, pp. 140–41 (SP 25/65, p. 253).

living accommodations, some of which had been pre-empted by officers and soldiers for their own use.[10] Such accommodations were eagerly sought after by Parliament members and other officials. Sir John Hippesley, M.P. for Cockermouth, had lived in Milton's lodgings before he was assigned to them. In the matter of lodging status, Parliament was not to be denied its priority over the Council of State. On May 9 it indirectly answered the Council's claim for Milton by voting that their Whitehall committee should "accommodate members of Parliament with lodgings in Whitehall, the Mews, and Somerset House . . . and to put forth such other persons and families as they shall think fit." [11] Even after this statement, the Council took special action on Milton's behalf. On June 11, as Masson points out, the Council directed a formidable committee of the Council to wait upon the Parliamentary committee to insist on Milton's keeping his lodgings near the Council's daily activities. In their official record the Council makes no mention of Milton's blindness; they were very emphatic about "the employment which he is in to this Council, which necessitates him to reside near the Council." [12] The intercession of the Council committee with the Parliamentary committee was evidently decisive: Milton stayed on at Whitehall. The persistence with which the Council supported him, and the decisive victory on this issue over Parliamentary wishes, show Milton as a vivid, cherished personality in the midst of the executive body of the nation.

COUNCIL AT THE HELM: THE MONTH BEFORE WORCESTER

August 3–September 3, 1651

The activities of the Council of State in the month before Worcester reveal as no other record the timely and resourceful support given to Cromwell to annihilate the Scotch threat once and for all. Invasion impended, supported by the magic of the king's name, which Charles and his generals counted on to bring thousands of new troops to his colors. The first aim of the Council was to arouse the militia of the various counties against the invader. By the Militia Act passed on August 12 the Council had the right to nominate militia commissioners in each county, the commissioners to call together foot and horse, to assess the citizens one full month's pay for troops, the citizens in turn to be reimbursed by Parliament.[1] The response of the various counties to these acts was prompt and vigorous. No royalist pamphleteer broke through the censorship to assert that the prerogative to control the militia was the king's

[10] Masson, IV, 316. [11] Masson, IV, 316.
[12] Masson, IV, 315; *CSPD*, 1651, p. 246 (SP 25/20, p. 26).
[1] *Acts and Ordinances of the Interregnum*, II, 551–52.

only. Even Charles himself at this juncture made no such claim. Milton's assertion in *Eikonoklastes* that the control of the militia could not be separated from the control of the funds to support it seemed at this moment fully vindicated. Perhaps the response of the citizens was due less to their support of the Commonwealth than to their resistance against a foreign army. Backed by Parliament's new laws, the Council issued a stream of instructions to the various militia commissioners. On August 7 the Council wrote to the commissioners of militia in York, Lancaster, Chester, Salop, Stafford, Derby, and Nottingham: "That Scots' army, which ours could not provoke to fight in Scotland, is now marching towards England . . . and though the army with the Lord General in Fife will soon be in their rear, we desire you, for preservation of the county and to give impediment to the enemy, to draw together to some convenient rendezvous what forces of horse and foot you can of the late militia there, to be ready to join Major-Gen. Harrison's forces already there. . . . Your charges in this work Parliament will reimburse." [2] It is significant that the Council refers to "the late militia" as the nucleus from which the commissioners will build their new militia to join with Harrison's troops. On August 8 the Council wrote again, urging frequent meetings of their troops; the militia must be ready to fall upon the rear of the enemy; to identify their agents sent amongst the people to join with royalist sympathizers; to "suppress the first tendency towards insurrection"; to send to the Council names of "such [citizens] as you find refractory." [3] The response to these messages, combining threat with exhortation and promise of ready funds, showed that the Council had accurately gauged both the response of the militia commissioners and the citizen soldiers to whom they appealed.

Meanwhile an amazing range of problems confronted the Council daily. On August 10, Speaker Lenthall being "at some distance," and finding from the messenger that a letter for him from Cromwell dealt with the Scots marching into England, the Council thought it appropriate to open the letter.[4] On the same day the Council considered reasons sub-

[2] *CSPD*, 1651, p. 307. [3] *CSPD*, 1651, p. 310.

[4] This is Letter CLXXX, dated at Leith August 6 (*Letters and Speeches*, ed. Lomas, II, 213–15). The enemy was now poised, as Carlyle says, "for a stroke at the heart of the Commonwealth itself." Cromwell urges Lenthall to do all possible to check the enemy's advance until his own troops can catch up with them. He understood not only the danger he was facing but the dismay that might agitate his colleagues at home: "I do apprehend that if he goes for England, being some few days march before us, it will trouble some men's thoughts." Cromwell reminds Lenthall of the strategy before Preston, "when England was much more unsteady than now, and when a much more considerable army of theirs, unfoiled, invaded you, and we had but a weak force to make resistance . . . we chose rather to put ourselves between their army and Scotland."

mitted by Thomas Violet of the Mint Committee, why farthings and half farthings should be minted, to consist of "fine rose" copper or tin. Such small pieces "ministers means of frugality, where poor men can have a farthing or half farthing's worth, and are not constrained to buy more of anything than they stand in need of."[5] On August 11, a committee of Whitelocke, Grey, St. John, Mildmay, Pickering, and Alderman Allein, was chosen to meet with the Common Council of London and inform them "of the invasion of this land by the King of Scots"; to advise alerting forces for the common defense and prevent correspondence or assistance to the invaders. The over-all strategy of the new war was a daily consideration in the Council's discussion. Couriers arriving and departing daily kept touch with all commanders. The Scots had deserted their own country in a foolhardy attempt to conquer England. Lambert with 3,000 horse and dragoons is to harass their rear; Harrison is to attack the van; Desborow and Heane to march to Reading. On August 12 the Council ordered distributed an act (passed by Parliament that very day), prohibiting any communication by the citizens with the Scotch king. The movement of all former supporters of the king were severely restricted. On August 12 the Council sent a letter to Thomas Lord Fairfax, asserting their confidence ("we are very well assured that you have not been wanting") in his efforts to defend Hull should it be attacked. "We give you this intimation . . . not doubting but you have that and all things else in your thoughts necessary in this juncture for the common safety."[6] In 1650 Fairfax had refused to march against Scotland. Would he now fail to defend England, particularly the city of which he was the governor? Between the lines the reader senses a plea to Fairfax, an appeal: We need you desperately. Whatever faults you have found with this Commonwealth, don't forsake us in this moment of danger.

The daily record of the Council's activities shows prompt and decisive national action on many fronts. While Cromwell was advancing into England in pursuit of the Scots' army, the Council anticipated daily the needs of his strategy. The members were determined that militia support of Cromwell would not be diminished by failure to pay the troops on time. On August 13, only the day following Parliament's authorization, the Council asked one of its committees to draw up a bill "for paying militia officers and others employed in the several counties." Meanwhile the Council did not hesitate to use tactics of terror against Charles' adherents in the population. On August 13 it ordered the proclamation forbidding correspondence with Charles to be read in public places in London, "proclaimed by beat of drum and sound of trumpet." On the 14th the Council had word for the first time that Charles had entered

[5] *CSPD*, 1651, p. 313.

[6] *CSPD*, 1651, pp. 315, 318, 323–24.

England with his army. On August 15 some suspected adherents of Charles, already seized, were released on bond on condition that they appear before the Council when summoned. On the same day the Council sent forth a letter congratulating Colonel Danvers, governor of Stafford, for his diligence in filling up the ranks of the militia of Cheshire. Between the lines of the record one reads the question: "What shall we do if Cromwell suffers a defeat?" In five orders on August 15 alone troops were ordered to rendezvous in and around London, Westminster, Southwark. Horses had been seized beyond the number needed for the militia: They might be of use to the enemy in the event of an uprising. On August 18 the Council sent to the various militia commanders a summary of events and preparation. The army of the enemy, about 12,000 men, was now between Preston and Wigan. Few men along the way had joined the enemy. Most people along the march had fled from the Scots' forces. On the other hand, many in the country had joined Cromwell's forces as he had marched south. On the 14th his army had quartered at Branspeth. To assist the Lord General, directs the Council, rendezvous your men at the place appointed in this letter. Provide commissions for new officers as needed. The persuasion of prompt pay concerned the Council week after week. "Procure a month's pay for each officer and soldier, and let every soldier have a week's pay in hand." On the 18th also a letter to Lambert and Harrison: Slow down the march of the enemy, so that Cromwell can catch up and join forces with you. On the 18th a letter to the absent Sir Henry Vane, saying, in effect: "Affairs of war and state are urgent. We need you. At the earliest moment possible, come back to our midst."

Chapter XIX

WORCESTER AND AFTER: CROMWELL'S DILEMMA

September–December, 1651

On June 28, 1651, writing from Scotland to the father-in-law of his son Richard, Cromwell said, "I hear my Son hath exceeded his allowance, and is in debt. Truly I cannot commend him therein; wisdom requiring his living within compass. . . . Indeed I cannot think I do well to feed a voluptuous humour in my Son, if he should make pleasures the business of his life, in a time when some precious Saints are bleeding, and breathing out their last, for the safety of the rest." Cromwell recalls the words of Uriah to David, "My Lord Joab, and the servants of my father, are encamped in the open fields: shall I then come into mine house to eat and to drink and lie with my wife?" [1] The letter reveals Cromwell as an indulgent father, providing an allowance for a married son living beyond his means and soon to become a father. Between the lines runs a tone of sad irony that his son should be living a comfortable life while soldiers are dying for the promise of a New Jerusalem on English soil. However far his fame has now reached, Cromwell knows as any man a father's helplessness in such a dilemma. He cannot but feel the distance between his son's potential accomplishments and his own magical rise. Already it must have been apparent to Cromwell, as Mrs. Hutchinson was later to write, that Richard "became not greatness." Oliver wrote to Mayor: "God forbid that his being my son should be his allowance to live not pleasingly to our Heavenly Father, who hath raised me out of the dust to what I am!" [2] As few other passages in his letters, this sentence reveals Cromwell's just sense of his own genius, not only as a general undefeated on the battlefield, but also as a mover and shaker in his country's civil destiny. Even in the earliest days of the Civil War, Cromwell had never felt himself a professional soldier. The prophet in him was more decisive in his leadership than his skill as a military tactician. When other men faltered, as Morley has written, "Hope shone in him like a pillar of fire." [3]

In July, 1651, unable to dislodge Leslie in his mountain fastnesses, Cromwell in a shift of strategy had crossed the Solway Firth. On August 2 he had captured Perth, thus cutting off the Scots from their supplies in the North, but deliberately laying England open to invasion for the sake of bringing the war to a final issue. "I do apprehend," wrote Cromwell to Lenthall on August 4, "that if he [the enemy] goes for England . . . it will trouble some men's thoughts, and may occasion some inconveniences." [4] It was time, thought Cromwell, to wreak utter destruction on the Scots. To bring them to battle on English soil instead of in their mountain fortresses was a military advantage to him greater than the magic name of Charles II to the enemy. Even half-hearted Englishmen would go to battle to defend their soil against the invader. The Council of State, realizing the psychological advantage of resistance to impending invasion and the still more pressing advantage of ready cash for the militia, was meanwhile making certain that once the enemy was on the run, no one, lord or commoner, would escape into Scotland again. As

[1] II Samuel 11:11; *Letters and Speeches*, ed. Lomas, II, 209–10. Richard Cromwell's father-in-law was Richard Mayor.
[2] *Ibid.*, II, 209. [3] John Morley, *Oliver Cromwell* (New York, 1900), p. 319.
[4] *Letters and Speeches*, II, 214.

Leslie marched south, he found to his dismay that the English were not flocking to the banners of Scotland's monarch. On August 17 the Earl of Derby joined the Scots army at Wyre Water, bringing to Charles' banner 250 foot and sixty horse. The army marched southward through Lancashire, turning toward the Welsh border, where royalist sympathizers were more numerous than in the midland counties. On August 25 Colonel Robert Lilburne, still waiting for Cromwell's own regiment of foot to join his horse, discovered that the Earl of Derby was advancing from Preston toward Manchester, where five hundred royalists were planning to join his forces. Lilburne retreated to Wigan, hoping to postpone an engagement with Derby until the regiment of foot had joined his command. In the battle that followed that day 1500 of Derby's horse and foot engaged Lilburne's cavalry. The end was a total defeat of the royalists, who suffered irreparable losses in dead and wounded; about four hundred were taken prisoner, though Derby himself escaped and joined the royal banner. Charles, meanwhile, was taken aback by the reception accorded him, especially from Colonel Mackworth, the governor of Shrewsbury, who refused to surrender the town or even to address him except as the "Commander-in-Chief of the Scottish Army." On August 22 Charles' army, spiritless and exhausted, marched into Worcester. Still acting as though the country would rise to his support, Charles held to his course, issuing an order for all men between sixteen and sixty to attend a rendezvous in defence of king and country at Pitchcroft meadow along the Severn. He sent forth also a proclamation that in national decisions on religion he would be governed by the Covenant; that he would pay arrears of any deserters from Cromwell's army; that he would favor a law granting forgiveness (except for Cromwell, Ireton, and others) to all who would disavow allegiance to the present government. But Charles' promises and proclamation fell on deaf ears. No one appeared at the Pitchcroft rendezvous, and Cromwell's army was fast approaching Worcester.[5]

In the battle that followed, on the afternoon and evening of September 3, just a year after the victory at Dunbar, Cromwell's army put the enemy to utter rout. The new republic's forces outnumbered its foes, about thirty thousand to fifteen or sixteen thousand, men less zealous and united than its own. Two bridges of boats enabled him to cross the Teme and the Severn in the afternoon, attacking the enemy forces stationed behind hedges to the south of the city. "The dispute was long and very near at hand," wrote Cromwell, "and often at push of pike, and from one defence to another." The Scots resisted tenaciously and bravely, but they were no match for the superior numbers and discipline of their

[5] I am here following Gardiner, *Commonwealth and Protectorate,* II, 32–41.

foes. Driven back into Worcester, they yielded gradually street after street and finally Fort Royal itself. "When we took the Fort," wrote Cromwell, "we turned his own guns upon him." Cromwell rode up and down at the risk of his life, offering quarter to his enemies. The battle was "as stiff a contest, for four of five hours," he wrote, "as ever I have seen." [6] When the horse of the enemy tried to escape, they found fresh militia men stationed at every bridge, every road. Cromwell reported six or seven thousand prisoners. "Indeed it was a stiff business; yet I do not think we lost two-hundred men." [7] The leaders of the Scots, Hamilton, Leslie, Middleton, Massie, and Derby, were wounded or taken prisoner. Only Charles, who had fought bravely and well at the head of his troops, miraculously escaped.

Cromwell's reports on the victory at Worcester are full of decorum and reserve. He praises the new militia, which he has already sent home again, as one good work of the new government, a sign that the Commonwealth is gradually finding acceptance among the people. It is the Lord's pleasure "to establish the nation and the change of the government, by making the people so willing to the defence thereof." As for the victory, the utter destruction of the enemy's resistance and leadership (without mention of the escape of Charles), "the dimensions of this mercy are above my thoughts. It is, for aught I know, a crowning mercy." [8] As always in Cromwell's letters, victory is a sign of the Lord's approval rather than the result of complex forces he may have analyzed in the quietness of his meditations. In eight years of military action he had not lost a battle. His genius in selecting men "of a spirit," men on fire with the fervor of fanaticism, raised to greater heights on the battlefield than ever possible in civilian life, was this selection of men like Harrison and Lambert and Lilburne his best and truest weapon? For the first time in English history the son of a butcher like Harrison might become a captain, a colonel, a major-general. The eight dragoons of Lambert's forces who crossed the Severn on a single plank left between the piers; the party of horsemen who followed them, wading or swimming, and drove the Scots off, holding the head for the bridge of boats that would later reach to the enemy side, who were these men? How had their powers expanded, little by little, or by swift reaches, like Cromwell's own? The miracle of growth is nowhere more evident but inexplicable than in Cromwell's own life. "As he grew into place and authority," wrote Clarendon, "his partes

[6] *Letters and Speeches,* II, 223–24. Harrison wrote with satisfaction (Whitelocke, *Memorials* [Oxford, 1853], III, 348) that "lords, knights, and gentlemen, were then plucking [*sic*] out of holes by the soldiers." Of the slaughter: "What with the dead bodies of men and the dead horses of the enemy filling the streets, there was such a nastiness that a man could hardly abide the town."

[7] *Ibid.,* II, 224, 225.

[8] *Ibid.,* II, 225–26.

seemed to be renew[d], as if he had concealed facultyes till he had occasion to use them." [9] With the victory at Worcester, the warrior phase of Cromwell's life had come to a decisive end; the more baffling work of civil leadership loomed ahead of him.

On October 2, a month later, Cromwell wrote to John Cotton inserting a narrative, probably the *Official Narrative of Worcester Battle.* "How shall we behave ourselves after such mercies?" he asked. "What is the Lord a-doing? What prophecies are now fulfilling?" From these lines we have a sense of Cromwell's struggle to know how to use his great name in civil dilemmas. Battles that changed the course of England's history had been decided in a few hours; and no one was immune to the feeling that greatness on the field of battle was somehow a surer test of a man's worth than any achievement in civil life. Milton's saying, "War makes many great whom peace makes small," was a sentiment no Puritan leader could yet apply to Cromwell. "I am a poor weak creature," he wrote to Cotton, "and not worthy the name of a worm; yet accepted to serve the Lord and His people." One cannot doubt the honesty of Cromwell's mood of self-abasement in this passage; but such a mood and such descriptions of his interior life as "my inordinate passions, my unskillfulness and everyway unfitness to my work," [10] were no barrier to a realistic estimate of his superiority to the men around him; no barrier either to his growing determination that eight years of campaigning for his country should not now end in frustration of the army's civil hopes.

Cromwell was not yet ready to impose his will on England's civil destiny; but a settlement of some kind, in which the Rump Parliament would yield its authority to a new representative, could not, he thought, be long postponed. Sometime in December, at Cromwell's insistence, a conference of leaders was called at Speaker Lenthall's house in Chancery Lane. Fortunately Whitelocke has preserved the essence if not all the details of the discussion. Among those present were Fleetwood, Desborough, Whalley, and Harrison for the army; Widdrington, St. John, Whitelocke, and Lenthall himself for the Rump. The discussion was frank and forceful, coming almost at once to a sharp division. Whitelocke himself posed the issue: What kind of settlement do Cromwell and his associates wish? Do they want a republic, an "absolute" republic, or a republic with "any mixture of monarchy"? Cromwell at once spoke up, saying, "My lord commissioner Whitelocke hath put us upon the right point." But in restating the issue Cromwell added a sentence the significance of which could not have been lost upon the group: "Whether a republic or a mixed monarchical government will be best to be settled;

[9] *Characters*, ed. David Nichol Smith (Oxford: University Press, 1953), p. 140.
[10] *Letters and Speeches*, II, 241.

and if anything monarchical, then in whom that power shall be placed?" Widdrington's answer was bold and forthright: He preferred a mixed monarchical government because it was "most suitable to the laws and people of this nation."[11] Moreover, coming directly to the point of Cromwell's question, Widdrington asserted that the king chosen should be in his judgment one of the sons of Charles I. Without directly attacking this position, Fleetwood reminded the company that it would be difficult indeed to make a choice between a kingdom and a republic. But St. John emphatically supported Widdrington. Unless the settlement incorporates something of kingly power, he insisted, it might "shake the foundation of our laws and the liberties of the people." Speaker Lenthall promptly concurred; any government without a tincture of monarchy "will breed a strange confusion." At this point Desborough broke in passionately, "I beseech you, my lord, why may not this as well as other nations be governed in the way of a republic?" To this angry question Whitelocke replied with sober patience: "The laws of England are so interwoven with the power and practice of monarchy, that to settle a government without something of monarchy in it, would make so great an alteration in the proceedings of our law, that you have scarce time to rectify, nor can we well foresee, the inconveniences which will arise thereby."[12] To the triumphant soldiers who had adventured their lives in a hundred charges for the Good Old Cause, such an analysis as that of Whitelocke, which English history has fully justified, was no more than a name and a shadow.

Thus the debate wavered between triumphant soldiers and the liberal lawyers of the new republic: the soldiers with no or little sense of the thousand ties of custom and law they had severed with the fall and execution of Charles. Whalley now spoke on the point of interwoven laws raised by Whitelocke: Of these laws he knew nothing, but he bluntly favored a republic. Moreover, he asked, if a monarchy were chosen, whom would they choose? Prince Charles they had fought on the battlefield; and the Duke of York was also their enemy. To this thrust Widdrington replied that the king's third son, the Duke of Gloucester, had not carried arms against the Commonwealth and was too young to have been corrupted by royalist tenets. But Whitelocke was willing to accept even Prince Charles. Could they not set a day by which he or the Duke of York must declare for the Parliament upon terms consonant with their liberties, both civil and religious? Cromwell then spoke against Whitelocke indirectly by saying, "That will be a business of more than ordinary difficulty," but granted that if a settlement could incorporate "somewhat with monarchical power," it might well be "very effectual."

[11] Whitelocke, *Memorials,* III, 373.

[12] *Ibid.*, III, 373.

Thus the debate ended, with Cromwell speaking twice in tentative favor of monarchical government, while his favored officers stood united against any monarchy at all; this despite the fact, wrote Whitelocke, that each one of them "was a monarch in his regiment or company." [13] From the debate, especially from Cromwell's last words, it was apparent he would not hear of bringing back any one of the house of Stuart. But did this mean he would not himself accept the throne? In Whitelocke's view Cromwell had called the conference to know men's minds. After a long debate it dissolved without taking any position on the baffling problem before them. The enemy was prostrate, Scotland and Ireland subdued; but the debate showed the victors sharply divided about a national settlement.

CHAPTER XX

GERRARD WINSTANLEY AND HIS *LAW OF FREEDOM*

February 20, 1652

THOUGH *Law of Freedom in a Platform* appeared early in 1652, its "Epistle Dedicatory," addressed to Cromwell, was dated November 5, 1651, two months after the victory at Worcester, when Cromwell's ascendancy was at the height of its persuasion. "It was intended for your view above two years ago," wrote Winstanley, "but the disorder of the Times caused me to lay it aside, with a thought never to bring it to light." [1] In the spring of 1649, then, Winstanley had been too discouraged to act. But then he had heard that Peters and other leaders had urged men to search the Scriptures for patterns of reformation. Moreover the passage from the Scriptures, *Thou shalt not bury thy talent in the earth,* "was like fire in my bones." He went to work again, gathered up his scattered papers, and compiled his *Law of Freedom.* Cromwell now needed his help and that of every man. The enemy was not beaten by a single person only, nor by the officers only, but also by the common man for whom he now speaks. Liberty recovered from the Conqueror was for all, not for the few. Nor was it possible to annihilate tyranny with the sword only. Indeed, says Winstanley, "as the Sword pulls down Kingly Power with one hand, the Kings old Law builds up Monarchy again with the other." [2] Winstanley puts a candle now by

[13] *Ibid.,* III, 373–74.

[1] E655(8), February 20, 1652, p. 11.

[2] *Ibid.,* p. 7.

Cromwell's door, realizing that he, Cromwell, has power in his hand to act for the freedom of all Englishmen. Do not be deceived by my poor language, says Winstanley; study the substance, and there you will find beauty.

There is no record that Cromwell ever replied to Winstanley's epistle, or read his rustic utopia even enough to call it a "paper shot," as he was to denominate Harrington's utopia some years later.[3] Nevertheless, it is impossible to imagine, reading *The Law of Freedom* three centuries after, that a mind like that of Cromwell, Milton, Ludlow, or Overton could have struggled with the ideas of Winstanley's utopia and come away unchanged. At no other long moment in English history were so many men eager to bridge the gap between vision and reality, as in the time of Puritan dynamics. Winstanley was a unique offshoot of the Puritan zeal for utopia, however defined: the momentary visitation of grace upon one's soul; the expectant silence of a Quaker meeting; the liberty to know and utter according to conscience; or the bright flame of a commonwealth, where the leader might salute a friend on a London street, as one equal to another.

1. PROMISES UNFULFILLED

In his "Epistle Dedicatory" Winstanley sets forth with relentless clarity the unfulfilled promises of the revolution in which his friends have engaged both as civilians and as soldiers. The clergy, and even some of the officers, still persecute men for their opinions. Even as in the days of the bishops, men are yet "made sinners for a word." Moreover, do not the people still pay tithes upon their property to support the clergy, who preach doctrines men cannot understand? Do not the lawyers still "sit in the Conquerors Chair"? As in centuries past the lords of the manor still require fines and heriots. They monopolize the use of the common land themselves, forbidding the commoners the free use of this land unless the commoners pay them rent. "So that," says Winstanley, "the poor are kept poor still, and the Common Freedom of the Earth is kept from them, and the poor have no more relief then they had when the King (or Conqueror) was in power."[1] England has cast out kingly power, abolished the House of Lords, and established a free commonwealth. Yet the benefits of such a revolution are on paper only, though there is enough land in England, maintains Winstanley, to support ten times as many people as now use it. Some citizens must beg to support themselves or work at such low wages as to force them to "starve, or steal, and so be hanged out of the way, as men not fit to live in the earth, before they

[3] *Milton in the Puritan Revolution*, p. 305.

[1] E655(8), pp. 6, 7–8.

must be suffered to plant the waste land for their livelihood." [2] We were promised annual parliaments, but now "the current of succeeding Parliaments is stopt." Still another injustice, says Winstanley, has been the disposition of the lands taken away from the crown and the bishops. The people gave no consent to the sale of this land, the possession of which was their birthright. The buying and selling of land owned by the state, possession of which, in Winstanley's view, was the birthright of all, was the most grievous injustice of all.

To Winstanley, England in late 1651 was at the most crucial turning point in her history. Never before had one man possessed as much power as Cromwell to set free the disinherited commoners and remove the injustices of centuries. The alternatives of action from which Cromwell had to choose, a decision which would affect not only England, but other countries as well, Winstanley set forth thus:

> And now you have the Power of the Land in your hand, you must do one of these two things: First, either set the Land free to the oppressed Commoners, who assisted you, and payd the Army their wages: and then you will fulfil the Scriptures and your own Engagements, and so take the possession of your deserved Honor.
>
> Or secondly, you must onely remove the Conquerors Power out of the Kings hand into other mens, maintaining the old Laws still: And then your Wisdom and Honor is blasted for ever; and you will either lose your self, or lay the Foundation of greater Slavery to posterity then you ever knew.
>
> You know that while the King was in the height of his oppressing Power, the People onely whispered in private Chambers against him: But afterwards it was preached upon the house tops, That he was a Tyrant and a Traytor to *Englands* peace; and he had his overturn.
>
> The righteous Power in the Creation is the same still: If you, and those in power with you, should be found walking in the Kings steps, can you secure your selves or posterities from an overturn? Surely No.
>
> The Spirit of the whole Creation (who is God) is about the Reformation of the World, and he will go forward in his work: For if he would not spare Kings, who have sat so long at his right hand, governing the World, neither will he regard you, unless your ways be found more righteous then the Kings.
>
> You have the eyes of the People all the Land over, nay I think I may say all neighboring Nations over, waiting to see what you will do.[3]

The main trends of Winstanley's argument in *The Law of Freedom* are inherent in this passage. The real tyranny to him was not the king as a person, but the laws which his ancestors had instituted to perpetuate

[2] *Ibid.*, p. 9.

[3] *Ibid.*, p. 4.

their economic power over the commoners. If Cromwell did not reverse this injustice, now centuries deep, he would be overthrown even as Charles I. Winstanley could not imagine that the commoners of England will live on generation after generation without possessing a large share of the earth and its fruits. To Winstanley such a progression of history was the inevitable outcome of God's true reformation.

2. THE CURSE OF BUYING AND SELLING

The most alarming element of Winstanley's proposals for his new government was his proscription of buying and selling. "When Mankinde began to buy and sell," wrote Winstanley, "then did he fall from his Innocency; for then they began to oppress and cozen one another of their Creation Birth-right." [1] Winstanley must have realized that such a statement, in the midst of analysis otherwise intelligible and, to some extent, highly acceptable to Cromwell, would appear the offshoot of a demented mind. But Winstanley's relentless fanaticism would not permit him to soften the extremity of the measures he proposed, even in his "Epistle Dedicatory." When man began to buy and sell the land, inequalities took root, and from inequalities came misery and wars, which ever since have plagued mankind. Nor can wars cease, insisted Winstanley, until inequalities in the ownership of property have been removed. For one man to be richer than his brother is a social calamity: "For Riches," insists Winstanley, "make men vain-glorious, proud, and to oppress their Brethren; and are the occasion of wars." A man cannot become rich, he cannot amass an estate by which he receives hundreds and thousands of pounds a year, unless other men labor for him. "All rich men," says Winstanley, "live at ease, feeding and clothing themselves by the labors of other men, not by their own, which is their shame, and not their Nobility; for it is a more blessed thing to give then to receive: But rich men receive all they have from the laborers hand, and what they give, they give away other mens labors, not their own." [2] This extreme attack on the incentives and machinery of community organization to which the English, rich and poor, had been accustomed for centuries, in itself may have alienated Cromwell and other cultivated readers. Winstanley often anticipates so skillfully the response of his reader that many of his extreme suggestions appear for the moment entirely reasonable. But such a proposal as the abolition of buying and selling, whatever its philosophical merit and justification in extreme Christianity, was a judgment few literate Englishmen could analyze without inflammatory resistance.

At the end of his "Epistle" Winstanley makes it clear that he does not

[1] E655(8), February 20, 1652, p. 12. [2] *Ibid.*, p. 12.

propose an immediate adoption of his utopia by all the people of England. He proposes only that the land belonging to the Commonwealth, the commons and wastelands, those lands taken out of the oppressors' hands, may be turned over to the common people who have struggled to overthrow kingly power. Let those who wish, says Winstanley, remain in the community of buying and selling according to their custom. Let others who wish join hands in creating a new society within the old, a society in which for the first time in England there will be no buying and selling. Then, should it prove successful, members of the old society will freely and voluntarily join it.[3] Though he makes this separation between the proposed experimental society and the old one, Winstanley speaks thereafter as if it is inevitable that the experimental society will be so crowningly successful that it will become the model of social organization for the whole land.

3. THE UTOPIA IN BRIEF

Winstanley's proposal is a communistic state without money, without tithes, without hereditary titles, without inequality of income. To be governed democratically by suffrage of all men over twenty, including drunkards and sinful people, the Commonwealth is to gather all classes under its wing, even, after a brief period, the royalists. Parliament members, in fact all officials of the Commonwealth, are to be chosen annually, for Winstanley has a pronounced dread of much power residing long in the same hands. To abolish old oppressive laws, to order the planting and reaping of the crops and the gathering of them into communal storehouses, where each may go and secure freely what he needs; to establish a suitable postal system; to raise an army—these shall be the duties of the Parliament. Each parish is to elect three overseers, a peacemaker, a master technician, a master of the common store; no one, claims Winstanley, will lack abundant food and clothing. Anticipating the inevitable query, "And are you going to feed the idle people too?" Winstanley makes the following provisions. An idle person is first to be admonished by the overseer, then, after a month of recalcitrance, to be whipped; if he still persists in idleness, he is to lose his freedom for one year and to serve under the taskmaster, or jailer. In spite of his hatred of priests, Winstanley would allow a kind of state church to continue in his ideal England. The ministers would, however, be elected annually; they would be required to learn a trade like other workers, to work for the same wages as other men; and their function would be to lecture on philosophical, scientific, and historical as well as religious subjects, man's struggle

[3] *Ibid.*, p. 14.

for economic freedom to be emphasized.[1] Such in brief was the "socialist effusion" which, in the words of Gardiner, "was too far removed from the actual world to move Cromwell either to approval or indignation." [2]

In his additional preface, "To the Friendly and Unbyassed Reader," Winstanley assumes a more reasonable and conciliatory tone than in his preface to Cromwell. He hastens to make clear that he is not proposing community of wives or households of more than one family.

> *Every Family shall live apart, as now they do; every man shall enjoy his own Wife, and every Woman her own husband, as now they do; every Trade shall be improved to more excellency then now it is; all children shall be educated, and be trained up in subjection to parents and elder people more then now they are: The Earth shall be planted, and the fruits reaped, and carried into Store-houses by common assistance of every Family: The riches of the Store-houses shall be the Common Stock to every Family: There shall be no idle person nor Begger in the Land.*[3]

What Winstanley proposes, then, is not the pure communism of Plato, in which no child knows his own father and every father takes a paternal interest in each boy; nor does the community have halls where a number of families dine together, as pictured by Thomas More. Each family in Winstanley's utopia owns its own house and controls its own children. Though rejecting communal ownership of children as in Plato, Winstanley asserts community responsibility for the education of each child. Winstanley applies communism to the ownership of land, the organization of labor in planting and harvesting of crops, and the storage of crops in storehouses. As he considers one after another elements of his utopia, Winstanley gradually individualizes his utopian blueprint. I find no internal evidence that Winstanley had read Plato, Campanella, More, or Comenius. The only utopian model Winstanley cites is the commonwealth of Israel. From the Bible and his own thoughts alone, he claims, was derived his dream for an English government that would carry the principles of Christianity, especially "Love thy neighbor as thyself," at long last into practice.

4. SABBATH DAY: SECRETS OF THE CREATION

In Winstanley's utopian England the role of the minister, elected annually by the people of each parish, is crucial to the flowering of civilized customs. One day in seven the people meet to refresh their fellowship and renew their allegiance to their country. The minister brings to his flock news of commonwealth affairs; then he reads portions of the law,

[1] I am here following my *Milton in the Puritan Revolution,* pp. 319–20.
[2] Gardiner, *History of the Commonwealth and Protectorate,* II, 79.
[3] E655(8), February 20, 1652, p. 15.

that the youth may be instructed and all citizens better prepared to defend their laws. On the seventh day, also presumably under the leadership of the minister, citizens make speeches about governments of other ages, such as the commonwealth of Israel and the tyrannies and slavery of ancient times. But on the sabbath day Winstanley would have also speeches and discussions about science: medicine, astronomy, navigation, botany. "Men may come to see into the nature of the fixed and wandring stars," writes Winstanley, "those great powers of God in the heavens above; and hereby men will come to know the secrets of Nature and Creation, within which all true knowledg is wrapped up, and the light in man must arise to search it out."[1] To study nature is to unravel the mind of God. Nor would the sabbath day omit discussions of the nature of man, "of his darkness and of his light, of his weakness and of his strength, of his love and of his envy, of his sorrow and of his joy, of his inward and outward bondages."[2] It is true, says Winstanley, that ministers of the present age discourse about the nature of man, but all too often speaking from their imagination. How would the ministers speak about the nature of man from experience? Winstanley does not say; presumably he means in terms of chemistry or biology rather than in terms of philosophy or ethics. In terms of an approach to a scientific method, Winstanley was often primitive and hesitant, asserting principles rather than methods; there is no evidence that he had ever read Bacon or Harvey or Gilbert or Copernicus. But he is convinced that people can come to know God only through a rationalistic inspection of the Creation. When a true commonwealth appears, and everyone is certain of a livelihood, then the discovery of the secrets of nature will advance apace. Only when the bondage of kingship has disappeared will knowledge no longer be the monopoly of the privileged few. Only then, asserts Winstanley, "will *knowledg cover the Earth, as the Waters cover the Seas.*" Thus the minister himself, to discover God and preach him to the people, must become a man without fancies, without guesses, patiently searching out the secrets of the creation. To Winstanley, had he known the researches of Harvey on circulation of the blood, the great anatomist would be the ideal man to lead a discussion of the nature of man on the sabbath day.

Nowhere does Winstanley show the revolutionary nature of his religious beliefs more than in his definition of the Deity in terms of observable phenomena. "To know the secrets of nature," he wrote, "is to know the works of God; And to know the works of God within the Creation, is to know God himself, for God dwels in every visible work or body." When a man studies a flower to know the secrets of its inner life, he is studying God himself. When man learns the secrets of the stars or

[1] E655(8), February 20, 1652, pp. 56–57. [2] *Ibid.*, p. 57.

the secrets of beasts and birds or studies his own body to know the principles of anatomy, he is unfolding the essence of God. "What other knowledg have you of God," asks Winstanley, "but what you have within the circle of the Creation?" When Winstanley speaks of knowledge of God, he always means, then, sensory knowledge of nature's works: "God manifests himself in actual knowledge, not in imagination; he is still in motion, either in bodies upon earth, or in the bodies in the heavens." To Winstanley there is no greater hindrance to man's intellectual growth than the habit of imagining what God is "beyond the Creation, or what he will be in a spiritual demonstration after a man is dead." Such a process, says Winstanley, is to "build castles in the air, or tells us of a world beyond the Moon, and beyond the Sun, meerly to blinde the reason of man." Thus men to try to attain knowledge of others have written or spoken instead of believing what they can actually observe. The use of imagination instead of observation in the search for knowledge is to Winstanley "the cause of all evil, and sorrows in the world." [3]

Winstanley has anticipated the replies to this definition of God and sensory verification as the way to true knowledge. He has anticipated attacks on what men will call his materialistic outlook. Traditional professors of religion will criticize his view of a minister's function as follows: *"This is a low and carnal ministry indeed, this leads men to know nothing, but the knowledge of the earth, and the secrets of nature."* [4] For those ministers who believe that the way to find God is to leave this world and go to heaven, Winstanley has only scorn and contempt. Those who call a knowledge of the earth a low and carnal knowledge, says Winstanley, are the ones who strive most to know the earth and profit from its fruits. The very ones who scorn a materialistic conception of religion are those who believe in buying and selling material things, "counting your self a happy man, if you be rich, and a miserable man if you be poor." Do not the ministers of the Commonwealth preach for money in order to enjoy the earth? Soldiers fight for the earth; lawyers work for the earth. Even the "professors strive to get Earth, that they may live in plenty by other mens labors." The ministers are constantly saying, *"Heaven after death is a place of glory, where you shall enjoy God face to face."* But, says Winstanley, he notices that such men are most reluctant "to leave the Earth to go thither." [5]

To Winstanley no sect of his day, even the Quakers, had set forth a definition of God he could accept. When he speaks of "professors," he usually means the appointed priests of the parishes, whatever their persuasion or the authority of their appointment; he does not mention Independents or Presbyterians or Anglicans. His views represent, then, a

[3] Quoted passages are from *The Law of Freedom,* p. 58. [4] *Ibid.,* p. 58.
[5] *Ibid.,* p. 59.

rejection of the prevailing ideas of the Deity, whatever their sectarian allegiance. By the words "divining Doctrine" which Winstanley's spirit "hath waded deep to finde the bottom of," he means the doctrine of guessing or imagining the nature of God, heaven, and hell. This doctrine, says Winstanley, "does not speak the truth, as it is hid in every body, but it leaves the notional knowledge of the thing as it is. And imagins, studies, or thinks what may be, and so runs the hazzard true or false: And this Divinity is always speaking words to deceive the simple, that he may make them work for him, and maintain him, but he never comes to action himself to do as he would be done by." [6] The nature and effects of this doctrine Winstanley sets forth as follows:

> First he [the minister] takes upon him to tell you the meaning of other mens words, and writing by his studying or imagining what another mans knowledge might be, and by thus doing darkens knowledge, and wrongs the spirit of the Authors who did write and speak those things which he takes upon him to interpret.
>
> Secondly he takes upon him, to foretell what shall befall a man after he is dead, and what that world is beyond the Sun, and beyond the Moon, &c. And if any man tell him there is no reason for what you say, he answers you must not judge of heavenly and spiritual things by reason, but you must believe what is told you, whether it be reason or no.[7]

Such a doctrine to Winstanley cannot be the expression of a strong and independent spirit; only a weak mind and a sick personality could accept it, one who does not understand his own manhood. Such a weak man "runs into fancies." If his religious passion runs into joyousness, he feels kinship with God as a personality; if he is sorrowful or pessimistic by nature, he begins to think of Satan as a person; he even fancies a hell in which he will burn, crying out that God has forsaken him; such a man, driven by imaginary truths, may in his terror take his own life. These are the effects of the divining doctrine, leaving a man bereft of his senses, imagining a heaven or a hell that does not exist. Winstanley has long since left behind any attempt to build up a doctrine that produces such effects, driving some men to madness, others to suicide, and turning all from the pursuit of well grounded knowledge. This way of thought cannot bring to man's mind the true nature of God in his creation; nor can it be the doctrine, says Winstanley, of Christ the savior of man.

5. FATHERHOOD AND HELPLESSNESS

The image of fatherhood as the essence of both authority and love recurs insistently in *Law of Freedom*. From fatherhood in the first family

[6] *Ibid.*, p. 60.　　[7] *Ibid.*, p. 60.

sprang all government. A father loved his children, fed and clothed them, directed them. In the image of the father lies the key to Winstanley's conception of original human nature; he cannot imagine a father who treats his children partially or unequally; who does not have a special concern for the youngest and weakest child; who does not exert his authority over them with tenderness. In fact, insists Winstanley, whose applications of democratic theory are more extreme and romantic than those of any contemporary, the children chose him to be their ruler. "How could this be?" one asks. "They could not even speak." They could not speak, it is true, Winstanley replies, "yet their weakness and simplicity did speak, and chose their Father to be their Overseer." [1] To Winstanley it was impossible for the average man or woman to resist the responses of love to the condition of helplessness. The helplessness of the child shapes the response of the father, choosing the father to be his guardian, to love him and care for him. The father of a family is in fact, continues Winstanley, the first and most important officer of the Commonwealth, and the children having chosen him by "joynt consent." Whatever the benign and loving authority of the average father, not all children become virtuous citizens: "Some are wise, some foolish, some subtil and cunning to deceive, others plain-hearted, some strong, some weak, some rash, angry, some milde and quiet-spirited." [2] Hence the people in each parish must choose one or several overseers to keep the peace, that the law may be preserved. As a father may punish a recalcitrant child, so the Commonwealth punishes an unruly citizen.

In his analysis of the duties of Parliament in a commonwealth, Winstanley turns again to his metaphor of fatherhood. Like a father the Parliament should remove all burdens from the people, succoring the weak and afflicted, removing injustices from the oppressed citizens. All too often in the past the Parliament has forgotten its duty toward the weak, having been corrupted by kingly power and intimidated by kingly frowns, respecting persons rather than justice; at such times the Parliament has despised the weak and vulnerable, contrary to a father's duty. Indeed, asks Winstanley, "hath not Parliaments sat, and rose again, and made Laws to strengthen the Tyrant in his Throne, and to strengthen the rich and the strong by those Laws, and left oppression upon the backs of the oppressed still?" [3] But now Parliament, having overthrown the tyrant with the aid of the commoners, must return to its true role as a father and provide for the poor, setting them to work planting crops and reaping grain, using the lands recovered from the king, the bishops, the lords of the manor: the wastelands, the chases, the forests, the abbey lands, and all those properties withheld from the English people by Wil-

[1] E655(8), February 20, 1652, p. 34. [2] *Ibid.*, p. 34. [3] *Ibid.*, p. 51.

liam the Conqueror. Such a national action would be the expression of a true Parliamentary father of the people. Like an honest father Parliament will not beguile its children with false promises; rather it "will fill our bellies, and clothe our backs with good actions of Freedom, and give to the oppressed childrens children their birth-right portion, which is Freedom in the Commonwealths Land, which the Kingly Law and Power, our cruel step-fathers and step-mothers, have kept from us and our fathers for many years past." [4] In a country where there is enough land for everyone, this is the slavery that the poor rightfully complain of. Kingly government has corrupted men until "covetousness and pride rule as King in one brother over another." Parliament as a father to its people should prohibit the buying and selling of the land, "which is all the childrens Birth-Right, and the price of their labors, monies, and blood." Let Parliament make a declaration that all its new laws must have the approval of those people who have been oppressed. Parliament is not to dally with its citizens, "but as a Father is ready to help his children out of misery." [5] Thus time after time Winstanley returns to his image of the Parliament as father and the citizens as children dependent upon a father's love and protection.

6. THIS CHEATING WORLD

Late in the treatise, addressing himself to the victorious Commonwealth army (and mainly, one feels, to Cromwell), Winstanley confronts them with his stabbing doubts and admonitions. Now that they have defeated the enemy on the battlefield, are they going to set up kingly laws again? If so, insists Winstanley, "King *Charls* hath conquered you and your posterity by policy, and won the field of you, though you seemingly have cut off His Head." [1] The power of kingly government is not in the king's body, but in his authority, his laws, his will. By their engagements, continues Winstanley, the army has promised those people freedom who helped rid the country of tyranny, which is a tree of many branches. Will members of the army itself now "reserve some part of the Kingly Power to advance their own particular Interest"? If so, the friends of the Commonwealth may be under a worse slavery than that of the king they have rejected. Moreover, such officers are not true Commonwealth soldiers; they are much worse tyrants, in fact, than those royalists they have cast out. The admonitions of Winstanley at this point take on the tone of a biting personal grievance. A tyrant soldier or officer "takes the possession of the Land to himself, and calls it his, and none of mine, and tells me he cannot in Conscience let me enjoy the Freedom of the Earth with him, because it is another man's right." [2]

[4] *Ibid.*, p. 51. [5] *Ibid.*, pp. 53, 54. [1] E655(8), p. 66. [2] *Ibid.*, p. 66.

7. THE DIVIDED PSYCHE: LAW AND HARMONY

In his analysis of the law of nature Winstanley postulates two hostile forces struggling for dominance in man's heart. One force of the law of nature is that power of life common to men and animals, including responses to a rash and greedy love of self, like the foolish actions of children or animals. Such a mindless action is called "*the law in the members warring against the law of the minde.*" The other force of the law of nature is represented by man's power of reflection, his ability to judge the destructive or benign effects of his actions, his capacity for temperance in eating, speaking, and acting. This power of reflection and judgment Winstanley calls "*the light in man, The reasonable power, Or the law of the minde.*" When a man uses the law of the mind and observes both the self-approbation and the dismay which certain actions and ideas bring him, his heart overcomes the rashness of his impulses and his personality reaches a high plateau of insight and harmony which Winstanley calls the "*testimony of a mans own conscience.*" The two hostile elements of man's personality, both a part of the law of nature, are in perpetual warfare with each other, each gaining allies from man's internal and external experiences, even as the dark struggles with the light, enlarging or diminishing its dominance. This struggle Winstanley pictures thus: "*The strong man armed, keeps the heart of man, till a stronger then he came, and cast him out.*" [1] This analysis of man's inner turmoil rejects emphatically the Calvinist view of man's essential depravity. On the other hand Winstanley's view of inner contradictions in man assumes no easy improvement in man's nature in proportion to the buffeting of beneficent forces. In an enlightened society, enriched by universal education and inspired daily by the vast range of community concern, the heart of man would still experience a constant warfare in his soul's field of battle.

The written law in any nation is to Winstanley a reflection of the relative power of reason and rashness in the minds of its lawmakers. When a wise man rules, the laws he puts into writing will preserve the peace of the land and curb and reduce the elements of irrationality and covetousness among the citizens. Good laws are passed on from one generation to another, such as the laws of Israel, written down by Moses and preserved for posterity. The preservation of good laws, however, has at times been wavering and uncertain, especially in times of warfare and conquest. When a kingdom is conquered, the new written law is likely to reflect not the support of peace and freedom, but rather the greed of the conqueror's friends. By skillful framing of laws, conquerors have taken away the land of the people and given much of the country's earth into

[1] Quoted passages are from *The Law of Freedom*, p. 78.

the hands of favorites. In the long history of kingship, according to Winstanley, the laws have generally been unfavorable to the common people. Kingship is hostile to a well governed land: Instead of setting up a law of righteousness, the law of kingship represents a retreat from righteous action. The precepts of the Bible, insists Winstanley, call for wholesome laws, consonant with the teaching of Christ. The true law of God, if translated into the written law, would make the earth the common property, unite Jew and Gentile in a brotherhood, and change the kingdoms of the world into commonwealths.

In the history of English law-making the common people have labored under heavy grievances. From the days of the Conquest, claims Winstanley, "the inferior people were successively of the rank of the conquered ones . . . servants and slaves." [2] They could not vote, nor could they hold office. Through the help of some statesmanlike members of Parliament, it is true, the commons had "here a line, and there a line of freedome inserted into their laws; as those good lines of freedom in *Magna Charta.*" [3] The new laws passed by the Commonwealth have not been of real benefit: "Though they be washed with Commonwealths water, their countenance is still withered." [4] The habit of keeping the proceedings of the law in French and Latin, says Winstanley, has been a heavy grievance: "Many have been imprisoned, whipped, banished, lost their estates and lives by that law which they were ignorant of." [5] Moreover, being unable to read the law, the citizens are helpless victims of the lawyers, whose interest it is to stir up as many lawsuits between man and man as possible. Often the lawyers cheat their clients out of their estates, always upholding the kingly interest. But, says Winstanley, in a moment of deep discouragement, suppose the laws are written at long last in English? What then? If the kingly bondage is still retained, such a change will do no good at all: It will "rather increase our sorrow, by our knowledge of our bondage." Thus Winstanley wavers between hope and despair in his vision of England's future: a realist who has looked into the darkest depths of England's ills, realizing their tenacity centuries deep; a visionary, too, aware of the vast explosion of knowledge in his own life and vistas of revolutionary change in generations of Englishmen to come.

At the end of *The Law of Freedom* Winstanley inserts a table of sixty-two pithy laws by which his utopia is governed. In this table Winstanley finds himself reverting to many basic personal freedoms inherent in the English law he has attacked as an inheritance from the Conquest. Some laws reflect a traditional harshness, such as the edict requiring the Biblical punishment of an eye for an eye, a limb for a limb, a life for a

[2] *Ibid.*, p. 76. [3] *Ibid.*, p. 77. [4] *Ibid.*, pp. 77–78. [5] *Ibid.*, p. 80.

life. On the economic aspect of utopian life, Winstanley provides laws for planting and harvesting, every family to serve as a team, keeping its tools ready for tilling, reaping, and threshing. Every young man is to learn a trade in seven years of apprenticeship, suffering penalties if he refuses to work: admonition to be followed by whipping and probation under the official taskmaster. Winstanley sets forth severe penalties also for any man who "calls the Earth his, and not his brothers," [6] for any man who gives or takes hire for labor, or persuades any person to buy or sell. Only the state may buy and sell; only the state may use gold and silver currently in dealing with other nations. Those men who have lost their freedom for offences against the state shall not revile the laws. Though in several places Winstanley limits freedom of speech, in matters of religious expression he is as extreme a tolerationist as Richard Overton or Roger Williams: "No man shall be troubled for his judgment or practice in the things of his God, so he live quiet in the Land." [7] Any one who uses weapons against the state shall die a traitor's death. Men and maidens shall marry whom they wish, for love only. At the marriage ceremony the two people give their vows to each other without the presence of a minister. When a woman is with child outside of wedlock, the father is required by law to marry her. If a man violates a woman against her wishes, he shall suffer the death penalty. (Winstanley says nothing about divorce.) Who may have a servant in this utopia? Only those who have themselves worked seven years as servants. At time of burial the officers of the parish accompany the corpse to the grave; but no man shall pronounce an exhortation.

Thus Winstanley: disciple of a strange Christ, beckoning in vain to utopian salvation. In an age when a thousand reformers sought to trace heavenly patterns, when inspired soldiers and officers risked their lives in cavalry charge or push of pike, each man shaped his own utopia: a justified union with God's purposes, as in Cromwell's letters after his victories; as in Milton's loftiest dream, "to leave something so written to aftertimes, as they should not willingly let it die"; as in Bunyan's cry, "Behold, thou art fair, my love." To many Puritans utopia was in part the achievement of holiness, however momentary, and the assurance of a Christ warm and loving and indwelling. To thousands of Independent soldiers, as to one part of Milton, utopia was a commonwealth of men in plain clothes, stripped clean of the lordly manners and customs of aristocrats and kings. To Bradford and Winthrop across the seas, utopia was a new world, clean and dangerous, a world uncontaminated by the presence of popery in nave, window, ritual, and altar; a world undis-

[6] *Ibid.*, p. 84.

[7] *Ibid.*, p. 81.

tracted by beauty of dress or the delicate tracery of fan vaulting in King's College Chapel.

But Winstanley rejects all contemporary definitions of utopia. The God of the other Puritans of his day is to him a stranger, though he and they had read the same Bible, analyzed the same commonwealth of Israel, which Milton was to claim in *Paradise Regained* was a better teacher of political ideals than the classics of Greece and Rome. From these classics Winstanley learned nothing; nor did he learn anything from Plato, Campanella, Bacon, or Comenius. Though he was closest to Bacon in scientific method and to Comenius in educational theory, he rejected all secular learning for an intense study of the Bible only. No more strange, deluded visionary than Winstanley emerged from the boiling agitation of his time. Whereas other searchers applied Biblical meaning to holy life, to sexual restraints, to the nature of heaven and hell, to the conquest of enemies, to the identification of witches, to laws forbidding adultery, swearing, blasphemy, to the justification of manhood suffrage, freedom of conscience, Winstanley alone justified from the Bible an equal birthright for every man in the earth and its fruits. Bradford's rugged realism in his account of the Pilgrims' rejection of communistic enterprise on the American scene is at a remote pole from Winstanley's passionate beliefs.[8] Winstanley was curiously unaware of the tenacity of economic custom centuries deep, of the thousand strong threads that bound all Englishmen, beggar or lord, to the buying and selling and owning habits of their fathers. But to Winstanley the promises of the Gospel were a sham without equality among men: not equality of social station only, but equality of property as well. A man like Milton, educated among the beautiful towers of Cambridge, released from all manual toil, with leisure supplied to him as he said "out of the sweat of other men," was in a sense a product of that inequality of property that Winstanley thought of as the essence of the world's wrongs. The visions that animated the poets and dreamers and painters of England and other lands, indeed the whole creative fervor of Renaissance life, was based in a sense on the leisure of the few gifted ones supported by the labor of humble men. But for Winstanley equality of manual labor as well as time for intellectual labor was pregnant with the beauty of love for one another, the only beauty, he thought, suffused with the love of Christ. "I tell you Jesus Christ is the head Leveller," he wrote. "Christ comes to you riding upon these clouds."

[8] William Bradford, *History of Plimouth Plantation* (Boston, 1901), p. 163.

Chapter XXI

THE NEW STATE CHURCH: DOUBTS AND EVASIONS

February, 1652

In the early months of 1652 it became more apparent than ever to Cromwell and his followers that in some form they would have to continue the established church. To abolish it as Milton wished was unthinkable, if only because the tithes that supported it were too closely interwoven with the economic life of the land to permit their abolition. Moreover, the livings of nine thousand parish ministers the Puritans could use to support the new republic, as the monarchy had used them by and large to uphold royalist principles. "All [sects]," wrote Roger Williams, in *The Bloody Tenent Yet More Bloody,* "Court the Magistrate for his Sword, & his Money." [1] But assuming the necessity of continuance, two thorny questions remained to be settled by Parliament: How were fit ministers, acceptable to the Commonwealth, to be selected? More important, what dissenting private groups or personal beliefs would the Commonwealth tolerate? Cromwell's impulsive statement, that *"he had rather that* Mahumetanism *were permitted amongst us, then that one of Gods Children should be persecuted,"* [2] was a belief more easily translated into polemic custom around the campfires than into the legal structure of the new republic.

Cromwell had already chosen his man, the learned John Owen, now dean of Christ Church, who had served as his chaplain in Ireland, to cope with the complexities of the state church problem. Owen was a man of solid intellectual distinction in a worldly sense, sweetness of countenance, moderation of discourse. Without mention of the bloody deed, Owen had preached before Parliament the day after the execution of Charles, on the subject, "A Discourse about Toleration and the Duty of the Civil Magistrate." He had preached again before the Commons after the battle of Worcester; and on February 6 of the new year he had preached at Ireton's funeral. On February 11 Owen and his friends presented to the Commons *Proposals for the Furtherance and Propagation of the Gospel,* made public March 31 as *The Humble Proposals of*

[1] E661(6), April 28, 1652, p. 315.

[2] *The Fourth Paper Presented by Major Butler,* E658(9), preface, "To the Truly Christian Reader."

Mr. Owen, Mr. Nye . . . and Other Ministers.[3] By these proposals Parliament would maintain the established church while permitting limited toleration of dissident voluntary sects. There were provisions to eject recalcitrant ministers, also to try and approve new ones. No new minister was to be approved without bringing testimony of his "Piety, and soundnesse in the Faith" from twelve persons, eight of whom would be ministers. In addition to these testimonies, an examination and judgment by a committee of county ministers would be required. Finally, a Parliamentary committee from one of six national circuits was to "examine, judge, and approve" of those ministers selected by county committees. The Parliamentary committee would also have the power to "eject all such persons as shall be found unfit for the Ministery, or teaching of Schooles." Dissenting groups not having churches would be required to meet "in places publikely knowne" and give notice to the magistrate of their presence at the appointed places.[4]

One of the first to take issue with the *Proposals* was Roger Williams, who had arrived in England early in 1652. In a letter written to Winthrop in 1654 Williams shows that during his time in England he had been on familiar terms with Milton: "The Secretary of the Council, (Mr. Milton) for my Dutch I read him, read me many more languages."[5] On April 28, 1652, Williams sent forth *The Bloody Tenent Yet More Bloody,* a bold and uncompromising assertion of his principles, prefaced by an address to Parliament and followed by "An Appendix to the Cleargie of the Four Great Parties." Again, as in *The Bloudy Tenent* (1644), Williams claims for Papist and Arminian outcasts complete freedom of conscience, praising the citizenship of conscientious Catholics, calling upon his countrymen to have full faith in Christian persuasion, none in unchristian persecution. The priests of all religions he condemns as "the greatest *peace-breakers* in the *world* . . . they . . . never rest stirring up *Princes* and people against any that shall appose their own *religion* and *conscience,* that is in plaine *English,* their *profits, honours* and

[3] E658(12). It was this tract that Williams replied to in "An Appendix" of *The Bloody Tenent Yet More Bloody.* The same fifteen proposals appeared at the end of *The Fourth Paper Presented by Major Butler,* E658(9), which appeared March 30.

[4] E658(12), pp. 3, 4. As Gardiner has pointed out (*Commonwealth and Protectorate,* II, 97), Owen's scheme was somewhat less liberal in tolerationist principles than the officers' *Agreement of the People* (Wolfe, *Leveller Manifestoes,* pp. 234 ff.). Unlike Owen's scheme, the *Agreement* said, "We desire not tithes," but did not specify a way to support the established church. The *Agreement* would have permitted unitarians like Biddle, but excluded "Popery or Prelacy" and by implication the Jews as well.

[5] *Milton in the Puritan Revolution,* p. 91.

bellies."[6] In his address to Parliament, though he has high praise for their achievements, Williams warns them against losing their zeal in the moment of victory, allowing their former fine professions to "prove but a fading colour."[7] Let them now surpass all other statesmen in the extension of toleration to Papists, Arminians, and all other dissenters; let them guard against the shipwreck of souls on the rock of the bloody tenet.

In his "Appendix to the Cleargy of the Four Great Parties," which he designates as the Catholic, the Episcopal, the Presbyterian, and the Independent, Williams analyzes with styptic clarity the persecution inherent in the fifteen recommendations set forth in *The Humble Proposals.* These proposals demonstrate what mercy to souls, asserts Williams, may be expected from the Independents themselves. By these arrangements hundreds, perhaps thousands, of Presbyterian and Episcopalian clergymen will be ejected against the consent of their parishioners and to the sorrow of a multitude of citizens. As for preaching without ordination, yes, the proposals allow it, but only upon swallowing a like bitter pill, an *approbation* in which two ministers must concur. If a man's conscience forbids him to attend the established church, the proposals permit him to worship in private, provided that he notify the magistrate, who may, no one knows how soon, become his prosecutor; thus, concludes Williams, do the proposals require him to deliver himself up to his enemies. To allow freedom within slavery, to use plummet, line, rule, and square to circumscribe man's soaring spirit—such, Williams claims, is the contradiction of the new model. All this is but "*Winding Staires* and *back dores*" to that persecution the Independents have universally deplored.[8] Fresh from his counterattack on John Cotton, Williams shrewdly evaluates the *Proposals* as a reflection of Massachusetts state-and-church relationship: liberty of conscience accepted in theory but forbidden in practice. Themselves exiled by the prelates, the Massachusetts divines had in turn harried Williams and his fellow-dissenters out of the land. On the unraveling of such a familiar pattern Williams could speak with wary precision.

Williams was now in a strategic position to aid his cause. Not only was he a close friend of Sir Henry Vane, the most powerful member of the Rump; he talked frequently with Cromwell himself. From the preface of *The Fourth Paper Presented by Major Butler,* which appeared March 30, it is evident that Williams was present at a meeting of the committee in which Cromwell had made his blunt statement about preferring the practice of Mohammedanism to persecution of one child of God.[9] In

[6] *Ibid.,* p. 92. [7] E661(6), sig. C. [8] E661(6), p. 319.
[9] E658(9), "To the Truly Christian Reader."

The Fourth Paper Williams appeals directly to Parliament "to proclaim a true and absolute *Soul-freedom* to all the people of the Land impartially; so that no person be forced to *pray* nor *pay,* otherwise then as his Soul believeth and consenteth."[10] The extremity of tolerationist zeal to which Williams subscribed appears in his passionate utterances about the Jews. Let us make way, he exhorts, "for their free and peaceable Habitation amongst us."[11] Are they not the people most beloved of God and most favored by his promises? Moreover, if it were not for the Jews, would Christian people have a savior? The English nation bears on its conscience a deep load of guilt for its treatment of the Jews. Williams does not omit or deny the Christian simplification of the ages, that the Jews killed Christ; but to Williams the burden of guilt lay with centuries of oppression by the Christians, not with Jewish penance for a single death. If a great commonwealth wants to establish soul freedom, runs Williams' reasoning, it will find ways and means to succor the consciences of all citizens, not Gentiles only. Thus, with Richard Overton and one or two other zealots, Williams took the most extreme tolerationist stand of his generation, whereas Milton, as we shall see, was quite hostile to toleration of Catholics and neutral to the plight of the Jews.

Toward the end of March a new and ominous danger alarmed Williams and confirmed his fears. The "Principles of Christian Religion" mentioned in Article 14 of *The Humble Proposals*[12] were not to be left to each minister's private interpretation; they had already been set down in fifteen fundamentals by Owen and his colleagues, though a copy of them had not yet come to Williams' hands.[13] Not only, then, must each state minister meet the approval of other ministers; he must swear to define Christianity in fifteen specifics, as Parliament's ecclesiastical officers should prescribe. Williams expresses hope that the Committee will retract this new threat to private conscience. If not this, will not some "Faithfull Witnesses (against such *Graven Images*)" speak out in this emergency? This appeal, in the last sentence of *The Fourth Paper,* would normally have caught and held the attention of his friends Vane and Milton. From the preface to his sonnet to Cromwell, it is clear that Milton was watching impending events with trepidation. He was now im-

[10] E658(9), p. 17. For proof of Williams' authorship, see below, n. 13.

[11] E658(9), p. 18.

[12] E658(12), p. 6 (March 30, 1652); E658(9), p. 23. The same words appear in Article 13 of the later version published December 2, E683(12), p. 4.

[13] *The Fourth Paper,* E658(9), p. 23. The initials "R.W." appear in two places in this pamphlet; but a more emphatic acknowledgement of Williams' authorship (hitherto unnoticed) appears in the marginal note on p. 14: "*The full debate of this point, may be seen in that great Controversie of the* Bloody Tenet, *between Mr.* Cotton *and my self.*"

pelled to act in the way he thought his words would carry most weight.

As the meetings of the Committee continued through March and April, Milton found it impossible not to speak his mind as Williams had spoken his. Milton opposed a state church with more resolute thoroughness and consistency than that with which he upheld the principle of toleration. As shown later in *Christian Doctrine,* he was opposed to a professional ministry even though supported by voluntary offerings. Whether or not Milton was unrealistic enough to believe that in the surge of revolutionary action abolition of the state church was now a possibility we cannot tell. A national church that used the magistrate's power to collect salary tithes was to Milton tyranny enough. But reliance upon the secular power to coerce dissenting conscience was an even darker evil of which many of Milton's contemporaries had bitter memories; twenty thousand such men and women had fled to the wilds of America to escape the long arm of persecution by the prelates. In such a background of events and ideas, with Williams' pamphlet and the prospect of the ministers' Fifteen Fundamentals before him, Milton resolved to appeal to Cromwell, who was a member of the key committee; his personal prestige might outweigh all. It is likely that Milton had heard of Cromwell's decisive testimony about *"one of Gods Children,"* perhaps from Williams himself. Yet in Milton's mind Cromwell's stand was still a matter of doubt. Might he not for politic purposes maintain a state church that by enforcing the Fifteen Fundamentals would nullify the extreme tolerationist tenets he had so often expressed in the army councils? Well, if Cromwell wavered, Harry Vane would not. In Vane there was no retreat on *this* principle.

To appeal to Cromwell, Milton then wrote two complimentary sonnets that reflect his intense anxiety for the cause at stake. Even in the heading of the sonnet to Cromwell he shows his resolution to make his appeal unmistakable: "To the Lord General Cromwell May 1652. On the proposalls of certaine ministers at the Committee for Propagation of the Gospell." After complimenting Cromwell on his military and civil achievements, Milton warns that "new foes aries, threatening to bind our souls with secular chaines." Then, as though Cromwell cannot fail to want the widest liberty of conscience, he concludes:

> Helpe us to save free Conscience from the paw
> Of hireling wolves whose Gospell is their maw.[14]

In these lines Milton shows that, like Williams, he fears a denial of toleration by a state church erected by his own party. Independents, as well as prelates and Presbyterians, will persecute Protestant consciences.

In the sonnet to Vane Milton reserves his highest tribute for Vane's

[14] *Poetical Works,* ed. H. C. Beeching (Oxford, 1930), p. 88.

understanding of the exact relationship that should exist between church and state:

> Both spiritual powre & civill, what each meanes
> What severs each thou 'hast learnt, which few have don.
> The bounds of either sword to thee wee ow.
> Therfore on thy firme hand religion leanes
> In peace, & reck'ns thee her eldest son.[15]

The sonnet to Vane was presented to him on July 8.[16] Though dictated to different amanuenses, the two poems must have been written, therefore, within a few days or weeks of each other. It is plain that Milton is recommending Vane's advice to Cromwell in the most unequivocal manner possible. The two sonnets reflect both his fears and his hope of deliverance from England's religious perils. But his appeal, like so many others, ended in frustration; neither Milton's advice nor any other convinced Cromwell that the state church should not be maintained.[17] The decision of the Rump, which was to come in March, 1653, to use civil power to support the church, could hardly have been taken without Cromwell's approval.

Milton was too keen an analyst to err in selecting Vane as the repository of tolerationist confidence. Though we have no statement from Vane himself about the ministers' proposals, his brother Charles was on the committee that protested against them, and Milton's sonnet is itself evidence that Vane was sharply antagonistic to the coercion inherent in the proposed legislation.[18] To this day Vane's own religious views remain vague and misty; but on the question of toleration of Protestant dissent he was clear and consistent from youth to death. To Vane, as to Williams, American intolerance had been a rough, unforgettable training school. As the twenty-three-year-old governor of Massachusetts he had encouraged Mrs. Anne Hutchinson to expound her strange antinomian theories, half believed them himself, protected her against incipient persecution.[19] On the issue of tolerating Mrs. Hutchinson, Winthrop in April, 1637, had defeated him for the governorship; whereupon Vane returned to England. In November, Winthrop and the orthodox ministers

[15] *Ibid.*, p. 88.

[16] George Sikes, *Life and Death of Sir Henry Vane* (1662; UTSL), p. 96.

[17] In this crisis Milton had timely support from Needham. In *Mercurius Politicus* for April 22–29, 1652, E662(2), appeared this passage: "To erect a power called *Ecclesiastick* in equipage with the *Civill*, to bear sway, and bind mens consciences to certain notions ordained for orthodox . . . opposing Christ in his way, whose kingdom being not of this world."

[18] I am here following my *Milton in the Puritan Revolution*, pp. 94–95.

[19] Thomas Hutchinson, *The History of the Province of Massachusetts Bay* (2 vols., 1765–67), I, 55 ff.

banished Mrs. Hutchinson from Massachusetts, accusing her of "speaking in derogation of the ministers among us," breaking the peace of the state. To her objection, "That's a matter of conscience, Sir," Winthrop replied, "Your conscience you must keep or it must be kept for you."[20] The verbatim report of her examination[21] illuminates more clearly than Winthrop's cautious journal the persecuting, witch-burning psychology against which Vane rebelled; one reads the drama even yet with shame and dismay.

Through his long leadership in the Long Parliament Vane had supported all extreme tolerationist measures for Protestant consciences. In *The Bloudy Tenent* Williams alludes to a "heavenly speech" on toleration, evidently by his friend Vane. Baillie regretfully reported that "the great shott of Cromwell and Vane is to have a libertie for all religions, without any exceptions," and that Vane "whom we trusted most, had given us many signs of his alteratione; twyce at our table prolixlie, earnestlie, and passionatelie had reasoned for a full libertie of conscience to all religions."[22] In 1647 the unitarian John Biddle had prefaced an explanation of his views by an appeal to Vane for help against persecution: "My adversaries . . . [have] instigated the Magistrate against me, hoping by his sword, (not that of the Spirit) to uphold their Will-worship. . . . It will be your part, Honoured Sir . . . to examine the businesse impartially, and to be an helper in the truth."[23] Vane rose in Parliament and asked that Biddle be freed.[24] Like Williams, he was unwilling to persecute even the Catholics.[25]

On the issue of freedom for Catholic or Jewish consciences, however, Vane made no full statements such as those of Roger Williams. Indeed, on the question of the readmission of the Jews to England, a question much discussed in the early months of 1652, Vane was silent. Though he made no plea for Catholic conscience, Vane did attempt to protect Catholics from persecution. On June 1, 1652, when the Commons took up the question of Irish Catholics, "not to compel any of the Recusants in this Nation to their Worship, or Divine Service, contrary to their Consciences," Vane voted against coercion.[26] On the same day, however, without division, the House voted not to tolerate "Exercise of the Popish

[20] *Ibid.*, II, 483. [21] *Ibid.*, II, 482–520.

[22] *Milton in the Puritan Revolution*, p. 95; Baillie, *Letters and Journals* (3 vols., Edinburgh, 1841), II, 230, 235.

[23] *Twelve Arguments Drawn Out of Scripture* (September 6, 1647), E406(1), pp. 4, 5.

[24] Article on Biddle, *DNB*.

[25] James Hosmer, *Young Sir Henry Vane* (New York, 1888), p. 369.

[26] *Commons' Journals*, VII, 138.

Religion in *Ireland*"![27] Only a zealot prepared to lose all his influence over his contemporaries would have voted for toleration of the mass, particularly in royalist Ireland. But Williams' analysis of English persecution of Irish consciences in *The Hireling Ministry None of Christs*, published while he was intermittently a guest at Vane's house, and obviously written to crystallize opposition to Owen's scheme of a state church, suggests that Williams' plea for Irish consciences was not unwelcome to Vane. Certainly Vane was more sympathetic to Papists than Milton or Cromwell. On the other hand, so far as the evidence goes, Vane never spoke out for readmission of the Jews, as did Cromwell, or made any specific mention of their right to liberty of conscience, as did Williams.

In a sense Milton's position on ecclesiastical reform was more extreme than that of Cromwell or even Vane: He wanted no state church at all. Moreover, his ideal was a ministry which earned its living by secular means and preached on the Sabbath as a service freely bestowed upon the flock.

Milton undoubtedly knew how remote this ideal was from realization even under Cromwell. But there was still a chance to enlarge tolerationist views within the new state church. In the new state ministry Milton

[27] *Ibid.*, VII, 138. Lingard states (*History of England* [14 vols., London, 1825], XI, 179) that Vane spoke in favor of a Catholic petition on June 30, 1652. The *Commons Journals* for that day, however, show that Sir Henry Vane, Senior, voted against the reading of the petition. The motion to read the petition carried by vote of 33–28, but the petition itself was denied. I cannot find any record of the younger Vane's vote on this issue.

As Lingard points out, the petition, mild and moderate enough, asking for "*such clemency and compassion . . . as in the judgment of this honourable House may consist with the publike peace*," may be found in John Austin's *Christian Moderator*, E1313(2), pp. 59–62. Austin's tracts contain some of the most searching pleas for toleration of Catholic conscience the Puritan Revolution produced. See the first part of the *Christian Moderator*, E640(1), August, 1651, and the third part, E705(15), July 14, 1653; in the latter Austin deals with the oath of abjuration.

A case cited by Lingard from *Christian Moderator* shows the savagery of Parliament's treatment of the Papists. A Catholic orphan girl appealed to the commissioners for sequestration at Haberdashers Hall for relief from the sentence against her, payment of two-thirds of her estate to the state. Having served as a maid for seventeen years, she had saved twenty pounds (at an annual wage of seven nobles), and deposited her money with a friend. The commissioners discovered her estate and appropriated two-thirds of it, 13 pounds, 6 shillings, 4 pence. The sequestrators said "they had not power to give her any releef, more than the bare thirds, unless she would take the oath of *Abjuration*." See *Christian Moderator*, E1313(2), p. 82. Austin's remarkable tracts deserve more attention than they have thus far received.

and Vane wanted the widest diversity of views and the fewest restrictions on the conscience of the individual preacher. But within the framework of the state church, how was heresy to be defined? Milton's answer was that no Protestant, even one denying the Trinity, could be considered a heretic. His country should not use civil power to coerce the conscience of a single Protestant. Catholic conscience, however, was another matter: That he would not allow even in the saying of mass in a private home. As for Jewish conscience in the new republic, Milton, as we shall see, was ambivalent and withdrawn, whereas Williams wanted free and full toleration. The state church in his view could not rightfully persecute any conscience, whether that of Protestant, Jew, or Catholic.

Chapter XXII

APPEALS FOR A NEW JERUSALEM

March, 1652

On March 30 Rogers Williams in *The Fourth Paper* had set forth the thorniest of all questions to the tolerationists of his day: "Whether it be not the duty of the Magistrate to permit the Jews, whose conversion we look for, to live freely and peaceably amongst us?" [1] Only ten days before, on March 20, Captain Robert Norwood had anticipated this question and given his answer: "Yes; because we would, if under their power, that they should tolerate us." [2] Perhaps as many as a dozen wrestlers with the problem in Milton's day would have answered in the affirmative, most of them obscure pamphleteers; of this small company, all but two or three justified their recommendations by unrealistic assumptions, as Williams did in his expectation of the Jews' conversion to Christianity. Milton, as we shall see, made no appeal for toleration of the Jews, vehement as he was in his sallies for the free conscience of all Protestants. Cromwell, however, was a staunch advocate of the return of the Jews to England and the freedom of their consciences. He was one of the number who had already given assurances to Manasseh Ben Israel, the renowned Jewish leader of Amsterdam. "It is made known to me," Manasseh had written, addressing the Parliament, "and to others of our Nation... that you do vouchsafe to help us, not onely by your prayers." [3]

[1] E658(9), p. 3.

[2] *Proposals for Propagation of the Gospel* (March 20, 1652), E656(21), p. 17.

[3] "Epistle Dedicatory," *The Hope of Israel,* 2nd ed., tr. Moses Wall (December 2, 1651), E650(1).

Manasseh's appeal, *The Hope of Israel,* had been translated into English by Moses Wall, who, like Williams, hoped for the conversion of the Jews, despite Manasseh's insistence that such an expectation was illusory; Manasseh cites, indeed, instances of Spanish priests who defected to Judaism during the Inquisition. Wall's purpose, aside from his hope of conversion and his admiration of Manasseh, who "may wel be set for a pattern to us Christians," is to remove the hatred of the Christians "from off that people . . . who are beloved for their Fathers sakes." [4] For the first time in centuries, then, at the birth of the new republic, the Jews of the continent could look with hope toward a new settlement on English soil.

One of the few extreme advocates of toleration for the Jews was Edward Nicholas, who had sent forth *An Apologie for the Honorable Nation of the Jews* in February, 1649. Unlike most critics, Nicholas would not admit that the Jews were in any measure responsible for their plight; he blamed alone "the rage of men in all countries," [5] as in the expulsion of 120,000 from Spain in 1493. On the score that the Jews killed Christ, Nicholas was the only apologist of his day who denied that a whole people as such could have been guilty of the execution of Jesus: "It is apparent in the Gospel, that that action was done by the Elders, chief Priests, and Scribes . . . and not that the whole Nation were guilty." [6] Let the English not follow the lead of Papist persecutors of the Jews: "I hope better things of our Nation." [7] Of all nations, should not England be the first to welcome the persecuted and the afflicted? Such an action would be a great example to other nations who have wronged the Jews. "It is not tollerable . . . to adde affliction to the afflicted, as we do in continuing Laws in force against them." [8] At no point did Nicholas hedge or retreat. He did not mention the possibility of conversion to Christianity; he did not point, as Williams had, to the talent of the Jews for accumulating wealth; and unlike Milton, whose father was a money-lender, he did not repeat the old refrain of Jewish usury. As for blood heritage, asks Nicholas, what race can claim more honorable descent? Were they not ennobled by God himself? How can kings or princes, popes or cardinals, claim ancestors superior to those of the Jews, "the most honorable Nation of the world"? [9] Nicholas' position, if not unique among the Englishmen of his time, he supported by a more rounded and complete analysis of principles than any contemporary except Cunaeus.

On January 28, 1653, appeared Clement Barksdale's translation of Petrus Cunaeus' *Of the Common-Wealth of the Hebrews.* In Cunaeus'

[4] "Translator to the Reader," E650(1), sigs. A4v, B.
[5] February 21, 1649, E544(16), p. 11.
[6] *Ibid.,* p. 6.
[7] *Ibid.,* p. 11.
[8] *Ibid.,* p. 8.
[9] *Ibid.,* p. 4.

long treatise, he is able to visualize the virtues of the Hebrews in clearer historical perspective than any other contemporary. In military valor they were inferior to no nation: "They alwaies rose higher by their overthrows, were enriched by their losses, and the keenness of their enemies sword put the more courage in them." [10] Moreover, did not the patriarchs and the prophets and Christ himself come from this nation? Like Nicholas, Cunaeus asks, "What Nobility could be greater?" [11] True they have declined in vigor under persecution and deprivation. What people could maintain their spirit that "For so many years, through the whole world, have been wearyed out with so great scorn and contumely? whom Children, in contempt, have pulled by the sleeve, and men by the beard?" [12] Alone among his contemporaries, Cunaeus blames the faults of the Jewish people upon conditions, not inherent perverseness. Under the Roman pagans they suffered ghastly persecution. In one moment of history alone, Titus sentenced four thousand to death in the pestilent airs of Sardinia, another four thousand to the beasts. Trajan, mildest of the Roman emperors, forbade them to read the law. What a body of learning has come down to the Gentiles with the help of Hebrew scholars! To the Hebrews we owe the preservation of the Bible. "How many *Errata's* had stoln into the Holy Scriptures, had the custody thereof been committed only to such as *Lactantius, Austin, Gregory, Chrysostom,* most holy men indeed, but unskillful of the Hebrew tongue . . . This was the Jews only study, and their sole care, to vindicate the Books of *Moses.*" [13] They counted not words and verses only, but the number of letters in each book; only by their diligence has the Bible been preserved.

In the relentless searching of the Gospels few ironies made deeper impressions on some minds than the plight of the Jews. Even a few sailors of England's far-flung ships echoed the views of Nicholas. On March 19, 1652, a sailor of the ship Phoenix, resting at Leghorn, described a visit he had made with friends to a local synagogue. There they found a man who could speak a little English: *"We . . . asked him the meaning of such and such things."* Then the writer asks: Is it possible that England will continue laws in force against the Jews when the Pope tolerates them, the Turks, the Duke of Florence? [14] In *A Bosome Opened to the Jews,* William Tomlinson noted the irony of praying for outcasts one is not willing to embrace in his own land. He would not have England "a rejecter of them being strangers in the time of their calamity, they seeking to come in and live peaceably among us." [15] In *A Brief Answer* Thomas Collier asked, "Must we take it into our hands, and become Executioners

[10] E1311(2), sig. A6. [11] *Ibid.*, p. 165. [12] *Ibid.*, p. 166.
[13] *Ibid.*, pp. 168–69.
[14] *Severall Proceedings* (April 29–May 6, 1652), E794(33), p. 2128.
[15] January 12, 1656, 669f20(22).

upon those poor dispersed people, let Turks and Indies do that, and not us who profess to know God in Christ." Almost alone among the commentators of his day, Collier considered Christ more Jew than Christian: "Our salvation came from them, our Jesus was one of them." [16] Such attitudes toward the Jews, if not foreign to Milton's outlook, found no expression in his letters, pamphlets, or poems.

Other thinkers who favored readmission of the Jews wrote with varying degrees of caution and reserve. Milton's friend John Dury, for example, evidently in response to Hartlib's request, wrote *A Case of Conscience, Whether It Be Lawful to Admit Jews into a Christian Common-Wealth.* The tract is signed January 8, 1656. Dury's first impulse is a generous affirmative: "A People in misery and distresse . . . there is no

[16] February 4, 1656, E866(1), pp. 4, 17. A strange fanatic and reported epileptic named Thomas Taney, a goldsmith in the Strand, claimed that the Lord spoke to him on November 23, 1649, changing his name from Thomas to Theauraujohn; whereupon Taney circumcised himself and claimed to be a prophet for both Jews and Christians. On April 25, 1650, Taney announced, in *I Proclaim from the Lord of Hosts,* 669f15(28), the return of the Jews to Jerusalem and the building of a new utopia there. The most complete statement of Taney's Ranter philosophy appeared in *Theauraujohn High Priest to the Jewes,* E656(10), March 15, 1651. "I am inferior unto no man," he wrote. Also: *"I turn my face from no man upon Earth."* In the same pamphlet Taney asserted (p. 5): "All Religion is a ly, and a cheat, a deceat; for there is but one Truth & that is Love, & that devoureth, not neither destroyeth any man, but lives in its own fire . . . Now if you be in the Gospel of Light, you must see none poor, neither in need, neither can you be in true Love, unless all have an enjoyment as your selves, and none want; for God is light, filling all his Creation with the Beames of his fulness." In *Theaurau John,* August 13, 1651, he asserted that God spoke through him (E640[8], p. 7): "The eternal Spirit renued in me dictating it self into your understanding." Like other Ranters, Taney attacked the clergymen of Oxford and Cambridge, pointing out that the apostles were humble, unlearned men. Taney was proud of his imprisonment (E656[10]), pp. 7–8: "The Prisons were alwayes the Prophets Schools." Several years later, on December 30, 1654, Taney set fire to a tent which he had erected in Lambeth and then threw into the fire (Gardiner, III, 235–36) a sword, a pistol, and a saddle, claiming that these symbols were the gods of England. On the same day Taney (*Commons Journals,* VII, 410) tried to invade the House of Commons, in front of which he drew his sword, "struck at divers Persons; and ran with his Sword against the Door of the House." According to *The Weekly Intelligencer* for January 2–9 (E823[2]), John ran with drawn sword at Mr. Cooper, the door keeper, and "slashed the cloaks of the standers by." When brought to the bar of the House, where he defiantly kept his hat on until ordered to remove it, Taney admitted that people were about to stone him because he had set fire to his tent and burned his Bible. He insisted that he had drawn his sword at the door of the House because a man had jostled him there. The House committed him to the Gatehouse for drawing his sword, burning his Bible, and affirming that the Bible was not the word of God.

doubt, but they may lawfully be received into any civil Societie."[17] Moreover, continues Dury, our indebtedness to them is far-reaching: "We have the Oracles of God by their meanes, preserved and conveyed to us, and the . . . accomplishment of . . . all the promises, whereof we desire, that they may be made partakers again with us . . . to shew that mercie to them which he [Jesus] hath shewed to us." It may even be a sin to refuse them admittance. But toward the end of his pamphlet Dury's doubts begin to mount. He warns Hartlib that Jews "aspire to have . . . riches and power over others, where ever they can get it"; he fears "their covetous practices and biting usury." The state, he concludes, *"doth wisely to goe warily, and by degrees, in the business of receiving them."*[18] Dury is aware that the Commonwealth hopes to profit by the international experience of some Jewish business men; but in his judgment the basis for admitting them should be rather "out of Christian love and compassion towards them." Thus, in contrast to Williams and Nicholas, Dury has many reservations. He is willing to grant the Jews liberty of conscience, provided they worship in their own tongue, do not blaspheme, proselyte, or "profane the Christian Sabbath."

Unlike Milton, therefore, Dury at least put himself on record as desiring a limited toleration of Jewish conscience. Another friend of Milton, Moses Wall, translated Manasseh Ben Israel's book, *The Hope of Israel,* saying, "Do not think I aime by this Translation, to propagate or commend Judaisme . . . through Grace I have better learned the truth, as it is in Jesus."[19] But Wall wrote to "remove our sinfull hatred from off that people, whose are the Promises, and who are beloved for their Fathers sakes."[20] Despite Manasseh's blunt warning against any such possibility, Wall and other writers hoped for the conversion of the Jews. Wall speaks of his great admiration for Manasseh, whose life embodies a model for Christian people.[21] The Parliamentarian Edward Spenser was willing also to admit the Jews to England, but conditionally: "My consent ye shall have, that you and your people shall live in *England,* and have meeting places to worship *Adonai,* but no place for sacrifices." Spenser doubts that England will permit circumcision or marriage to Christians. Moreover, a third part of each Jew's estate will be forfeit to the state at his death; another third is to be used for the maintenance of converted Jews![22]

[17] June 27, 1656, E882(11), p. 3. [18] *Ibid.*, pp. 7, 8, 9.
[19] E650(1), "The Translator to the Reader," sig, B1. [20] *Ibid.*
[21] *Ibid.*
[22] *An Epistle to the Learned Manasseh Ben Israel* (1650), British Museum, 701.a.40, pp. 11, 15–16.

At the far right of England's commentators on the Jews were men with whom Milton and Dury had nothing in common; nevertheless such commentators carried on the resistless march of folk superstition; they were a political force that even the champions of free Jewish conscience could not ignore. In his preface to the translation of Josephus, *History of the Latter Times of the Jews,* June 2, 1652, James Howell repeated the ancient accusations: Jews over the centuries had poisoned wells, counterfeited coins, falsified seals, crucified Christian children. The Jews look strange, have "*uncouth looks and odd cast of eye . . . likewise that rankish kinde of sent . . . which is observed to be inherent . . . I wish that England may not be troubled with that sent again.*" [23] William Prynne came forth in 1651 with two formidable volumes against the Jews, recapitulating the ancient grievances and conjuring up a new Jewish plot "*to seduce us unto Judaism,* to which many are now inclined." [24] Like Prynne, the anonymous writer of *Anglo-Judaeus* justifies the hostile treatment of Jews by English kings, attacks Manasseh for his appeal to Cromwell, accuses them of usury. "Lower we cannot prize any one of most abject condition," asserts the writer, "then by comparing him to a *Jew*." The author of this tract dedicated his volume to Cromwell, signing his epistle "W.H." [25] The strange royalist Arise Evans, who urged Cromwell repeatedly to set Charles II on his rightful throne, wrote that if kingship were not restored, the Jews would be to blame.[26] In his desire to resettle the Jews in England, granting them freedom of conscience, Cromwell found a steady resistance among some of his closest colleagues in the Council of State. Only Hugh Peters was a militant worker for the return of the Jews. Lambert was silent. Harrison was silent. Milton was silent. Dury was sure of the case for the return of the Jews by test of conscience but doubtful by the tests of expediency.

Despite the agitation for freedom of Jewish conscience in 1652 and 1656, Milton at no time spoke out decisively on this issue, the most searching tolerationist dilemma of his age. This fact is particularly striking when we reflect upon the agitation carried on by Williams in the early months of 1652 and the strenuous efforts made by Cromwell to secure readmission of the Jews to England. Milton's very aloofness from such a

[23] E1427, Epistle Dedicatory, "To Englands Imperial Chamber, the Renowned City of London," sig. [A6v].

[24] *A Short Demurrer to the Jews* (January 7, 1656), E483(1), and *The Second Part of a Short Demurrer to the Jews* (March 30, 1656), E483(2). The passage quoted is from E483(1), pp. 83–84.

[25] January 8, 1656, E863(3), p. 47.

[26] *An Eccho to the Voice from Heaven* (March 24, 1653), E1304(3), p. 135.

vital controversy is in itself a fact that deserves exploration and interpretation.

The nearest approach to a statement of Milton's attitude toward liberty for Jewish conscience is in *Observations on the Articles of Peace with the Irish Rebels.* By an official assignment of the Council of State, March 28, 1649, Milton had been called upon to justify the policies of the new republic, answering in part *A Necessary Representation* of the Belfast Presbytery, which the Council had ordered printed with the *Articles of Peace.* The Presbytery accused the new republic of embracing "even Paganisme, and Judaisme in the Armes of Toleration." Though Milton calls this charge "A most audacious calumny," he hastens to make a qualification: "And yet while we detest *Judaism,* we know ourselves commanded by *St. Paul, Rom.* II. to respect the *Jews,* and by all means to endeavor their conversion." [27] When Milton writes, "we detest *Judaism,*" he uses words repeated nowhere else in his writings. Nor do we find elsewhere in Milton Paul's admonition "to respect the Jews" or work for their conversion, though this injunction is found prominently in Williams (in *The Fourth Paper,* for example, as the leading justification). How, Williams had asked, can we hope to convert the Jews to Christianity if we forbid them to live in the land? But Milton did not expand the idea of conversion here or elsewhere. One can only conclude that he was interpreting the official attitude of the new republic, respect for the Jewish people, without denying all complaints against the Jews or committing the government to the universal toleration mentioned by the horrified Belfast Presbyterians.

Denial of Jewish liberty of conscience had been based on accusations centuries old in folk and intellectual custom. Milton resorts only rarely to these traditional slurs. In *Doctrine and Discipline,* it is true, he had written of the Jews: "Their hearts were set upon usury, and are to this day, no Nation more." [28] This accusation is particularly striking in view of the money-lending career of Milton's father and Milton's statement that his own livelihood had come "out of the sweat of other men." [29] Though he is very ambivalent on the subject, Milton elsewhere upholds usury, saying that it is not "against the word of God, nor the rule of charity." [30] In *Christian Doctrine* he asserts that usury is not to be ascribed to the "hardheartedness of the Jews." Moreover, God "would not have permitted the Israelites to lend upon usury to strangers" if it were wrong.[31] So that this attack upon the Jews, so common in Milton's time,

[27] Columbia, XVI, 238, 264. [28] *Complete Prose,* II, 289.
[29] *Church-Government,* in *Complete Prose,* I, 804.
[30] *Complete Prose,* II, 322. [31] Columbia, XVII, 39, 341.

indirectly referred to in Williams' statement "their known Industry in inriching themselves," Milton never took seriously enough in his own thinking to expand or justify.

The most persistent cause for persecution of the Jews has been the recurring simplification of the ages, "The Jews killed Christ," a charge repeated by Williams in *The Fourth Paper.* At no point does Milton expand or support this charge against the Jews as grounds for forbidding them home in England or denying them liberty of conscience. Milton refers most directly in *Second Defence* to the responsibility of the Hebrews for the death of Christ, when he says that by the clearest signs they might have identified him.[32] Milton refers obliquely to the recurring accusation to illustrate a distinction in his *Art of Logic:* "Long ago the proegumenic cause of the death of Christ was the ignorant zeal of the Jews; the procatarctic cause was the violation of the sabbath and the seditious assemblies with which he was charged."[33] Such a statement shows that Milton from time to time fell into the pattern of age-old rhetoric which had justified for centuries persecution of Jewish conscience. But his judgments of the Jews possess none of the blazing fury that dominate his passionate utterances against the Papists. He was not a champion of the Jews, like Edward Nicholas and William Tomlinson; but neither was he a fanatic opponent of their liberty of conscience, like William Prynne and James Howell.

The limits of Milton's toleration, then, are clearly defined in his undeviating hostility toward freedom of Catholic conscience; and his failure to speak for the Jews can only be interpreted, in the light of contemporary agitation, as a reluctance to permit them freedom of worship. Even the royalist Sir Thomas Browne was more outspoken for Jewish conscience than Milton, pointing out that "the persecution of fifteen hundred yeares hath but confirmed them [the Jews] in their errour." Was not persecution, asked Browne, the basis of the Anglican faith? "None can more justly boast of persecutions, and glory in the number and valour of Martyrs."[34] Milton's failure to speak for the Jews sprang from a tolerationist psyche unique among his contemporaries, informed by a vast learning, untouched by superstition, influenced by a reluctance yet to be unraveled. Though like his fellows Milton separated the Jew Jesus from the Christian Jesus, he never fell into the habit of separating as two spe-

[32] *Second Defence,* below, p. 600. In *Paradise Lost* Milton inserted one of the most persistent of all contradictions in the history of Christianity (XII, 413–14) "naild to the Cross / By his own Nation." Punishment of death by crucifixion was a Roman, not an Hebraic custom.

[33] Columbia, XI, 37.

[34] Sir Thomas Browne, *Religio Medici,* I, 25, in *Works,* ed. Simon Wilkin (4 vols., London, 1835–36), II, 37.

cies the Jews of the Bible from the Jews of his own time. He was an Old Testament Christian, more at home with the fire of the prophets than with the revolutionary love of the New Testament. He could not portray the meek and loving Christ in *Paradise Regained,* even as the Puritans could not glean their battle cries from the Gospels. But even a prolonged preoccupation with Old Testament Judaism did not induce Milton to take his stand with Richard Overton and Roger Williams for liberty of Jewish conscience.

CHAPTER XXIII

ENGLAND IN 1653

IN 1653 the memory of Charles I and his execution was in the minds of most Englishmen still green and ineffaceable. The magic of the king's name, to the average illiterate rustic as well as to the aristocrat forfeiting a part of his wealth to the inexorable new republic, was a reality no glorious victories of Cromwell could dispel. The average Englishman felt that he had a property in the king, a property enhanced rather than diminished by death itself. The fact that Charles II had been humiliated on the battlefield at Worcester, and was now again an exile in France, in no sense diminished the magic of the king's name. Pious Englishmen of rigorous morality in their private lives could forgive with scarcely a murmur of dissent Charles' daily pursuit of lovely and willing ladies; such a life in no sense reduced the identification they felt with his rightful crown and person. If it was true, as Milton claimed, that Charles I had undermined the people's liberties more dangerously than any other monarch, this was irrelevant to the maintenance of the precious symbol. "Oh why are you so foolish as to cry up a king?" cried Milton, in 1660, when the catastrophe of monarchy was fast descending upon him. In his attitude toward kingship Milton belonged, not to the Puritans or the Cavaliers of 1653, but to the American era more than a century hence, the era of Jefferson and Franklin and Paine. No one of Milton's day was less representative than he of the possessiveness the average Englishman felt for the king's person as the symbol of national unity.

In the absence of kingship a constitutional as well as psychological vacuum existed that Cromwell and his associates tried in vain to fill. It was this vacuum that Cromwell had in mind when he said to Whitelocke, in 1652, "What if a man should take upon him to be king?" It was this vacuum that finally brought the word *Protector* into being in 1653. Other practical problems of government, the financing of the army, the war against the Dutch, the expansion of vital committees, the relief of poor creditors, even the organization of the state church, could be solved by vigorous and efficient administration. But reverence for kingship pervaded all classes, a magic with roots centuries old which neither the Commonwealth nor the Protectorate could strike down.

1. THE PROTECTORATE IN 1653: EXPENDITURES AND INCOME

By the end of 1653 the Long Parliament and its Barebones successor had raised over £6,000,000 by confiscating and selling the lands and properties of their enemies. Sale of the king's goods had brought £108,990; bishops' lands, £675,603; Dean and Chapters' lands, £503,179; fee farms, £1,469,087; king's lands, £1,993,951; compositions, £1,304,957.[1] In taking over the lands of some seven hundred royalists, the government had the lands sequestrated, that is, put in the hands of county committees, who sold leases and collected rents and penalties of money payments. On each royalist the republic imposed an additional levy of one-fifth of the delinquent's personal estate and one-twentieth of his real estate. Many royalists compounded for their estates, that is, bought them back for payment of a fine, varying from one-half to one-tenth of their value, the proportion determined by the government's conception of the extent of their delinquency. Many purchasers who invested in confiscated properties exploited their tenant laborers to the utmost, rejecting traditional patterns of concern for servants and laborers for the prospect of quick return on their investments.[2] The confiscations of 1652 seemed the only sure way to finance the war against Holland. Many of the royalists named in the bill had been reduced to dire straits by the sudden calamity. Of this action Cromwell later said, "Poor men were driven like flocks of sheep by forty in a morning to confiscation of goods and estates, without any man being able to give a reason why two of them should forfeit a shilling."[3] As Christopher Hill justly writes, "it was an upheaval comparable with the dissolution of the monasteries."[4] The rents in the social fabric were in fact pervasive, and irreparable for decades to come.

[1] Maurice P. Ashley, *Financial and Commercial Policy under the Cromwellian Protectorate* (London, 1934), p. 41. These figures have now been further analyzed and corrected by H. J. Habakkuk, "Public Finance and the Sale of Confiscated Property during the Interregnum," *Economic History Review,* 2nd series, Vol. XV, No. 1, 1962, pp. 70–88.

[2] Christopher Hill, *Century of Revolution,* p. 146.

[3] Firth, *Oliver Cromwell,* p. 310. The bill was finally passed November 18, 1652. Gardiner (*Commonwealth and Protectorate,* II, 200) estimated 618 persons. See *Commons Journals,* VII, 192, 196–202, 204–209, for names of some 687 persons inserted in the bill.

[4] Hill, p. 146.

The army expenses for a year amounted to £1,500,000; the navy expenses about £1,000,000. In 1652 an additional £300,000 had been voted to build thirty new frigates. Total expenses in 1652–53 came nearer to £3,000,000 than ever before.[5] On November 24, 1653, when a new assessment bill requiring monthly payments by each county and town, totaling £120,000 for the nation, was introduced in Parliament, it met with formidable opposition, but was finally passed in somewhat altered form.[6] The assessment of counties and towns, together with the excise tax and the customs, brought an annual income of approximately £1,800,000.[7] Even with the capital at hand from compositions, fines, sales of royalist lands, the Protectorate, like the Commonwealth, was always running into deficits. The maw of war was never closed. The government of Cromwell, like that of Elizabeth, encouraged English piracy at sea in order to increase its revenues.

2. IN 1653: THE LOT OF THE LABORER

In 1653 the population of England was four to five million persons.[1] Of these perhaps 400,000 lived in London.[2] Life for the laborer was easier in 1653 than in preceding years. The price of wheat by the quarter had fallen from 65*s.* 6*d.* in 1649 to 25*s.* 2½*d.* in 1653.[3] Nevertheless more than half the population was illiterate, ill fed, and ill housed, forced to work at eight, ten, or twelve pence a day. Skilled laborers received slightly higher wages: Generally a freemason was paid one shilling eight pence, a bricklayer one and eight, a plumber one and six, a man hewing

[5] Firth, *Oliver Cromwell,* p. 309; Gardiner, *Commonwealth and Protectorate,* II, 199; and Ashley, *Financial and Commercial Policy,* p. 42.

[6] Gardiner, *Commonwealth and Protectorate,* II, 311–12. [7] Ashley, p. 42.

[1] See a summary of the estimates, which vary widely, in W. K. Jordan, *Philanthropy in England* (London: Allen and Unwin, 1959). No studies have been made for 1650–60. King estimated (*Natural and Political Observations,* ed. George Barnett [Baltimore: Johns Hopkins Press, 1936], p. 31) 5,500,000 persons in England in 1688; Thorold Rogers (*Six Centuries of Work and Wages* [2 vols., London, 1884], I, 463) estimates 2,500,000 in 1603, and roughly follows King in estimating 5,500,000 by 1702. Jordan estimates 4,200,000 in 1600.

[2] Estimates vary widely. Jordan (*The Charities of London* [London: George Allen and Unwin, 1960], p. 16) estimates 350,000 by 1642. King (*Natural and Political Observations,* p. 26) estimates 530,000 in 1688. If these estimates are fairly accurate, London must have housed over 400,000 people in 1653. Charles Creighton, in a memorable and vivid analysis, "The Population of Old London" (*Blackwood's Edinburgh Magazine,* CXLIX [1891], pp. 477–96) estimates 339,824 in 1634 and 460,000 in 1661.

[3] James E. Thorold Rogers, *History of Agriculture and Prices in England* (7 vols., Oxford, 1866–1902), V, 827.

timber one and three.[4] The average laborer's daily hire of twelve pence could buy one of the following: a half pound of beef, two chickens, two dozen eggs, two pounds of butter, a pound of currants, a pound of sugar, or a pound and a half of salt. About half of the worker's annual income of some nineteen pounds he paid out for food. Fuel was dear, a shilling for a sack of charcoal.[5] The cost of a horse, eleven pounds, would have taken more than half of the average worker's income for the year. The purchase of a sheep, about eleven shillings, required an investment of eleven working days. While the average laborer could not have earned more than fifteen or sixteen pounds a year, his bare expenses amounted to eighteen or nineteen pounds:[6]

Cottage and garden	24 shillings a year
Food	9 pounds, 1 shilling a year
Fuel	26 shillings a year
Clothing	6 pounds, 9 shillings a year
Tools	15 shillings a year
TOTAL	18 pounds, 15 shillings

At best, then, the life of the laborer was precarious; he was always on the verge of want for the very necessities of existence.

The laborer's real economic lot may be further clarified by comparing the income of his class with that of other occupations. No records exist for 1653 comparable to the classifications made by Gregory King in 1696 for the year 1688; neither the proportionate nor the actual incomes, however, could have been strikingly different in 1653 from those of 1688, when King estimated that the income of laboring people was fifteen pounds a year, cottagers and paupers six pounds a year, common soldiers fourteen pounds a year.[7] In 1688 a lord received 2800 pounds, a bishop 1300, a knight 650, a country gentleman 280, a merchant 400, a lawyer 140, a clergyman 45 to 60 pounds, a freehold farmer 50, and an artisan 40. In his late years Milton had an income of 200 pounds a year, approximately ten times as much as the laborers of his day. King estimated that laboring classes comprised 849,000 families in 1688, as compared with 511,586 families of the better classes; the laboring classes in King's view decreased the wealth of the kingdom; the professional, aristocratic, and business classes increased the wealth. The total income of the laboring classes King estimated as approximately 9,000,000 pounds, or about one-

[4] *Ibid.*, VI, 642.

[5] *Ibid.*, VI, 322, 445, 290, 375; in London the best ale and beer in December, 1654, was selling at eight shillings a barrel (*Weekly Intelligencer,* January 2–9, 1655, E823[2], p. 153).

[6] *Milton in the Puritan Revolution*, p. 12.

[7] *Natural and Political Observations, 1696,* ed. George E. Barnett, p. 31.

fifth of the total national income.[8] In 1653 the proportion of earnings received by laborers could not have exceeded this percentage. The scanty harvests of the 1640's had intensified the complaints of the poor. Despite increase in earnings of as much as fifty per cent, real wages fell in 1648–50. The years 1653–55, however, as Christopher Hill points out, were the most prosperous years of the era, and real wages rose sharply, largely because the price of wheat was lowest in the century. But for the laborer this was only a momentary lull. Even in these years the prices of many basic commodities, among them cheese, beef, and eggs, in relation to his daily wage gave him no advantage in increased earnings.

Such records of food costs and wages describe only in a pale sense the miseries which the laboring class endured. For the poor classes, comprising perhaps sixty per cent of the population, life expectancy was somewhat under thirty-five years. Justices of the peace in Devon fixed wages for women workers between the ages of eighteen and thirty years only. From this record it appears that the justices did not think women over thirty-five would be qualified physically for a laboring job.[9]

In 1653 many philanthropic citizens sought to relieve the privations of the poor with bequests of many kinds. Not the church or the nobles or the government, but wealthy merchants, especially the great merchants of London, relieved the miseries of the poor most generously and imaginatively. In the early 1650's, of total gifts to the London poor amounting to around £42,000 annually, Wilbur K. Jordan found that the great merchants gave 56.53%, or about £23,700 each year.[10] Jordan has estimated that some 7391 individual donors to all charities in London during 1640–1660 gave a total of £1,889,211.[11] Of these donors 438 were great merchants, 2,239 lesser merchants, 1087 tradesmen, 180 clergymen, 141 upper gentry, 388 lower gentry. About 1,100 of the donors were women. The proportion of benefactions for the poor to the total of all gifts was about thirty-nine per cent in London, forty-three per cent in the country as a whole.[12]

3. CHARLES II: DESTINY AND MYTH

In March, 1653, Charles II was twenty-two years old, a brown-haired, gray-eyed man about six feet tall, sallow in complexion, graceful in carriage, affable in manner, quick and accurate in judgment of men. On formal occasions he wore a purple cloak adorned with a silver star and a purple scarf and garter. The Faithorne engraving of about 1651 shows

[8] *Ibid.*
[9] Hill, *Century of Revolution,* p. 25.
[10] Wilbur K. Jordan, *Charities of London,* p. 425.
[11] *Ibid.,* p. 47.
[12] *Ibid.,* p. 426; Wilbur K. Jordan, *Philanthropy in England,* p. 254.

him with long curly hair reaching below his shoulders, a white lace collar around his throat, and a white scarf across his chest. His large gray eyes in this portrait are wary and commanding rather than gay or serious. Lines are already forming around his curving lips and thin mustache. In the Champaigne portrait of 1653 (in which he wears gold-decorated armor and a red sash) his long black curls fall on a blue collar trimmed with white lace. The gray eyes have a brownish cast. The eyelids droop slightly; the lower lip protrudes above the upper.

Of a robust constitution, Charles loved horses, hunting, yachting; he loved late hours, gay dances, and romantic trysts. The almost daily pursuit of mistresses was his chief delight. It is recorded that "in the year 1650, to the many fornications and adulteries which he then committed, [he] added the perpetration of an attempt upon a modest and virtuous lady," calling upon himself the displeasure even of his staunchest friends.[1] About a year before, on April 9, 1649, Lucy Barlow had given birth in Rotterdam to a son whom Charles immediately acknowledged as his own (and afterward made Duke of Monmouth), though his fatherhood was doubtful. His liaison with Mrs. Barlow had probably begun during the week of July 9–18, 1648, about two months after Charles' eighteenth birthday. Notwithstanding the urgent appeals of Hyde and Ormond, Charles did not break off the relationship until 1651.[2]

Nothing better portrays Charles than his escape after the battle of Worcester, September 3, 1651, in which he had borne himself with conspicuous bravery.[3] "After that the battle was so absolutely lost," said Charles, "as to be beyond hope of recovery, I began to think of the best way of saving myself . . . If I could possibly, I would get to London."[4] When with sixty men he had escaped from Worcester, leaving his shattered army behind, he was seized with a fit of remorse for fleeing. Pulling up and speaking to his fellow-Cavaliers, he proposed that they return and attempt to rally the Scottish horse for a new charge: If they could not turn the battle into victory, they would die with honor on the field.[5]

[1] Osmund Airy, *Charles II* (London, 1904), p. 95. [2] *Ibid.*, pp. 51, 71.

[3] One witness wrote (*Boscobel Tracts*, ed. John Hughes, London, 1857), p. 144: "Certainly a braver prince never lived, having in the day of the fight hazarded his person much more than any officer of his army, riding from regiment to regiment, and leading them on upon service with all the encouragement (calling every officer by his name) which the example and exhortation of a magnanimous general could afford."

[4] *King Charles Preserved* (London: The Rodale Press, 1956), p. 7.

[5] *Cf.* Thomas Blount, *Boscobel* (1662; UTSL), pp. 21–22: "Before His Majesty was come to *Barbon's bridge*, about half a mile out of *Worcester*, He made several Stands, faced about and desired the *Duke of Buckingham*, *Lord Wilmot*, and other of his Commanders, that they might rally and try the fortune of war once more;

Brave as he was, Charles was at a remote pole from this spirit of martyrdom. He soon yielded to the persuasions of his followers and made his escape from thousands of Puritan soldiers and citizens eager to capture a "tall man, above two yards high, with dark brown hair scarcely to be distinguished from black" at a reward of £1,000.[6] In the next forty days of wandering he was to be recognized by forty or fifty people, many of whom gave him shelter; yet no one betrayed him. As Clarendon wrote of the "miraculous deliverance," he stayed in "poor houses of poor men," almost all of them loyal Roman Catholics.[7] Charles took with him Richard Penderell, one of six brothers of whom he later said: "I chose to trust them, because I knew they had hiding holes for priests." [8] At White Ladies, about twenty-five miles from Worcester, he took leave of all his followers except Wilmot.

Then began a series of narrow escapes in which Charles showed remarkable resourcefulness and quickness of mind. His first precaution had been to disguise himself as a Puritan rustic by cutting off his hair to make himself a Roundhead. He dressed himself in a leather doublet with pewter buttons, green trousers, a pair of old shoes "cut and slashed to give ease to his feet." [9] At Bridport he acted as a groom to Colonel Wyndham. The ostler said, "You are welcome, I know you very well." "Where did you know me?" Charles asked. "At Exeter; I lived two years in an inn there." Charles instantly fell into step with his new friend's memory: "And so did I," he said, "in the service of Master Porter. I am glad I have met with a countryman; but I see that you are so busy that you have no time to drink with me: when I come back from London we'll talk of old stories." Another time, having a new shoe put on his horse, he asked the blacksmith if there was any news. The blacksmith replied, "There is no news since the good news of the beating the rogues the Scotch," but unfortunately he had no news that "that rogue Charles Stuart had been taken." To which Charles replied, "If that rogue were taken, he deserves to be hanged more than the rest for bringing in the Scots." The blacksmith replied, "You speak like an honest man," so well had Charles kept his disguise in both dress and manner.[10] A relaxed,

But at the Bridge a serious consultation was held, and then perceiving many of the Troopers to throw off their Arms and shift for themselves, they were all of opinion, the day was irrecoverably lost, and that their only remaining work was to save the King from those ravenous woolves and Regicides."

[6] Airy, *Charles II*, p. 102.

[7] Clarendon, *History of the Rebellion*, ed. W. Dunn Macray (6 vols., Oxford, 1888), V, 194 ff.

[8] *King Charles Preserved*, p. 11. [9] *Boscobel* (1662), p. 52.

[10] Airy, *Charles II*, pp. 103–104. Talking with a "country-fellow" in a buttery hatch, Charles found that the man had fought at Worcester under the command

quick-witted man, nimble and imaginative in any emergency, grateful to his death for the timely protection humble subjects had given him.

Charles was not a man to grieve over his new throneless state or the brave royalists who had died under his banners at Worcester. Burnet wrote that he lost the battle "with too much indifference." Once back on the Continent, he was thrust again into a life without daily purpose or national significance. No passion for divine right or sense of historic role ennobled his aims or reflections, as they had the outlook of his father. No praise from his friends or councilors could make him think well of himself, convinced as he was that "no body did serve him out of love." [11] In Charles' manner men found a softness and charm that made it easy to speak to him. Yet he trusted no one, and as Savile has written, "He would slide from an asking Face, and could guess very well" what favor a man was about to ask. He never expected from his listener the magnanimity that he lacked himself. Though he had a sharp, clear intelligence in judging men, he could not bring himself to wrestle with great books or kingly ideas. As a youth he had had Thomas Hobbes as his instructor in mathematics. He understood mechanics and navigation and the architecture of ships. But the years of ease and the pursuit of pleasure to which he devoted himself had created a state of mind in which taking his ease or receiving his mistress was almost the only persistent aim of his waking hours. As Savile wrote, "The Power of Nature was too strong for the Dignity of his Calling, which generally yielded as often as there was a contest." [12] His loyalty to individuals, especially to those who had helped him in distress, was tenacious and imaginative; his loyalty to the national welfare, however defined, was spasmodic and unpredictable. One can picture Milton finding common ground with many a royalist in Restoration London, men like Waller, Clarendon, Hobbes, Cowley, Boyle: But it is impossible to imagine Charles and Milton talking

---

of Major Broughton in his own regiment of guards and had seen the king in action. Charles' story of this encounter runs as follows (*King Charles Preserved,* pp. 25–26): "I asked him what a kind of man I was? To which he answered by describing exactly both my cloaths and my horse; and then looking upon me, he told me that the King was at least three fingers taller than I. Upon which I made what haste I could out of the buttery, for fear he should indeed know me."

[11] *Characters . . . of the Seventeenth Century,* ed. David Nichol Smith (Oxford, 1918), pp. 219, 220.

[12] *Ibid.,* pp. 213, 214. Savile also wrote (*A Character of King Charles the Second,* London, 1927, p. 27): "It may be said that his Inclinations to Love were the Effects of Health, and a good Constitution, with as little mixture of the *Seraphick* part as ever Man had: And though from that Foundation Men often raise their Passions; I am apt to think his stayed as much as any Man's ever did in the *lower Region.*"

affably and easily together. No two men in all England were more remote from each other than they in the definition of life's essence, whether of one incandescent moment or the central purpose of years and decades.

4. THE EARL OF CLARENDON

In 1653 the Earl of Clarendon was forty-five years old, a chubby man of glowing brown eyes, aquiline nose, and tufted chin, his curled hair scarce reaching below his white collar. Living in Paris near Charles II, Clarendon was secretary of state and one of a committee of four to whom Charles trusted all his main decisions. As ten years before at Oxford, though always his own man, Clarendon had won the complete confidence of the father, so now he found himself on the son's right hand, despite the extreme distrust of both Presbyterians and Catholics, who had urged Charles to dismiss him. A decade before Clarendon had urged the father not to send the young prince to France; now, in the light of the absolutist influence of the French court, the hostility of the Catholic queen mother, Henrietta Maria, and Charles' joyous pursuit of mistresses, all his fears were confirmed; even his place as trusted daily adviser did not reconcile him to the wastage abhorrent to his Anglican conscience and his vision of constitutional monarchy. In 1653 Sir Robert Grenville made the absurd accusation that Clarendon was in communication with Cromwell: a charge scornfully rejected without serious investigation by Charles himself.[1]

As a young man Clarendon had been a cherished friend to some of the choice spirits of the age, among them Jonson, Selden, Carew, May, Waller, and Hales. From these men he "formed his studies, and mended his understanding; and by [their] gentleness and sweetness of behaviour, and justice, and example, he formed his manners, subdued that pride, and suppressed that heat and passion he was naturally inclined to be transported with." [2] But Clarendon's favorite spirit was Lord Falkland, killed at age thirty-four fighting for the king at Newbury. Clarendon's character of Falkland is also a portrait of himself, the surest reflection of the values by which he lived. Living seventeen miles from Oxford, Falkland had grown up on familiar terms with the best minds of the great colleges; indeed, wrote Clarendon, Falkland's very house "was a University bounde in a lesser volume." [3] So passionate was Falkland to learn

[1] Thomas H. Lister, *Life and Administration of Edward, First Earl of Clarendon* (3 vols., London, 1838), I, 380–84.

[2] *Life of Edward, Earl of Clarendon* (2 vols., Oxford, 1857), I, 27. Hereafter cited as Clarendon, Autobiography.

[3] *Characters,* ed. David Nichol Smith (Oxford, 1918), p. 73.

Greek that he resolved not to visit his beloved London until he could read the Greek historians. In Clarendon's mind, as in that of his greatest contemporaries (even Milton thought it meet to practice swordsmanship and wear his sword daily), the true intellectual was seldom a separate personality from the brave soldier. Of Falkland, Clarendon wrote: "In the morninge before the battell, as alwayes upon Action, he was very cheerefull, and putt himselfe into the first ranke of the Ld Byrons Regiment, who was then advancinge upon the enimy, who had lyned the Hedges on both sydes with Musqueteers, from whence he was shott with a Musquett on the lower parte of the belly." [4] An ideal man, Falkland: a man of flowing courtesy, largeness of spirit, range of knowledge, epitome of England's fruit of aristocratic greatness. Clarendon shaped himself consciously in the image of Falkland and other rare spirits. To kings as well as to lords and commoners, he was a man eagerly sought after but reluctant to serve, never petitioning, as had the great Verulam, for place or preferment. At age thirty-four Clarendon became Secretary of State to Charles at Oxford; but only after such reluctance to replace his old friend Nicholas that Charles was in great agitation at the prospect of his not serving at all.

Clarendon's portrait of himself as a young man is as full of honest self-praise as that of Milton in *Second Defence* and *Pro Se Defensio*. His idea of marriage, however remote from that of a man like Milton or Hutchinson, was worldly and honorable by the custom of the day. His first impulse to marry, he wrote of himself, had "no other passion in it than an appetite to a convenient estate." The lady with the estate and young Hyde soon parted company. Not long afterward he did marry, in order to concentrate on the study of law "and to call home all straggling and wandering appetites, which naturally produce irresolution and inconstancy in the mind." His manners, at first given to disputation, mended rapidly; he soon became "affable and courteous to all kinds of persons." [5] He found that he had a genius for shaping enduring friendships. He never overcame entirely his outbursts of anger, particularly in his years of power after the Restoration. But Evelyn wrote of Clarendon: "True he was of a jolly temper, after the old English fashion." [6] He took delight in obliging his friends and spending money on hospitality. He found that men, great or lesser, trusted him: "His integrity was ever without blem-

[4] *Ibid.*, p. 86.

[5] Clarendon, Autobiography, I, 10, 11, 64. These passages are cited by Sir Charles Firth in "Edward Hyde Earl of Clarendon," pp. 16, 17, in *Oxford Lectures on History,* 1904–1923.

[6] *Diary of John Evelyn*, ed. E. S. De Beer (6 vols., Oxford: Clarendon Press, 1955), IV, 339.

ish, and believed to be above temptation."[7] He was ambitious to raise himself in the scale of men by the development of his talents and a richer personality rather than by the influence of the great. Indeed the great men of his time cherished his company and the flow of his fancy more eagerly than he cherished theirs.

Clarendon was no unquestioning royalist such as the later Strafford or the Earl of Montrose. The rule of law was always to him superior to the prerogative of the king, but he would define the law in his own way. In 1641 Clarendon had been shocked to hear Henry Marten say, "I do not think one man wise enough to govern us all."[8] It is plain from his own account that Clarendon did not yet visualize the depth and fierceness of the revolutionary surge against either the church or the crown. If bishops were not preserved, he thought the monarchy could not well survive. In his own mind he represented the best traditions of the English constitution as exemplified in the reigns of Elizabeth and James. In the early years of the Long Parliament he had acted to abolish the marshal's court and helped to prepare the articles of impeachment against Strafford; but his loyalty to the Anglican Church and possibly his personal loyalty to archbishop Laud led him to oppose the Parliamentary consideration of the London petition against the bishops. Step by step thereafter he separated himself from Pym's party and finally joined the king at Oxford. Clarendon told Henry Marten that he "had no relation to the court, and was only concerned to maintain the government and preserve the law."[9] He was in despair at Charles' violation of privilege in his attempted arrest of the Five Members. He would kiss the king's hand (an action unthinkable to Milton and Ludlow or Cromwell); yet he was reported to have plucked Charles I familiarly by the cloak.[10] To Clarendon the law justified Charles' indivisible claim to the militia. In May, 1642, when the Commons appointed lieutenants of militia in each county, he withdrew from the House. Yet Clarendon saw more clearly than most of Charles' advisers the danger of using the militia against the Parliament. With a surer touch than any man of his day Clarendon unraveled the subtle ambivalences in men's choices for king or Parliament. He saw that a man like Edmund Verney would die with the king while a part of his heart lay

[7] Clarendon, Autobiography, I, 64.

[8] Clarendon, Autobiography, I, 76. *Cf.* Ludlow's extreme statement of the issue (*Memoirs,* I, 206–07): "Whether the King should govern as a god by his will, and the nation be governed by force like beasts: or whether the people should be governed by laws made by themselves, and live under a government derived from their own consent."

[9] *Ibid.*

[10] Wood, *Athenae Oxonienses,* ed. Philip Bliss (4 vols., London, 1820), III, col. 1021.

with the Commons. "I do not like the quarrel," Verney told Clarendon, "and do heartily wish that the king would yield and consent to what they desire; so that my conscience is only concerned in honour and in gratitude to follow my master. I have eaten his bread, and served him near thirty years, and will not do so base a thing as to forsake him." [11] Verney hated the bishops, but no royalist leader as yet knew his feeling. Two months later he died for Charles at Edgehill. It is not likely Clarendon would have died for personal loyalty to his king alone. Of the king's two bodies,[12] one that of Charles as a man and one that of Charles as the embodiment of the monarchial image, Clarendon gave unswerving allegiance only to the latter. His ideal was a constitution that would weld diverse elements of the population together, with the king the dominant power and indispensable symbol of that constitution. He did not at first probe the opposing beliefs of the day deeply enough, however, to see that reconciliation by means of diplomacy was not possible in the face of Charles' intransigence and the enhanced hostility of the Parliamentary party.

Clarendon's antagonist in the conferences on the militia at Uxbridge was Bulstrode Whitelocke. Clarendon had declared that the militia "by the law of England is in the king only." [13] But Whitelocke, in his speech of May, 1642 (one of the most balanced statements in the whole controversy), had maintained that the power of the militia was neither wholly in the king nor wholly in the Commons. Parliament could not constitutionally direct the militia to act; the king could not direct it to act without money from the Commons. If the king wished, he had the right to carry on a war against a foreign enemy at his own expense. Whitelocke maintained that the power of the militia was not in the king only because "the power of money is solely in this house; and without the power of money to pay the soldiers the power of the militia will be of little force." [14] But the key dilemma of the moment was this: Where lay

[11] Clarendon, Autobiography, I, 135.

[12] See Ernst H. Kantorowicz, *The King's Two Bodies* (Princeton: Princeton University Press, 1957), pp. 13, 446–50. In their *Declaration* of May 27, 1642 (*An Exact Collection,* 1643, ed. Husbands, p. 304), though Parliament "acknowledged that the King is the fountain of Justice and protection," they asserted that "the Acts of Justice and protection are not exercised in his own person, nor depend upon his pleasure but by his Courts . . . therefore if judgements should be given by them against the Kings will and personall Command, yet are they the Kings Judgement."

[13] Whitelocke, *Memorials,* I, 381. When Pembroke urged Charles I to grant Parliament power over the militia for a time (March 9, 1642), Charles replied (Gardiner, *History,* X, 172): "By God! not for an hour."

[14] *Ibid.,* I, 161. In their *Declaration* defending the Militia Ordinance (*An Exact Collection,* 1643, p. 304), Parliament asserted that "although the Law doe

the power when the king and Parliament were at arms against each other?

Unlike Whitelocke and Clarendon, Milton had little use for constitutional precedent. In *Eikonoklastes* he wrote:

> As for the sole power of the *Militia,* which he claimes as a Right no less undoubted then the Crown, it hath bin oft anough told him, that he hath no more authority over the Sword then over the Law; over the Law he hath none, either to establish or to abrogate, to interpret, or to execute, but onely by his Courts and in his Courts, wherof the Parliament is the highest.[15]

How, Milton asked, can the sword be placed in the king's hands without the consent of Parliament? Was not the law superior to the sword and was not Parliament the ultimate interpreter of the law? Clarendon stood by precedent, which clearly designated the king as commander of the militia, and modern scholarship unanimously supports his claim. Whitelocke concurred; but he declared that the king could act only when the Commons had granted the needed subsidy. Milton despised decision by precedents, justifying his judgments unhesitatingly by the law of nature when the statutes of the realm did not support his conclusions. The fact was indeed that no exact precedent existed in English history in which king and Parliament were at war with each other, each claiming the right to appoint commanders of militia in the various counties.

Clarendon pierced men's motives more incisively and justly than any man of his time. He was painfully honest about the men of his own persuasion, as in his portrait of Edmund Waller. On the other hand, he was sometimes harsh and erroneous; he accused Whitelocke of giving allegiance to the Parliament only because all his property was in those counties controlled by the Parliamentary forces; he was a man, wrote Clarendon, "who could not bear or submit to be undone." [16] The religious source of Cromwell's fervor was a mystery to Clarendon. But what other royalist could have written of Oliver: "His partes seemed to be renew[d], as if he had concealed facultyes till he had occasion to use them"? [17] Religion to Clarendon was the essence of gradation, ritual, tradition, aristocratic grace, involving no upheaval or conversion in early life, as in the boyhood years of Vane, Cromwell, and Hutchinson, all of whom were men of that substance Clarendon believed necessary to superior creative

---

affirme it [the militia] to bee in the King, yet it doth not exclude those in whom the Law hath placed a power for that purpose, as in the Courts of Justice, the Sheriffs and other Officers and Ministers of those Courts."

[15] *Complete Prose,* III, 454.

[16] Clarendon, *History of the Rebellion,* VIII, 248; ed. Macray, III, 497.

[17] *Characters,* p. 140.

and intellectual ends. To Milton, whose life span exactly paralleled that of Clarendon, religion embodied an explosive compulsion to judge anew from first principles every institution of his day, whether political, theological, or economic.[18] Religion was to Milton a fresh search for new truth, or old truths neglected; for Clarendon religion was the assurance of old truths as embodied in the unchanging Anglican way. No more than Laud could he understand the compulsion that sent men from the gracious arms of the church to the wilds of New England.

5. JEREMY TAYLOR

In 1653 Jeremy Taylor, forty years old, son of a barber, Cambridge graduate, and royalist extraordinary, was living in London, where John Evelyn heard him preach on April 8, 1654.[1] Taylor had been chaplain to Laud and chaplain in ordinary to Charles I, who had given him his watch at the time of his execution. In the action before Cardigan Castle in 1645, the Puritan army had taken him prisoner but soon released him. From 1645 to 1653 Taylor had taught at Newton Hall, Golden Grove, Carmathenshire, where he had written *Liberty of Prophesying* (1647), *Holy Dying* (1650), and *Holy Living* (1651). "He was a person of great humility," wrote Wood, "had nothing in him of pride and humour, but was courteous and affable and of easy access."[2] Humane as he was, Taylor preached no full sermons on the plight of the poor or ways of relieving their distress either in Wales or in London. He addressed himself in the main, as did Milton, to the spiritual and intellectual dilemmas of well bred men like himself. He was, however, more charitable and less combative than Milton. "There was a generous ferment in his blood and spirits," said George Rust, "that set his fancy bravely a work." Despite his life-long association with leaders of the king's party, Taylor did not defer to social rank: "He weighed men's reasons," said Rust, "and not their names."[3] Personal piety to Taylor, as to Bunyan, was of deeper

[18] *Cf.* Milton's statement in *Areopagitica* (*Complete Prose,* II, 550): "If other things as great in the Church, and in the rule of life both economicall and politicall be not lookt into and reform'd, we have lookt so long upon the blaze that *Zuinglius* and *Calvin* hath beacon'd up to us, that we are stark blind." How contemptuous Clarendon was of Milton's political outlook appeared in a letter of August 23, 1652 (French, *Life Records,* III, 248–49), in which he wrote of *A Defence:* "So impious and scurrilous a Pamphlett as that written by Milton hath founde the way into Germany (wher we hope it founde the same exemplary reproch and judgement, it mett in ffrance)."

[1] *The Diary of John Evelyn,* ed. E.S. de Beer (6 vols., Oxford: Clarendon, 1955), III, 149.

[2] *Athenae Oxonienses,* ed. Anthony à Wood, III, col. 785.

[3] *The Whole Works of the Right Rev. Jeremy Taylor,* ed. Reginald Heber and Charles P. Eden (10 vols., London, 1847–54), I, cccxxiv–cccxxv. For a balanced

concern than the wages of the laborer, imprisonment for debt, or the contradictions between the pomp of kingship and the daily life of the lowly Jesus. Unlike Taylor, Milton combined piety with a searching application of Christian ideals to royalist assumptions of social superiority.

In 1647 Taylor had sent forth one of the great classics of his time, *A Discourse on the Liberty of Prophesying*. To Taylor the true test of a man's religion was not his opinions but his actions. Believe what he would, Papist or Anabaptist, let him live in the land without hindrance, without persecution. "Only let not men be hasty," wrote Taylor, "in calling every dislik'd opinion by the name of Heresy, and when they have resolved, that they will call it so, let them use the erring person like a brother, not beat him like a dog, or convince him with a gibbet."[4] No man can avoid the conclusions to which his mind leads him; and no state can invade a man's mind and require it to work as the state wishes. "If his error be not voluntary, and part of an ill life, then because he lives a good life, he is a good man, and therefore no Heretick."[5] Are there not such good men, devout in search, compassionate in action, in every hated sect?

Can anyone speak with finality on the definition of heresy? To frame such a definition, one must be able to interpret the Bible with unerring insight. But what man or group of men is thus infallible? Not the pope, answers Taylor, or the great councils of the church, or any tradition, or the church fathers. With no infallible guide to support him, each reader must depend upon his own reason, but, says Taylor, "the variety of humane understandings is so great, that what is plaine and apparent to one, is difficult and obscure to another."[6] If a believer would not be prescribed to in his search for truth, he should not attempt to make a final interpretation for his brother to accept. Taylor returns again and again to his primary principle: "In matters speculative . . . all determinations are fallible."[7] Therefore it is not possible for the church, the monarch, or the individual to define heresy with invincible assurance.

In his analysis of the search for Biblical truth, Taylor demolishes one by one the reasons given for persecution of the sects. No answer to Laud's persecution of the Puritans is more compelling than that given by his own chaplain in *Liberty of Prophesying*. In a more scholarly and complete, but less passionate, way, Taylor retraces the arguments of Overton and Williams, stopping short of their open stand for the freedom of both Catholic and Jewish conscience. Yet Taylor's pacific language often belies the extremities of his principles. "To tolerate," he writes, "is not to

---

view of Taylor's treatment of the theme of poverty, see Douglas Bush, *English Literature of the Earlier Seventeenth Century* (1962), p. 334.

[4] *Liberty of Prophesying* (1647), Epistle [separately paged], p. 29.

[5] *Liberty of Prophesying* (1647), p. 28. [6] *Ibid.*, p. 171. [7] *Ibid.*, p. 211.

persecute. And the question whether the Prince may tollerate divers perswasions, is no more then whether he may lawfully persecute any man for not being of his opinion." [8] Taylor argues at length against the Anabaptist rejection of infant baptism; but even this hated sect he would not restrain or persecute. The Anabaptists differ from us in this one particular. Why should we condemn or kill or persecute them for this one difference only? Even the Anabaptists, like all other sects, should have the liberty of prophesying.

The pages of Taylor breathe a charity lacking in many of his Puritan contemporaries, lacking in Prynne, Edwards, Feake, Rutherford, Thomas Young, Stephen Marshall; lacking in Milton himself. In a later edition of *Liberty of Prophesying* Taylor added at the very end a Jewish legend that embodies the spirit of his great work: One sunset time, as Abraham sat at the door of his tent, an old man came toward him, stooped with the weight of a hundred years. As his custom was, Abraham welcomed him inside his tent, washed his feet, and gave him food. When the old man asked no blessing on his meat, Abraham asked, "Do you not worship God in heaven?" The old man replied, "I worship only fire," whereupon Abraham became so angry he pushed the old man into the night. God then spoke to Abraham, saying, "Where is the stranger?" Abraham replied, "Because he does not worship thee, I sent him away." God answered, "I have suffered him these hundred years, although he dishonoured me, and couldst thou not endure him one night?" Abraham went out of his tent, finally found the old man, brought him back, and gave him hospitality for the night.[9]

CHAPTER XXIV

LOVE AND MARRIAGE: SATIRE AND PROTEST

In the daily flow of pamphlets from London presses, few authors of Milton's time dealt, as he had done in *Doctrine and Discipline,* with the desperation of the unsophisticated, idealistic husband in facing some of the intimate dilemmas of sexual life. Nowhere do we find a record of the intimate feelings of the submissive, unhappy wife. But beneath the façade of Puritan dialectic seethed a whole world undocu-

[8] *Ibid.*, p. 214.

[9] This story was not inserted in *Liberty of Prophesying* until the second edition, 1657. For analysis of its origin and versions, see Reginald Heber, *Life of the Right Reverend Jeremy Taylor* (2 vols., London, 1824), II, 279–84.

mented in any direct sense. Only in such handbooks of the day as *The Card of Courtship* do we find even an artificial reflection of manners and customs and social dilemmas in which every young mechanic, soldier, or Oxford student was involved. Except for targets of satire like Henry Marten, the sexual habits of most Puritan leaders remain as much of a mystery now as in the time of Cromwell and Vane. On the subject of sexual life outside of marriage, only such satirical sheets as *Mercurius Democritus* and *Mercurius Fumigosus* were daring enough to describe in blunt terms the night life of London. The author of these sheets was possibly Richard Overton, the only Puritan satirist who combined political sophistication with racy humor and reliance for circulation on the blunt sexual image.

1. COURTSHIP AND ALIMONY

On January 14, 1653, appeared *The Card of Courtship: or, The Language of Love,* a book of advice in the form of conversations, letters, songs, sonnets, the substance of which men and women in love might wish to express themselves. The editor inscribes his "Epistle Dedicatory" to "*longing Virgins, amorous Batchelors, blithe Widows, kinde Wives, and flexible Husbands.*" Near the end of the tract the author even sets down a series of suggestive subscriptions, such as "Yours in an unalterable affection," "Yours inseparably," "Your obliged kinsman," and "The humble admirer of your incomparable beauty." [1] The opening dialogue presents Amandus in conversation with Julietta on the subject of choosing a husband, Julietta's father having generously foregone his own right to select one for her. In a second discourse Eugenia and Flavia discuss the problem of marrying elderly men for their money. "Alas," cries Flavia, "our sex is most wretched; no sooner born, but nurs'd up from our Infancy in continual slavery; no sooner able to pray for our selves, but they braile and hud us with sowre awe of parents, that we dare not offer to bate our desires." Men may express their passions at pleasure, but women "must rake up our affections in the ashes of a burnt heart, not daring to sigh without excuse of the spleen." [2] In still another conversation a wife named Armelina, in love with a suburban gentleman, asks a prostitute's advice on how to win his love without arousing her husband's suspicions. "If he [the husband] chance steal upon you," says the courtesan, "let him find/ Some book lie open, 'gainst an unchast mind." In still another dialogue Antonio beseeches favors of intimacy from his neighbor's daughter Beatrice. Beatrice exclaims, "Can I believe you love me, when you seek the shipwrack of my honour?" [3] The editor also in-

[1] E1308(2), p. 167. [2] *Ibid.,* pp. 4–5. [3] *Ibid.,* pp. 8, 9

cludes *"Instructions (directed by the Author primarily to the vulgar, yet he exempts not some Gentlemen) how to demean themselves to their Mistresses."* When a lover finds his mistress unfaithful, how does he most fittingly take leave of her? The editor advises a letter ending as follows: "I now as perfectly hate you, as heretofore I dotingly affected you (to perpetuate your memory) I will fix this Epitaph upon your Tombe." [4] The epitaph follows, dealing a shattering ignominy to the faithless one.

The harsh realities of one unhappy marriage (the husband a Puritan leader) appear in *Alimony Arraign'd, or the Remonstrance and Humble Appeal of Thomas Ivie, Esq.* In 1652 Thomas Ivie had sent forth an appeal to Cromwell against the decision of the Court of Chancery to grant his second wife alimony. Having gone on a mission to Madras on behalf of the East India Company, Ivie claimed to have built the fort of St. George and the town of Madrassopotan, rectifying abuses that had injured English trade.[5] Upon his return to England the first news he had was of the death of his first wife, at that time on her way to meet him in London. Ivie does not specify the date of his return to England or the date of his wife's death. But in October, 1649, he had taken to wife a widow, Mrs. Theodosia Garret, daughter of Mr. David Stepkins. At the time of the marriage Ivie had agreed in writing to the financial arrangements dictated by the father: a jointure of £1000 per annum and a cash advance of £1000, also gifts to Theodosia of £1200 in jewels. Within eighteen months after the marriage, Ivie asserted, he had spent upon his wife an additional £3000, of which £600 had gone for clothing and £500 in ready money. He had maintained Theodosia with coach and horses and her choice of furniture, beds, linen, clothes. To satisfy her demands, Ivie claims, he was reduced to borrowing great sums of money. Finally, to reduce his expenses, he proposed moving into the country. Unwilling to accompany him, Theodosia continued her high life in London with women equally gay and prodigal in spending. In his petition Ivie asserted that his wife had said to two of her gentlemen friends, Snelling and Killigrew, "that her first Husband had done the part of a man, twelve times the marriage night, But that this Husband had done but eight." [6] When relations between husband and wife came to a breaking point, Mrs. Ivie appealed for alimony to the Court of Chancery. Since his wife had accused him of having the pox, Ivie in May, 1651, went to two physicians to clear himself of this accusation. In his petition to Cromwell he sets down two statements, each signed by two physicians and a surgeon, asserting that he had *"no Symptom or*

[4] *Ibid.*, pp. 14, 37. [5] June 17, 1654, E231(3), p. 2. [6] *Ibid.*, p. 23.

Token thereof [of the dread disease]."[7] According to Ivie, his wife had meanwhile engaged in a plot to accuse Jane Gilbert, her maid, of being with child by him. After many hardships and examinations by midwives and physicians, who disagreed in their conclusions about the pregnancy, Jane Gilbert died. Meanwhile the Court of Chancery, on July 24, 1652, had granted Mrs. Ivie alimony of £300 per year.[8] From this decision Ivie had appealed, first to Parliament and then to Cromwell himself.

2. THE EYES OF *FUMIGOSUS*

On June 7, 1654, appeared the first number of *Mercurius Fumigosus,* a satirical weekly that continued to appear until October 3, 1655. Fumigosus was similar in format and tone to *Man in the Moone,* discontinued in June, 1650, and *Mercurius Democritus,* discontinued in February, 1654 (except for several issues in 1659). In these journals worked a mind alive to incongruities, a mind in many ways like that of Richard Overton and now and then reminiscent of John Birkenhead. One has the impression of a journalist of acute and prodigal skill working hastily on a low level of his talent. The political temper of *Fumigosus* is neither royalist nor Commonwealth. His main aim is, quite evidently, to sell his pamphlet to people eager to explore the low life of London, its streets teeming with whores, beggars, peddlers; its smells of urine and excrement; its vast range of street cries; its tolling of bells and moan of horns along the Thames.

Each number of *Fumigosus* opens with a series of verses, of which the following, in Number 4, June 28, 1654, is typical:

> *Of low Mountains, high Dells and Vales,*
> *Of lying* Truth's, *and of true Tales,*
> *Of Lamb-like* Lyons, *Lyon Lambs,*
> *Of Civill* Wolves, *and of Ewe-Rams.*
> *Of water* Windmills, *Land* Weather-cocks,
> *Of Maids in* shirts, *and Men in* smocks.
> *Of Horn-mad* Cucks, *and jealous* Citts,
> *Of Midsommer Women in mad Fitts,*
> *Of* Money *and of* Machiavell,
> *My* Muse *prepareth now to tell.*[1]

A second feature of the weekly *Fumigosus* is a passage of racy wit, like the following from the same Number 4:

> Ding dong Bell; He that wants *Money,* had as good be in Hell: The madded World methinks is just like a *Multiplying Glass,* the more I look,

[7] *Ibid.,* p. 15. [8] *Ibid.,* p. 31. [1] June 21–28, 1654, E745(4), p. 25.

the more *Whimseys* I discover, the more Covetousness, the more Pride, the more deceit I discerne; methinks now I behold a Paradise of *Anticks,* O bedlam world! when every Trull, and greasy Kitchin Maid, with gold and silver Lace is overlaid, whilst mournfull Vertue clad in vailes of Night, eates her own sighs, and drinks her Tears down-right . . . every one complains, but who amends; all grows worse and worse still; one changes his God, another his Religion, another his Wife. . . . Oh fie upon't! I am as weary, as asham'd of rehearsing the follies incident to this mad Age.[2]

A third element of satire in *Fumigosus* is a fanciful story about a contemporary writer or celebrity, as in the following passage:

On Midsummer-Eve, as *Nick Culpeppers Ghost* passed along the bank-side, he being walking towards *Hide-park* to gather *Fern-seed* going by the *Bear garden Ditch,* all the *Bears* roared so loud against him, that the very *sound* of their roaring, shook down the top of *Pauls* Steeple and part of the body of the Church; the same Night a bed of fresh Roses miraculously sprung up in the *Bear-garden* Ditch.[3]

Another such passage personifies objects familiar to the Londoner's eye:

The Golden Weather-cock upon *Pauls Steeple* the last Night challenged the Cock on *Grantham Steeple,* to fight a Duel upon *St. Michaels Mount* in *Cornwall* next *Islington faire Day* come Twelve-Moneth, being the 36 day of the moneth of Michalmas, falling out just upon *Whitson-pope Monday* about six a clock in the morning after dinner, many rich Guilded Coaches are preparing at the *Taylors,* to goe out to see this *Cock-fighting,* most of the Citizens that the last *may* rid into *Hide-parke,* ride thither in water Sedans drawn by tame Sea-asses.[4]

An unfailing ingredient of *Fumigosus* is the imagery of sexual appetite, often analyzed as the religious exuberance of a strange sect such as the Family of Love:

Two loving Sisters being a little *over-heat* by a zealous *Jack-Smith,* basely deluded them into the *Devils Neckenger* to be *Dipt,* and whilst he was praying with them in the *water,* he appointed his Brother, to come and steal away their Clothes, which was cunningly performed, the religious *Dipper* having provided a Harbour on purpose not farr off to cover the *nakedness* of his two Female *Converts,* whom the very same Night he altring his judgment; miraculously turned them from their *new Dipping,* into the *Family of Love,* they (as he bragged to his Associates) that Night *Exercising* in a *Cafe,* or *B--dy House,* all as *naked as ever they were born:* Oh shame to Religion![5]

In his department called "The Weekly Intelligence" *Fumigosus* introduces a number of news stories, some of them playful and fanciful,

[2] *Ibid.,* pp. 25–26. [3] *Ibid.,* p. 27. [4] June 7, 1654, E740(5), p. 6.
[5] June 28–July 5, 1654, E745(11), p. 40.

often with a satirical slash at the Quakers or Ranters, such as the following:

> Many *Quakers* are seen every day walking *London* streets almost stark naked, in the day time; amongst the rest, one Mr. *Murford* a Quaker attended some houres at *White-hall* bare-foot, and bare-headed, but being brought before His Highness, he said;
> *The Saints are abused, and thou must right us: The World is proud, but thou must abase and humble it;* and, quoth he, *Wee the Spirituall and self-denying People are villified, but thou must right us from being wronged.* And so without moving his hat, he departed.[6]

Now and then *Fumigosus* includes some actual happenings, however exaggerated. In No. 43 the satirist reports: "Mr. *Rogers,* Prisoner at *Lambeth House,* Preacheth every Sunday through the Prison gates, and great concourse of People flock to heare him." [7]

Only rarely in *Mercurius Fumigosus* does the satirist show sympathy with the plight of the poor, the hardships of prison life, or civil liberties as interpreted by John Lilburne from his master Edward Coke. But in *Mercurius Democritus,* predecessor of *Fumigosus,* these strains of protest find a recurrent voice. The only difference between a ship and a prison, such as the Counter hole, writes *Democritus,* is that "the one is moving misery; and the other a standing one." In the Counter you can hear "the hideous ratling of chains, hand-cuffs, bolts, Guives and fetters." There one meets people in all stages of misery:

> One wringing his hands; another laughing; another swearing and cursing; one blaming Destiny; another, Luck; another, Fortune that brought him hither; one crying out of his evill wife: another of his false friend; another of his hard Creditor, that all like the Devil, and the seven deadly sins, laboured to bring him to that place of horror, whilest Lawyers and Jaylors like promethian Vultures gnaw asunder the very heart-strings of the poor persecuted prisoners . . . you may perceive the Plague Sores of the Law.[8]

One prisoner, plagued by vermin, kicks his bedfellow in the teeth, a sight to Democritus "more sad then any other object in the world." Another, fetching a pot of water to a fellow-prisoner, makes several motions toward a fellow-prisoner as if to make a gift, then flings it in his face. The buffeted one shakes off the water, looks about him, but says not a word. To escape momentarily from the horror, *Democritus* returns "to my merry Cue of laughter." But in his account of the Counter, he cries out, "Oh! the Torments of the Hole!" [9]

[6] March 21–28, 1655, E830(26), p. 338.

[7] *Ibid.,* p. 338. As *Fumigosus* states, Rogers was at this time a prisoner at Lambeth House. See account of him in *DNB.*

[8] November 9, 1653–January 25, 1654, E727(7), p. 447.

[9] *Ibid.,* p. 448.

From time to time appeared a single burst of social protest, such as *Mercurius Radamanthus,* evidently by the same hand that sent forth *Democritus* and *Fumigosus.* In *Radamanthus* the satirist deals at length with violations of fundamental liberties derived from Magna Charta and now endangered by lawyers' greed. "If it be any poore mans unhappy fortune," wrote Radamanthus, "to fall into the jawes of these savage monsters, hee is then rack't and pull'd for their extorting Fees, as they tearm it, so that for want of halfe a Crown, a poor man shall be kept in their Clutches, till he is utterly ruined: how long O ye Judges!"[10] To one of their clerks a poor man must pay eight pence for eight lines of handwriting on a single sheet; a shilling to a lawyer for merely signing his name. A poor man cannot even deliver a petition to the Upper Bench without paying the clerk half a crown. When a man is imprisoned in the Counter, he must pay the jailor almost twenty shillings for merely "turning the Key, as they call it." On top of these injustices is the most bitter grievance of all, the law's delay:

> Two or three poore men have been suing here for a Legacy, which was given by a Noble man long since deceased, and is detained from them by a Potent Adversary; so that it's foure years since their Suit began, and cannot yet get an Answer; assoone as his Contempts are twenty shillings, he forthwith pays that and then runs into contempts again; so that all the mony for Costs goes into the Clerks purses, and the Client would gladly now buy him a Brokers Suit to put on his back, if he could get money, which though it be deare enough, yet is cheaper and far better; for this may keep him warme, the other will starve backe and belly, to warm only a company of proud Clerks.[11]

And the poor prisoners kept in jail for debt in many places throughout the nation, like those in Norwich kept in prison for debt as many as thirty years. Radamanthus appeals to Parliament: It has the power to destroy the wicked ones and enact wholesome laws to protect the nation from their villainies.

Such a wrathful social protest from *Radamanthus* had few parallels in *Democritus* or *Fumigosus.* In *Fumigosus* the author skillfully turned each journalistic device of the day to his purpose, not giving up for a single page his dependence on racy imagery frowned upon by the Protectorate in a rather gloomy London, where all the theatres were closed and games on Sunday forbidden. No issue of *Fumigosus* appeared without some shocking images of ladies of the night: "A Lady of *Pleasure* the last night being *painting* her *Naked Breasts* for a *Nocturnall jobb,* so poysoned her heart, that she hath never been accounted honest since."[12]

[10] June 27, 1653, E702(14), p. 2. [11] *Ibid.,* p. 5.
[12] December 27, 1654–January 3, 1655, E821(15), p. 247.

Scarcely a page of *Fumigosus* is without the blunt, joyous appeal of the sexual image: Among the writers of the day, none except Richard Overton could have mustered such a continuous flow of metaphor, crude humor, and confrontation of incongruities. But if Overton was the author, he was a man now without fiery hope of social betterment, selling his wits for bread, unable to muster even a paragraph of his appeals for toleration in *The Araignement of Mr. Persecution* or his ringing defenses of the Levellers in *The Hunting of the Foxes.*

3. ON PURITAN INCONGRUITIES: JOHN BIRKENHEAD

On June 23, 1653, appeared one of a series of unique satirical pamphlets, this one entitled *Bibliotheca Parliamenti.* The royalist author, probably Sir John Birkenhead, was a satirist of remarkable talent and insight, touching upon a wide range of incongruities in Puritan life, political, social, and psychological. In each of his half dozen lists of imaginary books, acts of Parliament, and "cases of conscience" Birkenhead attacked both key personalities and central assumptions of the Commonwealth and Protectorate. *Bibliotheca Parliamenti* is divided into three sections: "Books to Be Sold in Little-*Brittaine,"* in which there are forty imaginary book titles; twenty-one "Acts and Orders"; and finally, twenty-one invented "Cases of Conscience." [1] Though his satire of sexual behavior alone assured him of a wide audience, Birkenhead puts his finger unerringly on the weaknesses of Puritan leaders and the dangers to the country inherent in their political actions.

Birkenhead is most successful in his attack on recognizable traits of Cromwell and his colleagues. Oliver's visage was a main target of satire: "An Act forbidding any to stamp the Lord Generals image on Gingerbread, lest the valour of it should bite the children by the tongues," and "Whether *Cromwel* hath not gotten a patent for brimstone, which makes his nose so fiery, and Tiffanies so seldom worn." [2] Henry Marten, Hugh Peters, and Thomas Scot are frequent targets of Birkenhead's attacks: *"Carnis Resurrectio,* or the exaltation of the flesh, by the power of the Spirit, to the comfort of the dejected; held forth in a close conference over the Butchers wife, by *Hugh Peters,"* and *"Inverecundus Moechus,* Or the Sin of Adultery Made Plain in a Midnight-Dialogue, by Mr. *Scot."* Elsewhere Birkenhead writes, "Ordered that a convenient place be nominated, where *Harry Martin* may keep a Regiment of Whores, for the better propagating of the Saints." [3] Of Cromwell's invented sexual aberrations Birkenhead writes as follows:

[1] June 23, 1653, E702(8), pp. 1, 4, 6. [2] *Ibid.,* p. 6. [3] *Ibid.,* pp. 1, 4, 5.

> *Annus tenebrosus,* or the further propagation of Heathenism amongst Christians, as it was held forth in a private conference by my Lord General to the Lady, whereby she became fully satisfied, and he much eased. Published to prevent imperfect relations, by *W. Dell* an eye-witness thereof.[4]

Birkenhead poked fun at Independency, the "mother of heresies," in such a title as the following: *"Daemonologie,* or the history of Independency, in two books, by Dr. *Nathaniel* Homes." Birkenhead dwells at length on the cost of maintaining the armed forces, with a glance at the latest levy:

> *The artificial Changeling,* a Tract proving our Army good Arithmeticians, since they can do any additional sum, amounting to 120000 *l.* and upwards; but the peoples grievances are set forth in the end, because the souldiery are so well skil'd in multiplication and addition, but know not how to subtract.[5]

Birkenhead poses many other ironic dilemmas of tender conscience such as the following: Since a strict censorship exists, is a man allowed to print, as Birkenhead does, the names of books that never existed? Did malignants plot with the Spaniards to invade England in 1588? Is an everlasting army better than an everlasting Parliament?

At times Birkenhead loses his sense of discrimination in such a cruel personal stab as this one: "The art of hearing without ears; by *Will. Prynne."* [6] In an earlier pamphlet, September 20, 1652, Birkenhead portrays the Puritans as hostile to learning: "An Act that the Library of *Oxford* be sealed up, lest men should read and grow wise." [7] Birkenhead is keenly aware of changes in social position in the general upheaval: "A double Act that the Lady *Cromwel,* and the lady *Fleetwood,* may have new faces, sutable to their new Coaches." [8] The satirist keeps reminding Harrison of his humble social origin: "Whether Major Generall *Harrison* be bound to give no Quarter, because his Father is a Butcher?" [9] Of the assumed saintliness of the Independent leaders, Birkenhead writes as follows: "Whether the letters of Maj. Gen. *Harrison* may not be inserted

[4] *Ibid.,* pp. 3–4.

[5] *Ibid.,* p. 4. To Birkenhead Parliament men are likely to be spiritually inferior (*Paul's Church-Yard, Centuria Secunda,* February, 1652, E652[14 *], p. [8]): "Whether the worme of Conscience dare bite a Parliament man?" On the question of the Engagement, Birkenhead poses this question (*ibid.,* p. [8]): "Whether the Great Pox may be called the *Ingagement,* since so many *well-affected* have lately *engaged?"*

[6] *Bibliotheca Parliamenti* (May 3, 1653), E693(19), p. 1.

[7] *Paul's Church-Yard, Centuria Tertia,* E675(12), p. 23.

[8] *Ibid.,* p. 24.

[9] *Paul's Church-Yard, Centuria Secunda,* February, 1652, E652(14 *), sig. B4.

into the Apocrypha, since they smell as much of Scripture phrase as the Maccabees?"[10] In many of his stabbing questions Birkenhead puts his finger on political dilemmas still unresolved. He puts a question for tender consciences: "Whether the House of Commons be a Widow, a Wife, a Maid, or a Common-wealth? . . . Whether it yet appeares that his late *Majesty* had reason to deny them the *Militia?*" Birkenhead proposes "An Act for admitting *Jewes* into *England,* with a short Proviso for banishing the Cavaliers." The nostalgia for kingship is a recurrent note in Birkenhead's pamphlets: "Whether twelve years are sufficient to try how we can live without a King?" Of Christmas celebrations, so hated by the Puritans, Birkenhead wrote, "Whether Cavaleers may have one Christmas in twelve years, when the *States* keepe Christmas all the yeare long?" and "Whether Master *Peters* did justly preach against Christmas Pyes the same day he eate two Mince-pies to his dinner?"[11]

Birkenhead's references to contemporary writers make an illuminating commentary. Is there a duller poet in all England than George Wither? See his *Aristotles* works in *English Meeter!* Such a pitiful poet! See his book *Pseudo Propheta, or The Pittiful Parliament.*[12] Even after his break with the Independents, John Lilburne was no hero to Birkenhead: "Severall *Readings* on the Statute of *Magna Charta,* by *John Lilburne;* with a Treatise of the best way of boyling *Soap.*"[13] Birkenhead's one reference to Milton's *A Defence* appeared first in *Paul's Church-Yard,* dated by Thomason July 24, 1651: *"Pro populo Anglicano.* Proving that Kings had many Evills, because the Kings-Evill was so often cur'd."[14] This mention shows no knowledge of Milton's place or importance in the new Commonwealth. But the very range of personalities and ideas named by Birkenhead show in general an astonishing curiosity about the Puritan personalities of his day. Nowhere can one find a more perceptive or concentrated cross section of the Puritan world as seen by a gifted royalist mind than in Birkenhead's pamphlets.

[10] *Paul's Church-Yard,* E675(12), p. 18. [11] E652(14 *), pp. [7], [3].

[12] *Paul's Church-Yard* (July 24, 1651), E637(15), p. [5]; June 23, 1653, E702(8), p. 1.

[13] E637(15), p. [2].

[14] *Ibid.,* p. [4]. This reference is overlooked by William R. Parker in *Milton's Contemporary Reputation,* where he cites (p. 97) only the 1659 edition of this pamphlet.

Chapter XXV

DISSOLUTION OF THE RUMP

April 20, 1653

By April, 1653, many members of the Long Parliament had sat in the Commons over twelve years. Originally a fairly representative body, elected in November, 1640, the Commons had been purged by the army of some 143 of its recalcitrant members on December 6, 1648.[1] Even at that time radicals like Harrison had pleaded against a purge and for a dissolution of the Commons to be followed by an election based on the wider rights of suffrage described in the *Agreement of the People*. The Rump was a determined body of some seventy-five resolute men, by no means pliable to Cromwell and his officers. Though elevated to power by the army, it was determined to maintain the fiction of the traditional superiority of civil to military authority. On February 6, 1649, claiming supreme power, the Rump had abolished the House of Lords; on February 7, kingship itself. A week later, on February 14, the Rump nominated the forty-one members of the newly erected Council of State.[2] Since that time, now four years past, the forces of the Commonwealth had routed the royalists, conquered Ireland and Scotland. During these victorious years the Rump resisted every hint or persuasion by Cromwell and his officers that it dissolve itself in favor of a newly elected Commons.

The Rump was the creation of an illegal military action; without representing a cross section of partisan views, it embodied in its deliberations, however, the traditional forms of Parliamentary procedure. Though a creature, as it were, of army power, it was a link to constitutional fabric and ritual centuries old. It is certain that Cromwell realized more clearly than any of his officers the dangers to England's constitutional fabric of the dissolution he had so long debated.

1. GRIEVANCES BEFORE THE FALL

Despite Cromwell's victories and many promises of reformation, the English people as a whole had no fewer grievances in 1653 than at the time of the king's execution. Prices of necessities were higher than ever.

[1] Gardiner, *Great Civil War,* IV, 270–73.

[2] Gardiner, *Commonwealth and Protectorate,* I, 3, 5.

"What a miserable quarter have poor people yet for *Coals,*" exclaimed *Mercurius Democritus,* "notwithstanding the late Proclamation to sell at 12.d. the Bushell? O *yee Chandlers, Ingrossers,* and *Hoarders* of *Coals,* what do you mean to do!" [3] Instructive and creative as ever, seeking reforms untouchable by the vortex of party strife, Samuel Hartlib sent forth in February *A Design for Plentie,* calling for the planting of fruit trees on the common lands throughout the nation, every town to appoint officers each year to see that trees were planted on the commons and the fruit gathered "given to the poor, & necessitous people of every Town, unto which they do belong." [4] A fruit tree, says Hartlib, enriches a country many times more than an oak tree. An oak tree after three hundred years of growth may be only worth five or six pounds. A good fruit tree within four years will yield the same profit "four or five times doubled." On January 31 friends of Christopher Love sent forth his *Scripture Rules to be Observed in Buying and Selling.* "Do not in buying a commodity," wrote Love, "work upon the necessity of a poor man, that hath need of money; this is a great sin in Tradesmen; they know that a poor man wants money, and he must sell off his ware, or else he cannot buy bread for his familie." Love also warned against broken promises in the setting of prices, against counterfeit money, against selling "stuffe to paint Harlots faces," against the deferring of payments, against hoarding of scarce commodities, against the buying of stolen goods, against imposing upon the ignorance of a simple person in a business exchange. Nor will the true Christian, asserted Love, buy or sell his fellow-man.[5]

Voices from all levels of society burst through the bounds of fear and censorship to give vent to their disappointment with the Rump, its committees, and its disregard of traditional freedoms. "It is not the being of a Parliament that makes the Nation happy," wrote the author of *The Only Right Rule,* "but their maintaining of the fundamentall Rights and Liberties." [6] Others were troubled that the petitions of the poor were neglected, "buried in oblivion as an old almanack out of date." [7] You complained against King Charles, wrote the author of *Vox Plebis,* for harboring traitors against the state. But what of traitors in the midst of the Commons? They are free to come and go. "The late Kings prerogative was a far better plea then your privilege." You claim that the king

[3] January 19, 1653, E684(30), pp. 321–22. [4] E686(5), p. 6.

[5] January 31, 1653, 669f16(84). Even in this constructive broadside, when the reader least expects the usual symbols of intolerance, Love inserts an injunction against the buying and selling of "monuments of Idolatry as Crosses, and Beads, and Images, and Crucifixes."

[6] January 28, 1653, E684(33), pp. 2–3.

[7] *For the Right Honourable Captaine General Cromwell,* February 18, 1653, E687(8), p. 3. See below, p. 212.

should have obeyed the laws, asserts the writer. Should not you also go by the rule of law and not by the rule of your own wills? "We looked for liberty, but behold slavery!"[8] The author protests with biting vehemence against the arbitrary power of the Rump's committees. Is there any county or city, he asks, where some citizens have not been imprisoned by the destructive authority of these committees? Among the critics of the early months of 1653, only George Wither voiced a fear of the dominance of military might over civil authority. In his eulogy of Thomas Westrow, he wrote:

> The *SWORD,* hath now, obtain'd the *soveraign pow'r,*
> Let it, Oh *LORD!* protect, and not devou'r.[9]

Thus none of the protesting voices, even Wither, spoke for the Rump's continuance. But what civilian leadership was to take its place? No elected Parliament, however broad its representation, could satisfy at once the army's demands for drastic reforms and the country's need for the coherence of ancient customs.

In this time of disillusionment mild or keen, the friends of the Commonwealth were its severest critics. On February 18 appeared a short tract titled *For the Right Honourable Captaine General Cromwel, Major General Harrison, and the Rest of that Noble Race of the Souldiery . . . Instrumental in Seeking the Relief of Captives, the Free-Born Subjects of this Nation. A Few Humble Proposals.* Each of the twenty-five complaints ends with the Biblical injunction, "Judge ye." The pamphleteer's grievances are political and religious in emphasis, rather than economic. A main target is the continuance of tithes and suits at law to maintain them. Among the main complaints were the following:

> Whether the Parliaments Acts for Tythes, with treble Dammages, and Imprisonment without Baile or Main-prize, be not more oppression tenfold then all the Bishops Canons, judge ye. . . .
>
> Whether the Civil sword in things of a Divine Nature, doth not make hypocrites threefold the servants of Satan, and cursed of God for their lame and blinde service, judge ye. . . .
>
> Whether all the Priests both of the old and new stamp in this Land, be not the same as when they were under the Papistical and Prelatical government, judge ye. . . .

[8] April 18, 1653, E691(13), pp. 4–5, 3. On April 11 appeared a broadside, *Poor Out-cast Childrens Song and Cry,* 669f16(93), pleading for relief for poor children, containing the lines:

> Grave Senators, that sit on high,
> Let not poor English Children die,
> and droop on Dunghils with lamenting notes:
> An Act for Poor's Relief, they say,
> Is coming forth; why's this delay?

[9] *Westrow Revived,* January 3, 1653, E1479(4), p. 68.

> Whether it be not a Case of justice and equity, that all people ought to be left free in themselves, how much or how little a portion they give to their Minister, forasmuch as the said Minister is left free to himself, how much or how little a portion of the word of God he preacheth to the people, judge ye. . . .
>
> Whether the tenth of the rich mans land, or the labour of the poor man, his Servants, Cattel and Seed, be Tythed, judge ye. . . .
>
> Whether the noisome swarmes of Lawyers, with their dependencies, be not a sufficient store for *France, Spaine, Holland, Poland, Swedland, Denmark, Scotland,* and *Ireland,* except the people are made of envy, hypocrisie, and deceit, as in *England,* judge ye. . . .
>
> Whether were we furthest from Reformation during the time the Bishops sent their Spannel-like Pursevants to hunt for Tithes, or now the Parliament hath taken that power off, transmitting it unto a Committee, termed a Committee of Plundred Ministers, who, with their blood-hound-like Messengers, hunt not only for Tithes, but for (the very lives of some men, in taking away their livelihood, by their covetous, idolatrous, oppressive practice, enforcing them to pay) treble dammages, which whether it be not sore oppression and Extortion, judge ye. . . .
>
> Whether it is not cruelty in the higest [*sic*], to increase the rich man by oppressing the poor, judge ye.[10]

Thus the religious radicals, supporters of the government, set forth their grievances against the settled order of rich man and poor man, tithes and courts, lawyers and inequities. Now that they were in power, the Independents could not in a few years put to flight against the grip of custom the injustices of centuries. It was easier for the critics of the Rump to identify their grievances than to trace the steps, one by one, by which the revolution could be channeled into legal machinery reluctantly acceptable to the nation at large.

In early April Cromwell met almost daily with both officers and civilian leaders to discuss the thorny dilemma of the Rump's desire to preserve its present identity or continue its members as a part of the new representative.[11] Yet Cromwell himself held back from military dissolution of the Rump. Even in the days preceding the crucial action of April 20, Cromwell "seemed to reprove" his officers for urging immediate action. On April 6, on the other hand, Whitelocke reported, "Upon discourse with Cromwell, I still found him in distaste with the parliament and hastening their dissolution." [12] Day by day the Rump postponed its decision to name the time on which they would dissolve themselves and call a new

[10] February 18, 1653, E687(8), pp. 2, 3, 4, 5, 6, 7.

[11] See Masson, IV, 407–11, and below, p. 213, n. 1. *The Weekly Intelligencer* for April 12–19, E691(17), reported (p. 816) that the Rump's main aim in composing the bill was "to fill the House again with Persons of the same spirit, and temper as themselves, and by these proxyes to perpetuate their own sitting."

[12] Whitelocke, *Memorials,* IV, 2.

Parliament. On April 19 Cromwell met with a number of the Rump's leaders and several officers at his lodgings at Whitehall. Whitelocke and Widdrington, more emphatically than other Rump colleagues, told Cromwell that it was "a most dangerous thing to dissolve the present parliament and to set up any other government, and that it would neither be warrantable in conscience or wisdom so to do." [13] One of the most respected lawyers in the land, Whitelocke had refused to serve on the High Court of Justice that had tried Charles I. Though he continued to serve Cromwell and the Commonwealth as a member of the Rump and the Council of State, his integrity was unimpeachable. Many Rumpers opposed Whitelocke's views on this occasion, siding with the officers in their demand for an immediate dissolution; among these Oliver St. John was the most emphatic. Early next morning, April 20, Whitelocke came again to Cromwell's lodgings, where only a few officers and Parliament colleagues were in attendance. When the trend of the discussion assumed an early dissolution, it was proposed that forty persons, half officers and half members of the Rump, should be named by the Parliament to carry on until a new Parliament could be elected. Whitelocke was opposed to this proposal. He thought that England "would be in a desperate condition after the parliament should be dissolved." [14] As long as the Rump continued, in Whitelocke's view, some links with the constitutional past still held an alternative to chaos.

2. DECISION IN ANGER: THE DISSOLUTION

April 20, 1653

As the discussion at Cromwell's house continued that morning, Whitelocke and a few friends pleading for delay, the officers for action, Harrison sent word to Cromwell from the Commons that the members were hurrying through a bill to fill up vacancies in the House, the bill [1] to

[13] *Ibid.*, IV, 4. [14] *Ibid.*, IV, 5.

[1] No copy of the bill has survived. The various parties recognized that to send out a call for a full and free Parliament would mean that a large number of Presbyterians would be returned. Such a Parliament might easily mean the overthrow of the Commonwealth and the return of the Stuarts. As it finally emerged, however, the bill eventually provided not only for the dissolution of itself, but also for the continuation of its members in the next Parliament. It provided further that the Rump's own committee should superintend the elections of the new members and judgment of their qualifications. Cromwell considered the bill pernicious in its intention to perpetuate the Rump membership and its control over the selection of new members. See Masson, IV, 407–11. Cromwell's last act before leaving the House (Ludlow, I, 355), was to snatch the actual bill from the hand of the clerk and put it under his cloak.

which Cromwell had objected and which the leaders of the Commons had promised to hold in abeyance. Anger at what he considered a betrayal roused Cromwell to action. He summoned soldiers to accompany him from Whitehall to the House and stationed them at the street approaches to the House, also at the doors and in the lobby.[2] Taking his seat in the Commons, Cromwell waited; he was dressed in plain black clothes and gray stockings. Fifty-three members were present. Debate on the bill continued. There was still time. Then Cromwell called Harrison to his side, saying that he thought the time ripe for a dissolution. As Gardiner points out, even Harrison was somewhat appalled at Cromwell's momentous decision. "Sir," he said to Cromwell, "the work is very great and dangerous." "You say well," said Cromwell, and sat down until the Speaker was about to put the hated bill to a final vote. Then he said to Harrison, "This is the time: I must do it." [3]

Then he rose as if to speak to the question. Before him sat some of the great personalities of his time: Sir Henry Vane, Sir Peter Wentworth, Algernon Sidney, Henry Marten, Bulstrode Whitelocke, Colonel John Hutchinson. At first Cromwell spoke in a commendatory vein of the Rump's patriotic achievements. Then the tone of his language changed: He attacked them for "their injustice, delays of justice, self-interest," for their desire to perpetuate themselves.[4] Sir Peter Wentworth, stung by this blow, rose to protest against Cromwell's diatribe, "the more horrid," he said, "in that it came from their servant whom they had so highly trusted and obliged." Wentworth cried, "It is a strange language this; unusual within the walls of Parliament this! And from a trusted servant too; and one whom we have so highly honored; and one . . ." His eyes blazing, Cromwell turned upon Wentworth and Marten: "Some of you are whoremasters," he said, looking from one to the other, "living in open contempt of God's Commandments." [5] By this time Cromwell had put on his hat and was striding from one place to another, now and then stamping his feet, looking at the people he attacked: "Others are drunkards," pointing to inoffensive Mr. Chaloner, who sometimes had a cup too much. Finally he cried, "Come! Come! I will put an end to your prating. You are no Parliament. I say you are no Parliament. I will put an end to your sit-

[2] Whitelocke, *Memorials,* IV, 5.

[3] Ludlow, *Memoirs,* I, 352; Masson, IV, 411; Gardiner, II, 262. A curious point: Ludlow uses no punctuation after the word *time.* Masson uses a colon, Carlyle a semicolon, Gardiner a period.

[4] *Sydney Papers,* ed. Robert W. Blencoe (London, 1825), pp. 139–40. Cromwell added (Blencoe, p. 140): "Perhaps you thinke this is not Parlementary language, I confesse it is not, neither are you to expect any such from me."

[5] Masson, IV, 412; Carlyle, *Letters,* ed. Lomas, II, 264–65; Gardiner, *Commonwealth and Protectorate,* II, 262–63.

ting." Turning to Harrison, he said, "Call them in; call them in."[6] At Harrison's orders, the door opened, and some thirty or forty soldiers, led by Lieutenant Colonel Worsley, entered the House. At this point Vane intervened, rising to speak: "This is not honest," he cried, "yea it is against morality and common honesty." Whereupon Cromwell cried, "O Sir Henry Vane! Sir Henry Vane! The Lord deliver me from Sir Henry Vane!"[7] As Whitelocke points out, many a man in the Rump Parliament carried a sword, but there was no resistance to Cromwell or his musketeers. "We did not hear a dog bark at their going!" said Cromwell at a later time.[8]

3. AFTERMATH: PROPHECY AND JUSTIFICATION

Two days later, on April 22, appeared a justification of Cromwell's dire action, entitled *A Declaration of the Lord General and His Councel of Officers*. Recalling the Lord's favor in the conquest of Ireland and Scotland, the glorious victory at Worcester, the *Declaration* asserted Oliver and his officers had waited in vain for a speedy redress of grievances from the Rump, and the creation of a new commonwealth in which righteousness and justice would prevail. In August, 1652, they had presented a petition for which the Rump returned thanks but on the issues of which they had taken no action in the months that followed. When finally forced to discuss a bill for dissolution of themselves, they had "resolved to make use of it to recruite the House with Persons of the same Spirit and temper, thereby to perpetuate their own sitting."[1] Petitions were presented to the House for continuance of the Rump which the *Declaration* asserts were encouraged by its members "if not set on foot by many of them." Finally, after various meetings with members of the Commons, the officers had come to the conclusion that "this Parliament, through the corruption of some, the jealousie of others . . . and negligence of many, would never answer those ends which God, his People, and the whole Nation expected."[2] The *Declaration* recalls the promise made to Cromwell but broken on the morning of April 20, that the Rump would take no action as yet on the bill they preferred. The *Declaration* does not mention the ousting of the Rump by military force. It says only: "We

[6] Masson, IV, 412; Gardiner, II, 262, 263. Speaker Lenthall kept his seat, as did Algernon Sidney, until Harrison (Blencoe, p. 141) "pulled the Speaker by the gowne" and "Harrison and Wortley [Worsley] putt theyr hands upon Sydney's shoulders.

[7] Masson, IV, 412; Gardiner, *Commonwealth and Protectorate,* II, 263. A slightly different account appears in Carlyle, *Letters,* ed. Lomas, II, 265.

[8] Carlyle, *Letters,* ed. Lomas, II, 266. [1] E692(6), p. 5. [2] *Ibid.*

have been necessitated, though with much reluctancy, to put an end to this Parliament." The officers and their chief have sought the advice of the Lord night and day, "that we may obtain grace from him, and seeing we have made so often mention of his Name, that we may not do the least dishonour thereunto." [3] In closing its account of their proceedings, Cromwell and his Council authorized all judges, mayors, and all other state officers to continue in their customary duties. But hereafter no legal custom in England could remain indifferent to that new power that with a file of soldiers could reduce to impotence the very seat of civil authority.

On April 24 John Spittlehouse set forth his tract, *The Army Vindicated in Their Late Dissolution of the Parliament.* To Spittlehouse there was no hope that the sighs and groans of the people could be eased by the Rump Parliament. Had not its members been elected long ago under a kingship now extinguished? Its very basis had been an army action, and it had continued in power only by permission of the army. Of all their electors, none except the members of the army had been loyal to them. Yet now it attempts to domineer over the only power that upheld them. In what group of Englishmen, asks Spittlehouse, does one find the true Commonwealth for which the war was fought? Not in the Presbyterians, who gave up before the task of reformation was half finished. It would be folly to admit either Presbyterians or royalists to any new Parliament. As the true power for reformation in England, concludes Spittlehouse, let the army elect a Parliament! [4] In the army, as in no other body, resides the true Commonwealth for which the war was fought. In the army resides the true spirit of the Congregational churches. The army had gloriously subdued all the enemies of the Commonwealth in England, Scotland, and Ireland. They have deeply engaged themselves in many protestations for a settlement of righteousness. They are stationed in all parts of the nation, ready to act for the public safety. Spittlehouse includes in his recommendations a plan of election of a new representative, voting to be by commissioned officers only.[5] Thus the plan Spittlehouse outlined would have created a House of Commons made up entirely of officers, triumphant in the Lord's cause on the battlefield, however shallow their knowledge of law and Parliamentary custom in earlier eras. It was a bold plan, representing the only realities of power that could prevent a return to monarchy, a plan that anticipated the dismissals of Parliaments to come and rule by major generals in 1655.

On May 16 appeared a justification of Cromwell's action quite remote from Spittlehouse's apology for God's soldiers donning the mantles of statesmen and legislators; *A Letter Written to a Gentleman in the Coun-*

[3] *Ibid.*, pp. 8, 10. [4] E693(1), p. 8. [5] *Ibid.*, p. 11.

try, Touching the Dissolution of the Late Parliament. The letter was probably written by John Hall, brilliant and precocious, then twenty-six years old, of St. John's College, Cambridge. A friend of Henry More, Thomas Stanley, Thomas Hobbes, and Samuel Hartlib, Hall had become a propagandist for the Commonwealth, serving the Council of State,[6] which directed him to accompany Cromwell to Scotland in 1650. In 1651 he had written *A Gagg to Loves Advocate,* a justification of Love's trial and execution. Like Needham, Hall had written diatribes against monarchy and the Presbyterians; like Needham, he knew the classics so thoroughly that he cited parallels of the contemporary scene with the happenings of Greece and Rome. Hall's values are for the most part secular and realistic; he exhibits none of the Fifth Monarchy fervor and little of the Independent's appeal to victory as proof of God's signal favor.

Alone among his contemporaries, Hall spoke of the dissolution of the Rump as the greatest of all revolutions, "without *contestation,* without effusion of *blood,* and, for any thing I can perceive, without the least resentment of those whom it generally concerns."[7] Like other sympathetic critics, Hall calls attention to the conquest of Ireland and Scotland, all in three years, a feat which six centuries of monarchs could not encompass. Hall acknowledges the Rump's leadership in these conquests. He also acknowledges "that there have been among them as *brave* men, as *wise* and worthy *Patriots,* as any Nation ever had."[8] But the Rump's control of great wealth from the sale of the bishops' lands, the deans and chapters, together with the lands belonging to the king, the queen, and the princes, and finally the property of the delinquents—the sale of all these lands, releasing great sums of money subject to Parliamentary action, led to unexampled corruption, the machinery of which Hall describes as follows:

> You must needs think there was very notable carriage in this Businesse, as to the Profit of the *Commonwealth.* For first, 3 *d. per* pound must be allowed in point of purchase; Then you had *Registers* (who constantly dispatched by Deputie) at *high* Fees, and their *Under-Officers* as *cunning* and as *ravenous* as those of the *old* Courts. Then must *march* forth an *Army* of ignorant and unlearned *Surveyors,* and these at 20 sh. *per diem,* to return Surveys sometimes low, in the favour of some noble Gentleman, in whose eye it was to purchase, and sometimes excessively high, for to over-ballance the other; (besides the *Kings* Lands, which being allotted for the payment of the *Souldiery,* were commonly over-valued by one

[6] Masson, IV, 88. Masson (IV, 520–23) follows Thomason in ascribing the tract to Milton, based partly on the passage (E697[2], p. 19): "I am no *Member* of their *Councills* and by a late infirmity lesse able to attend them." For summary of various ascriptions, see French, III, 327–28.

[7] E697(2), p. 1.

[8] *Ibid.,* p. 6.

half,) whilst in the mean time a single *Mathematician* did properly all their work to their hands; and all this, besides a pestilent sort of people called *Messengers,* &c. who *intangled* rights, *disturbed* the people, and carried on the businesse so excellently well, that possibly much about one half might by their endeavours be brought into the Coffers of the Commonwealth.

After the return of this Survey, so laudably perform'd as I have described to you, an honest *Member* casts a *sheeps-eye* at such a Manour. Marry then he goes to *Gurney-house,* sends in *his name,* and tels them he was to attend the Parliament immediately; upon that he is called in, though other people had been design'd, and other businesse directed for that time; and by his *authority,* or *friends* at the Table (for he that had a hand in placing them there, must needs have favour from them) makes a Contract as low as possible, gets it may be so long time, as that he may pay for the Manour out of the *Mansion-house,* or the *Woods;* and by this means it is incredible to what Estates some have raised themselves. One of them who was a Brewers Clark, his man was heard to say, That he thank'd God his Master had now 800 l. a year. Another Gentleman having not an over-considerable Fortune before, hath made it 10. or 12000 l. a year, and hath been heard to say, (as I am informed) That he had more Land than any man in *England.* Another comming out of a *Draper's* shop at *York,* hath convey'd himself into an Estate in Possession and Reversion of above 5000 l. a year. But examples of this kind are innumerable.[9]

So long as the country was at war at home and abroad, continues Hall, these injustices could be absorbed. But once peace had settled on the land, they came to be aware that Parliament had not acted to remove the inequities and injustices, quite apart from the amassing of individual fortunes from the sale of public lands. Then it became apparent that these men, who had held power so long, did not want to relinquish it. To Hall there was nothing more destructive "than the Continuation of many men in the same power, especially unlimited and supreme."[10] Like other critics, Hall asserts that the Rump had no true authority to rule, having been elected under a kingship now no more. Though they engaged in many actions "to the eternall Renown of the Nation," many "diseases grew upon them."

Hall agrees that the action of Cromwell in the dissolution was "somewhat *rough,* and *Barbarous,"* but absolves him on the ground that a great spirit may be excused for such passionate outbursts.

At the end of his tract Hall asks whether the new government will bring more happiness to England than a continuation of the Rump would have

[9] *Ibid.,* pp. 7–8. One reason why Milton probably could not have written *A Letter* is that he never analyzes the situation in terms of economic details, as in this passage. Yet he may have dictated parts of the tract to Hall or some other friend.

[10] *Ibid.,* p. 10.

done. To his own question Hall returns a cautious answer. He urges his reader not to expect swift and remarkable reforms: "I am no *Member* of their *Councills,*" he writes, "and by a late infirmity lesse able to attend them, yet if I can believe any thing; or understand Men when they make the clearest *professions,* they intend all noble things." [11]

Milton was too closely identified with the Rump Parliament as an official of the Council of State to have been wholly sympathetic with Cromwell's abrupt and contemptuous dismissal. It is impossible to associate the harsh characterizations Milton inserted in his *Character of the Long Parliament* with his views of the Rump in 1653. No doubt many of the same harsh and fraudulent practices which Milton described (probably in 1648, when he had completed four books of the *History of Britain*) continued through the years to 1653. No doubt many citizens were still "tossed up and down after miserable Attendance from one Committee to another with Petitions in their hands." No doubt also "were their Friends confiscate in their Enemies." Even the harsh accusation, "the Ravening Seizure of innumerable Thieves in Office," [12] might in his mind have been justified in 1653 as applied to minor officials who served the numerous committees.

In the *Character of the Long Parliament* appears Milton's conclusion that Englishmen in general make wonderful soldiers but poor statesmen. Also he wrote that the English leaders in general lack the knowledge and examples of the greatest men of ancient times. But we cannot imagine Milton writing such statements in 1653 about the leaders of the Rump Parliament. Had he felt such an extreme distrust of men he met and talked with daily, he would have been forced to resign his post. We can only conclude, therefore, that Milton had mixed feelings about the abrupt dismissal of many men whom he trusted and admired as selfless and dedicated patriots. Only the year before, Milton had recommended Vane in a sonnet to Cromwell as a statesman who had the best understanding of the relationship of church and state. Now Sir Henry Vane had been singled out by Cromwell for one of his most blunt and derisive denunciations. Unlike men like Hutchinson and Vane, however, Milton did not retire from active political life when Cromwell dismissed the Rump. The fact that he continued to work for the Council of State shows that whatever his dismay at Cromwell's action or his loyalty to members of the Rump abruptly driven out, he would stand by Cromwell as the last great hope for the creation of the Commonwealth he cherished.

One important criticism of the Long Parliament inserted in his *Character of the Long Parliament* we find Milton anticipating in 1652. In the

[11] *Ibid.*, pp. 13, 14, 19.

[12] Columbia, XVIII, 250.

Character Milton writes that some members of the Long Parliament "had been called from Shops and Ware-houses, without other Merit, to sit in Supreme Councels and Committees." These men, accustomed to the huckstering habits of the commercial world, "fell to Huckster the Commonwealth."[13] We cannot imagine that Milton would have voiced such an accusation against the Rump as a whole in 1653. But in his conversations with Mylius in 1652, Milton excused in part the baffling and needless delays of the Commons and the Council by saying that many of their members had come to government office from the habits and psychology of the business world.

But Milton's high regard for the Rump was to be shown again in 1660, when the officers recalled the members of the Rump to make a valiant resistance against restoration of kingship. Milton's last stand for a commonwealth, *The Readie & Easie Way,* which appeared only a few weeks before the king's restoration, suggested a perpetual senate to preserve England in liberty. By this suggestion Milton evidently meant the surviving members of the Rump Parliament.

Chapter XXVI

FIRST DAYS OF LILBURNE'S TRIAL

July 13–15, 1653

The first days of Lilburne's trial threw into bold contrast the traditional courtroom procedure observed in ordinary jury trials even during the Commonwealth and Protectorate, and the departure from these customs in special high courts such as those that had tried and convicted Charles I and Christopher Love. The Rump Parliament had continued in power after Pride's Purge for four years. Unconstitutional body that it was, the Rump had not attempted to suspend trial by jury throughout the land; nor had the government in the brief ten weeks since its inception proposed any bold departure from the jury principle, however eager Cromwell was for reforms of the legal code. For several centuries trial by jury, though violated or distorted in particular cases, had stood at the center of English jurisprudence. The new edition of Coke's *Institutes,* as ordered printed by Parliament in 1641, had emphasized afresh the legal traditions surrounding and supporting trial by jury. When, therefore, in June, 1653,

[13] *Ibid.,* XVIII, 249.

Cromwell generously permitted Lilburne trial by jury, he actually put the Rump and the Protectorate on trial, with the most resourceful courtroom orator in all England as the key prosecutor. After Lilburne's acquittal on August 20, the jury was questioned by the Council of State and Lilburne was kept in prison. Each of these actions symbolized a defeat for the new Protectorate full of portent for the future.

On January 15, 1652, Lilburne had been sentenced by the Rump Parliament to banishment from England, Scotland, and Ireland, "and not to return into any of them, upon pain of being proceeded against as a Felon; and, in case of such Return, shall suffer Death, accordingly." [1] Lilburne was also sentenced to pay three thousand pounds to the state, two thousand pounds damages to Sir Arthur Haslerig, whom he had falsely accused, and five hundred pounds each to four of the commissioners for compounding, who had, he asserted, connived with Sir Arthur. Lilburne's crime was his support of a false accusation against Sir Arthur made by Josiah Primate, a London leather merchant whose petition had been presented on December 23, at which time the Commons had appointed a committee of fifty members, among them Whitelocke, Pickering, Marten, Vane, and Harrison, to examine the evidence.[2] In his petition Primate claimed that he had been in possession of seams of coal in Harraton, of Durham County, in 1647, 1648, and 1649, in which he and his tenants had invested two thousand pounds. These seams of coal, which had been worked by undertenants George Lilburne, uncle of John, and George Gray, had brought Primate an income of five thousand pounds a year.[3] But in September, 1649, claimed the petition,

[1] *Commons Journals,* VII, 73. [2] *Ibid.,* VII, 72, 55.

[3] *Ibid.,* VII, 71. In his *Just Reproof to Haberdashers-Hall,* E638(12), July 30, 1651, Lilburne had inserted a petition by Primate to the Commissioner for Compounding much more complete than the petition recorded in the *Commons Journals.* In this statement (*Reproof,* pp. 7–8) Primate asserted that his lease of the collieries extended back to 1628 (*Calendar of the Committee for Compounding* [5 vols., London, 1889–92], III, 2128) and that his share by the assignment of Sir John Hedworth (for forty-one years) was three-fourths. [The remaining fourth did therefore actually belong to the delinquent Thomas Wray, and the Durham Committee was within its rights in compounding that portion of the income.] On the day before the sequestration, asserts Primate (*Reproof,* p. 19) he had appealed in vain to the Committee to require Wray to show his title to the mines: "It would not be permitted by sir Arthur Haselrige that the said *Wray* should show any title thereunto." Between 1642 and 1647 work on the various seams had been interrupted by flooding and in 1648 by a disastrous fire that had taken fifty lives. But the years 1647 and 1649 had been prosperous, due to the investment of two thousand pounds by the undertenants in clearing the mines of water. In his statement Primate asserts that his losses from the unwarranted seizure by Sir Arthur amount to fifteen pounds a day; he petitions for the return of his property to him and his undertenants.

Sir Arthur had induced Colonel Francis Wren and Colonel George Fenwick of the Durham Committee to join with him in violently sequestering Primate's collieries. When Primate appealed to the Commissioners for Compounding in London, Sir Arthur attended every session and overawed the Commissioners, who sustained his seizure of the Harraton collieries. Now that the issue was settled, why was Lilburne banished? He had acted only as counsel for Primate and his uncle, George Lilburne. He had been active in distributing and signing Primate's petition, and in August, 1651, he had written a violent pamphlet against Sir Arthur and the decision of the Commissioners for Compounding. Yet Lilburne himself had been charged with no crime. The sentence of the Rump, not of any court of law, passed against him without an opportunity to defend himself, to produce witnesses, or to be represented by counsel, was an astonishing repudiation of traditional forms to which it is hard to imagine that men like Whitelocke and Vane willingly gave consent. On January 20, when Lilburne was called to the floor of the House to receive judgment against him, he obstinately refused to kneel.[4] By February Lilburne had crossed to Holland, not to return until June 14, 1653.

In late April or early May, 1653, when Lilburne learned of the dissolution of the Rump, he decided at once to return to England. In *The Banished Mans Suit,* written on the day of his return to London, June 14, Lilburne claimed he had "made many humble addresses to your Excellency" since the Rump's dissolution for a pass to return to his native land, hoping to live there peaceably, "in an utter obscurity and uselessness to my generation."[5] That very morning, asserted Lilburne, his wife and his friend William Kiffin had waited upon Cromwell several hours; but the Protector had been too occupied with affairs of state to see them. On June 16, still at large, Lilburne sent forth to Cromwell and the Council of State *A Second Address,* a petition more formal in tone than its predecessor, asserting that the Parliament which had sentenced him, now dissolved, had not tried him according to any statute in existence; nor had it allowed him liberty of defense.[6] On June 20, now a prisoner in Newgate, Lilburne issued *A Third Address.* Why is he considered "a person so abominable, that he is unfit to live or breath in this Commonwealth"?[7] Lilburne demanded that the act passed by the Rump against him should be suspended; that he might have liberty of peacefully petitioning the government for the repeal of the Rump's condemnation; and finally, that he be freed from

[4] *Commons Journals,* VII, 74. [5] 669f17(16). [6] 669f17(20).
[7] 669f17(22).

prison and be permitted to live in England in quiet submission to the Commonwealth.

When Lilburne found that his trial had been fixed to begin on June 20, he was alarmed. As subsequent events showed, he needed time to rally his followers to his defense. Also the new Nominated Parliament was not yet in session; it was to meet for the first time on Monday, July 4. When his request for a delay of his trial was granted, Lilburne and his colleagues (both Richard Overton and Thomas Prince were active in assisting him) issued almost daily petitions and manifestoes. On June 22 appeared Lilburne's *Defensive Declaration,* in which he denied having any treasonable association with royalist agents abroad, particularly Captain Wendy Oxford. Moreover, declared Lilburne, "I never writ a line in my life to the King." [8] On June 24 came forth a petition to Parliament stressing trial by jury, reprinted in substantial part from the Leveller petition of January 20, 1652, at the time of Lilburne's banishment.[9] On June 25 appeared the *Humble Petition of Diverse Afflicted Women,* protesting against the impending trial, addressing the Parliament not yet met, concerned lest "your new Authority should lay its foundation in his innocent blood." [10] On July 1 Lilburne issued *The Prisoner's Most Mournful Cry,* addressed to John Fowke, Lord Mayor of London, who had committed him to prison. In this pamphlet Lilburne violently attacked the new government, asserting that "they have destroyed and rooted up by the roots, by their swords, wills, & pleasures, all the formal setled legal Power and Government of this ancient free Nation." [11] On July 2 appeared the second edition of Lilburne's *Plea in Law* against the Rump's action of January 30, 1652, reminding his readers that a jury trial is the right of every citizen under the Magna Charta, the Petition of Right, and the act that abolished the Star Chamber.[12] By such daily outbursts Lilburne rallied his old supporters, meanwhile appealing from one authority to another: from Cromwell and his Council of State to the new Parliament; from the new Parliament to thousands of his followers aroused to protest by his inflammatory manifestoes. The trial was now due to open July 13. Every device of propaganda Lilburne knew he had put into action to influence the outcome of the new crisis in his turbulent career.

When the trial opened at the Old Bailey on Wednesday, July 13,

[8] E702(2), p. 11. On the same day, June 22, was published *A Jury-Mans Judgement,* E702(6), effectively reviewing Lilburne's case, stressing right of trial by jury, asserting that (p. 14) *"Parliaments* have *not power* over *Fundamental Law,* and especially over this Tryall by *twelve men."*

[9] 669f17(24); 669f16(37), January 23, 1652.

[10] 669f17(26).

[11] E703(12), p. 3.

[12] E703(12X), p. 2.

Lilburne, as was his wont, contested every step in the court procedure, questioning indeed the very first command of the court to raise his right hand. What, he asked, was the legal significance of this traditional action? Convinced finally that raising of his hand was no threat to him, Lilburne said he was ready to answer the indictment. Was he guilty or not guilty? But Lilburne would not answer this question without first being permitted to speak against what he termed the illegality of the indictment. Nor would he plead guilty or not guilty until he had had an opportunity to put into writing errors in the indictment. Without a copy of the document, he could not examine and analyze it. Therefore the first step of the court, he said, was to grant him a copy of the indictment and to assign him learned counsel to advise him. In asking and securing from the court a copy of the indictment, Lilburne as usual called upon the authority of Coke.[13] Whatever his justification in theory, no other prisoner before an English bar had been granted hitherto a copy of the indictment.[14] Of the judges of the court, Lord Chief Baron Wilde was the most sympathetic to Lilburne's pleas. Not only was Lilburne granted a copy of the indictment, but eventually he was granted the privilege of presenting to the court exceptions to the indictment even though he had still not pleaded guilty or not guilty. Thus in the very opening session of his trial Lilburne forced his judges to disregard the threat of Cromwell's overwhelming power and grant him protection of ancient legal forms. His exceptions to the indictment took so much time that on the third day of the trial he had still not completed his presentations. On Friday, July 15, pleading for still more time in which to present his exceptions, Lilburne said, "The failing in one word, might cost him his life." To this plea the judges finally yielded.[15]

The trial was carried on at times amid tumultuous demonstrations by the spectators, which numbered three to four thousand. Lilburne himself was often interrupted by the clerk and the judges. Men and women spectators also interrupted in support of Lilburne, and Lilburne claimed the right of a spectator at a trial to give evidence at any time. According to Lilburne one of the judges, Alderman Atkins, was so intimidated by

[13] *Triall of Mr. John Lilburne* (July 13 [sic], 1653), E708(3), pp. 1–2. The writer claims that Lilburne read aloud passages from Coke's *The Third Part of the Institutes,* pp. 29, 34, 137, 230. The accused one, asserts Coke (1644 ed., p. 34), may "require a copy of so much of the Indictment, as shall be necessary for the framing of his plea, which also ought to be granted. . . The Indictment is commonly found in the absence of the party, and yet it is the foundation of the rest of the proceeding."

[14] Gardiner, *Commonwealth and Protectorate,* II, 295.

[15] *Triall,* E708(3), p. 6.

the actions of Lilburne's followers that he called out to Colonel Okey to send some troops of horse to protect his person.[16]

The record of the trial as printed by Lilburne and his friends is filled with curious revelations. So often did Lilburne himself interrupt the judges or prosecutor that the clerk asked to have him gagged. When the judges complained about the loss of time imposed by Lilburne's constant haggling over the legality of courtroom procedure, Lilburne replied, "It is you who trifle away time, and not I." Why was it, Lilburne complained, that the prosecutor Prideaux was permitted to sit on the judges' bench with his hat on his head? Why should the prosecutor be permitted to sit side by side with those who pronounced judgment? The prisoner complained that the Earl of Strafford himself had been given more respect and more legal consideration than he, John Lilburne. Nevertheless, asserted Lilburne, one of the judges, Baron Wilde, had treated him fairly, and one of the most learned barristers in England, John Maynard, had set his hand to his exceptions to the indictment. After securing a copy of the indictment and presenting his exceptions to it, Lilburne demanded the right of *oyer*.[17] Essentially the right of oyer meant that Lilburne and his counsel had a right to analyze in court the very law which had condemned him to banishment. Was this law in itself legal? In this approach Lilburne held a great advantage, inasmuch as the Rump Parliament which had sentenced him to banishment was not a freely elected one. Moreover, it had now been dispersed by Cromwell himself, and a new Parliament had taken its place. How, then, asked Lilburne in effect, could any law passed by the Rump Parliament be binding upon the present government or its citizens?

When Lilburne demanded oyer, he claimed that the court had a right to judge the Parliamentary action on which his conviction was grounded. "My Counsel commands me to insist," he said, "and dwell upon the demand of Oyer as my right, and as the chiefest shield, and buckler I have to defend my life." When he was interrupted again and again by the Lord Mayor, Mr. Lee the recorder, Attorney General Prideaux, and a Mr. Hall to whom Lilburne always refers as "mumbling Mr. *Hall*," he cried out:

> My Lord rob me not of my Birthright, the benefit of the Law, nor interrupt me not, but give me free liberty to speak for my life; and my Lord, if you will be so audacious and unjust in the face of this great auditory of People, to deny me, and rob me of all the rules of Justice, and right, and will forcably stop my mouth, and not suffer me freely to speak for my life according to Law, I will cry out and appeal to the People.[18]

[16] *Ibid.*, p. 25. [17] *Ibid.*, pp. 16, 18, 19, 21, 23, 24, 43. [18] *Ibid.*, p. 17.

It is evident from this passage, as in the record of the whole trial, that Lilburne did not hesitate in this trial as in his trial of 1649 to appeal not only to the jury but to the audience of supporters. On the question of oyer Lilburne and his judges debated long and bitterly. Lilburne was finally persuaded to deliver a copy of his exceptions to the indictment, even though he had insisted that his demand for oyer should be satisfied before debate on the exceptions by his counsel. This agreement was not put into writing by members of the court, but by friends of Lilburne who signed their names to the statement to show its authenticity. On July 16 Lilburne had still not pleaded guilty or not guilty, insisting that other matters, such as the debating of the exceptions and the privilege of oyer, be first completed. Lilburne's courtroom strategy, his appeal to laws known but irregularly observed, had been spectacularly successful. The court decided upon a recess until August 10. Lilburne was acquitted on August 20, to the tumultuous acclamation of his followers. But in actual fact the issue had never been in doubt since the first two days of the trial and the court's reluctant assent to Lilburne's citations from Sir Edward Coke.

Chapter XXVII

THE NEW PROTECTORATE ON TRIAL

1. FALL OF THE SAINTS: DECEMBER, 1653

Cromwell's first attempt to bring together a new Parliament was by nomination of the Congregational churches of each county. From those thus nominated, 140 were chosen by the Council of Officers; of these, five of the nominees represented Scotland and six Ireland. All the men chosen were Puritan leaders whose godliness was well known; whether or not they had any knowledge of law or Parliamentary traditions was an irrelevant concern.* It was hoped that Henry Vane would become a member; to the reign of the saints about to begin, he was said to prefer a heavenly setting. The new Parliament met first on July 4, when Cromwell addressed them, his vision glowing, his hopes ecstatic.

By December, 1653, it had become evident that the Nominated Parliament could no longer act cohesively to carry forward the burden of legislation that Cromwell and his officers could conscientiously approve. The Saints of the Commons, inspired in part by Christopher

* For a full account of the ways in which the new Parliamentarians were nominated, see Austin Woolrych, "The Calling of Barebone's Parliament," *English Historical Review,* Vol. LXXX, No. 316 (July, 1965), pp. 492–515.

Feake, supported measures that would have disrupted the traditions of legal procedure and the patronage of the church that Cromwell was now eager to let stand. On the morning of December 12, the supporters of the Commonwealth, convinced that Parliament should now abdicate and return its power to Cromwell, assembled "an hour or more"[1] early at the House. Various members accused the saintly opposition of wanting the officers to give up their salaries; of hindering necessary levies of money; of wanting to destroy the state ministry; of destroying property by "attempting to take off the Power of Patrons to present to Church-livings"; of desiring "total Alteration of the laws."[2] The theme of various speeches by Commonwealth supporters was that such opposition made it impossible to legislate with security or consistent purpose. Finally it was moved by Sir Charles Wolseley *"that the sitting of this Parlament any longer as now Constituted, will not be for the good of the Commonwealth; and that therefore it is requisite to deliver up unto the Lord General* Cromwell, *the Powers which they received from Him."*[3] The

[1] *A True Narrative of the Cause and Manner of the Dissolution of the Late Parliament,* December 12, 1653, E724(11), p 1. *An Answer to a Paper Entitled A True Narrative,* E725(20), is much less factual in detail than *A True Narrative.* The author of *An Answer* does not dispute the chain of events on the crucial morning of December 12 as described in *A True Narrative.* Rather his purpose is to give the events an interpretation favorable to Cromwell's party. Supporters of the government, asserts the author (p. 8), speaking of the Saints' attitude toward the ministry, tried to show "how unjust and cruel it was to turn out the good and bad together, and put many godly, painfull, faithfull Teachers, out of their Freeholds, to seek a subsistence for them and their Families." The author's key characterization of the psychology of the Saints runs as follows (p. 9): "I cannot but mention the confidence was taken by One of his own Opinion, as that he said, He spake it not, but the Lord in him; which had it been believed, All reasoning had ceased, and every man must have yeilded present obedience to what he had promulged."

The document that best represents the Saints' view of the dissolution is *An Exact Relation of the Proceedings and Transactions of the Late Parliament* (December 12, 1653), E729(6), written, according to Sir Charles Firth, by Barebones himself. The cry about taking away property, says the author (p. 18–19), is completely without foundation: "Oh the Parliament men, many of them are such as would destroy all property: As if they had none themselves, when as though all of them had not very bulkie Estates, yet they had free Estates, and were not of broken Fortunes, or such as owed great summes of money." Barebones reminds the reader of former Parliamentary action in selling the lands of bishops, deans, and chapters. Was this destroying property? Was a former Parliament destroying property when it took away "the fifth and twentieth part of Persons Estates for the good of the whole?" *An Exact Relation* is an indispensable document in gaining a rounded picture of the issues behind the dissolution.

[2] *A True Narrative,* pp. 1–2.

[3] *A True State of the Case,* February 8, 1654, E728(5), p. 22. The writer quotes accurately (except for "is requisite" instead of "was requisite") from the *Com-*

motion was supported by Colonel Sydenham and others, but opposed by members of the opposition, who were rapidly increasing their numbers as the clock ticked on. Instead of putting the measure to a vote, however, the speaker rose from his place and led about forty supporters of Cromwell out of the chamber and down to Whitehall, leaving behind a minority variously estimated as twenty-seven to thirty-five.[4] The minority was drawing up a protest against such scandalous action when Colonel Goffe and Lieutenant Colonel White appeared at the door of the House. The officers urged the members to leave the House, "pressing it often." The members refused, urging the officers to withdraw "unless they had command to put them forth." [5] Despite protests, the officers then called in their men to disperse the resistant members. The precedent set by Cromwell's soldiers at Pride's Purge in 1648 and again by Cromwell himself in dismissing the Rump Parliament April 20, 1653, was by now a pattern more inimical to orderly government than England had experienced from a long line of kings, including the hated Charles I.

When the forty members reached Whitehall, they hastened to subscribe in writing to Wolseley's motion. Shortly afterward, though Cromwell showed surprise when he received them, he did not reject their abdication. As the days passed, the number of signers gradually increased to eighty, thus lending the authority of a majority to a dubious manipulation of power. No one was more forthright about this than Cromwell himself. "My power, again by this resignation," he said afterward, "was as boundless and unlimited as before; all things being subjected to arbitrariness, and a person having power over the three nations boundlessly." [6] The way was now clear for the adoption of the *Instrument of Government* long favored by Lambert and his fellow-officers, and not submitted for discussion or approval to any civilian body. Even so, Cromwell's military commands, and not the wording of the *Instrument*, were the basis of his power as head of the state. Though Cromwell and his officers again rejected the title of *king*, it was soon apparent that much of the ritual and pomp of kingship would now attach itself to the title of *Lord Protector*.

---

mons Journals, which record, however (VII, 363), adds the following: "And that Motion being seconded by several other Members; the House rose: And the Speaker, with many of the Members of the House, departed out of the House to *Whitehall;* where they, being the greater Number of the Members sitting in Parliament, did, by a Writing under their Hands, resign unto his Excellency their said Powers: And Mr. Speaker, attended with the Members, did present the same to his Excellency, accordingly."

[4] I am here following Gardiner's *Commonwealth and Protectorate*, II, 326.

[5] *A True Narrative*, p. 3.

[6] *Commonwealth and Protectorate*, II, 329 n.

2. THE *INSTRUMENT* AND ITS CRITICS

As Gardiner points out, the principle of a written constitution as embodied in the *Instrument* owed much to the Levellers and their agitation for *The Agreement of the People.* Nevertheless the prerogatives of Parliament were by the *Instrument* reduced almost to nullity in favor of power in the Protector's hands. The first two articles of the *Instrument* (adopted by Cromwell and his officers December 14–15) read as follows:

> I. That the Supreme Legislative Authority of the Commonwealth of England, Scotland, and Ireland, and the Dominions thereunto belonging, shall be and reside in one Person, and the People assembled in Parliament; the Style of which Person shall be The Lord Protector of the Commonwealth of England, Scotland, and Ireland.
>
> II. That the Exercise of the chief Magistracy, and the Administration of the Government over the said Countries and Dominions, and the People thereof, shall be in the Lord Protector, assisted with a Council, the Number whereof shall not exceed 21, nor be less than 13.[1]

Whatever the actual power of his monarchical predecessors, none had claimed such absolute dominion as these two articles gave to Cromwell. Moreover under the *Instrument* Cromwell was given control of the militia in times when Parliament was not sitting, "with the Advice and Consent of the major Part of the Council." The limitation of the Protector's power was lodged not in Parliament but in the Council of State. The office of Lord Protector was to be elective, not hereditary. The *Instrument* provided freedom of doctrine and worship to all Protestants professing faith in Christ, but the usual prohibition against Catholics appears in the phrase, "provided this Liberty be not extended to Popery nor Prelacy." The rights of Jewish conscience, as in *The Agreement of the People,* were nowhere mentioned. Nor did the new constitution permit freedom of worship to those who "hold forth and practise Licentiousness."[2] What such wicked fellows as Henry Marten and Peter Wentworth thought of this prohibition even *Mercurius Democritus* omitted to report.

The Council of State selected by the new government was one that could not have had Milton's full sanction, if only because such men as Vane, Bradshaw, and Overton were conspicuous by their absence. In *Second Defence* he was pointedly to choose Bradshaw and Overton as among the great patriots he had served with. Nevertheless the new Council under the Protectorate did include nine men he was to single out for spe-

[1] *Acts and Ordinances,* II, 813. Unlike its predecessors, the Council of State was a permanent body. Its members held office for life. See Hill, *Century of Revolution,* p. 136.

[2] *Ibid.,* II, 813, 822.

cial praise: Cromwell, Charles Fleetwood, Henry Lawrence, Sir Gilbert Pickering, William Sydenham, Walter Strickland, John Desborough, Edward Montague, and John Lambert. Of the new Council none except Cromwell was a fiery reformer like Thomas Harrison, with a gift for speaking God's thoughts and making them good with his sword. On December 21 Harrison, having refused to serve the new government, had been forced to lay down his commission.[3] With such a man as Harrison, however remarkable, Milton had little in common except the assurance of God's approval for his actions. Perhaps Milton would have concurred with Roger Williams' judgment of Harrison, in a letter to Winthrop, July 12, 1654: "Surely, Sir, he is a very gallant, most deserving, heavenly man, but most high flown for the kingdom of the saints, and the fifth-monarchy now risen, and their sun never to set again."[4] In his new Council of State, Cromwell needed prophets less than men of steady application to business: The Protectorate now needed consolidation of the Commonwealth's gains, not new vistas of revolution.

On February 2 appeared at Leith a pamphlet written to justify a Commonwealth already fallen: *The Survey of Policy,* by Peter English, with a prefatory letter by David Pierson to Lambert and Lilburne and an "Epistle Dedicatory" to Cromwell. The principles set forth opposed the undeviating royalism of Salmasius with a somewhat cautious and contradictory defense of democratic rule. "As the Legislative power *radically,* is in the People, so by Nature they ought to choose their own Governours and Rulers. But nature being contaminated, all men upon that accompt are not fit to make choice of their Rulers." Yet, asserts the author, a democracy is to be preferred to monarchy and aristocracy, which restrict men's capabilities. Only "Democracy giveth people their full liberty which they had in the state of perfection, in so much as they are capable of it."[5] Every man who wishes should be free to preach the gospel. The author of *The Survey* uses none of the bitter rhetoric found in Milton's

[3] "Harrison . . . is an honest man," said Cromwell, "and aims at good things, yet from the impatience of his spirit will not wait the Lord's leisure, but hurries me on to that which he and all honest men will have cause to repent." See Ludlow, *Memoirs* (2 vols., Oxford, 1894), I, 346.

[4] James Knowles, *Memoir of Roger Williams* (Boston, 1834), p. 263. Williams' comments on the crisis are very instructive. Though Harrison has been second in the nation in late months, says Williams, he is now not permitted beyond five miles from his father's house in Staffordshire. Though Vane has retired into Lincolnshire, he is "daily missed and courted for his assistance." Williams notes with satisfaction that in the Barebones Parliament fifty-six members were against priests and tithes as opposed to fifty-four members of the opposite persuasion. On this key issue, central to his political beliefs, Milton must have been as sympathetic as Williams to the fifty-six members. Yet he made no comment about this crucial action in December, 1653, or afterward.

[5] E727(17), sig. [A4], p. 170.

Defence or *Second Defence.* He demonstrates the traditional limitations on the king's power in England and Scotland which Salmasius seems unaware of. At no point does English claim that Great Britain now has a democracy. But if it is a trend toward democracy, it is justified, because only in a democratic form of government does the average citizen have a chance to reach a higher level of manly action.

A strong justification for the turn of events, *A True State of the Case of the Commonwealth,* did not appear until February 8. The word *Protectorate* does not appear on the title page. Though the fire of the author's metaphor blazes but seldom in this pamphlet, his writing takes on a sharper sting and clarity as his argument advances; certainly he puts the issue in perspective more comprehensively and skillfully than any fellow-propagandist. As fully as anyone of his time, this man spoke for Milton from the same classical sources to which Milton appealed. Even the phrasing and diction of this pamphlet are often difficult to distinguish from those of Milton. The writer's main aim is to show that the Protectorate embodies the substance of the main aims for which the war was fought. We did not fight, continues the champion, for a particular form of government. "As for the King himself, there appeared not the least intentions to cast him off, till he had quite cast off the People."[6] Who could see any possibility of coming to agreement with such a man? Between the lines one reads the questions the writer knows people are thinking: "What is the difference between a Protector and a king? Does Cromwell not dress now as a king, put on the robes of a monarch, surround himself with kingly ritual?" The author's next task is to justify the dissolution of the Rump, which had made no move to provide for a new Parliament until army action was imminent; some members, indeed, had a design to "have perpetuated the Power in their own Hands." Even so, asserts the critic, the evil of the biennial Parliaments which the Rump proposed was "discernable to every eye, and would have proved a remedy worse than the disease."[7] The fatal weakness of the Rump's Biennial Bill was that it would have concentrated executive and legislative power in the same hands.

As for the Parliament of the Saints, asserts the writer, their actions from the first were doomed to failure. These men were not subject to any ordinary measurement of manhood or statesmanship. Who could deny or confirm the messages they received from Christ himself, directing the setting up of a Fifth Monarchy upon earth? "The business of Government," wrote the author, "is not conversant about the inward graces and

[6] E728(5), p. 5. The internal evidence in this pamphlet is overwhelming that Needham was its author.

[7] *Ibid.*, p. 9.

Qualifications of men." The Saints were so unrealistic as to oppose levies of money for the army at home and the maintenance of warships abroad. Soldiers they despised as *Janisaries* and *"Pensioners of Babylon."* Moreover, they stood for a total eradication and not a reform of the old laws of England. In all discussion of differences, they were stiff and unyielding: "They un-sainted every man, whose Conscience was not of the same size with their own, and condemned all as Enemies to Reformation, who kept not an even pace with Themselves in the House." [8] In the field of state religion, they were not content with the removal of scandalous ministers; they wanted all ministers dispossessed of their livings and put to work earning their subsistence, as did their secular fellow-men. In the midst of such utopian fantasies, no work of the Parliament could go forward; differences hardened between the Saints of the Parliament and their opponents; so much so, asserts the writer, that the two parties might have been men from different nations. Had the Saints not been ousted and the power of government returned to Cromwell, the great cause for which men had fought and worked would have been frustrated forever.

The author is not content with justifying the dissolutions of two Parliaments within eight months; he devotes more than a third of his pamphlet to an analysis of the benefits and virtues of the new *Instrument of Government*. It gives assurance of a succession of Parliaments in which members from all counties were represented. The Protector is to have no power of negative voice such as kings had possessed: If he does not give his consent within twenty days, the act in question becomes law without his approval. But Parliament cannot alter the government as described in the *Instrument*. "Some power," asserts the author, "should pass a Decree upon the wavering humors of the People, and say to this Nation, as the Almighty himself said once to the unruly Sea; *Here shall be thy Bounds, hitherto shalt thou come, and no further*." [9] As for the militia,

[8] *Ibid.*, pp. 25, 20, 19, 14.

[9] *Ibid.*, p. 34. As in many articles in *Mercurius Politicus*, Needham contrasts in *The True State* the bearable difficulties of the Commonwealth and Protectorate with the alternative of the return of Charles II. The young Charles, insists the writer (p. 48), is "by bloud almost a stranger to this Nation, being by the Mother a *French-man*, and now unquestionably such by his education in that Court, where he hath alwaies before his eyes that patern of absolute Power which bewitched his Father." Charles' very religion is suspect. He renounced his allegiance to the Presbyterians of Scotland, and there is (p. 49) "ground enough to believe him sufficiently affected, if not sworn to Popery." If Charles should return, he would bring with him followers (p. 49) "which will like Locusts devour the whole Land before them." In such an event no man's life or property will be safe. One word against the king would be justification for execution and confiscation of his property (pp. 50–51): "Our Wives and Children, our Estates and Fortunes, would all

he continues, the king had claimed power over it as his absolute right. In the new constitution this kingly claim is wholly overthrown; the Protector may direct the militia during Parliament's sitting only with Parliamentary consent; and at other times only with the consent of a majority of the Council of State. Parliament has all its traditional powers of legislation, but now subject to no veto: It appoints magistrates and officers of the state, oversees the national ministry, votes appropriations, acts as a court of last appeal. The Protector's powers were expressly limited by the *Instrument*. Parliament elected members of the Council of State, which body in turn elected a new Protector upon the death of the incumbent one. Needham's analysis of the new constitution is on the whole the most judicious and impartial of his day. The principle of a written constitution made possible a more exact delineation of powers and duties than any government had hitherto possessed. While the Protectorate in effect gave the nation the semblance of a king, it provided checks and balances that anticipated the American Constitution to come. But over the creation and application of the *Instrument* hovered the overwhelming aura of Cromwell. Whatever the written word might trace in beautiful theory, its life tenure depended on a single great man with a sword at his side and many doubts about the future in his heart.

3. MARCH OF EVENTS: LAWS AND COMMITMENTS

January–September, 1654

In the eight months that followed the dissolution of the Barebones Parliament, December 12, 1653, Oliver and his Council ruled the land without a Parliament. Acts and ordinances were passed by proclamation of the leader and his Council. Significantly enough, on January 19, 1654, an ordinance was passed canceling the requirement to sign the Engagement. The Engagement, it is true, had been an oath taken to support the Commonwealth, and the Commonwealth was now no more. But the new ordinance opened with an acknowledgment of the failure of the very principle of loyalty oaths and Engagements: They "have proved burthens and snares to tender Consciences, and yet have been exacted under several penalties." [1] The penalties for not taking the Engagement were held void by the new ordinance. But for the tender consciences of the Papists, the new Protectorate had no more concern than its predecessors. Another

be exposed as a sacrifice to the boundles ambition and cruelty of a race of Tyrants; it would enervate the natural vigor and courage of the People, and exceedingly debase the honor of this free Nation."

[1] *Acts and Ordinances,* II, 830.

ordinance of January 19 provided a continuation of the penalties under Elizabeth and James I for adherence to the Pope and membership in the Catholic church. As in the preceding century, to worship God as a Catholic was still tantamount to high treason.

On March 17 an ordinance was passed for the continuation of the excise: two shillings for every barrel of beer or ale ("of above six shillings the Barrel"); two pounds for every imported tun of wine vinegar; five shillings on every hundredweight of foreign soap; five shillings on imported dyed silk ("for every twentie shillings in value, to bee paid by the first buyer").[2] Three days later, on March 20, an ordinance was passed for approval of preachers in state churches. Commissioners of approbation were headed by Francis Rous, Thomas Goodwin, and John Owen. In this crisis no timely Miltonic sonnet appealed to Cromwell to resist a state ministry's tyranny over conscience; nor did Williams send forth a pamphlet, as in 1652, to oppose the new hirelings. On March 22 a new ordinance continued the decision of the preceding Parliament, "An Act for Impresting of Sea-men."[3] No records of the day trace the inarticulate dismay of English youth carried off the streets to serve on Oliver's ships. On March 31 Oliver passed an ordinance revising the act of October 5, 1653, "for the Relief of Creditors and poor Prisoners."[4] Judges by the new ordinance were forbidden to proceed to the sale of property belonging to prisoners until April 20, 1655. In an ordinance passed on March 31, 1654, Oliver and his Council prohibited cock fighting on the grounds that such matches are "commonly accompanied with Gaming, Drinking, Swearing, Quarreling, and other dissolute Practices, to the Dishonor of God, and do often produce the ruine of Persons and their Families."[5] Thus Oliver kept the myth of sainthood as a governmental concern, while the realities of power kept to the traditional channels of law and custom, now upheld by men at arms.

On April 11 an ordinance was passed putting into execution *An Act Prohibiting the Planting of Tobacco in England.* On April 12 Cromwell and his Council passed "an Ordinance of Pardon and Grace to the People of Scotland," making the Scots respectable citizens again on condition that they pay stated amounts of money to the public treasury. On May 26 the Protectorate passed "an Ordinance for Relief of Debtors in Scotland in some Cases of Extremity." On June 9 another ordinance was passed "for relief of Creditors and Poor Prisoners." Unable to secure convictions of its enemies in trials by jury, the Protectorate on June 13 passed another ordinance "for Establishing a High Court of Justice." Some time in June a Catholic priest was executed in London for no other

[2] *Ibid.*, II, 846–49. [3] *Ibid.*, II, 855–58. [4] *Ibid.*, II, 860–61.
[5] *Ibid.*, II, 861.

crime than following his faith and occupation. Though Cromwell wished to pardon him, he was opposed by the Council of State. On June 29 an ordinance was passed prohibiting challenges and duels. The strategy of the Protectorate to avoid large crowds found expression on July 4 in an ordinance "prohibiting Horse-Races for Six Moneths." Still another ordinance for "the Relief of Creditors and Poor Prisoners" became law on August 11. On August 21 was passed one of Cromwell's favorite reforms, *An Ordinance for the better Regulating and Limiting and Jurisdiction of the High Court of Chancery*. The ordinance fixed and simplified the process of law and the conditions by which the defendant could be arraigned. The office of register in chancery was forbidden to execute its orders by deputies. Each register was to receive only the fee named in the bill itself. On September 2 the government passed *An Ordinance for appointing Visitors for the Universities*.[6]

4. FOREIGN POLICY: HOLLAND AND SWEDEN

In his role as Lord Protector, Cromwell now had a freer hand to resolve dilemmas in foreign policies as well as in domestic ones. On November 18, 1653, Oliver had presented to the Council of State a suggested draft for a treaty of peace with the United Provinces. Some of the suggested stipulations were too harsh to form the basis of conciliation. The draft treaty stipulated, for example, that the States General could not elevate the young Prince of Orange to any position of command, military or civil. Upon meeting an English vessel, a Dutch ship was required to strike its flag, lower its topsail, and admit English officers to inspect its decks and cargo. Such a proposed indignity could not possibly meet with Dutch approval, whatever the great victories of the English over them. On December 5 the Dutch commissioners broke off negotiations and asked for passports to their native land. Upon his accession to the Protectorate, Cromwell felt a need to bring the victorious war against Holland to a close. Adopting a conciliatory policy, he agreed to relinquish the treaty requirement that the Dutch acknowledge that they had initiated the war. The treaty with the Dutch was finally signed on April 5, and peace was restored between the two nations. On the same day, April 5, John Dury was dispatched to attempt an establishment of a Protestant league which would initiate an alliance with the Dutch Republic.[1]

[6] *Ibid.*, II, 70, 898, 911, 917, 937, 941, 943, 949, 1026.

[1] Gardiner, *Commonwealth and Protectorate,* III, 62 ff. *A Perfect Account* for April 5–12, 1654, E733(1), p. 1360, reported that "The peace with Holland being concluded . . . our Merchants are lading of goods on shipboard, as fast as Lighters can be gotten to carry them where the ships ride at anchor. We likewise hear of the like preparations in Holland for transporting of goods of several sorts hither."

On November 6, 1653, Whitelocke had set sail for Sweden to assume his new post as ambassador to that kingdom.[2] On December 23 Queen Christina had received him in her palace in an elaborate ceremony of which Whitelocke gives a vivid account in his *Journal*. Whitelocke's own dress befitted the magnificent occasion; his suit "was of black English cloth, of an exceedingly fine sort, the cloak lined with the same cloth, and that and the suit set with very fair rich diamond buttons; his hatband of diamonds answerable; and all of the value of £1000."[3] Whitelocke describes the whole ceremony with satisfaction; it showed a proper respect for gradations in men and position. As for the queen, she sat at the far end of the room on a crimson chair covered with a crimson canopy. As Whitelocke walked forward, he took off his hat, after which the queen took off her cap of black velvet. Rising from her seat, she came forward to greet Whitelocke. Her dress was of plain gray; her petticoat swept the floor. Over her dress she wore a man's jacket, also of plain gray, which reached to her knees. On the left side of her jacket she wore decorations, one of them tied with a crimson ribbon. Around her neck she wore a black scarf, the kind soldiers and seamen had worn in former times. Her braided hair hung loose under her black velvet cap.[4] This ceremony, like others that followed, Whitelocke describes with affectionate completeness.

On January 5 Whitelocke had a private audience with Queen Christina, the dialogue of which he made a record of in his *Journal*. Part of it reads as follows:

> *Queen*. Hath your General a wife and children?
>
> *Whitelocke*. He hath a wife and five children.
>
> *Qu*. What family were he and his wife of?
>
> *Wh*. He was of the family of a baron, and his wife the like from Bourchiers.
>
> *Qu*. Of what parts are his children?
>
> *Wh*. His two sons and three daughters are all of good parts and liberal education.
>
> *Qu*. Some unworthy mention and mistakes have been made to me of them.
>
> *Wh*. Your Majesty knows that to be frequent; but from me you shall have nothing but truth.
>
> *Qu*. Much of the story of your General hath some parallel with that of my ancestor Gustavus the First, who, from a private gentleman of a noble family, was advanced to the title of Marshal of Sweden, because he had risen up and rescued his country from the bondage and oppression which the King of Denmark had put upon them, and expelled that king; and for his reward he was at last elected King of Sweden, and I believe that your General will be King of England in conclusion.

[2] Bulstrode Whitelocke, *Journal of the Swedish Embassy,* ed. Charles Morton (2 vols., London, 1855), I, 108.

[3] *Ibid.,* I, 229.

[4] *Ibid.,* I, 231–32.

Wh. Pardon me, Madam, that cannot be, because England is resolved into a Commonwealth; and my General hath already sufficient power and greatness as General of all their forces both by sea and land, which may content him.[5]

When Whitelocke learned that a treaty with Denmark had been agreed upon, he did not press Christina for an alliance against that country. His main efforts were directed toward a treaty governing commercial exchange between the two countries. This treaty was signed on April 11. Whitelocke left Sweden soon after, before Queen Christina's abdication [6] on June 6 or the coronation of Charles X as her successor.

5. CROMWELL IN 1654

In January 1654, Cromwell was fifty-four years old, two inches under six feet, a tall man among Englishmen of his era. For the past ten years he had lived a soldier's life in bivouac or camp or on the battlefield. On many occasions Cromwell knelt in prayer with fellow officers long into the night. The Lord spoke to his victorious prophets. His victories were signs to Cromwell that the Lord held the Good Old Cause in his hand. "If I were ten years younger," Cromwell reportedly said, "there is not a king in Europe I would not make to tremble." [1] Often now, in early 1654, he still wore a plain cloth suit such as that in which he received the abdication of the Barebones parliamentarians. Years before, in the Long Parliament, Warwick had remembered him as wearing linen none too clean, with "a speck or two of blood upon his little band." In those years as now, his countenance was "swoln and reddish, his voice sharp and untunable, and his eloquence full of fervor." [2] But as the years marched and his name gathered magic, Cromwell's talents expanded with the confrontation of new dilemmas, "as if," wrote Clarendon, "he had concealed facultyes till he had occasion to use them." [3] In his new part as Lord Protector, Cromwell's appearance was majestic, his presence full of grace and charm, warts and big nose notwithstanding.

[5] *Ibid.*, I, 285.

[6] *The Weekly Intelligencer* (April 18–25, 1654), wrote of Queen Christina: "She doth overcome her Sex in the constancy of her Temper, and in the election of a single life. She doth overcome most Kings in Knowledg, Power, and magnificence, but in Resigning her Soveraign Authority at so young a Age, she doth overcome the condition of Mortality, and shews herself most worthy of that incomprehensible Crown to which only she aspires."

[1] Charles Firth, *Oliver Cromwell* (World Classics ed., Oxford, 1900), p. 304.

[2] *Memoires* (1701), pp. 247–48.

[3] *Characters of the Seventeenth Century,* ed. David Nichol Smith (Oxford, 1918), p. 141.

Few men of his day were warm as Cromwell in his affection for his fellows. He found it easy to like men, to put his arm around a friend, to throw a pillow at Ludlow's head, to jump from his horse as he often did and engage in games or horseplay with common soldiers. One never forgets the picture of Cromwell's inking Marten's face with the same pen he had used in signing the death warrant of Charles I: a gesture of contempt for the king as well as an escape from the moment's tension.[4] A fearless man, given to sudden bursts of generosity toward his enemies, Cromwell would often ride up and down the lines to offer quarter to royalist soldiers close to annihilation. Beneath his horseplay, his impulsive affection, his fervent interpretation of God's wishes, worked a mind of immense talent in the handling of men. The vast range of Cromwell's subtlety in his persuasion of minds no biographer has yet traced with rounded vision or a sure hand. In all moments of crisis he possessed an uncanny awareness of the complex man or group he must persuade. He may have found it justifiable, as Huntington claimed, "to play the knave with a knave." [5] Did he also play the knave with honest men for the sake of the Lord's gain? No man was more aware than Cromwell of the great barriers he had leaped in climbing to the pinnacle of power and honor in his own land. "Our Heavenly Father . . ." he wrote to Major, "hath raised me from the dust to what I am!" [6] Cromwell's mastery of ideas in private was always less successful than his grappling with concrete issues when he met men face to face. In talking with ministers, he could quote the Bible with aptness and accuracy. In talking with common soldiers, he was full of gaiety, buffoonery, and that electric energy of identification with the man he sought to win, all this without for a moment forfeiting the persuasion of his leadership magic. "He seemed exceeding open hearted," wrote Baxter, "by a familiar Rustick affected Carriage, (especially to his Soldiers in sporting with them)." [7] As Protector, Cromwell sometimes went hawking on Hounslow Heath. There one day he met the royalist Sir James Long, "fell in love with his company," and commanded Long to wear his sword and meet him by appointment on the hawking field.[8] At ease with men, as much at home as Bunyan with Biblical language, Cromwell was an immature wrestler with the republican ideas of Greece and Rome,[9] ideas which Hobbes rightly thought the

[4] *DNB* article on Henry Marten.

[5] Robert Huntington, *Sundry Reasons* (August 11, 1648), E458(3), p. 14.

[6] Carlyle, *Letters,* ed. Lomas, II, 209. Clarendon notes that Cromwell raised himself to a great height without the aid "of estate, allyance or frendshipps." (*Characters,* p. 139).

[7] *Reliquae Baxterianae* (1696), p. 99. [8] Aubrey, *Brief Lives* (1898), II, 37.

[9] When Cromwell read Harrington's *Oceana,* he saw no relation between classical sources and England's dilemmas. He was said to have declared that "the Gentle-

intellectuals of the Puritan cause had absorbed at Oxford and Cambridge and turned against their king.

Cruel and ruthless as he was at Drogheda, Cromwell normally had no heart for mass murder of his enemies. It was often proposed that the Puritan army engage in a massacre of the royalist leaders of the population as the only sure way to maintain the Commonwealth. But such murderous proposals Cromwell could never for a moment consent to. "He was not a man of bloode," wrote Clarendon.[10]

6. BUNYAN: WRESTLER WITH DOUBT

In January, 1654, John Bunyan, twenty-six years old, still living at Elstow, was attending St. John's church in Bedford and had come to know John Gifford.[1] Slowly and painfully, prayer by prayer, as Bunyan's dialogue with God unfolded, his enormous energy played forth each day over the promises of Scripture. Already God had raised him from the dust to a small pinnacle of hope; but every day brought a new banishment into a cavern of despair. When he had almost given up the hope of ever attaining the full life of the spirit, he thought again of the passage, "Look at the generations of old and see; did ever any trust in the Lord, and was confounded?"[2] Repeating the words to himself, Bunyan decided to read from Genesis through Revelation to see if any man in the Bible who believed in God had been confounded. But where was this promise in the good book? Bunyan needed the reassurance, the authority of the printed word. He had no doubt that he could find the passage soon; but find it he could not, though he asked help from one religious man, then another. Over a year later, Bunyan found the words he so cherished in one of the books of the Apocrypha, Ecclesiasticus. But no sooner was one promise fulfilled in Bunyan's life than a new doubt began to gnaw at his spirit; no man of the day sought a daily intimacy with the divine more fervently than Bunyan. Much as he trusted his God, he still felt confounded and bereft. One feels that Milton had no doubt that his God, however abstract and untouchable, was ever at his side; but Bunyan was never quite sure, even until his last days. His self-reproach, his doubts, beset him daily; only now and then a chink in the darkness let in a stream of light that transformed his spirit with joyous assurance. Not so with Milton: His sense of God's approval was constant and unshakable.

---

man had like to trapan him out of his Power, but that what he got by the Sword he would not quit for a little paper Shot." See *Milton in the Puritan Revolution,* p. 305.

[10] *Characters,* ed. David Nichol Smith, p. 140.

[1] John Brown, *John Bunyan* (Boston and New York, 1885), p. 92.

[2] *Grace Abounding,* ed. G. B. Harrison (Everyman, 1928), p. 23.

7. HENRY MARTEN: PURITAN EXTRAORDINARY

In January, 1654, Henry Marten was fifty-two years old, a fading power since the dissolution of the Rump but outspoken and irrepressible as ever. No member of the Commons had been more fanatical than Marten in bringing Charles I to judgment. In his political views he was a consistent supporter of the Levellers, of the poor who petitioned redress, of those who favored the widest toleration of religious beliefs. But Marten's private life was an embarrassment to the Independents. When Cromwell, in turning out the Rump, had fixed his glance on Marten and Wentworth and said, "Some of you are whoremasters," he spoke for personal piety as a superior virtue to zeal for secular reformation. Long ago Charles I had condemned Marten for his wenching. Seeing Marten in Hyde Park one day, the king had exclaimed: "Let that ugly rascall be gonne out of the parke, that whore-master, or els I will not see the sport." [1] In the news sheets of the day, *Mercurius Democritus* and *Mercurius Fumigosis,* Marten was almost a weekly target of satirical thrusts, such as, "You may know what *exercise* he hath been at, by his wide stradling." [2] In his nightly search (assisted by emissaries) for ladies of delight, Marten was a scandal to his Puritan colleagues in the Commons. In this sense, as Aubrey writes, "he was as far from a Puritane as light from darknesse." [3]

Marten's gift for exuberant humor and repartee made him a favorite of both his constituents of Berks and his colleagues in the Commons. Aubrey records that Cromwell on one occasion addressed Marten as "*Sir* Harry Martin," whereat Marten rose and bowed, saying, "I thanke *your majestie,* I alwayes thought when you were *king,* that I should be knighted." On another occasion, when Marten attacked old Sir Henry Vane and concluded by saying, "*But for young Sir Harry Vane*—" several cried out, "What have you to say to young Sir Harry?" Marten replied: "*Why! if young Sir Harry lives to be old; he will be old Sir Harry!*" [4] Marten's ready wit, his pithy analysis of issues, his relentless honesty, often won over the whole House to his views. As Aubrey writes, Marten was never arrogant, covetous, or proud in his manner; he was "a great

[1] Aubrey, *Brief Lives* (1898), II, 44. What relation such comments may have had to the realities of Marten's life is of course unknown.

[2] *The Royall Diurnall,* April 14, 1650, E598(16), sig. G2v.

[3] Aubrey, *Brief Lives* (1898), II, 44. The Puritan writers of the period have left no record of the sexual habits of their leaders. But William Walwyn found some leading Independents of the London congregations quite outspoken in their discussions of frequency of marital intercourse in the lives of their friends. See *Walwyns Just Defence* (1649; UTSL), pp. 32–33.

[4] Aubrey, II, 45.

cultor of justice, and did always in the house take the part of the oppressed."[5]

8. HARRISON: ECSTASY AND SAINTHOOD

In January, 1654, Thomas Harrison, forty-eight years old, son of a Staffordshire butcher, was a major general in Cromwell's army and one of the great revolutionary forces of his time. "Of a Sanguine Complexion," Baxter wrote of him, "naturally of such a vivacity, hilarity and alacrity as another Man hath when he hath drunken a Cup too much."[1] Harrison would not often debate religious issues; but he would break forth in a fervent and graceful flow of language, almost in an ecstasy, in conversations with his fellows around the campfires. Or when the enemy broke ranks and began to run, as at Langport, he would speak in a torrent of rapturous praise for the victory of God's soldiers. To Harrison, as to most Puritan soldiers, there was no conflict between the lightning-like calculations of combat with pike and sword, as at Appleby in 1648, and the frenzied flow of gratitude for the Lord's presence.[2] Harrison was the darling of the Barebones Parliament, frequently preaching in churches attended by the Saints. When the Commons voted fifty-six to fifty-four in favor of the abolition of priests and tithes, Harrison was in enthusiastic agreement. Impatient for reform, sympathetic with Leveller principles, he was less bound by economic and political custom of privilege than either Cromwell or Milton. But at this crisis, as at no other in these tumultuous months, we expect Milton to name Harrison and support the Saints. Like Harrison, Milton was in theory unwilling to let established custom stand in the way of religious reforms. Even at this crucial point, however, Milton did not support Harrison and the Saints in their stand for those state principles he believed in most passionately.

9. JOHN HUTCHINSON: PURITAN ARISTOCRAT

In January, 1654, Colonel John Hutchinson, thirty-nine years old, was living at his home in Nottinghamshire. A member of the first two Councils of State under the Commonwealth, Hutchinson had retired into private life with the dissolution of the Rump in 1653. Like many other members of the Rump, like Milton himself, Hutchinson never lost his

[5] *Ibid.*, II, 44–45.

[1] *Reliquiae Baxterianae* (1696), p. 57.

[2] *"By God I have leaped over a Wall,"* said Harrison on the scaffold, *"by God I have run'd through a Troop, and by my God I will go through this death, and he will make it easie to me."* See *A Compleat Collection of the Lives, Speeches, Private Passages, Letters and Prayers of Those Persons Lately Executed* (1661; UTSL), p. 21.

allegiance to that resolute body. Though Hutchinson is idealized in his wife's biography of him, elements of his personality emerge with unique distinctness from her writings. "He was of a middle stature," she wrote, "of a slender and exactly well-proportioned shape in all parts, his complexion fair, his hair of light brown, very thick set in his youth, softer than the finest silk, and curling into loose great rings at the ends; his eyes of a lively grey, well-shaped and full of life and vigour." [1] Though a strong Puritan, Hutchinson cherished the graces of an aristocratic life. He was a graceful dancer, was skilled in fencing, loved music and, according to his wife, Lucy, played the violin with masterly skill. Hutchinson loved also the aristocratic habit of practicing with guns and bows and arrows. Unlike most Puritans and unlike Milton himself, Hutchinson had a keen appreciation of paintings, sculptures, and engravings. While in London he always sought out the most gifted artists. Like a true aristocrat he took much pride in his country estate, in planting fruit trees, in opening up new springs of water, and making fish ponds. For a time, writes Mrs. Hutchinson, he delighted in hawking; but she reports with quiet satisfaction that he soon gave it up.

Lucy Hutchinson was too much in love with her husband to paint his portrait with justice. To her "he from a child was wise, and sought to by many that might have been his fathers for counsel." At the summit of his values was a daily preoccupation with the virtues of Christianity, which Lucy defines as "that universal habit of grace which is wrought in a soul by the regenerating Spirit of God, whereby the whole creature is resigned up into the divine will and love." Christianity was to Hutchinson "the fountain of all his virtues, and diffusing itself in every stream." To Hutchinson, as to Milton, Jerusalem was ever a more sacred fountain than Athens or Rome. Nevertheless, Hutchinson, like Walwyn and Milton, did not reject the pagan authors. Indeed Christianity and pagan virtues were fused in his intellectual equipment. Cicero, Plutarch, and Seneca had fresh meaning when studied side by side with the Bible. In such a mingling the pagan authors "are regenerated, and take a new name and nature." [2]

In her husband Lucy Hutchinson could find no fault. "He had a native majesty," she wrote, "that struck an awe of him into the hearts of men, and a sweet greatness that commanded love." In his relations with his family he achieved in Lucy's mind a pinnacle of perfection: "He was as kind a father, as dear a brother, as good a master, and as faithful a friend as the world had." [3] Whatever Hutchinson's faults the portrait of a

[1] Lucy Hutchinson, *Memoirs of the Life of Colonel Hutchinson* (Everyman ed., London, 1908), p. 18.

[2] *Ibid.*, p. 20, 21.

[3] *Ibid.*, p. 22, 25.

disciplined and creative personality, lacking the leadership of Harrison in war and the creative powers of a Milton or a Marvell in the world of letters, emerges from Lucy's biography. Every Puritan who had attended Oxford or Cambridge experienced a unique mingling of boyhood interpretations of Christianity with his new knowledge of Greek and Roman values. In the disciplines of the creative arts, of moral, political, and historical theory, Rome and Greece were indispensable. In the battlefields of the Civil War it was fervency of religious belief that won the day. As a Puritan personality Hutchinson achieved a rare greatness of spirit without reaching a pinnacle in art or war or leadership in civic virtues.

10. HARTLIB: CURIOSITY AND PUBLIC WELFARE

In 1653 and 1654 Samuel Hartlib, friend of Milton, Dury, and Comenius, was living at Angel Court near Charing Cross, a man whom Pepys was to describe in 1655 as the "master of innumerable curiosities." Hartlib kept a diary of ideas, events, impressions of people, inventions, social improvements of many kinds.[1] He sought the creative fruits of remarkable minds, concentrating on ideas for social improvement that would not alienate any faction. Let the poor from every parish be gathered into colonies on inclosures of wasteland and common land. Let physicians serve poor people without compensation. Hartlib adds news about noted people, many of them, such as Henry More, his familiar friends. Dr. Harvey is so ill it is not likely he will recover. Robert Boyle has a great fancy for keeping bees on his estate in Ireland. Only rarely does Hartlib introduce a note about his personal life: In late April of 1653, he writes, his sight became cloudy and weak. From Sir Cheney Culpeper Hartlib has heard about a new invention of a combination wagon and coach that can accomodate fourteen passengers. Who is the best musician of the world? Is is not Henry Lawes, who often plays the Irish harp at the bedside of Cromwell himself? When were the streets of Paris and London paved for the first time? No more than a hundred years ago. Hartlib hopes that the cleaning of streets will now go forward, creating another beneficient precedent. At the end of many entries in his diary Hartlib gives the name of the person who gave him the information. From his own son Hartlib learned that Lady Selby of Berwick was a

[1] These notations by Hartlib are taken from his unpublished diary, *Ephemerides,* edited in part by George H. Turnbull before his death, and now by Professor W. H. G. Armytage of Sheffield University. For some interesting sidelights on Hartlib's philanthropic gifts to younger scholars, see Pamela Barnett, *Theodore Haak, F.R.S.* (Mouton & Co., The Hague, 1962).

lovely, virtuous lady and skillful surgeon, fondly admired by Cromwell himself. If a new library went up, supported by gifts from the public, as at Manchester, Hartlib recorded it. He had found out that in a will made December 16, 1651, Humphrey Chetham had named three ministers who would choose books for the new library. A friend of Hartlib's and great lover of curiosities was Sir Kenelm Digby, who was engaged in 1654 in seeking out ships on the ocean floor and bringing up valuables, especially iron. From one ship alone Digby had brought up metals valued at two to three thousand pounds. Then, a note on oranges: Hartlib has seen orange trees in Surrey that would put a Spanish grower to shame. Improvements in agriculture have a special fascination for Hartlib. Could not those lands be exempt from taxes on which the government might plant fruit trees and gooseberries in all hedges, the berries in turn to be turned into wine and marketed by the state?

11. NEW HERESIES AND STRANGE EVENTS
January–March, 1654

The flow of pamphlets during the early months of the Protectorate revealed a startling variety of strange religious behavior. On January 4 appeared a pamphlet entitled *The First New Persecution,* describing the barbarous treatment of two itinerant women at Sidney Sussex College on their way through Cambridge. Students gathered around them to mock and ridicule their lowly intelligence. "How many gods are there?" the students asked. "But one God," was the reply. When the students responded derisively, the women called them anti-Christs and denominated the college as *"a Cage of unclean Birds, and the Synagogue of Satan."* [1] Upon complaint to the mayor of Cambridge, Mr. Pickering, that the two women were engaged in preaching, a constable was dispatched to bring them before him. The mayor asked where they had come from and where they had lodged last night. The women replied that they were strangers and did not know the name of the place, but they had paid for their lodging and had come away. "What are your names?" asked the mayor. The women answered, "Our names are written in the book of life." When the mayor asked, "What are your husbands' names?" the women replied, "We have no husband but Jesus Christ, and he sent us." At this strange talk the mayor flew into a rage, called them whores, and ordered them from his house. As they were leaving, he gave the constable a warrant to take them to the market cross and whip them until the blood came. At this point, continues the narrative, the women fell on their knees and

[1] E725(19), p. 4

asked the Lord to forgive the mayor. This reply so infuriated the mayor that he sent three of his sergeants to see that the constable carried out the threatened torture. At the market cross the executioner commanded the women to take off their clothing. Upon their refusal he stripped them to the waist, placed their arms in the whipping post, and executed punishment upon them. During the torture, according to the account, the women cried, "The Lord be blessed! The Lord be praised!" At the end of the punishment they fell on their knees and prayed God to forgive the executioner. Finally the two women were taken to the edge of town and thrust out, "no man," runs the account, "so much as giving them *a cup of cold water*."[2]

On January 12 William Erbery sent forth a new affirmation of his belief in the Fifth Monarchy: *An Olive-Leaf: Or, Some Peaceable Considerations to the Christian Meeting at Christs-Church in London.* Erbery is in favor of supporting the new Protectorate. He hopes that Mr. Rogers and Mr. Powell and their flocks will seek a unification with other Englishmen to stabilize the civil government. Erbery asks, in effect, "Can men devoted to spiritual growth and following Christ's example reject any kind of civil government?" Is monarchy in a king any more against the reign of Christ than aristocracy in a Parliament? Will not Christ when he comes to reign put down all authority and rule, not only monarchical authority, but aristocratic power and democratic rule? In the great Fifth Monarchy to come, says Erbery, there will be no parties of Presbyterian, Independent, or Anabaptist. Such names as Cavalier, Roundhead, and Romanist will no longer be heard in that ideal commonwealth.[3]

On January 7, when Vavasor Powell appeared before the Council of State, he was attended by a group of followers, one of them a woman named Anna Trapnel. Sitting before a fire in a small room near the Council chamber as Mr. Powell came forth, she was "seized upon by the Lord."[4] Praying and singing, Mrs. Trapnel was carried down into the lodging of a Mr. Roberts, who tended the Whitehall ordinary. Her strength failing, she took to bed at eleven that night. For five days and nights afterward, until January 12, she ate and drank almost nothing, now and then taking a little toast in small beer or taking a sip of beer, sometimes only washing her mouth with it. For seven more days she continued thus, twelve days in all. Mrs. Trapnel lay in bed with her eyes shut, meanwhile speaking and singing as in a trance for some hours each day.[5] Many people of various social stations came to see her and

[2] *Ibid.*, p. 6. [3] E726(5).
[4] *The Cry of a Stone,* February 20, 1654, E730(3), p. 1.
[5] See also *Strange and Wonderful News from Whitehall,* March 16, 1654, E224(3).

hear her speak, among them Colonel Sydenham, Colonel West, Colonel Bennet and his wife, members of the dissolved Parliament, Christopher Feake, Lady Darcy, and Lady Vermuyden. In the last seven days of her trance, a record was made of Mrs. Trapnel's account of herself. She was the daughter of William Trapnel, a shipwright, and as a child had lived in Stepney Parish. The last words uttered by her mother upon her death bed had been, "Lord! Double thy spirit upon my child." [6] Seven years ago she had been ill with a severe fever, at which time the Lord said to her, "After two days I will revive thee, the third day I will raise thee up." Thus it happened, and Mrs. Trapnel felt henceforth that she was a special instrument of God's grace "for the refreshing of afflicted and tempted ones, inwardly and outwardly." Finally the Lord assured Anna that not only individual men and women but also "the universality of Saints shall have discoveries of God through thee." This message of assurance was only the beginning of miraculous happenings in Mrs. Trapnel's life. She was a prophetess for the army when it entered London, to find the shops closed, the windows shut up: "I had many Visions, that the Lord was doing great things for this Nation." In such a manner Mrs. Trapnel spoke on and on, day after day, identifying her prayers and visions with the victories of the Commonwealth, great battles at sea, Cromwell's marches in Scotland and the victory at Dunbar. At times Satan entered into her and moved her to blaspheme, to cast herself into a well, or to destroy herself with a knife. After many terrible assaults, during which she suffered from fever and ague, she shut herself up and prayed for a "humble, broken, melting frame of Spirit." [7] The Lord heard her plea and rescued her from despair. Whatever the deficiencies of rationality, the narrative of Anna Trapnel is one of the most graphic and compelling in the vast range of religious phenomena in the Puritan era.[8] In Trapnel's visions and self-upbraidings one finds a relentless candor. However remote from rational inquiry her thoughts and actions, a sharply etched portrait of a unique spirit caught up in visions, cast down by shame and torment, emerges from her story.

On January 14 appeared *The Perfect Pharise under Monkish Holines*, a skillful attack on Quakerism by five Newcastle ministers led by Thomas Weld. The method of the critics is to pinpoint one by one the doctrines of the Quakers and marshal the most telling arguments against each tenet. The intellectual positions of Quakerism, even as distorted by the authors' interpretations, have a partial validity confirmed by many

[6] *The Cry of a Stone*, p. 3. [7] *Ibid.*, pp. 3, 5, 9.

[8] See also *A Legacy for Saints*, July 24, 1654, E806(1), a more complete account of Trapnel's life with a preface by John Proud and Caleb Ingold, members of Trapnel's church in Great All Hallows, London. At the time the two men wrote the preface, May 9, 1654, Trapnel was a prisoner in Bridewell.

Quaker statements. Some of the main Quaker heresies the authors set down as follows:

1. *Equality with God.*
2. *There is no distinction of persons in the God head.*
3. *The soul is a part of the Divine Essence.*
4. *Christ is in every man.*
5. *No real Saint but he that is perfect, and perfectly holy in this life, and doth not sin.*
6. *Every man in the world hath a light within him sufficient to guide him to salvation, without the help of any outward light or discovery.*
7. *There is no need of any outward teaching by reading or hearing the Scriptures opened or applied.*
8. *The Scriptures are not the word of God, but a declaration of the conditions of them that spoke them forth.*
9. *There is no mediate Call to the Ministry.*
10. *The spirits are not to be tryed by Scripture.*
11. *They cry down Baptisme with water . . . as being but types and shadows ceasing upon the appearance of Christ within them.*

In the application of these principles, continued the authors, the Quakers believe in the following practices:

1. *Not to salute any.*
2. *Not giving any outward token of reverence to Magistrate, Parent, Master, or any other.*
3. *That no man must have the title of Master.*

Of all contemporary attacks, this one has more perceptive clarifications of Quaker doctrine than any other. The authors patiently quote such leaders as Fox, Naylor, Farnsworth, and Bateman, and compare their heresies with sound doctrinal conclusions gleaned from the Scriptures.[9]

On January 29 James Naylor sent forth his *Lamentacion . . . over the Ruines of This Oppressed Nacion*, together with George Fox's *Warning to the Rulers of England*. The two leaders had intended to distribute their tract to each member of the Commons, but the dissolution of December 12 had frustrated their plan. Who speaks in Naylor's message, in Fox's? Not they themselves, claimed the two leaders, but the spirit of the Lord in them. "Oh *England!*" cried Naylor, "how is thy expectation failed now after all thy travails? the People to whom Oppression and Unrighteousness hath been a Burden, have long waited for Deliverance, from one year to another, but none comes."[10] The laws are impotent, the courts themselves full of iniquity. The men now in power are indeed the choicest of the land; but they have failed, those who have

[9] E726(7), pp. 3, 5, 6, 7, 14, 17, 20, 22, 26, 28, 29, 31, 33, 34.
[10] E727(9), p. 3.

cried most loudly for the rule of Christ have brought forth nothing but wind. Meanwhile, for preaching the truth, for witnessing Christ in their consciences, men are still cast into dark holes, without a hearing, without a trial. Many have gone forth without earthly possessions to speak God's love to the world; but many of these have been whipped and beaten and stoned, with nothing charged against them except that they were strangers with no known habitations. In his *Warning to the Rulers of England,* Fox strikes a quieter vein than Naylor, deploring the persecution by law of consciences informed by the inner light. In the consciences, not in the Bible, lives the Eternal Word. It existed before any language; indeed it "breaks in pieces all Languages and tramples upon them and brings all into one Language, for that which keeps in many Languages keeps in confusion." [11] To no language or Scripture would Fox appeal, to no original Hebrew or Greek, but only to the Word written in man's conscience. To make a law against freedom of conscience was to make a law against God himself.

On February 6 another Quaker leader, William Deusbery, published *A True Prophecy of the Mighty Day of the Lord.* In Deusbery one finds neither the fire of Naylor's diction nor the subtleties of Fox's ideas. Despite the pacifism inherent in Quaker doctrine, Deusbery rejoices in the Lord's apocalyptic overthrow not only of the king, Lords, and bishops, but also of the Barebones Parliament itself. Because none of these, asserts Deusbery, would obey the light of conscience, the Lord brought them to dust. Now, adds the author, if you will not obey "the light in your consciences," a similar fate awaits you. He appeals thus to the new regime: "O be valiant for the Truth upon Earth, ye Rulers of *England,* and give over building up *Sion* with Blood, and *Jerusalem* with iniquity." [12] Must ministers possess secular knowledge in order to serve God? There is no Scripture for this; no Scripture for baptism; no Scripture either for particular doctrines, or for churches which you allow no one to enter except yourselves. Deusbery pleads for the rejection of all sects and doctrines: "Come out of *Babylon,* all Forms, and Observations, and Traditions, which are set up by the will of man." [13] Trust only to the light of conscience, and persecute no man for his peculiar vision. Thus Deusbery, like so many of his contemporaries: He omits to advise the state how nine thousand parish ministers, supported by church traditions and tithe customs centuries old, can suddenly reject all such forms and benefits, and follow the inner light, some men leaving families behind, as many wandering Quakers did, as Christian was to do in *Pilgrim's Progress,* preaching only from the mysterious vision within.

In its issue of January 31–February 8, the *Weekly Intelligencer* re-

[11] *Ibid.*, p. 17. [12] E727(19), p. 8. [13] *Ibid.*, p. 16.

ported that a group of Quakers not far from Newcastle had tried on February 3 to interrupt the minister's Sunday morning sermon. A melee ensued. The parishioners attacked the Quakers, almost killing two of them. Frightened by the attack, the Quakers dropped to their knees and began to tremble. At this sight some parishioners were struck with remorse and began to accuse each other for attacking such harmless people. When the sermon ended, the minister was asked to discuss issues with the Quakers; many parishioners, however, opposed such a concession and made some insulting comments to the proposers. At this point another melee broke out, this time between the two groups of the congregation. Many joined in, and by the end of the fight scarcely a man remained who was not injured in head or hand.[14] Whether apocryphal or not, this news story reflects the widespread explosive response to Quaker doctrines, the fearless pacifism of the Quakers (whatever their trembling in moments of persecution), and the divided sentiments of a normal congregation toward a sportsmanlike consideration of strange religious ideas in an era of sharp and painful divisions among orthodox believers.[15]

In the early months of the Protectorate the mystic royalist Arise Evans was busy again with prophecies and visions. In March, 1652, in *An Eccho to the Voice from Heaven,* Evans had prophesied that "God will bring in the king," and that after Cromwell there would be "a King again in *England.*" [16] On May 16, 1653, less than a month after Cromwell had dissolved the Rump, Evans had petitioned Cromwell and his officers to place Charles II upon the throne of England! [17] On May 26, 1653, according to his own statement in his preface to *The Bloudy Vision of John Farly,* Evans had delivered a petition for Charles to the Council of the Army, and had disputed with the officers some four hours, setting forth in speech much more than he had ever put in print. Only a few days before the December 12 dissolution, Evans had sent forth his *Bloudy Vision of John Farly Interpreted by Arise Evans,* saying in his preface, *"Why do not ye bend the strength of your prayers for* Charls your right *King,* and his party, that they may enjoy their rights again?" [18] Evans demanded to know what had become of all the properties taken from the king and the church. What had become of the crown lands?

By February, 1654, however, Evans' prophecies had began to exalt the

[14] E728(2), p. 153. [15] See Cromwell's proclamation, below, p. 269.

[16] E1304(2), pp. 88, 116.

[17] 669f17(7). Evans admonishes Cromwell and his associates that "without their conjunction to their Native and right King, there is no hope of peace, certainty, or safety to this Nation, nor to your selves (most Noble Worthies), whose actions are glorious, though as yet much imperfect."

[18] December 10, 1653, E1498, the preface, sig. A5 (dated at the end September 13, 1653).

bright vistas of a Cromwellian England. On February 9 appeared *The Declaration of Arise Evans,* a pamphlet boasting of his former prophecies and reminding his readers how many of his prophecies have come true. Had he not foretold the death of Charles I? Had not God through him "declared the most remarkable things that befel these kingdoms since the wars began"? Now a glorious future awaits the new Protectorate. Evans exhorts his reader "to submit to OLIVER your supream Governor and Lord Protector." [19] On February 15 appeared a new tract exalting Cromwell, *The Great and Bloody Visions,* in which Evans interpreted two trances of John Farly. In one vision Farly saw a newly sown wheat field, on which were gathered a circle of white doves, with a dove of surpassing brightness alone in the center. To Evans the milk white doves in the field were the saintly leaders who had supported Cromwell; the dove alone and brightest of all is the great leader himself, who "in due time will shine like the Sun over all the earth." [20] Evans' stated confidence in his prophetic powers was boundless. He compares himself indeed to Saul of Tarsus. "I hope I shall be cleer from the blood of this Generation," he wrote, "being sent of God to declare the things hereafter mentioned." [21] Many events had proved that God spoke his will through his prophet Evans.

Of all the strange offshoots of religious behavior, a belief in witchcraft was one of the few that could claim common acceptance among the various sects from left to right. In its issue of February 21–27, *Perfect Occurrences* reported that a certain Frances Beard had been tried at the Old Bailey for bewitching a child on Thames Street. Some four months previously the child had been stricken lame in the left leg, then in the right arm, "sometimes lying raging and speechless, and at other times foaming at the mouth." Some weeks after the child had been taken ill, she saw Frances Beard come walking along the street, whereupon she began to scream and made certain signs which the parents interpreted as accusations that Mistress Beard had caused her illness. The parents at once had Mistress Beard arrested and brought before a justice of the peace, who committed her to Newgate to await trial for bewitching a child. When she was accused and tried at the Old Bailey, witnesses testified against her. Officials who examined her asserted that they found "three long teats near her privie Parts, which she said were only the Pyles." [22] This evidence to the court appeared to be overwhelming; Mistress Beard was convicted of witchcraft and cast again into prison, along with others who were likely to suffer execution.

[19] E224(1), pp. 1, 4. [20] E224(2), p. 8. [21] *Declaration,* E224(1), p. 1.
[22] E730(11), p. 16.

Chapter XXVIII

MOULIN'S *CLAMOR* AND MILTON'S *SECOND DEFENCE*

August, 1652–May, 1654

THE *Cry of the Royal Blood,* which had appeared in August, 1652, was an attack too formidable for Milton to let pass, whatever the agony of blindness and the press of his daily duties for the Council of State. Less scholarly and more bitter in tone than *Defensio Regia,* the *Clamor* contained many biting personal references to Milton that in his mind called for a harsh and bitter rebuttal. Moreover, the king worship of the author, Pierre Du Moulin, was to Milton more blatant and superstitious than that of Salmasius. "The majesty of kings," wrote Du Moulin in his opening sentences, "has been sacred in all ages, since it is the image of the divine, the well-being of the people, and the life of the laws." [1] Compared to execution of Charles, the crime of the Jews against Christ was only the shadow of evil. The Jews were blinded to the glory of Christ; the regicides, however, understood full well the legal rights of their sovereign and their responsibility to him. The English struck down not only their king but their church as well. Such action was a mortal danger, as the great Salmasius had proved, to all Protestant monarchies in Europe. Who was to defend such treason? Who was to answer the great Salmasius? Selden, claims Du Moulin, refused the task, and the universities had been purged of many learned men by the tyrannical republic. Only one republican was found who could write Latin, a certain John Milton: "Who he was and where he came from was in doubt, whether a man, or a worm voided from the dung pit." [2] A seditious man, this Milton. Had he not been expelled from Cambridge? Had he not championed divorce initiated by either husband or wife? From the overthrow of marriages Milton had turned to the toppling of kingdoms, justifying the regicides in their unprecedented crime, saying in effect, "I did it." In the loathsome book *Eikonoklastes* he "reviles the sacred spirit of King Charles." [3] Finally, in his slanderous reply to Salmasius, Milton attempts

[1] Tr. Paul Blackford; *Clamor* (1652), p. 1: "Cum omnibus saeculis sacra fuerit Regum Majestas, utpote Divinae imago, populi salus, & vita legum."

[2] Tr. Blackford, Appendix D, below, p. 1050; *Clamor* (1652), pp. 8–9: "Quis & unde dubium, homone [sic] an vermis heri è sterquilinio editus."

[3] Tr. Blackford, Appendix D, below, p. 1051; *Clamor* (1652), p. 10: "Sanctis Caroli Regis Manibus teterrimus carnifex insultat."

to ennoble the horrible crime of the republicans with accents of justice and the pious strain of religious justification.

Du Moulin is acutely aware that his task is a humbler one than that of the great Salmasius: "For who wielded a brush after Apelles?" Later he asks, "Who would dare follow you?" Moulin writes for the relatively unlearned readers. They also should be exhorted to raise their cries to heaven against the parricides. In addressing them and defending kingship, he can reply to Milton in kind, dealing him insult for insult, blow for blow. "Do you, you dung-heap, you blockhead, do you dare to gnaw away at men of Salmasius' calibre?" [4] A man like Milton does not deserve a reply to the graceful and eloquent rhythms of the master scholar. Salmasius' dignity does not permit him to descend into the pit of brawling indignities which Milton's methods have made necessary.

In the series of verses at the end of *Clamor,* Moulin inserts the harshest epithets against Milton that any enemy had yet loosened against him. "Seize him! Quick! Quick!" cries Moulin. "Bind him hands and feet! I owe him the sacred rites of the scourge. First, prod with a goad, this future disciple to a gallows, this great bulwark of the people, this prop of Parliament." [5] In the pages that follow Moulin calls Milton a great *stinking pestilence,* an *impious tormentor,* a *gallows slave,* a *dark pettifogger.* To Moulin Milton is an ulcer to the church and a poison to religion. In his contest with Salmasius he is like a mouse scourging an elephant, a frog reviling a panther, an ape scoffing at a bear. What! Milton teaching Salmasius how to write Latin! He is like a pig teaching Minerva, a Thersites teaching Nestor. As an enemy of the public, Milton is "more savage than Busiris, more fierce than a tigress seeking her whelps," yet "less warlike than a scared rabbit . . . fouler than a toad, filthier than a prostitute." [6] Moulin's battery of epithets against Milton

[4] Tr. Blackford, Appendix D, below, p. 1078; *Clamor* (1652), p. 163:

> Ten sterquilinium, ten cucurbitae caput,
> Ausum Monarchas rodere, ten *Salmasios?*

[5] Tr. Blackford, Appendix D, below, p. 1078; *Clamor* (1652), p. 162:

> Eho nefandum carnificem Lorarii
> Corripite jam jam, quadrupedem constringite;
> Solemne debeo Virgidemiae sacrum.
> Hunc vos futurum discipulum cruci, prius
> Stimulis forate, grande praesidium popli,
> Columen Senatus.

[6] Tr. Blackford, Appendix D, below, p. 1080; *Clamor* (1652), p. 169:

> . . . saevior Busiride,
> Quaerente catulos tygride concitatior,
> Idem es fugaci imbellior cuniculo,
> Populo execranti simia contemptior,
> Minor pediclo, turpior bufonibus,
> Summaenianis nuribus inquinatior.

was without precedent in his fiercest polemic experience and unthinkable in the relatively sedate prose of the learned Salmasius. To Moulin, Milton is "shriller than a parricide feeding upon vipers . . . viler than Cromwell, more damned than Ravaillac." It is only in the light of such epithets that the reader can understand the harshness of Milton's replies to *Clamor* in the pages of *Second Defence.*

In the chapters that follow, Moulin recounts in horrified accents the crimes of the English rebels that Milton has justified. Nothing could be more remote from the sober analysis of a royalist like Clarendon, for example, than Moulin's historical simplifications and exhortative manner. "As if the gates of law and shame had been broken," he writes, "the torrent of rebellion overflooded itself and inundated three kingdoms equally with one deluge." [7] The queen driven to exile; the rise of the Independents in army and Parliament; Cromwell, "worst of tormentors put fear into the best of kings"; the high court of justice recruited from the most savage opponents of the king, including the dregs of London, barkeepers, mechanics, cobblers, soldiers from the army long hostile to kingship; the revolutionary demands of the Parliament, the accusation of the king; the farce of a trial; the London ministers pleading in vain for the king's life; the incendiary Hugh Peters, an adulterer who had forsworn the ministry, urging the king's death from the pulpit.

One virtue of the *Clamor* is its frequent quotations of English sources neglected in the main by Salmasius in *Defensio Regia.* In his account of the actual trial of Charles, Moulin's narrative suddenly takes on a dignity incompatible with his many diatribes against the lawless Independents, especially when he quotes Charles' reply to Bradshaw's statement that Charles had been called into court by authority of the English people, by whom he has been elected. The king replied, says Moulin, as follows:

> The kingdom had by no means devolved upon him by an election, but by a succession of above a thousand years; that he asserted the rights of the English people more fully and better by rejecting an authority unlawful and set up at pleasure than they by asserting the same. If they would boast of the authority of the Parliament, there was no one here (he glanced around at the standing crowd) to be seen from the ranks of the lords, without which he denied that a Parliament could be set up; also a king, who might issue a judgment about a king, ought to be present. But neither one house of the Parliament nor the other, nor any other court in the whole world, had the right to force the king of England into line,

[7] Tr. Blackford; *Clamor* (1652), p. 25: "Inde quasi ruptis legum & pudoris repagulis, effudit se rebellionis torrens, triaque Regna uno diluvio pariter inundavit."

> much less a few seditious judges conferring upon themselves the authority of the lower house which they themselves had trampled down.[8]

Moulin describes not inelegantly the demeanor of the king before the court; his courtesy to his enemies, even in the shadow of condemnation, and Bradshaw's repeated refusals to hear him speak in his own defense; his refusals to reply to the charges against him, denying that any peers existed by whom legally his case might be judged: "He ordered them in turn to give a reason for having usurped power against their king; with him life was at a small price compared with reputation, conscience, laws, and the liberty of the people, all of which were being destroyed in their own defence in the presence of such judges." Were not all actions in Parliament, Charles had asked, taken in the name of the king? The House of Commons was not permitted to act as a court to punish the meanest citizen, much less the king himself. When for the third time Bradshaw ordered the captive led away from the tribunal, the king had said, "Remember it is your king from whom you turn your ears." What justice, he had asked, could the people as a whole expect from these men when they denied the king himself leave to speak in his own defense?

The insults that the king suffered from the soldiers and other onlookers Moulin describes without exaggeration: the soldiers spitting on his clothes, one man spitting on his face; soldiers blowing smoke in his face as he passed along, throwing their broken pipes at his feet; profane soldiers night and day invading his chambers, laughing at his prayers, jeering and mocking his devotions, distracting him with questions. On the fatal day, when he was led from St. James' palace to Whitehall, walking about five hundred steps through the park between, continues Moulin, he "seemed rather to fly than to walk to his death, complaining to the spear-armed guards for their slowness." On the scaffold, obliged to speak only to his enemies, he denied the accusations against him once more, saying, "I never conscripted an army before my enemies took up arms against me." Charles' confession of guilt on the scaffold for his part in the fall of Strafford draws high praise from Moulin. After the fatal stroke, asserts Moulin, the enemies of the king smeared their hands with his blood, dipped their staffs in his blood, carried away the bloody chips around the block. Even the bloody hairs of his head were carried away and sold. These gory happenings were no doubt exaggerated by royalist writers; but in the main the most unbiased sources have substantiated the story as repeated by Moulin, a story far more vivid and detailed than had appeared in Salmasius' *Defensio Regia*. It is significant that Milton

[8] Tr. Blackford, Appendix D, below, p. 1060; *Clamor* (1652), p. 58.

makes no attempt in *Second Defence* to deny the general authenticity of Moulin's account of the trial and execution of Charles.

MILTON SENDS FORTH *A SECOND DEFENCE*
May 30, 1654

Almost two years elapsed before Milton was able to send forth his response to *The Cry of the Royal Blood*. *A Second Defence* is not a point-by-point or chapter-by-chapter rebuttal of Milton's antagonist, as in *Eikonoklastes* and *A Defence*. To have replied in this accepted manner of the day would have meant rewriting many of the arguments he had set forth in these two tracts.[1] Rather, therefore, Milton selects from his opponent's onslaughts those he feels most obligated to reply to. In making such a selection, he felt bound to answer first the many personal insults scattered through *The Cry of the Royal Blood,* Vlacq's dedicatory preface to Charles II, and Moulin's verses, "In Impurissimum Nebulonem Johannem Miltonum," printed at the end of *The Cry*.[2] The result of this method of selection and reply is a much more self-centered polemic than any prose work Milton had hitherto written except *Doctrine and Discipline of Divorce.* Milton opens his tract with a pious thankfulness to God that he was born in a time of crisis, a time that called forth the greatest deeds of magnanimity and valor yet known in the world, deeds that delivered the state from the dominance of one man and the church from abject slavery. In the struggle, continues Milton, he is proud that he was selected by the republic to reply to the great Salmasius, in which task he overwhelmed his antagonist and forced him to retire from the polemic battlefield with his will to reply shattered and his reputation in ruins. Victorious over Salmasius, who was now silent forever, Milton imagined that his task was at an end. Some indeed would lay the guilt of Salmasius' death upon Milton himself. In this passing reference to Salmasius, Milton writes, "I shall not impute his death as a crime to him, as he imputed my blindness to me."[3] This reference to Milton's blindness is suggestive of the prevailing tone of *Second Defence,* which is more in the tradition of personal justification than the elaboration of principles which Milton had concentrated on in his reply to *Defensio Regia.*

At the beginning of his tract Milton feels at a great disadvantage because he does not know who his opponent is. "You there!" he cries,

[1] See Milton's own statement, below, p. 549. For preface and notes to text of *Second Defence* by Donald A. Roberts, see below, pp. 538–686.

[2] *Clamor* (1654), pp. 162–72.

[3] *Second Defence,* below, p. 559.

"Who are you? A man or a nobody? Surely the basest of men—not even slaves—are without a name. Shall I then always contend with those who are nameless?" In order to reply to the bitter personal attacks of his antagonist, Milton must identify his opponent. How resourcefully he tried to do this we still do not know. Certainly he selected More as his target on relatively weak evidence. "For either he has been basely hired," continues Milton, "and, after the fashion of Salmasius, has sold this Cry of his to the royal blood," or he desires to conceal a scandalous life. Then, without any evidence so far discovered, Milton names More as his antagonist. More was vulnerable to bitter satire. Milton writes, "He happened to have conceived a passion for a certain maidservant of his host, and although she not long afterwards married another, he did not cease to pursue her. The neighbors had often noticed that they entered all by themselves a certain summerhouse in the garden."[4]

A Second Defence opens, then, with two strains of rhetoric, one on a high level of moral and patriotic justification of his task, and the other in the strain of personal vilification of his imagined opponent. On the other hand, no prose Milton wrote except the troubled and unlovely passages of *Pro Se Defensio* is as bitter and on the whole unjustified as his attacks on More in *A Second Defence.* No passages in Milton's prose are richer in autobiography and self-revelation than those of *A Second Defence.*

We are indebted to Moulin's attacks on Milton's person for the autobiographical replies, which help us to visualize Milton more clearly than any other passages he wrote about himself in prose or verse. When, says Milton, his opponent can find nothing to blame in his life or in his manners, he casts aspersion upon his personal appearance and upbraids him for his blindness. At first Moulin calls him "A monster, dreadful, ugly, huge, deprived of sight." But immediately, says Milton, he corrects himself by saying, "Yet not huge, for there is nothing more feeble, bloodless, and pinched." It is true, says Milton, that he is not a tall man, but he is rather of middle height than diminutive. But "why is that stature called small which is great enough for virtue?"[5] In his younger years, says Milton, he was skilled in the use of the sword and practiced its use daily. In those years he thought himself a match for any man, however much stronger than he, and able to protect himself against any insult that might pass between two men. Now, years later, says Milton, he has the same strength and eager spirit of his younger years. The only difference is that now he is blind. Yet his eyes are

[4] *Second Defence,* below, pp. 560, 563, 565–66.
[5] *Second Defence,* below, pp. 582, 583.

without any cloudiness of color, clear and bright as the eyes of those with perfect vision. In his appearance of a seeing person, continues Milton, he is indeed a dissembler, but a dissembler against his will. Though his antagonist has spoken of him as "nothing more bloodless," he is so youthful looking that almost everyone would think him ten years younger than forty.[6]

When *Second Defence* appeared, Milton had been blind almost two years, since about February 28, 1652.[7] Already he envisioned himself as a part of the community of blind men who live in the light of God's special favor and concern. This divine protection makes those who are blind secure against the slings and arrows of angry men, so much so, says Milton, that the darkness of blindness seems to have come from the overreaching of heavenly wings.[8] At this point Milton anticipates the passage in his invocation to light in which all the sufferings of the blind have a divine compensation in the extended powers of inward illumination:

> So much the rather thou, celestial Light,
> Shine inward, and the mind through all her powers
> Irradiate, there plant eyes, all mist from thence
> Purge and disperse, that I may see and tell
> Of things invisible to mortal sight.[9]

Milton also reminds his antagonist of the great blind heroes of Israel, Greece, and Rome. There was Isaac himself, who experienced many years of blindness. Who more memorable in Greek life and literature than the blind Tiresias, the prophet Phineus, or Timoleon of Corinth? Thus does Milton dwell on his blindness as a benefit conferred by God amid his suffering: "... let no one mourn for my eyes, which were lost in the cause of honor." Blindness indeed is a suffering tolerable, even friendly, compared to many other evils. "Not blindness but the inability to endure blindness is a source of misery."[10] Like the prophets of old, says Milton, he is not without honor in his own country. Because he is thus handicapped, the state has taken away none of his dignity or any public office he held while he could see. It does not diminish in any way the work or the favors which it assigned to him. Indeed, as did the Athenians in ancient times, the state has given him a maintenance in the Prytaneum—that is, provided quarters for him and his family at Whitehall, the center of government.[11] In such passages on the significance of

[6] At the time Milton wrote *Second Defence* he was forty-five years old. When Milton wrote " 'Ere half my days," he was over forty. It is a curious fact that in references to his age Milton consistently makes himself appear younger than he actually was.

[7] French, *Life Records,* III, 197.

[8] *Second Defence,* below, p. 590.

[9] *Paradise Lost,* III, 51–55.

[10] *Second Defence,* below, pp. 591, 584.

[11] *Ibid.,* below, p. 591.

his blindness and the honor he holds in the state, Milton rises to a high eloquence in the midst of his self-praise. But a moment later he is reduced, alas, to the hurling of epithets at an antagonist still unknown.

Moulin's attempt to diminish his stature both as a physical personality and as a leader of the English rebels, a kind of characterization the learned Salmasius had not attempted, has struck Milton at a sensitive point. His answer is an autobiographical sketch in *Second Defence,* a deliberate attempt to show his high place in the world of learned and creative men. Milton does not claim a gentle birth for his father, nor does he even mention the elder Milton's accomplishments. The undeviating integrity of his father and the charitable activities of his mother are significant of the values he held to be most precious. A proud sense of his own worth and the honor he owes his parents animate Milton in these passages, so much so that for the moment his antagonist fades into the background. So intense had been his desire for learning, he writes, that from the time he was twelve he rarely went to bed before midnight. As for his years at Cambridge (years aloof from all profligate conduct), Milton asserts that he had the admiration of the fellow students he most cherished. The significance of the five years of meditation and growth at Horton, in which Milton read *in the order of time,* he passes by with no more than a sentence. In telling of his tour abroad, he feels it necessary to show that his social position was high enough to require the services of a servant. Such a symbol of his place in the world of men was much less revealing, however, than his reference to Sir Henry Wotton's letter of good wishes and advice of importance to a young man traveling in Europe. By his mention of Thomas, Viscount Scudamore of Sligo, Milton shows that he was not unacceptable in social rank to high circles of aristocratic life. In his many references to learned men in *Second Defence,* particularly Holstentius, Manso, and Gaddi, Milton portrays himself as a highly respected and eagerly sought visitor among the most advanced circles of the countries which he visited. Moreover, though he had spoken with complete freedom and without embarrassment about his Protestant convictions, he had been warmly welcomed by Catholic scholars.[12]

Milton traces with some care the itinerary of his continental tour beginning with his trip from London to Paris in late April or early May, 1638. In Paris he called upon the English ambassador, Lord Scudamore, and through Scudamore met Hugo Grotius, then ambassador from Sweden to the French nation. From Paris, Milton traveled south to Nice, thence by ship to Genoa. After visiting Leghorn and Pisa, he came to Florence, where he spent two months, August and September, 1638. One of the enigmas of Milton's recollections of Italy is his failure to mention

[12] See *Second Defence,* below, pp. 612–16.

any of the great paintings or works of sculpture which he must have seen in Florence. But we know from *Areopagitica* that he did visit Galileo, then in his seventy-eighth year and blind: "There it was that I found and visited the famous *Galileo* grown old, a prisoner to the Inquisition, for thinking in Astronomy otherwise then the Franciscan and Dominican licencers thought."[13] From Florence Milton traveled to Venice, thence to Rome, where he stayed another two months. Next he traveled south in a leisurely manner to Naples, where he was entertained by the illustrious Giovanni Battista Manso, who showed Milton over the city and visited him several times at his own lodgings. Intending to pass over into Sicily and Greece, Milton had tidings of the civil war impending in England. Of the decision not to go to Greece he wrote, "I thought it base that I should travel abroad at my ease for the cultivation of my mind, while my fellow-citizens at home were fighting for liberty."[14] Yet Milton did not at once return to England. Instead he went on to Rome and again to Florence, where he spent another two months. Later he stayed another month in Venice. Crossing to Switzerland by way of Milan and the Pennine Alps, he stopped at Geneva. There he spent some weeks conferring daily with John Diodati, the great professor of divinity. Passing then into France, he came to Paris and thence to London, having been away from England a year and three months.

That part of the autobiography in which Milton describes the conditions that brought forth his earliest prose works is on the whole a factual and balanced narrative. Milton shows that he was more fully prepared than most of his contemporaries to participate in the revolution at hand. The ritual of the Anglican service which he had loved in his youth was now completely subordinate to the need for expelling the bishops from their power and reforming both state and church. He had studied the moral, legal, and religious justification by which man could remove himself from every kind of slavery. Milton's tracing of his early polemic agitation in *Second Defence* is pointed and economical: his five antiprelatical tracts, the first of which traces the fundamentals of church reform; his divorce tracts, dealing with the pressing need for reform of marriage laws; and his *Areopagitica,* tracing the dire need for freedom of printed ideas and removal of censorship. Thus far (until 1649), said Milton, he had written nothing about the rights of kings, nor had he discussed this subject until the king had been vanquished in war and pronounced an enemy by Parliament and condemned by the High Court of Justice. Only then, says Milton, incited by Presbyterian ministers who had formerly condemned Charles in a most bitter fashion, had he undertaken to justify Charles' trial and execution.[15]

[13] *Complete Prose,* II, 538; Masson, I, 788.

[14] *Second Defence,* below, pp. 617–20.

[15] *Ibid.,* below, pp. 620–26.

Milton is proudly boastful of his services to the state and the church. He has supported himself while writing for the cause of reform, not petitioning any body of men for subsistence but depending upon his own limited private fortune. Neither the Commonwealth nor the church gave him either honors or subsidies. "Other men gained for themselves advantages, other men secured offices at no cost to themselves. As for me, no man has ever seen me soliciting aught through my friends, clinging with suppliant expression to the doors of Parliament, or loitering in the hallways of the lower assemblies." [16] This passage realistically represents Milton's patriotic outlook and contribution to the state. He was a self-subsidized reformer. Unlike his predecessors John Donne and Francis Bacon he had not petitioned great men of the court for favors or advancement. Another patriotic endeavor on Milton's part, he says, was the writing of the history of his own nation from remotest times, four books of which he had finished by January, 1649. One must grant in perspective the realism of Milton's assessment of his motives and accomplishments in the reforms he thought imperative. A poet by choice, he had injected himself into reformation on many fronts, thinking like Dante that a man cannot become a really great poet without acting the part of a fearless citizen and patriot. The Council of State of the new republic invited him, says Milton, to serve his nation in the field of foreign affairs. When *Eikon Basilike* appeared, written with great malice against the new republic, Milton was ordered by the Council to answer it. Milton's book, *Eikonoklastes,* was no insult to the king, as Moulin claims, but rather a projection of Milton's conviction that he should serve Queen Truth rather than King Charles.

A little more than midway through *Second Defence,* Milton reveals that he has other purposes than merely replying to his antagonist. He is uneasy about the events of the Protectorate, which had been proclaimed December 16, 1653.[17] Between his autobiographical passages and his praise of civil and military heroes, Milton inserts, as if for Cromwell's attention, a panegyric of John Bradshaw, who has been attacked, it is true, by Moulin as the wicked president of the High Court of Justice which tried the king. Bradshaw had been twice appointed president of the Council of State, but he had been outside the government since April 20, 1653, when Cromwell had dissolved the Rump Parliament. Hours after dismissing the Rump, Cromwell had entered the offices of the Council of State and said, "Gentlemen, if you are met here as private persons, you shall not be disturbed; but if as a Council of State, this is no place for you; and since you cannot but know what was done at the

[16] *Ibid.,* below, p. 627.

[17] *Instrument of Government, Acts and Ordinances,* II, 813–22; see also Gardiner, *Commonwealth and Protectorate,* II, 330.

House in the morning, so take notice that the Parliament is dissolved." On that occasion Bradshaw had answered Cromwell with composure and resolution. "Sir," he had said, "we have heard what you did at the House in the morning, and before many hours all England will hear it; but, Sir, you are mistaken to think that the Parliament is dissolved; for no power under heaven can dissolve them but themselves; therefore take you notice of that."[18] On December 16, 1653, when Cromwell had been installed as Protector, Bradshaw had refused to support him. At the time Milton wrote *Second Defence,* however, the break between Bradshaw and Cromwell was not yet irrevocable. Bradshaw had not yet declared, as he was later to do, that "if he was to have a master, he preferred Charles to Oliver."[19] Milton's insertion of high praise for Bradshaw reflects a personal loyalty he was evidently eager to place on record. Milton describes Bradshaw as "the most faithful of friends, and, in every change of fortune, the most to be relied upon." To Milton, Bradshaw is a rounded man in the great tradition:

> No man more quickly and freely recognizes those who deserve well of him, whoever they may be, nor pursues them with greater kindness. Sometimes it is the godly, sometimes the learned, sometimes men famed for any kind of genius, sometimes, too, soldiers and heroes, reduced to poverty, whom he assists out of his own resources. If they are in no need, he yet honors and welcomes them gladly. He is wont always to shout the praises of other men, to be silent about his own.[20]

No man more than Bradshaw, asserts Milton, is ready to forgive his political enemies or defend the cause of the oppressed. No threats can turn him aside from the habit of intrepid support of friends or rectitude of action. Though it is true that Bradshaw is a special target in Moulin's *Clamor,* Milton's character of him in *Second Defence* is so detailed and personal in tone as to make the reader think it was intended for Cromwell's perusal rather than Moulin's.

On still other issues Milton makes clear he is dissatisfied with Cromwell's rule. He advises the Protector to abrogate more old laws than create new ones. The education of youth in England is still woefully deficient. The country as a whole needs to take many steps forward in this vital peacetime concern. In a society of intellectually curious men, says Milton, Cromwell should provide the citizens a wide liberty of publishing their ideas without the interference of the censor. Returning to the strain of *Areopagitica,* he declares that nothing more than freedom of the press would contribute toward the expansion of truth and the propagation of knowledge. Nor should the learning of choice spirits

[18] Gardiner, *Commonwealth and Protectorate,* II, 265. [19] *Ibid.,* III, 186.
[20] *Second Defence,* below, pp. 638–39.

be restricted by the narrowmindedness and the censure of lesser minds. "May you always take the side of those," exhorts Milton, "who think that not just their own party or faction, but all citizens equally have an equal right to freedom in the state." [21] In the paragraph that follows, addressed to his fellow-countrymen, he introduces a sentence possibly directed at Cromwell rather than at the citizens in general: "Many men has war made great whom peace makes small."

Later in *Second Defence,* in the midst of his panegyric to Cromwell, Milton again writes as the protagonist of those leaders no longer at Cromwell's right hand. He deliberately turns aside to address Thomas Fairfax, whom he compares to Scipio Africanus of old. "You have defeated, not only the enemy, but ambition as well, and the thirst for glory which conquers all the most eminent men," he writes, "and you are reaping the reward of your virtues and noble deeds amid that most delightful and glorious retirement which is the end of all labors and human action, even the greatest." [22] Could Fairfax have retired, had he not left Cromwell at the helm of state, pillar of liberty? Milton is less than ingenuous when he thus suggests that Fairfax is satisfied with the turn of events. But his insertion of praise to Fairfax in the midst of his address to Cromwell is a pointed reminder of Milton's own scale of values in his evaluation of the Protectorate.

Toward the end of *Second Defence,* after his naming of Whitelocke, Pickering, Strickland, Sydenham, Sidney, Montague, and Lawrence, two of whom had withdrawn from active service in the Protectorate, Milton's admonitions to Cromwell take on a new directness. He is still deeply troubled that no sharp separation has been made between church and state:

> I would have you leave the church to the church and shrewdly relieve yourself and the government of half your burden . . . and not permit two powers, utterly diverse, the civil and the ecclesiastical, to make harlots of each other while appearing to strengthen, by their mingled and spurious riches, actually to undermine and at length destroy each other. I would have you remove all power from the church (but power will never be absent so long as money, the poison of the church, the quinsy of truth, extorted by force even from those who are unwilling, remains the price of preaching the Gospel). I would have you drive from the temple the money-changers, who buy and sell, not doves, but the Dove, the Holy Spirit Himself.[23]

No passage Milton wrote concentrates in so short a space his fundamental opposition to state payment of ministers, especially payment forcibly extracted from those who did wish to support the church. Such

[21] *Ibid.*, p. 679. [22] *Ibid.*, below, p. 669. [23] *Ibid.*, below, p. 678.

a system, asserts Milton, is an affront to the very essence of Christianity.

Milton is not content with this sharp admonition to Cromwell on the point of his deepest convictions. Sir Henry Vane is present even though Milton does not name him. Vane, to whom Milton had addressed his sonnet of July, 1652, is now an outsider of the state he helped so actively to create. "Sir Henry Vane! Sir Henry Vane!"[24] Cromwell had cried on that historic occasion of April 20, 1653. "The Lord deliver me from Sir Henry Vane!" Vane's name is such a striking omission in Milton's list of noble republicans that no sophisticated reader would have overlooked its significance.

The admonitions Milton addresses to his fellow-countrymen at the end of *Second Defence* show his profound belief in the equation of private with political morality. Only the arts of peace, not those of war, asserts Milton, can make England a more virtuous nation. But the foundation of political virtue exerted in time of peace is freedom from those vices which make the soul a slave. Not even Cromwell or Brutus himself could save a nation from inward corruption. However much some people cry for liberty, they are slaves without knowing it. Just as "to be free is precisely the same as to be pious, wise, just, and temperate, careful of one's property, aloof from another's, and thus finally to be magnanimous and brave, so to be the opposite to these qualities is the same as to be a slave."[25] At this point Milton comes to one of his most unrealistic exhortations addressed to his fellow-countrymen: "You, therefore, who wish to remain free, either be wise at the outset, or recover your senses as soon as possible."[26] Such passages reveal as no others in his prose Milton's contempt for those men who are slaves to their passions, men he thought were generally found among the lower classes. Unless one is master of his passions, he does not deserve political freedom: "Such is the decree of law and of nature herself, that he who cannot control himself . . . should not be his own master."[27] In the midst of such unrealistic exhortations, Milton inserts a passage on the principle of a wider suffrage supported by the Levellers: "For why should anyone then claim for you freedom to vote or the power of sending to Parliament whomever you prefer? So that each of you could elect in the cities men of his own faction . . . however unworthy . . . ?"[28] To Milton it was axiomatic that wicked men, slaves to their passions, would elect to office men of their own unbridled desires. Except in the last great poems, no more profound statement of distrust of democratic action was to come from Milton's pen.

[24] Gardiner, *Commonwealth and Protectorate*, II, 263.
[25] *Second Defence*, below, p. 684.
[26] *Ibid.*, below, p. 684.
[27] *Ibid.*, below, p. 684.
[28] *Ibid.*, below, p. 682.

Chapter XXIX

THE MARCH OF EVENTS

1654–1655

THE Nominated Parliament, which had first met July 4, 1653, had resigned its powers to Cromwell December 12. On September 3, 1654, the first Parliament under the *Instrument of Government* met at Westminster. By the *Instrument* the suffrage electing the new Parliamentarians had been more severely restricted than under the monarchy or the Commonwealth. Royalists of course had been disqualified. In the boroughs, where the influence of Puritan sympathizers was likely to be strongest, the franchise had been left untouched (or augmented by the admission of the free burgesses). Even so, the vote in the boroughs had been very small; in Colchester, the total number of men voting in 1654 was only two hundred. In the counties, where the influence of the royalists was strong, the vote had been no longer allowed to the forty-shilling freeholder; the franchise had been limited to those possessing real estate or personal property valued at two hundred pounds.[1] Under such restrictions, the new Parliament contained a sizable number of Presbyterians, men of substance whom Cromwell hoped would support his program. Of the fifty-six radicals who had voted against tithes and a state ministry in the Barebones Parliament, only four were returned to the Parliament that met September 3, 1654.[2]

It soon became evident, however, that even with this Parliament Cromwell was to face thorny dilemmas. In his mind they had no right to challenge either his prerogative or any part of the *Instrument of Government*. Before his first speech in the Painted Chamber, September 4, he had to some minds displayed almost kingly arrogance, first, in not speaking to them in the House, second, in surrounding his coach with a hundred officers and soldiers who marched with bared heads on the way to the Chamber. In the days that followed several new members of the Commons asked embarrassing questions: Was the House prepared to leave all supervision of the law to one man? Was no man to have free speech to attack the title of Protector? Was Oliver to be

[1] Gardiner, *Constitutional Documents,* p. 141; Gardiner, *Commonwealth and Protectorate,* III, 172–78.

[2] Gardiner, *Commonwealth and Protectorate,* III, 176.

sole judge of election returns? Many of the London clergy, in their prayers of Sunday, September 10, pleaded for the Lord's support of their Parliament; only a few prayed for the Protector. Was Oliver's power not to be limited as Parliament thought fit? Could the members of the Council of State not be elected by the Commons every three years? To a republican like Bradshaw, a master like Charles was more acceptable than a dictator like Cromwell. Most members, however, preferred Oliver if he could subordinate his own role to that of Parliament. Harrison introduced a note of violence by asserting he would petition the Commons to resist tyranny, for which cause he himself would rally twenty thousand men. For this bold threat Harrison was arrested and soon on his way from Staffordshire to London to answer for his sedition.[3]

Such challenges to his authority under the *Instrument of Government* Cromwell could not long ignore. Whatever his deficiencies in the art of government, he possessed an uncanny sense of the timely moment to impose his will on the turbulent tide of England's upheaval. On September 12, speaking to Parliament again in the Painted Chamber, he struck again and again with the hammer of his will. "I said you were a free Parliament," he told them. "And so you are, whilst you own the government and authority that called you hither." As Cromwell spoke, he was aware of the lack of that magic a king's name might have had in the reconciliation of warring factions. But he reminded them both of his birth and his experience in civil affairs: "I was by birth a gentleman, living neither in any considerable height, nor yet in obscurity. I have been called . . . to serve in Parliaments."[4] He justified again the dissolution of the Rump. Had he not insisted, many times over, that they put an end to their sitting? When the Barebones Parliament had resigned its power to him, "power . . . boundless and unlimited as before," he had sought with his colleagues a way to reconcile parties through a new constitution, the Instrument of Government. By the *Instrument* no Parliament could make itself perpetual, abolish freedom of conscience, or be denied, while it is sitting, equal power over the militia with the Protector. Would the members agree to uphold the fundamentals of the *Instrument?* If so, concluded the Protector, let them sign the statement prepared for them in the lobby outside the door of the House. When the members examined the document, called the Recognition, about 145 of them signed it at once, reconciled to working within the framework of the new constitution, whatever their private doubts or reservations.[5]

[3] *Ibid.,* III, 181–88.
[4] Abbott, III, 451–52.
[5] *Ibid.,* III, 453, 455, 463.

Four months later, on January 22, 1655, Cromwell came again before the Parliament, spoke for two hours, and in the last sentence of his speech announced its dissolution. "Instead of seasonable providing for the Army," said Oliver, "you have laboured to overthrow the government, and the Army is now upon free quarter." [6] On January 5 the House had voted less than half of the moneys necessary to meet military and naval expenses, a decrease that would have reduced the daily pay of the cavalry soldier to two shillings and of the foot soldier to eight pence. In the eyes of the Protector this vote alone made the position of Parliament untenable. "What signified," Oliver had said earlier, "a provision against perpetuating Parliaments if this power of the militia be solely in them?" [7] The underlying reality of the army's role in English affairs, its purge of the Long Parliament, its creation of the *Instrument of Government,* its support of the Protector, Cromwell could not speak of. To him the army was the means God had placed in his hands to bring forth in England extraordinary fruits "as have not been known in the world these 1000. years." [8] In the last minutes of his speech Cromwell assured his hearers that he could raise money by his power of the *Instrument of Government,* by that same power that brought together the Parliament then assembled in the Painted Chamber.

Though the dismissal of Parliaments alienated old friends and Commonwealth followers of every persuasion, such cleavages were not so dangerous to the Protectorate as royalist plans for an insurrection. About these plans, through his highly efficient network of spies, Cromwell was fully informed; he even had a letter in Charles' own handwriting encouraging an insurrection, which had been set for February 13, 1655. This letter Cromwell showed to the Lord Mayor, aldermen, and members of the Common Council to elicit their raising of a new London militia. He also ordered all suspects arrested and all horses in London seized. Though the uprising was postponed, Cromwell's vigorous preparations continued unabated. On February 24 he issued an edict forbidding horse races for six months, to avoid public gatherings; he knew through his spies the movements of royalist exiles who were charged with inducing the gentry to gather to raise the king's standard at the various city gates on the new time agreed upon, March 8. But to the average royalist the risk to life and property of such a rising was too great to engage in in the teeth of Cromwell's overwhelming police power and force of disciplined troops.[9] The only rising of importance, that led in Wiltshire by Colonel

[6] *Ibid.,* III, 593.
[7] Gardiner, *Commonwealth and Protectorate,* III, 243, 246.
[8] Abbott, III, 592–93.
[9] Gardiner, *Commonwealth and Protectorate,* III, 277–82.

John Penruddock on March 11 and 12, was put down with prompt action. In the trials at Salisbury on April 11 and 12 six of the prisoners were found guilty of treason; of these three were executed. At Exeter following the trial on April 18, of twenty-six prisoners seven were hanged; two prisoners, Penruddock and Grove, were beheaded. The uprising was at an end. Only 139 persons were named as participating in the rising, mainly gentlemen and their servants and associates. On March 24 the Protector announced to the militia commissioners in London that the danger was over, and the militia would not be called out.[10] Thus the crisis passed; the new threat to the Protectorate faded away.

Penruddock's rising was a warning to Cromwell that only a still more watchful vigilance than he had hitherto exercised could keep his power intact. The assumption of a pervasive passive civil loyalty, however reluctant among some groups, was no longer possible. Only military watchfulness subject to his command could he be certain of. A new militia of volunteers loyal to the Protectorate was therefore organized in each county. The counties of England were then divided into ten (later eleven) districts, to each of which Cromwell assigned a major general, under orders "to endeavor the suppressing all Tumults, Insurrections, Rebellion, and other unlawful Assemblies."[11] The twenty-one heads of Cromwell's "Instructions to the Major Generals" were in the main subordinate to this first command. Cavaliers were to be under close surveillance. Each member of a family having servants was required to register with the local militia, a duplicate list to be kept in London. Any person who had fought against the Commonwealth or Protectorate (or had come from abroad) was to register and give notice of any change of residence. Gatherings at stage plays, cock fights, bear baitings, and horse races were prohibited. The major generals and their deputies were to disarm suspicious persons, track down robbers, enforce laws against scandalous ministers, drunkenness, swearing, and breaking of the Sabbath. In the London district all gambling dens and houses of prostitution were to be sought out and suppressed. Cromwell's officers were in effect, then, to watch over the morality as well as the movements of the citizens within their districts.[12] A measure more likely to arouse hostil-

[10] Abbott, III, 648–49, 658–59, 670–71, 689, 696–97, 705.

[11] *Ibid.*, III, 844. For a thorough and illuminating analysis, see David Underdown, *Royalist Conspiracy in England* (New Haven: Yale University Press, 1960), pp. 159–77, "The Major Generals."

[12] *Ibid.*, III, 844–48. In the first part of his long and compelling article, "Cromwell and the Insurrection of 1655," *English Historical Review* (No. X, April, 1888, 323–50), Sir Charles Firth effectively refuted the theory that Cromwell "patched up" the insurrection to conciliate the army and consolidate his power. Firth shows that the idea of appointing major-generals had indeed come from the officers but not until "after or during the insurrection of March 1655."

ity and resistance can scarcely be imagined; but it imposed for the time being a civil quiet (and a protection against uprisings) which Cromwell thought necessary to the Protectorate's survival.

Meanwhile freedom of conscience, to Cromwell the most precious of all liberties, he had to interpret anew in the light of persistent Quaker agitation. On February 15 Oliver issued *A Proclamation Prohibiting the Disturbing of Ministers and other Christians in their Assemblies and Meetings,* a broadside filled with Oliver's flowing fervor and Biblical diction. God's enemies in the land have been overthrown. The Protector speaks with pride of the English as a religious people, of "a free and uninterrupted Passage of the Gospel running through the midst of Us... A Mercy that is the Price of much Blood." Every Protestant is protected by the state in his right to worship unmolested in his own way, and this right must be held inviolate. Yet all men must "profess with sobriety, their Light and Knowledge." The preachers of the state ministry have a right also to freedom of expression, to freedom from interruptions by those bitter people who have lately sprung up in the land, attending sermons and interrupting the preachers. Among these are Quakers and Ranters, who pretend indeed to great piety and claim for themselves the right to exercise their own kind of worship. But their interruptions of sermons are contrary to the just freedoms of the various ministers and their congregations. Such men and women must forbear or be esteemed "Disturbers of the Civil Peace" and liable to prosecution.[13] Thus *A Proclamation,* which begins with the roll of mercies, reminds its readers of the coming of peace, reasserts freedom of conscience, but ends with a pointed threat against the lowly Quakers, many of whom had already suffered imprisonment without trial.

A number of Quaker meetings had been broken up by Cromwell's zealous officers, among them Colonel Hacker in his command in Leicestershire. Arrested and brought before Hacker, George Fox had refused to sign a paper engaging himself not to take up arms against the Protectorate, declaring that he was opposed to all use of weapons in any cause. Carried to London at Hacker's orders by a Captain Drury, lodged at the Mermaid, and next day brought before the Protector, Fox acceded to the demand of Cromwell not "to take up a carnal sword or weapon" against the government, since this was indeed in agreement with his own

[13] February 15, 1655, 669f19(68). On the heresies of the day one of the best summaries is that of Baxter, *Reliquiae Baxterianae* (1696), pp. 74–79. Baxter wrote (p. 116) that the Quakers "acted the Parts of Men in Raptures, and spake in the manner of Men inspired, and every where railed against Tythes and Ministers." On occasion in Presbyterian services Quakers would interrupt the minister and cry out, *"Come down thou Deceiver, thou Hireling, thou Dog!"*

principles.[14] In this confrontation with the Protector Fox preached a little sermon, attacking the ministers as "hireling priests." Cromwell found himself very sympathetic to Fox as a personality, recognizing that this man, whatever his bold words, was no threat at all to the civil powers. He said to Fox, "Come again to my house, for if thou and I were but an hour of a day together, we should be nearer one to the other." According to Fox, Cromwell said that "he wished me no more ill than he did his own soul." [15] Shown the Protector's dining hall and told that he might eat and sup there, he refused. Fox departed with assurance from Cromwell that he was free to address meetings wherever he wished to, whether in London or in other parts of the country. This permission Cromwell gave to Fox despite the fact that Quaker meetings had been prohibited by order of the government a few days previously.[16]

Meanwhile, about May 16 had come news of the persecution of the Protestant Vaudois in two Piedmontese valleys of the Alps west of Turin, the Pellice and the Chisone. The Vaudois peasants had been Protestants since the thirteenth century, when they had adopted the doctrines taught by the Waldenses, who were followers of Peter Waldo. In the seventeenth century they had modified their ascetic doctrines in favor of the theories of Calvin. Though subject to persecution from time to time, in 1561 they had been granted toleration by Duke Philibert Emanuel, a toleration limited, however, to the two valleys of the Alps. The toleration was not extended to communities such as La Torre, Luserna, or San Giovanni of the Pellice Valley.[17] Between 1638 and 1648 a number of Catholic missionaries were sent into the Protestant valleys. The Waldenses had retaliated with various violent acts including the burning of a mission house in Villar. In 1653 the government had sent forth an edict confirming the toleration privileges of 1561 to all those Protestants who lived within the communities then named. In response to this action the Waldenses rebuilt the mission house they had burnt.[18] It was decided, however, that missionaries would remain in the Protestant valleys, and the doctrines of the Catholic Church would be

[14] Abbott, III, 639. Whatever its distortions, Fox's colorful account of this conversation is invaluable. Before meeting the Protector, wrote Fox (*Journal*, ed. Norman Penney [London, 1924], p. 105), "I was moved of the Lord to write a paper *To the Protector by the Name of Oliver Cromwell,* wherein I did in the presence of the Lord God declare that I did deny the wearing or drawing of a carnal sword, or any other outward weapon, against him or any man: and that I was sent of God to stand a witness against all violence, and against the works of darkness."

[15] Fox, *Journal,* p. 106.

[16] Gardiner, *Commonwealth and Protectorate,* III, 262–63.

[17] *Ibid.,* IV, 178.

[18] *Ibid.,* IV, 178–79.

taught there. The Vaudois continued to extend their activities as traders into the towns outside the limits imposed upon them. They also purchased farms in the country to the south. In January, 1655, had come a crisis in which the duchess decided to enforce the agreement of 1561, ordering the Protestants to leave the towns of Luserna, Lusernetta, San Giovanni, La Torre, Bibiana, Fenile, Campiglione, Bricherasio, and San Secondo within three days upon threat of death and forfeiture of their property (unless they agreed either to become Catholics or to sell their property to Catholics). Determined to enforce her edict, the duchess on April 6 sent the Marquis of Pianezza from Turin with a body of soldiers which was gradually enlarged into a considerable force as it passed through various towns in which troops were already quartered. The marquis found that the Vaudois had deserted most of the villages in the plain. At La Torre, however, he was faced with a body of Waldenses who had refused to move from their homes. Nor would they now provide shelter for the troops of the Marquis.[19]

In the fighting that followed, beginning April 17 and continuing until April 24, the fiery resistance of the Vaudois precipitated burnings of houses, killings, and tortures that even the fiercest soldiers in sane moments could not have anticipated. In the massacres of April 24, 150 women and children were cruelly tortured; the soldiers "chopped off the heads of some and dashed the brains of others against the Rocks." When some prisoners refused to attend mass, the soldiers "hanged some, and nailed the feet of others to trees, with their heads hanging toward the ground." [20] Women, elderly people, and children were slain with indiscriminate fury. A heavy snow began to fall, slowing the flight of the victims, felling them with cold and weakness, and in some cases precipitating avalanches that swept them to their deaths. The exact number killed is not known.[21] According to an official tabulation cited by Gardiner, in the two communities of Villar and Bobbio, of 884 persons

[19] *Ibid.*, IV, 180–81.

[20] Samuel Morland, *History of the Evangelical Churches of the Valleys of Piemont* (1658; BML), p. 330. Morland includes many pictures and descriptions of the massacres. He writes (pp. 344, 341) that soldiers "took many small children and tender Infants, and flung them down the Precipices." One Guliemo Roche on May 8 stabbed the ears and feet of a servant to Jacopo Michalino of Bobbio, then "cut off his privy Members, and . . . applied a burning candle to the wound."

[21] Morland lists the names of the ones massacred village by village (pp. 362–79), a total of around 257. He also gives the names (pp. 380–83) of around 113 of the victims who died in prison. Masson (V, 39) states that the names of three hundred murdered victims are on record. Abbott (III, 707) estimates "two or three hundred."

seventy-five were prisoners of the duchess' troops, fifty-five were refugees in France. Of the remaining 759, 274 had been killed, thirty-six had been swept to death by an avalanche, and 449 had renounced their Protestantism for adherence to the Catholicism of their persecutors.[22]

At a time when England was splintered into many contending political and theological factions, the massacre of the Vaudois was a means of temporary unification. The news of the persecution roused biting anger in every Protestant breast, whether Quaker, Presbyterian, Ranter, or Anglican. A day of fasting and prayer was appointed for May 30 in London and in the rest of the country for June 14. Cromwell and his Council appointed a day of humiliation. Addresses to Cromwell came forth from many London congregations and from army officers in Ireland. Unprecedented collections of over 38,000 pounds were made to relieve the suffering of the Vaudois, Cromwell himself contributing 2000 pounds. The Protector sent forth letters of protest to the Duke of Savoy, the King of Sweden, to Cardinal Mazarin, to the King of Denmark, to the Protestant cities of Switzerland, to the United Provinces. Cromwell was so aroused by the cruelties in Piedmont that he was ready to act for the protection of the Savoy Protestants and wished to join the Netherlands in interceding for them. He sent a special commissioner, Samuel Morland, an associate of Whitelocke in his mission to Sweden, to proceed to the scene of the massacre and make him a detailed report. Morland left London on the 26th of May and talked with the French king and Mazarin on June 1. Thence he continued to Rivoli, not far from Turin, in which city he arrived on June 21.[23] Morland's subsequent reports to Cromwell intensified the resentment that for the moment united all English factions.

In the midst of unprecedented toil on state letters related to the Piedmont massacres,[24] Milton wrote one of his most passionate sonnets:

> Avenge, O Lord, thy slaughtered saints, whose bones
> Lie scattered on the Alpine mountains cold,
> Ev'n them who kept thy truth so pure of old
> When all our fathers worshiped stocks and stones,
> Forget not; in thy book record their groans
> Who were thy sheep, and in their ancient fold
> Slain by the bloody Piemontese that rolled
> Mother with infant down the rocks. Their moans
> The vales redoubled to the hills, and they
> To heav'n. Their martyred blood and ashes sow

[22] Gardiner, *Commonwealth and Protectorate,* IV, 185.

[23] Masson, V, 40–42.

[24] Milton's state letters in this emergency and the historical background will be fully treated in Volume V of the *Complete Prose.*

O'er all th' Italian fields, where still doth sway
The triple tyrant, that from these may grow
A hundredfold, who, having learnt thy way,
Early may fly the Babylonian woe.[25]

The fervor of Milton's spirit echoes throughout the poem; no longer is he a sectarian, a champion of Independency crying out against the Anglicans or the Presbyterians. The enraged Protestant citizen calls out to the Lord to avenge his own, forgetting for the moment, like most Englishmen, the wars against the Irish and the massacres at Drogheda.

Cromwell's regime in 1655 seemed stable and secure; never had the name of an English ruler possessed such magic with the crowned heads of Europe or such assurance of military prowess at home. His ships at sea were as much feared and respected as his troops upon the land. In coping with the multitude of administrative details, Cromwell was prompt and resourceful, even in the smallest matters. What English king would have received a strange fanatic like George Fox and invited him to sup in the royal dining hall? Cromwell liked strange people, especially fanatics in religion, with whom he felt a kinship. When he imprisoned his old comrades, like Major-General Harrison, he did so with reluctance.

Cromwell was now alienated from many of his closest associates of the years of the Commonwealth. Vane and Hutchinson had refused to serve in any Parliament after the dissolution of the Rump. Sidney and Bradshaw now stood aloof. Robert Overton was under suspicion. On December 13, when Ludlow had last spoken to the Protector, he had declared that if he saw a way to appear "in behalf of the people, I cannot consent to tie my own hands before-hand."[26] After an exchange of blunt talk between the two men in the presence of Lambert, Sydenham, Montague, Strickland, and Fleetwood, Cromwell allowed Ludlow his liberty.

[25] Douglas Bush, *Complete Poetical Works of John Milton,* p. 198. Of this sonnet Bush writes: "Milton's combined invective and prayer has often been likened to the imprecations of the Hebrew prophets, and it is in fact cast in biblical language, harsh, compassionate, simple, and fervent."

[26] Ludlow, *Memoirs,* I, 434. Few accounts of Cromwell's old associates are as illuminating as that of Ludlow's trip to England and his subsequent conversation with Cromwell. Ludlow (I, 426–27) was especially indignant that Lord Fitz-Williams, "a civil person, tho a papist," who had fought against the Parliament at Preston, should assure him that he would be glad to speak on Ludlow's behalf to Cromwell, whom he called "his Highness the Lord Protector." Ludlow adds: "I gave him my thanks for his civility, but thought it a strange revolution of affairs, that the interest of a gentleman who had been Lieutenant-General in the army of the Irish rebels, should be so much greater than mine in the General of the army of the Commonwealth."

Despite the fact that the jury had acquitted Lilburne on August 20, he had been imprisoned, first in Jersey, and next at Dover Castle. Even though Lilburne had declared himself a Quaker, Cromwell would not release him. Feake, Rogers, and Biddle were also in prison, men whose heresies Cromwell could well forgive in soldiers under discipline. But in a civil regime, such men were too persuasive and inflammatory to be allowed abroad. Thus, despite his belief in toleration, Cromwell had to impose sanctions on the free speaking he loved so well. One may well imagine that his Council of State, including the Areopagitican John Milton, approved, reluctantly as Cromwell himself, of the Protector's repressive measures.

CHAPTER XXX

MILTON AND *PRO SE DEFENSIO*

August 8, 1655

BEFORE *Pro Se Defensio* appeared, August 8, 1655, Milton had received information at various times for three years past that Alexander More was not the author of *Regii Sanguinis Clamor*. As early as October, 1652, when Vlacq had attacked Milton in his preface to *Clamor*, comparing him to a "monster horrible, deformed, huge, and sightless,"[1] Vlacq had written to Hartlib saying that "Mr. Morus was not the author of the Book."[2] Hartlib had replied on October 29, saying,

[1] *Clamor* (1652), preface to Charles: *"Monstrum horrendum, informe, ingens, cui lumen ademptum."* See translation of *Clamor* by Paul Blackford, below, p. 1045. Adrian Vlacq: printer and publisher at the Hague. See below, pp. 1088–93,

[2] French, *Life Records,* III, 270; Masson, IV, 627. Indispensable new information on the Milton-More controversy, as well as authoritative analysis, will be found in Kester Svendsen's edition of *Pro Se Defensio,* below, pages 687–825. See especially the preface, below, pp. 687–93, and the following notes: p. 689, n. 3 (sources); p. 704, n. 17; p. 708, n. 24; p. 710, n. 28; p. 713, n. 33; p. 722, n. 55 (Pelletta); p. 727, n. 66 (Spanheim); p. 747, n. 117 (Pontia); p. 753, n. 132 (articles against More); p. 757, n. 140 (Geneva sources); p. 777, n. 199 (various women involved with More); p. 779, n. 200; p. 781, n. 207 (Hotton); p. 784, n. 216 (More's testimonials); p. 785, n. 217 (testimonials); p. 798, n. 244; p. 805, n. 269 (Elisabeth Guerrett). For further details see Svendsen's "Milton's *Pro Se Defensio* and Alexander More," University of Texas *Studies in Literature and Language,* I (1959), 11–29; "Milton and Alexander More: New Documents," *JEGP,* LX, No. 4 (October, 1961), 796–807.

"I am glad you have told me that Morus is not the author of that most vile and scandalous book." [3] Vlacq had reminded Hartlib that Phillips had made the same error in his *Responsio* of attributing the *Clamor* to More. Meanwhile, however, Milton had heard repeated reports from the continent that More was the author of *Clamor*. Much as Milton trusted Hartlib, who had no doubt relayed Vlacq's emphatic assurance, Milton did not trust Hartlib's sources of information. He had gone ahead with *Defensio Secunda*, picturing More as the guilty author of *Clamor*. But in April, 1654, only one month before *Secunda* appeared, Hartlib had two emphatic letters from Dury which again asserted More's innocence. Dury's letter of April 14 read in part as follows: "I have understood from one of the Ministers of Middelburg of my acquaintance who is very familiar with Mr. Moore that hee is not the author of that booke." [4] In the matter of Pontia, asserts Dury, a court of justice has just declared More completely innocent, and Dury knows that Milton would not want to make a mistake and spread reports about a man who is blameless. How passionate Dury felt about More's innocence appears from a second letter to Hartlib dated April 19 in which Dury reports that he has conferred with a Reverend Hotton, who knew More well and assured him that the author was not he. Dury ended his letter by saying, "You may let Mr. Milton know of this lest hee should wrong the innocent & wrong his owne Credit by spreading false reports." [5] By the time Dury's letter reached England and Hartlib had spoken about it to Milton, *Defensio Secunda* was already in the press. It was too late for Milton to draw back now, even had he been convinced by this latest evidence that he had made indeed a tragic blunder.

Meanwhile, in the weeks preceding May 20, William Nieuport, the Dutch ambassador in London, had been working on More's behalf to prevent publication of *Second Defence*. On June 23, 1654, Nieuport wrote to More saying that he had communicated More's message to Thurloe imploring him to speak to Oliver himself. Not content with this, Nieuport had asked two of his friends, who were well acquainted with Milton, to urge him not to publish *Second Defence*.[6] Shortly afterward

[3] Vlacq's preface, "Typographus pro Se-ipso," in *Defensio Secunda* (Hague, 1654; PUL), sigs. [8*]-[8v*]; Masson, IV, 627. For full analysis of Milton's dilemma, see Kester Svendsen, preface to *Pro Se Defensio*, below, pp. 687–693, and his illuminating notes to *Pro Se*, especially nn. 8, 10, 17, 32, 39, 45.

[4] Turnbull, *Hartlib, Dury and Comenius*, p. 42.

[5] *Life Records*, III, 370; Turnbull, pp. 42–43.

[6] Milton's own story of the Nieuport action on More's behalf (below, p. 740) fully confirms the Nieuport letter, which More (below, p. 1101) reprinted in full in *Fides Publica*. See also Masson, IV, 632–33.

the gentlemen brought Nieuport word that Milton had so strong a belief that More was the real author of the *Clamor* that these men, though friends of Milton as well as Nieuport, "could by no means dissuade him." The only concession Milton made was "to assure us that he would let nothing proceed from his pen of an unbecoming nature, or in any way prejudicial to the States of the United Provinces." [7] Nieuport sent to Thurloe a copy of More's letter, still hoping for intervention on the part of Oliver himself. But just about this time (May 20) occurred the Gerard-Vowel plot against Oliver's life, which so absorbed Cromwell and his associates that they could not give the matter attention. Meanwhile, continues Nieuport, Milton published his *Defensio Secunda.* It is evident that Nieuport found himself not only deeply sympathetic to More's position but convinced of the truth of his statements. On August 7, 1654, a friend of More's wrote him from London that *Second Defence* was out and that it was impossible to suppress it. When Milton had been told that More was not the author of the *Clamor,* he had answered that at least he was sure that More had caused it to be printed and that More had written the preface. Moreover, said Milton, there were far worse things that he could have put in the book, but he was reserving them for another blast at More. Thus all More's attempts both to convince Milton and to prevent publication by intercession of friends or formal intervention of the Dutch ambassador ended in frustration. Copies of the book had already appeared in Holland before August 7. Thurloe reported on July 3 that "two or three copies of Milton against the famous Professor Morus" had appeared at the Hague. According to Thurloe, More was doing all he could to suppress the book. Meanwhile Madame de Saumaise had ordered a number of More's letters to be published "to render him so much the more ridiculous." Thurloe also wrote that More now denied he was the author of the preface to the *Clamor*. But, insisted Thurloe, "we know very well the contrary." [8] Vlacq was now determined to reprint *Defensio Secunda,* together with the *Clamor,* in one volume, with a preface replying to Milton's attack on him in *Secunda.*

A few months later, in October, 1654, appeared More's reply to Milton, *Fides Publica,* flatly denying his authorship of *Clamor* and calling upon the true author to make himself known. The circumstances of More's reply threw into bold relief both Milton's attack and More's passionate new declarations of his innocence. Vlacq reprinted *Second Defence* in the same volume with More's *Fides*. Though *Second Defence* preceded *Fides* in the volume, two prefaces attacking Milton, one by Dr. George Crantz, friend of Salmasius, and one by Vlacq, preceded the reprint of *Second Defence*. Crantz at once deals Milton an ugly blow with the charge that

[7] Masson, IV, 632.

[8] *Ibid.,* III, 634. See below, p. 740.

he has set forth the heresy that "the doctrine of the Gospels and of our Lord Jesus Christ concerning divorce is diabolical." Though the great Salmasius is no more, continues Crantz, his reply to Milton lives, and Milton "will learn that the dead also bite." [9] Admitting More's hasty temper, his arrogance, his combativeness, Crantz extols his talents without once referring to the main point at issue, whether More did or did not write *Clamor*. Vlacq, however, in his preface, "The Printer in His Own Behalf," emphatically asserts More's innocence, recalling that he had written Hartlib two years before that More was not the author, and quoting Hartlib's letter in reply of October 29, 1652. Why had Milton made no serious inquiry to find out if More was the author? He had chosen rather to thunder savagely against More when, asserts Vlacq, he was certain More was not really the guilty one. Why is Milton "eager to impose upon the whole world and to defame a neighbor with calumnies and the blackest lies"? [10] Who was the author, if not More? Vlacq asserts that he still does not know who wrote the *Clamor*. His defence of himself against Milton's hasty barbs is a document of pith, dignity, and moderation.

In some of his charges against More, Milton was on firm ground. As subsequent events were to prove, More did receive the manuscript sheets of *Clamor* from Salmasius, who in turn had received them from Moulin. More did supervise the printing of the *Clamor*. More did write the epistle to Charles which opened the book, "Carolo II. Dei Gratia Magnae Britanniae, Franciae & Hiberniae Regi," in which appeared the characterization of Milton as "Monstrum horrendum." All other parts of *Clamor* were written by du Moulin himself, who was to reveal in 1670 that he had feared violent action against himself by the Commonwealth if he had made his authorship known in 1652.[11] These true charges against More Milton tried to make equivalent to a full responsibility for the authorship of the *Clamor*.

In the opening pages of *Pro Se* Milton attempts to set in perspective his own part in the establishment and support of the new English republic, thus by inference diminishing the stature of his opponent. Had he not stood forth among all Englishmen in praising his country's liberators and condemning the tyranny they had overthrown? God had chosen him in signal favor to speak for his country's freedom. And now, in another crisis, called to a meaner task, though blind and infirm and stricken by two deaths in his family, he will not falter; like Scipio Africanus, he will not fail the state or his own expectations of himself (*mihimet nunc non defuero*). Nor in this polemic, claims Milton, re-

[9] *Defensio Secunda* (Hague, 1654), "Lectori." [10] *Ibid.*, sig. [8v*].
[11] This information appears in Masson, V, 214–22.

ferring to his promise to Nieuport, shall anything indecorous or discreditable appear from his pen; within him is a complete conviction of moral uprightness. Whatever expectations of him possess the minds of his noblest contemporaries, when the fury of his enemies falls on him alone, he will not fail. In such passages of open and passionate self-praise, Milton asserts his superiority to his enemy. In the past he has recounted the noble deeds of English leaders; now he must stoop to searching out the hiding places of nameless attackers pitted against himself. Could a man of such stature as he engage in a pamphlet defence from unworthy or mistaken motives? Thus Milton's unspoken question to his readers. He alone stands out against a new and ignominious blow at the champions of liberty.

On the sixth page of his *Pro Se* Milton boldly accuses More of being "the author of that most clamorous lampoon" against him. The lampoon ("In Impurissimum Nebulonem Johannem Miltonum, Parricidarum & Parricidii Advocatum") had appeared at the end of the *Clamor* and was only ten pages in length.[12] Even in this first assertion of More's guilt Milton significantly omits an outright accusation that More is the author of the *Clamor* itself. But no other person has come to light who could have written such an outcry! The very fact that the *Clamor* does not displease More Milton uses as a partial proof of his guilt. Moreover, writes Milton, "he who published that clamor must be considered its author."[13] This first doubtful and doubting accusation of authorship Milton weakens by linking it at once with More's debaucheries. A libel, suggests Milton, is hard to prove because it can be composed without witnesses; debaucheries are another matter; they require companions and accomplices. Almost immediately Milton again admits the uncertainty of his accusation when he writes, "unless I make it plain that you are the author of that infamous libel against us, or that you have *shown sufficient cause why you should be deservedly considered the author,"*[14] he will admit defeat and withdraw from the conflict, dishonored and disgraced.

Milton's stubborn identification of More's authorship of the *Clamor* with his writing of its accompanying lampoon in verse against Milton mars the effectiveness of his rhetoric throughout *Pro Se.* Only after this weak, ambivalent accusation does Milton come finally to an outright declaration that More is the author. He supports this declaration with the strong claim of a persistent report from the continent which was, says Milton, unanimous and invariable. Such a report, says Milton, "is called the voice of the people, which was believed by the ancients to be a

[12] *Clamor* (1652), pp. 162–72. [13] *Pro Se Defensio,* below, p. 701.
[14] *Ibid.,* below, p. 702 [my italics].

goddess and is called by us today the voice of God"! [15] Moreover, continues Milton, in two years he has met with no person, either Englishman or foreigner, who did not agree that More was the author of the *Clamor*. In his conversations with people from home and abroad, says Milton, no one else was named as the author of *Clamor* except More. The nearest approach to verification of such evidence appears in a letter written from Leyden September 27, 1652, containing the sentence, "Nor of greater moment is that book of More's entitled *The Cry of the Royal Blood to Heaven*." [16] Much more important evidence, from Milton's point of view, appears in an undated letter from Amsterdam which begins thus: "It is very certain that almost everyone throughout these parts considers More as the author of that book which is entitled *The Cry of the Royal Blood;* for he himself corrected the sheets as they were taken from the press, and some copies display More's name subscribed to the dedication, of which he was likewise the author." [17] Milton does not claim that this letter was published in an English or Dutch newspaper. Another letter he quotes is similarly anonymous and undated: "A certain man of the first rank said to me at the Hague that he had *The Cry of the Royal Blood,* with that very epistle of More's." [18] Even these accusations do not claim specifically that More wrote the *Cry*. Of these letters which Milton quotes, only the one from Leyden, September 27, 1652, claims directly that the *Clamor* itself is More's work. One letter does make the statement that More tried to get a printer for the *Clamor* before Vlacq accepted it. Realizing the weakness of his charges against More, Milton claims that he has other proof of More's authorship which he is not at liberty to divulge. If it were possible for him to set forth his evidence, More would be blasted beyond hope. But some time in the future, says Milton, he hopes that these witnesses will "publicly offer their names to the service of so great a truth." [19] Such an appeal to witnesses who cannot speak is in itself one of the many signs of weakness in Milton's case against More. As in all his pamphlets, Milton is continually aware of the response of the acute and gifted reader to his argument. Hence his uneasiness now in the presence of his own rhetoric. At no time does he offer what he himself would consider indisputable proof of More's authorship.

The most damning evidence against Milton's position lies in two letters from Dury written in late April, 1654, two years later than the letter from Leyden on which Milton bases his accusation of More's guilt. At no time in the *Pro Se* does Milton take into account the time sequence of these letters, in which Dury at first accepts More's guilt, based upon many re-

[15] *Ibid.*, below, p. 704.
[16] *Ibid.*, below, p. 710.
[17] *Ibid.*, below, p. 717.
[18] *Ibid.*, below, p. 717.
[19] *Ibid.*, below, p. 718.

ports, and then writes emphatically that More is not the guilty one. These two letters against his own position Milton boldly quotes on pages 16 and 17 of the *Pro Se*. Each of them emphatically states that More is not the author of the *Cry*. It is evident that Dury has great confidence in his informant and believes that Milton will be eager to correct the error that he, Dury, has also made. The two letters by Dury, written within a week of each other, show the extreme urgency that Dury felt to set straight the record of a man he had falsely accused. Milton, however, dismisses this late evidence of a reputable informant by attacking Dury's source of information. Such a man as Mr. Hotton is not to be trusted because, as Milton writes, he is "most devoted to the royalist faction, most inimical to us, and on terms of secrecy with More." [20] Milton impatiently asks, where did Hotton get his information? Did not the report he submits to Dury come from More himself and not from Hotton's personal knowledge? Therefore, says Milton, Hotton is not to be trusted, since it is evident that he received his information only from More and not from an unbiased source. In such a manner does Milton reject the evidence presented by Dury, whose fairness and impartiality most leaders of Milton's time, whether royalist or Puritan, gladly acknowledged.

Milton's condemnations of More for allegedly writing *Clamor* are the least persuasive of all the polemic in his career. Instead of presenting evidence to convict his opponent, Milton challenges him time after time to present proof of his innocence. At one point he reduces More's defense of himself to a few statements of satirical dialogue:

> But now, it would appear, you mean to reduce the whole affair to a few words: "I am not," you say, "the author of that *Cry*." You do not convince me. "The matter is clear, it is evident: and to affirm it with further arguments would be more foolish than to match mortal light with the sun's radiance." Leave off the bombast; say something at last. "I myself deny it as much as I am able." Yet once more; once threateningly and imperiously; now wretchedly. "My friends are not silent." Out of your mouth. "Preachers admonish." On your credit. "Ambassadors confirm." Out of your letters. But what is all this save that singular denial of yours made in the beginning, "I am not the author"? [21]

It is true that More does not present evidence that he is not the author. The only conclusive way for More to have proved his own innocence was to identify the real author, as he might well have done. It is highly to More's credit as a staunch royalist that he did not name Moulin as the real author when he was under fire from Milton's polemic batteries. But by those legal principles which Milton himself subscribed to, More was to be adjudged innocent until proven guilty.

[20] *Ibid.*, below, p. 709.

[21] *Ibid.*, below, p. 745.

Nowhere in *Pro Se* is Milton more grievously unfair to More than in those pages in which he defines the word *author*. Whether he was the author, the editor, or the publisher, of *Clamor,* More was equally reprehensible. Indeed if More was no more than an ally and assistant (*socium & administratum*) in getting out the book, he was as guilty as if he had written the whole tract. Had More written one line of the *Clamor* or one versicle of the epistle to Charles II or the rhymed attack on Milton at the end? If so, he was as guilty as if he had written every word of the book. If More had assisted in procuring the composition of *Clamor,* he was guilty. Milton's justification for this strange position is two citations from Justinian, one of which reads: "If any, to the infamy of another, shall write, compose, or publish any libel or poem or history, or with evil intent shall cause any such to be done, &c." [22] The most extreme statement of this analysis of More's guilt is as follows:

> I shall yield to you . . . [for the sake of argument] that you are not the author of this libel titled *The Cry of the Royal Blood.* And yet, as perchance you now expect, you shall not escape thus. . . . If I find that you wrote or contributed one page of this book, or even one versicle, if I find that you published it, or procured or persuaded anyone to publish it, or that you were in charge of its publication, or even lent yourself to the smallest part of the work, seeing that no one else comes forth, for me you alone will be the author of the whole work, the culprit and the crier.[23]

Thus Milton, writing, one feels, in haste and desperation, perhaps convinced (if at any time in his career) that he has made a tragic blunder, but seeing no way by which he can now withdraw his accusation. It seems certain that Milton felt more deeply wounded by the verses, "In Impurissimum Nebulonem Johannem Miltonum Parriciduram & Parricidii Advocatum," which Milton refers to only as *infame carmen,* than by any other part of *Clamor.* And had not More affixed his signature to the epistle to Charles II in various copies of the volume, according to many witnesses? But whether or not such copies actually carried More's signatures remains uncertain to this day.

One of the main aims of Milton's rhetorical strategy in replying to More is to shift the argument away from his opponent as the supposed author of *Clamor* to More as the guilty fornicator and adulterer; to More also as the "preaching wolf" with the "goatish voice." Fortunately for Milton's strategy the burden of the testimonials in both *Fides Publica* and *Supplementum* dealt with More's character and reputation as a man and a minister, not with his writing of *Clamor.* As long as Milton is dealing with his main accusation, that More had a hand in writing *Clamor,* he is uneasy and unconvincing; but as soon as he touches More's affair

[22] *Ibid.,* below, p. 713.

[23] *Ibid.,* below, pp. 712–13.

with Claudia Peletta, he is completely at ease, having evidence at hand (evidently from Thurloe's investigators as well as from other sources) that More is vulnerable to this attack. Even in the first hundred pages of the Latin *Pro Se,* no more than thirty-five contain allusions to More's participation in the writing of *Clamor;* in the last half of the book (some one hundred pages) no more than ten deal in part with the question of More's authorship. The more vehemently More defended himself with character testimonials, the less space Milton needed to give to the charge of authorship he knew by this time to be utterly untrue. Milton's analysis of More's personal life, like most statements in other prose tracts, is largely quite accurate, like those details he gives about the execution of Charles I. But his main grievance against More, that he had written the *Clamor,* is flimsy and unconvincing from the opening fusillade. In the *Commonplace Book* Milton had quoted with approval the idea that a lie is justified when it is told for the benefit of one's country. Convinced at first of More's guilt, bit by bit persuaded he might be mistaken, unwilling to acknowledge his error in *Second Defence,* did Milton believe his duty as spokesman for the Commonwealth was to demolish More's reputation, whether or not he had written one versicle of the poem against him or one line of the attacks on the Commonwealth?

Though Milton writes, "I am singularly secure," no tract he had thus far sent forth represented less conviction of a just cause or reach for greatness than *Pro Se.* His very shrillness, his thickets of scornful sexual epithets, his praise of his own integrity, accent his desperation. Not only is the prose of *Pro Se* Milton's left hand in style (the poorest of his Latin compositions); *Pro Se* is the shrunken left hand of his patriotic spirit, his zeal for a New Jerusalem, his dream of greatness for himself. "He alone is to be called great," writes Milton, "who performs great deeds, or teaches how they may be done, or writes about them in terms becoming their greatness."[24] By this definition of greatness *Pro Se* is only a polemic wasteland. No memorable thoughts spring forth; no portraits of his great contemporaries, as in *Second Defence;* no revelations of a unique torment, as in *Doctrine and Discipline;* no burning, unforgettable images, as in *Areopagitica.*

No historian is equal to the task of placing the elements of Milton's genius in perspective. But if the soaring autobiographical passages of *Paradise Lost* reach heights no other English poet save Shakespeare has risen to, the prose of Milton's *Pro Se* least represents his capacious spirit. In this tract Milton was bound by the grip of polemic custom in

[24] *Ibid.,* below p. 774.

a patriotic cause, even as Cromwell on the battlefield could not avoid the ugly necessities of push of pike and slash of sword and the death of the young for the sake of the Lord of Hosts. In *Pro Se* Milton is a dwarf of himself. But even while composing *Pro Se,* he brought forth from a deep well of his poetic depths "Avenge, O Lord, thy slaughtered saints." In daily associations, as in his writing, Milton was driven by diverse passions, no less whole and harmonious than those of Cromwell, Hobbes, Marvell, or Rembrandt. In his daily relations with the Council of State, it is clear that Milton's humbler talents of diplomacy in defence of the state were cherished by many of his most distinguished contemporaries. The infinite patience and courtesy embodied in Milton's long series of conversations with Mylius in 1651–1652, are in themselves a revelation of Milton's capacity for imaginative service to the state.[25] Nor can one omit to recall, in assessing the elements of Milton's genius, the dauntless courage with which he was to face the extinction of the Commonwealth a few years later, his resolution, if none would hear him, to say with the prophet, "*O earth, earth, earth!* to tell the very soil it self, what her perverse inhabitants are deaf to." [26] At this moment Milton spoke from the deepest commitment of his spirit, not counting for a moment the prospect of a life cut too short to complete the great epic of his dreams.

Now forty-seven years old, at the height of his powers, the burden of his richest music, his soaring poetic dreams, still untraced and untallied, Milton does strike off in *Pro Se* one passage that probes a deep vein of his creative powers. When More writes, "To this mushroom lately sprung from the earth, what man or men have I opposed?" Milton replies, "You err, More, and know not me. To me it was always preferable to grow slowly, and as if by the silent lapse of time." [27] This passage describes Milton's uncanny sense of his own readiness for great achievement; he felt he needed more time for ripening than other great poets. Even for "Lycidas," written in his twenty-ninth year, he had felt he was not ready. In Emerson's characterization of greatness as "a long scale of degrees" he described a process in Milton's psyche that never flagged or halted. Involved as he had been now for fifteen years in the quest for a utopian England, the expansion of his poetic powers, as *Paradise Lost* was to prove, had not slackened or withered, but step by step, year by year, had gathered riches. Meanwhile his left hand struck out again and again in passionate defense of a dream he must have known embodied now only a fragment of his early hopes. Yet another side of him was still green, still growing and blossoming, making ready for the great tasks to come.

[25] French, *Life Records,* III, 74–89, 91–109, 111–13, 115–18, etc.

[26] *Readie & Easie Way* (2nd ed., 1660), pp. 106–107.

[27] *Ibid.,* below p. 819.

A DEFENCE OF THE PEOPLE OF ENGLAND

February 24, 1651

PREFACE AND NOTES BY WILLIAM J. GRACE
TRANSLATION BY DONALD C. MACKENZIE

Considering his fame as writer of *The Tenure* and *Eikonoklastes,* it is not surprising that Milton should have been assigned to answer the long attack upon the regicides contained in Salmasius' *Defensio Regia,* which was published no later than mid-November, 1649.[1] Although Thomason dated his copy May 11,[2] copies must have been in England considerably before that date, for on January 8, 1650, the Council of State ordered Milton to prepare something "in answer to the Booke of Saltmatius, and when hee hath done itt bring itt to the Councell."[3] Milton had completed the task by mid-December, 1650, for on December 23 the Council ordered it to be printed,[4] and on December 31 it was entered in the *Stationers' Registers.*[5] On the following Monday, February 24, 1651,[6] was published Milton's "answer to the Booke of Saltmatius," the *Joannis MiltonI Angli Pro Populo Anglicano Defensio contra Claudii Anonymi, alias Salmasii, Defensionem Destructivam, Londini, Typis Du-Gardianis, Anno Domini, 1651.*[7] It had required about a year to compose, and, as Masson observes, it is the publication of this work which deserves precedence in Milton's life of this year.[8] On June 18 he received the formal thanks of the Council.[9]

The edition of *Regia* used by Milton is a folio, containing the royal

[1] See Falconer F. Madan, "Milton, Salmasius, and Dugard," *The Library,* fourth Series, IV (1923–24), 137, and his "Revised Bibliography of Salmasius's *Defensio Regia* and Milton's *Pro Populo Anglicano Defensio," The Library,* fifth series, IX (1954), 101–103.

[2] Thomason, I, 743, mistakenly catalogued in 1649, rather than 1650.

[3] French, II, 286.

[4] French, II, 334–35.

[5] French, II, 335.

[6] French, II, 350.

[7] For abbreviated descriptions of all known editions, see Madan articles, above, n. 1. For full bibliographical descriptions of authorized editions, see below, Appendix G, pp. 1140 ff.

[8] Masson, IV, 312.

[9] *Ibid.,* IV, 321–22.

arms, a copy of which is contained in the McAlpin collection, Union Theological Seminary, New York, and is the one referred to in the present work. The title page of Salmasius' book reads: *DEFENSIO REGIA, Pro CAROLO I. AD Serenissimum Magnae Britaniae Regem CAROLUM II. Filium natu majorem, Heredem & Successorem legitimum. Sumptibus Regiis* Anno 1649. For bibliographical analysis of this edition of *Regia,* see below, p. 295.

Kathryn A. McEuen of Brooklyn College has translated the *Defensio Regia* of Salmasius, and we are indebted to her for kindly allowing us to make use of her material. For selections from her translation of *Regia,* see below, pp. 986–1035. Paul Blackford of Western Illinois University made available to us his doctoral thesis, containing a fresh translation of Milton's *A Defence,* with textual notes.

If the text of *A Defence* is considered from the point of view of its intellectual contents, unembarrassed by Milton's rhetorical devices and by seventeenth-century personal vituperation, a clear and cogent argument arises which can be examined on its merits. It may well be maintained, in opposition to Hanford, that *A Defence* "rises" to principles.[10] This does not mean that *A Defence* does not possess serious deficiencies in argument, but these deficiencies result from limitations exterior to the internal logic of the argument. Nor does it mean that Milton's premises would necessarily gain acceptance.

Milton's technique in *A Defence* is not that of modern propaganda or psychological warfare. In spite of the fact that *A Defence* was directed to a continental audience and composed in Latin, Milton's arguments are not slanted toward doubtful or neutral opinion. Outside of the persistent effort to destroy the prestige of Salmasius, Milton's arguments are partisan and are directed to strengthening the convictions of those already convinced. At times *A Defence,* in spite of its somber and weighty materials, reads like the rounds of an athletic contest. Partisanship is absolute, and the champion insults and exults over his foe, reviles him with rhetorically delicious insults before resuming the next point, the next combat.

Today this method of dialectic would seem, if not psychologically distasteful, certainly intellectually wasteful.[11] But for Milton's govern-

[10] *A Milton Handbook* (New York, 1946), p. 110: "But Milton seldom rises to principles, confining himself rather to point by point replies to his opponents." In 1658 Milton spoke (*A Defence,* 1658 [CUL], p. 171) of the world's reception of *A Defence* as "my zealous labor's fruit—the highest that I for my part had set before me in this life."

[11] Actually Milton's interpretation follows classical precedent. *Cf.* Sir Maurice Bowra, *The Greek Experience* (New York: New American Library, 1961), p. 88: "The Athenians had almost no laws of libel or slander, and their political debates were as candid and vituperative as their private and forensic quarrels."

mental supporters these personal insults and heavy thunderbolts seemed essentially part of a great contest.

In accord with this partisanship, Milton assumes (without feeling any necessity for proof) the unmitigated guilt of Charles I. In explaining the methods of Milton's argument, the historical appraisal of the activities and motives of Charles I can be conveniently bypassed. The absolute assumption of the king's guilt was Milton's propaganda position.[12] The main intellectual content of the treatise is concerned not with Charles I himself, but with the moral justification of the rights of a people to remove a tyrant.

Many of Milton's arguments are based on authority, particularly the authority of the Scriptures. Milton assumes throughout *A Defence* that the words of Scripture, at least as he interprets them, are final and unquestionable. He also assumes that they are consistent.[13] But since there can be considerable room for disagreement as to what the Scriptures exactly connote, a great deal of *A Defence* becomes a matter of Scriptural exegesis. A number of Milton's interpretations seem narrow, private, or quaint. He assumes, for example, that God was essentially a republican; that God gave the Jews kings as a kind of ironic and vindictive punishment for their lack of judgment in not adhering to republican principles. He supports his thesis by detailed exegesis of the Old Testament.

But however documented the argument may be, the portrait of God engaged in politics is somewhat anthropomorphic and wayward. Amusingly enough, God in support of Israel's republican principles appears rather royalistic and absolute.[14] The weakness in Milton's biblical arguments arises, as is so often the case with Scriptural exegesis, from making its applications limited and technical. The Bible is a collection of an entire national literature, ranging all the way from narrow legalisms to sublime poetry. It cannot easily be quoted with effect as a treatise on law or politics. It could scarcely serve as a precedent for legal procedure even in Puritan seventeenth-century England.

Milton's references to classical authorities partake for the modern reader of the same type of weakness as the Scriptural exegesis, although

[12] Milton in *A Defence* (below, p. 330) speaks of "a deed so excellent." He considers the trial of Charles I as "legal process" and that future generations should not "be deprived of the advantage of such a good example."

[13] A very interesting though quaint example is the account of Samuel and his sons. On the somewhat slender evidence of this and other passages, Milton concludes (below, p. 370): "This evidence all proves that the Israelites were given a king by God in his wrath."

[14] In *A Defence* (below, p. 367), in opposition to Salmasius' insistence on the kingship of Christ (in the temporal as well as the spiritual sense), Milton tends to reverse himself. At any rate his Arianism in denying the royal divinity of Christ at this point is merely implicit.

quite a few of the classical quotations actually deal with principles of law. Sometimes, however, Milton actually appeals to passages of imaginative literature within the classics for statement of legal principle. Milton brings together an impressive set of classical quotations directed against tyranny; he even brings together definitions of tyranny; but, either because the classics did not furnish such examples, or because Milton was not interested, he does not cull quotations from the classics to show what juridical procedure a people is to follow when it has been determined that tyranny is present.

Milton's lack of concern with legal precedent and procedure may be viewed as a basic weakness in his argumentation. During the centuries intervening from Milton's time, Anglo-Saxon tradition has been so concerned with the "rule of law" and with the careful statement of such law through legislation and court decision that the modern reader feels that there is a basic flaw in Milton's approach. But Milton's contemporaries did not necessarily feel this flaw. Actually for Milton and many of his contemporaries Scriptural exegesis was a kind of legal precedent, no less germane to this kind of argument than constitutional law.[15]

II

It must be borne in mind that the problem of establishing legal precedent for the execution of a king, even his removal, was a novel issue in Milton's time. Salmasius' *Defensio Regia* is concerned with expressing European shock at the execution of Charles I; *A Defence* is concerned with justifying the punishment.

Milton in attempting to meet the thorny problem of legal precedent falls back upon the law of nature.[16] "If you must know by what right,

[15] Hugo Grotius, whom Milton met in Paris, makes thousands of references to Scripture in formulating the foundations of international law. Milton maintains that the Gospel does not clash with reason or the law of nations (*A Defence*, 1658, p. 42): "Nec evangelii doctrina cum ratione aut cum iure gentium pugnat." Milton has always been of the opinion that the law of God agrees exactly with the law of nature (*A Defence*, 1658, p. 74): "Quamquam in ea sum opinione, Salmasie, semperque fui, legem Dei cum lege naturae optime consentire."

[16] It is interesting to note how Milton enters some untried ground in other contexts regarding the law of nature. In dealing with divorce in the *Tetrachordon*, Milton finds himself obliged to take marriage outside the realm of the natural law: "Though marriage be most agreeable to holiness, to purity and justice, yet it is not a natural, but a civil and ordain'd relation" (*Complete Prose*, II, 601). But in playing down the marriage bond, Milton exalts a principle which he always identifies with the natural law, that of natural leadership. He accepts a situation where a husband contentedly yields to a wife exceeding him in "prudence and dexterity." "For then a superior and more natural law comes in, that the wiser should govern the less wise, whether male or female" (*Complete Prose*, II, 589).

under what law—under that law which God himself and nature hath appointed that all things for the safety of the commonwealth should be deemed lawful and righteous."[17]

A certain superficial agreement, of course, existed in the use of the term "law of nature." The natural law was *unwritten* law dealing with first principles that theoretically were discernible by *all* men. In this sense a classically educated Puritan like Milton is apt to put aside theological assumptions in favor of the tradition that has come down through Plato, Cicero, and the Stoics. But even here unresolved difficulties existed. Could corrupted natural man perceive these unwritten truths or, if he could, had he the resources, without "grace," to apply them? Did "all men" really mean all men, or only all "regenerate" men? Hobbes' concept of the law of nature as a jungle from which only by the construction of a powerful state could one hope to escape was more consistent with the original concept of the essential corruption of the natural man than Milton's "nature, the mild mother of us all."[18] Was the natural law an ideal theory to which men might ultimately aspire, or did it signify a kind of universal conscience operating in the hearts of all men, which might be perversely transgressed but not without the subject's knowledge of what he was doing?

Milton's position is nearer to that of medieval Catholicism than it is to Calvinism in these matters. Milton says that the word *nature* means "either the essence of a thing or that general law which is the origin of everything and under which everything acts."[19] In thinking of *essence* as *nature*—essence cannot be changed—Milton is close to Thomistic tradition.[20] As far as "essence" being corrupted, Milton states in *Christian Doctrine:*

[17] *A Defence,* below, pp. 317–18.

[18] Milton has argued at the beginning of Book II of *A Defence* (below, pp. 341–42) that nothing could be more inhumane than to maintain that tyrannical kings are consistent with the natural law. Are such, he asks, (below, p. 342) assigned to us by "the gentle kindness of mother nature"? Milton's references to "nature" are almost invariably optimistic. The lady in Comus speaks of "most innocent nature." Once, however, in "On the Morning of Christ's Nativity," Milton approximated the Calvinist position: "Nature" hiding her *"guilty* front with innocent snow."

[19] *Christian Doctrine,* Columbia, XIV, 27.

[20] The word *nature* is often used in the seventeenth century without Calvinist associations. Arthur Lovejoy speaks of the "epistemological primitivism" of the period (Arthur O. Lovejoy and George Boas, *Primitivism and Related Ideas in Antiquity,* Baltimore, 1935, p. 253): "Notably in the 17th and 18th centuries it was to become a commonplace that men's minds as nature made them, *i.e.* illuminated with the 'pure light of nature' undimmed by sophistications arising from intellectual vanity, saw most clearly the simple and fundamental truths which man needed to know."

> There can be no doubt that for the purpose of vindicating the justice of God, especially in his calling of mankind, it is much better to allow man (whether as a remnant of his primitive state, or as restored through the operation of grace whereby he is called) some portion of free will in respect of good works, or at least of good endeavors . . . For if our personal religion were not in some degree dependent on ourselves, and in our power, God could not properly enter into a covenant with us, neither could we perform, much less swear to perform, the conditions of that covenant.[21]

But Milton's principal argument against kingship is based upon the "Law of Nature" rather than on Scripture. "Puritan" John Milton took the law of nature seriously and was not a strict Calvinist, believing neither in the essential corruption of the "natural" man nor in an unqualified predestination. He states in *The Christian Doctrine:* "If then God reject none but the disobedient and unbelieving, he undoubtedly gives grace to all, though not in equal measure, yet sufficient for attaining knowledge of the truth and final salvation." [22] Among Milton's special assumptions about the law of nature is that a free people is not bound by any statute of preceding Parliaments, but by the law of nature only, which is the only law of laws truly and properly fundamental to all mankind. It is to this law that any reforming Parliament or people must have recourse.[23] What is superior by nature should rule what is inferior, even if it is necessary to use force:

> Indeed by the laws of nature every good king always accounts the senate or the people not only his peers but his betters. But a tyrant being by nature inferior to all men, whoever is stronger than he ought to be accounted equal and superior to him. For even as nature of old taught men from force and violence to betake themselves to law, so whenever law is set at naught, the same dictate of nature must necessarily prompt us to betake ourselves to force again.[24]

According to Arthur Barker, interpreting certain passages in the *Tetrachordon,* Milton thinks of a primary and a secondary law of nature.[25] "Prime nature"—nature before the Fall—"has made us all equal, made

[21] *Christian Doctrine,* Columbia, XV, 213–14. [22] *Ibid.,* XIV, 147.

[23] *The Readie & Easie Way* (second ed., 1660), pp. 9–10.

[24] *A Defence,* below, p. 466. "Profecto jure naturali rex quisque bonus senatum vel populum habet sibi semper et parem at superiorem: Tyrannus autem cum natura infimus omnium sit, nemo non illi par atque superior existimandus est, quicunque viribus plus valet. Quemadmodum enim a vi olim ad leges duce natura deventum est, ita, ubi leges pro nihilo habentur, necessario, eadem etiam duce, ad vim est redeundum" (*A Defence,* 1658, p. 110).

[25] Arthur Barker, *Milton and the Puritan Dilemma* (Toronto: University of Toronto, 1942), pp. 114 ff.

us equal coheirs by common right and dominion over all creatures." But because of the subsequent decay from original righteousness, nature "suffered not only divorce but all that which by civilians is termed 'the secondary law of nature and of nations.' " The secondary law of nature is an imperfect expression of the original law of nature. Under the Gospel, however, there is a "second fresh penciling of the eternal law by the spirit in the hearts of believers, a renewing of law originally engraven in Adam's breast." The law of nature, therefore, sometimes refers to the law as it would apply to the regenerate in a Christian commonwealth. In this sense it is only the regenerate who are capable of the *natural* liberty which is the end of just government. But the law of nature, in a secondary sense, may apply to the natural right of any people, Christian or otherwise, to freedom from tyranny—but not necessarily to the right of natural liberty—a very different matter.[26]

The regenerate, following a higher law of nature, are not necessarily subject to the magistrates. What this wise and virtuous minority does (in *A Defence*, it is the army) is in accordance with the law of nature and, therefore, representative of the people.[27] Milton is not concerned with explaining to outsiders by what criteria, juridical or otherwise, the wisdom and virtue of such a minority can be determined and proved. When Salmasius asks pertinently, "Who excluded the lords from the parliament, was it the people?" Milton's answer is flatly, "Ay, it was the people." When Salmasius presses with persistence, "Was it the people that maimed the House of Commons by driving away some of its members?" Milton replies, "Yes, I say it was the people." [28]

III

Before the all-important relationship of the ruler to natural law can be clarified in Milton and Salmasius, their conflicting interpretations of the word *people* have to be clarified.

Basically, for Salmasius, people are the subjects whom the sovereign governs. For Milton, people are the better part who are regenerate and in conformity to the will of God. Actually Salmasius, in following the principle of divine right, is in one sense more democratic than Milton, because people include everyone but the king, whereas in Milton, when definition

[26] *Ibid.*, p. 190.

[27] *Cf.* below, p. 457. "For whatsoever the better, that is, the sounder part of the legislature did, in which the true powers of the people resided, why may not the people be said to have done it? What if the majority of the legislature should choose to be slaves, or to set the government for sale, ought not the minority prevent this and keep their liberty, if it be in their power?"

[28] *A Defence*, below, p. 457.

is forced upon him, people constitute an élite class. Milton sometimes speaks of *people* in the popular historical sense of a collective organism, as distinct from its individual members or élite groupings, especially in his quotations and historical citations. And Salmasius, on the other hand, often thinks of the people as a special cultural group in a sense the reverse of Milton's—the lower classes, *plebs* rather than *populus,* as in his unique reference to the Levellers.[29] Salmasius makes it clear that *people* in his sense are not just an aggregate of individuals; [30] Salmasius thinks of *people* as transcending individuals; he has a sense of *people* as we might have in the word *corporation* or in "suing a corporation as a legal person." He is closer than Milton to the medieval juridical *communitas*. A people exists for Salmasius independently of the individuals who compose it.

Both Milton and Salmasius, regarding the relationship of people to government, share in varying degrees of theological determinism. According to Salmasius, good rulers are given as a reward to people; tyrants, as punishment. Both kings and tyrants, viewed as God's instruments, would seem equally to be carrying out the duties of predestination. Milton argues in one case that, if Salmasius can justify the Emperor Nero as one of the "powers that be," to whom, regardless of his immorality, as *de facto* sovereign, obedience is owed, then why not to the de facto Cromwell? [31] Salmasius argues his predestination so far as to claim that, in the case of the ballot, God himself directs the votes and opinions of men to what he has in mind, actually "rigs" elections! [32]

Milton at times argues like Salmasius, but from a reverse point of view. God, Milton argues, allowed the Jews to depart from a theocratic republic, and institute kings—*as a punishment for their obduracy.*

Allowing for these differences in the use of the word *people,* we may ask what natural law demands in the way of status and qualifications for the ruler.

Milton finds the origin of kingship in personal character. He had always been conscious of the supposed natural right of the superior to rule the inferior. He states this in many places and in a great variety of ways. Like Aristotle, he did not believe in an even distribution of rights, but in a distribution according to merit. Merit, of course, did not depend on purely natural talent, but more especially upon the acceptance of divine truth (generally given, of course, a sectarian interpretation).

Salmasius also supports the basis of leadership in natural law, but on a very different principle from that of Milton. His concept is based on the "natural" status of the father and is, in this sense, much closer to the ancient Roman law (the *patria potestas*). Salmasius, following Aristotle,

[29] "Peraequatores" in *Regia* (1649), p. 182, l. 25. [30] *Ibid.,* p. 168, ll. 1 ff.
[31] See *A Defence,* below, p. 384 [32] *Regia* (1649), p. 172, ll. 4–5.

traces the growth of the state from the union of villages, following the laws of kinship. The family leads to the growth of the village, and the villages lead to the state following the authority of the father, on a primogeniture basis. Kings, as derived from fathers, follow the original historical pattern. Salmasius would not agree with Hobbes that it was originally fear that gathered men together into societies, but rather it was fear *in the first place* that had scattered them from their natural historical pattern of father-king relationship.[33]

Kings, according to Milton, do not fall within the law of nature.[34] Salmasius maintains the opposite. Salmasius adheres completely to the theory of "rex legibus solutus" which a Catholic theologian like Bellarmine no less than a Milton denies.[35] But in Salmasius a king is "above" the law only in the sense that no human agency may punish him. In fact, Salmasius emphatically states that "All antiquity holds that a king was unbound by laws, as much secular as those instituted by Christ."[36] But a king can be punished only by God. If the king is unfettered by laws, he ought not to judge by this that he is above the laws, that he may live more unrestricted than others who seem bound by them. Kings are merely men who return to the same dust with the others.[37] "Fears have been imposed upon the kings of all nations, but not so as to bind them by fear of trial and execution."[38]

In refuting a Salmasian analogy between a king and a father, Milton insists that "Our fathers begot and made us; our king made not us, but we him. Nature gave the people fathers, but the people gave itself a king."[39]

But Milton in supporting this argument had a thorny point to meet in the exegesis of the Hebrew Scriptures regarding kings. Did the Hebrew kings receive their appointments from God, as Salmasius insisted? Milton from his reading of Hebrew history is forced to admit the possibility of a king being appointed by God, but at the same time he insists that such a king, like all other kings, is bound by covenants, implicit contracts

[33] *Ibid.*, p. 175, l. 28 ff.: "Haec prima origo regalis regiminis, & ab his principiis repetenda, ut maxime naturalis, ratio & causa monarchici imperii."

[34] *A Defence,* below, p. 342. Kings are imposed on men not by nature, asserts Milton, but by crime, superstition, cowardice. In equating the law of nature with that of Scripture, Milton contends, following St. Chrysostom, that St. Paul "does not say that there is no prince but of God. He says there is no power but of God." A "power" falls within the law of nature; a "prince" does not.

[35] *Cf.* Courtney Murray, "St. Robert Bellarmine on the Indirect Power," *Theological Studies,* IX:4 (December, 1948), 527.

[36] *Regia* (1649), p. 159, ll. 32–33. In Salmasius' view, the king is never free, however, from moral, as distinct from legal, responsibility.

[37] *Ibid.*, p. 338, ll. 11–12. [38] *Ibid.*, p. 43, ll. 18–19.

[39] *A Defence* (1658), p. 2: "Pater nos genuit; at non rex nos, sed nos regem creavimus."

between king and people. These covenants apparently grew out of the secondary law of nature previously described. They are necessary in the secular state as a result of the fall of man. The absolute law of God does not abolish the rights of the people.

What are the implications in this debate relative to the law of nature? Obviously Milton conceived of the law of nature as an implicit code of abstract justice superior to that of the state.[40] Although the law of nature was distinct in Roman thought from the law of nations which, though unwritten like the law of nature, was based on custom rather than on abstract universal reason, Milton himself finds a perfect correlation among the law of nature, the law of nations, and the law of Scripture. Salmasius, in constantly asking by what law the king was condemned, means *by what written law*. For Milton, the answer is the unwritten law of nature. This thesis infuriated Salmasius, who finds in it a blank wall. "The English rascals dare to say that, when the written law fails, recourse should be made to natural law." [41]

If Salmasius had maintained that the king is "loosed from the law," had not Milton argued that the *people*, the righteous minority, were *above* the law? Milton's basic innovation in *A Defence* is his insistence upon the rights of a minority, if it is "right," to take matters into its own hands. His justification for his point of view lies in the special interpretation that he gives to the law of nature.

William J. Grace
Fordham University

[40] *Cf.* Don M. Wolfe, *Milton in the Puritan Revolution* (New York, 1941), p. 308.

[41] *Regia* (1649), p. 166, ll. 32–34.

ROBERT W. AYERS

TEXTUAL NOTE: *PRO POPULO ANGLICANO DEFENSIO*

The *Defensio,* first published in London by Dugard in quarto, February 24, 1651, was speedily reprinted by others. By spring there were several editions, and no later than October, probably even August of the same year, Dugard himself published a folio "Editio emendatior," larger in format and imposing in appearance. Milton continued to think well of the patriotic act which the *Defensio* constituted, with the consequence that he published a much revised edition in duodecimo, probably in October, 1658.[1]

The present translation [2] is based primarily upon the Columbia University Library copy, B823M64 X5 1658, of the 1658 edition (Madan No. 14), which Milton designates as the final form of the work. Collation: 12mo: A-G^{12}, H^{10} [$5 (-A1, title page) signed]; 94 leaves; pp. [16] 1-171 [1]. Contents: [A1], title page (verso blank); A2-[A8], Preface; [A8v], blank; [A9]-[H10], the work; [H10v], errata. This copy has been collated with British Museum copy E.1900.(1), and Houghton Library (Harvard) copy 14496.13.25*. Occasional use has also been made of Princeton University Library copy EX 3859.37.15 of variant 1 of the third issue of the first edition (1651, quarto, Madan No. 1), and of Pierpont Morgan Library copy W4D of the second edition (1651, folio, Madan No. 2). Complete descriptions of all authorized editions will be found below, Appendix H, pp. 1140–44.

ROBERT W. AYERS
Georgetown University

[1] For dates and bibliographical data, see below, Appendix H, pp. 1140–44.

[2] In the translation of *A Defence* the page numerals of the original Latin text have been inserted in brackets after the English equivalent. This practice has been followed through the volume in all translations of Latin originals. Placement of such bracketed page numerals can, of course, be only approximate, but it was felt that such pagination would be very useful to future scholars.

TRANSLATOR'S NOTE

Essays on the principles of translating are many, and another is not needed here. There is wide agreement that translators can but be traitors; yet the reluctant traitor aims at fidelity. The goal is in one part relatively simple—to reproduce the logical content of the original. The success or failure of this part of the translator's work can be measured with objectivity and reasonable ease by any competent judge. In a volume of this length errors caused by ignorance or carelessness may have survived: if this is so, the translator's protests that he did his best are no excuse, and he can but cry *mea culpa*.

Logical content, however, is not everything, even in a prose polemic, especially in one by a master artist. The words themselves have connotations not suggested by their rough equivalents in another language. Arrangements of words in an inflected language cannot be reproduced in English; and Latin usage encourages a degree of balancing and subordination of clauses not found in English.

Milton came as close as anyone could to writing Latin in English: one thinks of parts of the *Areopagitica*. Few of us will probably regret that this example was not generally followed. The translator has aimed at fidelity in tone and style, but not at the expense of failing to write English—not Milton's English, of course. Such an attempt would demand unusual learning and audacity. Nor are we using modern colloquialism, which would be quite inappropriate for a text considered so serious by its author.

No one style, in fact, can handle the variety of styles in Milton's Latin. At times it is senatorial rhetoric, and we hear again Cicero against Catiline or Antony. At times it is Plautine comedy, earthy in its humor and delighting in puns. At times the dominant tone is the satirist's *saeva indignatio*. A modern classicist, indeed, can only marvel at the width of Milton's classical learning. He knew and used the vocabulary and phraseology of Latin authors from the beginning down to his own day. In the volume before us Milton strikes down his opponent with Olympian thunderbolts; he thumbs his nose at the pedant with a schoolboy's impudence; he pierces him with the rapier of wit.

But, above all, fierce indignation! Is this pedant and poltroon Salmasius to challenge with impunity the liberties of the people of England? This *Gallus*—how can one reproduce it? Gallus, a Frenchman? Gallus, a cock crowing on his dunghill? Gallus, a eunuch priest of Cybele? Milton means all these. The flexibility and range of Milton's style defies as it challenges the translator. One can but vary the mood of the English version to reflect the changes in the Latin. One can but try, knowing that success is beyond reach, and the only question is the degree of treachery involved.

DONALD C. MACKENZIE

Williams College

JOANNIS MILTONI
Angli
PRO POPULO ANGLICANO
DEFENSIO

Contra *Claudii Anonymi*, aliàs *Salmasii*, Defensionem REGIAM.

LONDINI,
Typis *Du-Gardianis*. Anno Domini 1651.

Joannis Miltoni
ANGLI
PRO
Populo Anglicano
DEFENSIO
Contra *Claudii Anonymi*, aliàs
SALMASII
DEFENSIONEM REGIAM.

Editio correctior & auctior, ab Autore denuo recognita.

LONDINI,
Typis *Neucombianis*, Anno Dom. 1658.

PREFACE[1]

I AM afraid that it would seem as if I deserve the title of a verbose as well as an inept defender of the people of England, if I were to be as full of words and as lacking in substance as Salmasius ap-

[1] In its organization Milton's *A Defence* follows that of Salmasius' *Defensio Regia.* Both works consist of a preface followed by twelve "books." In his own preface Milton attempts to answer some of the main points discussed by Salmasius in the preface to *Defensio Regia.*

The leading ideas of Salmasius' preface may be summarized as follows: (1) No such deed as this "parricide . . . committed by a nefarious conspiracy of impious men" has ever been known. The act will serve as a bad example for the future. (2) The perpetrators of the crime deserve the hatred and abuse of all types of people; they are willing both to overthrow the kingdom and to subvert its laws. (3) They never intended to set up a popular government. Instead of one king they have set up forty tyrants. The English "triumvirs," leaders of the faction against the king, retained the kingdom for themselves, selecting thirty-seven accomplices in tyranny to share the power and oppress the citizens in servitude. They deprived the kings and nobles of liberty and even of life. (4) They think only *they* govern fairly. They adopted the name of *Independents,* since they wished to depend upon no one, and wished all to depend upon them! (5) All kings are onerous to them. They actually killed a king whose "piety, justice, religion, and clemency was second to none among the ancient kings." His only harm was that he reigned, not that he reigned badly. (6) If they had really wished a republic, they would have left the government, once the king was removed, to the bishops, nobles, and representatives of the people. The bishops and nobles, both ancient orders, were debarred. (7) The bishops had been retained even during the Reformation; it seemed that they were necessary! Many Presbyterians admitted the fact. As long as there was an episcopacy, a thousand baleful sects and heresies did not sprout in England (among the most offensive sects are the Brownists and the Independents). (8) The Independents are the very ones who first banished the bishops, and then the nobles, from Parliament, and soon deprived the king of his kingdom and his life. Their real wish was to set up not a democracy but a tyranny. (9) The control of affairs has returned to *one* [Cromwell]. He is king in everything but name. The legitimate king did not commit even a hundredth part of *their* crimes in violating human and divine laws. These men have abrogated laws and assumed powers that the real king did not have. The whole affair of the condemnation and killing of the king was contrary to the laws of the land. (10) The men now in power have overthrown a government of a thousand years' standing. They have established a tyranny deceitfully called "popular" government. "Is it a democracy, in which forty nefarious men, slayers of the king, have the highest authority over affairs, an authority from which it is impossible to appeal?" (11) Power [sovereignty] cannot reside in the people when no appeal is possible from the forty tyrants, when the people cannot make laws or create magistrates. (12) The tyrannical acts of the leaders

peared to many in his defense of the king.[2] Nevertheless, since not even in the treatment of an ordinary subject should one be so hasty as to fail to employ some introduction appropriate to the importance of the work he is undertaking, I too hope that, if in my discourse on this subject of paramount importance I neither neglect nor overdo an introduction, I may reach my two main ends: That so far as it in me lies, I may in no way fail this cause, which is most noble and deserving of eternal remembrance, and that I may be held to have myself avoided the futility and redundance which I censured in my opponent.

My discourse, indeed, will be of matters neither small nor mean: [3] a king in all his power, ruling according to his lust after he had over-

---

of the rebel army include: keeping the king in prison, seizing the city by arms, filling the homes of the citizens with soldiers, plundering the treasury, putting members of Parliament in chains. They gave judicial power, especially over the king, to the lower house . . . abrogated old laws, set up new laws, punished crimes arbitrarily. (13) The Independents desire only to command, not to obey, and will not subject themselves to any magistrate or to any law. If they had their way, they would exterminate all kings within ten years. (14) The blood of the king of England summons to its revenge all wearers of crowns. Suitable revenge consists in restoring the son to the throne and punishing those "most savage beasts," the Independents.

[2] Normally Milton refutes Salmasius in the order of the points made by his opponent. The quotations by Salmasius are usually consecutive. Although more often than not Milton quotes directly, he frequently paraphrases, omitting words and phrases that in a modern manuscript would be indicated by the use of three or four dots. Milton's quotations are generally fair; but sometimes, in the heat of polemics, he overlooks the fulness of Salmasius' meaning and makes Salmasius' thinking appear more petty and trivial than it really is.

Salmasius tends to be repetitive. His method is to make each book a unit in itself, sometimes incorporating references, quotations, and arguments he has previously used which he considers germane to the new consideration of his subject. In spite of this verbosity, he makes a number of telling points not lacking in substance, but weakened by his constant insistence on Divine Right.

[3] Milton's point-by-point refutation of his opponent prevents him from giving *A Defence* its own structure and emphasis. Among other critics, Samuel L. Wolff and James Holly Hanford have deplored the structure and sequence of argument Milton accepted from his opponent. Wolff writes ("Milton's 'Advocatum Nescio Quem,'" *MLQ*, II, December 4, 1941, 559): *"A Defence* . . . does not attract the reader to its own contents; rather it distracts him from them by keeping him conscious that they are for the most part prescribed from without." Hanford writes (*A Milton Handbook*, New York, 1946, p. 110): "Milton seldom rises to principles, confining himself to point by point replies to his opponent." Actually, however, if the text of the *Defensio* is considered from the point of view of its intellectual content, unembarrassed by Milton's rhetorical views and by seventeenth-century personal vituperation, a clear and cogent argument does emerge which can be examined on its merits. As I have shown above (pp. 286–91),

thrown our laws and oppressed our religion, at length overcome in battle by his own people which had served a long term of slavery; after that put under guard; and, when neither in word nor deed had he given the slightest ground for hope of his improvement, condemned to capital punishment by the highest court of the realm and beheaded before the very gates of the palace.[4] I shall also explain (which will greatly aid in freeing men's minds from the burden of superstition) what law it was, and in particular what law of our people, in accordance with which this judgment and execution took place; and I shall easily defend my fellow-citizens, those brave and upright men who have deserved so well of the citizens and peoples of all the world, from the most unjust slanders of native or foreign calumniators, and particularly from the revilings of this vain sophist who acts as leader and cheerleader of the rest. For what majesty of an high-enthroned king ever shone with brilliance such as that which [A2] flashed forth from the people of England when they had shaken off this ancient and enduring superstition,[5] and caused the king himself (or rather that

---

Milton's argument does grapple with principles, whether or not one can accept their application to the actions of the Independents.

Milton's skill as a debater in the technical sense is of a high order. He is agile and versatile, but comprehensive rather than selective. One of the many examples of his technique is the argument (see below, p. 384) in which he turns Salmasius' contention that Christians obeyed Nero's *de facto* government into support of the principle that Christians should likewise obey the *de facto* government of Cromwell.

[4] Milton disregards the assumption that Charles stepped to the scaffold from a window of the Banqueting House of Whitehall. See Gardiner, *Great Civil War* (4 vols., London, 1905), IV, 321.

[5] Throughout *A Defence* Milton assumes that the powers attributed to Charles I actually reside in the people of England. Milton states (below, pp. 317–18) that the king was punished "by that law of Nature and of God which holds that whatever is for the safety of the state is right and just." In the present treatise Milton does not face the juridical issue of who has the legal right, or what legal machinery can be devised, to determine what things are for the safety of the state and how the law of nature is to be interpreted.

Salmasius is deeply skeptical that the oligarchy ruling England ("the forty nefarious men") represents the people. On the surface they have transferred authority to the people, but in actual fact, he contends, they have appropriated it to themselves. See *Defensio Regia* (1649 folio; UTSL), p. 7, ll. 4–10. Hereafter cited as *Regia, 1649.*

Salmasius questions the meaning of the statement that the voice of the people is the voice of God (*Regia,* 1649, p. 28). *People* includes kings and leaders. Later Salmasius writes (*Regia,* 1649, p. 169, ll. 28–35): "It is fitting before all things to know what they wish to be understood by the name of people. The *'people'* is

enemy who had once been king, and who alone among men asserted a divine right of freedom from punishment) to be caught in the meshes of his own laws and to tremble at the bar of justice? Finally, did they shrink from inflicting on his guilty person the same penalty he would

---

generally divided into nobles and common people . . . If they interpreted people in this sense which includes all kinds and conditions of men, they might talk less aimlessly."

Neither Milton nor Salmasius presses the concept of "people" in a juridical sense, in the same way that we speak of a corporation as a "person." Salmasius himself frequently thinks of people merely as a crowd of disorderly plebeians; Milton as often equates "people" with his own selective minority of better citizens. Salmasius writes that nothing is more fickle than the common people (*Regia,* 1649, p. 170, ll. 17–18); that they have as many heads as persons (*Regia,* 1649, p. 214, l. 6); that no one is known as people in England except a crowd of workmen and artisans (*Regia,* 1649, p. 290, ll. 5–6).

As viewed by the Independents, asserts Salmasius, the people consisted partly of soldiers, partly of the unlearned and stupid mass. The "mass" itself is inclined to revolution; they believe that they are cured of their malady if they change their bed.

Again and again Salmasius returns to his concept of the English Independents as a vulgar mass (*Regia,* 1649, p. 51, l. 39; p. 52, ll. 1–5): "But who is that people in whom the advocate of crime [John Cook] wishes the power of creating the king to reside? Is it not a crowd of workmen of the lowest class? Among the Israelites the power of appointing a king was not given to the dregs, the filth of a people. The elders of the people alone had this right, long aged in experience, proved in wisdom, and powerful in the Sanhedrin."

Actually Salmasius, in spite of his snobbery, in following the principle of royal right is theoretically more democratic than Milton, at least more universal, because people include everyone but the king, whereas in Milton, when definition is forced upon him, people are an élite class, regenerate and in conformity to the will of God. But complications arise when both writers use the term "people" broadly. Milton sometimes speaks of the people in the more popular historical sense of a universal organism distinct from its individual members or elite grouping (especially in his quotations and historical citings), and Salmasius often thinks of the people as a special cultural group—the lower classes (the "people of England"), *plebs* rather than *populus,* as in his unique reference to Levellers ("Peraequatores," *Regia,* 1649, p. 182, ll. 24 ff.).

The views of both men are at times complicated by theological determinism. According to Salmasius, good kings are given to the people (to all individuals, to good individuals only, to the corporation that transcends the aggregate of individuals?), tyrants as a punishment. Both, as God's instruments, would seem to be doing their duty. Salmasius goes so far as to say (*Regia,* 1649, p. 172, ll. 4–5) that God himself directs the votes and opinions of men to what He has in mind (*i.e.,* rigs elections). Then how could men reject kings, it might be asked? Milton at times argues like Salmasius, but in reverse. God allowed the Jews to depart from a theocratic republic, and institute kings, as a punishment for their obduracy. But, it might be asked, weren't the Jews in so doing and in being punished, fulfilling the Will of God?

have inflicted on any other man? But why do I proclaim as if performed by the people these deeds which, as I may say, in their very nature send forth a voice and bear witness to the presence of God in every place?

It is God who, whenever his infinite wisdom wills it, is wont to overthrow haughty and unruly kings who exalt themselves above the measure of mankind, and he often destroys them utterly with their whole house. It was by his evident will that we were unexpectedly encouraged to hope for that security and liberty which had been well-nigh lost to us: We followed him as our leader; and with reverence for the traces of the divine presence at every step we entered on a path surrounded by no shadows, but rather illumined, pointed out to us, and revealed by his guidance. To treat worthily of all these great events, and to compose a memorial which every nation and every age may perhaps read, would be (if I were to rely on my diligence alone, whatever it may be, and my strength alone) but a vain hope. What elevated and splendid discourse, what outstanding talent, could be capable of sustaining such a burden?—especially when in all the centuries hardly one person can be discovered able to write with distinction about the deeds of famous men or states. Should any man believe that any words or language of his could match these great and wonderful deeds performed evidently by almighty God himself rather than by mortal men?

Even though the leaders of our state have authorized me to undertake this task,[6] and desired that it be my duty to furnish the deeds they so gloriously performed under God's guidance with a defence against jealous slanders (a duty second in importance to theirs alone, and one in which the sword and implements of war are of no avail, but which requires other weapons); and, although I take great pride in their decision that by their wishes I before all others should be the one to take on this enviable task for the noble liberators of my country (because indeed from early youth I eagerly pursued studies which impelled me to celebrate, if not to perform, the loftiest actions) [A2v], it is nevertheless a fact that, despite all such encouragements, I lose heart and turn to aid from on high. I call on almighty God, giver of all gifts, to grant that just as success and righteousness attended those

[6] On January 8, 1650, Milton was ordered by the Council of State to prepare "something in answer to the Booke of Saltmatius, and when hee hath done itt bring itt to the Councell." See French, *Life Records,* II, 286.

famous men who led us to liberty, who crushed in line of battle the insolence of the king and the passion of the tyrant, and who then by a memorable punishment put an end to them forever, and that just as I alone, when the king rose again as it were from the dead and in his posthumous volume commended himself to the people by new slyness and meretricious arguments, did recently overcome and do away with him,[7] so I may now with good success and in very truth refute and bring to naught the ill-tempered lies of this barbarous rhetorician [Salmasius].

Though Salmasius is a foreigner and—deny it as often as he will—a grammarian,[8] he is yet not content with the rewards of his trade and would prefer to be a great busybody; he dares to meddle with government, and that not his own, although to so great an undertaking he brings neither moderation nor understanding nor any other suitable talent, but only arrogance and his grammarian's lore. If his present writings, composed in a kind of Latin, had been published in England in our language, I believe they would hardly have seemed to anyone worth the trouble of answering, for some would despise them as hackneyed arguments refuted over and over again long ago, and others, even royalists, would spurn them as foully tyrannical and not to be borne by the vilest of slaves. Now, however, when he makes his turgid pages current among foreigners who know nothing of our affairs, it is necessary that those who misunderstand our situation should be instructed, and that Salmasius, who so often yields to his great passion for calumny, should be treated himself as he treats others. Some may wonder why we have suffered him to go in triumph so long rejoicing unassailed in our universal silence: [9] As for others I know not, but for

[7] This refers to Milton's *Eikonoklastes,* written in answer to the *Eikon Basilike,* the "posthumous volume" popularly attributed to Charles I. See *Complete Prose,* III, 335–601.

[8] Milton's reference to Salmasius as a "grammarian" is one of contempt. The term signifies "elementary school teacher," as well as "philologist" and "annotator." Among his voluminous works Salmasius edited several Roman historians, which earned his call to Leyden in 1631. Milton's slur is belied by the fact that Salmasius was the most famous scholar of Europe, sought after not only by great universities of his day but also by kings and queens. Almost any city in Europe, including London before 1641, would have considered it a great honor to have the privilege of supporting Salmasius in the style befitting a prince.

[9] Milton's reply actually took twenty months. We know that a copy of Salmasius' work had appeared in England by May 11, 1649 (French, *Life Records,* II, 246). We know also that *A Defence* was entered in the *Stationers' Registers* on December 1, 1650. J. Milton French (*Life Records,* II, 350–51) places the actual date of publication on February 24, 1651.

myself I can say with assurance that if I had been granted leisure and strength enough for writing it would have been no long laborious task to find words and arguments for the defence of a cause so just.[10]

But in the precarious health [11] I still enjoy I must work at intervals [A3] and hardly for an hour at a time, though the task calls for continuous study and composition. Therefore, even though I may be unable to herald worthily the praises of those noble fellow citizens who preserved our country and whose deathless deeds now resound through the whole world, I may still hope it will be no great task for me to justify and defend them against the arrogance of this tiresome pedant and his foolish professorial talk. Surely nature and law would have been badly looked after if slavery were eloquent and freedom dumb, if tyrants had advocates [6] but those who can master them had none. It would be sad if the very reason which we enjoy by gift of God did not furnish far more arguments for preserving men, setting them free, and as far as nature allows making them equal one to another, than for grinding them down and ruining them utterly under a single despot.

Let us then approach this cause so righteous with hearts lifted up by a sure faith that on the other side stand deception, lies, ignorance and savagery, on our side light, truth, reason, and the hopes and teachings of all the great ages of mankind.[12]

* * * * * * *

[10] In presenting "a cause so just," Milton does not follow any technique of modern propaganda or psychological warfare. Although the *Defensio* was directed to a continental audience (there were many more editions abroad than at home) and composed in Latin, Milton's arguments are not addressed to doubtful or neutral opinion. Outside of the persistent effort to destroy the prestige of Salmasius, Milton's arguments are partisan and are directed to strengthening the convictions of those already convinced. Partisanship is absolute; the champion insults and exults over his foe, and reviles him with rhetorically delicious insults before going to the next point. In accord with this partisanship, Milton assumes (without feeling any necessity for proof) the unmitigated guilt of Charles I. The main intellectual content of the treatise is concerned not with Charles I but with the moral justification of the right of the people to remove a tyrant.

[11] Milton later wrote in *Defensio Secunda* (1654, p. 47; below, pp. 587–88): ". . . cum datum mihi publice esset illud in defensionem regiam negotium, eodemque tempore & adversa simul valetudine, & oculo jam pene altero amisso conflictarer." See also French, *Life Records,* II, 290.

[12] William R. Parker in *Milton's Contemporary Reputation* (Columbus: Ohio State University Press, 1940), p. 86, refers to a report in the *Mercurius Politicus,* No. 56, June 27–July 3, 1651, p. 890, that Milton's book "hath been burnt at Thoulouse, by an arrest of that parliament." A subsequent publication of that

Well then, I have given preface enough, and since our business is with critics let us see first what the title of such an elegant work has to say: *A Royal Defence of Charles the First, to Charles the Second.*[13] You undertake a great task obviously, whoever you are, in defending a father to his son: It will be a wonder if you do not win your case. But now, Salmasius, though you take refuge in anonymity as elsewhere you did under a false name, I summon you before another court and other judges, where perhaps you will not hear those cheers and bravos which you strove for so desperately in your own literary exercises. Why indeed is this defence of the king directed to the king his son? No torture is needed, for the defendant confesses. "At the king's expense," Salmasius says.[14] Your discourse is hired, then, and at a high price.

So you were unwilling to defend Charles the father, best of kings in your judgment, before Charles the son, poorest of kings, without some royal recompense. Being a sly old rogue you did not wish to be a laughing-stock, and so you called it a "Royal" Defence: for after you had sold it the defence was no longer yours but rightly royal,

---

journal (July 3–10, 1651, pp. 914–15) includes Paris as well as Toulouse. The reporter adds "and by this policy of the Court, in burning the Book, will make it a Martyr, whose ashes will be scattered far and wide, and the Cause and the Book be more inquisitively desired." *Cf.* J. Milton French, "Milton, Needham, and *Mercurius Politicus,*" *SP,* XXIII (1936), 236–52. According to Parker (p. 35), "Ten or eleven reprints appeared on the continent, but two editions seemed to suffice for England until Milton himself revised it in 1658. All but two of these editions, at home and abroad, were confined to 1651; and after 1652 they ceased."

[13] The title page of Salmasius' book reads: *DEFENSIO REGIA, I. Pro CAROLO AD Serenissimum Magnae Britaniae Regem CAROLUM II Filium natu majorem, Heredem & Successorem legitimum. Sumptibus Regiis* Anno 1649.

[14] The title page contains the phrase "Sumptibus Regiis," which means "at the king's expense." J. Milton French (*Life Records,* II, 247) quotes a passage from *Claudii Salmasii Ad Johannem Miltonum Responsio, Opus Posthumum* (1660; PUL), p. 21 (hereafter cited as *Opus Posthumum, 1660*) to the effect that this phrase was used so that the book would be protected against prohibition of publication by reverence for the king's name. In all subsequent editions that same phrase was added like an amulet. In the same work (p. 270) Salmasius denies again that he ever got any reward for his work. W. McNeill, in "Milton and Salmasius," *English Historical Review,* LXXX, No. 314 (January, 1965), 107–108, notes a holograph of Sir William Boswell, English ambassador at The Hague, dated March, 1649. The text of the letter shows a warm appreciation for Salmasius' desire to write on behalf of Charles I, but it promises no sum of money for his efforts. The letter does not prove, of course, that Salmasius did not later receive a monetary payment.

bought indeed for an hundred sovereigns,[15] a fat reward from a starving king. I speak of what is known: I know who [A3v] brought the coins to your house, who carried that beaded purse; [16] I know who saw you stretch forth your greedy hands, pretending to embrace the king's chaplain, who had been sent with the gift, but actually embracing the gift itself; and indeed when you had received but a single payment the whole treasury was nearly drained. Here comes the man, though: the stage door creaks and the actor strides on to the boards:

> Give heed, keep silence, and see what the Eunuch wants.[17]
> Whatever he is, his approach is unusually tragic.

"Our ears have just been dealt a fearful wound, and our minds a worse, by a horrible message about the murder among the English in the person of the king, a murder committed by the wicked plot of sacrilegious men." [18] Surely that horrible message must have had a sword far longer than the one Peter drew,[19] or else these must have been most hare-like ears [20] to be wounded at such a distance, for the message could not even annoy any but the most stupid ears. What harm is done you, which of you is hurt, if we inflict on our enemies and foes, whether commoners, nobles, or kings, the penalty of death? Give up what concerns you not, Salmasius, for I have a "message" to send about you which is "horrible" indeed, and I shall be surprised if it does not deal a more "fearful wound" to the ears of all gram-

[15] We translate Milton's "Jacobaeis" as "sovereigns," in order to preserve his pun on *Jacobus* (James) and *jacobus* as a popular name for the sovereign, a coin first struck during the reign of James I, and valued then at about twenty shillings. *Translator's note.*

[16] Milton asserts here that he knows who delivered payment for the *Defensio Regia* to Salmasius without naming the messenger. Masson (IV, 255) identifies the man as Dr. *George* Morley, later bishop of Worcester and then of Winchester. In *Opus Posthumum* (1660), p. 270, Salmasius denies that he received any reward. Salmasius identifies the messenger as a Reverend William Morley (not *George* Morley) and states that the stuff about the sovereigns *(Jacobuses)* is nonsense. See J. Milton French, "Some Notes on Milton," *N&Q,* CLXXVIII (February 10, 1945), 52–55.

[17] Terence, *Eunuchus,* Prologue, ll. 44–45, in *Terence,* tr. John Sargeaunt (2 vols., Cambridge: Loeb Classical Library, 1939), I, 238–39.

[18] *Regia* (1649), p. 1, ll. 1–6.

[19] At the arrest of Jesus. See John 18:10; Matthew 26:51; Mark 14:47; Luke 22:50.

[20] hare-like ears: Actually a pun, *aures auritissimae,* which can hardly be reproduced in English.

marians and critics who are sensitive to polish and learning. This message concerns the murder among the Dutch in the person of Aristarchus,[21] committed by the wicked barbarism of Salmasius. You, the mighty critic, when hired at the king's expense to write the king's defence, not only failed to rouse the sympathy of any but fools with your most unnatural introduction which resembled nothing so much as the senseless wailing of women hired to mourn at funerals, but, furthermore, with your opening period you roused to laughter those who had hardly finished reading its manifold improprieties.[22] What, I ask you, is "committing murder in the person of the king," what is "in the person of the king"? [23] When was Latin ever spoken like that?

Unless perhaps you are telling us about some pretender like the false-Philip [24] who assumed the guise of king and carried out some murder or other among the English: In this you may have spoken more truly than you thought, for a tyrant, like [A4] a king upon the stage, is but the ghost or mask of a king, and not a true king. However, for rustic errors of speech of this sort in which you are so rich through-

[21] Greek grammarian and critic (ca. 220–145 B.C.).

[22] According to Henry J. Todd, *Poetical Works of John Milton* (6 vols., London, 1826), I, 125, as quoted by J. Milton French in *Life Records,* II, 248, a copy of Salmasius' book formerly existed, "the margins of which are said to be decorated with barbarisms and solecisms detected by Milton."

[23] *Regia* (1649), p. 1, ll. 3–4: "de parricidio apud Anglos in persona Regis." Milton questions Salmasius' use of *persona* as equivalent to *person.* Nor does Milton accept *persona* to mean *body.* The purest meaning of the word judged from its derivation would be *mask.* The word came to mean by transference "the part or character which one sustains in the world." It also comes to mean "a person or personage. Dr. Mackenzie observes: "Milton rightly objects not only to the sense in which Salmasius uses *persona,* but also to his phrase *in persona Regis.* Even if *persona* were equivalent to *corpus* the phrase would hardly be Latin: *in corpore Regis* would be a solecism in this context."

This is one of a number of places in which Milton attacks the Latinity of Salmasius (see below, note 53). In this particular instance, Milton overlooks the *juridical* meaning Salmasius gives the word *person.* Salmasius argues in book VIII of the *Defensio Regia* that a king has two aspects, one natural, one political. His political aspect cannot be killed or wounded (*cf.* the concept of the crown in contemporary British jurisprudence). For Salmasius power divorced from the person is chimerical. The political and natural bodies are in one person, and power (sovereignty) cannot be separated from the person (*Regia,* 1649, p. 216, ll. 15–16). "Majesty is inseparable from the person" (*Regia,* 1649, p. 217, ll. 26–27). The Independents are so greatly insane, he argues, "that they separate the person of the king from his power" (*Regia,* 1649, p. 215, ll. 14–16).

[24] the false Philip: Andriscus, a slave whose claim to be the son of King Perseus of Macedon stirred up the Fourth Macedonian War, 149–148 B.C.

out you shall be chastised not by me, for I have no time, but by your fellow pedagogues, to whom I deliver you for ridicule and caning.[25]

There is something worse to follow: You state that the decree of our highest magistrates concerning the king was the action of a foul conspiracy of sacrilegious men. Do you, a wretched scoundrel, so describe the deeds and decrees of what was but lately the strongest of realms, and is now, being a commonwealth, so much the stronger? No king (until now) even could be induced to pronounce or publish any heavier charge against the actions of those men. It is then with justice that the highest council of Holland, true descendants of the old liberators of their country, have by their edict condemned to oblivion this defence of tyranny, so ruinous to the freedom of all peoples; [26] its author every free state should ban or cast out from her borders, and particularly that state which at the public cost supports one so ungrateful and so foully hostile to the commonwealth.[27] For he attacks the very foundations and the basis in justice of that commonwealth as he does ours; he attempts indeed to weaken and subvert both at a single blow, and reviles with his abuse the great champions of liberty there under our names.

Consider now, most illustrious council of the Federated Netherlands, and weigh in your hearts who it was that incited this partisan

[25] caning: It is unfortunate that while Milton castigates Salmasius' solecism in the use of *persona,* he is himself culpable in his use of *vapulandum.* Dr. Mackenzie: "The proper form to express what Milton clearly intended is *verberandum:* see J. E. Sandys, *A History of Classical Scholarship* (3 vols., New York: Harper, 1958), II, 286."

[26] According to Francis F. Madan, Walter Strickland, the Parliamentary resident at The Hague, applied to the Estates of Holland and West Friesland for the suppression of Salmasius' *Defensio Regia* on November 6, 1649. The Estates concerned issued on January 17 an order suppressing the *Defensio.* J. Milton French (*Life Records,* II, 277) places the confiscation December 21–28. See Francis F. Madan, "A Revised Bibliography of Salmasius' *Defensio Regia* and Milton's *Pro Populo Anglicano Defensio,*" *The Library,* Fifth Series, Vol. IX, No. 2 (June, 1954), 101.

[27] Milton chides his fellow-commonwealthsmen in Holland for their maintenance of a writer as hostile to their republican premises as to those of the Independents. Salmasius went to Leyden in 1631 to fill the university chair vacated by Scaliger. He was not to teach, but to "shed on the university the honor of his name, illustrate it by his writings, and adorn it by his presence." Salmasius remained in Leyden until 1650, when he was called to the court of Christina of Sweden as her private tutor. For a fairly full biographical account, see Masson, IV, 162 ff. As Kathryn McEuen has shown, however, contrary to Masson's statements, Salmasius did not lose favor with Queen Christina because of Milton's attacks on him in *A Defence.* See below, pp. 968–69.

of royal authority to write, who it was that lately began to act the king amongst you. Consider what plots, attacks and disturbances followed throughout Holland, and what the case would now be, how slavery was prepared for you and a new ruler, and how that liberty which had been won by so many years of toil and battle would now have perished from your midst had not the most providential death of that headstrong youth [28] allowed it to breathe again.

But our friend continues his bombast and fashions wondrous tragedies: "Those to whom this awful news"—of Salmasius' murderous barbarisms no doubt—"comes, suddenly their hair stands on end [29] with horror and their voices stick in their throats, just as if they had been struck by a thunderbolt." [30] It will be news to the scientists [A4v] that thunderbolts stand hair on end, but everyone knows that mean and cowardly hearts are smitten even by the report of some great deed, and then clearly reveal themselves the fools they were before. "Some did not check their tears"—little women of the court, I suppose, or some others yet more effeminate, among them Salmasius himself, by a novel metamorphosis become a Salmacis,[31] attempting by his fountain of false tears distilled by lamplight to draw the strength from manly hearts. I therefore warn and caution:

> Lest wicked Salmacis should sap one's strength with waters
> strong to harm,
> And he who came a man should leave unmanned, touched
> by the water's melting charm.[32]

[28] Milton refers to the death of William II, Stadtholder of Orange, on November 6, 1650, at the age of twenty-four. William had married Mary, eldest daughter of Charles I, on May 12, 1641. In 1648 the sons of Charles I, James and Charles II, took refuge in the Netherlands. Revulsion in the Netherlands at the execution of Charles I created tension with the Commonwealth government bordering on war, though both countries were eager to avoid it for commercial reasons. Antagonism toward the Commonwealth, however, induced William II to make plans with Mazarin and Charles II which would have led to the increase of his power in the United Provinces and supposedly to the restoration of the Stuarts.

[29] hair stands on end: Virgil, *Aeneid,* IV, 280, in *Virgil,* revised ed., tr. H. Rushton Fairclough (2 vols., Cambridge: Loeb Classical Library, 1960), I, 414–15.

[30] *Regia* (1649), p. 1, ll. 6–10.

[31] A reference to Ovid, *Metamorphoses,* IV. Salmacis was the Carian fountain in which Hermaphroditus, son of Hermes and Aphrodite, was bathing when the nymph of the fountain whose love he had rejected prayed that she might be united to him forever. See Ovid, *Metamorphoses,* tr. Frank Justus Miller (2 vols., Cambridge: Loeb Classical Library, 1951), I, 198–99.

[32] Ovid, *Metamorphoses,* IV, 285–86, and 385–86.

"Those more bravely spirited"—for it seems he cannot even speak of brave and spirited souls in decent language—"burned with such a flame of indignation that they could scarce control themselves." [33] For such madmen we care not a fig, and such threats we rout and put to flight with that true courage which is master of itself. "Everyone surely cursed the authors of such a crime." [34] Their voices, however, as you were just saying, stuck in their throats, and I wish they had remained stuck until now, if it is our exiles of whom you speak, for we know well that their mouths are ever full of nothing but curses and threats which all good men do indeed hate but hardly fear. So far as other persons are concerned, it is not to be believed that anyone was found, particularly in a free people, so born to slavery that when the account of the king's punishment had reached him he would speak against us or accuse our action. On the contrary, we must suppose that all good men called all these events good, and even gave thanks to God as the giver of a model of justice so clear and lofty, and of such a wholesome warning to other rulers.

Those ferocious and flint-hearted men,[35] then, who weep for some strange sad slaughter, and with them their jingling spokesman who is the weakest since the world first heard and knew the name of king, may with our blessing weep and weep again. What lad fresh from school, or what fat friar from any cloister, would not have declaimed on this royal ruin with greater skill and even in better Latin than this royal advocate? I would be foolish indeed to pursue his childish [A5] ravings thus closely in the whole volume, although since he swells enormously with haughty pride that would be a pleasant task, were it not that he shields himself by such a rude barbaric structure of a book, and like Terence's soldier [36] lurks behind the ranks. This is surely a crafty plan, for thus the boldest foe would die of boredom in censuring each detail before he had confuted the last of them. I did wish to furnish at this time some example, at least to the extent of this prelude, and to give my sagacious readers an immediate taste of the man, so that we may discover from this one-page appetizer how well our host will treat us with his other fine dainties: What a mass of childish follies will be heaped up in the whole work of an author

[33] *Regia* (1649), p. 1, l. 12. [34] *Regia* (1649), p. 1, ll. 13–14.

[35] See Tibullus, *Elegies,* I, 10, 2, tr. J. P. Postgate, in *Catullus, Tibullus, and Pervigilium Veneris* (Cambridge: Loeb Classical Library, 1950), pp. 244–45.

[36] Terence, *Eunuchus,* 781.

who put so many of them at the very beginning where they had the least business. From this point on I shall disregard with pleasure this vocal composer of speeches fit only for mackerel.[37]

In so far as our affairs are concerned, however, there is no doubt that what has been publicly written and proclaimed by the authority of Parliament will have more weight with all upright and wise foreigners than the insulting lies of this single most impudent manikin, who, under hire to our exiles and the foes of their country, has no hesitation in scraping up and writing down the sheerest falsehoods when any of those to whom he had hired his services dictates to him or propagates his slander. To reveal to all his utter lack of conscience in writing anything at all, true or false, holy or unholy, I need summon no witness other than Salmasius himself. In his *Apparatus contra Primatum Papae* he writes:

> There are very weighty reasons why the church should return from Episcopacy to the apostolic institution of elders; from Episcopacy were introduced into the church evils far worse than the schisms which were once feared: the disease which from that source spread through the churches plagued the whole body of the church with a wretched tyranny and even subjugated rulers and monarchs themselves; there would be a greater benefit for the church if the whole hierarchy were abolished than only its head the pope (p. 196). The Episcopacy and the papacy could be cast out with great advantage; removal of the Episcopacy would drag down the papacy itself which is chiefly based on it [A5v] (p. 171). There are special reasons why it should be removed in the kingdoms which have already given up the papacy.

He sees

> no reasons why it should be retained there; the reformation which in this respect is incomplete seems but partial; no

[37] The word *scomber* (mackerel) was an epithet of abuse widely used by Roman poets. See Catullus, 95, 8 (*Catullus, Tibullus, and Pervigilium Veneris,* tr. F. W. Cornish [Cambridge: Loeb Classical Library, 1950], p. 168); Persius, *Satires,* I, 43 (*Juvenal and Persius,* tr. G. G. Ramsay [London and New York: Loeb Classical Library, 1924], p. 320); Martial, *Epigrams,* III, 50, 9 (Martial, *Epigrams,* tr. Walter C. A. Ker [2 vols., Cambridge: Loeb Classical Library, 1947], I, 194).

> reason or probable cause can be advanced for the need or possibility of preserving Episcopacy after abolition of the papacy (p. 197).[38]

Although four years ago he wrote this and much more to the same effect, he is now so vain and impudent as to dare seriously to accuse the English Parliament on this topic, that it moved not only to cast the bishops from the upper house,[39] but also to dispense with them entirely.[40] What is this? The very same Episcopacy he now upholds and recommends by use of the identical proofs and reasonings which in that former volume he had thoroughly exposed: bishops are now of course necessary and must by all means be kept, to prevent the burgeoning in England of a thousand pestilent sects and doctrines! [41]

[38] These quotations are derived from Salmasius' *Librorum de Primatu Papae, Pars Prima, Cum Apparatu Accedere de eodem Primatu, Nili & Barlaami Tractatus* (Leyden, 1645; NYPL). Elsewhere Milton uses variants in referring to the title of Salmasius' work. Here it is *Apparatus contra Primatum Papae;* below, p. 336, it is *Apparatus de Primatu;* below, pp. 348, 365, 398, it is *Apparatus ad Primatum.* Hereafter referred to as *De Primatu.*

The quotations attributed to Salmasius are partly paraphrase and direct quotation from several different pages. On p. 196 Salmasius states: "In Papa autem omnis mora stat ne Ecclesia novis illis stat dogmatibus & erroribus repurgetur, ac tota reformetur tam in capite ipso quam in membris." Nearer in meaning to the sense of lines 10–12 of the quotation is Salmasius' statement (p. 197): "De Episcopatu ipso proprias etiam habet is causas, cur removeri quodque debeat ab Ecclesiae regimine in illis regnis, ac rebuspublicis quae iam Papatui renunciarunt." On p. 171 is contained the substance of Milton's phrase about the Episcopacy dragging down the papacy with it: "Posse Episcopatum cum Papatu ipso tolli bono iure, idque cum summo bono Ecclesiae, ea quae praecesserunt, declarant. Et sublato quidem Episcopatu ruere ipsum Papatum super illo utpote fundatum & inaedificatum, certo est certius."

Milton's references to p. 197 contain literal quotations; but he omits Salmasius' statement that "Episcopacy strengthens the way and prepares the steps toward Papal monarchy" ("Episcopatus viam muniit & gradum fecit ad Papalem monarchiam"). Salmasius' statements quoted by Milton are: "Non integra videri potest nec plena reformatio quae hac parte imperfecta sit" and "Nihil afferri potest rationis aut causae probabilis cur sublato Papatu retineri debeat aut possit Episcopatus."

[39] An ordinance was passed on October 9, 1646, for "the abolishing of Archbishops and Bishops within the Kingdom of England and Dominion of Wales and for settling of their Lands and Possessions upon Trustees for the use of the Commonwealth." See Sir Charles H. Firth and R. S. Rait, *Acts and Ordinances of the Interregnum* (3 vols., London, 1911), I, 879–80.

[40] The Bishops Exclusion Bill received royal assent February 13, 1642. See Gardiner, *History of England,* X, 165, and *Complete Prose,* I, 179–80.

[41] *Cf. Regia* (1649), pp. 4, ll. 32–39; 5, l. 1: "The bishops had been retained even during the Reformation; it seemed that they were necessary . . . many

What a tricky turncoat you are! Do you carry your shameless vacillation to such lengths even where religion is concerned, or I might say in betrayal of the church? [42] That church it was whose holiest ordinances you apparently upheld with so much bluster for the sole purpose of overthrowing them at your convenience with greater scandal and mockery. It is known to all that when Parliament was most desirous of reforming our church like other churches and had decided wholly to abolish Episcopacy, then the king first forbade it and next went to war with us for this reason above all; and this war finally caused his own downfall.

Go and boast of being the king's advocate, you who now openly betray and attack the cause of the church, which you had yourself supported, so that you may stoutly defend the king: that church must stamp you with her heaviest censure. In what concerns the constitution of our commonwealth, however, now that you a half-pint peregrinatory professor have turned from your pigeonholes and carpetbags stuffed with a mass of nonsense, which you might better have been putting in order, and have chosen to become a nasty busybody in the affairs of a country where you have no business—on this subject I shall reply shortly to you, or rather to any wiser man than you.

Our form of government is such as our circumstances and schisms permit; it is not the most desirable, but only as good as the stubborn

---

Presbyterians admitting it, because as long as there was an Episcopacy, a thousand baleful sects and heresies did not sprout in England, and among them that most offensive one whose name is Brownists and Independents. They are the very ones who first banished the bishops, and then the nobles from Parliament, and soon deprived the king of his kingdom and his life."

[42] Salmasius' attitude toward bishops is somewhat equivocal. He believes that kings actually have ecclesiastical power, citing the fact (*Regia,* 1649, p. 229, ll. 29–30) that Moses appointed Aaron high priest. He terms Henry VII a "hybrid *person*" because he had both ecclesiastical and secular power. He calls to witness (*Regia,* 1649, p. 230, l. 39) the great jurist, Edward Coke. He quotes (*Regia,* 1649, p. 231, ll. 21–23) a statute of Edward III to the effect that kings "anointed by sacred oil" have spiritual jurisdiction.

But Salmasius does not strongly defend bishops, except to note (*Regia,* 1649, p. 264, ll. 7–9) that the pride of the bishops could not be compared with the pride of the Puritans. He argues on two occasions (*Regia,* 1649, pp. 263, ll. 30–34; 302, ll. 19–21) that the king found the bishops already established when he ascended the throne. The king did not make them. He had to protect them, lest he deny his inaugural oath.

Salmasius argues in his Preface (*Regia,* 1649, p. 4, ll. 33–37) that a thousand pestilent heresies did not sprout in England as long as the Episcopacy remained —that even the Presbyterians admitted this fact.

struggles of the wicked citizens allow it to be. If, however, a country harassed by faction and protecting herself by arms regards only the sound and upright side [A6], passing over or shutting out the others, whether commons or nobles, she maintains justice well enough, and this too even though she has learned by her own woes to suffer no longer a king or his lords. Your attack on the Supreme Council and the President of that Council simply makes you ridiculous, for the Council you dream of is not supreme,[43] but rather appointed for a specified time by the authority of Parliament and composed of forty men from its ranks; and any one of these may be chosen president by the votes of the rest. It has always been the practice for the Parliament, which is our Senate, to appoint a few of its members when it seemed necessary, to whom was granted the right to meet in any suitable place and conduct as it were a smaller Senate.[44] Often the most serious business was assigned and entrusted to them for speedier and less public settlement: the supervision and oversight of the fleet, army, treasury, and indeed any task of peace or war. This, whether called a council or something else, may be new in name but is in fact of long standing, and without it no state at all can be well governed.

As to the punishment of the king and the change in our form of government, you must stop that bawling and pouring forth of your poisonous venom [45] until I can join battle with you and show chapter by chapter, despite any opposition of yours, by what law, right, and judgment these things were done. If you still demand "By what right or what law?", my reply is "By that law of Nature [46] and of God which

[43] On February 13, 1648, an "Act for Constituting a Council of State for the Commonwealth of England" was passed, which contained sixteen provisions. Milton is technically correct in stating that the "Council you dream of is not supreme." There are two exceptions to the *carte blanche* which the act otherwise provides: (1) "You are alsoe to observe and putt in execution such further orders as you shall receive from tyme to tyme from the Parliament." (2) "The power hereby Comitted to this Counsell of State shall continue for the space of one whole yeare from the day of passing hereof, unlesse it be otherwise ordered by the Parliament." See Firth, *Acts and Ordinances,* II, 4.

[44] Salmasius' version is that they have established a tyranny deceitfully called "popular" government. He asks (*Regia,* 1649, p. 6, ll. 38 ff.): "Is it a democracy in which forty nefarious men, slayers of the king, have the highest authority over affairs, from which it is not permitted to make appeal?"

[45] *Cf.* Cicero, *De Amicitia,* xxiii, 87, in *De Senectute, De Amicitia, De Divinatione,* tr. William A. Falconer (Cambridge: Loeb Classical Library, 1953), pp. 194–95.

[46] Milton's final appeal is always to the "law of nature." Salmasius also appeals

holds that whatever is for the safety of the state is right and just."[47] This was the answer of wise men of old to such as you. You make it an accusation that we abolished laws in force for so many years, but

---

to the law of nature, deducing conclusions contradictory to those of Milton. Salmasius would accede to Milton's statement that the safety of the people is the highest law. But according to Salmasius' interpretation of natural law, it is particularly the function of the king to provide such safety, just as rulers do among bees or rams in the insect or animal kingdom. "The English parricides" maintain that the right of majesty (sovereignty) resides in the people by origin and the force of its very nature, whereas for Salmasius the law of nature places sovereignty in the person of the king.

Salmasius argues (*Regia,* 1649, p. 101, ll. 21 ff.) that kings are provided by the law of nature, although the Jews were taught the necessity for kingship by the prophets of God. Rulers are meant by nature to excel others in wisdom and strength (a principle with which Milton would agree, Christ being the perfect ruler; see below, n. 91). By the law of nature the king is to his people as a father to his family. Salmasius contends (*Regia,* 1649, p. 5, ll. 10–13) that the Independents and Brownists based their claims to power on the "law of nature" as a "splendid pretext" by which to embrace "tyranny."

[47] Milton maintains emphatically that the law of nature is above the king but is not bothered by the complications of this theory in regard to written law and constitutional procedures. He never defines who or what body, actual or proposed, can legitimately determine when the king has violated the law of nature to which he is subject.

Milton's scattered examples from history fall short of coming to grips with Salmasius' objection, arising out of the history of the Israelite kings (*Regia,* 1649, p. 37, ll. 2–4): "Nec exemplum ullius in his posterioribus Judaeae & Israëlis regibus afferri potest qui judicium capitis subierit aut in jus vocatus sit ex ulla criminis causa." This idea, a common inference especially through Books II and VII of the *Regia,* is paraphrased by Milton (see below, p. 356): "there can be cited no instance of any king called to the bar and condemned to die."

In answering Salmasius' paraphrased question (see below, p. 345), "what law provides for his (*i.e.,* the king's) punishment," Milton says "the same law that provides for the punishment of others." The "same" law is the law of nature. But obviously Salmasius has in mind, in this context, a written law fortified by juridical procedure and precedent, while Milton has in mind an unwritten abstract justice. In fact, Salmasius observes (*Regia,* 1649, p. 166, ll. 32–34): "The English rascals dare to say that when the written law fails, recourse should be made to natural law." Salmasius' question and Milton's reply run along parallel lines that do not meet.

In his generalized "Salmasian" question Milton implies that Salmasius believes that kings may go unpunished. Salmasius states (*Regia,* 1649, p. 159, ll. 32–33), "All antiquity held that a king was unbound by laws, as much secular as those instituted by Christ." But the king can be punished only by God. In a particularly moving passage at the end of the *Regia,* p. 337, ll. 35 ff., Salmasius warns about the eternal judge from whom nothing can be hidden. If the king is unfettered by laws, he ought not to judge by this that he is above the laws, that he may live more unrestricted than others who seem bound by them. Kings are merely men who return to the same dust with the others.

you fail to state whether they were good or bad.[48] If you had, no one would have listened to you, for "Olus, what are our laws to you?" [49] I wish they had abolished more laws—and more legal tricksters too —for then they would have done more for Christianity, and for the people too. You rage because "the Manii,[50] sons of the soil, not even noble in their own country or known to their own kinsmen, thought these matters theirs to decide." [51] You should have remembered the teaching not of Scripture alone but also of the poet: [52]

> God has the power to lift
> The lowest to the heights [A6v],
> To disclose what lies hid.

You must learn too that of those you call "hardly noble" some yield to none of your persuasion or kind in nobility, while others are self-made men who follow the course of true nobility through toil and rectitude, and bear comparison with the noblest of men. These latter had rather be called sons of the soil, provided it be their own, and exert themselves at home, than suffer hunger in a foreign land as slave to the whim or purse of a master, and live as you do—a merchant of hot air, a homeless, houseless, worthless man of straw.[53] Even from this

[48] Salmasius points out (*Regia,* 1649, p. 5, ll. 10–11) that the Independents claim that authority resides in the people according to the principle of natural law: "Plebis nomen in quo supremam auctoritatem quasi de iure naturali residere affirmant."

[49] Milton mocks Salmasius, as Martial mocks Olus in *Epigrams,* VII, 10.

[50] The Manii were proverbially paupers of obscure lineage. See Persius, *Satires,* VI, 56 ff.

[51] *Cf. Regia* (1649), p. 6, ll. 33–34: "At idem Manios aliquos, terrae filios, vix domi nobiles, vix suis notos, licere sibi credidisse quis ferat?" Salmasius previously stated that it was less intolerable when a Julius Caesar or a Cornelius Sulla overturned the state by strength or bravery. His snobbery toward the "terrae filios" brings out Milton's ire.

[52] the poet: Horace, *Odes,* I, 34; in *The Odes and Epodes,* tr. C. E. Bennett (London: Loeb Classical Library, 1925), pp. 90–91.

[53] Milton's calling Salmasius "a homeless, houseless, worthless man of straw" is a fair example of the rough treatment he accords Salmasius, though generally his abuse is more specific than this.

One set of charges revolves around Salmasius' reputation as a Latin scholar. Salmasius in *Regia* (1649), p. 269, ll. 38–39, says that a grammarian does not knowingly make a solecism, but Milton alleges that there are many such in Salmasius. He characterizes Salmasius (below, p. 336) as a "filthy foreigner and solecist, and a reproach to fellow pedagogues in morals and syntax alike." Milton even ridicules him (below, p. 338) as one who thumbs anthologies and dictionaries,

wandering life you would have to be transferred to the guardianship of your relatives [54] were it not for your only accomplishment of knowing how to blabber out before strangers some empty speeches and other nonsense for a high price. You censure our magistrates for admitting the dregs of all the sects: but why not admit them? It is for the church to drive them from the congregation of the faithful, not for the magistrates to force them from the state, so long at least as they break none of their country's laws. Men first came together to form a state in order to live in safety and freedom without violence or wrong;

---

as (below, p. 339) a "boring little weevil," as one who (below, p. 339) is said "to smell of the classroom."

When Milton comes to specific examples, he does not make a strong case. In the Preface (above, p. 312) Milton refers to Salmasius' "murderous barbarisms" in a general way, and (above, p. 313) compares Salmasius' Latinity unfavorably with that of a lad fresh from school. He is accused (below, p. 349) of being a solecist also in regard to Hebrew. With this possible exception and that below, p. 457 (see note), Milton deliberately or unconsciously misunderstands Salmasius' meaning, as in Milton's reference to *persona* in the Preface (above, p. 310). Milton exaggerates (below, pp. 404–405) Salmasius' use of "the Christ of the Lord" meaning the "anointed of the Lord." Salmasius does not necessarily use the name of Christ "cheap" even if his usage is somewhat pedantic.

Another set of charges revolves around Salmasius' alleged inconsistencies and contradictions. Here Milton's case is stronger, though he is not always scrupulously fair to Salmasius. Normally he makes a strong case in showing inconsistencies between what Salmasius says in the *Defensio Regia* and what he has said in previous publications (see note to Preface, above, p. 314). But he is not always effective in dealing with Salmasius' alleged internal contradictions.

Milton cites (below, p. 387) an alleged contradiction, which actually arises from Milton's confusing Salmasius' position that a king is not bound by any laws (he cannot be brought to judgment, punished) but should observe the law (in this sense he is bound by the highest tribunal, that of God). The alleged inconsistencies (below, pp. 367, 452) can be similarly explained. In regard to Salmasius' argument quoted below, p. 424, Milton states (below, p. 426) that "nothing more unfortunate could, I believe, have befallen kings than to have you as their advocate." But Salmasius' contention that the king should have "associates in power" does not necessarily compromise his doctrine of royal right, for Salmasius certainly does not mean by "associates" equals.

On the other hand, Milton catches Salmasius (below, p. 531) in one open contradiction. He also makes a reasonable allegation on the point raised below, p. 355, that Salmasius "pleads my case." Examples could be multiplied, but Milton has far from a perfect score, and he is not justified in saying, as he does below, p. 355, that "you really need no opponent, for you are always so opposed to yourself."

[54] guardianship of your relatives: Under Roman law madmen and spendthrifts (*furiosi* and *prodigi*) were committed to the guardianship of the *agnati*, kinsmen exclusively through the male line.

they founded a church to live in holiness and piety: The former has laws and the latter doctrine, which is quite different, and it is for this reason that war has followed war throughout our Christian world for so many years: namely, that magistrates and church are confused as to their jurisdictions.[55]

On this account particularly we cannot bear popery, for we know that it is less a religion than a priestly despotism under the cloak of

[55] See in this connection *Complete Prose,* I, 199–203, dealing with Milton's *Reason of Church-Government* (1642).

Milton's concept of the relationship of church and state is intimately bound up with the concept of the law of nature as outlined below, p. 327, n. 9. He rejected an ecclesiastical hierarchy, but accepted an hierarchy of secular rule among men according to the law of nature.

Milton takes the view that men are founders of the state. The church has no direct business with the state. The English civil war was fought, according to Milton, over the issue of the bishops, of church interference in the secular order. His opposition to the papacy lies in the charge that it is basically a secular order using the disguise of a church. Milton's whole drive is in the direction of isolating the spiritual order from the political. On the other hand, the scriptural exegesis of Salmasius causes Milton to have to face the problem of the theocratic state. Milton seems to have considered the theocratic state ideal for the Hebrews. God allowed the Jews to depart from a theocracy only as a punishment for their obduracy. The Hebrew republic apparently comes from God, but the kings from wilful men (below, p. 370)

Milton, in a long exegesis (below, p. 376) of the "render-unto-Caesar-the-things-that-are-Caesar's" passage, contends that (below, p. 376) "we too are by the intervention of Christ free, either as citizens or Christians, and therefore it is no part of a king's right to exact heavy tribute from those who are his sons and free men." Here again Milton says that the state has no direct relation to the elect and the regenerate. Christ merely paid Caesar's tribute as a matter of expediency in order to leave his main mission unimpeded.

If Milton had been less anti-Catholic or if his reading in the field of political philosophy had been less restricted, he would have discovered that Cardinal Bellarmine would have supplied many views parallel to his own on the subject of royal absolutism and the proper juridical position of a Christian church. Milton would have enjoyed Bellarmine's treatise against the royal absolutism of James I, whom Milton also attacks in Book II of the *Defensio*. Milton, too, might have been pleasantly surprised by Bellarmine's definition of the limitation of papal power as well as of royal authority. According to Courtney Murray, "St. Robert Bellarmine on the Indirect Power," *Theological Studies,* IX:4 (December, 1948), p. 499, the basic premise in Bellarmine's view of the papacy "is that the Church's power is single, and solely spiritual, that she is not by divine right any merely temporal jurisdiction." Murray interprets this to mean that the church has no power directly and immediately to produce juridical effects within the temporal order. Milton would have been surprised by Bellarmine's explanation of the origin of papal *political* power which, in substance, is Milton's own (*Theological Studies,* p. 505): "Dominion is not founded on grace or faith, but on free will and reason; nor does it derive from divine law, but from the law of nations."

religion, arrayed in the spoils of temporal power which it has violently appropriated in defiance of the clear teaching of Christ. No Independents such as you alone imagine them have ever been seen among us, except for those who refuse to recognize any orders or synods as higher than the individual churches, and who feel as you do that all such should be uprooted as offshoots of the hierarchy or rather its very stem. For this belief they are called Independents by the ignorant.[56] Finally I see that you are acting so as to stir up against us not only the hatred of all kings and rulers, but also the fiercest of wars. Once, though for a very different reason, King Mithridates [57] stirred up all the kings [A7] against the Romans and spread very similar lies: that the Romans planned the destruction of all their kingdoms, regarded no rights of man or God, had from the start gained everything by force of arms, and were brigands and sworn foes of royal power. So wrote Mithridates to King Arsaces. But what impudence

[56] Salmasius, as might be expected, depicts the Independents in a very unflattering way. He constantly refers to their *bulldog* ("Molossian") fierceness. His indictment in *Defensio Regia* is a long one. He alleges the following: (1) The "Independents" are well named because (p. 10, ll. 7–13) the principal axiom of this wicked sect is that no one should be subject to magistrates, kings, and laws. (2) They are hypocrites, affecting sanctity in the midst of an act of crime (p. 269, ll. 35–37). Outside the church they procure all things evil for the same person (Charles) whom they prayed for in the chapel (p. 88, ll. 1–4). (3) They have broken faith a thousand times (p. 300, ll. 18–19). Salmasius does not regard the Independents as men who may have empirically "muddled through" to their final position. Rather he regards them as long-term devious planners (p. 16, ll. 12–13): "By plan and reason they committed the crime meditated for a long time before." He even accuses them (p. 256, ll. 3–5) of complicity in the escape of Charles in order to put him in a false position. In particular, they violated the covenant with the Scots concerning care for the sovereignty (p. 254, ll. 21–26; p. 300, ll. 18–23). (4) The churches of the Independents are "unlimited" (p. 267, ll. 37–38). No secure and unmixed tenet can be elicited from any of them (p. 268, ll. 6–7). By claiming inspiration, the leader of the Independents has disguised God's holy spirit for deceiving the English nation (*Regia,* p. 269, ll. 12–14). (5) They sought to destroy the king in order to destroy the kingdom; they did not seek to preserve the kingdom from a bad king (p. 28, ll. 28–32). If anyone asks what cause made Charles a tyrant, the answer is easy (p. 305, ll. 6–8): the victorious army of the Independents! The principal count in the indictment can be summarized in Salmasius' words (p. 23, ll. 34–39): "They changed the ancient rule of a kingdom accustomed to be governed by one ruler into another rule held by several tyrants, against justice, against the statutes of the kingdom, against the faith of their oath, against the solemn pact of the Covenant, which originated between the two kingdoms, and in which it was clearly provided that the majesty of the king should be observed by all with courtesy, and his person protected."

[57] The "letter" of Mithridates is to be found in a fragment of Sallust, *Histories,* in *Sallust,* tr. J. C. Rolfe (London: Loeb Classical Library, 1921), pp. 432–41.

could have led you from playing the part of a prattling orator in your classroom to think that by sounding an attack you could rouse even a boy-king with your voice so foul and quavering that surely its trumpeting could never have moved even Homer's mice to fight the frogs.[58] I have then no fear of any war or danger which a wretch like you can stir up against us among the kings abroad with your weakly-raging eloquence, when you tell them, surely in jest, that we play football with the heads of kings, roll diadems like hoops, and treat imperial sceptres as carelessly as baubles. Your foolish head would best top a bauble if you think to turn kings and rulers to war by such childish talk. You call next upon all the nations, who will, I know, pay little heed to your words. Then you summon to the king's side the villainous and savage scum of Ireland, which in itself shows your criminal madness and how far you surpass most of your fellow men in wicked thoughtless rage, not scrupling to seek the aid and friendship of an accursed race from whose unholy alliance, stained as it is with the blood of so many of our worthiest citizens, even the king himself always drew back, or so pretended. That very treachery and cruelty which he did his best to hide and tried in every way to put from him, you, you worst of two-legged rogues, fearing neither God nor man, do not hesitate to adopt of your own free will before all the world. So be it! Arm yourself then for the king's defence with these Irish patrons on your side.[59]

First, you take a very necessary precaution, lest someone should

[58] The mock-epic on the battle of the frogs and mice was in antiquity attributed to Homer.

[59] For a discussion of the background of the Irish revolt see *Complete Prose,* I, 168–70. Salmasius denies (*Regia,* 1649, p. 321, ll. 22 ff.) Charles' responsibility for the disasters that befell English Protestants in Ireland. The slaughter of what Salmasius called "many thousand Reformed" in Ireland was not committed by Charles' order or command. Salmasius cites Charles' own evidence, and, in particular, the "incomparable" *Eikon Basilike,* in defense of his innocence. Salmasius does not mention the dubious intrigues Charles engaged in to maintain royal support among Irish Catholics at the same time that he was wooing Scotch Presbyterians and other groups. See C. V. Wedgwood, "Scotland and Ireland, August–November, 1641," in *The King's Peace, 1637–1641* (London: Collins, 1955), pp. 453–85.

Salmasius asks in reference to the Cromwell who, preparatory to his Irish expedition, was conveyed by a "six-team chariot drawn by white horses, accompanied by a retinue of eighty of the nobles" (*Regia,* 1649, p. 133, ll. 33 ff.), what evil did the Irish deserve at the hands of the regime, the Irish now persecuted in war, whose cities are burnt and who are everywhere slaughtered (*Regia,* 1649, p. 298, ll. 37–39)?

suppose you are about to snatch all the prizes for eloquence from Cicero or Demosthenes, for you say that you see "no need to proceed [A7v] like an orator." You are wise in seeing no need for what you cannot accomplish; who that has met you ever expected you to be an orator? You do not and cannot ever publish anything requiring toil, clarity, or taste, but like a second Crispinus[60] or that Greekling Tzetzes,[61] care not for quality, but only quantity, for writing well is beyond your scope. This case, you say, will be tried before the whole world as audience sitting as it were on the bench. This so pleases me that I long for an adversary who is skilled and prudent, not an unpractised ignoramus like you. Your peroration is clearly tragic, drawn I suppose from Ajax the Lash-Wielder:[62] "their injustice, impiety, treachery and cruelty I will publish to heaven and earth; I will hand the guilty leaders over to posterity, and prosecute the culprits to the end."[63] What flowery rhetoric! You dull, stupid, ranting, wrangling advocate, born only to pull apart or copy good writers, did you really think you could create anything which would live? You whom the next generation will seize and hurl to oblivion, you may be sure, along with all your worthless works. It may be, though, that this royal defence will draw some life from my reply, and will be read again after long-neglected obsolescence. I might ask the great state of Holland to cast it from their vaults, for it is no asset, and let it fly abroad on whatever wind it will. But if I can show to all the empty lying folly which it contains, it will I think be the more strictly suppressed the more widely it circulates. Now let us see how he "prosecutes his culprits to the end."[A8]

[60] Plotius Crispinus, at whose garrulity Horace sneers as Milton sneers at that of Salmasius. See Horace, *Satires,* I, i, 120, in Horace, *Satires, Epistles, and Ars Poetica,* tr. H. Rushton Fairclough (Cambridge: Loeb Classical Library, 1947), pp. 14–15.

[61] A Byzantine scholar of the twelfth century. In *A Short History of Classical Scholarship* (3 vols., Cambridge, 1903–1908), Sir John E. Sandys writes of the author that he (I, 409) "is dull as a writer and untrustworthy as an authority." Milton's acquaintance with Tzetzes is attested by his marginalia on Euripides and Lycophron.

[62] The Ajax of Sophocles, who went mad with rage when Odysseus wore Achilles' armor, and ran among the sheep, killing them with his scourge in the vain notion that they were Agamemnon and his men.

[63] Milton is quoting from *Defensio Regia* (1649), p. 13, ll. 1–4. Salmasius adds that the culprits are guilty of a crime for which there is no precedent in the past and for which there will probably not be one in the future. Milton ignores this point.

CHAPTER I [1]

SINCE an empty windbag like you, Salmasius, thought it an additional source of pride and arrogance that the king of Great Britain was indeed the defender of the faith and you were the defender of the king, I shall grant that the king and you were equally deserving of these titles; for the king has so defended his faith—and you the king—that each appears, in fact, to have ruined his case. This I shall demonstrate at various later points, and particularly in this first chapter. On page twelve of your preface you said: "A cause so good and just needs no rhetorical coloring, for merely to state how the affair was carried out is to defend the king." [2] Since in this whole chapter where you promise that straightforward account, you neither state clearly how the affair was carried out nor avoid the use

[1] The main arguments of Salmasius in *Regia,* book I, pp. 14–28, run as follows: 1. The memory of man cannot recall such a heinous deed as the execution of the king. The deed was parricide because the origin of kings makes them paternal, the fathers of their country. 2. This deed was committed by a so-called Christian country, professing itself Reformed. What makes this deed particularly bad is that it was done deliberately, with premeditation, and with no subsequent repentance. 3. The perpetrators became "king." Their rule is as grievous as that of any king can be. 4. The ignominy heaped upon the king was unprecedented, actually hurting the cause of the leaders of the Independent faction. 5. An attempt was made to make the act seem legal. "Is there any force more violent than that which is disguised under the name and color of justice?" The death of the king had already been determined upon, so the show of legality was merely a cloak. 6. Because they have denied the divine right of kings, the leaders have opposed themselves to God. They have rendered the Christian religion contemptible. They have denied the right of natural succession, keeping the son from the throne. 7. The upper house had dissented from the punishment of the king; the lower house consented only after the "thinking ones" had been driven out.

These acts constitute tyranny. Charles' judges were seditiously-minded against all kings; they are guilty of parricide and the overthrow of divine, natural, national, public, and private laws. They are responsible for the upheaval of the State, oppression of the liberty of the people, abolition of Parliament, extermination of the nobility, embezzlement of the public treasury, breaking of the Solemn Covenant, preventing royal succession, and setting up a military government. They have established an unfortunate and dangerous precedent. The accusations against the king were forced, a matter of research, so that he might be got rid of, apparently legally, in order that the leaders of the faction might usurp the kingdom.

[2] *Regia* (1649), p. 12, ll. 20–22.

of such rhetorical coloring as you can manage, it is clear that if we follow your own judgment, the king's cause will be neither good nor just. You must not, however, claim what none would concede, that is, any ability at rhetorical narration, for as narrator you cannot rightly play the part of orator, historian, or even the meanest advocate. Instead, like some brazen hawker at a country fair, you stirred up great hope for the future with your first words, not with any intention of ever telling the promised tale, but rather that you might peddle your faded dyes and lie-filled vials to as many readers as possible. For "when you are to speak of the deed you feel encircled and alarmed by so many monstrous novelties that you know not how to begin, pursue, and conclude your account." [3]

Is this what you call a plain tale? I can explain this difficulty: First you feel alarmed by the great number of your [1] own monstrous lies, and then not so much that your empty head is encircled by all these foolish trifles as that it is actually set whirling by them, so that you neither know now, nor ever did, what should at any time be said "first or later or in conclusion." "Amid the difficulties hampering the expression of the enormity of a crime so unparalleled this phrase alone comes readily to mind and must be continually reiterated," that is, "never has the sun itself seen a wickeder deed." [4] The sun, good teacher, has seen much which escaped Bernardus,[5] but it is wise for you to bring it in so often, not to reveal our crimes but to add some badly needed warmth to the chilly reception your defence will meet.

"Kings," you say, "are coeval with the sun's creation." [6] May the gods and goddesses grant you a warm day, Damasippus,[7] to sun yourself, for your own inspiration lacks fire; and one might otherwise think you a shady sort of teacher. Indeed, you are wholly in the dark in failing to distinguish the rights of a father from those of a king; by calling kings fathers of their country,[8] you think this metaphor

[3] *Regia* (1649), p. 14, ll. 1–4. [4] *Regia* (1649), p. 14, ll. 4–9.

[5] Paul Blackford suggests that it may be a Latinized form of "barnard" or "bernard," the cony-catching pamphleteers' term for a "lurking cozener." "The Bernard counterfeits many parts in one, and is now a drunken man, anon in another humor . . . only to blind the cozen . . . the more easily to beguile him" (Dekker, "The Belman of London," *Works,* 1885, III, 126). *Translator's note.*

[6] *Regia* (1649), p. 14, ll. 13–14.

[7] Damasippus: Mentioned in Horace, *Satires,* II, iii, 16.

[8] *Regia* (1649), p. 14, l. 20: *Ut patres veri, ita reges qui pro patribus sunt . . .*

has forced me to apply right off to kings whatever I might admit of fathers. Fathers and kings are very different things: Our fathers begot us, but our kings did not, and it is we, rather, who created the king.[9] It is nature which gave the people fathers, and the people who gave themselves a king; the people therefore do not exist for the king, but the king for the people. We endure a father though he be harsh and strict, and we endure such a king too; but we do not endure even a father who is tyrannical. If a father kill his son he shall pay with his life: shall not then a king too be subject to this same most just of laws if he has destroyed the people who are his sons? This is the more true since a father cannot abjure his position as father, while a king can easily make himself neither a father nor a king.

If as you say the "next" consideration is "the nature of the deed," then to you, you foreigner most ignorant of our affairs, I now speak as a native eye-witness: it was a king who was neither "good" nor "just" nor "compassionate" nor "God-fearing" nor "dutiful" nor "peace-loving," to use your words, whom we "removed from our midst," [10] but rather a foe of nearly ten years' standing, and the ravager, not the father, of his country. "Such an act has been performed before": This you admit, for you dare not try to deny it! "But never," you say, "by Protestants against a Protestant king." [11] [2] Can he really be called Protestant who in writing to the pope hailed him as "Most Holy

[9] Here we meet Milton's favorite principle of jurisprudence—the *law of nature.* A father falls within the law of nature; a king does not. In this way, Milton attacks Salmasius' presumed false analogy. "By *nature* then the king is no more sacred than the nobles or the people's magistrates . . . [italics added]" says Milton (see below, p. 426). Salmasius' analogy between the power of kings and the power of fathers is attacked again on p. 428. On p. 422, Milton states his belief that "the law of God does most closely agree with the law of nature." By implication he agrees with Salmasius' explanation of the laws of nature (often merely referred to as "nature") on p. 424. "The law of nature . . . is that reason innate in all men's minds which considers the welfare of every people where men enjoy mutual satisfaction and association. It cannot secure that common welfare, unless it decide who should rule, since there are persons who must be ruled." But Milton goes on to deny that the law of nature insists that one person (a king) must rule.

[10] *Regia* (1649), p. 14, ll. 29–30.

[11] *Regia* (1649), p. 15, ll. 25–28: Milton's quoted material is a summarized paraphrase rather than a direct quotation. Such a crime, says Salmasius, might have been committed by Gentiles, infidels, Romans, Turks, but not by Christians. Even more strongly, such a crime would not be committed by the reformed subjects of a reformed king: "Sed quis unquam audivit, quis legit, haereditarium regem legitimum, regnum possidentem, Christianum, Reformatum, accusatum à suis subjectis, causam capitis dicere coactum, condemnatum, securi percussum?"

Father," and who was always more kindly disposed toward Papists than toward the Orthodox? [12] Whatever he may have been, however, he was not the first even of his own household to be removed by Protestants. Was not his grandmother Mary deposed, banished, and at last executed by Protestants,[13] without any complaint even from the Scottish Protestants? Indeed it would be true to say that they lent a hand. When there have been so few "Protestant" kings we need not wonder that none of them has been put to death in this way; but deny, if you dare, that it is right to drive from the realm a wicked king or tyrant, or to punish him as he deserves.[14] Exactly this was the opinion

[12] A famous letter, headed "Sanctissime Pater," was written by the then Prince Charles in reply to one from the Pope of April 20, 1623, concerning negotiations then taking place for marriage of Charles to the Infanta of Spain. I have found it in William Prynne's *Popish Royall Favourite* (1643), pp. 40–41, and *Hidden Workes of Darkenese* (1645), pp. 38–39. In the first of these volumes (pp. 36, 41–42) Prynne indicates that the letter had previously been printed widely in various languages.

[13] Milton reminds Salmasius that another crowned head, Mary, Queen of Scots, was beheaded by Protestants as well as Charles I. It is an interesting comment on the intellectual climate of the seventeenth century that the execution of Charles seemed so novel and earth-shaking. Foreign governments had some awareness that Charles' execution signified much more than that of the Scottish queen, who was not executed by her own subjects, that this execution was the sign of a very real and revolutionary social change—the emergence of that Puritan middle class so praised by Milton (see below, p. 471) to political power.

[14] Salmasius is just as opposed to tyranny in itself as is Milton, but he takes pains to point out what he thinks are the differences between a king and a magistrate. A magistrate may be punished, but a king may not. A tyrannical magistrate is one thing, a tyrannical king another. Once a magistrate has been created, he has real power over the people who created him. The people ought to be subject to the magistrate, just as soldiers to the leader whom they elected to command them (*Regia,* 1649, p. 59, ll. 7–8), or as clerics to the bishop whom they have created (*Regia,* 1649, p. 146, ll. 17–18).

It has been asserted that Charles was merely the chief magistrate of the people, the president of the English parliament (*Regia,* 1649, p. 184, ll. 20–21). But a magistrate does not necessarily govern for life or have hereditary power. He does not possess divine right. Under kingly rule, the people transfer all sovereignty and may not recover it (*Regia,* 1649, p. 148, ll. 3–9). This is not true of magistrates (*Regia,* 1649, p. 146, ll. 34–37). The king, unlike the magistrate, does not have an equal or superior in the kingdom (*Regia,* 1649, p. 153, ll. 18–19). If two rule at the same time, by this very fact they are not really kings, because they do not have what is especially kingly—the right not to be judged by anyone (*Regia,* 1649, p. 154, ll. 3–5). A king is bound by no one but God and is bound to render account of his acts to no one but God (*Regia,* 1649, p. 130, ll. 14–15). Sovereignty ceases to be the people's once it begins to be the king's (*Regia,* 1649, p. 145, ll. 37–39). The safety of the government always demands that the

of the great divines who were the very instruments of the reformation of the church.

You admit that countless kings have died a lamentable death, one by the "sword," another by "poison," or in a dismal "cell" or by the "hangman's noose," but what seems to you most wretched of all, and as it were portentous, is for a king to be brought to trial, "made to defend himself on a capital charge, condemned, and beheaded." [15] You witless mortal, will you tell me whether it is not kinder, fairer, and more in accordance with the laws of all our states, to bring to trial one accused of any crime, let him defend himself, and should he be found guilty, lead him to the execution he has deserved, after granting him, upon condemnation, time for repentance or for resolution, than to slaughter him like a beast without trial in the hour of his capture? What defendant who had the choice would not prefer the former punishment? Should not the manner of punishing his people which is considered more temperate for a king, be held also more temperate for a people in punishing their king, and even more acceptable to the king himself? Your choice was for the king to be destroyed in secret and without witnesses, so that future generations might be deprived of the advantage of such a good example, or that those responsible for this glorious deed might seem to have fled the light of day and to have earned the disapproval of the laws and of justice herself.

You heighten the affair by saying that it was not in any sedition or secession of the nobles, or any mad rebellion [3] of the soldiers or the populace, not in hatred or fear or lust for power or blind impetuosity of soul that the deed was done, but rather that it was thought out after long and careful deliberation. How wise you were to turn from law to grammar-school! You base your abuse on what are called the accidents of the affair, which in themselves have no weight, though as yet you have failed to show whether the deed itself merits censure or praise. See how easily I can attack you: If the deed was fair and noble, those who performed it deserve the greater praise in acting for the right alone, unmastered by passion; while if it was hard and painful, in moving not by blind impulse but on careful deliberation. That these

---

sovereignty given by the people to the ruler should never return to them (*Regia*, 1649, p. 147, ll. 31 ff.). A king's name was sometimes given to magistrates, but this was a historical error. The king is essentially different from a magistrate, because the one has sovereign power, the other not.

[15] *Regia* (1649), p. 15, ll. 21–28.

deeds were inspired by God is my belief when I recall the unexpected zeal and unity with which the whole army, joined by a great part of the citizenry, sent forth a single cry from almost every district of the realm for the punishment of that king who was the cause of all their woes. Be that as it may, it is certain that whether magistrates or people be considered,[16] none ever undertook with loftier, or, as their very foes confess, with calmer heart a deed so excellent and so worthy of even the most heroic days of old. Their action endowed with new nobility the laws, the courts, which henceforth were restored to all alike, and above all the figure of justice herself, making her after this notable decision more glorious and precious than she had ever been before.[17]

[16] Salmasius is quoted by Milton (see below, p. 457) as stating: "The form of government introduced by them is not popular but military." Milton makes at that point a rather partisan definition of the "people." "I say it was the people, for why should I not say that the act of the better, the sound part of the Parliament, in which resides the real power of the people, was the act of the people?"

Although Milton offers no specific criteria for defining "the sound part," their status above and beyond the written law is generally assumed in his work. Although all men are born into a state of natural liberty, only the regenerate manage to maintain it (see below, p. 343, and p. 422, n. 2). This minority, this spiritual elite, embodies "the people," from whom all jurisdiction flows. Milton thinks in oligarchic rather than in democratic terms. In commenting on Milton's *Readie & Easie Way* Hanford states (*A Milton Handbook,* New York, 1946, pp. 126–27) that "Milton's scheme is partly modeled on the government of the Netherlands, partly on the ideal commonwealth of Plato, with its aristocratic rule by the guardian class."

[17] "Their action endowed with new nobility . . . the figure of justice herself"; Milton, even allowing for his rhetorical flight, is possessed of a sense of awe and wonder over the execution of the king. The novelty of the issue in the seventeenth century must be kept in mind. Salmasius squarely raised the issue of legal precedent: "In accordance with what law, under what system of right, in respect of what judgments are these things done" (*Regia,* 1649, p. 29, ll. 5–8). Salmasius obviously has Milton at a disadvantage, for there was little or nothing in the way of legal precedent, though there had been considerable philosophical speculation about the rights of a people as against a tyrant. According to Wilfrid Parsons, "St. Thomas Aquinas and Popular Sovereignty," *Thought* (September, 1941), St. Thomas maintained that the ruler held his authority from God, it is true, but through the community of which he is a representative. St. Thomas points out the unwritten contract between ruler and people. Since the grant of authority "reposes primarily upon this contract, obviously the people can revoke the authority when the contract has been broken by the ruler even when it has subjected itself to him in perpetuity." St. Thomas, of course, writes on a theoretical level. The Middle Ages did not offer a juridical procedure (the papal interdict several times mentioned by Salmasius was more of a boycott than a legal procedure) for the revocation of such authority. See further, G. P. Gooch,

By this time I have suffered through three pages of this chapter and still have found no trace of the clear account he promised. He bemoans our teaching "that when a king's government is injurious and vexatious he may rightly be deposed; led by such teaching," he says, "they would not have spared the life of a king who was better than their own in a thousand ways." [18] Mark the man's shrewdness! I want you to tell me how this follows, unless you admit that a king who is in a thousand ways better than ours would still govern injuriously and vexatiously, and this would lead you to make the king you defend worse in a thousand ways than those who govern injuriously and vexatiously, and turn him, I suppose, into the worst of all tyrants. Blessed be ye, O kings, who have so active an advocate!

Now begins his tale. "They racked him with diverse tortures." With what ones, tell us! "They transferred him from jail to jail" [4]—rightly, for the former tyrant was now a prisoner of war—"frequently changing the guards"—lest they transfer their allegiance. "At times they held out to him hope of freedom, at times even of a restoration by means of a covenant." [19] Clearly then our plan had not been fixed far beforehand, nor had we long been snatching at any "means and opportunities" of casting off our king.[20] We had demanded certain things of him long before, when he had almost subdued us, since without them the people could have had no hope of freedom or safety; and it was these very same things which we humbly begged of him when he was a prisoner, not one time only, but thrice or more,[21]

English Democratic Ideas of the Seventeenth Century (Cambridge, 1927), p. 8.

[18] *Regia* (1649), p. 16, ll. 26–29. [19] *Regia* (1649), p. 16, ll. 36–38.

[20] Salmasius insists strongly that the Independents had long planned, rather than drifted into, the execution of the king. They sinned "deliberately and rationally" (*Regia*, 1649, p. 16, l. 3); a long time before (*Regia,* 1649, p. 16, ll. 12–13): "Consilio & ratione meditatum diu ante facinus peregerunt."

[21] Charles, now a captive of the Parliamentarians to whom the Scots had surrendered him, was conducted to his new prison at Holmby. At Holmby Charles made new proposals. He was ready to confirm the Presbyterian government for the space of three years, on condition of liberty of worship for himself and his household; on condition that twenty divines of his nomination be added to the assembly at Westminster; and that the final settlement of religion at the expiration of that period be made in the regular way by himself and the two Houses. He was willing that the command of the army and navy be vested in persons to be named by them, on condition that after ten years it might revert to the crown; if these things were accorded, he would pledge himself to give full satisfaction with respect to the war in Ireland.

and were each time refused. It was when hope of his compliance was at an end that Parliament passed that famous decree against sending further requests to the king; not when first he became tyrannical, but when his condition became incurable.

Later, however, certain members embraced a changed policy, and on finding a suitable opportunity sponsored a motion for sending proposals to the king once more. In criminal madness they equalled that Roman Senate which voted, despite the protests of Cicero and all the wiser men, to send envoys to Antony; [22] and their end would likewise have been the same, had not almighty God granted a different outcome, reducing the Romans to slavery but assuring us of our freedom. For though the king had conceded nothing more than before which could lead to the establishment of peace and a true settlement, these members nevertheless decided that they had gained satisfaction from the king. That part of the House, therefore, which was uncorrupted, on seeing themselves and the commonwealth betrayed sought the aid of the army, which was ever brave and loyal to the state. In this affair my belief is, though I hesitate to express it, that our troops [23] were

---

At this point developments outran the expectations of both the king and the Presbyterians. The army, at first casually, then with mature deliberation, emerged at the centre of power—a process that arose partly from a concrete situation, grievances of veterans' arrears in pay and other matters, partly from an ideological ferment (the ferment is expertly analyzed in A. S. P. Woodhouse, *Puritanism and Liberty* [Chicago: University of Chicago Press, 1951], pp. 23–35). For the attitude and decisive influence of the army see below, p. 333, n. 24. See also Gardiner, *The Great Civil War* (4 vols., London, 1894), III, 274–96; Merritt Y. Hughes, introduction to *Complete Prose,* III, 6–9, 22–31; Wolfe, *Leveller Manifestoes* (New York: Thomas Nelson, 1944), pp. 46–64; Haller and Davies, *Leveller Tracts* (New York: Columbia University Press, 1945), pp. 33–87.

[22] send envoys to Antony: Milton refers to the debate in the Roman Senate on the first four days of January, 43 B.C. Cicero's protests are contained in his *Fifth* and *Sixth Philippics*. See *Philippics,* tr. Walter C. A. Ker (Cambridge: Loeb Classical Library, 1951), pp. 253–334.

[23] On December 6, 1648, Colonel Pride, whose troops were stationed in the lobby of the House, arrested some forty-one Presbyterian members as they approached the Commons to participate in the duties of the day. Four other members were later put under restraint, and some ninety-six others were forbidden to enter the House, making a total of 143 members excluded by Pride's Purge. On December 7 seventy-eight members were present in what came to be known henceforth as the Rump Parliament. On December 14, fifty-seven were present, on December 20, fifty-one members on the second division of the day. See Gardiner, *Great Civil War,* IV, 270–74; *Commons Journals,* VI, 95, 97, 101.

On January 6, 1649 the Rump Parliament passed an act without the concurrence of the Lords setting up a High Court of Justice for the trial of King

wiser than our legislators, and saved the commonwealth by arms when the others had nearly destroyed it by their votes.[24]

Salmasius then relates many lamentable events, doing so with such lack of skill that he seems not to arouse but to beg for pity. He grieves that "our king suffered capital punishment in a manner none had ever done before" [25]—and this though our author had frequently said that no king at all had ever suffered capital punishment. Is this your custom, you lout, to compare the manner of doing deeds when there are no deeds to compare? "The king," he says, "was executed as a bandit, assassin, murderer, traitor and tyrant." Is this [5] your defence of the king, or your judgment of him, which is indeed much harsher than the one we passed? What led you suddenly to speak out on our side? He complains that "the king's head was cut off by masked executioners": [26] what can we do with this fellow? Earlier he complained of "murder being done in the person of the king," and now of its being done in the person of an executioner. Why should I continue with the rest of his paltry lies about the "blows" and "kicks" of common soldiers, the "charging of fourpence to see the corpse"? These matters simply proclaim the chicken-hearted stupidity of an unsuccessful

---

Charles, who, asserted the act, "hath had a wicked design totally to subvert the ancient and fundamental laws and liberties of this nation." See Gardiner, *Great Civil War,* IV, 288–91; Gardiner, *Constitutional Documents,* pp. 357–58; *Commons Journals,* VI, 113.

[24] The constant target of Salmasius is the army. "If anyone ask what cause made Charles a tyrant, it is easy to answer the victorious army of the Independents!" (*Regia,* 1649, p. 305, ll. 6–8). The army had offered a secure refuge to the religious and political opponents of Presbyterianism. The "votes" that Milton refers to are those of the Presbyterian members. As early as 1647 they had passed measures to reduce the power of the army. Among other things, it was voted that no commission should be granted to any member of the lower House, or to any individual who refused to take the Solemn League and Covenant, or to anyone whose conscience forbade him to conform to the Presbyterian scheme of church government.

[25] *Regia* (1649), p. 17, ll. 4–5.

[26] *Regia* (1649), p. 17, ll. 5 ff. This is the beginning of a long passage in Salmasius with which Milton deals in parts. Salmasius does not actually complain about the masked executioners to whom Milton alludes three sentences later. Salmasius ironically questions the value of the executioners in masks when so many *unmasked* executioners were present supported by so many armed infantry and cavalry! According to Salmasius, those who groaned or wept at the piteous spectacle of the king's execution were flogged by the soldiers. Salmasius' passage is much more poignant than Milton's remark about not making a single reader any sadder suggests. Milton argues rather at a tangent in bringing up the alleged questionable Latinity of *persona* again (see above, p. 310, n. 23).

dabbler in letters, without making a single reader any sadder. Son Charles would have done much better to hire one of the gang of buffoons who sing their little elegies to the crowd on street-corners rather than to have called in to mourn his father's misfortune this lamentable, or rather laughable, declaimer who has so little taste or savor that his very tears lack any grain of salt.[27]

His tale is told now, and what he does next is hard to say, so swollen and turbid is the flow of his discourse! Now he is in a passion, now he yawns, and puts no limit on his chatter, even repeating ten times matters for which one telling would be too much! I do believe that the improvised effusions of any blabbermouth who makes rhymes while standing on one leg would be far more deserving of publication than these; so unworthy are they of a serious reply from me.

Why mention his praise of a "protector of religion" who made war on the church to keep in it those foes of religion and tyrants, the bishops? How could he preserve the "purity of religion" [28] who had himself submitted to the corrupt teaching and rites of the bishops? I would like you to state the heresies of those "sects" to which is granted, you say, "a license to hold those sacrilegious assemblies" which even Holland forbids. But there is now none more sacrilegious than you with your assumption of the worst license of all, namely that of incessant slander!

"They could have done the state no greater injury than by removing its master." [29] Learn now, you rascal house-born slave, that unless you remove the master, you destroy the state, for it is some private property, and not a commonwealth [6], which owns a master. "Then they persecute with every injustice those pastors who detest their deed." [30] In order that all may know what these pastors are [31] I shall speak briefly: they are the very men who taught with tongue and pen that the king must be opposed by force, who never ceased to curse continually, like Deborah against Meroz,[32] all those who failed to furnish arms or money or men for this war, and who ranted to

[27] salt: Salt was commonly employed by the ancients as a symbol of wit in speech or writing.

[28] *Regia* (1649), p. 21, ll. 13–17.

[29] *Regia* (1649), p. 21, ll. 21–23.

[30] *Regia,* 1649, p. 21, ll. 25–27.

[31] Milton refers here to the Presbyterian ministers who favored war against the king but drew back from the prospect of bringing him to trial. See *Second Defence,* below, p. 626; and *The Tenure,* in *Complete Prose,* III, 255.

[32] Judges 5:23.

their congregations that this war was not against a king but against a tyrant worse than Saul or Ahab and more like Nero than that wretch himself. Upon the removal of the bishops and priests whom they had hotly attacked as pluralists and absentees, they rushed at top speed to occupy two or three of the richest benefices apiece, so that it is now a common tale how these shameless shepherds[33] have flocked from their own cures to other cares. Neither decency nor reverence for God could check their madly raging avarice until the most scandalous notoriety in the church had heaped on them the very burning shame which they themselves had used a little earlier to brand the priests. Since their greed is not yet sated and their hearts, restless for power, are now accustomed to incite riot and to hate peace, they never cease their seditious attacks against the present government as formerly against the king. This righteous king was, they now say, cruelly killed, although he is the same whom a little while ago they heaped with every curse and, as by God's will, handed over to Parliament so that he might be stripped of all his royal power and crushed in a sacred war. Now they say that the schismatics are not wiped out! This is surely a ridiculous request to make of the magistrates, who have thus far never been able in any way to root out the two worst heresies in the church from the very ranks of the tribe of ministers themselves, namely avarice and ambition. Those sects among us which they attack are certainly obscure, while those they follow are notorious and far more dangerous to the church of God, having been headed by Simon Magus and Diotrephes.[34] Vile though these men are, however, we are so far from persecuting them that we are indeed too gentle with such schismatics who daily plot against the state.

Now you are angry, you truant cockerel, since according to your snarling speech the English are "fiercer than their native bulldogs,"[35]

[33] shameless shepherds: Milton here enjoys a pun based on *greges . . . pastores . . . egregii.*

[34] Simon Magus and Diotrephes were early heresiarchs who receive New Testament mention (Acts 8:9; III John 9).

[35] The best known "classical" dog was the huge Molossian, "whose open jaws, strong teeth, and loud bark are described by Lucretius, V, 1063" (see *Oxford Classical Dictionary,* p. 294). *Molossian* could be said to be Salmasius' favorite adjective. In the English setting the nearest thing to "Molossian" is "bulldog." Salmasius' repeated use of the phrase exasperates Milton. On p. 452 below, Milton asks, "Does your madness affect your voice, too, so that like a cuckoo you must forever sing the same song?" Milton answers Salmasius in kind: If Sal-

and had no regard for "the lawful successor and heir" [7] to the crown, nor "the youngest son," nor for "the Queen of Bohemia." [36] You shall furnish your own answer: "When the government is changed from monarchy to some other form, no succession is allowed among those who supervise the new regime" (*Apparatus de Primatu*).[37] You say that "a little part of one realm" was responsible for all these innovations "in the three kingdoms": [38] if they were true, they would deserve to rule the rest, as men rule women. "These are the men who took it on themselves to change the ancient form of government into a new one under many tyrants." [39] Their action was right and propitious; you cannot censure them without showing yourself at once a filthy foreigner and a solecist,[40] and a reproach to your fellow pedagogues in your morals and syntax alike. "The English will never wash out this stain": [41] it is rather you, blot and stain though you are on all grammarians, who could never sully the fair name and living renown of Englishmen.[42] For with such firmness of heart as has scarcely been recorded before they fought and conquered not only their enemies in arms, but the inwardly hostile or superstitious beliefs of the mob as well, and each won for himself for the future the name of liberator in every land; the people dared to perform in common such an act as in other lands is thought possible only for great-hearted men of old.

What "the Protestants and the early Christians" [43] did or would

---

masius speaks of the "mad dogs of England," Milton refers to Salmasius' wife as a "barking bitch" (see below, p. 380). By the end of Book V, Milton exclaims, "Here is Salmasius' shrewdest thrust, his seal perhaps, or his motto, forced on us for the sixth time" (see below, p. 451). Many other such passages appear in later books. In *Regia* (1649), p. 280, l. 26, Salmasius refers to the "molossica feritate" of the Independents; the same phrase is used again in *Regia* (1649), p. 300, l. 9, in reference to the writings of Charles' accusers and judges.

[36] *Regia* (1649), p. 22, ll. 6–14.

[37] Salmasius' passage in *De Primatu* runs as follows: "Novam formam induit Respublica cuius status & ordo mutatur per alios atq; alios gubernatores quos accipit, non successores eosdem sibi conservat, qui diversi sunt generis, atque ordinis, & disparis potestatis." See *Librorum de Primatu Papae: Pars Prima cum Apparatu* (Leyden, 1645; NYPL), p. 127, ll. 8–11.

[38] Apparently a paraphrase of *Regia* (1649), p. 23, ll. 10–13.

[39] *Regia* (1649), p. 23, ll. 34–35.

[40] solecist: Salmasius' Latin reads "regimen regni . . . in alium qui." Thus neuter nouns are followed by masculine pronouns.

[41] *Regia* (1649), p. 24, ll. 16–18. [42] *Regia* (1649), p. 24, ll. 24–25.

[43] Milton's chief purpose in quoting from Salmasius' works, as at this point from the *De Primatu* (called by Milton here *Apparatus*) is to justify his often

have done in such a case I shall relate when the time for treating of legality has come, and so avoid your mistake of outdoing in loquacity all the babblers and Battuses.[44] You ask how you are going to reply to "the Jesuits"[45] in our behalf: rather mind your own business, you renegade, and blush for your own crimes which force the church to blush for you, now that you have turned from your late loud fierce attack on the primacy of the pope[46] and on the bishops to be an Episcopal sycophant. You admit that "some Protestants" unnamed by you (but since you call them worse by far than the Jesuits I shall state their names: Luther, for example, and Zwingli, Calvin, Bucer, Pa-

---

repeated charge of inconsistency and self-contradiction. He particularly takes issue with the references of Salmasius to church history.

On p. 348 below, the *De Primatu* is quoted again to show that Salmasius, now using the "commonwealth of bees" to support a monarchy, previously condemned the same example when used to support the rule of the pope. On p. 364 below, Salmasius is shown to have reversed himself from the position taken in the *De Primatu* that God gave the Israelites a king as a punishment for having abandoned the pure worship of God. On p. 368 below, the *De Primatu* is quoted to show that Salmasius previously had not considered Moses as master or sole ruler of the Israelites.

The work of Salmasius refuting the Jesuit Petavius is quoted as showing that Salmasius maintained that the pope and the bishops could be driven from the church because they were tyrants. But, according to Milton, Salmasius does not take a similar position in regard to the king (see below, p. 397). Two references, on p. 391 and p. 429, are made to the same passage in the book against Petavius. Salmasius is accused of reversing his stand that conflict between the nobles and the kings is a lighter evil than certain ruin under a tyrant king.

[44] Battuses: a babbler whom Mercury turned into stone for betraying his theft (Ovid, *Metamorphoses,* II, 688) of Apollo's cattle.

[45] Salmasius asks the question (*Regia,* 1649, p. 25, ll. 38–39) "How shall we answer the Jesuits?" He says the Independents are far worse than the Jesuits (*Regia,* 1649, p. 26, l. 13). The reason is simple: The Jesuits are simply interested in removing a tyrannical king, not in destroying a kingdom. The Independents want all kings exterminated. Salmasius enjoys making this needling comparison of the Jesuits with the Independents. He makes it again in *Regia* (1649), p. 276, ll. 9–13. It was particularly from these two sources, he alleges, that the "detestable doctrine" arose among the English that it is permitted, according to law, to kill a tyrant.

[46] Milton refers to the book published by Salmasius under the pseudonym of Walo Messalinus (see below, p. 391, n. 75). In a long passage at the end of book VI (*Regia,* 1649, p. 98, ll. 31 ff.) Salmasius argues that Loyola had disseminated the doctrine that kings are subject to the pope, and that the Independents had amplified this doctrine to mean that no one was subject to a king. The pope exercised his controls by releasing subjects from their oath of fealty to the king (*Regia,* 1649, p. 96, l. 28, and *Regia,* 1649, p. 100, l. 26). For the Catholic position see above, p. 330, n. 17, and below, p. 340, n. 4.

raeus, and many more) [47] taught that tyrants "should be deposed, but left it to a court of wise and learned to decide who is a tyrant."

"But who were these English judges? Were they wise, learned, of pre-eminent worth or birth?" [48] I should say that a people which has felt the weight of slavery's yoke [8] on its neck may be wise, learned, and noble enough to know what should be done with its own tyrant, without asking the advice of foreigners or pedagogues. Not only did the Parliaments of England and Scotland show both by their words and their express deeds that this king was a tyrant, but there was also agreement from well-nigh the whole people of both realms, until later the schemes and lies of the bishops brought about a separation into two factions. What if God has wished that those who carry out his decrees against the most powerful monarchs of this world, just as those who share in the light of the Gospel, should include few wise or learned men, few who are powerful or noble? Thus, through those who are not such, he might destroy those who are, so that the flesh boast not before him.

Who are you to yelp thus? A scholar, I suppose, who till old age has spent his time thumbing anthologies and dictionaries and glossaries, instead of reading through good authors with judgment and profit; and so all your talk is of manuscripts and variant readings, of displaced or corrupt passages: you reveal that you have never tasted a drop of honest scholarship. Are you wise? You who brawl about the tiniest trifles and make them the matter of your beggar's wars; you who,

[47] The same list of theologians, with the exception of Paraeus, is mentioned again by Milton on p. 396 below. He alleges that these theologians are viewed as "Brownists" by Salmasius because they maintain that a single tyrant unbound by law "cannot with impunity break down all discipline and trample on all men's traditions." This is simply an inference on the part of Milton; actually Salmasius does not mention them.

Huldreich Zwingli (1448–1531) preached against fasting, veneration of saints, celibacy of priests, maintained that the holy spirit alone was necessary to make the word of God intelligible, and that there was no need of church, councils, or Pope in the matter. Martin Bucer (1491–1551) sought, after Zwingli's death, for a compromise that would unite the Lutherans with the Swiss followers of Zwingli. In 1549 he was appointed Regius Professor of divinity at Cambridge, and was consulted in the revision of the Book of Common Prayer. Milton uses him as an authority in dealing with divorce. See *Complete Prose*, II, 422–77. David Paraeus (1548–1622) of Heidelberg pleaded for a reconciliation of Lutheranism and Calvinism.

[48] *Regia* (1649), p. 26, ll. 16–17.

though yourself ignorant and untrained, abuse astronomers and physicians of good repute in their own fields; you who would, if you could, deny fire and water to anyone who tried to rob you of your petty fame for restoring any little word or letter in some manuscript?

Despite all this you are angry and show your teeth because everyone calls you pedagogue. Hammond,[49] lately the best-loved chaplain of this king, is called by you in some trifling book or other a worthless rascal, since he called you pedagogue; I do believe you would have set about heaping the same abuse on the king himself, and withdrawing this whole defence, if you had heard that he agreed with his chaplain's judgment of you. See now how, as one of those Englishmen whom you presume to name "mad, ignorant, base and wicked,"[50] I personally despise and mock you; for it would be far beneath the dignity of the English nation herself to take any general notice of such a boring little weevil as you. Writhe and struggle in any way you will, up or down or roundabout, you are still but a pedagogue, [9] and, as though you had made to some divinity a prayer more foolish than that of Midas himself,[51] whatever you touch smells of the classroom—except when it is ungrammatical.

Any man then "from that plebeian scum" which you so criticize, (for I shall not debase, by any form of comparison with you, our true nobility, whose intellect, character, and position are well evidenced by their mighty deeds)—any man from that plebeian scum, I say, who has learned this one thing only, that he was born not for kings but for his God and country, is to be considered far more learned than you, far wiser, far more upright and more serviceable in every walk of life: he is learned without much reading, while you have read without profit, and with all your skill in languages and scanning or scribbling of tomes are but a brute beast at the end.

[49] Dr. Henry Hammond (1605–1660) was made royal chaplain in 1644 (*DNB*). Colonel Hammond, governor of the Isle of Wight, who had custody of Charles I during 1647 was his nephew.

[50] *Regia* (1649), p. 26, l. 18. Although Milton temporarily identifies himself with what Salmasius calls "the plebeian scum," he later takes a more conservative position. Below, p. 471, he admits that Salmasius' description of the populace as "blind and brutish, without skill in ruling, the most fickle of men, the emptiest, the unsteadiest, and most inconstant" may be true of the dregs of the populace. This is not true, he says, of the middle class, "which produces the greatest amount of good sense and knowledge of affairs."

[51] Midas: Ovid, *Metamorphoses,* XI, 102 ff.

CHAPTER II[1]

The argument that a thing is what it is believed to be when all men agree in holding the same opinion of it was said by Salmasius in the conclusion of his last chapter to be of overwhelming weight on his side,[2] and, although he was far astray in applying it to a point of fact, I may very well use it against him in my treatment of the legal rights of kings. While he defines a king (if what is described as unlimited in the whole world can actually be termed a definition) as one whose power is supreme in the kingdom and responsible to none but God, one who may do as he will and is not subject to the laws,[3] I shall be able to prove the opposite, not merely by my own theories and evidence but by his as well; that is, no nation or people of any size—for we need not plod through all the jungles of savagery—no nation, I say, has ever granted such rights or power to its king that he should not be subject to the laws, that he might do as he will, that he should judge all and be judged by none.[4] Indeed I am

[1] In book II of the *Regia,* 1649, pp. 29–52, Salmasius asks these questions: Who is a king? By whom, by what authority, for what crime, by what jury was the king condemned? Salmasius' main assertions are these: 1. A king is one who has supreme authority in the kingdom, who is answerable only to God; who, unfettered by laws, gives laws; who judges all and is judged by none. 2. This concept of kingship is supported by the experience of the Israelites and by the authority of the Roman writers, especially Sallust and Cicero. 3. A king was not given to the Israelites as a punishment, because Moses had foretold the establishment of kings. From intercourse with other nations, the Jews must have known what the kings of these nations were like when the Israelites were asking for a similar king for themselves. 4. When the Israelites asked for a king, Samuel thought an injury was being done to him and his sons. In warning the Israelites (that some kings might be tyrants), Samuel did not describe their first king or any king in particular, but what any king might be in the future. 5. David did not kill Saul (tyrants must not be killed), though the opportunity was his, because Saul was king and anointed of God. 6. Charles is compared to the ancient Jewish kings. Kings can do what they please, without fear of laws and judgments. God alone is the avenger of the unjust king.

[2] *Regia* (1649), p. 28, ll. 14–17.

[3] *Regia* (1649), p. 29, ll. 9–12. Salmasius adds further that a king is permitted to do what he likes. He is one who gives laws but does not receive them; moreover he is one who judges all but is judged by none.

[4] Courtney Murray's comment ("St. Robert Bellarmine on the Indirect Power," *Theological Studies,* IX:4 [December, 1948], p. 527) is of interest here and

sure that no one ever lived in any nation whatsoever, except this Salmasius alone, [10] who was so servile in heart as to uphold as royal prerogatives all the monstrous misdeeds of tyrants. Many of those among us most favorable toward the king have ever been guiltless of a belief so base, and we may easily see from some of his own earlier works that his opinion on these matters was far different before he was bribed. It is indeed clear that no free man in any free state, much less in the renowned university of the great Dutch republic,[5] could have written books so slavish in spirit and design that they seem rather to emanate from some slave factory or auction block. If a king may by his royal right do whatever he will, a doctrine which even that villainous Antoninus Caracalla did not dare believe unhesitatingly upon the incestuous urging of his step-mother Julia,[6] then surely there is not now and never was anyone who should be termed tyrant.

When he has violated all the laws of God and man he will be none the less a king and guiltless by his royal right. For what wrong has this just man committed? He has simply exercised his rights over his own subjects. Nothing that a king can do to his subjects is so fearful or cruel or mad as to justify any complaint or remonstrance that the king has exceeded his rights. Are you a beast, that you assert that this right of kings is based on the common practice of mankind or rather on the

---

throws light on Milton's problem of finding legal precedent for the execution of a king. "Now, the king did indeed acknowledge himself as bound by law; the concept of the irresponsible king, *rex legibus solutus,* was a later development and a piece of neo-paganism. However, the medieval problem was how to keep the king obedient to the law, how to compel him to do his duty of justice, how to punish his breaches of duty, how to get rid of him if he were incorrigible or useless. Basically, it is a problem of the institutionalization of society; and in a mature society it is solved by the creation of institutions within the political order that will serve to insure the supremacy of law and its due processes against the encroachments of force, wielded either by the ruler or other agencies. This is an exigence of rationality itself, a demand of the autonomy of the political order when developed to maturity, that it should be 'directed and corrected' from within itself, by the operation of its own political institutions. So a mature man is directed and corrected from within; it is the child that is under complete tutelage. Murray concludes (p. 527): "The political defect of the Middle Ages was that there were no effectively organized political institutions that could contrive to keep the monarch subject to law, or to do away with him if he became a tyrant."

[5] *I.e.,* at the University of Leyden.

[6] Antoninus Caracalla: For this apocryphal tale see Spartianus, "Vita Caracalli," X, 2, in *Scriptores Historiae Augustae,* tr. David Magie (3 vols., London: Loeb Classical Library, 1921), II, 27–29.

law of nature? [7] Should you be called human, you who are so hostile and inhumane to all men, and who thus attempt to rob and ruin mankind made in the image of God, in order to show that the cruel and implacable masters imposed on nations by superstition, crime, cowardice in some cases, or treachery, are actually furnished and assigned them by the gentle kindness of mother nature? When your vicious teaching [8] has made them far fiercer than they were before, you not only proceed to urge them to grind all men under foot and for the future treat men with even sharper scorn, but also seek in the most

[7] Milton on several occasions accuses Salmasius of arguing against himself (see above, p. 317, n. 46). Salmasius tends to trap himself by insisting on the most extreme version of the doctrine of divine right at the same time that he wants to insist that Cromwell has established a tyranny in England. In such a quotation from the apostle (*Regia,* 1649, p. 215, ll. 26–27) as "for he who resists power, resists the thing accomplished of God," Salmasius is logically bound to accept not only a Nero but a Cromwell as well. If all power ordained in the age should have honor (*Regia,* 1649, p. 93, ll. 13–16), any *status quo* can be justified. In a classic example (below, p. 384) Milton drives home the dilemma of Salmasius. He asks Salmasius why he does not accept the present government of England since it is an established power.

[8] What Milton calls Salmasius' "vicious teaching" actually is a doctrine stated in the most exaggerated terms. Salmasius even says of Christ that "he could have been born under the most flourishing and powerful rulers of all who ever existed, but he chose rather to assume human nature under a tyrant" (*Regia,* 1649, p. 53, ll. 9–12). He quotes Jeremiah 27:6 in regard to Nebuchadnezzar: "And now I have given all these lands into the hands of Nebuchadnezzar, King of Babylon, my servant." Though an oppressor of the Jews, he was an instrument of God. Salmasius argues that a tyrant is often the scourge of God; when he has done his service, he, in turn, is broken (*Regia,* 1649, p. 77, ll. 6–7).

The prophets were opposed to any uprising against kings (*Regia,* 1649, p. 78, ll. 10–11). A subject cannot accuse a king any more than a slave his master (*Regia,* 1649, p. 164, ll. 20–21). "For all laws, human and divine, constantly establish that a king, even ruling badly, must be endured." (*Regia,* 1649, p. 248, ll. 14–16).

The judgment of kings is reserved to God (*Regia,* 1649, p. 62, ll. 14–16). Salmasius declares the principle that "it is permitted by law for a tyrant to be killed" is abominable. He attributes the spreading of this opinion in England to the Jesuits and Independents (*Regia,* 1649, p. 98, ll. 36–37; p. 100, ll. 5–7).

In justice to Salmasius, it should be noted that the punishment of a tyrant by God was not merely a personal theory of his but a strongly held common belief. God is supposed to search the secret conscience. So much the more should kings be aware of God's wrath. From God not even a wicked crime conceived of in the mind can be hidden. "If the king is unfettered by laws, he ought not to judge by this that he is above laws and that he lives more unrestricted than others who appear to be bound by them." (*Regia,* 1649, p. 337, ll. 39 ff.). While kings have sovereignty over others, who are men like themselves, they return to dust like other men, having played their special role in the theatre of the world (*Regia,* 1649, p. 338, ll. 7 ff.).

foolish and wicked manner possible to provide them with weapons against the people in the form of natural law and royal right and even laws of the people themselves. You might well do the opposite of old Dionysius [9] and turn from pedagogy to tyranny, to gain not that royal right of maltreating whom you will, but the other one of dying miserably, so that like Tiberius shut up on Capri [10] you will be free to feel yourself dying a daily death through your own choice.

Let us however look somewhat more closely at the nature of this royal right. [11] Such, as you say, was the judgment of all the East and West alike. I shall not repeat for you the words of Aristotle and Cicero,[11] who are surely our most reliable authorities, and who said in the *Politics* and the speech *On the Provinces* respectively that the peoples of Asia readily endure slavery, while the Jews and Syrians were born for it.[12] I confess that those who long for liberty or can enjoy it are but few—only the wise, that is, and the brave; while most men prefer just masters so long as they are in fact just. But God was never so angered against all mankind, and no people was ever so hopeless or so senseless, that they wished to impose on themselves and their children the requirement of this most cruel law, namely of enduring masters who were unjust and insupportable.

You cite particularly "the words of that king in Ecclesiastes who was famous for his wisdom," [13] and so we too appeal to divine law, leaving this king for consideration later, when we shall better understand his opinion. Give ear to God himself, Deuteronomy 17: "When thou art come into the land which the Lord thy God giveth thee, and shalt say I will set a king over me, like as all the nations that are about me." [14] I want everyone to note this point particularly, that

[9] Dionysius the younger, tyrant of Syracuse, who after his defeat is said to have become a schoolmaster. See Cicero, *Tusculan Disputations,* III, xii, 27, in *Tusculan Disputations,* tr. J. E. King (Cambridge: Loeb Classical Library, 1950), pp. 258–59.

[10] For Tiberius' letter see Tacitus, *Annals,* VI, 6, and Suetonius, "Tiberius," lxvii, in *Suetonius,* tr. J. C. Rolfe (2 vols., London: Loeb Classical Library, 1920), pp. 388–89.

[11] Aristotle, *Politics,* 1285 a 20 (III, 14), tr. H. Rackham (London and New York: Loeb Classical Library, 1932), pp. 248, and Cicero, *The Speeches,* tr. R. Gardiner (London and New York: Loeb Classical Library, 1958), X, 550–51.

[12] This passage is noteworthy in emphasizing Milton's view that those desirous of liberty form an élite group. See below, p. 457.

[13] *Regia* (1649), p. 29, ll. 24–25.

[14] Deuteronomy 17:14. Harris F. Fletcher in *The Use of the Bible in Milton's Prose, Studies in Language and Literature* (Urbana, 1929), XIV, 43–49, shows

God himself bears witness to the right possessed by almost all peoples and nations of enjoying whatever form of government they wish, or of changing from one to another; this God asserts specifically of the Hebrews and does not deny of other nations. A republican form of government, moreover, as being better adapted to our human circumstances than monarchy, seemed to God more advantageous for his chosen people; he set up a republic for them and granted their request for a monarchy only after long reluctance. To show that he had left to the people the choice of being governed by one man or by many, provided that this government be just, God also established laws for the prospective king, if they should definitely desire one, and in these laws warned him against "multiplying for himself horses or wives or riches," so that he might understand that he had no rights against others when apart from the law he could make no decisions as to his own position. He was likewise bidden to copy with his own hand "all the provisions of this law," and when written "to keep them, that his heart be not lifted up above his brethren." This account makes it very clear that the king as well as the people was bound by these laws. Josephus, [12] an excellent interpreter of his people's laws, a man of wide experience in the administration of his own commonwealth and far superior to a thousand of those swindling rabbis, writes to much the same effect in book IV of his *Antiquities:* [15] Ἀριστοκρατία μὲν οὖν κράτιστον etc.: that is, he says, "aristocracy is the best form of government, and therefore you should seek no other, for it is enough to have God as governor. If however you are so bent on having a king, let him rely more on God and on the law than on his own wisdom, and let him be prevented from aiming at greater power than suits your best interests." This is part of what Josephus writes on this passage in Deuteronomy. Secondly, Philo Judaeus,[16] a writer of weight and a

---

that Milton uses for his Latin quotations from the Bible the Latin version of Tremellius-Junius. In using Tremellius-Junius, Milton quoted verbatim or varied only slightly from it with two exceptions in which he appears to have used the Vulgate.

[15] Josephus: "Jewish Antiquities," IV, 223, in *Josephus,* tr. H. St. J. Thackeray (9 vols., Cambridge: Loeb Classical Library, 1957), IV, 582–83. This is a commentary on Deuteronomy 17:14, which Milton had previously quoted.

[16] Philo Judaeus, *De Specialibus Legibus,* IV, 185, and *Legum Allegoria,* III, 79–80. The reference is actually to the third book, not to the second as Milton states. See *Philo,* tr. F. H. Colson *et al.* (10 vols., Cambridge: Loeb Classical Library, 1956), VIII, 122–23, and I, 352–53.

contemporary of Josephus, who wrote a lengthy commentary on all the Mosaic law and was most learned in its lore, explains this chapter of the law in his volume of the creation of rulers; he says there that the king is not subject to the laws only in the way in which any public enemy may be spoken of as not subject to the laws. Τοὺς ἐπὶ λύμῃ καὶ ζημίᾳ τῶν ὑπηκόων, etc.: that is, he says, "those who seize great power for the ruin and destruction of the people are to be termed not kings but foes, for their acts are the acts of irreconcilable foes; indeed those who do wrong under the pretence of ruling are worse than open enemies, as the latter can easily be repelled, while it is hard to lay bare the wicked craft of the former." Why then should they not be considered as enemies when they are discovered? So too in the second volume of his *Allegories of the Law;* king and tyrant are contraries; and again, a king not only compels but complies.[17]

It may however be said that these remarks are all very true; a king more than anyone else should obey the laws: but if he does the reverse, what law provides for his punishment? To that I answer, the same law that provides for the punishment of others, for I find no exceptions.[18] There is no specific law either about the punishment of priests, or even of the minor magistrates, all of whom might with equal justice and propriety claim freedom from the penalty for any crime, on the ground that there is no statute providing for their punishment. None of them, though, has claimed such freedom, nor is it likely that anyone would grant it them for such a reason. Thus far God's own law has taught us that a king should obey the laws and not exalt himself above the rest who are also his brethren.

Let us see next whether Ecclesiastes advocates a contrary doctrine (chapter VIII, verse 1, etc.) [13]: "I counsel thee to keep the king's commandment, and that in regard of the oath of God. Be not hasty to

[17] A king not only compels but complies: That Philo does not write this in the *Legum Allegoria* is evident from a close examination of that book. That Philo writes it at all, in the context which Milton implies, seems extremely doubtful, for Philo looked upon kingship as of divine origin, and upon the king as the representative of God upon earth, subject only to the laws of God and nature, a point of view entirely foreign to the words which Milton attributes to him.

[18] Milton here states his principle quite clearly—the king has no special position in regard to the law. As usual, he does not go into the problem of what juridical apparatus can be applied to a king who is a lawbreaker. Milton did not even see the necessity for speculating on what juridical apparatus can be applied in a "commonwealth" to determine when the decisions of a state are "sound" or in keeping with law.

go out of his sight; stand not in an evil thing: for he doeth whatsoever pleaseth him. Where the word of a king is, there is power; and who may say unto him, What doest thou?" There is general agreement that in this passage Ecclesiastes is instructing neither the Great Sanhedrin nor the Senate but private persons. He commands observance of the king's orders, especially because of the oath of God; but who gives his oath to a king unless the king in turn swears by the laws of God and of his country? So in Joshua 1, 17, the Reubenites and Gadites promise to obey Joshua: "According as we hearkened unto Moses in all things, so will we hearken unto thee; so but God be with thee as he was with Moses." You see that a qualification is stated; and hearken unto Ecclesiastes himself again when he says "the quiet words of wise men ought to be heard rather than the shouting of him that ruleth among fools." Of what else does he warn us? "Stand not in an evil thing; for he doeth whatsoever pleaseth him." He does certainly do so to wicked men who persist in their wickedness, being armed with the power of the law, and he can treat them with clemency or harshness as he will. This has no sound of tyranny, nor is there anything to make a good man tremble.

"Where the word of a king is, there is power; and who may say to him, What doest thou?" [19] Yet we read of one who said to his king not only "What hast thou done?" but also "Thou hast done foolishly" (I Samuel 13). But you may say that Samuel was no ordinary man. I cast in your teeth your own words, though they come somewhat later, on page 49: "What was there extraordinary in Saul or David?" you ask.[20] In the same way I ask what there was extraordinary in Samuel? He was a prophet, but so are those today who follow his example, for they act according to the will of God whether manifest or innate: all this you admit below on page 50.[21] In his wisdom then Ecclesiastes here warns private citizens against contending with their king: for it is wholly ruinous to strive even with a man of wealth or

[19] Ecclesiastes 8:4.

[20] *Regia* (1649), p. 49, ll. 1–2. Part of the sentence—*ad regnum vocatione*—is not translated by Milton. "Extraordinary" is in reference not to character but to "calling to the kingship."

[21] It is hard to see from the context on p. 50 what "admission" of Salmasius' Milton has in mind. Salmasius admits the operation of "secondary" causes implicitly or overtly, under the control of man, but which God either orders or permits, and which are attributed to him. Milton's point seems to be that there is nothing more extraordinary in being called to the throne directly by God than indirectly by God through the people.

power in any form. Are we for this reason to suppose that the nobles, all the other magistrates, or the whole people will not even dare to murmur when the king wishes to indulge in madness, or that when he is witless, wicked and passionate, devising the ruin of all the righteous, they will not resist and oppose him, fearing that he may undertake the overthrow of all the establishments of God and man and ravage the whole realm with robbery, fire and sword, since he is so little subject to the laws as to be permitted what he wills? You are still smeared, Sir Knight,[22] with the slave-market slime of Cappadocia [14]; and every free nation, if ever again you dare set foot in one, should either ban you as a monster of depravity to the ends of the earth, or else send you, as a candidate for slavery to replace an ass in a mill, under the solemn obligation of grinding in your place under some most foolish tyrant, if they ever let you loose. What could be said or repeated that would be too fierce or foolish to apply to you?

Now continue! When the children of Israel sought a king from God, they said they wished to be governed by him with the same authority as all the other peoples which enjoyed that form of government. But Virgil bears witness that the kings of the east used to rule with supreme authority and unlimited power:

> In no such way doth Egypt nor great Lydia,
> Nor Parthia's hosts nor Median Hydaspes
> Yield reverence to their king.[23]

In the first place it is of no concern to us what sort of king the Israelites wanted, particularly since God was wroth at their desire for a king, not in accordance with divine law but in imitation of the gentiles, and he was wroth furthermore that they desired a king at all. Secondly we cannot think that an unjust king, not subject to the laws, was the desire of the very people who could not endure the rule of the sons of Samuel, though these were bound by laws, and who had recourse to monarchy only to escape the greed of these sons. Lastly your Vir-

[22] Martial, *Epigrams,* X, 76, 5. Milton's Latin in the rest of the sentence would, like the translation, seem obscure to a reader who failed to recognize the allusion to Terence, *Andria,* 199 ff. There a master threatens to send his slave to replace an ass in the task of grinding in a mill. The master adds that if he ever lets his slave loose he will take the slave's place himself. The idea, of course, is as if one were to say, "I'll be hanged if I ever let you go."

[23] Virgil, *Georgics,* IV, 210–12, in *Virgil,* tr. H. Rushton Fairclough (2 vols., Cambridge: Loeb Classical Library, 1950), I, 210–11.

gilian citation [24] does not prove that eastern kings ruled with absolute power, for even Virgil's bees, more respectful toward their kings than the Egyptians or Medes, nevertheless by his own account live under mighty laws, and therefore not under kings bound by no laws.

But see how little malice I bear you! Though most men think you a scoundrel, I shall show that you have only assumed the disguise of a scoundrel. In your *Apparatus ad Primatum Papae* you say that some scholars at Trent used the example of the bees to support the rule of the pope, and this it is which you borrowed with equally evil design.[25] Now that you have turned scoundrel you shall be answered by the very reply you made to them when you were honest, and by your own hand be stripped of the scoundrel's disguise.

"The government of the bees is a commonwealth, and is so described by scientists; the king they have is harmless, and is more a leader than a tyrant; he does not flog or prod [15] or kill his subject bees." It is then no wonder they respect him so. It was a bad day for you when you brought in those bees, for by contrast with their triple teeth you are shown to be a toothless drone. Aristotle, however, a deep student of politics, says that the Asiatic type of monarchy, which he calls barbaric, was *κατὰ νόμον* or in accordance with law [26] (*Politics*, III),[27] and indeed when he lists five species of monarchy, he writes that four of them are in accordance with law and have the approval of the people, but these monarchies are none the less tyrannical in so far as they are granted, even at the desire of the people, power so extensive; but the kingdom of Sparta seems to be the best example of a kingdom, since all things in that community are not in the power of the king. The fifth type he calls *παμβασιλεία* [28] ["absolute autocracy"], and here alone he discovers that right of ruling as they please which you ascribe to all kings; but where or when such government has ever existed he does not say, and seems to have mentioned it only to show that it is irrational, unjust, and wholly tyrannical.

You say that Samuel expounded to them the rights of kings so as to

24 Virgil, *Georgics,* IV, 210–12. For the reference below to Virgil's bees, see *Georgics,* IV, 154.

25 This is a quotation from Salmasius, *De Primatu,* p. 211, ll. 28 ff.

26 Milton prints Greek followed by a Latin paraphrase. The Greek has been retained and the paraphrase translated.

27 *Politics*: 1285 a 25 (III, 9).

28 Might be rendered as "absolute autocracy." The word is rare, perhaps only used by Aristotle on political theory.

discourage them from choosing a king; [29] but what was his source? Not surely the law of God, for we have seen that it drew a far different picture of the rights of kings, and neither was it God himself speaking through Samuel, for God disapproved and censured it and thought it vicious. The prophet then was not maintaining that these royal rights were a divine grant but rather a most depraved method of government usurped by the pride of kings and their lust for rule! This is not what kings should do, but what they wish to, and he was showing the people the procedure of the priestly sons of Eli, using the same word which on page 33 you, being a solecist in Hebrew too, call Mishpat.[30] In I Samuel 2:13 he wrote "the manner of those priests with the people was this," namely, ungodly, hateful, and tyrannical, and so their manner was not a right but a wrong. In this same way did the early fathers explain this passage; of them one will serve as well as many, namely Sulpicius Severus,[31] contemporary and friend of Jerome, judged by Augustine to be a man of great learning and wisdom. In his *Sacred History* he states that Samuel explains to the people the nature of royal despotism and the pride of power. Surely royal rights are not despotism and pride, but rather, as Sallust states [16],[32] the rights and power of kings are granted so that liberty may be preserved and the commonwealth strengthened, and later are changed into despotism and pride. Such is the explanation of this passage by all orthodox theologians and jurisconsults, and as you might have learned from

[29] Salmasius argues that Samuel wished to dissuade the Israelites from choosing a king, because under judges a just and lenient rule was possible, but, under a king, unique power is exercised, often with the greatest injustice. In other words, according to Salmasius, Samuel was keenly aware of what divine right meant and warned the Israelites about its possible consequences. See *Regia* (1649), p. 33, ll. 38 ff.

[30] This Hebrew word might roughly be transcribed into Anglicized "mishpoth." It means "rule" or "law." It can also mean "lawful procedure." Salmasius is not a solecist here as Milton alleges. Milton wants the word to mean "procedure" rather than "law." Salmasius wants the word to mean the "right" that follows from an "office." Salmasius argues on page 33 of the *Regia*, 1649, alluded to, that Samuel insists that if the Jews select a king, they run the unavoidable risk of having a king who may transgress and run into excesses, but these must be considered as legitimate as far as the law is concerned and must be endured.

[31] Sulpicius Severus, *Historia Sacra,* I, 32, in *A Select Library of Nicene and Post-Nicene Fathers of the Christian Church,* Second Series, ed. Philip Schaff and Henry Wace (14 vols., New York, 1890–1900), XI, 86 (hereafter cited as *Fathers, N. and P.N. 2*).

[32] Sallust: *Jugurtha,* XXXI, 26.

Sichardus,[33] by many of the rabbis too, and no rabbi ever held that this passage treated of an absolute right of kings.[34]

On page 106, chapter 5 below, you complain that not only Clement of Alexandria [35] but everyone else too has gone astray, and say that you alone have hit the mark. What utter impudence or folly it is to oppose all authorities, particularly the orthodox, and change those customs of kings, which God himself has wholly damned, into a royal right, using as your argument the fair name of right, though you admit that this right of yours mainly consists in robberies and wrongs, violence and insult. Was any man ever so legally independent as to have permission to steal and rob, subvert and confound everything? Did the Romans ever say, as you maintain, that anyone acted thus by his own right? In Sallust,[36] Gaius Memmius, tribune of the people, attacked the pride of the nobles and their freedom from the punishment of their crimes, saying that "to do what one wishes with impunity is to be a king." This phrase delighted you, and you immediately added it to your assets, but unless you had been sound asleep you would never have touched it. Was he supporting the rights of kings? Or was he not rather attacking the sloth of the plebs for allowing the nobles to play the tyrant with impunity, and for enduring once again the same royal practices which their ancestors had by their own right cast out of the realm with the king himself? You should have sought Cicero's advice; he could have shown you how to understand Sallust better, and Samuel too. In the *Pro Rabirio* [37] he says: "We all know

[33] Wilhelm Schickhard, German Orientalist (1592–1635), author of *Jus Regium Hebraeorum e Tenebris Rabbinicis Erutum*. See *Commonplace Book*, in *Complete Prose*, I, 460.

[34] Milton is correct—and for a good historical reason. The written Hebrew commentaries started a long time after the rule of kings had stopped. The *Mishnah*, the first set of commentaries, was orally preserved but not actually written down until about 100 A.D. The Pharisees were opposed to the kingly domination of Maccabees, and the only absolute power they recognized was that of divine law. Strictly theocrats, they accepted the Maccabees only as an expediency.

[35] *Regia*, 1649, p. 106, ll. 21–23. Salmasius quotes Clement of Alexandria to the effect that "to a people seeking a king a humane master is not promised, but an obstinate tyrant." He adds: "In this matter all are in error, not only Clement."

[36] Sallust: *Catiline*, VI, 7.

[37] Cicero, *Pro C. Rabirio Postumo*, XI, 29, in *The Speeches*, tr. N. H. Watts (London: Loeb Classical Library, 1931), pp. 392–93.

the habits of kings; these are their orders: 'Heed and obey my words.' " In the same speech he quotes from the poet's similar sentiments, which he calls not the rights but the habits of kings, and advises us to read and ponder, "not so much for our pleasure as in order to learn what to guard against and avoid." See how Sallust has treated you, when you thought to make this foe of tyrants into an advocate of their rights. You may be sure that this royal right is shaky and is hastening its own ruin when like a drowning man it clutches at any straws [17], and tries to support itself by such evidence and authorities as hasten the ruin which perhaps might otherwise have been postponed.

"Summum ius" you call *"summa iniuria,"* [38] and this applies particularly to kings, for, in the use of their full rights, their acts are those ascribed by Samuel to the rights of a king." [39] This is a wretched right that you can defend only by the greatest wrongdoing, when forced to consider its logical conclusion. Full rights are when one demands the full extent of the law, standing on its letter to the detriment of justice, or when one quibbles over the interpretation of the statutes with evil intent; this being the source, according to Cicero, of the old axiom. Since however it is certain that all rights spring from the fount of justice, you must be a villain if you say that "for a king to be unjust, harsh, violent and a robber, or as bad as the worst that ever was, is his royal right according to the prophet's recommendation to his people." [40] What right, be it interpreted strictly or mildly, be it written or unwritten, can possibly lead to wrongdoing?

That you may not think to admit this of other men but deny it of kings, I can bring against you one who was himself a king and who maintains that such royal rights are execrable both in his own sight and in that of God. Psalm 94, "Shall the throne of iniquity have fellowship with thee, that frameth mischief by law?" Think not then to wrong God so cruelly, and make him appear to teach that the perverse and wicked deeds of kings are their royal rights, when he specifically shows his abhorrence of the society of wicked kings for their bringing upon their people every trial and tribulation under the claim of royal rights. Do not bring a false charge against the prophet of God; for in

[38] *Summum ius . . . summa iniuria:* Cicero, *De Officiis,* I, X, 33, in *De Officiis,* tr. Walter Miller (Cambridge: Loeb Classical Library, 1951), pp. 34–35.
[39] *Regia* (1649), p. 30, ll. 32–35. [40] *Regia* (1649), p. 30, ll. 20–21.

thinking that in this passage he is an advocate of the rights of kings you present us with no true Samuel, but, like the witch,[41] summon an insubstantial ghost, though I am sure that not even her hell-sprung Samuel was such a liar as to name what you call royal rights anything but unbridled tyranny. We read of rights granted to crime, and you admit "it was the worst kings who used to employ the licence which was their right."[42] This right which you have brought in to destroy mankind has been proved by us to be no grant of God, and as we shall show later it is of the devil. "This licence" you say "lets one be able to do what he will," [18][43] and you advance Cicero as author of this right. I am always glad to cite your authorities, for usually you ruin yourself by your own witnesses. Hear then the words of Cicero's *Fourth Philippic:*[44] "What better cause for war is there than to ward off slavery, that condition which is most wretched even though the master may not be cruel, for he has the power to be if he wishes?" He has the power of violence, that is, for, if Cicero were speaking of rights, he would contradict himself and make the just cause of war unjust. What you describe then are not royal rights, but the wrong, force, and violence of kings. You pass from royal to private licence: a private citizen may be a liar or ungrateful. So may a king, but what then? May kings also steal, kill, and commit adultery with impunity? Does it make any difference so far as the seriousness of the wrong is concerned whether a king or a brigand or some foreign foe kills, plunders, and enslaves a people? We ought certainly with equal right to drive off and take vengeance on the former as on the latter, since both are hostile and ruinous to human society, or even on a king particularly, since though he has received from us so many services and honors he yet betrays the safety of the people which had been entrusted to him on oath.

You finally admit that "Moses gives the laws by which a king, whenever one may be chosen, should govern, although these differ from the rights established by Samuel."[45] This contradicts your earlier statement in two ways: for you said the king was not bound

[41] The Witch of Endor summoned Samuel from the dead at Saul's request (I Samuel 28:7–25).

[42] *Regia* (1649), p. 31, ll. 8–9. This passage occurs in a context where Cicero rather than Samuel is the authority under discussion.

[43] *Regia* (1649), p. 31, l. 9.

[44] Cicero's *Fourth Philippic:* Not the fourth but the eighth—VIII, iv, 12.

[45] *Regia* (1649), p. 32, ll. 32–35.

by any laws, and now you say he is; and also you make the laws of Moses contrary to those of Samuel, which is ridiculous. But the prophet says: "You shall be slaves to the king." [46] Though I did not deny that they were slaves, still they were slaves not because of the rights of the king but rather because of the unjust usurpation of many of their kings. The prophet warned them beforehand that their stubbornness in that request would result in their own punishment, not through any rights of the king but through their own deserts. If however a king not subject to the laws might do what he wished, the king would be far more than a master, and his people far lower than the lowest of all slaves. Even a foreign-born slave used to have God's law as his bulwark against a master who acted unjustly; and will then this whole people, even a free nation, find on earth no law or bulwark as a refuge against wounds and affliction and despoilment, and be freed from the slavery of the kings of Egypt only to be handed over to one of the brethren [19] to be crushed, if he wishes, under a heavier yoke? Since this accords neither with divine law nor with reason, no one can doubt that the prophet told of the habits and not the rights of kings; and not even the habits of all kings, but only of most.

You then turn to the rabbis and cite two of them with no better luck than you had before, for it is obvious that the chapter about the king which Rabbi Joses spoke of as containing the rights of kings is in Deuteronomy and not in Samuel; and Rabbi Judas [47] declared quite correctly, contradicting you, that the passage in Samuel concerns only his putting fear into the people. For what is clearly injustice to be named and taught as right is a destructive procedure, unless perhaps it is called right in irony. Here verse 18 is appropriate: "And ye shall cry out in that day because of your king which ye shall have chosen you; and the Lord will not hear you in that day." Such was the punishment awaiting those headstrong people who in opposition to God's will wished to have a king granted them. These words how-

[46] I Samuel 8:17.

[47] Rabbi Joses . . . Rabbi Judas: Perhaps Jose Ben Halafta, second century Talmudist, and Judah Ben Ilai, second century codifier of the Mishnah. For a full discussion of whether Milton read the Rabbinical Hebrew in such a work as Buxtorf's rabbinical Bible or depended on such contemporary commentators as Lightfoot, Pococke, and Whitgift for his knowledge of Rabbinical glosses see Harris F. Fletcher, *Milton's Rabbinical Readings* (Urbana, 1930), and George N. Conklin, *Biblical Criticism and Heresy in Milton* (New York: King's Crown Press, 1949).

ever do not prevent their trying prayer or anything else, and if the people may cry out to God against their king, they may equally undertake any other honorable means of freeing themselves from tyranny. Who indeed under the pressure of any evil thus cries out to God to the neglect of all his other duties, and sinks down in idle prayers?

But whatever the truth may be, what has all this to do with our rights or those of our kings? We never opposed God's will in seeking a king nor did we receive one by his grant, but rather followed the rights of peoples and established our own government without God's mandate or prohibition either. In such a case I see no reason why it should not be a tribute to our courage and increase our fame to have deposed our king, when the Israelites indeed found themselves accused for having sought one. The very facts speak for themselves: God heard the prayers we sent up against our king when we had one and set us free, while he commanded those who, having none, importuned one from him, to be slaves, until after their return from Babylon they reverted to their former means of government.

Next, in yet another ill-omened undertaking, you begin to give lessons on the Talmud. In a desire to prove that a king is not judged you show from the Codex of the Sanhedrin [48] that "the king neither [20] judges nor is judged," [49] but this conflicts with the request of that people who sought a king for the very reason that he might judge them. You try in vain to cover this over, and tell us indeed that it should be understood of kings who ruled after the captivity; [50] but listen to Maimonides,[51] who gives this definition of the difference between the kings of Israel and Judah: "the descendants of David judge and are judged," but says neither is true of the Israelites. You are

[48] "Tract Sanhedrin" of the *Babylonian Talmud*. See edition of Michael L. Rodkinson, (20 vols., New York, 1896–1903), VII, VIII (XV, XVI), 43.

[49] *Regia* (1649), p. 34, ll. 21–25.

[50] *Regia* (1649), pp. 34–35: "Certum quidem est Maimonidem hanc ponere inter reges Israëlis & reges Judaeorum ex Davidis posteris differentiam, quod reges familiae Davidis judicarent, & judicarentur, testimonium adversus eos dicerent alii, ipsique in alios dicerent, Reges autem Israëlis judicandi potestatem non habuisse nec etiam judicari potuisse." A few lines earlier Salmasius (p. 34, ll. 34–35) stated that the people asked for a king to judge them, referring to I Kings 8 for his authority.

[51] *Maimonides:* a twelfth century scholar with whose works in the Buxtorf edition Milton shows some acquaintance, as evidenced by quotation in *Doctrine and Discipline of Divorce*. See *Complete Prose,* II, 257.

your own foe and by your arguments with yourself or your Rabbis you plead my case.

You say that this "did not apply to the first kings," for it is said in verse 17: "Ye shall be his slaves"; by custom clearly, and not by right, or if it was by right, as a penalty for seeking a king; and although they did not pay the penalty under this or that particular king, still they did under most of them generally, and that is a matter not relevant to our concerns. You really need no opponent, for you are always so opposed to yourself. You say on my behalf that Aristobulus first and then Jannaeus surnamed Alexander [52] did not receive that royal right from the Sanhedrin which is the guardian and interpreter of rights, but rather by a gradual usurpation on their own account against the opposition of the council. To please these kings that fine tale about "Gabriel smiting" the leaders of the Sanhedrin was made up, and this great right of the king not to be judged, on which you seem to depend so much, was by your own confession derived from that old wives' tale or even worse, being but a rabbinical fable.[53]

That Hebrew kings can be judged and even condemned to the lash is shown at length by Sichard [54] from the rabbinical writings; and it is to him that you owe all this matter, though you are not ashamed to howl against him. We read, on the contrary, that Saul [55] himself made trial of the lot for the stake of his life along with his son Jonathan, and obeyed his own decree. When Uzziah [56] too was judged a leper and cast from the temple by the priests like one of the people, he yielded and ceased being king; but had he refused to leave the temple, give up his office, and live apart, asserting that royal right of not being bound by the laws, do you think the Jews and their priests would have allowed the temple to be defiled, the laws broken, and the whole people endangered by infection? Shall laws then have force against a leprous

[52] Josephus, *Jewish Antiquities,* XIII, 11.

[53] The material to which Milton refers and partly summarizes is contained in *Regia,* 1649, p. 36, ll. 15 ff. Salmasius himself classifies the story of "Gabriel smiting" among "nugae . . . & fabulae Rabbinicae."

[54] Sichard: See above, p. 350, n. 33.

[55] When Saul asked the Lord's counsel as to whether the Israelites should attack the Philistines and received no answer, he thought that the Israelites had offended the Lord and that a sacrifice should be made. Then he cast lots between himself and his son Jonathan and Jonathan was taken, but the people would not allow the sacrifice. See I Samuel 14:37–45.

[56] II Kings 15:5.

king, and none against a tyrant? Is anyone so mad or foolish as to think that although the law has warnings and provisions against the injury of a people by infection from a diseased king, there is yet no legal remedy for the far more serious case when a godless, [21] unjust, and cruel king plunders and tortures and kills his people and wholly ruins the state?

Then you say that "there can be cited no instance of any king called before the bar and condemned to die." [57] This argument, so Sichardus wisely answers, is as if someone should discourse as follows: "The Emperor was never summoned before the elector: therefore, if the Elector Palatine should set a day for the Emperor's trial, the latter need not plead in court"; but nonetheless the Golden Bull of Charles IV [58] shows that he made himself and his successors subject to such proceedings. Why should we wonder that when the condition of the people is corrupt so much has been allowed to kings, since so many private citizens have by wealth or favor gained impunity for the worst of crimes? That state of being ἀνυπεύθυνον, however, or being dependent on no one and accountable to no man, which you describe as peculiar to royal majesty, is said by Aristotle, *Politics,* IV, 10,[59] to be particularly tyrannical and not to be borne in a free country. You

[57] This is apparently a paraphase of the *Regia* (1649), p. 37, ll. 2–4: "Nec exemplum ullius in his posteribus Judaeae & Israëlis regibus offeri potest qui judicium capitis subierit aut in jus vocatus sit ex ulla criminis causa." Actually Milton's quotation makes Salmasius' statement seem more sweeping than it is. Salmasius' context is strictly Israelite history in reference to the kings between Saul and Joachim. Milton, however, draws the inference, not inconsistent with Salmasius' general intention, "that no instance can be cited." Salmasius would undoubtedly add "in the case of a *true* king," not merely one possessing the name, or a chief magistrate whose title is that of king but who never actually derived royal right from the people, the right the prophet Samuel is alleged to have had in mind when he warned the Israelites about what kingly power really meant.

[58] A "Golden Bull" was the general designation of any charter decorated with a golden seal or *bulla.* The name has, in practice, been restricted to a few documents of unusual political importance, particularly the Golden Bull of Charles IV to which Milton alludes. The main object of this bull was to provide a set of rules for the election of the German kings, or kings of the Romans, as they are called in this document. In its final form the bull was issued at the diet of Metz on December 25, 1356. The text of the golden bull consists of a prologue and thirty-one chapters. The chief result of the bull was to add greatly to the power of the electors. The work of summoning the electors and of presiding over the deliberations fell to the archbishop of Mainz, but if he failed to discharge this duty, the electors were to assemble without summons within three months of the death of the king. No admission is made in the bull that the election of a king needs confirmation from the pope.

[59] *Politics,* IV, 10: *Politics,* 1295 a 20 (actually IV, 8).

bring on Antony, the most cruel of tyrants and the subverter of the Roman republic, as your authority, and a very suitable one he is, for saying that a king cannot rightly be held accountable for his deeds; and yet Antony, when preparing to march against the Parthians, called before him Herod to defend himself on a charge of murder, and it is thought that he would have punished even the king, had not that king used his gold to bribe him. So then Antony's assertion of royal power and your royal defence are derived from a single source! And *rightly so,* you say, "for kings owe their thrones to no other man, but hold them as the grant of God." [60] Tell me then who these kings are, for I deny that such kings have ever existed. In the first case, Saul would never have been king [61] unless the people had wished for one in defiance of God's will; and, though declared king at Mizpah, he yet lived as little more than a private citizen, following his father's flocks, until at Gilgal he was for a second time created king by the people. Was not David too, though anointed by God, anointed later by Judah at Hebron, and then by all the Hebrews, who still waited until a covenant had been completed (II Samuel 5:1, and I Chronicles 11). A covenant however binds kings and limits them. Solomon, you say, "sat on the throne of God and pleased all men" (I Chronicles 29) [22], and so there was some importance in pleasing the people. Jehoiadah appointed Joash king,[62] but at that time also arranged a covenant between king and people (II Kings 11). These kings, as well as the rest of the descendants of David, were, I confess, appointed both by God and by the people; [63] but all others everywhere I assert to have been appointed by the people alone, and it is for you to show their appointment by God, except in the way in which all things great and small are said to be made and appointed by God. It is then in a very

[60] *Regia* (1649), p. 39, ll. 30–31. [61] I Samuel, 10:24.

[62] Athaliah, mother of Ahaziah, after the latter's death destroyed all the royal line except Joash, then an infant, who was hidden by his sister Jehosheba. Seven years later, Jehoiadah, the high priest, conspired with nobles and magistrates, killed Athaliah, and put Joash on the throne (II Kings 11–12).

[63] Milton had a thorny point to meet in the exegesis of the Hebrew scriptures regarding kings. Did the Hebrew kings receive their appointments from God as Salmasius insisted? Milton from his reading of Hebrew history is forced to admit the possibility of a king being appointed by God, but at the same time he insists that such a king, like all other kings, is bound by *covenants,* implicit contracts between king and people (see below, p. 359). These covenants apparently grew out of the secondary law of nature (see below, p. 442, n. 2). They are necessary in the secular state as a result of the fall of man. The absolute law of God does not abolish the rights of the people. The king is under law as well as under God. The people are judges of guilty rulers (see pp. 358 and 359).

special manner that the throne of David is called the throne of God; the thrones of other kings are God's only as all other things are his. This you should have learned from verses 11 and 12 of the same chapter: "All that is in the heaven and in the earth is thine; thine is the kingdom, O Lord. Both riches and honor come of thee, and power and might." The reason for this frequent repetition is not to make kings swell with pride but to warn them that though they may think themselves gods there is yet a God over them to whom they owe all. From this we may easily understand the teaching of the Essenes and of the poets,[64] that kings are accompanied by God and stem from Jove; for that the lesser magistrates too, even the judges, are from that same God was established by king Solomon himself, Proverbs 8, 15, 16, and as Homer declared in the *Iliad,* I, 238–39, "judges who guard the laws from God." Furthermore all of us alike are of God and his children.

This absolute right of God, then, does not abolish the rights of the people, nor prevent all other kings not appointed by God from owing their rule to the people alone, to whom therefore they are accountable. This fact, even though the mob is wont to flatter its kings, is recognized by kings themselves, both good ones like Homer's Sarpedon,[65] and wicked tyrants like those of the poet. "Glaucus, why is it that we two are honored above all others in Lycia, and all men look on us as Gods?" [23] He answers his own question—*because the brilliance of our valor exceeds that of others: let us then do battle stoutly, lest our Lycians call us cowards.* By these words he indicates both that the office of king is granted by the people, and that an account must be rendered to the people of the conduct of war. Wicked kings on the other hand, in order to strike terror into their people, make public proclamation that God is the source of royal rule, though their private prayers are directed to no divinity but Fortune. The famous lines from Horace are appropriate:

> The rugged Dacians and the vagrant Scyths,
> The mothers of barbarian kings,

[64] The Essenes were pre-Christian monastic Jews, of whom what little was formerly known (before the discovery of the Dead Sea Scrolls) came from Philo and Josephus. Since Milton has been using these authors in the present chapter, we may assume that they are the source of his knowledge of the Essenes. The "poets" referred to in the passage are undoubtedly Solomon and Homer who are next quoted.

[65] *Iliad,* XII, 310 ff., tr. A. T. Murray (2 vols., Cambridge: Loeb Classical Library, 1946), I, 566–67 ff.

And despots robed in purple
All tremble at thy power,
Lest with thy cruel heel thou crush
Their palaces, and the subject throng
Should fly to arms, arouse their laggard friends,
And cast all despotism to the ground.[66]

If therefore kings today rule by divine sanction, by that same sanction do the people maintain their freedom, for all things indeed have their source and sanction in God. To both these points Scripture bears witness; that kings rule through him and are by him hurled from their thrones, but nonetheless we see each of these done far more often by the people than by God. The rights of the people, then, just as those of the king, whatever they are, are derived from God. Wherever the people have set up their kings without the direct intervention of God they can by the same right of theirs cast them down. The hand of God is more evident in the ouster than in the establishment of a tyrant, and more of his favor rests on a people when they disown an unjust king than on a king who grinds down his unoffending subjects.

The people [67] furthermore do with God's approval judge their guilty rulers: for He conferred this office on his chosen ones when, in Psalm 149, he says that those who sing the praises of Christ their king shall cast in chains the kings of the gentiles, all of whom the Gospel terms tyrants, and apply the letter of the law to those who boast of their freedom from all statutes and laws. Let none be so stupid, none so wicked, as to believe that kings, who are often but lazy louts, are so dear to God that the whole world must depend upon their whim and be ruled by it; or that because of their influence and, on their account, the whole human race, which I might almost call divine, is to be placed and numbered with the most irrational and worthless of animals. [24]

Well now, to keep busy you bring on Marcus Aurelius as a supporter of tyrants, though you would have been better off to let Aurelius lie.[68] I know not whether he said that God alone was the judge of

[66] Horace, *Odes,* I, XXXV, 9 ff.

[67] By "the people" Milton means "the sound part"—not people in a collective sense, for the phrase "chosen ones" follows significantly, implying more than the merely historical meaning of the "chosen people."

[68] Salmasius states that Marcus Aurelius has wisely and knowingly said that magistrates judge in regard to private persons, princes in regard to magistrates, God in regard to princes (*Regia,* 1649, p. 40, ll. 17–18).

tyrants; but Xiphilinus,[69] whom you quote on autarchy, does state that God alone can be the judge of autarchies, though I do not agree that in that context autarchy means monarchy, and I believe it less each time I read what goes before. Indeed anyone who has read the passage might wonder how that incongruous and suddenly ingrafted idea could fit in or what it could mean: particularly since Marcus Aurelius was the best of emperors and, so Capitolinus reports,[70] treated the people as had been done when the state was free; and there is no doubt that at that time the rights of the people had been paramount. That same ruler tells in the first volume of his *Life* [71] of his reverence for Thrasea, Helvidius, Cato, Dio, Brutus and all tyrannicides or men who wished for that honor, and he tells also of his design for a commonwealth governed by just laws with equal rights for all: not Marcus Aurelius, so the fourth book states, but the law is master. He knew that everything belonged to the Senate and people, and said that he was so far from having anything of his own that his very habitation belonged to them, or so Xiphilinus has it: [72] to such a degree did he avoid making his royal right the grounds for any usurpation. On his deathbed [73] he recommended his son to the Romans as successor on condition of his worth, and did not therefore claim that unlimited and imaginary right of ruling as though such right, which is indeed your autarchy, were delivered by God to pass from hand to hand. All the history of Greece and Rome, you insist, is full of examples—though nowhere can this be seen—and all the history of the Jews; but still you add that for the most part the Jews were little pleased with royal power. Indeed you have seen before, and will again, that the Greeks and Romans were exceedingly little pleased with tyrants, and so were the Jews, as we might read if that work of Samuel in which he defined the rights of the kingdom, which is men-

[69] *Regia* (1649), p. 40, ll. 18–19. Joannes Xiphilinus, eleventh-century epitomizer of Dio Cassius. See Dio Cassius, *Dio's Roman History,* LXXII (LXXI), 3, 4 (*Dio's Roman History,* tr. Ernest Cary [9 vols., London: Loeb Classical Library, 1914], IX, 5), or Boissevain's edition, III, 252. Salmasius, Milton indicates, has perverted Xiphilinus' meaning.

[70] Capitolinus, "Vita M. Antonini," *Scriptores Historiae Augustae,* XII, 1.

[71] Marcus Aurelius Antoninus, I, 14, in *Communings with Himself,* rev. and tr. Charles R. Haines (London: Loeb Classical Library, 1916), pp. 10–11.

[72] Dio Cassius, LXXII (LXXI), 33, 2, or Boissevain's edition, III, 273.

[73] On his deathbed: Xiphilinus, in his "Epitome of Book LXXII" of Dio Cassius' *Roman History,* states that Marcus Aurelius commended his son Commodus to many Romans, including members of the Senate.

tioned in I Samuel 10, were extant—a book which, so the Jewish scholars relate, was torn up or burned by the kings so that they might exercise with greater impunity their tyranny over their subjects.

Take a look around now and see if you can seize some prey: King David finally is your candidate for the rack, and you twist his words in Psalm 17 when he says "let my sentence come forth from thy presence": therefore, so Barnachmoni [74] has it, [25] "none but God judges a king." But rather it seems more likely that David wrote these words when he was being harassed by Saul and, though already anointed of God, did not refuse even the judgment of Jonathan. In I Samuel 20 he says: "If there be iniquity in me, slay me thyself," and later, like any other falsely accused by men, he appeals to the judgment of the Lord, as is clear from what follows: "Thine eyes behold the thing that is right, for thou hast searched mine heart," etc. What has all this to do with the judgment of kings or with courts? Surely the rights of kings are most dangerously undermined and weakened by those who reveal that they are based and built on such shifty supports.

Now comes that old argument which is the masterpiece of our courtiers: "Against thee only have I sinned," in Psalm 51:6.[75] As though king David repenting in bitter grief and tears, lying in sackcloth and ashes on the ground, and humbly imploring God for mercy, had actually spoken these words with any thought of the rights of kings, when he considered himself hardly deserving the rights of a slave! Did he believe that all God's people, his own brothers, were so contemptible in comparison with him that to murder, defile, or rob them could be no crime for him? [76] Far be such arrogance and unseemly ignorance

[74] Rabbi Mose ben Nachman (Hebrew), Bar Nachman (Aramaic), Bar Nachmoni (Latin), or Nacmanides (Greek) was born around 1195 in Gerona, Spain, and died in 1370 in Akko, Palestine. An authority on law, he wrote a cabbalistic commentary on the Bible. His Neo-Platonic views were opposed to those of the now better known contemporary Rabbi Mose Bar Maimon (Aramaic, Rambam; or Greek, Maimonides), who was Aristotelian. His mystical thought has long remained influential in Eastern Jewish thought. Salmasius quotes him in regard to Psalm XVII (*Regia,* 1649, p. 40, ll. 23–25): "Ex quo probat Bar-Nachmoni, ut iam viris doctis notatum est, *quod nulla creatura judicat regem nisi Deus.*"

[75] Psalm 51:6: Milton's numbering of the verse agrees with the Latin text of Junius-Tremellius, rather than with that of the Authorized Version (51:4).

[76] *Regia* (1649), p. 40, ll. 27–30. Salmasius maintains (*Regia,* 1649, p. 42, ll. 27–30) that Scripture itself confirms the fact that God granted a king to the petitioning Israelites not as a tyrant or punishment but as something salutary and good. Salmasius does not assume that a king must be a tyrant; the tyrant is an

of himself or his kindred from so revered a ruler. "Against thee only have I sinned" then clearly is to be taken as "against thee in particular."[77] Apart from this however it is plain that the words of the psalmist and his emotionally charged thoughts are little suited and not to be used for the exposition of the law. But, you say, "He was never brought to the bar nor did he defend himself on a capital charge before the Sanhedrin."[78] To be sure: for how could his deed be brought to light when it had been carried out in such solitary secrecy that, as happens with dark matters in such a court, there were hardly more than one or two who had known of it for a number of years, as appears from II Samuel 12: "Thou didst it secretly?" And what if the Sanhedrin had grown slack in the punishment of private citizens as well: would anyone conclude that they were not liable to punishment? The reason for their inaction here is obvious: he had passed judgment on himself, saying in the fifth verse, "The man that has done this thing shall surely die." To which the prophet immediately answered "Thou art the man"—which shows him liable to death in the prophet's eyes. God however exercised his power and his wondrous mercy towards David, freeing that king both from his guilt and from the very sentence of death he had pronounced against himself [26],[79] and saying to him in verse 13, "Thou shall not die."

---

exception. But if he is a tyrant, he must be endured. While he states that a father would not give his son a serpent instead of an eel when he asked for food (*Regia,* 1649, p. 41, ll. 29–30), Salmasius is also attached to the idea that God scourges the people for their sins through tyrants (*Regia,* 1649, p. 58, ll. 4–6).

[77] *Regia* (1649), p. 40, ll. 30–31. Salmasius argues that this verse is to be interpreted to mean that David offended only God (as distinct from other men or the law of the land) and that only God would be the judge of his transgression.

[78] *Regia* (1649), p. 40, ll. 34–36. Salmasius argues that, while David added adultery to homicide, God sent a prophet to him who reproached him for his sin and confounded him with shame.

[79] II Samuel 12:1-7 relates how Nathan told David the story of the wayfaring man who came into the city where a poor man and a rich man lived, the one with but a single sheep, which he loved as a daughter, the other with many flocks. And the rich man failed to take of his own flocks to entertain the traveller, but killed the poor man's single sheep. The story angered David, who said to Nathan:

> As the Lord liveth, the man that has done this thing shall surely die . . .
> And Nathan said to David:
> Thou art the man.

In II Samuel 12:13:

> And David said unto Nathan, I have sinned against the Lord.
> And Nathan said to David, The Lord also hath put away thy sin ; thou shalt not die.

You next run wild against some bloodthirsty advocate,[80] and are intent on refuting his peroration. He can look to that himself; my business is to finish with all speed. There are however some points which I cannot pass by, particularly your remarkable inconsistencies. On page 30 you state that the Israelites do not speak out against having a king who is unjust and given to violence and pillage or as bad as can be, but on page 42 you twit the advocate for maintaining that they sought a tyrant, and ask indignantly whether they wished to jump from frying pan to fire and taste the cruelty of the worst of tyrants rather than suffer the continuance of the wicked judges with whom they were already familiar.[81] You said before that the Hebrews preferred tyrants to judges, and here judges to tyrants: "There was nothing they wanted less than a tyrant." The advocate will answer you from your own book, for by your account every king is by his royal right a tyrant.

What follows is fine: "At that time the supreme power belonged to the people, for they rejected the judges and chose a king." [82] Bear

[80] As Samuel L. Wolff points out ("Milton's 'Advocatum Nescio Quem': Milton, Salmasius and John Cook," *MLQ,* II, 4 [December, 1941], 599), "some bloodthirsty advocate" is John Cook (1608–1660) of Gray's Inn, the solicitor general appointed by the High Court of Justice which tried Charles I. Wolff writes (p. 559), "Though associated with three other counsel, Cook was sole active prosecutor in open court; he presented (20 January 1649) the official charge against the king, and made from day to day the several motions which mark the progress of the trial, including the motion (23 January) for 'sentence and judgment.' "

According to Wolff, Cook had composed a speech to be delivered at the trial by way of summing up for the prosecution. But the king refused to acknowledge the jurisdiction of the court. On February 9 (ten days after the king's death), Cook published the speech, with additions, as a pamphlet of forty-three pages octavo, under the title *King Charles His Case, or, an Appeal to all Rational Men Concerning His Tryal at the High Court of Justice, Being for the Most Part That Which Was Intended To Have Been Delivered at the Bar If the King had Pleaded to the Charge* (McAl).

Salmasius found in Cook's pamphlet (Wolff, p. 600) a "convenient repertory of matter to refute." Only chapters 6, 7, 10, are quite free from references to it. The *Defensio Regia* is like an extended form of the king's plea or defence, and Milton's *A Defence* is like a rebuttal of Salmasius' plea against Cook.

[81] *Regia* (1649), p. 30; p. 42, ll. 4–6. Salmasius is not so inconsistent as Milton makes it appear. He maintains that in seeking a king the Israelites are not seeking a tyrant. But if the king happens to be a tyrant, they must not proceed against him but leave his punishment to God. Although Milton sometimes really catches Salmasius in self-contradiction and in an internal lack of logic (see below p. 364), in this particular case he is "straining."

[82] *Regia* (1649), p. 42, ll. 15–19.

that in mind when I ask you to repeat it later. You deny "that God in his anger gave the Israelites a king to be a tyrant or as a penalty for them, but for their own advantage and well-being." [83] All this, though, is easily refuted: why did they cry out against that king they had chosen unless the power of a king was an evil, not perhaps in itself, but because usually, as in fact the prophet here warns, it turns to arrogance and despotism. If still I have not convinced you, you must at least recognize your own words and signature, and blush to do so. *Apparatus ad Primatum Papae:* "God in his anger which had been kindled by their sins gave them a king, for they had rejected God as their king. So, too, as a penalty for its sin in abandoning the pure worship of God was the church delivered over to the despotism, worse than royal, of one mortal ruler." [84] If then your parallel is true, either God gave a king to the Israelites as a penalty and an evil institution, or he gave a pope to the church as a reward and a good institution. What can be more frivolous and less sensible than this fellow? Who would trust him even in trifles when in matters of such weight he is so careless about his assertions and so soon denies them?

On page 29 you say that "by the decision of East and West alike, amongst all nations a king is above the law," [27] while on page 43 that "all the kings of the East ruled in accordance with statute and legal right, and even the kings of Egypt were bound by the law in great affairs and small," [85] while your promise at the start of this very chapter was that you would prove that all kings were above the law and made laws but were not held by them. I really must pardon you, for you are either mad or on our side: what you are doing is obviously not defending the king but attacking and making fun of him. Otherwise Catullus' phrase [86] in reverse would fit you neatly, for you are as much the worst of advocates as anyone ever was the best of poets. Unless that same dullness which you say "sank" the

[83] *Regia* (1649), p. 42, ll. 27–30.

[84] Milton's quotation is a paraphrase of several statements of Salmasius contained in the *De Primatu,* p. 230, ll. 22–29: "Iratus Deus regem illis dedit cum animum addidisset prius regem a Samuele petendi, offensus eorum peccatis, & quod se dereliquissent, & Deum habere regem ac Dominum renuissent. Tum dixit Deus ad Samuelem, *Audi vocem populi in omnibus quae loquuntur tibi, non enim te abjecerunt, sed me ne regnem super eos.* Ita certe Ecclesia ubi peccata & vitia atque abusus in ea abundarunt, quasi in poenam eius delicti quod a puro Dei cultu desciverat, variisque implicaverit erroribus in unius mortalis Monarchae plusquam regium dominatum."

[85] A paraphrase of lines 2–7 of p. 43 of the *Regia* (1649).

[86] Catullus, 49.

advocate has in fact blinded you instead, you must feel that you have yourself become a dull brute.

You now admit [87] that "laws have been imposed on the kings of all nations, but not so as to bind them by fear of trial and execution." [88] The latter you have proved neither from Scripture nor from any trustworthy author. Here is a brief explanation for you: to give civil laws to men not subject to laws is foolish and laughable; to punish all others while granting one man impunity for every crime, despite the fact that the law allows no exceptions, is the height of injustice. These two errors are not made by wise lawgivers, much less by God. In order to

[87] *Regia* (1649), p. 43, ll. 15–19. Part of the quotation is missing to the effect that laws were given to kings, even in antiquity, which they were to observe if they wished to reign well and be good.

[88] One of the strongest points that Salmasius makes in the course of the *Defensio Regia* concerns the constitutionality of the king's trial and condemnation. Salmasius asserts that "forty brigands" abrogated all civil and criminal laws which had been observed for many years and substituted others at will (*Regia,* 1649, p. 6, ll. 22–24). They preferred to kill the king through "processes" of law rather than through direct violence (*Regia,* 1649, p. 19, l. 20). But there is no force more violent or more unjust than that which is disguised under the name of justice (*Regia,* 1649, p. 19, ll. 30–31).

First of all, there was no legitimate Parliament. Without the king, Parliament is merely two Houses (*Regia,* 1649, p. 313, l. 20). Since the whole Parliament does not have power without the king's consent, a small part of Parliament could not assume for itself what was not permitted to the whole House (*Regia,* 1649, p. 278, l. 10). The whole House did not have power, and therefore it could not transfer it, for what it does not have, it cannot give (*Regia,* 1649, p. 278, ll. 11–12).

Secondly, the judges did not have authority. The king alone, Salmasius maintains, possesses the whole authority to make judges and to order them to judge (*Regia,* 1649, p. 279, ll. 14–17). A judge merely assigned by a judge does not have the power to give judgment (*Regia,* 1649, p. 284, l. 36). He asks wherefore are the leaders of the army made supreme judges of England (*Regia,* 1649, p. 279, ll. 29–30). Soldiers who could not render judgment, legitimate and valid, concerning a workman of the lowest class, condemned the king himself to death (*Regia,* 1649, p. 280, ll. 13–15).

The trial was illegal, among other reasons, because Parliament had been truncated, the House of Lords being removed entirely, and the House of Commons being purged again of all who opposed the oligarchy, part being put in chains, part taking to flight (*Regia,* 1649, p. 23, ll. 28–30). Those who were permitted to remain in it were either promoters of the faction against the king or its special authors (*Regia,* 1649, p. 23, ll. 31–32). Assuming a king could be tried, he must be tried by those of equal rank (*Regia,* 1649, p. 288, ll. 19–21); but a king cannot commit treason against his subjects and his vassals (*Regia,* 1649, p. 320, ll. 29–31). What right had the judges over a king who was also King of Scotland and Ireland (*Regia,* 1649, p. 291, ll. 21–22)? Charles was falsely accused and executed for a crime never before heard of or known (*Regia,* 1649, p. 326, ll. 26–27).

show all that you have failed to prove in any way from the works of the Hebrews what you had undertaken to prove in this chapter, you freely admit that "some of their teachers deny that their fathers should have recognized any king but God, though such a king was given to punish them." [89] With these teachers I cast my vote.[90]

It is neither fitting nor proper for a man to be king unless he be far superior to all the rest; [91] where there are many equals, and in most

[89] *Regia* (1649), p. 44, ll. 1–3.

[90] This is the most outrightly theocratic statement in *A Defence*. But Milton does not press the point that the only king that should be recognized is God. He may have assented to the idea in a general way without considering the complexities attached even to the simplest versions of theocracy on the operative level.

[91] This is a favorite Miltonic doctrine of "natural" leadership. The "naturally" superior should govern. But Milton did not come to grips with the problem of how juridically such natural leadership could be discovered and verified. Like Aristotle, he did not believe in the even distribution of rights, but in a distribution of rights according to merit. Merit, of course, did not depend on merely natural talent, but more especially upon the acceptance of divine truth (generally given a sectarian interpretation). In the *Defensio* there is an area of unresolved tension between statements that sound broadly democratic and other statements that sound decidedly aristocratic. Milton's rejection of feudalism does not imply a rejection of one of the cardinal ideas of feudalism—that of hierarchy. Obviously Milton dislikes the juridical form in which this concept was expressed in the Roman Catholic Church; he had been deeply aware of the possibilities of ecclesiastical tyranny in the church of archbishop Laud. But one of the main reasons for Milton's opposition to feudalism is based on his assumption that there was no close connection between *official* hierarchy and the *genuine* hierarchy of natural law.

As Don Wolfe points out, "The conception of a leader holding his position by virtue of his superior integrity alone dwelt in Milton's mind persistently, from youth to old age" ("Milton's Conception of the Ruler," *SP*, XXIII: 2, April, 1936, p. 253). Milton, in speaking of Julius Caesar (see below p. 449), offers an argument that would well confirm Milton's own support of Oliver Cromwell: "If indeed I had wished any tyrant spared it would have been he, for although he forcibly established his rule in the republic yet he did perhaps best deserve to rule." A dangerous principle could thus conceivably arise, that power belongs, independently of legal precedent, to the man of talent, of *virtù*, to an enlightened dictator. Salmasius contends that the law of nature cannot procure the common good unless it can ascertain who shall have a *right* to govern.

Milton's principal argument against kingship is based upon his concept of the law of nature. Kings, according to Milton, do not fall within the law of nature. Cruel and implacable masters are not assigned by the gentleness of mother nature (see above p. 342). Milton, who at times equates the law of nature with that of nations and of Scripture, contends, quoting Chrysostom (see below, pp. 382–83) that St. Paul's phrase ("For there is no power but of God") refers to the position of power itself, not to the possessor of it. In other words, St. Paul does not say that there is no *prince* but of God. St. Paul says there is no *power* but of God. The

states there are very many, I hold that they should rule alike and in turn. Everyone agrees that it is most improper for all to be slaves of *one* who is their equal, often their inferior, and usually a fool.

It is no "recommendation of royal government" to say that Christ was sprung of royal stock, any more than to call Christ their descendant is a recommendation of the worst of kings. "The Messiah is king." This we recognize, it brings us joy, and we pray for his speedy advent: for he is worthy and there is none like him or resembling him. [28] But, until that time, we are right in believing that to entrust the royal sway to men unworthy and undeserving, as has mostly been the case, has brought mankind more harm than good. This does not mean that all kings are tyrants, but to avoid seeming obstinate I will suppose with you that it did: What good does that admission do you? "These two consequences follow," you say, "that we must call God the king of tyrants and indeed the greatest of tyrants himself." [92] Although the first of these consequences does not follow, what usually happens in your whole volume does follow: you continually contradict both Scripture and yourself, for you had said in your previous paragraph that "there is one God who is king of all things and himself created them." But he also created tyrants and demons, and by your judgment of him he is king of these too. We spit out your second point and would have your blasphemous mouth stopped for calling God the greatest of tyrants because, as you keep saying, he is spoken of as king and lord of tyrants.

Then too you do little to help the king's business by pretending that Moses was "a king with supreme power." [93] He may indeed have been,

---

semantic inference, a very interesting one not fully explored by Milton, is that a "power" falls within the law of nature but that a "prince" is outside of it.

Interestingly enough, Milton allows (p. 428 below) that a monarchy is possible provided that the sole ruler is the best of men and fully deserving of the crown. But the only person who meets these requirements "is the son of God whose coming we look for."

[92] Milton refers to two passages of Salmasius. "What should be thought of kingly government as the greatest evil to the state, when the Messiah himself is called a king in Scripture?" (*Regia,* 1649, p. 44, ll. 14–15). "If all kings are tyrants, as the Advocate of England's public enemies says, God himself should be called king of tyrants, and even the greatest tyrant himself, since he was the first and supreme tyrant" (*Regia,* 1649, p. 44, ll. 34–37).

[93] *Regia* (1649), p. 44, l. 39. Salmasius asks, "But then was not Moses himself king?" Milton interprets this to mean king "with supreme power." The interpretation is correct, but the quotation is not exact.

and so might any other who like Moses could bring our affairs before God (Exodus 18:19); but not even Moses, who was so to speak the very companion of God, could do as he would with God's people. What are his own words? "This people comes to me to enquire of God"; and not then to receive the commands of Moses. Jethro continues: "Be thou for the people to God-ward, and thou shalt teach them about the laws of God." Moses again says (Deuteronomy 4:5), "I have taught you statutes and judgments, even as the Lord my God commanded me." It is for this reason that in Numbers 12 [94] he is called "faithful in all God's house." At this time then Jehovah was king over the people and Moses but the interpreter of Jehovah the king. You must therefore be wicked and sacrilegious if without authority you dare to hand over from God to man that supreme power which Moses possessed, not in its absolute form, but only in a derived and intermediary sense during the very presence of God. You reach the height of your wickedness in saying here that Moses was king with supreme power, when in *Apparatus ad Primatum,* page 230, you had said that "he ruled the people jointly with seventy elders and was rather the first citizen [29] than master." [95] If then he was king (as indeed he was) and the best of kings, and, as you insist, had the royal power in its highest degree, but still, as you admit, was neither master nor sole ruler of the people, then it follows of necessity that even those kings who are endowed with the highest authority do not by their highest rights as kings become masters, nor should they, by themselves, rule their people, much less rule them as they will. How shamelessly you lie about a command of God "concerning their immediate appointment of a king when they should have entered the Holy Land" (Deuteronomy 17); [96] like an

[94] Numbers 12:7.

[95] *De Primatu,* p. 230, ll. 16–18: "Ab eo tempore non solus Moses Populum judicavit, sed una cum iis in commune ius reddidit, & primus eorum fuit, non dominus."

[96] Deuteronomy 17:14. Salmasius' omission of the phrase quoted by Milton ("*When* thou shalt say, I will set a king over me . . .") alters the possible sense of the Scripture, for, with the phrase included, the choosing of the king seems to be at the discretion of the Israelites. With this provision included, God is not necessarily expressing his own will but merely foreseeing the future. The following verse (15) to the effect that God will choose the king from the number of brothers whom the Israelites will set up *could* be construed to mean that the Israelites are merely constituting a king s*elected* by God. This would help Salmasius' position, but actually Salmasius' Latin, *regem sibi constituerant,* does not take in the whole sense of verse 15, a strange omission since it would be helpful to Salmasius' interpretation. *Cf. Regia* (1649), p. 45, l. 8.

old fox you omit what goes before: "When thou shalt say, I will set a king over me." Remember also those words which I now ask you to repeat. You said on page 42 "the people had then the most complete power." Once again you must decide whether you prefer to be taken as mad or impious. "Since God," you say, "had so long before decided that a royal government should be established as the most suitable form for that people,[97] how can the following story fit in with his decision? The prophet opposed it, and God dealt with him as if he himself did not favor it." The fellow sees that he has become ensnarled and tripped up; notice now with what spite against the prophet and impiety towards God he tries to escape the trap: "We must consider here that it was Samuel whose sons were then judging the people, and whom the people were disowning for their corrupt decisions, and that Samuel did not wish the people to cast off his own sons: in order to please his prophet, God agreed that what the people wished found little favor in his eyes." [98] Put your enigmas in plain language, you wretch: Samuel hoodwinked the people—and God, Samuel! It is then not the advocate but you who are the crazy madman to abandon the fear of God to honor a king. Do you think that Samuel was one [99] to prefer his sons' greed and ambition to his country's safety and esteem, or, when his people sought what was right and proper, to deceive them with such craft and cunning and teach them lies instead of truth? Or that God would do any man a favor in an affair so base, or would deal falsely with his people? The rights of kings were therefore not what the prophet explained to the people, or else those rights were, as God and his prophet bore witness, evil, burdensome, full of violence, without profit, and a costly waste to the state; or finally, as would be criminal to suggest, both God and the prophet [30] tried to cheat the people. God indeed gives evidence throughout of his great displeasure at their request for a king—thus in verse 7: "They have not rejected thee, but they have rejected me, that I should not reign over them, according to all the works which they have done wherewith they have forsaken me, and served other gods." The meaning clearly is that it is a form of idolatry to ask for a king who demands that he be worshipped and granted honors like those of a god. Indeed he who

[97] *Regia* (1649), p. 45, ll. 9–12. Salmasius has been quoting Deuteronomy to the effect that God instructed the Israelites through Moses to choose a king as soon as they came into the promised land.

[98] *Regia* (1649), p. 45, ll. 21–28.

[99] I Samuel 8.

sets an earthly master over him and above all the laws is near to establishing a strange god for himself, one seldom reasonable, usually a brute beast who has scattered reason to the winds. Thus in I Samuel 10:19 we read: "And ye have this day rejected your God, who himself saved you out of all your adversities and your tribulation, and ye have said unto him, Nay, but set a king over us"; and in 12,12: You sought a king "when Jehovah was your king"; and in 17: "See that your wickedness is great, which ye have done in the sight of the Lord, in asking you a king." Hosea too speaks of a king with contempt in Chapter 13, 10–11: "Where is thy king? Let him now save thee in thy cities. Where are thy judges? For that thou saidst, give me a king and princes, I gave thee a king in mine anger." That hero Gideon also, himself greater than a king, said: "I will not rule over you, neither shall my son rule over you; the Lord shall rule over you" (Judges 8); [100] just as if he had been teaching them that it was not for any man, but for God alone, to rule over men.[101]

For this reason the Jewish commonwealth, where God alone holds sway, is called a theocracy by Josephus [102] in his refutation of the Egyptian Apion, who like you was a grammarian and a blasphemer. When at last the Jewish people came to their senses they complained that it had been ruinous for them to have other kings than God (Isaiah 26:13). This evidence all proves that the Israelites were given a king by God in his wrath.

Your account of the tyrant Abimelech [103] would make anyone laugh: It was said of him, when he was killed partly by a stone hurled

[100] Judges 8:23.

[101] Milton contends throughout his Scriptural exegesis that the right sort of government for the Jews was a theocracy and that they were punished for departing from this ideal situation by having kings. Though the Bible can be quoted as a treatise on law or politics only with difficulty, yet for Milton and many of his contemporaries Scriptural exegesis served the purposes of legal precedent. The great contemporary and acquaintance of Milton, Hugo Grotius, makes thousands of references to Scripture in formulating the foundations of international law. Milton himself maintains that the teachings of the gospel do not clash with reason or the law of nations (see below, p. 383). He believes that (p. 422) "the law of God does most closely agree with the law of nature."

[102] called a theocracy by Josephus: Josephus, *Contra Apion,* II, 165.

[103] the tyrant Abimelech: *Cf.* Judges 9:53–54.

> And a certain woman cast a piece of a millstone upon Abimelech's head and all to brake his skull. Then he called hastily unto the young man his armor-bearer, and said unto him, Draw thy sword and slay me, that men say not of me, A woman slew him, And his young man thrust him through, and he died. . . . Thus God rendered the wickedness of Abimelech, which he did unto his father, in slaying his seventy brethren.

by a woman and partly by the sword of his armor-bearer, "that God paid back the sin of Abimelech." [104] This account you say strongly indicates that "God alone is the judge and punisher of kings." Say rather of tyrants, knaves, and bastards, if this be so: whoever has usurped power by any action has forthwith gained royal rights over his subjects and escaped punishment; the means of defence will melt away in the hands of the magistrates, [31] and the people no longer will dare to raise a murmur. I suppose if some strong brigand thus died in battle we must say that God alone is the punisher of brigands, or if he had been condemned and slain by the executioner's hand it was not God who repaid his sin. You never read that the judges of the Jews were ever brought to trial, although you freely admit on page 47 that "in an aristocracy even the prince may and should be brought to trial for any transgression." [105] If so, why not a tyrant in a monarchy? Because God paid back the sin of Abimelech! But the woman paid it back too, and so did the armor-bearer, over both of whom he boasted his royal rights. Suppose a magistrate had paid it back? Does he not wield the sword of God to repay evil with evil?

From this "very weighty" argument about the death of Abimelech he turns, as is his wont, to words of abuse, pouring forth nothing but mud and slime from his mouth and proving neither from Scripture nor the rabbis any of the things he had promised to prove: he has not shown at all that the king is above the laws, nor why he alone of men should not be punished for his sins. On the contrary he becomes entangled in his own evidence and through his own labors demonstrates the superior truth of the opinion opposite to his. Having had little success with arguments, he tries to stir up hatred against us by the worst of all charges, suggesting that we had cruelly murdered the best and most harmless of kings.

He asks, "Was Solomon himself a better king than Charles the First?" [106] There were, I admit, some who did not hesitate to compare James, his father, with Solomon, and indeed to prefer the former's descent. Solomon was the son of David, who was originally Saul's musician: James was the son of the Earl of Darnley, who is said by Buchanan [107] to have caught David the musician [108] on a nocturnal visit

[104] *Regia* (1649), p. 48, ll. 19–21. [105] *Regia* (1649), p. 47, ll. 15–17.

[106] *Regia* (1649), p. 51, l. 6.

[107] *Cf.* George Buchanan, *History of Scotland* (1582; UTSL), fols. 210–210v; (2 vols., London, 1722), II, 309–10.

[108] David the Musician: David Riccio (or Rizzio), secretary to Mary Queen of Scots, James I's mother. Darnley's complicity in the murder of Riccio is

to his queen's bedroom when he had slipped the bolt, and killed David on the spot. For such a reason was the ancestry of King James more illustrious, and he was called a second Solomon; though the account leaves it to the reader to determine whether he could claim David the musician as sire.

I still do not see how it could have occurred to you to compare Charles with Solomon. It is that same Charles you praise so highly whose obstinacy, greed, and cruelty, whose fierce tyranny over all good and God-fearing men, [32] whose wars, arsons, brigandage, and countless killings of his wretched subjects his own son Charles is at this very moment confessing and lamenting before the people of Scotland on that stool for public repentance, and even giving up any claim to that royal right of yours.

But if you like parallels so well, let us compare Charles with Solomon. The reign of Solomon began with the well-earned punishment of his brother: that of Charles with his father's death; for I do not use the word murder,[109] although all the signs of poison were in evidence upon his father's body, because the blame for that fell upon Buckingham: but Charles did not only absolve that slayer of the king and of his father from all blame in the highest council of state, but also dissolved Parliament to keep the whole affair from any Parliamentary investigation. Solomon "oppressed the people with heavy taxes": at least he spent them on God's temple and public buildings, while Charles spent his on debauchery. Solomon was lured to idolatry by many wives; Charles by one. Solomon was lured to crime, but it is not said that he lured others: Charles not only lured others by the richest rewards of a corrupt church, but also compelled them by edicts and

---

generally accepted, but Mary's affair with Riccio is based only on Darnley's evidence, which, in turn, may have sprung from the latter's well-founded jealousy of Riccio, who had taken Darnley's place as the queen's political adviser, a jealousy encouraged by Mary's political opponents among the Scotch nobility (*DNB*).

[109] It was at one time generally believed that George Villiers, first Duke of Buckingham, had poisoned James I. In 1882 Dr. Norman Chevers maintained that there was no medical evidence for such a belief (in a pamphlet "Did James the First of England Die from the Effects of Poison?"). S. R. Gardiner (*History of England,* V, 313–14) added that Buckingham had no motive for such an act. Hugh Ross Williamson, contending that new medical evidence contradicts Chevers (*George Villiers, First Duke of Buckingham* [London, 1940] pp. 171–74), argues that Buckingham had lost the favor of James and had gained that of Charles. (I am indebted to Dr. Paul Blackford for this information.)

ecclesiastical regulations to erect those altars which are abhorred by all Protestants, and to worship crucifixes painted on the walls and hanging over these altars. But for this Solomon was not condemned by his people to die. I say that it does not follow that the people should not have condemned him, and there may have been many reasons why the people did not think it expedient. Undoubtedly they soon showed in word and deed what their rights were, when ten tribes drove out Solomon's son; and, had he not made a hasty retreat, might well have crushed with stones a king who had done no more than threaten them. [33]

CHAPTER III [1]

Having by now sufficiently argued and demonstrated that the kings of Moses' nation were by God's command subject to all the laws which bound their people, that there are found no records of any exemptions, that it is an unsupported and irrational lie to say that these kings "could with impunity do as they pleased," "could not be punished by the people," and that "their judgment was

[1] Salmasius summarizes in book III (*Regia,* 1649), pp. 53–73, the divine right of kings as he sees it based on the divine law of the ancient covenant. The question remains: Did Christ set up a new covenant?

1. The answer, based on quotations from the New Testament, is that Christ himself lived under tyrants and ordered his followers to obey them. 2. The apostles handed down the same teaching, received from their master. 3. Just as kings are the servants and ministers of God, so the subjects of a king are his servants and ministers. But the new saints have a different opinion. When they have slain their king, they think they have merely slain their minister. 4. Paul exhorts that all kings, good or bad, be honored. This evangelical rule is supported by Peter and Irenaeus. 5. God gives the type of ruler suitable to a nation. A king may be given to chastise a nation or to be useful to it. There are three types of kings: those kind and eager for the public good; those severe and quick to punish transgressions; those proud, cruel, and tyrannical. 6. Tertullian, Origen, Ambrose, Augustine, and Jerome are quoted to further the cause of submission to whatever kind of ruler is in power. A special point is made of David's statement: "Against Thee only have I sinned." This is interpreted to mean that David could be punished only by God. 7. On account of the perversity of the English people, God permitted a good king (Charles) to be taken away from them and that his place should be taken by many tyrants and hypocrites! 8. Subjects cannot be released from the oath which they take to the king, and, therefore, cannot reject him or take up arms against him or kill him.

reserved by God for his own tribunal,"[2] let us see whether the Gospel advocates what the Law did not command and indeed advised against. Let us see whether the Gospel, God's proclamation of our freedom, subjects us to the slavery of those kings and tyrants from whose wilful despotism the old law, though it countenanced slavery to some degree, had set God's people free.

You base your first argument on the person of Christ,[3] who took upon himself, as we all know, the form not only of a subject but even of a slave,[4] so that we might be free. I do not speak of inward freedom only and omit political freedom. The prophecy of his advent foretold by Mary his mother, "He hath scattered the proud in the imagination of their hearts; he hath put down the mighty from their seats, and exalted them of low degree,"[5] must indeed be but idle talk if his advent is instead to strengthen tyrants on their thrones and subject all Christians to their savage power.

By his birth, his slavery, and his suffering under tyranny he has won for us all proper freedom. Christ did not prevent, but rather made all the more possible either our endurance of slavery, when that must be, without dismay, or our worthy struggle for freedom. Thus in I Corinthians 7,[6] Paul makes this assertion not of religious liberty alone, but also of political: "Are you called slave? Care not for that; but if you can become free, then use your freedom. You are bought for a price; be not the slaves of men." It is then vain for you

[2] *Regia* (1649), p. 52, ll. 24–31. Milton takes excerpts from the concluding paragraph of the second book of Salmasius. The paragraph reads in full as follows: "Sic igitur hoc caput concludam ex iure quod Scripturae divinae auctoritate regibus afferitur, non omnia quidem regi esse facienda quae facere potest, praecipue si inhonesta sint, si perniciosa, si ea per leges ab ipso positas facere non liceat, sed omnino tamen id ei licere quod potest, citra legum aut judiciorum metum, & cum impunitate maxima, ut qui solum habeat judicem suorum delictorum ac vindicem Deum."

[3] *Regia* (1649), p. 53, ll. 9–12. Salmasius argues that Christ chose to assume human nature under the tyrant Augustus when he could have been born in a free and flourishing republic. He ordered his followers to obey tyrants as He himself obeyed. Salmasius quotes Luke 22:25 in support of his stand: "And he said unto them, The kings of the Gentiles exercise lordship over them; and they that exercise authority upon them are called benefactors."

[4] The present translation uses "slave" rather than "servant." *Servus* by itself means slave. Milton consciously contrasts "slave" and "free" (*servus* and *liberus*), and the states of slavery and freedom. Although "slave" in the context may offend our ears, we should hesitate to revise what Milton chose to say. The Greek of the New Testament (δοῦλος) even more emphatically means "slave."

[5] Luke 1:51–52.

[6] I Corinthians 7:21–23.

to urge us to slavery from Christ's example, for, at the cost of his own slavery, he put our political freedom on a firm foundation. In our place he assumed the form of a slave, but never failed [34] to preserve the heart of a liberator: and therefore his doctrines on the rights of kings were, as I shall show, far different from those taught by you, who, even in a free state, have undertaken the novel task of giving instruction in the rights not merely of kings but of tyrants, maintaining that when tyranny of any sort, inherited or self-created or accidental, has fallen to the lot of a nation, that nation is, by the requirements of religion as well as of necessity, subjected to slavery.

As usual, however, I can turn your own evidence against you. When certain Galilean collectors were demanding two drachmas from him, Christ asked Peter, in Matthew 17,[7] from whom it was that earthly kings collected tribute or poll-taxes, and whether from their own children or from foreigners. From foreigners, said Peter. Then, said Christ, "the children are free; but that we may not irk them do you pay them for me and for yourself." This passage keeps the commentators busy with explanations of the identity of the persons to whom they paid these two drachmas; some say to the priests for the Temple, others to the emperor, while I believe it was to Herod, who had appropriated the Temple revenues. Josephus [8] tells how a number of taxes which had been exacted by Herod and his sons were later discontinued by Agrippa. This tax here, however, which in itself was small, was burdensome when combined with many others; the two drachmas of which Christ speaks must certainly have been burdensome, and indeed earlier under the republic poor citizens had paid no tax. For these reasons Christ took the opportunity of censuring the injustice of Herod, under whose sway he was: for though the other rulers of the earth, at least those desirous of being called fathers of their country, used to demand heavy taxes not from their sons (that is, their own citizens) but from foreigners and particularly those conquered in war, Herod on the other hand oppressed his own sons rather than foreigners. But in any case, whether you grant that we should here interpret 'sons' as those citizens who are the subjects of kings, or whether, like Augustine,[9] you take them to be the sons of

[7] Matthew 17:24–27. [8] *Jewish Antiquities,* XIX, 6, 3.

[9] This usage is so widespread in Augustine as to make individual citation superfluous. The reference is to the general idea of St. Augustine's *De Civitate Dei;* that is, that Christians are citizens of a heavenly city.

God, namely the faithful and the whole body of Christians, it cannot be doubted that if Peter was a son, and accordingly free, then we too are by the intervention of Christ free, either as citizens or as Christians, and therefore it is no part of a king's right to exact heavy tribute from those who are his sons and free men.

Christ indeed testifies that he made payment not because he was obligated to do so but to avoid causing trouble for himself as a private citizen by angering the collectors, knowing as he did that in the course of his life on earth he had a far different duty and task to perform. Since therefore Christ denied that it was a king's right to impose burdensome taxation on free men, [35] it is clear that he denied all the more strongly his right to rob, plunder, kill or torture his own subjects, and more particularly Christians. Because on other occasions too he seemed to speak in similar manner of rights of kings, there were those who began to suspect that he did not consider the licence of tyrants to be the right of kings. It was then with some reason that the Pharisees would probe his mind with such questions and would say, as they began their queries on royal rights, that he cared for no one nor regarded any man's position; and it was also with reason that he grew angry when such questions were asked him. See Matthew 22.[10] What if some fellow tried to attack you by stealth or ensnare you in your talk and provoke you to a statement to be used against you later, and, in a country ruled by a king, question you as to the rights of a king? I suppose you would not become angered with such a questioner? From this then one may deduce that his judgment as to royal rights was not one which kings loved. The same point can be easily inferred from his reply, which seems designed to drive off his questioners rather than to instruct them. He asked for a tribute coin and inquired: "Whose likeness is this? Caesar's. Render therefore unto Caesar the things which are Caesar's; and unto God the things that are God's." But who is not aware that what belongs to the people must be rendered to the people? Render to all what you owe, says Paul in *Romans* 13,[11] and therefore render not all things to Caesar. Our freedom belongs not to Caesar, but is rather a gift from God himself given us at birth, and to surrender it to any Caesar, when we did not receive it of him, would be an act of shame most unworthy of man's origin. If any person should gaze upon a man's face and features and inquire whose likeness was found there, would it not be easy for

[10] Matthew 22:15–21. [11] Romans 13:7.

anyone to reply, the likeness of God? Since therefore we are God's own, and indeed his children, we are for this reason his property alone, and accordingly cannot without wickedness and extreme sacrilege deliver ourselves as slaves to Caesar, that is to a man, and a man who is unjust, unrighteous, and a tyrant.

Our Lord however has left it a question what belongs to Caesar and what to God: for, if that coin was the same as the didrachm usually given to God, as was certainly the case later under Vespasian, then Christ did not settle the dispute but actually made it worse, since it is impossible to deliver the same object at once to God and to Caesar. But perhaps he defined what was Caesar's, that is, the coin stamped with his likeness: How does this bring either Caesar or you more than a penny's profit? For Christ either assigned to Caesar nothing but that one denarius and gave us title to all other things, or else, if he assigned to Caesar whatever coinage is struck with his name, [36] he would be giving well-nigh all our possessions to Caesar, and would be inconsistent with his former assertion that his payment of but two didrachms to the kings for Peter and himself was not because of any actual obligation.

Finally, the grounds of your argument are weak: Money does not carry the ruler's portrait to show that it belongs to him, but to show that it is pure, and to prevent anyone from daring to counterfeit it when it is stamped with his likeness. For if an inscription were so powerful in regard to royal rights, then surely kings could by the mere inscription of their names make all our property immediately theirs; and on the other hand if all our property is theirs already, as you maintain, then that coin is not due to Caesar because it bears his name or likeness, but because, even without the stamp of his likeness, it was legally his before. Thus it is plain that in this passage Christ did not so much wish to advise us in this involved and doubtful fashion about duties towards kings or Caesars as to accuse the hypocritical Pharisees of wicked spite. Tell me, when the Pharisees later informed him that Herod was plotting against his life, did they get from him a meek submissive answer to take back to the tyrant? Instead he told them "Go and say to that fox," [12] thus intimating that the right by which kings lay snares for their subjects is not that of a king but of a fox.

But yet "he allowed himself to suffer the penalty of death under a

[12] Luke 13:32.

tyrant."[13] How else was that possible, if not under a tyrant? "Under a tyrant he suffered punishment," thus, I suppose, becoming a supporting witness for all the most unjust features of kingly rights: you really are a wonderful casuist! Although it was to set us free and not to sell us into bondage that Christ made himself a slave, it is true that he lived in that guise; he did not, however, yield anything to royal rights beyond what was just and good.

Now let us see what were his teachings on this matter. The sons of Zebedee,[14] when they claimed the highest rank in the kingdom of Christ, which they vainly imagined would soon be set up on earth, were so reproved by Christ as to warn all [37] believers of his will concerning the rights of office and of civil power to be established among them. "Ye know," he said, "that the princes of the Gentiles exercise dominion over them, and they that are great exercise authority upon them. But it shall not be so among you: but whosoever will be great among you, let him be your minister; and whosoever will be chief among you, let him be your servant."[15] Unless you were mad, could you have believed that these statements helped your case, or that by such arguments you made us consider our kings as lords of all? May our enemies in the field be men like this, though we are well able to conquer armed foes too; men who, like you, will wander blindly and unarmed into the hostile fort while thinking it their own; for, in your folly, you always bring up as the strongest support for your case whatever ruins it for you most completely.

"The Israelites kept seeking a king 'such as all these peoples had' "! God dissuaded them in many words here summarized by Christ: "Ye know that the princes of the Gentiles exercise dominion over them."[16] When they sought one still, God gave them a king despite his anger. Christ gave a warning to prevent a Christian people from seeking a master at all, as do the gentiles: "But it shall not be so among you." What could be clearer? Among you there will be no haughty tyranny of kings, not even though they be called by the fair name of *Euergetes*[17] or benefactors; but instead whoever would be great among you (and who is greater than the chief?) must be your minister, and whoever would be first or chief must be your servant. And so the advo-

[13] *Regia* (1649), p. 53, l. 16.

[14] Matthew 20:20–21.

[15] Matthew 20:25–27.

[16] Luke 22:25.

[17] *Euergetes:* The title of *Euergetes* or "benefactor" was sometimes adopted by or awarded to Hellenistic rulers as, for example, Ptolemy Euergetes I & II.

cate you attack [18] was not in error but had Christ's authority in saying that a Christian king is the minister of the people, as indeed all good magistrates are. Amongst Christians, then, there will either be no king at all, or else one who is the servant of all; for clearly one cannot wish to dominate and remain a Christian.[19]

Even Moses, who established laws which were in a sense slavish, did not rule the people insolently, but rather bore their burdens, and carried the people in his bosom as a nurse does a suckling (Numbers 11): [20] but a nurse is a servant. Plato taught [21] that magistrates should be termed not the masters but the servants and helpers of the people, and the people not the servants but the maintainers of the magistrates, since they maintain even royal magistrates by food and wages.

[18] John Cook. See above, p. 363, n. 80.

[19] In *Milton: Man and Thinker* (New York, 1925), p. 188, Saurat remarks that "had men remained in their normal state, no government would have been necessary. The origin of government is in the fall. Consequently, for true regenerate men government is not needed." This is the view Saurat attributes to Milton. The tendency in sectarian Protestantism (going back through Calvin and Luther to late Augustinianism) was to consider the state as a consequence of the fall. The Thomistic tradition considered the state as a necessary correlative to man's nature whether he had fallen or not. In the one view, the state is a coercive rod of chastisement over unregenerate men, punishing them for their own good; in the other, the state is an expression of man's nature and needs, whether fallen or not.

Alexander Passerin D'Entrèves in *The Medieval Contribution to Political Thought* (Oxford, 1939), pp. 22–23, summarizes the problem thus: "It has been rightly remarked that the different manner of conceiving the necessity and foundation of the state, before and after St. Thomas, derives from a different conception of human nature; instead of considering the state as an institution which may well be necessary and divinely appointed, but only in view of the actual conditions of corrupt mankind, Thomas Aquinas follows Aristotle in deriving the idea of the state from the very nature of man. But here again the idea of the natural law, and the conception of the harmonious correspondence between the natural and the revealed order which is expressed, provided a solid ground for further developments. For the Aristotelian conception, with its insistence upon the fulfilment and end of human nature, contained at the bottom a challenge to the Christian idea of the existence of higher and ultimate values, and of the inadequacy of merely human means for their fulfilment. The natural order, which comprises and sufficiently justifies political experience, is for St. Thomas only a condition and a means for the existence of a higher order, as natural law is but a part of the eternal law of God. If *gratia non tollit naturam,* certainly also, *natura non tollit gratiam,* and nature requires to be perfected by grace. Thus the action and value of the state, as part of the natural order, must be considered in the general frame of the divine direction of the world, and is entirely subservient to that direction." See below, p. 422, n. 2, relative to the "law of nature."

[20] Numbers 11:12.

[21] *Laws,* IV, 715.

These same magistrates are called by Aristotle [22] the guardians and ministers [38] of the laws, and by Plato both guardians and servants. The apostle indeed calls them ministers of God,[23] but this in no way prevents their also being ministers of the laws and of the people, for both laws and magistrates exist for the people.

You, however, keep bawling out that this is "the opinion of the mad dogs of England." [24] I would not have thought that the English were dogs if such a mongrel as you had not yelped at them with such unnatural barking: God save us, the master of St. Loup,[25] the sainted Wolf himself, complains that the dogs are mad! Once St. Germain,[26] whose colleague was that Loup of Troyes, did on his own authority strip our sinful king Vortigern of his kingdom, and surely St. Loup must scorn such as you, master not of St. Loup but of some blackguard land-louper, lower than Martial's snake-master.[27] You have at home a barking bitch [28] who rules your wretched wolf-mastership, rails at your rank, and contradicts you shrilly; so naturally you want to force royal tyranny on others after being used to suffer so slavishly a woman's tyranny at home. Whether then you are wolf-master or your wolf-bitch masters you, whether you are wolf or were-wolf, you will surely be sport for the English hounds: but there is no time now for a wolf-hunt, and so let us leave the woods and return to the king's highway.

Lately you wrote against all primacy in the church, while now you call on "Peter as prince of the apostolic group." [29] Who could trust a manikin with such wobbling principles? What are Peter's words: "Submit yourselves to every ordinance of man for the Lord's sake: whether it be to the king, as supreme; or unto governors, as unto them that are sent by him for the punishment of evildoers and for the praise of them that do well: for so is the will of God." [30] Peter wrote this to men who were not merely private citizens but even foreigners

[22] *Politics*, 1287 a 22 (III, 16). [23] Romans 13:4.

[24] *Regia* (1649), p. 53, ll. 27–28.

[25] St. Loup was the name of Salmasius' estate in Burgundy.

[26] *Cf.* Nennius, *Historia Britonum*, xlvii–xlviii; *History of the Britons*, tr. A. W. Wade-Evans (London: S.P.C.K., 1938), pp. 69–71.

[27] *Martial*, I, 41, 7.

[28] a barking bitch: Milton writes *Lycisca*, the name of a bitch in Virgil's *Eclogues*, 3, 18, and in Ovid, *Metamorphoses*, 3, 220. It is applied to a woman by Juvenal, 6, 122, in *Juvenal and Persius*, tr. G. G. Ramsay (London: Loeb Classical Library, 1924), pp. 92–93.

[29] *Regia* (1649), p. 54, l. 24. [30] I Peter 2:13–15.

scattered and wandering through most of Asia Minor, who could have no rights in their places of sojourn but those of hospitality. Do you think that freeborn and noble countrymen, that meetings of the native citizenry, assemblies and parliaments, are to be treated no differently in their own land than are scattered strangers on foreign soil? Or that within their country the same things are fitting for private citizens and for the senators and statesmen without whom even kings [39] cannot exist? But suppose Peter had written these words to neither foreigners nor private citizens, but to the Roman Senate itself: what would follow then? For no direction which is coupled with some reason can or should bind anyone beyond the scope of its reason. "Submit yourselves" ὑποτάγητε, which is, if you consider the force of the word, "in lower order" or "legally subject": as Aristotle says, ἡ γὰρ τάξις νόμος, or "order is law." [31] "Submit for the Lord's sake": why? Since both king and governor are appointed by God to punish those who do evil and honor those who do good. "For so is the will of God." That is, we should obey such as are here defined, for there is no mention here of others. See how appropriate is the reason for this command: and in verse 16 he adds "as free men," [32] and therefore not as slaves. What if some rule in the opposite way, bringing cruel torture and ruin to the good, but immunity, praise and prizes to sinners? Must we all be subject to such a one forever, not private citizens only, but leaders, officers, and even the Senate itself? Is not rather this government of men? Why then is man competent to establish what is right and sound for men, if he is not competent to abolish what is evil and ruinous for them?

But, you say, that very king whom they were ordered to obey was Nero, then tyrant at Rome, and, therefore, we too must submit to tyrants.[33] It is however questionable whether Nero or Claudius then ruled, and furthermore those ordered to obey were foreigners, scattered private individuals rather than consuls, praetors, or the Roman Senate.

We come to Paul now, since you claim over the apostles that right which you deny us over our kings, namely of granting the primacy to Peter and taking it away again. Paul wrote to the Romans, verse 13: [34] "Let every soul be subject unto the higher powers. For there is no power but of God: the powers that be are ordained of God." This Paul

[31] *Politics,* 1287 a 18 (III, 11).
[32] I Peter 2:16.
[33] *Regia* (1649), p. 55, ll. 15–16.
[34] Romans 13:1.

wrote to Romans, and not as did Peter to scattered foreigners, but still he wrote to those who were mainly private citizens and common folks: nevertheless his writings teach most brilliantly the whole manner, origin, and end of government, revealing the more clearly that the true and reasoned basis for our obedience [40] is far different from any slavery. "Let every soul," or in other words each man, "be subject." Chrysostom has satisfactorily explained the apostle's intention in this chapter: "Paul does this," he says, "to show that Christ set up his laws not to subvert the general form of government but to give it a firmer foundation." [35] Therefore he did not so act as to strengthen the most hateful tyranny of one man over all men by establishing Nero or any other tyrant beyond the power of law or penalty.

"Paul wrote also to teach that vain useless wars should not be undertaken"; [36] he does not then condemn wars waged against a tyrant, an enemy of his country within her borders, who is for that reason the more dangerous. "There was a common report among men of that time which libeled the apostles as traitorous revolutionaries whose every word and deed was aimed at the overthrow of the general laws: Paul stopped the mouths of those slanderers." [37] And so the apostles, unlike you, composed no briefs for tyrants; instead their teachings and their deeds were objects of suspicion to all tyrants, and required defence and explanation before them. Chrysostom has shown us the apostle's design; let us now look at Paul's words: "Let every soul be subject to the higher powers." [38] He did not state what these were; for he had no intention of abolishing the rights and institutions of the various countries or of allowing absolute sway to the lust of a single individual. Certainly all the best emperors were aware that the authority of the laws and the Senate far exceeded their own: so too in all civilized lands right has ever been the most sacred possession. Thus in Herodotus,[39] Pindar calls law the lord of all, and, in his hymns, Orpheus [40] hails it as king of gods as well as men: "Heavenly law I

[35] *Homilies on Romans*, 23 (in *A Select Library of the Nicene and Post-Nicene Fathers of the Christian Church*, ed. Philip Schaff, XI, 511; hereafter referred to as *Fathers, N. and P.N. 1*).

[36] Chrysostom, *loc. cit.*

[37] Chrysostom, *loc. cit.*

[38] Romans 13:1.

[39] Herodotus, *Histories*, III, 38, tr. A. D. Godley (4 vols., New York and London: Loeb Classical Library, 1921–24), II, 51.

[40] *Hymns*, LXIV (LXIII), 1–2, in *Orphica*, ed. Eugene Abel (Leipzig, 1885), pp. 91–92.

hail, the holy ruler of gods and men"; giving as his reason that law alone controls the destiny of all that lives. Plato in the *Laws* [41] says it is law which ought to be the most powerful in the state, and in his *Letters* [42] praises that form of government where law is ruler and king over men; and not men, tyrants over the law. This too is the judgment of Aristotle in the *Politics* [43] and of Cicero in the *Laws*,[44] [41] that the laws are as far superior to the magistrates as the magistrates are to the people. Since therefore the judgment of the wisest men and the institutions of the most experienced states show that the law is always considered the highest and ultimate power, and since the teachings of the Gospel accord with reason and with the laws of the nations, he is most truly subject to the higher powers who whole-heartedly obeys the laws and the magistrates who govern in accordance with the laws of the state. It is then not the people alone on whom such obedience is enjoined, but kings as well, who are in no way above the law.

"For there is no power but of God"; [45] that is, no form of state and no legitimate basis for the government of men. Then too the most ancient laws were ascribed to God as author, for law, as Cicero writes in the *Twelfth Philippic*,[46] is "nothing but that right reason derived from divine will which commands what is right and forbids what is wrong." The appointment of magistrates comes therefore from God, to the end that men may through their guidance live under law; but surely the choice of the form of government and of magistrates has always belonged to men in free nations. For this reason Peter calls both king and governors human foundations or creations [47]—so, too, Hosea 8: [48] "They have set up kings, but not by me; they have made princes, and I knew it not." It was only in this Hebrew state, where God's guidance could be sought in different ways, that the law ordered consultation with God on the appointment of a king: we other peoples

[41] Plato, *Laws*, IV, 715.

[42] *Epistles*, VIII, 354 c 1.

[43] *Politics*, 1287 a 20 (III, xi, 3).

[44] Cicero, *De Legibus*, III, 1, 2, in *De Re Publica, De Legibus*, tr. Clinton W. Keyes (Cambridge: Loeb Classical Library, 1951), pp. 460–61.

[45] Romans 13:1. In *Regia* (1649), p. 55, ll. 23–26, Salmasius says that this text explains why all supreme power should be obeyed and served. "Let every soul be subject to the higher powers. For there is no power but of God: the powers that be are ordained of God."

[46] *Twelfth Philippic:* Not the twelfth, but XI, xii, 28.

[47] I Peter 2:13.

[48] Hosea 8:4.

have no such instructions from God. At times either the very form of government itself, if it be unsound, or those in authority are both human and fiendish. Thus in Luke 4: [49] "All this power will I give thee, for that is delivered unto me; and to whomsoever I will I give it." Thus the fiend is termed prince of this world; and in Revelation 13 [50] the Dragon gave the beast his own dominion and throne and mighty power. Therefore we must here understand not powers of any kind whatever, but of the legitimate kind described below; we must understand the powers of office in themselves and not in every case those who exercise them at the moment. For this reason Chrysostom is very plain: "What is your opinion: is every ruler then appointed by God? [51] I believe not, for the apostle speaks not of any particular ruler [42], but of the position itself: he does not say that without God there is no ruler, but rather no rule." So speaks Chrysostom. "Whatever powers there be are ordained of God," and so the apostle would be understood to mean here legitimate powers; evil and vice, being disorder, cannot possibly be ordained and continue vicious, for this would imply the presence of two contraries, order and disorder.

"Whatever there be" you would take as "whatever now exist," which might make it easier for you to demonstrate that the Romans should have obeyed Nero, who then, so you suppose, was their ruler. This argument we can support, for think as ill as you wish of the government of England, you must admit that the English should be content with it, since it now exists and is ordained of God like Nero's government of old. And Nero, no less than Tiberius, had seized "an authority not his own through his mother's wiles," [52] so that you cannot say he gained it of right. This makes you all the more unprincipled and the subverter of your own beliefs, for you would have had the Romans obey the power which then existed, but will not have the English obey the power which now exists.

Surely no two things in all the world are more direct opposites of each other than a wretch like you who is usually in contradiction to your wretched self. But what can you do, poor fellow? This sharpness of yours has cut your kingling to ribbons, for I will force you to admit that in accordance with your own theory the present government of

[49] Luke 4:6. [50] Revelation 13:2.

[51] *Homilies on Romans,* XXIII (*Fathers, N. and P.N. 1,* ed. Philip Schaff, XI, 511).

[52] *Regia* (1649), p. 54, ll. 13–15.

England is ordained of God and therefore that all Englishmen within the borders of that state should obey that government. Hearken then all ye critics, and keep your hands off, for this is Salmasius' latest emendation of the Epistle to the Romans: he has discovered that the reading ought to be "the powers that now be," not "the powers that be," and this to prove that everyone should have obeyed the tyrant Nero, who was supposedly in power then. But, my good man, your purple patch has faded,[53] and you have ruined your beautiful explanation now just as you did the king a moment past. The letter which you say was written in the reign of Nero was in fact composed under Claudius,[54] an honest ruler and a decent man, as good scholars have decided on clear evidence; and even Nero had five excellent years, so that the oft-repeated argument is as false as it is common; [43] namely, that a tyrant must be obeyed because Paul told the Romans to obey Nero: this is discovered to be the clever lie of some ignoramus.

Whoever resists authority, that is lawful authority, resists the ordinance of God. This decree touches kings too, who resist the laws and the senate. But does he who resists an illegitimate authority, or the corrupter and subverter of a legitimate one, resist the ordinance of God? You would not have said so, I believe, if you were sane. The following verse removes all doubt that the apostle here speaks only of legitimate authority.[55] He makes it clear by his definition so that no one will go astray or discover here a mare's nest of foolish notions as to who the magistrates are who serve this power, or why he urges us to be obedient. "Rulers are not a terror to good works, but to evil; do that which is good, and thou shalt have praise of the same: for he is the minister of God to thee for good; he beareth not the sword in vain, for he is a revenger to execute wrath upon him that doth evil."

[53] Milton's point is based on Aristophanes, *Frogs,* 1200 ff., in *Aristophanes,* tr. Benjamin B. Rogers (3 vols., London: Loeb Classical Library, 1924), II, 408–409 ff.

[54] Salmasius argues (*Regia,* 1649, p. 60, ll. 12–21) that St. Paul in his Epistle to the Romans made the reference to "the powers that be" strictly universal, including rulers, good or bad, even Nero, who, according to Salmasius' reading of history, was emperor when the letter was written. According to Salmasius, St. Paul went to special pains to avoid the misunderstanding that "good" kings only should be obeyed. The interpretation, of course, is radically altered if St. Paul had Claudius Tiberius (10 B.C.–54 A.D.) in mind rather than Nero, as Milton insists.

[55] Romans 13:3–4.

Who but a knave denies or refuses to admit that he should willingly submit to such a power or to its minister? And this not merely to avoid his anger and wrath or in fear of punishment, but rather for the sake of his own conscience. Without magistrates and civil government there can be no state or human society or life itself. But whatever power or magistrate acts in the contrary manner is not truly ordained of God, and therefore we are not obliged or instructed to obey such a power or magistrate, nor debarred from wise opposition, inasmuch as we shall not be resisting the power or the magistrate here favorably depicted, but a cut-purse, a tyrant, and a foe; and if he must be termed magistrate simply because he has power and may seem appointed by God for our punishment, then by such reasoning the devil himself will be a magistrate. Clearly a single object has but a single accurate definition: and so if Paul here defines a magistrate, as indeed he does with great accuracy, he cannot by the same definition and the same words define a tyrant, who is the exact opposite. Therefore it appears that he wishes us to obey only the magistrate defined and described by him, and certainly not his opposite the tyrant.

"For this cause [44] ye pay tribute also," he adds as the reason for his command: and thus Chrysostom says "Why do we pay taxes to the king? Is it not as though we paid a fee for care and guidance to one who watches over us? And surely we would have paid him nothing had we not known from the start that such supervision was for our own good."[56] And so I come back to what I said before: since obedience is not required of us without qualification but with the addition of a reason, that reason which is added is to be the true measure of our obedience: if the reason applies but we do not obey, we shall be rebels; if we obey, but the reason does not apply, we shall be sluggish and servile.

"However," you say, "the English are in no sense free, for they are wicked scoundrels."[57] I have no wish to bring up the defects of the French, though they are under kings, nor to discount those of the English, but I can still say that their sins were taught them under the monarchy, like the Israelites in Egypt, and have not been im-

[56] Chrysostom, *Homilies on Romans,* XXIII, in *Fathers, N. and P.N. 1,* ed. Philip Schaff, XI, 513.

[57] *Regia* (1649), p. 56, ll. 18–20. Milton paraphrases Salmasius' rhetorical question: "Who indeed are less free than those who are bound by the chains of so many vices and outrages?"

mediately unlearned in the desert, even under the guidance of God. But there is much hope for most of them, not to enter on the praises of our good and reverent men who follow eagerly after truth, of whom we have as many as you can imagine anywhere. You say that a heavy yoke is laid upon the English; but what if it is laid on those who strove to put a yoke on the rest of the citizenry? On those deservedly subdued? The others I am sure have no objection to maintaining their freedom at their own expense after the public coffers have been emptied by the civil wars.

Now Salmasius descends to the hair-splitting of the rabbis. He denies that a king is bound by the laws, but proves on their authority, that a king is guilty of treason if he suffers his rights to be restricted:[58] and so a king is bound and not bound, guilty and not guilty: so often is Salmasius in contradiction to himself that to such a fellow opposition seems like a twin sister.

But God, you say, gave over many realms in slavery to Nebuchadnezzar. For a definite period, I confess, he did so (Jeremiah 27, 7), but I challenge you to show that he gave over the English as slaves to Charles Stuart even for half an hour; I would not deny that he permitted it, but I never heard that he gave them over. And on the other hand, if God enslaves a people whenever they have less power than a tyrant, why should he not also be said to liberate them when they have more power than a tyrant? Should Salmasius ascribe his tyranny to God, but not we our freedom? [45]

There is no evil in the state which God has not introduced (Amos 3):[59] hunger, disease, sedition, and public enemies; but is there one of these which the state will not strive with all its power to cast off? Although aware that they were introduced by God, it will rather get rid of them if it can, unless God in heaven has forbidden it. Why will it not eject tyrants likewise if it be the stronger? Shall we believe that one man's unbridled passion for the destruction of all is more divine than the power of the whole state for the good of all? Let so senseless a doctrine and so destructive a plague be far from all states and every gathering of freeborn men. Such a doctrine utterly subverts all civic life and for the sake of one or two tyrants debases all mankind to the level of beasts; for, when exalted over all the laws, these tyrants will exercise the same jurisdiction and dominion over men and beasts.

[58] *Regia* (1649), pp. 56, ll. 37–39; 57, l. 1.

[59] Amos 3:6.

I pass by at this time those foolish dilemmas of yours, to revel in which you invent someone who believes that that overriding power has its seat in the people; I do not hesitate, however, to assert that the authority of every magistrate comes from the people. Thus Cicero says in the *Pro Flacco:* [60] "Those wise and reverent ancestors of ours wished whatever the plebeians decreed or the people ordered to be so ordered or forbidden." Thus Lucius Crassus,[61] the great orator and then the leader of the Senate, whose cause he was upholding before the people: "Do not suffer our body to be at the bidding of anyone but your whole number, whom we can and should obey." For though the Senate directed the people, it was the people who had granted to the Senate that authority to guide and direct it. Thus it is that, in our reading, we find majesty more often ascribed to the Roman people than formerly to the kings. So Marcus Tullius in the *Pro Plancio:* [62] "The condition of freedom for a people, and particularly for this ruling people which dominates the world, is the ability to give or take away from anyone by its votes whatever it desires: we must accept the wishes of the people with good nature; if we think little of office we need not follow the bidding of the people, but if we seek office we must never cease to direct our prayers to them." Shall I shrink from calling a king the servant of the people, when that Roman Senate which ruled so many kings professed itself the people's servant? [46] You may admit the truth of this under the popular government when the law on kingship [63] had not yet handed over the power of the people to Augustus and his successors. Look at Tiberius, though he, according to you, and also in fact, was a tyrant in more ways than one: Yet even after that law on kingship, when he was called Lord by someone, he is reported by Suetonius [64] to have prohibited such an insulting form of address for the future. Are you aware of this? That very tyrant of yours considered it an insult to be called Lord. He it was who said in

[60] *Pro Flacco,* VII, 15, in *The Speeches,* tr. Louis E. Lord (Cambridge: Loeb Classical Library, 1956), pp. 382–83.

[61] Lucius Licinius Crassus, Roman orator and consul of the late second century, B.C., whose oratorical powers received mention by Cicero. For the story and quotation see *De Oratore,* I, lii, 225, tr. E. W. Sutton (2 vols., Cambridge: Loeb Classical Library, 1942), I, 158–59.

[62] *Pro Plancio,* IV, 11, in *The Speeches,* tr. N. H. Watts (London: Loeb Classical Library, 1923), pp. 418–19.

[63] *Lex Regia,* the practice of the emperors of assuming for life such powers as the "proconsulare imperium" and the "potestas tribunica."

[64] Suetonius, *Tiberius,* 27.

the Senate: "I have said to you here, and often in other places as well, that a good and useful ruler who has been endowed by you with such wide and unrestricted power should be obedient to the Senate, obedient for the most part to the whole citizenry, and often to private individuals; I am not ashamed of this statement, and both in the past and at the present moment I have found you kindly, just, and indulgent masters." [65] It will avail you nothing to call this the pretence of a practiced hypocrite; for who desires to seem to be other than he should be? This was the reason why other emperors, and not, as Tacitus writes,[66] Nero only, were wont to bow to the people in the Circus. Claudianus [67] writes of this in his poem *On the Sixth Consulship of Honorius:*

> With what unutterable majesty
> The king doth clothe his subjects when to all
> He openly appears, to render them
> Homage in turn, and royal purple stoops
> To honor the array in Circus sitting,
> While heaven above reechoes with the cheers
> The honored throng sends up from serried seats.

What else did the emperors of Rome mean by this adoration than to confess that even after the law on kingship the populace as a whole was still superior to them?

Actually this is just what I suspected at the very beginning, that your attention was devoted to the thumbing of dictionaries and the elaborate publication of a few bits of wearisome nonsense rather than to the careful study of good writers; and, being wholly without a trace of the wisdom of ancient writers, you suppose that matters which are found among the opinions of the great philosophers and have long been current among the sayings of the wisest statesmen are but the novel nightmares [47] of some "mad enthusiasts." You had better go and take Martin the cobbler and William the tanner,[68] whom you so scorn, as your companions and guides in darkness; though actually they could teach you much and solve such foolish riddles of yours as: "Is the people a servant in a democracy, when a king is in a mon-

[65] *Ibid.*, 29. [66] *Annals*, XVI, 4.

[67] *De Sexto Consulatu Honorii*, 611 ff.

[68] *Regia* (1649), p. 59, l. 14. "Who is the people?" Salmasius scornfully asks. "Is it Martin the cobbler, William the tanner, John the tailor?"

archy? Is all of it, or but a part?" [69] Then when they have acted as your Oedipus you should repay them by going to the devil as the Sphinx did; [70] otherwise I can see no end to your foolish riddles.

You ask, "When the apostle speaks of kings are we to understand that he means the people?" [71] Paul does indeed tell us to pray for kings (I Timothy 2:2), but he had told us above in verse 1 to pray for the people. But there are those among both kings and people for whom we are forbidden to pray. May I not lawfully punish one for whom I may not pray? What is to prevent it? You may retort that when Paul wrote those words the worst of men were ruling: This however is false, for Ludovicus Capellus [72] has successfully shown by irrefutable arguments that this epistle too was composed in the reign of Claudius. When Paul speaks of Nero he calls him not king but lion, meaning wild beast, and rejoices that he was snatched from his jaws (II Timothy 4).[73] It is our duty to pray not for beasts but for kings, so that we may lead lives of peace and quiet in all reverence and uprightness. Note that here emphasis is placed less on kings than on peace, reverence, and uprightness. What people, however, would not prefer to lead an upright life in anxiety, trouble, and to war in its own and its children's defence against a tyrant or an enemy alike, instead of leading under enemy or tyrant a life equally full of anxiety and trouble and shameful, slavish, and corrupt as well? Recall that according to Livy [74] the Samnites were familiar with both states, and rose in revolt because peace with slavery was worse than war with freedom.

Recall your own words too; for I summon you also as a witness repeatedly, not because of your importance, but to show all men how full of double dealing you are, how inconsistent, how much at the bidding of the king's cash. "Who," you ask, "would not choose to suffer the

[69] *Regia* (1649), p. 58, ll. 18–21, and 58, l. 33. Milton runs together the part of one long sentence with a subsequent short sentence, twelve lines removed from the previous quotation.

[70] Oedipus solved the riddle of the Sphinx, after which she cast herself to death from a rock.

[71] *Regia* (1649), p. 59, ll. 21–22.

[72] Louis Cappel, French Hebraist (1585–1658), author of *Critica Sacra* (Paris, 1650) and *Spicilegeum, seu Notae in Novum Testamentum* (Geneva, 1632), called the beginner of modern Biblical criticism. See George N. Conklin, *Biblical Criticism and Heresy in Milton* (New York: King's Crown Press, 1949), p. 15.

[73] II Timothy 4:17.

[74] *Livy,* X, xxxi, 14, in *Livy,* tr. B. O. Foster, Evan T. Sage, and Alfred C. Schlesinger (13 vols., London: Loeb Classical Library, 1919–24), IV, 478–81.

disputes usually arising in an aristocratic state from the rivalry of the nobles than the inevitable wretchedness and ruin found under a single ruler who is wont to give orders like a tyrant? The Roman people [48] preferred their republican government, tossed though it was by countless storms, to the unbearable yoke of the Caesars. A people which has taken on itself monarchical government to avoid sedition is often eager to revert to its former state when it has once discovered that the evil which it wished to avoid was actually less burdensome?"

These and other statements of yours are on page 412 of that discussion of Episcopacy published under the assumed name of Walo Messalinus [75] and written in opposition to the Jesuit Petavius, though you are more the Jesuit than he, and actually the worst of that crew. We have already considered the verdict of holy Scripture on this matter, and need not regret our careful investigation, because there is now no need to search all the massive volumes of the early fathers to discover what they thought. If they add anything not found in Scripture we may rightly reject their authority, such as it is.

Your citation from Irenaeus,[76] "By God's command are appointed kings of a nature suited to those they presently rule," [77] is in obvious conflict with Scripture. Though God had clearly stated that judges were better suited than kings to rule his people, still he left the matter wholly to the wishes and judgment of the people, so that they could if they wished exchange the aristocratic government which better suited them for the less suitable rule of a king. Then too we often read of a wicked king being given to a good people, and also the reverse, a

[75] Salmasius' work, *De Episcopis ac Presbyteris contra D. Petavium Loiolitam, Dissertatio Prima, Lugduni Batavorum* (Leyden, 1641; NYPL; hereafter referred to as *De Episcopis ac Presbyteris,* 1641) was published under the pseudonym of Walo Messalinus. The quoted material is from p. 412, ll. 28 ff. Dionysius Petavius or Denis Petau, S. J. (1583–1652), who was professor of Catholic dogma at the Sorbonne. A famous linguist, he edited Greek and Latin manuscripts. Historian and geographer as well, he was interested in the application of astronomical data to historical dates. His most important historical work was *Opus de Doctrina Temporum* (Paris, 1627). His *De Theologicis Dogmatibus* (Paris, 1644–50) particularly excited Salmasius. Petau was so important a scholar in his day that he was offered a cardinal's hat, but Louis XIII prevented his accepting it because the king was afraid such a distinguished man might have to leave France.

[76] *Regia* (1649), p. 62, ll. 18–19.

[77] Irenaeus, *Against Heresies,* V, 24, 3 (in *The Ante-Nicene Fathers,* ed. Alexander Roberts and James Donaldson, New York, 1899, I, 552; hereafter cited as *Fathers, A.N.*

good king to a wicked people. It is therefore a task for men of the utmost wisdom to discover what may be most suitable and advantageous for a people; certainly the same government is fitting neither for all peoples nor for one people at all times; now one form is better, now another, as the courage and industry of the citizens waxes or wanes. He who deprives a people of the power to choose whatever form of government they prefer surely deprives them of all that makes up civil liberty.

Next you cite Justin Martyr as rendering obedience to the Antonines,[78] the best of emperors; but who would not have obeyed rulers so outstanding and so mild? "How much worse," you say, "are we Christians today! They put up with a king of another faith." [79] They were of course private citizens and far inferior in power. "Now however papists will not endure a Protestant king [49], nor Protestants a papist." [80] You are wise to show yourself neither papist nor Protestant; you are generous too, for you freely grant what we did not ask, namely that today all Christians agree on this matter to which you alone with unrivalled insolence and wickedness are opposed, being far different from the fathers you praise: they used to write defences for Christians to pagan kings, while you write for the worst of papist kings against Christians and Protestants. Next you vainly drag in references from Athenagoras and Tertullian, explaining points already treated by the apostles themselves with much more clarity and directness. Even Tertullian is far from your position of wishing the king to

[78] *Regia* (1649), p. 62, ll. 24–29. In *Commonplace Book* (*Complete Prose,* I, 437) Milton writes: "What the early Christians decided about this, Justin Martyr, writing to the Emperor Antoninus Pius, makes clear in his belief, founded upon the teaching of Christ, that we should give to Caesar the things which are Caesar's and to God the things which are God's; 'therefore,' he says, 'we worship God alone, and in other matters we gladly serve you,' in which he plainly assigns 'worship' to God alone, and 'willing service' to kings. apolog: 2, p. 64."

Justin Martyr was born of pagan parents at Flavia Neapolis about the year 100. He wrote an *Apology* whose two parts are sometimes regarded as separate works with the same title, and *The Dialogue with Tryphon.* Of several other contemporary works attributed to him, some cannot definitely be considered his, while others certainly are not. In attempting to reconcile Christian with pagan culture, he consciously recognizes the truths of Greek philosophy as a preparation for those of Christianity, and in the process gives much valuable information about the life of the church in the second century. He was martyred under the prefect Rusticus between 163 and 167. See *Complete Prose,* I, 397, 632, and *Fathers, A.N.,* ed. Roberts and Donaldson, I, 159–308.

[79] *Regia* (1649), p. 64, ll. 2–4.

[80] *Regia* (1649), p. 64, ll. 5–6.

be a master; a fact which you either missed or wickedly concealed. In his *Apologeticum* he dared to write as a Christian to a pagan emperor, saying that it was wrong for the emperor to be called Lord. "Augustus," he says "the founder of the empire, did not even wish to be called Lord, which is a title of God: I shall call the emperor Lord, to be sure, but only when I am not forced to call him Lord in God's place: for I am not his slave and my only Lord is God." [81] In the same place we read: "How is the father of his country Lord?" Rejoice then in your Tertullian, whom you had better have left alone. You say he called the slayers of Domitian parricides.[82] He was right in this, for Domitian was slain by the treachery of his wife and slaves, by Parthenius and by Stephanus the guilty embezzler. If however the senate and the Roman people, just as formerly they judged Nero a public enemy and sought him for punishment, had punished Domitian in the ancient manner, should they, think you, be called parricides? Surely one who spoke of them thus would himself have earned punishment as you now have earned the gallows.

The reply to Irenaeus fits Origen as well.[83] Athanasius reports that it is sinful to summon the monarchs of the world before human tribunals.[84] Who reported this to Athanasius? In this I hear no voice of God. I shall believe in those rulers and kings who admit that this is untrue of them, rather than in Athanasius.

You next bring in Ambrose, who turned bishop from being proconsul and catechumen, with his ignorant if not fawning explanation of the words of David: "Against thee only have I sinned." [50] [85] It was his wish that all other men be servants of the emperor, that he might make the emperor his servant. The pride and more than popish pomp with which he treated the emperor Theodosius at Milan, passed sentence on him for the massacre at Thessalonica, and forbade his entry into the church, and also the revelation of his unlettered ignorance of Gospel

[81] *Apologeticum,* 34, in Tertullian, *Apology, De Spectaculis,* tr. T. R. Glover (London: Loeb Classical Library, 1931), pp. 156–59.

[82] *Regia* (1649), p. 67, ll. 1–2.

[83] *Regia* (1649), p. 67, l. 15. Salmasius remarks that, about the time Tertullian flourished, Origen began to be known.

[84] Salmasius (*Regia,* 1649, p. 67, ll. 34–35) makes a direct quotation from Athanasius' *Sermo de Cruce et Passione Domini: "Nam si reges terrae ad humana tribunalia in testes vocare nefarium est."* Athanasius argues that what is uncreated has superior power over what is created.

[85] *Regia* (1649), p. 68, ll. 11–19. The explanation is contained in St. Ambrose, *Letters,* LI, i, in *Fathers, N. and P. N. 2,* ed. Schaff and Wace, X, 450.

teaching, are well known to all.[86] He commanded the emperor to leave his audience chamber though the emperor had fallen at his feet, and when at length the emperor had been restored to communion and made offerings, drove him beyond the rails from his place at the altar, saying to him "O Emperor, the place within is reserved for priests alone, and may not be defiled by any others." Was this a teacher of the Gospel or a high priest of Moses' ritual? This fellow, using the tricks common to most ecclesiastics, sought to make the emperor lord of other men that he might himself lord it over the emperor. Thus it was that with these words he turned back Theodosius as though he were his servant. "You are emperor of your fellow-men and fellow-slaves; over all there is but one Lord and King and Creator." Fine indeed: The truth which had been concealed by the craft and flattery of the bishops was revealed by one man's bad temper, or to put it less harshly, ignorant zeal.

To Ambrose's lack of learning you add your own ignorance or heresy by eloquently denying on page 68 that "under the old covenant there could be remission of sin through the blood of Christ at that time when David confessed to God that he had sinned only against him." [87] The orthodox belief is that no sins were ever remitted save by the blood of the Lamb slain from the foundation of the world; [88] as to you, I know not the novel error which you follow, but surely the follower of that great theologian, though you keep referring to him, did not stray from the truth in his assertion that any of the people could have cried to God, with the same right as David, "Against thee only have I sinned."

Next you show off your Augustine and parade some churchmen of Hippo; [89] but your Augustinian citations cause no difficulty. Why should we not admit with the prophet Daniel that God changes circumstances, assigns kingdoms and takes them away, but still through the

86 Theodoret, *Church History,* V, 17, in ***Fathers, N. and P. N. 2,*** ed. Schaff and Wace, III, 143–45. Theodosius the Great (346–95) shared the rule of the Roman Empire with Gratian.

87 *Regia* (1649), p. 68, ll. 26–29.

88 Milton quotes loosely the text of Salmasius, who attacks a recent anonymous pamphleteer for maintaining that the action of David in seeking pardon from God might equally well have been adopted by any sinner of low degree. Salmasius scornfully denies (among much else) the possibility of the remission of sins through Christ before the incarnation, while Milton says the orthodox view is the reverse.

89 *Regia* (1649), p. 69, ll. 34 ff.

agency of men? If it was God alone who gave Charles his kingdom, it was he who took it away and gave it to the nobles and people. [51] If you say that obedience should for that reason have been tendered to Charles, you must now say that it should be tendered to our present magistrates, for you admit yourself that God also gave our magistrates that power which he gives to wicked kings as punishment for the sins of the people; and even by your own verdict our magistrates, being likewise appointed of God, can be removed from office by none but God himself.

Here too, then, as is your wont, you turn your blade against yourself and are your own assassin; there is justice here, for you are so far gone in shameless rascality and senseless fury that those upon whom, by all your arguments, no finger should be laid are by your own assertion said to be liable to pursuit in war by all their subjects. Ishmael the slayer of Gedaliah the governor was, you say, called parricide by Jerome, and rightly so; for with no justification he slew the governor of Judea and a good man.[90] The same Jerome writing on Ecclesiastes said that Solomon's warning to "keep the king's commandment" agrees with Paul's teaching; [91] and he should be praised for giving a less extreme interpretation of this passage than did his contemporaries. You will not come down to the period after Augustine, you say, to search out the opinions of scholars.

To make it clear to everyone, if, after all this, you actually have any supporters, that you can more easily lie than hold your peace, after a single paragraph you cannot help rushing into the utter darkness of Isidore of Seville, Gregory of Tours, and even Otto of Freising.[92] Had you but known how slight we consider their importance you would not have used a lie to advance their dubious testimony. Does anyone wish to know why he lacks courage to come down to the present times, why he lurks in hiding, why he disappears so suddenly? Here is the reason: He knows that he will have as many bitter foes as there are great teachers in the Protestant church. Just let him run the risk

[90] *Regia* (1649), p. 71, ll. 4–8. [91] *Regia* (1649), p. 71, ll. 19–23.

[92] Isidore of Seville (570–636), a Spanish encyclopedist and historian, distinguished himself in controversy with the Arians and was chosen archbishop of Seville in 609. St. Gregory of Tours (538–594), historian of the Franks, while aiming at impartiality, tended to excuse the crime of kings who protected the church. Otto of Freising, bishop of the city of the same name, wrote *Gesta Friderici Imperatoris,* and is the principal authority on the earlier part of the reign of Frederick I (1123–1190) surnamed Barbarossa.

and he will find how easily I shall confound and crush him as he struggles and scrapes his strength together, once I have formed my battle line of Luthers, Zwinglis, Calvins, Bucers, Martyrs and Paraeuses.[93] I shall even bring against you your colleagues from Leyden, whose academy and thriving republic, the ancient home of freedom, [52] the very fountainhead indeed of humane learning, could not purge your slavish spite and inborn rudeness. When you could find no orthodox theologian whom you might advantageously name as your supporter and were bereft of all Protestant assistance you were not ashamed to fly to the Sorbonne, though well aware that this popishly inclined institution carries no weight with the orthodox. We leave this foul defender of tyranny to be absorbed by the Sorbonne; we have no need for a chattel slave so worthless as to deny that a whole people is the equal of the worst of kings.

There is no use in your trying to ease yourself by transferring to the pope a belief accepted and maintained by all free nations, all faiths, all the body of the orthodox. It is true that when the pope and his bishops were weak and powerless he first appeared to advocate that filthy doctrine of yours; [94] but by such tricks he gradually gained great wealth and power and became himself the worst of tyrants. He did however attach them all securely to himself by persuading the people, whose minds he had long controlled by the bonds of superstition, that even the worst of kings could not be deposed unless the pope had himself released them from their oath of allegiance. But you avoid orthodox authors and try to bring the truth into disrepute by maintaining that what is well known as their unanimous opinion was a popish innovation.

It took great skill to avoid revealing yourself as neither papist nor Protestant but instead some sort of half-wild Edomite Herodian who worships and adores the most savage of tyrants as a heaven-sent Messiah. You say you have proved this to be in accordance with the teachings of the fathers of the first four centuries, the teachings which alone are to be considered as evangelical and Christian. This fellow is really shameless now: How much of their speech and writings could neither have been taught nor approved by Christ and the apostles?

[93] See above, p. 338, n. 47.

[94] "That filthy doctrine" is, of course, that kings, whether good or bad, whether just or tyrannical, are constituted by God, are judged by God alone, and are free from the laws which they themselves make (*Regia,* 1649, p. 71, ll. 29–32).

In how many points do all Protestants differ from the fathers? But what is it that you have proved from the fathers? "That even wicked kings are appointed by God." [53] [95] Let them be appointed, just as in a sense every evil is appointed by God. Are they then "to have none but God as their judge, to be above the law, to be liable neither by written or unwritten law, natural or divine law to trial by their subjects or before their subjects?" [96] Why so? Surely no law forbids this or grants kings exemption. Reason, justice, and morality command the punishment of all sinners without distinction. You have adduced no law written or unwritten, natural or divine which forbids this. Why then are not kings to be punished? "Because even when wicked they are appointed by God." Should I call you rascal or dolt or blockhead? You must be a knave to dare to teach the populace a belief so vicious, and a fool to rely on proofs so senseless. God said in Isaiah 54: [97] "I have created the slayer to destroy"; the slayer is therefore above the law: Turn and twist this as you will, you will find that the conclusion is equally valid in either case.

The pope too is appointed of God in the same way that tyrants are, and was given to the church for its sins, as I have shown before by your very own words: but still you assert that because he, like a tyrant, has raised his primacy to an unbearable peak of power, both he and his bishops as well may be driven out with more justice than they were appointed (*Walo Messalinus,* page 412).[98] You say that pope and bishops, though appointed by God in his anger, are to be driven from the church because they are tyrants; you deny that tyrants may be driven from the state, because they were appointed by God in his anger. What foolish nonsense: The pope has for his domain only the conscience, which he cannot injure against the will of any individual, but still you cry out that he, who cannot be an actual tyrant, should be driven out as the worst of tyrants; you contend, however, that an actual tyrant who controls our whole lives and property, without whom no pope could be tyrant over the church, should in every case

[95] *Regia* (1649), p. 73, ll. 28–29.

[96] *Regia* (1649), p. 73, ll. 29–32.

[97] Isaiah 54:16.

[98] Milton is quoting from Salmasius' work, *De Episcopis ac Presbyteris* (Leyden, 1641). The passage to which Milton refers is found on p. 411, l. 26, to p. 412, l. 5: "Si tam isti locales Episcopi Presbyterorum, eorumdemque olim etiam Episcoporum primates, quam ille localium omnium primas Episcoporum, fastu intolerabili in fastigium potestas haud ferendum, ac tyrannidi non absimilis, primatus suos evehant, meliore iure erunt tollendi quam fuere constituti."

be endured in a state. A comparison of these statements of yours shows so clearly your childish folly in maintaining either truth or falsehood that henceforth no one can fail to perceive your inconsequential ignorance and headlong heedlessness.

You offer an additional reason for your position: "Things would seem turned upside down." [99] This would be a welcome change, for it would be the end of mankind if the worst situations [54] were unalterable—a welcome change, I repeat, for the king's power would revert to the people from whose will and suffrage it first arose and was conferred on one of their number. It is the most even-handed justice to transfer power from him who causes injury to him who suffers it, for there can be no suitable third party to judge between men, since none would suffer the judgment of a foreigner. All men alike are bound by the law, and there can be nothing more equitable; then no man of flesh and blood would be a god. Whoever establishes such among men commits as great a crime against the state as against the church. Once again I can turn your own weapons against you.

You call the greatest heresy that by which a single man is thought to sit in Christ's place, for there are here the two marks of Antichrist: spiritual infallibility and temporal omnipotence (*Apparatus ad Primatum,* page 171).[100] Surely kings are not infallible? Why then should they be omnipotent? Or if they were, why should they be less ruinous to civil life than the pope to spiritual? Does God really have no care at all for civil life? If not, he certainly does not forbid us to care; and if he does, he wishes the same reformation of the state as of the church, especially since it has been found that in both spheres the attribution of infallibility and omnipotence to a human being is the root of all evils. He does not enjoin such patience in civil affairs that the state should put up with the cruelest of tyrants while the church should not; his injunctions are rather the opposite, in that he has left the church no weapons save patience, righteousness, prayer and Gospel teaching, but handed over to the state and with it all its officers not patience but laws, and arms to avenge wrong and violence.

This fellow's perverse and topsy-turvy mind rouses amazement or

[99] *Regia* (1649), p. 73, l. 33.

[100] *De Primatu,* p. 171, ll. 15–20. "Maxima primum hæresis & perniciossima ex ea delebitur, quo creditur unum hominem in loco Christi sedere qui non possit errare in rebus fidei, & supremam habere debeat potestatem supra omnes reges terrae. Signant, *infallibilitas* in spiritalibus, & *omnipotentia* in temporalibus."

laughter; in the church he is a true tyrannicide, a Helvidius or Thrasea,[101] while in the state he is a subservient satellite of every tyrant. If he be right, it is not we alone who were rebels in casting off our king, but all Protestants as well in casting off the mastery of the Pope against the will of their kings. But now for the present he has been long laid prostrate, smitten by his own missiles; it is his nature to keep well-supplied with weapons the hands of any foe who does not flag, [55] and to furnish the best of handles for rebuttal or ridicule. A man would sooner tire of thrashing him than he of presenting his back to the lash.

CHAPTER IV [1]

YOU, Salmasius, suppose that by this Royal Defence you have won great favor with kings and put all the rulers and lords of the earth in your debt, though, if they were to judge their own advantage and fortune by the standard of truth instead of your adulation, there is no one they should hate more than you, drive off and keep farther from their presence. In raising royal power immeasurably above the law, you manage to warn men far and wide of their unsuspected slavery, and you spur them on more sharply to awake with all speed from that hibernation in which they used to dream that they were free; you have warned them of what they had

[101] Mentioned in Xiphilinus' "Epitome of Book LXXII of Dio Cassius' *Roman History.*" See above p. 360, n. 69. Helvidius Priscus, put to death by Vespasian, and his father-in-law, Thrasea Paetus, put to death by Nero, were examples both of Stoic fortitude and of opposition to tyranny.

[1] In book IV (*Regia,* 1649, pp. 74–99) Salmasius examines the question whether Jews and Christians treated kings in the same manner. 1. David refrained from killing Saul, although he had the provocation and the opportunity, because Saul was the anointed of God. No one raised his hand against Solomon when he had broken the commands laid upon him. A revolt occurred under Jeroboam, but it was always disapproved of; and his successors were regarded as wicked and impious. In spite of the king's wickedness, the prophets did not advise revolt. God seemed to avenge the sin of Solomon (God is the avenger of kings) through bringing punishment upon his son. 2. But there is no parallel in Jewish history to the treatment that the English accorded Charles. The Jews did not even revolt when their king established a different religion. The revolt against Joram was not similar to that of the English against Charles, because that revolution was carried out at God's command. 3. Although the prophets corrected kings, they did not

not known, that they are slaves of kings. Thus they will consider that royal dominion is the less tolerable the more you convince them that such unlimited authority did not rise from their own sufferance but was of such character and extent from birth because of the very nature of the rights of kings. Therefore you and your defence, whether or not you convince the people, must be for the future a cause of ruin, doom, and curses for all kings. If you convince the people that royal rights are all-extensive, they will no longer endure royalty; if you do not convince them, they will no longer endure kings who wrongly claim as their right a power so illegal.

If such kings as have still taken no stand upon this point will listen to me and allow themselves to be limited by law, they will exchange their present precarious, unhealthy, and violent authority, filled with anxious fears, for one which is stable, peaceful, and enduring. If its proposer causes them to spurn advice [56] so beneficial to themselves and their kingdoms, they should realize that it stems not from me so much as from the wisest king of old. When Lycurgus the king of Sparta,[2] sprung from an ancient race of kings, saw that his relatives who controlled Argos and Messene had turned their rule into tyranny and destroyed both themselves and their states, he attempted to plan

judge them. In fact, they were often put to death by kings. Though many Jewish kings were wicked, none was put to death. 4. Even the good Jewish kings suffer in comparison with Charles, for David and Solomon were guilty of crimes of which Charles was not. 5. God evidently did not approve of rebellion against a king, no matter how wicked, for through His prophets He never commanded the people to rebel. After the time of the prophets, wicked kings ruled with impunity. 6. The teachings of the New Testament are the same as that of the Old Testament in this respect. Paul enjoined prayer for those in high places. Tertullian testifies that the Christians were not involved in conspiracies against the emperors, although such acts would have had some justification. They had the power and could have rebelled, but they submitted anyway. 7. All the church fathers advocate obeying one's master, no matter what kind he is. The principle concerning fidelity to kings has weakened in the centuries since the time of Christ. As long as the force of the evangelic and apostolic doctrine held, there were no regicides. Christians have deteriorated. 8. It is worse to abrogate a law than to break a law. The attitude toward the inviolability of kings began to change when the Pope assumed over kings the power of excommunication and interdiction. Kingly majesty was weakened from the time the Pope, as God's vicar on earth, sat in judgment over a king. When a bishop released the subjects from their oath of fealty to the king, regal power was impaired still more.

[2] Plato, *Epistles,* VIII, 354, in *Plato's Epistles,* tr. Glenn R. Morrow (Indianapolis: Library of Liberal Arts, 1962), p. 254. See the life in Plutarch, who ascribes the foundation of the ephorate to Theopompus. Herodotus, *Histories,* I, 65, ascribes it to Lycurgus.

for the safety of his country and the preservation of royal authority in his own family as long as possible by making the senate his colleague in ruling and by making the power of the ephors, which resembled that of a censor over the king, the bulwark of his realm. By this means he handed down to his descendants a kingdom unshaken for long ages. Perhaps, as some suppose, it was Theopompus, who ruled Sparta more than a century after Lycurgus, whose reasonableness was such as to raise the popular power of the ephors above his own, and who boasted of having thereby strengthened his realm and bequeathed it to his children in a greater and more enduring form. But at any rate our modern kings had here no mean example to imitate, and they can find in it distinguished authorship for unimpeachable advice. That a master superior to the law should be endured by all men in the person of any single man was never commanded by any law, nor could it be, for a law which overthrows all laws cannot itself be law. Therefore though the laws reject you as one who would overturn and destroy them all, you strive to renew the struggle in this chapter by means of examples. Let us make trial of them as well, for often examples reveal clearly what is not stated but merely hinted at by the laws themselves.

We shall begin with the Jews, who were best advised of the divine will, and then with you come down to the Christians. We shall however start at the earlier time when the Israelites, who had somehow come under a monarchy, cast from their necks that yoke of slavery. Eglon king of Moab [3] had subdued the Israelites in war and made his capital in their midst at Jericho; he did not despise the divine power, for when God's name was spoken he arose from his throne: the Israelites had been under Eglon for eighteen years and sent offerings to him as to their own king rather than an enemy. But while they openly rewarded him as their king they slew him by secret plots [57] as an enemy. Indeed Ehud his slayer is held to have acted at God's command. What could be higher recommendation for such a deed? For it is God's nature to encourage deeds upright and praiseworthy, not wicked and faithless and ferocious. We are not told, however, that he had any direct instruction from God. "The children of Israel cried unto the Lord," [4] and we too have cried; the Lord raised up a deliverer for them, and for us too. Their neighbor entered their household, and their enemy became their king; our king became our enemy,

[3] Judges 3:12–21. [4] Judges 3:15.

and so no longer king, for in no way can a foe of the state be its citizen: Antony was no longer considered consul, nor Nero emperor, when declared enemy by the Senate. As regards Antony this is clearly shown by Cicero in his *Fourth Philippic:* [5] "If Antony be consul, Brutus is our enemy: if Brutus be the deliverer of the republic, Antony is our enemy. Who but a brigand thinks that such a man is consul?" With equal justice, I maintain, none but a country's foes think a tyrant is her king. It matters not whether Eglon was a foreigner and our man a native, since they were both enemies and tyrants. If it was right for Ehud to slay the one, it was right for us to punish the other. Even the heroic Samson, though his countrymen reproached him saying, Judges 15,[6] "Knowest thou not that the Philistines are rulers over us?," still made war single-handed on his masters, and, whether prompted by God or by his own valor, slew at one stroke not one but a host of his country's tyrants, having first made prayer to God for his aid. Samson therefore thought it not impious but pious to kill those masters who were tyrants over his country, even though most of her citizens did not balk at slavery.

It may be said that David,[7] the king and prophet, would not slay Saul as being the Lord's anointed. But whatever David would not do is not forthwith forbidden us: David would not act, being a private citizen; must therefore a council, a Parliament, a whole people at once refuse? He would not kill his foe by treachery; shall a magistrate therefore refuse to punish a criminal by law? He would not kill a king; and shall a senate therefore fear to touch a tyrant? He had scruples as to the slaughter of the Lord's anointed; shall a people then scruple to condemn their own anointed, especially one whose anointing, [58] whether sacred or civil, had been washed off by continual warfare which had bathed him from head to foot in the blood of his citizens?

I do indeed recognize as the Lord's anointed those kings whom he anointed through his prophets, or like Cyrus (Isaiah 44) [8] named for a specific purpose; the rest I hold to be anointed of the people, or of the soldiers, or of their own supporters alone; and even if I granted that all kings are anointed of the Lord, you could never bring me to believe that this makes them superior to the law and beyond punishment for any of their crimes. What is the result of all this? David kept himself

[5] Cicero, *Philippics,* IV, iii, 8 ff.
[6] Judges 15:11.
[7] I Samuel 26:9.
[8] Isaiah 44:28.

and some private citizens from raising their hands against the Lord's anointed. But God himself forbade kings (Psalms 105) [9] to touch his own anointed, which is his own people. To the anointing, such as it is, of kings he preferred the anointing of his people. Is it therefore forbidden to punish even the faithful, if they have broken the law?

King Solomon came near to punishing capitally Abiathar [10] the anointed priest of the Lord, and finally spared him not because he was the Lord's anointed but because he was his father's friend. If therefore the high priest, who for the most part was chief magistrate as well, was not exempt from punishment through that sacred and civil anointing of God, how can a mere civil anointing exempt a tyrant? You may say that "Saul too was a tyrant who deserved death"; [11] true, but it does not follow from that fact that without popular support or magisterial command David was a proper and suitable person to slay Saul the king in any place whatever. And was Saul really a tyrant? I wish you would say so; indeed you do, though earlier you said in Chapter II, page 32, that "he was not a tyrant but a good and chosen king." [12]

Why should any paid informer or forger be publicly branded while you escape the same mark of shame? Their very rascality is far more straightforward than your writings and discussions of the most important subjects.

Thus, if it helps you, Saul was a good king, but if not, he suddenly becomes no good king but rather a tyrant; this is hardly surprising, for your shameless pandering to the sway of tyrants simply makes tyrants of all good kings.

And even David, who for various reasons which do not concern us here would not slay the king [59] [13] his father-in-law, had no hesitation in gathering forces in his own defence and attacking or besieging Saul's cities; and had he not known that its dwellers were opposed to him he would have garrisoned the town of Keilah against Saul. If Saul had tried to besiege that town, bring ladders to its walls, and himself

[9] *Cf.* Psalms 105:14–15. [10] I Kings 2:26.

[11] *Regia* (1649), p. 74, ll. 35 ff. Salmasius says that David did not kill the king, though Saul was a tyrant.

[12] Milton here catches Salmasius in a real contradiction! In *Regia* (1649), p. 32, ll. 7–10, Salmasius is arguing on the authority of Samuel that Saul was a good king. Saul is cited as an example of God's intentions to give the Israelites good kings rather than tyrants.

[13] I Samuel 23:1–12.

lead the attack, do you suppose David would have laid down his arms on the spot and betrayed his whole force to the anointed enemy? Hardly; he would have acted as we did, for when he was driven to it by his own extremity he promised extensive aid to the Philistines who were his country's foes, thus doing to Saul what I believe we would never have done to our own tyrant. I have long been disgusted and wearied with your lies: you pretend it is the English policy "to spare enemies rather than friends, and so they were not obliged to spare their king, since he was their friend." [14]

Who ever heard of this before you made it up, you prince of liars? We may however forgive you this: for you have not yet used in this chapter your best, though very shopworn, oratorical coloring, which is now for the fifth time, and will before the end of your book be ten times, hauled out of your cubby-holes and ointment boxes, namely that the English are "fiercer than their own mastiffs." [15]

It is not so much the English that are fiercer than their mastiffs, as you that are more ravenous than any mad dog in having the iron guts to keep coming back to your oft regurgitated matter.

David, you say, ordered the death of the Amalekite [16] who had, as he pretended, slain Saul; [17] but there is here no parallel of persons or actions. Unless David, because of his supposed defection to the Philistines and forming part of their forces, was therefore the more eagerly attempting to divert from himself suspicion of having pressed the murder of the king, I cannot myself believe that David had any reason for this harsh treatment other than that man himself reported that he gave the final blow to the king when the king was already mortally wounded and dying in pain. The very same action by Domitian,[18] when he executed Epaphroditus for helping Nero's suicide, is universally condemned.

Next, with unheard of rashness, you are not content to call the Lord's anointed the man [60] you had just named as "a tyrant driven by an evil spirit," but you even hail him as "the Christ of the Lord"; [19]

[14] *Regia* (1649), p. 75, ll. 13–15.
[15] *Regia* (1649), p. 75, l. 20.
[16] II Samuel 23:13–15.
[17] *Regia* (1649), p. 75, ll. 33 ff.
[18] Suetonius, *Domitianus*, XIV. For one account of this see below, p. 447.
[19] *Regia* (1649), p. 76, l. 1. Actually Salmasius is quoting I Samuel 26:9, the words of David to Abisai: "Kill him not; for who shall put forth his hand against the Lord's anointed, and shall be guiltless?" Milton is plainly unfair; he ignores the common usage of "christus" to mean anointed; he attributes to Salmasius himself the words of the Bible.

you hold the name of Christ so cheap that you do not shrink from applying that holy name even to a devil-driven tyrant.

I turn now to an instance in which one must be blind indeed not to see that the right of the people is more ancient than that of kings. When Solomon died [20] the people held an election at Sichem about the appointment of his son; Rehoboam went there as a candidate, to avoid seeming to claim the kingdom as an inheritance or to own a free people as he owned his father's cattle. The people stated conditions for his prospective reign, and the king asked for three days to consider them; the elders were consulted, and they gave him no advice as to his rights as king but rather told him to win over the people by flattering promises, since it was in their power to make him king or pass him by. He then consulted those of his own age who had been brought up with him from childhood; driven by some Salmasian gadfly they bellowed of nothing but king's rights and urged him to threaten whips and torture. Rehoboam followed their advice in his reply to the people, and so when all Israel saw that the king "hearkened not unto them," they immediately asserted their own freedom and the rights of the people in open and fearless language: "What portion have we in David? To your tents, O Israel! Now see to thine own house, David." After that they stoned Adoram when he was sent by the king, and would perhaps have made an example of the king himself had he not fled with all speed. He prepared a great host to subdue the Israelites: God forbade him saying: "Ye shall not go up nor fight against your brethren the children of Israel, for this thing is from me." So weigh this well! God was displeased before when the people wished a king, but would not hinder their right; now when the people did not wish Rehoboam as king, God not only granted the people this power, but also stopped the king when he undertook a war for this reason. God reproved him for it, instructing him that even those who had fallen away from him were none the less to be considered brothers instead of rebels.

Now pull yourself together! You say that all kings are of God and therefore the people must not resist even tyrants. [61] [21] In turn I assert that by God's testimony popular assemblies, elections, campaigns, votes and enactments are equally of God, and therefore on God's authority too it is equally forbidden for a king to resist the

[20] The material about Rehoboam is contained in I Kings 12:1–24.

[21] *Regia* (1649), p. 74, ll. 1–6.

people. Just as it is certain that kings today are of God and may therefore command obedience from the people, so it is certain that today free popular assemblies are of God and may therefore compel the compliance of their kings or cast them off, while they may not on this account make war on their people any more than did Rehoboam. Why then, you ask, did the Israelites not revolt from Solomon? Who but you would ask so foolish a question, when it has already been established that there is no punishment for a revolt from a tyrant? Solomon did fall into certain vices, but he did not therefore become a tyrant immediately: He balanced his vices by great virtues and services to the state. But suppose he had been a tyrant; a people is often unwilling or unable to remove a tyrant, and it is enough that it did when it could. You say that "Jeroboam's deed was always disapproved, his defection abominated, his followers considered rebels." I have often read of the censure of his defection, not from Rehoboam but from the true worship of God,[22] and I recall that his followers were indeed often termed wicked, but never rebels.

"Any act contrary to justice and law cannot," you say, "create a right." [23] What then becomes of the rights of kings? You state that "every day adulteries, murders, and thefts are committed without punishment." [24] Do you not see that you are now answering your own question why tyrants are so often unpunished? "Those kings were rebels, yet the prophets did not lead the people away from their obedience to them." [25] Then why, you wretched false prophet, would you seduce the English people from allegiance to their magistrates, though these may in your view be rebels? This crew of English brigands, you say, alleges that they were led to the undertaking of this crime so foul by a supposed voice from heaven.[26] That the English ever alleged any such thing is but one of your countless lying fictions. But I shall continue to deal with you through examples.

The great city of Lebnah [27] revolted from King Joram because he had forsaken God; therefore it is the king who was in revolt and not the city, which was not branded as rebellious but seems, if [62] you consider the reason which is appended, rather to be approved. "Such revolts should not be taken as examples." [28] Why then did you promise

[22] I Kings 14:7–16.

[23] *Regia* (1649), p. 77, ll. 13–15.

[24] *Regia* (1649), p. 77, ll. 13–15.

[25] *Regia* (1649), p. 78, ll. 11–13.

[26] *Regia* (1649), p. 78, ll. 25–27.

[27] II Kings 8:22.

[28] *Regia* (1649), p. 79, ll. 12–13.

with such bombast that in this whole chapter you would fight us to a finish with examples, when you can actually offer for examples nothing but empty denials without weight as proofs: when I adduce specific and substantial instances you deny that they should be used as examples. Who would not hoot you from the platform for such arguments? You challenged me to a contest of examples; I advanced my examples; and what do you do? You twist and turn and seek refuge in side issues; I shall go on and leave you.

Jehu killed a king [29] at the bidding of a prophet; he even had his rightful king Ahaziah killed. If God had not wished that a tyrant be slain by a citizen, and had this been a wicked and impious deed, why did he order it done? If he commanded it, it was surely permissible, praiseworthy, and noble. It was not however permissible and good to put a tyrant to death because God commanded it, but rather God commanded it because it was permissible and good. Athaliah had been ruler for seven years when the priest Jehoiada without scruple drove her from the realm and slaughtered her. You may say that she had seized a dominion to which she had no claim.[30] Did not Tiberius long afterwards seize a sovereignty which was not his? [31] But he and other tyrants of this sort were said by you above to have a right to obedience based on the teaching of Christ: [32] it would obviously be ridiculous if it were right to slay one who had unjustly assumed royal authority but wrong to slay one exercising it most evilly. You say that being a woman she could not legally reign: "Thou shalt set over thee a king" not a queen.[33] If it turns out like this I shall say "Thou shalt set over thee a king, not a tyrant" for there is more difference between king and tyrant than male and female.

The cowardly and idolatrous king Amaziah [34] was put to death not by any conspirators but, as is indeed more probable, by the nobles and the people; for as he fled from Jerusalem with none to help him

[29] See II Kings 9:1–27 for the account of Jehu and Athaliah.

[30] *Regia* (1649), p. 81, ll. 34–38.

[31] Tiberius (42 B.C.–37 A.D.) was the adopted son of Augustus. Agrippa Postumus was his only male descendant by blood to survive him, and had been banished in disgrace during Augustus' lifetime. The execution of Agrippa Postumus after Augustus' death may or may not have been carried out under standing orders of that ruler: see Tacitus, *Annals,* I, 6.

[32] *Regia* (1649), p. 53, ll. 17–20: "Agnovit non semel nec uno modo potestatem tunc imperantium quasi legitimam, cum tamen ex usurpatione nata foret primum, nec justius deinde exerceretur quam erat usurpata."

[33] *Regia* (1649), p. 81, ll. 38–39.

[34] II Kings 14:19.

he was pursued as far as Lachish. They are said to have decided on this after he had forsaken God, and we read of no investigation by his son Azariah of his father's death. You then use a lot of Rabbinical nonsense to show that the Hebrew king was over the Sanhedrin; but you disregard the actual words of king Zedekiah (*Jeremiah,* 38): [35] "The king is not he that [63] can do anything against you." Thus he spoke to the nobles, clearly confessing himself the inferior of his own council. "Perhaps," you say, "he dared deny them nothing from fear of sedition." [36]

How much, will you tell me, is that "perhaps" of yours worth, when your stoutest assertion carries no weight at all? What could be more capricious, inconsistent, unreliable than you? How often have I found you as diverse as patchwork, in disagreement, out of harmony, and at variance even with yourself?

Again you set up comparisons between Charles and the good kings of Judah. You speak of David especially as one to be abhorred, saying, "Take David who was both adulterer and murderer; you find nothing like this in Charles.[37] Take his son Solomon who was much spoken of as wise." [38] Who would not be indignant at hearing the names of great and holy men and kings besides thus bandied about by a foul worthless good-for-nothing? Dare you compare Charles with David, one full of superstitious fancies and a mere novice in the Christian faith with a king and a reverent prophet of God, a fool with a wise man, a coward with a hero, a sinner with a saint? [39] Can you praise the purity and continence of one who is known to have joined the Duke of Buckingham in every act of infamy? There is no need to investigate his more private habits and hidden retreats when even in the theatre he kisses women wantonly, enfolds their waists and, to mention no more openly, plays with the breasts of maids and mothers.

[35] Jeremiah 38:5.

[36] *Regia* (1649), p. 80, ll. 12–15.

[37] *Regia* (1649), p. 81, ll. 17–19.

[38] *Regia* (1649), p. 81, l. 20.

[39] In contrast to Milton, Salmasius finds Charles a good, pious, chaste, and religious ruler. In innocence and integrity of life he gave precedence to none of the rulers who then reigned. He was the first martyr king of England (*Regia,* 1649, p. 296, l. 6), and he sought only after the kingdom of Christ (*Regia,* 1649, p. 296, ll. 20–21). On several occasions he is compared to Christ (*Regia,* 1649, p. 20, ll. 17–21; p. 271, ll. 19 ff.). He lived to the pattern of Christ (*Regia,* 1649, p. 296, ll. 2–3). Of *Eikon Basilike* Salmasius wrote (*Regia,* 1649, p. 300, ll. 3–6): "His posthumous book breathes everywhere love toward God, charity toward his neighbor, benevolence towards his people, although for the great part undeserving and rebellious."

I warn you, you imitation Plutarch, to give up such foolish parallel lives for the future, lest I be forced to recount stories of Charles which I would otherwise gladly pass over.

By this time it is quite clear what things were attempted or carried out by the people against tyrants, and what justification they had, during the period when God himself governed the Jewish state in accordance with his will and his decrees as though he were visibly present. The following ages do not guide us by their own authority, but, because they acted in all cases according to the standards and manners of their forefathers, they merely furnish, by their imitation, support for ours. Thus when after the Babylonian captivity God gave them no new commands as to their government, they returned to the ancient Mosaic form [64] even though the royal line was not extinct. King Antiochus of Syria,[40] to whom they paid tribute, and his governors were resisted under the leadership of the Maccabaean high priests, since he had demanded what was not lawful; they asserted their freedom by force and henceforth gave the rule to the worthiest individuals, until Hyrcanus son of Simon, the brother of Judas Maccabaeus, ravaged the tomb of David and began to maintain a foreign army and to add a sort of royal authority to that of his priesthood, thus leading his son Aristobulus to be the first to claim a crown for himself.[41] Tyrant though he was, the people did not act or plot against him; and no wonder, for he ruled but a year. When he himself was stricken by a grave malady and repented of his deeds, he did not cease to long for death, until he died with that prayer on his lips. The next ruler was his brother Alexander.[42] You say that though he was a tyrant "none rose against him." [43] You might have been safe in your lies had Josephus perished and your Josippus alone survived, from whom you cull some useless Pharisaic maxims.[44]

[40] Antiochus III (223–187 B. C.) was a member of the Seleucid dynasty originating in a general of Alexander the Great. He was contemporary with Judas Maccabaeus.

[41] Aristobulus I (104–103 B. C.) was the successor to John Hyrcanus I (135–104). He extended Hasmonaean territory northward in Palestine and is said to have assumed the title of king, though on his coins, he appears, like Hyrcanus I, as a high priest.

[42] Alexander Jannaeus (103–76 B. C.), younger son of John Hyrcanus, Judaized the Peraea.

[43] *Regia* (1649), p. 82, l. 38.

[44] Milton's following account is to be found in Josephus, *Jewish Antiquities*, XIII, 372 ff. Josippus is quoted by Salmasius, *Regia* (1649), p. 83, l. 8. Alexan-

The actual facts are these: when he had misruled the state in war and peace, Alexander,[45] though guarded by a great band of Pisidian and Cilician mercenaries, could not prevent the people from nearly crushing him with palm and citron boughs as he was making the sacrifices, for they judged him unfit for this office. After that, a major war was waged on him for six years by the great majority of the people; when in it he had slain many thousand Jews and at last, being anxious for peace, asked what they would have him do, they all replied with one voice that he should die, and that they would hardly forgive him if he were dead.

To avoid by any means this account which fits your ends so ill, you cloaked your foul deception in a few Pharisaic aphorisms, when you should either have omitted this instance completely or else have faithfully recounted the actual events. Did you not like a sly old night prowler rely more on your lies than on the justice of your cause? Even those 800 Pharisees whose crucifixion Alexander ordered were among those who had taken up arms against him; with the rest they had unanimously sworn to put the king to death [65] if, as a beaten foe, he should fall into their hands. After her husband Alexander, Alexandra seized the crown as had Athaliah earlier;[46] this she did not of right, for as you just admitted yourself the laws did not allow a woman

der's wife offered his body either to be burnt or thrown to the dogs. Salmasius, anxious to show that the Pharisees had respect for their kings, uses Josippus as an authority for their reply to this offer. "It would be shameful to repay our master, the anointed of God, at the same time king and high priest, with this violence. Whatever evil he (the king) has done to us has been expiated by his death."

Josippon (Josippus) is a pseudonym for Joseph Ben Gorion, which may in turn be a pseudonym for an anonymous writer. The chronicle, probably dating to the tenth century, was first printed in Mantua in 1476. The name Josippus may have been designed intentionally to confuse the reader with that of Josephus. Josephus is a careful historian, checking his sources, making few mistakes and none intentionally. Josippus belongs to a legendary school of historians and merits the contempt with which Milton refers to him, "Your Josippus." That his work was widely read can be seen by the entries in NYPL for 1558, 1561, 1567, 1575, 1599, 1615 editions of the English translation: *A Compedious and Most Marveillous History of the Latter Tymes of the Jewes Commune Weale Beginnynge Where the Bible and Scriptures Leave Continuing to the Utter Subversion and Last Destruction of That Country and People: Written in Hebrew by Joseph Ben Gorion Translated into Englishe by Peter Morvyng, London.* Hereafter referred to as *De Bello Judaico.*

[45] Alexander Jannaeus, as above.

[46] Athaliah as mentioned on p. 357 above from the account in II Kings 11:1–3. Alexandra Salome reigned 76–69 B. C.

to reign. She did it partly through force as leader of the foreign mercenaries and partly through the favor of the Pharisees who had much power over the people, for she had won them over to herself by the argument that, while she should have the name of the ruler, they should possess the ruling power. Just so with us, the Scottish Presbyterians granted Charles the title of king on condition that they keep the actual control.[47] After the death of Alexandra, her sons Hyrcanus and Aristobulus quarreled over the kingdom, and the latter, being stronger and more diligent, drove his elder brother from the realm. When Pompey turned from the war with Mithridates against Syria, the Jews thought they had found in him finally an impartial judge of their freedom; they sent him an embassy on their own behalf. They renounced both brothers as kings, complaining of their enslavement by them; Pompey took the crown from Aristobulus and left to Hyrcanus his priesthood and that leadership which was sanctioned by ancient custom; henceforth he was called High Priest and Ethnarch.[48] Under Archilaeus, son of Herod, the Jews again sent a legation of 500 to Augustus Caesar to make grave accusations against the late Herod and Archilaeus; [49] the latter, so far as was in their power, they deprived of his dominion, and they begged Caesar to allow the Jewish people to live without a king. Caesar was somewhat moved by their

[47] Milton seems to speak in general terms here about the Scotch Presbyterians. The Scotch were prepared at all times to accept Charles as their king provided he would support Presbyterian discipline through taking the covenant and accepting the establishment of the Directory. In June and July, 1646, negotiations were carried on to this effect. Salmasius (*Regia,* 1649, p. 300, ll. 18–23) accuses the Independents of having broken the Covenant in which provision was made for the protection of the king's person and the solemn pact by which his sovereignty was guaranteed. Milton does not mention the fact that in July, 1647, successive addresses were made to Charles in the name of the military, expressive of the general wish to effect an accommodation, which should reconcile the rights of the throne with those of the people (Gardiner, *Great Civil War,* III, 316–33). The Independents, no less than the Presbyterians, considered coming to terms with Charles on the principle indicated by Milton.

[48] Aristobulus, younger son of Alexandra Salome (76–69), expelled his brother Hyrcanus, who fled to Aretas III of Arabia. Aretas was besieging Aristobulus in Jerusalem when Pompey intervened, stormed the city, and appointed Hyrcanus high priest of an ethnarchy comprising Galilee, Samarcitis, Judaea, and Peraea.

[49] Archilaeus (or Archelaus) received the kingdom of Judaea by the last will of his father, Herod the Great. Proclaimed king by the army, he submitted his claims to Augustus, who gave him the greater part of the kingdom with the title of Ethnarch. He suppressed a sedition of the Pharisees, killing nearly 3000 of them. He was deposed in A. D. 7.

prayers and appointed, not a king, but only an Ethnarch. After he [Archilaeus] had been Ethnarch for ten years the people in an embassy to Caesar accused him of tyranny; Caesar gave them a kindly hearing, summoned the accused to Rome, and, after he [Archilaeus] had been found guilty in his trial, exiled him to Vienne.[50]

Now answer me this; would not men who sought to have their kings accused, found guilty, and punished have preferred, if they had the power or been granted their choice, to find them guilty and punish them in person? You do not deny that later when the Roman governors were greedy and oppressive in their provincial administration, the people and their leaders frequently took up arms against them: as usual you invent the most foolish reasons for this: "They were not yet accustomed to the yoke"; [51] I suppose under Alexander [66], Herod, and his sons. Against C. Caesar and Petronius they were unwilling "to wage war." Wise men indeed, since they could not! Would you hear their own words? "Not wishing to wage war because we would not have been able." Are you like a hypocrite to ascribe to religion what the men themselves confess was due to their own impotence?

Then you make much ado about nothing in proving from the fathers, just as tediously as you had before, that we should pray for kings. For good kings, as no one denies. For wicked ones as long as there is hope for them; for robbers and enemies too—but rather that they may come to their senses, than ravage our fields or slaughter us utterly. We pray for both of these, but who would forbid us to punish the former by law and the latter by arms?

I pay no heed to your "Egyptian Liturgies"; [52] but as to the priest who, as you say, prayed that "Commodus might succeed his father," [53] it seems to me that he was not uttering a prayer but rather the direst curse against the Roman Empire.[54]

[50] Archelaus reigned briefly (4 B. C.–A. D. 6). After the Jews complained of his violation of the Mosaic law and of his cruelties, he was banished to Vienne.

[51] *Regia* (1649), p. 83, l. 20.

[52] *Regia* (1649), p. 86, l. 31: *Liturgiae Copticae, hoc est, Aegypticae* . . . Salmasius goes on to say that there are Coptic liturgies extant under the names of Basil, Gregory, and Cyril derived from ancient Egyptian sermons translated into Latin which Christian Egyptians use today who preserve the old ecclesiastical custom of praying for the Turkish emperor.

[53] *Regia* (1649), p. 87, ll. 15–16.

[54] Milton's low estimate of Commodus (161–192 A. D.) may be based on the fact that he largely ruled through favorites and degraded the Senate. He apparently became mentally deranged and regarded himself as the incarnation of Hercules. His advisers eventually caused him to be strangled.

"We," you say, "broke our repeated pledge given in solemn conclave to maintain the power and majesty of the king." [55] I shall await your fuller treatment of this point below, and join battle with you there. You revert to patristic commentaries, about which you must realize this in brief: Any statements of theirs unsupported by Scripture or sufficient proof of some sort are to me of no more weight than those of anyone else. You first bring on Tertullian, a writer hardly orthodox, known for his frequent errors, so that his evidence would be worthless, even if it supported you. But what does he say? He censures riot and rebellion; [56] so do we, but in so doing we would not immediately prejudice all the rights of the people, privileges, decrees, powers of all the magistrates save the king alone. The fathers are speaking of plots rashly undertaken through the madness of a mob, not of the summons of magistrates, Senate or Parliament to a people to take arms against a tyrant.

Thus your citation from Ambrose: [57] "Not to fight back, to weep, to groan, these are the protections of priests, and no one by himself or with a few others can say to the Emperor 'I like not your law': priests may not speak thus, and shall laymen be permitted?" [58] It is now clear of whom [67] he speaks; of priests and private citizens, not of magistrates: but it is also clear what a weak and unseasonable argument he [Ambrose] employs to herald the coming dispute between layman and priest over civil law itself.

Since you think us hard pressed and confuted by these instances from the early fathers, in that, however provoked, they began no war

[55] *Regia* (1649), p. 88, ll. 4–8: "I do not know whether the English conspiratorial poltroons prayed for their king, but it is evident that they never put forward in solemn assembly their fealty to his authority and majesty, which they afterwards violated in nefarious and sacrilegious, reckless action."

[56] Tertullian often refers to the acceptance by Christians of imperial rule, and to their recognition that the Roman emperor is appointed by God; for example, *Ad Scapulam,* chapter 2.

[57] St. Ambrose (*ca.* 340–397), bishop of Milan. See the entry in the *Commonplace Book* where Milton speaks of the "severe rebuke" that Ambrose gave the elder Theodosius "on account of the slaughter of the inhabitants of Thessalonica." See *Complete Prose,* I, 432, especially n. 10.

[58] Milton runs together as one two separate quotations by Salmasius from Ambrose—one from his *Oratio in Auxentium de Tradendis Basilicis,* the other from his *Epistle XXXII*. The first reads in full (Milton only quotes part): "Attacked, I have not known how to resist. I shall be able to grieve, to weep, to groan. Against armies, even Gothic soldiers, tears are my weapons. For such are the fortifications of the priest; otherwise I ought not nor can resist" (*Regia,* 1649, p. 91, ll. 21–24). The second is in *Regia* (1649), p. 91, ll. 11–13.

against the emperors, I shall show first that they had no power, then that they made war when they could; and finally that, even though they did not war when they could, they were in this respect men whose lives and customs do not deserve our imitation in matters so important. Everyone knows that on the fall of the Roman republic all the imperial strength and governmental control fell into Caesar's hands alone; every legion served only Caesar: the result was that, if the Senate to a man, the whole equestrian order, and all the populace had been eager for revolution, they might indeed have exposed themselves to slaughter, but could have done nothing at all towards the recovery of their freedom; for, even if they had done away with an emperor, the empire would still have remained. What then could the Christians have accomplished, who, though many in number, were scattered unarmed plebeians, for the most part men of the lowest classes. How many of them could a single legion have kept in order without difficulty? What powerful leaders had often attempted vainly to their own ruin and the destruction of their seasoned forces were these little men of the multitude to hope to carry out? About 300 years from the birth of Christ and 20 years more or less before Constantine, when Diocletian was emperor, only the Theban legion was Christian; and for this very reason was slain by the rest of the army at Octodurum in Gaul. They did not conspire with Cassius, Albinus, or Niger: [59] and does not Tertullian count it in their favor that they did not shed their blood for the infidel? It is then apparent that the Christians were unable to free themselves from the power of the emperors; that it would in no way have helped them to conspire with others while gentile emperors reigned.

I shall proceed to demonstrate that afterwards Christians warred [68] on tyrants, used arms in their own defence, and frequently punished the crimes of tyrants. First of all Constantine when a Christian crushed in war his colleague Licinius, the oppressor of the eastern Christians; indicating by this action that one magistrate can chastise another. For the sake of his subjects, he punished Licinius who ruled as his equal, and did not leave the vengeance to God alone.[60] If Con-

[59] Avidius Cassius rebelled against M. Aurelius. Clodius Albinus and Pescennius Niger were rivals of Septimus Severus for the throne. Salmasius, quoting from Tertullian's *Apologeticum,* said Christians had no part in these conspiracies (*Regia,* 1649, p. 88, ll. 30–31).

[60] At the conference of Carnuntum in 308 Constantine was called on to resign the title of Augustus and to become Caesar again under Licinius as second em-

stantine had likewise oppressed the people under his authority, Licinius could have decreed the same punishment for him.

Since this matter has been transferred from God to man, why is not the relationship of Parliament to Charles that of Constantine to Licinius? Constantine was put in office by the soldiers; Parliament by law—which made it the equal or indeed the superior of the king. The Arian Emperor Constans [61] was opposed with arms by the Byzantines as long as they could; when Hermogenes was sent with soldiers to drive from his church the orthodox bishop Paul, they attacked and defeated him [Hermogenes], burned the building to which he fled, and slew him half burned and wounded as he was. Constans threatened his brother Constantius with war if he did not return their bishoprics to Paul and Athanasius. See you how, when their bishop's office was at stake, these saintly fathers of yours did not scruple to urge war between brothers and against their king. Soon afterwards, when the Christian soldiery were making whom they would emperor, they slew Constans son of Constantine for his corrupt and haughty rule and gave the empire to Magnentius.[62] Were not indeed those who hailed Julian as Emperor, not yet an apostate but faithful and active, though Constantius their own emperor opposed this act, among those Christians whom you urge on us as examples? [63] When Constantius sharply

---

peror. Licinius married Constantine's sister in 313, but subsequently quarreled with Constantine and was defeated by him in battle in 314.

[61] Milton is confused about this episode in Roman history. The similarity in nomenclature between the people concerned may partly explain this—Constans, Constantius, and Constantinus, all sons of Constantine I surnamed "the Great." Constans, who was not an Arian as Milton states, was allotted Italy and Illyrium on the division of his father's empire, while Constantius was made emperor of the East, and Constantine II the emperor of the West. Constantius became sole emperor after 350. Of the sons of Constantine I, Constans and Constantine II were on the side of the Nicenes; Constantius, to whom had been allotted the East, was an Arianiser. Milton has confused Constans with Constantius. As the text below reads, Constans the "Arian" is compelling the return of bishoprics to the *orthodox* "Paul and Athanasius"! Constans was not an Arian. Rather it is Constans the *orthodox* compelling the *Arian,* Constantius, Emperor of the East! Constans restored Athanasius to his see in Alexandria in 346.

[62] His brother Constantine II attacked Constans in 340, but was defeated and killed. Constans, after his brother's death, is referred to as Emperor of the West. He was killed in the rebellion of Magnentius, in the Pyrenees, in 350.

[63] *Regia,* 1649, p. 91, ll. 23–26. Salmasius says that Christians obeyed faithfully such a tyrant. On p. 90, ll. 32–35 of the *Regia* (1649), Salmasius maintains that no Christians refused to reverence Julian or rebelled against him who had harassed them more than any pagan emperor.

forbade this act in a letter read to the people, they all cried that they had done as the governor, the army, and the civil officials had ordered. These same people declared war on Constantius and did their best to depose and kill him.

What of the Antiochenes, those notable Christians? I suppose they prayed for Julian in his apostasy, when they used to come up to him in public and heap abuse on him, ordering him by way of mockery to make a rope out of that long beard of his. [69] They proclaimed public thanksgiving, banquets, and rejoicing on news of his death, and do you suppose that their prayers for his life and health were profuse? Indeed it is said that he was killed by a fellow-soldier who was a Christian. The church historian Sozomen [64] certainly does not deny this, and indeed praises any such act: "It is not surprising that one of the soldiers had such thoughts, for down to this period not only Greeks but all men used to praise tyrannicides who did not hesitate to risk death for the liberty of all; and none should rashly censure this soldier who fought so hard for God and for the faith." These are the words of the contemporary writer Sozomen, a good and holy man; so that we can easily see what the other good men of this period thought on the subject.

When Ambrose himself was ordered by the emperor Valentinian II to leave Milan he would not obey,[65] but surrounded himself with an armed throng and defended his person and his church by arms against the royal prefects; thus daring to oppose the supreme power in contradiction to his own teaching. More than once at Constantinople the exile of Chrysostom caused dangerous revolts against Arcadius.[66] And so what the early Christians did against tyrants, what not only soldiers but the people, and the fathers themselves did by way of resistance or making war or stirring it up, right down to the time of Augustine, since you wish to go no further, I have set forth in brief.

[64] *Ecclesiastical History,* VI, 2, in *Fathers, N. and P. N. 2,* II, 346.

[65] Valentinian II (371–392) supported the Arians against Saint Ambrose, bishop of Milan (340?–397). Gratian, the younger son of Valentinian I, supported Ambrose. When Maximus, however, usurped supreme power in Gaul, Valentinian II sent Gregory to him to dissuade him from a descent on Italy. In 392 Valentinian II was assassinated, and Eugenius usurped power. See below, p. 418, n. 69.

[66] Arcadius (378–408), elder son of Theodosius the Great, was created Augustus in 383, succeeded his father in 395. He banished John Chrysostom, patriarch of Constantinople, in 404.

Of the murder by the patrician Maximus of Placidia's son Valentinian [67] for misconduct with his wife I say nothing; that the Emperor Avitus,[68] who discharged his soldiers and was wasting away in excesses, was quickly driven from power by the Roman Senate is not mentioned here. These events took place some years after Augustine's death. You may enjoy this gift from me and suppose I have related none of these tales; but even if the early Christians had obeyed their kings in every case and neither done nor wished to do anything against tyrants, I shall still show that they were not men on whose authority we should rely or from whom we can safely seek examples. Long before Constantine the body of Christians had lost much of their early [70] holiness and purity of faith and morals. After Constantine had endowed the church with huge resources and had begun to long for position and power and civil authority, everything rushed headlong to destruction. First luxury and laziness, then a throng of every heresy and vice, crowded into the church as though somewhere their cells had been opened. Thus jealousy, hatred, and strife became common everywhere; and finally there was as much dissension between these brothers bound by the dearest ties of faith as between the fiercest foes; no shame or sense of duty remained; whenever they wished, soldiers and army commanders set up new emperors or slew good and bad alike. What need to speak of men like Vetrannio or Maximus or Eugenius suddenly raised to power by the troops, of Gratian, best of rulers, or Valentinian II, by no means the worst, murdered by them.[69]

[67] Valentinian III, Emperor of the West (425–455), son of Constantius, was slain by followers of Aëtius whom Valentinian had himself slain the previous year. Petronius Maximus was proclaimed emperor immediately after Valentinian's murder (March 16, 455) and was himself murdered three months later.

[68] The only Roman emperor who meets Milton's description of discharging soldiers and "wasting away in excesses, who was driven from power by the Roman Senate" is Varius Avitus (A. D. 218–222), known as Heliogabalus (Elagabalus), a high priest of the Syrian cult of the sun god. His name was struck from the roll of Roman emperors. He discharged part of the army in order to finance his splendid ceremonials. He cannot be included in the events that took place "after Augustine's death" (d. 430). In fact, of the previous events mentioned, only the reference to Valentinian III took place after Augustine's death.

[69] Vetrannio died in 356 at Prusa, Asia Minor, reputed to be a very old man. The date of his birth is unknown. He was commanding general in Illyria and Pannonia when Magnentius revolted against Constantius in 350 A. D. He warned Constantius about the impending revolt. But, under pressure from the army with whom he was very popular, he briefly assumed the purple himself. On Christmas,

These were indeed the acts of soldiers and officers, but, nevertheless, Christians of the era you call so evangelical and ask us to imitate.

Now hear a few tales of the churchmen. Pastors and bishops and some of our admired fathers, leaders of their flocks, fought for bishoprics as for a tyrant's power. Throughout the city, in the church itself, and at the very altar, without any distinction, priest and layman battled to the death; they murdered and slew with great destruction on either side. Perhaps you remember Damasus and Urcisinus in the time of Ambrose.[70] There is no need to recall the riots at Byzantium and Antioch and those at Alexandria particularly led by Cyril, a father praised by you as an advocate of obedience.[71] In the battle in that city Theodosius' prefect Orestes was nearly killed by the monks.

Your impudence or carelessness would amaze anyone: "Down to Augustine and after his time history mentions no plot of any citizen or officer or group to kill their king or take arms against him"; [72] from famous histories [73] I have named both citizens and leaders who

---

350, he abdicated in favor of Constantius, and retired as a private citizen to Asia Minor.

The Eastern empire devolved upon Gratian (375–83) when the infant son of Valentinian I was proclaimed emperor under the title of Valentinian II. Gratian ceded it to Theodosius I in 379. Gratian was overthrown by Magnus Maximus II, who, by an agreement in 385 or 386, was recognized as Augustus and sole emperor in Gaul, Spain, and Britain, while Valentinian II had control over Italy and Illyricum. In 387 Maximus crossed the Alps and forced Valentinian II to flee to Theodosius, who subsequently defeated Maximus in 388. After the death of Maximus, Theodosius I conferred upon Valentinian II all that part of the empire his father (Valentinian I) had held. Arbogest slew Valentinian II and set up the grammarian Eugenius in his place in May, 392. Eugenius, in turn, was defeated and slain by Theodosius in September, 394.

[70] After the death of Pope Liberius in 366, two factions of clergy respectively supported Damasus and Ursinus (the latter name with four alternative spellings according to Espasa Calpe's *Diccionario Universal*—Ursinus, Urcinus, Urcisinus, Ursisinus—the last spellings may have originally been derogatory). The bishop of Tibur consecrated Ursinus as pope; the bishop of Ostia consecrated Damasus. Although Ursinus was banished to Cologne where he died in 381, the schism continued under the successor of Damasus, Zozinus.

[71] Milton apparently considers the two quotations that Salmasius makes from Cyril (*Regia,* p. 86, ll. 37 ff.; 87, ll. 2–9) as implying Salmasius' praise of him as an "advocate of obedience." Both quotations emphasize the importance of peace for the church, but there is no suggestion made in Salmasius of peace at all costs, of obedience in a slavish sense.

[72] *Regia,* 1649, p. 94, ll. 5–8.

[73] The church histories of Socrates Scholasticus and Sozomen.

with their own hands slew kings good and bad alike, and whole armies of Christians [71] and many bishops too who fought against their emperors! You call in fathers who advocate or boast of obedience to the king in many words; I call in those same fathers and others as well who in as many deeds cast off their obedience, even in lawful matters, and with arms defended themselves against the emperor, some using force and violence against his deputies, some who strove for bishoprics fighting civil wars with each other. But I suppose it was right for Christian to fight against Christian, citizen against citizen, for bishoprics, though wrong to fight for freedom, wife and child, or life itself against a tyrant. Such fathers would make anyone ashamed.

You drag in Augustine's dictum that "a master's power over his slaves and a king's power over his subjects" [74] are the same. I reply that, if Augustine spoke thus, he said what Christ and his Apostles never did, though he supports what is otherwise an evident falsehood by their authority alone; and furthermore, if he did speak thus, my cause is not injured, for of a master's power over his slaves he said in *The City of God,* book 19, chapter 14: "In the house of a just man who lives in accordance with the faith, even he who commands serves those he seems to command"; if, as you claim, he said the same of a king's power over his subjects and did not contradict himself, he stated that kings, especially good ones, do in fact serve those they seem to command: and in *The City of God,* IV, 4, he certainly made the statement that the power of a wicked king over his subjects and that of a robber over those he meets is the same: "Without justice what are kingdoms but great gangs of thieves, for gangs of thieves are themselves nothing but little kingdoms?" Look at your Augustinian derivation of that wondrous right of kings to dare what they will; how this power is one and the same as that of thieves, not of painters or poets.

The remaining three or four pages of this chapter are pure lies or the same old boring matter, as anyone may see from my rebuttal above. As to the pope, of whom you have so much beside the point to say, I would gladly have you shout yourself hoarse. As to your long harangue to catch the ignorant with the argument [72] that "every Christian obeyed his king, whether he were good or tyrannical, until

[74] *Regia* (1649), p. 93, ll. 6–8.

papal power began to be recognized as superior to royal, and freed subjects from their oath of allegiance," [75] I have demonstrated its utter falsehood by countless instances up to Augustine's time and beyond.

Your final statement [76] that Pope Zachary freed the French from their oath of allegiance is no nearer the truth.[77] Francis Hotman, a Frenchman and a lawyer who is most often cited, denies in Chapter 13 of his *Franco-gallia* [78] that Chilperic was deposed by papal authority or that the realm was offered to Pepin; [79] the affair was carried out in the great popular assembly according to its ancient right, as he proves from the oldest French records. Furthermore both the documents of the French and pope Zachary himself deny that there was any need to absolve the French from that oath. These French documents relate, on the testimony of Hotman and also of Girard,[80] the most famous historian of that people, that the ancient Franks had kept to themselves from the earliest days the right of choosing and deposing their kings as they saw fit. The only pledge which it was their custom to swear to the kings they appointed was to render them faithful obedience on condition that the kings, in turn, stood by the oath they swore

---

[75] Apparently this is a summary of Salmasius' position as stated in *Regia,* 1649, p. 96, ll. 16–28, rather than a direct quotation. Apostolic tradition, according to Salmasius, demanded reverence even for wicked kings. This tradition broke down when a power greater than kingly ("holiness"—the pope's title) became known to history. The Roman church introduced this in place of imperial rule. The pope punishes kings, deprives them of kingdoms, gives kingdoms to others, releases subjects from their oath of allegiance.

[76] *Regia,* 1649, p. 98, ll. 3–5. See below, p. 471, n. 81.

[77] In the *Commonplace Book* (*Complete Prose,* I, 444), Milton quotes Sigonius, *De Regno Italiae,* who gives an alternative version to the one supported by Milton here: "From Chilperic Pope Zacharias takes away his kingdom because of his idleness, thus freeing the Franks from the obligation of their oath of allegiance." Milton disagrees with Salmasius' interpretation that the pope first frees the people from their oath of fealty preparatory to deposing a king. According to Salmasius' interpretation of Zachary, the people can always depose a king, but the Pope alone may release them from an oath of fealty. Sigonius would have the release from the oath a consequence of the actual deposition.

[78] For an account of the *Franco-Gallia,* see *Complete Prose,* I, 459, n. 6.

[79] *Franco-Gallia,* pp. 90–97.

[80] Milton quotes Bernard de Girard (*ca.* 1535–1610) several times in the *Commonplace Book.* The work to which Milton refers is *L'Histoire de France.* The quotation in *Complete Prose,* I, 461, is pertinent here: "It should be noted that until the time of Hugh Capet all the kings of France were elected by the French, who kept for themselves this power, to choose, to exile, and to drive out their kings."

at the same time. Therefore if the kings have been the first to break faith by their maladministration of the state which has been entrusted to them there is no need for the pope to intervene when the kings, by their own faithlessness, have absolved the people of their oath. Finally, Pope Zachary, who, you say, claimed this authority, disclaimed it himself in the letter to the Franks which you cited,[81] and ascribed it [such authority] to the people. If "the ruler is liable to punishment by the people through whose favor he rules, if the populace appoints the king and can depose him," as the pope himself expresses it, it is most unlikely that the Franks wished to impair their ancient right by any later oath whatsoever, or ever obliged themselves to give up the privileges their fathers had enjoyed of giving all honor to good kings but removing bad ones; nor did they intend to render to tyrants the same obedience as to good kings. When a people is bound by such an oath [73] and their king turns tyrant or degenerates through his worthlessness, they are released from their bond by his faithlessness, by justice herself, and by the very law of nature; and so in the judgment of the pope himself there was nothing at all for the pope to release.

[81] St. Zacharias (pope, 741–752), according to Salmasius "the first high priest who dared release the French from their oath of fealty," encouraged the deposition of Childeric and, with his sanction, St. Boniface crowned Pippin king of the Franks at Soissons in 752.

The "letter cited" is described by Salmasius as "Epistola ad eosdem consilium petentes de Chilperico abdicando." The explicit quotation from the letter is contained in *Regia* (1649), p. 98, ll. 7–10: *"Principem, nempe, populo cuius beneficio regnum possidet obnoxium esse. Quaecumque enim habet potentiam, gloriam, divitias, dignitatem, a populo accipere, & plebi accepta referre necesse esse. Regem plebem constituere, eundem & destituere posse."* Salmasius equates this statement with the false doctrines of the fanatical Independents of England. Salmasius, who is simultaneously committed to attacking papal doctrine and Independency, maintains, however, that where an oath of fealty has been taken by the people to the king, the pope claims that he alone may release them from that oath. By this device the popes extended their political power though, it is implied, the papal theory of kingship was about as radical as that of the Independents.

CHAPTER V[1]

I now believe, as I have always done, Salmasius, that the law of God does most closely agree with the law of nature,[2] and therefore that I have sufficiently demonstrated what divine law has decreed concerning kings, and what has been the practice of God's people both Jewish and Christian. I have at the same time shown by this single demonstration what is most conformable to the law of nature. Nevertheless, since you suppose "that we can now be most

[1] In book V (*Regia,* 1649, pp. 100–129) Salmasius argues that two erroneous conceptions of kingship exist. One concept is that the pope has authority over the king. Another concept is that supreme authority resides in the people, to whom the king is minister and servant. The Independents subscribe to the second concept.

The main threads of Salmasius' argument run as follows: 1. The theory of kingship is founded on the law of nature, although the Independents maintain an opposite interpretation of the law of nature. The very nature of things demands that one person have authority, supreme authority, though he may share his powers with others, whose aid he needs in administering affairs. 2. The king has the same relation to his country as a father to his family. 3. Natural law demands stability of government. Rebellion against the existing government is detrimental to the state and brings about more trouble than the chance misdemeanors of a ruler. 4. The history of the Israelites, Diodorus' account of the Egyptian kings, Herodotus' history of the Persian king, the Greek and Roman writers all confirm this interpretation. All these authorities show that kings have been bound by no laws, but that good kings voluntarily submitted to them. 5. English history shows that three kings were killed in prison: Edward II, Richard II, and Henry VI. The death of Charles is contrasted with that of Julius Caesar and the emperor Nero. 6. In regard to the Jewish kings, there is no record of any one having been judged and condemned by the Sanhedrin. These kings could not be judged, for if they had been, there would have been no difference between them and the judges, and there would have been no point in changing the type of ruler from judges to kings. 7. In considering all the cases of kings slain wickedly or parricidally which may have occurred at any time anywhere, one can find nothing equivalent to that of Charles in the wickedness of the crime and in the method of carrying it out.

[2] As Arthur Barker has pointed out (*Milton and the Puritan Dilemma,* pp. 114 ff.), Milton thinks of a primary and a secondary law of nature. Basing his thinking on Selden's *De Jure Naturali Gentium,* Milton argued in the *Tetrachordon* (*Complete Prose,* II, 661) that

> prime nature made us all equal, made us equal coheirs by common right and dominion over all creatures

but, because of the imperfections and decay of man from original righteousness, nature

> suffered not only divorce but all that which by civilians is termed the 'secondary law of nature and of nations.'

powerfully refuted by the law of nature,"[3] I shall freely admit that what I formerly considered superfluous is now necessary. The result will be that, in this chapter, I shall make it perfectly clear that you are wrong and that there is nothing more in accord with the laws of nature than the punishment of tyrants.

If I fail in this, I shall grant you on the spot that by the laws of God as well they cannot be punished. My plan is not to compose at this time an elaborate discourse about nature and the origins of civil life. Men of learning have treated this topic at length in both Greek

---

The secondary law of nature is an imperfect expression of the original law of nature. Under the Gospel, however, there is a "secondary fresh pencilling of the eternal law by the spirit in the hearts of believers, a renewing of law originally engraven in Adam's breast" (Barker, p. 116). The law of nature, therefore, may refer to the law as it would apply to the regenerate in a Christian commonwealth. In this sense it is only the regenerate who are capable of the "natural" liberty which is the end of just government. The law of nature, in the secondary sense, may apply to the natural right of any people, Christian or otherwise, to freedom from tyranny—but not necessarily to the right of natural liberty, a very different matter (Barker, p. 190). The general belief of Independent Protestantism was that the authority of the magistrates (the king was only a superior kind of magistrate) derived from the secondary law of nature, of nature after the fall. After the fall men perceived that unrestrained violence meant destruction and so "agreed by common league to bind each other from mutual injury"; that because "no faith in all was found sufficiently binding," they deemed it necessary to establish "some authority that might restrain by force and punishment what was violated against the common right"; and that, because of the failings of magistrates, they limited the power of authority by laws and counsellors. It follows, as Milton states in *The Tenure* (*Complete Prose,* III, 202) that

> the power of king and magistrates is no thing else but what is derivative, transferred, and committed to them in trust from the people to the common good of them all, in whom the power yet remains fundamentally and cannot be taken from them without a violation of their natural birth right.

The regenerate need not be exposed to the jurisdiction of the magistrates; they are free by the indwelling of the spirit, they follow a higher law of nature than the secondary law resulting from the fall. Such a view is at the back of Milton's mind when he justifies, as he does in the *Defensio,* a spiritual élite, a minority, taking control in the face of ordinary legal and democratic procedures. The Miltonic thesis that only the wise can enjoy liberty is stated on p. 343 above. "I confess that those who long for liberty or can enjoy it are but a few, only the wise, that is, and the brave." On p. 457, below, Milton justifies the action of the army: "I say it was the people; for why should I not say that the act of the better, the sound part of the Parliament, in which resides the real power of the people, was the act of the people?" The people is, in fact, for Milton the sound and *regenerate* minority, who act according to the *primary* law of nature. For the background of Augustinian theology in regard to the relation of theories of the state to the fall see p. 379, n. 19 above.

[3] *Regia* (1649), p. 101, ll. 30–32.

and Latin. My aim is the greatest possible brevity, and, since I would gladly have avoided the task, I shall let you instead prove yourself false and be your own undoing. I shall therefore start from your own axiom and make it the basis of the rest of the discussion.

"The law of nature," you say, "is that reason innate in all men's minds which considers the welfare of every people where men enjoy mutual association. It cannot secure that common welfare, unless it decide who should rule, since there are persons who must be ruled."[4] This is clearly to prevent the strong from crushing the weak, allowing those whom their mutual safety and defence had brought together to be scattered by violence and outrage [74] and forced to revert to lives of savagery. Is this not your meaning, though you expressed it more wordily? Therefore

> of those who joined together it was necessary to choose some who excelled the rest in wisdom or bravery to hold evil-doers to their duty by force or by persuasion; often a single person of outstanding courage and judgment could accomplish this; sometimes it was more than one whose united counsel would bring it about. Generally, since one man cannot foresee and regulate everything himself, he must consult with several and admit others to a share in the government. Thus whether power be restricted to a single possessor or revert to a whole people, control does in fact always remain in the hands of several persons, for all the people cannot govern a state at the same time and all things cannot be governed by one man.[5]

Below too you state:

> The manner of government is equally natural whether it be through several or a few or one only, since it springs from the principles of this same nature, which forbids an indi-

[4] *Regia* (1649), p. 101, ll. 36 ff.

[5] *Regia* (1649), p. 102, ll. 8–12 correspond to Milton's quotation ending with "persuasion" (line 4). *Regia* (1649), p. 102, ll. 13–14 correspond to Milton's next sentence. A sentence from Salmasius is omitted, "Whence the titles *Duumvir* and *Triumvir* in small states, and even in larger ones." The quotation then follows *Regia*, 1649, p. 102, ll. 14–17, with the concluding part of Salmasius' sentence omitted, "by whom justice is exercised and what concerns war and peace is carried out." The quotation picks up again at *Regia,* 1649, p. 102, ll. 25–29, eight lines later.

vidual so to govern that he has no others as associates in power.[6]

Though I could have gathered as much from book III of Aristotle's *Politics,* I preferred to cite those gleanings you stole from Aristotle, as Prometheus did fire from Jove, to your own destruction and the overthrow of kings. Mull over as you will your definition of the law of nature, you will find there no place for the rights of kings as you describe them, and indeed no trace of them at all. "The law of nature," you say, "in arranging who should rule others, looks to the welfare of all peoples." [7] Not then of one person nor of the king. And so the king exists for the people: the people then are more important than the king and above him; and since the people are above him and more important, there can be no right of a king by which he, the inferior, can injure or enslave the people, his superior. Since a king has no right to do wrong, the rights of the people remain supreme; and so the right by which men first combined their judgment and strength for common defence before kings were created, and by which they placed one or more in charge of the rest to preserve the safety, peace, and freedom of all, is the same right by which they can check or depose either those [75] same persons who for their courage or judgment were put in command, or any others if through sloth, folly, wickedness or treachery they misgovern the state: For nature has always looked, as she now does, not to the dominion of one man or a few, but to the safety of all, whatever may become of the dominion of the one or the few.

Now who is it that the people choose? "Those" you say "who excel the rest in wisdom or bravery," that is those who seem by nature most fit to rule, "whose outstanding courage and judgment can accomplish" that task.[8] Thus there is by nature no right of succession, and no king but the one who surpasses all others in wisdom and bravery; the rest have become kings by force or favor contrary to nature, when they should rather have been slaves. For nature gives the wisest dominion

[6] *Regia* (1649), p. 103, ll. 4–9.

[7] *Regia* (1649), p. 101, 36 ff. Milton's quotation is an excerpt from a much longer sentence: "Clearly the very law of nature, the reasonableness of which is infused into the minds of all men, when it concerns the good of people universally, in so far as men enjoy society among themselves, cannot procure the common good, unless it arranges who ought to rule as well as determining who shall be ruled."

[8] *Regia* (1649), p. 102, ll. 8–10.

over those less wise, not a wicked man dominion over the good or a fool over the wise. Whoever takes away their dominion from such as these behaves altogether in conformity with nature. Listen to your own words as to nature's purpose in appointing the wisest king—"to hold evil-doers to their duty" [9] either to nature or the laws. Can he hold others to their duty who neglects or does not know his own duty, or acts against it?

Tell us any decree of nature which orders us not to observe nature's wisest regulations in public or civic affairs, to pay them no heed and to consider them of no moment, though nature is wont to accomplish great wonders to avoid the frustration of her ends in natural affairs where men are not concerned. Show us any rule of nature or natural justice which makes it right for lesser offenders to be punished but kings and rulers guilty of every crime to be immune, and, on the contrary, even in the midst of all their wickedness, to be honored and adored and treated as next to God himself.

You admit that "the mode of government itself, whether it be carried on by a number or a few or a single person, is equally natural." [10]

By nature then the king is no more sacred than the nobles or the people's magistrates, who may and should, as you granted freely above, be punished if they sin; and so you must admit the same of kings, who are appointed for the same good purpose. "Nature does not allow," you say, "an individual so to govern that he have no others as associates in power." [76] [11] She is then far from allowing a monarch, far from allowing one man, so to rule that all others are made the slaves of his own single dominion. In joining to the king associates in power "in whose hands the government always remains," you give him colleagues and equals, and you bring in those who may punish or depose him.[12] Thus in your usual manner, in attempting not indeed to exalt royal power but merely to base it on nature, you utterly destroy it: with the result that nothing more unfortunate could, I believe, have befallen kings than to have you as their advocate!

You luckless wretch, what darkness so befogged your brain that you were forced into this error, exposing and revealing to everyone

[9] *Regia* (1649), p. 102, l. 11. [10] Regia (1649), p. 103, ll. 4–5.

[11] *Regia* (1649), p. 103, 6–7.

[12] "Associates in power": *alios socios imperandi*. Salmasius does not imply that the associates share the sovereignty, but the administration, a point overlooked by Milton on p. 427 below.

by your own ignorant and ambitious attempt that vice and folly you had formerly concealed and masked so long, selling your services at the price of your own shame, and becoming so tamely the bond slave of your own derision? What was the divine anger, what were the penalties you had incurred, which brought your name into the open and put it on the tongues of men, leading you to defend so ostentatiously this abominable case with equal impudence and folly, and in defending betray it against your will through utter ignorance? Who could wish to see you more cruelly crushed or more wretched than you now are, when only folly or madness can save you from being the most wretched of men by dashing your hopes, and making the tyrants you support more hated and detested by all, for your inept and unwise defence? Thus rashly you array more enemies against them in proportion to your intentional grant to them of license to do evil and to rule unpunished.

I return now to your war with yourself. Being so criminal as to wish to give tyranny some basis in nature, you saw you must first extol monarchy above other forms of government, but, as usual, could not begin without some inconsistency. Having just said, "The manner of government, whether by several or a few or one only, is equally natural," you immediately tell us that "the manner of government administered by one man is the most natural of the three,"[13] despite your own recent statement that "nature does not allow an individual to be sole governor."[14] Accuse now whom you will of slaying tyrants, when you have by your own stupidity slaughtered all kings and kingship itself. Whether the government of one man or several is in fact the better [77] cannot be discussed here. Monarchy has indeed been praised by many famous men, provided that the sole ruler is the best of men and fully deserving of the crown; otherwise monarchy sinks most rapidly into the worst tyranny. As to your saying it was "patterned on the example of the one God,"[15] who, in fact, is worthy of

[13] On the basis of analogy to the exemplar, God, who alone established all things and so governs them (*Regia,* 1649, p. 103, ll. 12–14).

[14] Milton's method of quoting sometimes ignores the real meaning of Salmasius. Salmasius had asserted (*Regia,* 1649, p. 103, ll. 6–7) that nature did not allow an individual to be sole ruler in the sense that he should *not* have associates in administration. Salmasius makes an implicit distinction between a *gubernator* ("one who governs") and *socii imperandi* ("associates in administration"). They are not on the same level. But a *gubernator* should have *socii imperandi.*

[15] *Regia* (1649), p. 103, l. 13.

holding on earth power like that of God but some person who far surpasses all others and even resembles God in goodness and wisdom? The only such person, as I believe, is the son of God whose coming we look for. As to your forced comparison of kingdom with a family to allow an analogy of a king to a family head—it is true that a father should rule his family, since he begot or supports all its members. But none of this applies to a king—quite the opposite. You next set up for our imitation gregarious animals, birds particularly, including bees, for in your system of nature-study these are birds! "Bees have a king." [16] Those of Trent, I suppose, as you perhaps recall? The others, as you affirm, have republics. You should really give up this nonsense about bees; they belong to the Muses and hate insects like you and, as you see, refute you. "Quails are led by their Quail-Mother." [17] Set those snares for your own pelicans; we are not caught by such foolish fowling.

"The cock of the roost commands males as well as females." [18] Indeed this is your concern, not ours! How can this be? For you are yourself a Gallic cock and said to be rather cocky, but instead of commanding your mate, she commands and hen-pecks you; and if the cock is king of many hens while you are the slave of yours, you must be no cock of the roost but a mere dung-hill Frenchman! As far as books go, certainly no one has heaped up more dung than you, whose crowing over your heap deafens everyone; this is the one characteristic of the cock which you possess.[19] I promise to stuff you with chicken feed if by pecking through this whole dunghill of yours you can find me a single gem. But why give you chicken feed? For unlike Aesop's plain and simple cock you eat not that, and like Plautus' scoundrel seek rather gold for your scratchings; but with a different outcome [78] so far, for you unearthed one hundred gold sovereigns, though you deserved death by Euclio's stick far more than the poor little bird in Plautus.

To proceed: "Considerations of expediency and safety alike demand that whoever is once appointed to rule be kept in office." [20] No

16 *Regia* (1649), p. 103, ll. 23–24.

17 "Coturnices sub Ortygometra duce trans mare abeunt & inde ad nos redeunt" (*Regia*, 1649, p. 103, ll. 24–25). Milton omits the poetic association.

18 *Regia* (1649), p. 103, ll. 27–28.

19 Plautus, *Aulularia*, 465, tr. Paul Nixon (5 vols., London: Loeb Classical Library, 1937), I, 282–83. Milton plays with puns on *Gallus*, a Frenchman, and *gallus*, a cock, and related words.

20 *Regia* (1649), p. 103, ll. 33–35.

one denies this insofar as his preservation is consistent with the general safety, but that one should be preserved to the ruin of all is seen by everyone to be quite contrary to nature. You however wish to preserve at all costs "a bad king as well, or even the worst, for the evil brought on the state by his bad government is less than the slaughter arising from the sedition stirred up to remove him." [21] What has this to do with the natural rights of kings? I suppose you would say that if nature warns me to let myself be plundered by robbers or, when captured, to spend all my goods on ransom rather than be forced to fight for my life, that this constitutes a natural right of robbers? Nature bids the people yield at times to tyrants' violence or to circumstances; but are you going to base a natural right of tyrants on such extremities of sufferings of the people? Will you assert that the right granted the people by nature for their own preservation was actually granted the people by nature for the destruction of the people? Nature teaches us to choose the lesser of two evils and to endure while we must; will you set up for tyrants, though they may at times be the lesser evil, a natural right of doing evil with impunity?

Recall at least your former writings opposing the Jesuit on Episcopacy which I cited above in the third chapter and which clearly contradicts this.[22] There you assert that "the plots and quarrels and conflicts between nobles and people are a far lighter evil than the certain wretchedness and ruin under a single tyrannical king." [23] And even you then spoke the truth, for you were not yet raving; you had not yet been gilded by Charles' sovereigns or contracted this royal disease of gold fever. Were you anyone else I should say you had finally become ashamed of your foul lies, but you could easier burst than blush, and long ago lost all sense of shame in your greed for gold!

Perhaps you may recall that the palmiest days of the Roman republic were after the expulsion of the kings? [79] Could you forget the Dutch, whose republic, after they had driven out the Spanish king in long wars successfully waged, by glorious courage won her free-

[21] *Regia* (1649), p. 104, ll. 10–14.

[22] On pp. 390–91, above, Milton quoted Salmasius' work against Petavius, in which Salmasius found a republican form of government superior to that of a monarchy, and from the same work again on p. 397 above, a passage in which Salmasius contends that the pope may be driven out because of his tyranny.

[23] Salmasius, *De Episcopis ac Presbyteris* (Leyden, 1641), p. 412: "Quis non perferre mallet in republica Aristocratico regimine gubernata ex optimatum aemulatione dissentiones oriri solitas, quam ex uno monarcha tyrannico more imperare consueto certam miseriam ac perniciem?"

dom? Now at her own expense the republic supports you as a knight of the blackboard, not, we hope, that the Dutch youths may from your lying sophistry learn to be so foolish as to choose a return to Spanish slavery rather than fall heir to the glorious freedom of their fathers! Carry off these corrupt teachings to farthest Siberia and her frozen ocean, and go with them yourself to the devil!

Finally you take as example the English, who executed their tyrant Charles after he became their prisoner in war and proved incurable. You say that "by their conflict they mutilated an island which under her kings had been happy and luxurious." [24] Nearly ruined by luxury rather, to make it less conscious of its servitude, and with its laws annulled and its religion sold into bondage, when the English freed it from slavery. Behold this editor of Epictetus complete with Simplicius,[25] this sober Stoic, who finds that "an island steeped in luxury" is happy! [26] No such teaching, I am sure, ever issued from Zeno's porch.[27]

But what of that? Will you teach that kings may do what they will, but find yourself, the great Tomcat, forbidden to publish from your cat house as from some fine chateau, whatever philosophy you please? [28] But put on your mask again.

"Never was so much blood spilled, so many families destroyed, under any king." [29] But all this must be laid to Charles' account, not to the English people; he first raised a host of Irishmen against us and

[24] *Regia* (1649), p. 104, ll. 19–21.

[25] Salmasius had published *Simplicii Commentarius in Enchiridion Epicteti* (Leyden: 1640; NYPL).

[26] Zeno of Citium, of Phoenician descent (*ca.* 350 B. C.), was regarded as the founder of the Stoic school of philosophy.

[27] ". . . beatam sub regibus suis, & luxu copiisque . . ." (*Regia,* 1649, p. 104, l. 21).

[28] Milton here has another series of puns: *lupus, lupanar,* and *lyceum.*

[29] *Regia* (1649), p. 104, l. 24. When Milton writes here that the Irish had killed 200,000 English in Ulster alone, he reaches a new peak of exaggeration. In *Eikonoklastes,* Chapter XII, he had claimed that the Irish had killed 154,000 in Ulster alone. In the second edition of *Eikonoklastes* (1650) Milton asserted that "the total summ of that slaughter in all likelihood [was] fowr times as great." This would have made the Irish rebels guilty of 600,000 English deaths. Milton's contemporary John Temple estimated 300,000. According to Ferdinando Warner (whose analysis was accepted by Gardiner, *History of England,* X, 69), the actual number of English slaughtered in the Irish Revolt may have been four thousand; eight thousand more may have died of ill usage. See *Complete Prose,* I, 169, n. 7.

by his own warrant bade all Ireland rise against the English. Through their agency some 200,000 English were slain by him in the single province of Ulster, to say nothing of the rest. He tried to raise two armies to destroy the Parliament of England and the city of London, and performed many other hostile acts, before the magistrates or people raised a single soldier to defend the state. What teachings of law or religion ever instructed men to consider their own ease and the saving of money or blood or life more important than meeting the enemy? Does it matter whether the enemy be foreign or domestic? Either one threatens the state with the same bitter [80] and ruinous destruction. All Israel saw that without much shedding of blood she could not avenge the outrage and murder of the Levite's wife;[30] did they think that for this reason they must hold their peace, avoid civil war however fierce, or allow the death of a single poor woman to go unpunished? Surely if nature tells us to endure the tyranny of the worst of kings rather than risk the safety of many citizens in recovering our freedom, she also tells us to endure not only a king, who alone must in your opinion be endured, but also the dominion of the nobles or an oligarchy—or at times even a host of robbers or rebellious slaves. Fulvius and Rupilius [31] would not have fought the servile war after the slaughter of the praetors' armies, nor would Crassus have moved against Spartacus [32] when the consular forces had been wiped out, nor Pompey against the pirates.[33] The Romans would have yielded to slaves or pirates, on nature's command doubtless, to avoid spilling the blood of so many citizens. And so "this feeling" or any resembling it, you have never shown "to be implanted by nature in mankind"; and yet you continue to predict evil and to call down on us God's vengeance. I trust he will rather direct such vengeance against you and other such prophets, for we did but impose a well-deserved punishment on one who was our king in name alone, being in fact our fiercest foe, and we expiated the deaths of countless good citizens by the execution of their murderer.

You next say that monarchy is nearer to nature because "both

[30] Judges 14–21. The story of the Levite whose wife was violated and murdered by the men of Gibeah, Benjamites. He roused the Israelites to civil war against the offenders, in vengeance for the deed.

[31] Fulvius Flaccus and Rupilius, consuls in 134 and 132 B.C., fought against a slave revolt in Sicily.

[32] Crassus crushed the revolt of Spartacus in 71 B.C.

[33] Pompey routed the pirates in 67 B.C.

now and formerly more nations have adopted government by a king than by nobles or people." [34] I reply first that this has not happened on the urging of God or of nature. God would not have his people under a king's rule save with his opposition. What is commanded by nature and good sense may best be seen in the case of the wisest nations rather than the greatest number of them. Greeks and Romans, Italians and Carthaginians and many besides have of their own accord preferred government by nobles or people to that of a king; and surely these nations were more important than all the rest. Thus Sulpicius Severus reports that "the name of king has ever been hateful to nearly all free peoples." [35] In fact, however, all this, like what follows so copiously, being your usual footless repetition, is now irrelevant. [81]

I hasten to show by examples what I have established by reason, namely, that it is most in accordance with nature for tyrants to suffer any punishment, and that on nature's own instructions all peoples have often brought this about. Thus your shamelessness will be proclaimed and your foul licence in lying become known to all.

As your first example you cite the Egyptians; and indeed anyone might see that you are an outright gyp. "Nowhere in their history," you say, "is there an account of any king being slain by the people in a rebellion, nor was any war waged or action taken by the people to drive one from the throne." [36] What then of Osiris,[37] perhaps the first Egyptian king? Was he not slain by his brother Typho [38] and twenty-five other conspirators? Did not a great part of the people follow them and enter a great conflict with Isis and Horus, the king's wife and son? I omit Sesostris [39] who was nearly cut off by his brother's

[34] *Regia* (1649), p. 105, ll. 16–19.

[35] Sulpicius Severus, *Historia Sacra,* I, 32. *Cf. Commonplace Book,* in *Complete Prose,* I, 440.

[36] *Regia* (1649), p. 108, ll. 10 ff.

[37] Osiris was an agricultural deity of Syrian origin, venerated at Mendes, part of a triad consisting additionally of Isis and the child Orus. He was later identified at Memphis with two local gods of the dead, the hawk, Sotri, and the bull, Apis. Later, as god of the underworld, he becomes identified with the nightly progress of the sun.

[38] The giant Typhoeus or Typhon was identified with the god Set, god of the sirocco, of death, blight, of the eclipse of the sun and moon, and of the barren sea, the author of all evil and the murderer of his brother Osiris.

[39] Sesostris was evidently a mythical figure, satisfying the pride of Egyptians after contact with the great conquerors from Assyria and Persia. According to Diodorus, he conquered the whole world, including even Scythia and Ethiopia. He seems to be a compound of Set I and Rameses II in the XIXth Egyptian dynasty.

plots; Chemmis and Chephren too,[40] deservedly hated of the people, who threatened to tear them to pieces after death when they could not during their lives. Think you that men who dared to cut down the best of kings would have been restrained by the light of nature or any scruples from laying hands on the worst? Or that those who threatened to cast from their tombs kings who were dead and finally harmless, in a land where the humblest corpse was inviolate, would have feared to punish by nature's law kings who were alive and dyed with guilt, if only they had possessed the power? You, I know, might make such statements, however foolish they may be; but to prevent you from daring to make them I shall make you mute. Be it known then that many centuries before Chephren, Ammosis [41] ruled the Egyptians and was as bad a tyrant as ever was; the Egyptians put up with him patiently. You triumph: This is what you wish. But hear what comes next, O noble friend of truth, as I quote the words of Diodorus: "They endured their oppression for a time, for they had no means of resisting those who were stronger." [42] But when King Actisanes of Ethiopia began to wage war against Ammosis, many seized their opportunity and revolted, and after Ammosis had been easily subdued, Egypt was added to the Ethiopian realm. Here you see that, as soon as they could, the Egyptians took up arms against their tyrant, [82] joined forces with a foreign king to depose their own and his descendants, and preferred a good and temperate king like Actisanes, even though he was a foreigner, to their native tyrant. With remarkable unanimity these same Egyptians, when their tyrant Apries and his mercenaries had been defeated in battle under the leadership of Amasis, strangled him and handed over the realm to the noble Amasis.[43] Note this too:

[40] Cheops, in Herodotus, is the name of the king who built the great pyramid in Egypt. He reigned for fifty years and was succeeded by his brother, Chephren, who reigned fifty-six years and built the second pyramid.

[41] Amasis or Ammosis II (Greek forms of the name Ahmase, Ahmosis, meaning "the moon is born") reigned 570–526 B.C. Most of the information extant about him is found in Herodotus, II, 161 ff.

[42] Diodorus Siculus, I, ix, 2, in *Diodorus of Sicily,* tr. C. H. Oldfather (10 vols., London and New York: Loeb Classical Library, 1933–47), I, 206–207.

[43] According to Herodotus, II, 161, *et seq.,* troops on the way home after a disastrous expedition to Cyrene suspected they had been betrayed by Apries, the reigning king, so that he might increase his absolute power by the help of mercenaries. Amasis, sent by Apries to quell the revolt, was proclaimed king by the rebels. Apries was defeated, taken prisoner, and after three years was handed over to the populace, who strangled him.

Amasis for a time treated the captured king well and kept him in the palace itself, until, on the complaint of the people that he did wrong to support one who was his enemy and theirs too, he handed over the king to them, and they exacted the penalty I mentioned. This account is in Herodotus and Diodorus.[44] What more do you want? Do you not suppose that any tyrant would have preferred the axe to the noose? When later the Egyptians were brought into the Persian empire, you say they remained faithful: This is sheer lying, for they never stayed faithful to Persia, but rebelled four years after their subjection by Cambyses.[45] They were again mastered by Xerxes,[46] but soon revolted from his son Artaxerxes, and chose a certain Inarus [47] as their king. With him they were conquered but seceded again and made war on Artaxerxes Mnemon when they had made Tachus [48] king. They were however no more loyal to their own king, for, having taken the crown from the father, they gave it to his son Nectanebus, until at last Artaxerxes Ochus [49] brought them once more under Persian control. Even under the Macedonian kingdom they showed by deeds as far as they could that tyrants should be punished; they threw down the statues and likenesses of Ptolemy Physcon,[50] though with his mercenary armies he was so strong that they could not

44 Herodotus, II, 161 ff., and Diodorus, I, 21 ff., I, 53 ff.

45 Cambyses of Persia, son of Cyrus and of a daughter of Apries, the deposed king of Egypt, threatened an invasion of Egypt during the last years of the reign of usurper Amasis II, but the blow actually fell on his son, Psammetichus III, in 525 B.C. An account is to be found in Herodotus, III, 2, 4.

46 Xerxes I of Persia, son of Darius I, ascended throne, 485 B.C., was murdered in 464. He suppressed a revolt in Egypt in 486.

47 Artaxerxes I (465–425) put down a rebellion in Egypt led by Inarus (Inaros) after a long struggle (460–454) against a coalition of Egyptians and Athenians.

48 Artaxerxes II (404–359) surnamed Mnemon, the eldest son of Darius II, could not subdue a revolting Egypt. Two expeditions (385–383 and 374–372) both failed. Tachos (Teos) of Egypt secured a body of Greek mercenaries under Spartan king Argesilaus and a fleet under Athenian general Chabrias to fight the Persians. But Tachos offended Argesilaus, and his crown was given to his son Nekhtharheb (Latinized by Milton to Nectanebus), the last of the Pharaohs.

49 Artaxerxes III Ochus (359–338) caused two invasions of Egypt. The first in 346 failed. The second in 343 personally led by Ochus succeeded.

50 Ptolemy Physcon was Ptolemy VII (Euergetes II), put on the throne by Alexandrians and subsequently surnamed Physcon because of his bloated appearance. He was the younger brother of Ptolemy VI (Philometor) who reigned 181–145, with whom and his sister Cleopatra, he agreed to be a joint king. After numerous quarrels, he was made in 163, after Roman arbitration, separate king of Cyrenaica.

kill him. A tumult of the people drove into exile his son Alexander because he slew his mother; in turn his son Alexander [51] was for his cruel tyranny torn violently from the palace and killed in the public gymnasium by the people of Alexandria.[52] For his many misdeeds Ptolemy Auletes [53] too was driven from the realm.

Since these facts are so well known that a scholar could not, and one who professes to teach and expects credence in such important matters should not, be ignorant of them, everyone must think it a shame and a disgrace that such an unlettered [83] ignoramus struts so proudly as a scholar, bringing honest learning into disrepute, and goes about soliciting pay from kings and commonwealths, or that such a shameless liar is not branded with some extraordinary mark of shame and driven from all association and fellowship with men of virtue or learning.

Now that we have finished with Egypt, let us look at Ethiopia next. They believe their king is chosen by God and they worship him as if he were a God; but still when he is condemned by the priests he kills himself. This indeed, so Diodorus affirms,[54] is their way of punishing all other evil-doers; they do not perform executions themselves but send an attendant to bid the guilty die.

You come next to the Assyrians and to the Medes and Persians who were most attentive to their kings, maintaining that "the right of kings there was combined with a complete freedom to do what they would," thus contradicting the word of all historians. In particular Daniel tells us [55] that when king Nebuchadnezzar ruled too haughtily men drove him from their society and left him to the beasts. Their laws were not called those of the king but of the Medes and the Persians, in other words, of the people; and, since they were irrevocable, the kings too were bound by them. Thus Darius the Mede, despite every effort, was

[51] Ptolemy X reigned alone (Alexander I) in Egypt from 101–89 after the death of his mother, Cleopatra Kokke. He was expelled in 89 by a popular uprising.

[52] In 80 B.C. Ptolemy XI (Alexander II), son of Alexander I, assassinated his step-mother, Berenice, who had assumed government in Alexandria, and was immediately killed by the enraged people. With him the legitimate Ptolemaic family became extinct.

[53] Ptolemy XII (80–51), Philopator Philadelphus Neos Dionysus nicknamed Auletes ("the flute-player"). From 58 to 55, Auletes was in exile, driven out by popular rebellion. In 55 he killed his daughter, Berenice, ruler in Alexandria, and assumed power again.

[54] Diodorus, III, 5–6.

[55] *Cf.* Daniel 5:20; 20:21.

unable to take Daniel out of the hands of the satrap. "In those days," you say, "peoples thought it wicked to repudiate a king for abusing his rights." [56] But you are so wretchedly dull that, in the middle of all your talk praising the obedience and moderation of these people, you call attention of your own accord to the fact that Arbaces deprived Sardanapalus of his kingdom.[57] Arbaces did not act alone in this but had the aid of the priestly jurists and the people, and he acted mainly for this reason, that the king carried his abuse of royal rights not indeed to the point of cruelty but merely luxury and wantonness. Search through Herodotus, Ctesias,[58] and Diodorus and you will find, quite the reverse of what you say, that "For the most part these kingdoms were not destroyed by foreigners but by their own subjects." [59] The kings of Assyria were destroyed by the Medes, the Medes by the Persians, by their subjects in either case. You admit yourself "that Cyrus rebelled and despots seized power in various parts of the realm." [60] Is this the way you carry out your plan of asserting the rights of kings among the Medes and Persians, and the reverence of these people for the kings? What hellebore can cure such lunacy [84] as yours? [61]

"Herodotus," you say, "makes clear the rights of the Persian kings in ruling." [62] Cambyses, desiring to wed his sister, asked advice of the royal judges, men chosen "from the people," interpreters of the law, to whom all questions were submitted. What did they do? They said they found no law bidding brother marry his sister, but had found one

[56] *Regia* (1649), p. 109, ll. 23–24.

[57] According to Ctesias (Diodorus, II, 24 ff.), Arbaces was one of the generals of Sardanapulus, and said to be founder of the Median Empire. But consensus among historians is that there was no such historical personage.

Sardanapalus (Assur-bani-pal) last king of Assyria, died about 626 B.C. There is no historical evidence that Sardanapalus was deprived of his kingdom except for the fabulous Ctesias, accepted uncritically as an authority both by Milton and Salmasius.

[58] Ctesias may have been known to Milton from the *editio prima* of Stephanus (1566), reproduced at the end of his 1570 edition of Herodotus.

[59] *Regia* (1649), p. 109, ll. 24–26.

[60] Not a direct quotation but a paraphrase of *Regia* (1649), p. 109, ll. 34–35, and p. 109, ll. 29–30.

[61] This may be a pun on *Cyrus* and *Anticyra*. Anticyra was the name of two ancient towns, one in Phocis, the other in Thessaly, both of which were noted for their production of hellebore, chief cure among the ancients for madness.

[62] *Regia* (1649), p. 109, ll. 35–37. *Cf.* Herodotus, III, 31.

allowing the Persian king to do as he wishes. In the first place, if according to his rights the king might do anything, why was any other but the king himself needed as interpreter of the law? These wholly superfluous judges would have stayed anywhere rather than in the palace. Next, if the Persian king might do as he wished, it is incredible that Cambyses, who was most eager for power, was so unaware of it as to inquire from these judges what was permitted him. And what happened? Wishing either "to flatter the king," as you admit, or fearing what the tyrant might do to them, as Herodotus reports, they pretend to have discovered some very pliable law and thus satisfied him with a sop, which is not an unknown practice today with judges and jurists. You state that "the Persian Artabanus told Themistocles that there was no law among the Persians better than the one which provided that their king must be revered and worshipped." [63] This law on the worship of kings is a fine one for you to cite; it was condemned even by the early fathers: and Artabanus, the advocate of the law, is a fine one too, who soon afterwards slew with his own hands Xerxes, his king. These regicides you summon are fit guardians of kings: I suspect you are contriving some plots against kings. You cite the poet Claudianus as evidence for the obedience of the Persians.[64] I refer you however to their own deeds and histories, which are full of revolts of Persians, Medes, Bactrians and Babylonians, and of slayings of kings as well. Your next authority is Otanes the Persian,[65] who was the murderer of his own king Smerdis, and what in hatred of royal power he sets forth about the wrongs and crimes of kings, their violations of the law, their killing of the innocent, their lewdness and adultery, all this you would call rights of kings, and are reminded to renew your slander of Samuel.

To Homer's account of kings being descended from Jove I replied above; [85] [66] and I should as soon take Charles as King Philip for an interpreter of the law. Then you bring on some remains of a frag-

[63] *Regia* (1649), p. 110, ll. 6–10.

[64] *Regia* (1649), p. 110, ll. 13–14: "*quamvis crudelibus aeque parebant Dominis*" ("however cruel their masters, they equally obeyed them.")

[65] *Regia* (1649), p. 110, ll. 14–17. According to Salmasius, Otanes the Persian, when he is expressing his ideas on the best situation for a state, defines a monarch to be one who does with impunity what he likes. *Cf.* Herodotus, III, 79. Milton says correctly that Otanes' words are hostile to monarchy.

[66] *Regia* (1649), p. 110, ll. 26–29.

ment [67] of Diotogenes the Pythagorean,[68] but say nothing about what kind of king he speaks of. You must therefore listen to his preface, to which all that follows should be referred. "He should be king who is the most just of men; he is most just who adheres most closely to the law"; for without justice "there can be no king, nor without law justice." [69] This is in direct opposition to your royal right. The philosophy of Ecphantas, whom you have quoted,[70] is to the same effect: "He who undertakes to rule should be by nature pure and spotless," and later, "He who rules in accordance with virtue is called king and is one." Therefore the one you call king is no king according to the Pythagoreans. Hear now in turn what Plato wrote in his *Eighth Epistle:* [71] "Let the royal power be bound to account for its actions; the laws must govern both kings and other citizens if they have acted in opposition to them." I may add to this Aristotle, *Politics III*,[72] "It is neither expedient nor just that one be master of all when men are similar or equal; or that he be the law himself, whether laws exist or not; or that a good man be lord of other good men, or a bad man of bad men." Also book V chapter 10: "One whom the people does not wish becomes immediately not king but a tyrant." Note too Xenophon in his *Hiero:* [73] "States are so far from avenging the slaughter of their tyrants that they give great honor to tyrannicides and even set up

[67] The fragment is quoted by Stobaeus, XLVIII, 61, in Joannis Stobaei, *Anthologii Libri Duo Posteriores,* ed. Otto Hense (4 vols., Berlin, 1909), IV, 263.

[68] *Regia* (1649), p. 110, ll. 37–39: "Diotogenes Pythagoreus wrote in the *Librum de Regno* that, as God was universal in regard to the world, so the king had similar relationship to the state over which he presided." The *Librum* is a fragment conserved in the anthology of Stobaeus. The meaning of the statement seems a little obscure, but a comment by Louis Delatte in *Les Traités de la Royauté d'Ecphante, Diotogène et Sthénidas* (Paris, 1942, p. 254) helps to explain it. "Why is the king not a kind of high priest? It is the king, the best by nature and most honorable, who should be honored by the being, best by nature and most honorable on earth. There is, therefore, in effect a relationship between the world and the state, between God and the king, that Diotogenes expresses in mathematical language under two proportions:

$$\frac{\text{God}}{\text{World}} = \frac{\text{King}}{\text{City}} \quad \text{and} \quad \frac{\text{City}}{\text{World}} = \frac{\text{King''}.}{\text{God}}$$

[69] This quotation is found in Stobaeus, XLVIII, 64 (Hense, IV, p. 273, p. 276).

[70] *Regia* (1649), p. 111, ll. 13–16. [71] Plato, *Epistle* VIII, 355 d–e.

[72] Aristotle, *Politics,* III, 17 (1288 a 1); V, 10 (1313 a 14).

[73] Xenophon, *Hiero,* IV, 5, in *Scripta Minora,* tr. E. C. Marchant (Cambridge: Loeb Classical Library, 1946), pp. 26–27.

their statues in the temples." I may cite Marcus Tullius as an eye-witness: *Pro Milone,*[74] "The men of Greece grant divine honors to tyrannicides: What have I not seen at Athens and other Greek cities; what decrees honoring such men as gods, what hymns and chants? They are treated as wellnigh divine in immortality, worship, and remembrance." Finally Polybius, that most weighty author, writes in the sixth book of his *Histories:* [75] "When rulers begin to yield to their baser desires, the kingdom becomes a tyranny, and plots against the despots [86] are undertaken; the movers of these are not the worst citizens but the noblest and most magnanimous." I have offered but these few selections, though I have far more in store; more indeed than I can use.

You shift ground next from philosophers to poets, and I meet you there gladly. "Aeschylus alone could show that in Greece kings were limited by no law or courts; in his tragedy *Supplices* he calls the Argive king a ruler not subject to judgment." [76] You should know, since with each twist and turn you make I see better your rashness and lack of judgment, that we should consider not so much what the poet says, as who in the poem says it. Various figures appear, some good, some bad, some wise, some foolish, each speaking not the poet's opinions but what is appropriate for each person. The fifty daughters of Danaus had fled from Egypt to the Argive king as suppliants; they are praying for his protection against the Egyptian force following in their fleet; the king replies that he cannot give such protection without consulting the people first:

> I lack the power to give you this assurance
> Ere I take counsel with the folk in town.[77]

These wandering suppliant women feared the uncertainty of a popular vote and press the king with renewed blandishments:

> Thou art the state, thou art the people too,
> Being their unquestioned ruler.[78]

[74] Cicero, *Pro Milone*, 29, 80.

[75] Polybius, VI, 7, 7, in *The Histories,* tr. W. R. Paton (6 vols., London: Loeb Classical Library, 1925), III, 282–85.

[76] *Regia* (1649), p. 111, ll. 28–31.

[77] Aeschylus, *Supplices,* 368–69, in *Aeschylus,* tr. Herbert W. Smyth (2 vols., Cambridge: Loeb Classical Library), I, 40–41.

[78] *Ibid.,* 370–71.

The king replies:

> I have already told you that without the people's aid
> I would not do this thing, not even if I could.[79]

And thus he turns over the whole affair to the people:

> I go to call this country's habitants
> And to persuade that body.[80]

Then the people decree that aid should be given the Danaides, and these words of the joyful old Danaus follow:

> Rejoice, my children, for the inhabitants are kind, [87]
> And the full vote of the assembly hath been passed.[81]

Had I not revealed these matters, how rashly would this sciolist have determined the rights of kings among the Greeks from the mouths of women and wanderers and suppliants, though the king himself and the actual facts tell a far different tale.

We learn the same from Euripides' Orestes, who was himself king of the Argives on his father's death, and when brought to trial by the people for the murder of his mother pleaded his own case and was condemned to death by popular vote. The same Euripides also testifies in his *Supplices* that at Athens the royal power was bound by the laws. He has Theseus king of Athens speak thus:

> This city is not ruled by any single man,
> But she is free, and governed by her people.[82]

So says his son Demophoon, also king of Athens, in the same poet's *Heracleidae:*

> I rule not as a tyrant does barbarians,
> But if I act with justice I receive the same.[83]

That at Thebes the ancient rights of the king were no different is affirmed by Sophocles in his *Oedipus Tyrannus*, and thus both Tiresias and Creon reply to Oedipus with great spirit:

[79] *Ibid.*, 398–99. [80] *Ibid.*, 517–18.
[81] *Ibid.*, 600–601.
[82] Euripides, *Suppliants*, 404–405, in *Euripides,* tr. Arthur S. Way (4 vols., London: Loeb Classical Library, 1919), III, 532–33.
[83] Euripides, *Heracleidae*, 423–24.

I am in no respect your slave.

and

I too have my place in this our state;
It is not yours alone.[84]

And in the *Antigone* Haemon tells Creon:

That is no city which belongs to one.[85]

The Spartan kings indeed were often brought to trial and it is well known that they were sometimes punished by death: this is not strange, for the very Lycurgus who wrote their laws could have learned from Homer, whom he had read through with great care [88], that even in heroic times the kings' rights were no different. His Achilles did not hesitate, on learning that Agamemnon was the one who had brought ruin on the people who were then smitten by a plague, to call him before a crowded assembly of the Greeks and though a king himself to make a king subject to the judgment of his own people with these words:

People-devouring king, thou rulest over men of naught,
Else would Atreides now have made his last insult.[86]

That men of all ranks felt as did the heroes about royal rights can be witnessed by Alcaeus, the prince of lyricists: His songs, so pleasing in themselves, are reported by Horace to have pleased the people all the better for containing praise of those who had driven tyrants from their states.

The shades do marvel at each poet's lines,
Worthy of sacred silence to be heard:
But with a more attentive ear the close-packed mob
Drinks in the tales of war and tyranny deposed.[87]

To these I may add the similar opinion of Theognis, who flourished shortly before the descent of the Medes into Greece, when men distinguished for their wisdom flourished in numbers throughout all

[84] Sophocles, *Oedipus Tyrannus,* 410, 630, in *Sophocles,* tr. Francis Storr (2 vols., London: Loeb Classical Library, 1932), I, 40–41, 58–59.

[85] Sophocles, *Antigone,* 737.

[86] *Iliad,* I, 231–32.

[87] Horace, *Odes,* II, 13, 29–32.

Greece; he himself professes to have received from the sages the precepts embodied in his verse:

> Smite as you will the people-devouring tyrant,
> No need to fear any hatred of heaven for this.[88]

Surely this shows well enough what were the ancient rights of kings in Greece; let us turn to Rome. You stress that statement which is not Sallust's but that of C. Memmius in Sallust: "doing what you will with impunity": [89] I have answered this above. Sallust himself wrote the wise words: "The Romans had a rule of law, the rule being entitled royal" [90] but when "this was changed into despotism" they expelled it, as you know. Thus Cicero says in his *In Pisonem:* [91] "Am I to think him a consul who thinks our republic has no Senate? And am I to count him a consul without that council in whose absence the very kings themselves could not survive in Rome?" Do you hear that at Rome the king without the Senate was nothing? You object that "Tacitus says Romulus ruled the Romans at his pleasure." [92] Yes, for there was as yet no state but only an off-scouring of outcasts with no legal basis: Once all men lived without law, for there were no states. But Livy tells us that after Romulus, even though everyone wished for a king, having as yet not tasted the sweet fruits of freedom, "supreme power was left to the people, [89] to prevent their giving up more rights than they kept"; [93] and "this right was violently torn from them" by the Caesars, as the same historian says.[94] Servius Tullius ruled at first through a ruse, pretending to be the deputy of Tarquinius Priscus, but afterwards he himself put it to the people "whether their wish and decree was that he should rule," and finally, as Tacitus reports, "he gave his sanction to those laws which kings themselves were to obey." [95] Would he have thus impaired his own and his descendants' rights if he had thought before that the rights of kings were above the law? Tarquin the proud, the last of these kings, "was the first to

[88] Theognis, *Elegies A.*, 1181–82, in *The Elegies of Theognis,* ed. T. Hudson-Williams (London, 1910), p. 160.

[89] Salmasius' full statement reads (*Regia,* 1649, p. 112, ll. 30–33): "Their wisest historian, one who lived and wrote under the Republic, while it still flourished under the same laws for all and enjoyed its liberty, said 'to be able to do what you will with impunity is to be king.' "

[90] Sallust, *Jugurtha,* XXXI, 9.

[91] Cicero, *In Pisonem,* 10, 23.

[92] *Regia* (1649), p. 113, ll. 1–2. *Cf.* Tacitus, *Annals,* III, 26.

[93] Livy, *Roman History,* I, 17, 2–9.

[94] *Ibid.,* I, 46, 1.

[95] Tacitus, *Annals,* III, 26.

give up the custom of asking the Senate's advice on every question"; [96] for this and other crimes the people deprived L. Tarquin of royal power and exiled him with his wife and children. This is related mainly from Livy and Cicero, and you could hardly adduce better interpreters of the rights of kings among the Romans. So far as dictatorships are concerned, they were but temporary and never instituted save in public extremity, when they must be given up within six months. What you call the rights of the emperors was no right but sheer force; the empire was set up with no right save that of arms. But, you say, "Tacitus, who flourished under the rule of one man" wrote as follows: "The gods have given the emperor supreme authority, while the subjects are left with the glory of obedience." [97] You say not where he wrote this, knowing well that you had deceived your readers; but I nosed it out at once, even though I did not come on the exact spot at once. These are not the words of Tacitus, who was a noble writer most opposed to tyranny, but of a certain Roman knight M. Terentius in Tacitus, *Annals* VI, who, when on trial for his life, uttered this flattery of Tiberius amid other such expressions spoken in fear of execution by him. "The gods have given you supreme authority, while we are left with the glory of obedience." [98] You bring this forward as the opinion of Tacitus, for you would not choke on a dish of opinions you find useful though they were cooked up in any baker's or barber's shop or even in a torture chamber; so completely indiscriminate is your greed, whether from a desire to boast or an awareness of your weakness. If you had chosen to read Tacitus himself instead of copying so carelessly extracts from any source, he would have informed you of the source of this imperial right. "After the victory at Actium the form of government was overthrown and no trace of the old pure manners could be found; [90] equality was over and everyone looked to the orders of the emperor." [99] The same author would have told you in book III of his *Annals*,[100] whence come all your royal rights: When equality was ended and self-seeking violence began to take the place of decent moderation, then despotisms appeared and among many peoples remained forever." You might have learned the same from Dio [101] if your native superficiality and waywardness had let you

[96] Livy I, 49, 7. [97] *Regia* (1649), p. 112, ll. 33–36.
[98] Tacitus, *Annals*, VI, 8. [99] *Ibid.*, I, 3–4. [100] *Ibid.*, III, 26.
[101] Dio Cassius, LIII, 28, in *Dio's Roman History*, tr. Earnest Cary (9 vols., London: Loeb Classical Library, 1914), VII, 363.

study anything thoroughly. He relates in that fifty-third book which you cited that it was brought about partly by arms and partly by the treacherous pretence of Octavian Caesar that the emperors were not limited by law; for while Octavian promised before an assembly that he would give up the principate and obey the laws and commands of others, pretending to refuse the empire, he gradually seized it by keeping all the legions as his own to carry on the wars in his own provinces. This is no legal exemption from the laws but rather such forceful breaking of legal limitations as the gladiator Spartacus might have brought about, and a personal assumption of the title of *princeps* or emperor or *autokrator* as though God or natural law had subordinated all men and laws alike to him. Would you learn in some more detail of the origin of the rights of Caesar? At the bidding of Caesar, who had then gained supreme power through his criminal raising of forces against the republic, Mark Antony became consul and during the celebration of the Lupercalia at Rome, by an evident concert and to the accompaniment of the people's groaning and lamentation, placed a diadem on Caesar's brow. He then ordered it inscribed in the calendar for the Lupercalia that the consul Antony by popular command had offered a kingdom to C. Caesar. Of this Cicero said in his *Second Philippic:* "Was it for this that L. Tarquin was driven out and Sp. Cassius, Sp. Melius, M. Manlius were slain, that after those many centuries M. Antony should accomplish the impiety of appointing a king at Rome?" [102] Surely you deserve every torture and everlasting shame even more than did Antony himself, though you must not let this make you proud, since I do not compare so despicable a fellow as you with Antony in anything but wickedness; like the lewdest Lupercal you have attempted in this impious Lupercalia of yours [103] to bind the brows of all tyrants and not of one only with the headband of a ruler unbound by any law, a band which no law may unbind. If, in truth, one should believe the oracle of the Caesars themselves, for this is the name given their edict by the Christian emperors [91] Theodosius and Valens (*Codex* 1.14) [104] the power of the emperors

[102] Cicero, *Philippics,* II, xxxiv, 87.

[103] The series of puns in the Latin defies reproduction in the English.

[104] The edict referred to by Milton is quoted in the Codex of *Justiniani Sacratiss. Principis,* with the commentaries of Dionysius Gothofredus, "Secunda editio, plerisque locis emendata, & notis in tres posteriores libros aucta," by Eustathius Vignon and Jacobus Stoer (1595; UTSL). This volume is bound together with the *Corpus Juris Civilis* (1594) of Eustathius Vignon and Joannes Gymnicus. It was

depends on the power of law. Therefore by the judgment or oracle even of the Caesars themselves, the majesty of the ruler must be subordinated to that of the laws on which it depends. Thus when the imperial power was at its height Pliny wrote to Trajan in the *Panegyricus:* [105] "Domination and chieftainship are different in nature. Trajan avoids actual royal power and keeps it far from him, and occupies the position of leader lest there be a place for a master." Later he says: "All that I said of other rulers was for this purpose, that I may show how our father Trajan reforms and corrects the practices of a principate which the customs of many years had corrupted and depraved." Have you no shame in continually prating of what Pliny calls the depraved practices of the principate as the rights of kings? So much in brief of royal rights among the Romans. Everyone knows what they did to their tyrants, whether kings or emperors. They drove out Tarquin, and that in accordance with ancient custom; for, in the expulsion from the state of Agylla of the tyrant Mezentius, Rome's neighbor Etruria offered one ancient example, or else in the eighth book of his *Aeneid* Virgil, who was unsurpassed in the creation of what was appropriate, meant with this tale to show Caesar Octavian, even then Rome's ruler, what had been the rights of kings from immemorial ages among all nations.

> At last the weary citizens besiege in arms him and his house, while he rages furiously; they slay his comrades and set fire to his roof. Amid the slaughter he slips away in flight to the Rutulian domain and gains protection from the arms of his host Turnus. Thus all Tuscany blazed with righteous rage and in open warfare claims the king for punishment.[106]

You see here that not only did the citizens, burning in their righteous wrath, seek to slay the tyrant in a sudden onslaught, nor did they merely drive him from the realm, but actually undertook a war and dragged him back as a fugitive exile to face trial and execution. "But

---

published in Paris, "Cum Privilegio Christanissimi Galliarum Regis." The pertinent quotation is contained in Codex I.14, Arabic subdivision 4 (p. 89): "Adeo de auctoritate juris, nostra pendet auctoritas & revera majus imperio est, submittere legibus principatum. Et oraculo praesentis edicti, quod nobis licere non patimur, aliis indicamus." For a modern edition, see *Corpus Juris Civilis,* ed. Paul Kruger (3 vols., Weidmann, Berlin, 1954). *Cf. Complete Prose,* II, 399, 442. Milton has substituted Valens for Valentinian.

[105] Pliny, *Panegyricus,* XLV, 3; LIII, 1, in Pliny, *Panegyricus,* ed. Joannes Arnzenius (Amsterdam, 1638), pp. 208, 245.

[106] Virgil, *Aeneid,* VIII, 489–95.

how," you ask, "did they drive out Tarquin? Did they summon him to court? Not at all; they shut the gates against his coming." [107] A ridiculous point, for what else could they do but shut them against one who rushed on with [92] part of his army in attendance? Does it matter whether his sentence was exile or death, so long as one admits he paid the penalty? The foremost men of the age slew C. Caesar the tyrant in the Senate; and M. Tullius, himself the best of men and known as father of his country, praised this deed in the highest terms at various times and particularly in the *Second Philippic*. I shall rehearse a few instances. "All good men did what they could towards the slaying of Caesar; there were some without a plan, some without courage, some without opportunity, but none without the desire." [108] And later: "Was there ever a deed, as God is my witness, done not in this city alone but in the whole world, which was greater, more honorable, more worthy of eternal remembrance by mankind? I have no objection to being included in partnership in this plan along with the leaders, just as though it had been the Trojan Horse." [109] The words of the tragedian Seneca may apply to Romans as well as Greeks:

> Jove on his altar can receive no sacrifice
> Of higher worth, or richer, than an unjust king.[110]

For if you take these as the words of Hercules, in whose mouth they are placed, they show the judgment of the greatest Greek of his time; if you take them as the words of the poet who lived in Nero's age—and it is the custom of poets to place their own opinions in the mouths of their great characters—he indicates what he himself and all good men even in Nero's time thought should be done with tyrants; how righteous, how pleasing to the gods they held tyrannicide to be. Thus the best Romans did what they could to kill Domitian. This is set forth clearly by the younger Pliny in his *Panegyric* to the emperor Trajan: "It was a joy to hurl that haughty visage to the ground, to set on with the swords and swing the axe as if each blow brought him bloody torture: no one so checked his delight as to feel that the sight of his torn and bleeding joints and limbs, his grim and terrible statutes cast down and thrown into the flames, was anything but vengeance overdue." [111] Later he says: "Those men fail to love good

[107] *Regia* (1649), p. 117, ll. 32–35.
[108] Cicero, *Philippics*, II, xii, 29.
[109] *Ibid.*, II, xiii, 32.
[110] Seneca, *Hercules Furens*, 922–24.
[111] *Panegyricus*, LII, 4.

rulers as they should who fail to hate bad ones as they should."[112] He counts it one of Domitian's crimes that he slaughtered Epaphroditus for being in some way the slayer of Nero: "Has the vindication of Nero ceased to cause us pain? [93] Will he who punished his slayer allow criticism of his life and reputation?"[113] It is clear that he thought it well-nigh criminal not to have killed Nero, and the blackest of crimes to have punished his slayer. From this it is evident that all the outstanding Romans not only killed their tyrants by any means whatever when they could, but also, like the Greeks before them, held such a deed to be worthy of the highest praise: When through lack of power they could not bring a tyrant to trial in his lifetime, they did try him after death and condemn him according to the Valerian Law.[114] For when Valerius Publicola, the colleague of Junius Brutus, saw that tyrants surrounded by their soldiers could not be brought to trial, he had a law passed permitting them to be killed before trial in any way whatever; an accounting was to be rendered later. Thus when Cassius' sword had accomplished the death of C. Caligula which all had prayed for, Valerius Asiaticus,[115] a man of consular rank, cried out to the troops who were rioting over his death, 'Would it had been I who slew him,' even though he had not been there. At that same time the Senate voted to do away with the remembrance of the Caesars and to tear down their temples. So far were they from anger at Cassius. When shortly Claudius was hailed as emperor by the troops, they used a tribune of the people to forbid his acceptance of the principate, but the power of the army prevailed. The Senate declared Nero an enemy of the state and sought to punish him in the ancient manner: that form of punishment was to fix the neck of the stripped criminal in the stocks and beat his body with sticks until he died. See how much more gently and moderately the English treated their tyrant, even though many believed him responsible for spilling more blood than Nero himself. The Senate too condemned Domitian

[112] *Ibid.*, LIII, 2. [113] *Ibid.*, LIII, 4.

[114] Whatever the reasons for a Roman citizen's condemnation to capital punishment, he had the right to appeal (*provocare*) to the *Comitia Centuriata*, or, in the case of a fine, to the *Comitia Tributa*. The magistrate who disregarded such an appeal, unless there was a dictatorship or state of siege, was regarded as guilty of murder. Valerius Publicola (consul in 509 B.C.) initiated legislation which was much refined in the *Lex Valeria* (c. 300 B.C.). See *The Oxford Classical Dictionary*, p. 742, under the title "Provocatio."

[115] Dio Cassius, *Roman History*, LIX, 30, 2.

after his death, and was able to order the public removal and destruction of his statutes. Commodus was slain by his own household and not avenged by the Senate or the people, but rather declared an enemy, for they sought his corpse to punish it. The decree of the Senate on this affair is extant in Lampridius: "From the foe of the fatherland let the honors be stripped; let the murderer be dragged in the dust and mangled in the charnel-house; let the enemy of the gods and the slayer of the Senate be dragged in the dust with a hook." [116] The same men, in a crowded meeting of the Senate, sentenced the emperor Didius Julianus to death and ordered a tribune sent to slay him [94] in his palace; [117] and they also deposed Maximinus and declared him a public enemy. I may cite the very decree from Capitolinus: [118] "The consul asked 'Senators, what is your will as to the Maximini?' The answer was 'They are enemies, enemies of the state, and anyone who kills them will win a reward.' " Would you learn whether the Roman people and provinces obeyed the emperor Maximinus or the Senate? Hear what the same Capitolinus says: "The Senate sent letters to all the provinces to ask their support for the common welfare and freedom, and they all harkened. Everywhere the friends and officials, the governors and tribunes and soldiers of Maximinus were slain; a few cities stood by the public enemy." Herodian has the same account.[119]

Why say more about the Romans? Let us see now what were the rights of kings at that time in neighboring states. Among the Gauls thus king Ambiorix admitted "his power was such that the multitude had no less rights over him than he over them." He was then judged as much as judging. King Vercingetorix too was accused of treachery by his own people, according to Caesar in his account of the Gallic War.[120] "The power of the German kings was not unlimited or absolute; the leaders deliberate on smaller matters and all the people on more important ones. The king or chief is heeded more for his influence in persuasion than for his power of command; if his view is un-

[116] Lampridius, "Commodus," *Scriptores Historiae Augustae,* XVIII, 3.

[117] Spartianus, "Didius Julianus," *Scriptores Historiae Augustae,* VIII, 8.

[118] Capitolinus, "Maximini Duo," *Scriptores Historiae Augustae,* XVI, 4 and XXIII, 2–7.

[119] Herodian VIII, v, 8–9, *Herodian of Antioch's History of the Roman Empire,* tr. Edward C. Echols (Berkeley: University of California Press, 1961), pp. 206–207.

[120] Caesar, *Gallic War,* V, 27, 3, tr. H. J. Edwards (London: Loeb Classical Library, 1917), pp. 268–69.

popular they reject it by their uproar." So says Tacitus.[121] In fact you yourself admit that what you earlier described as wholly unheard-of was actually often done, and indeed "fifty kings of Scotland were either deposed or imprisoned or slain, and some even suffered public execution." [122] Why do you, as it were sneaking your tyrants out for burial like paupers under cover of darkness, keep shouting so loud that what was often done in Britain itself is unparalleled wickedness?

You go on to extol the reverence of Jews and Christians toward their tyrants, and join one lie to another, all of which I have exposed time and time again. Just now you were praising far and wide the obedience of the Assyrians and Persians, while now you count up their revolts; and now you give many reasons for the frequent revolts of those you said just before never revolted. You next return to your long abandoned account [95] of the punishment of our king so that you may now make up for any accidental oversight in making yourself foolish and absurd! You tell how "he was led through the members of his court." [123] I wish I knew what you mean by members of his court. You go over the sufferings of the Romans from turning the monarchy into a republic, regarding which I have shown above how shamefully you cheat yourself. When you used to refute the Jesuit by showing that "under aristocrats and people there are at worst uprisings, while under a tyrant ruin is sure," [124] are you now so foolishly venal as to dare to state that "the Romans drained those draughts of woe as punishments for their former ejection of their kings?" [125] Rather because King Charles later gave you 100 sovereigns was the reason why you allege the Romans paid for their expulsion of the kings. You say things went ill for the slayers of Julius Caesar. If indeed I had wished any tyrant spared it would have been he, for although he forcibly established his rule in the republic yet he did perhaps best deserve to rule. But I no more suppose that anyone was punished for slaying Caesar than that C. Antonius, the colleague of Cicero, was punished for killing Catiline; for, when later he was convicted on other charges, the tomb of Catiline, as Cicero says in the *Pro Flacco,*[126] was decked with flowers, because

[121] Tacitus, *Germania,* 11, in *Dialogues,* tr. William Peterson *et al.* (London: Loeb Classical Library, 1914), pp. 278–81.

[122] *Regia* (1649), p. 115, ll. 20–23.

[123] *Regia* (1649), p. 118, l. 6: *per Aulae suae membra.*

[124] This is a paraphrase from Salmasius, *De Episcopis ac Presbyteris* (Leyden, 1641), based on the previous long quotation on p. 428 above.

[125] *Regia* (1649), p. 118, ll. 15–16.

[126] Cicero, *Pro Flacco,* XXXVIII, 95.

Catiline's supporters rejoiced and kept claiming that Catiline's actions were now justified, in order to arouse bad feelings against those who had removed him.

These are tricks of scoundrels to frighten the best men from vengeance against tyrants and often from punishing even the worst criminals. It would be easy to refute you by showing how frequently success and good fortune came to the slayers of tyrants, if from that one could draw any sure conclusion as to the consequences of actions. You make the accusation that "the English imposed on their hereditary king not the punishment usual for the sacrifice of tyrants but for robbers or traitors." [127] In the first place I have no idea what heredity has to do with impunity for crimes; no man of sense can believe that it has any bearing. What you speak of next as barbarity should rather be ascribed to the kindness and moderation of the English, for, though being a tyrant involves every sort of wickedness toward the country, rapine, treachery and treason, still they considered it enough to punish their tyrant no more heavily than any ordinary brigand or common traitor. [96] You hope "some Harmodii or Thrasybuli will arise to avenge the tyrant's shades by our murder." [128] You will yield to despair and, cursed by all good men, end that life which suits you so well by hanging yourself long before you see Harmodii avenging tyrants by the blood of Harmodii. This may well happen to you, and no one could make a better forecast about such a knave as you: the other is impossible. You speak of thirty tyrants who rebelled under Gallienus.[129] If tyrant fights tyrant, are all who fight or slay a tyrant therefore tyrants themselves? You will never establish this, you slave on horseback, nor will Trebellius Pollio [130] your authority for it, who is about the lowest of historical writers. "If any of them were judged enemies by the Senate, this," you say, "was not a right but a revolt." [131] You remind us how emperors were made; it was indeed the revolt, the violence, and, to be brief, the madness of

[127] *Regia* (1649), p. 119, ll. 4–8.

[128] *Regia* (1649), p. 119, ll. 9–12. Harmodius was one of the tyrannicides who slew Hipparchus in 514 B.C.; Thrasybulus led the successful opposition to the oligarchy in Athens in 411 B.C.

[129] *Regia* (1649), p. 120, ll. 13–17.

[130] Trebellius Pollio is the reputed author of the "Tyranni Triginta" in the *Scriptores Historiae Augustae*.

[131] *Regia* (1649), p. 120, ll. 29–31: "Si qui hostes a Senatu aliquando judicati sunt, ut de Nero legimus, factio id fecit non ius, vis potentior maiorque eorum qui in eum conspiraverant."

Antony, rather than any right, which originally led the Emperors themselves to rebel against the Senate and people of Rome. "Galba," you say, "paid for his revolt against Nero." [132] Tell us then how Vespasian paid for his revolt against Vitellius.[133] "Charles," you say, "was as different from Nero as were these English butchers from those Roman Senators." [134] You deep-dyed knave, your praise is slander and your slander the highest praise!

But a few sentences above you wrote on this very question that "under the Emperors the Senate was an assembly of slaves in togas," [135] while now you say that the same Senate was an assembly of kings! If this be true, why are not kings, according to you, but slaves in togas? Fortunate are kings in having such a panegyrist, the lowest of humans and stupidest of beasts, unless I should call him unique in being the most erudite of asses! You would have the English Parliament resemble Nero rather than the Roman Senate.

This insatiable passion of yours for gluing together the most foolish comparisons compels me to correct you and show how like Nero Charles was. "Nero," you say, "killed his own mother" [136] with a sword; Charles used poison to kill his father and his king! To pass over other proofs, it must be that the one who snatched from the arms of the law the Duke who was guilty of the poisoning [97] was himself guilty too. Nero killed many thousand Christians, Charles many more. Suetonius bears witness that some praised Nero after he was dead, missed him much, for a long time decked his tomb with flowers in spring and summer, and threatened his foes with every evil; [137] there are those who are driven by the same disease to long for Charles and exalt him with the highest praise while you, a gibbet-knight, act as their chorus leader. "The English soldiers, fiercer than their own hounds, set up a new and unheard of court." [138] Here is Salmasius' shrewdest thrust, his seal perhaps, or his motto, forced on us now for the sixth time. *Fiercer than their own hounds*. Come, you rhetoricians and schoolmasters, and, if you are wise, pluck this lovely blossom so dear to Salmasius; in your notebooks and cabinet store this eloquent

[132] *Regia* (1649), p. 121, ll. 8–9.

[133] Roman emperor (A.D. 70–79) led a successful revolt against his predecessor, Vitellius, who was defeated and killed in 69.

[134] *Regia* (1649), p. 121, ll. 12–14.

[135] *Regia* (1649), p. 120, l. 38: *togatorum mancipiorum*.

[136] *Regia* (1649), p. 121, l. 24.

[137] Suetonius, *Nero*, 57.

[138] *Regia* (1649), p. 121, ll. 27–31.

fellow's colors lest they fade. Does your madness affect your voice too so that like a cuckoo you must forever sing the same song? What fatality is this? Madness is said to have turned Hecuba into a dog,[139] and now turns you, the Sire of St. Loup, into a cuckoo.

You now begin on a new self-contradiction! On page 113 above you stated that "the ruler is above the direction, as well as the compulsion, of the laws, and is bound by none of them at all." [140] Now you say you will speak below "about the difference between kings insofar as some have ruled with greater or lesser power than others." [141] You try to prove "by the most faultless argument" as you call it, though it is in fact the most foolish, "that kings could not be tried or condemned by their own subjects"; [142] you say "that there was no other distinction between judges and kings, but yet the Jews were led by disgust and hatred of judges to seek for kings." [143] But, because they could try and condemn those judges whose administration was corrupt, do you therefore suppose that in disgust and hatred of them they were led to seek for kings whom they could not punish or restrain if they overthrew all justice? So foolish an argument befits none but you. There was then some reason why they sought a king other than to have a master who was above the laws. It would be irrelevant to seek after it now, but whatever it may have been, both God and his prophet bear witness that it was by no means wise. You next bring heavy charges against those rabbis of yours [98] through whom you proved, according to your earliest boast, that the Hebrew king was not subject to judgment, because they report that he could be both judged and chastised: This very fact makes it as clear, as if you had confessed it, that you lied in your former statement of what you had proved through their evidence. Finally you stoop so low as to forget your defence of the king and stir up some wretched little squabbles about the number of Solomon's stables and how many horses he had in his stalls.[144] Then you revert from groom to squire, mouthing the same old moralistic

[139] The story of Hecuba is found in Ovid, *Metamorphoses,* XIII, 399 ff.

[140] Milton seems to misunderstand Salmasius' point here. Salmasius is talking about a *good* ruler in *Regia,* 1649, p. 113, ll. 18–22, the passage to which Milton refers. Salmasius' favorite point is implicit here that the good ruler obeys laws, even though he is freed from them. "Since it is the responsibility of the good ruler to command what is right for himself, no less than for his subjects, he does either freely, and can do neither with impunity, even though he is freed from the laws, whether they are *directives* or *sanctions,* as the term is" (Salmasius' italics).

[141] *Regia* (1649), p. 122, ll. 9–11.

[142] *Regia* (1649), p. 122, ll. 17–18.

[143] *Regia* (1649), p. 122, l. 39 ff.

[144] *Regia* (1649), p. 125, ll. 3 ff.

saws, or more truly you assume again the form of a crazy cuckoo you had before. "In these latter days," you bawl, "discipline has lost its strength and rules are broken";[145] this doubtless because a single tyrant unbound by any law cannot with impunity break down all discipline and trample on all men's traditions. You say this doctrine was brought by the Brownists into Protestant circles. So then Luther, Calvin, Zwingli, Bucer, and all the famous orthodox theologians are in your view Brownists.[146] The English are the less disturbed by your slanders when they hear you use the same insults in your raving about the great leaders of the church, and indeed about the whole reformed church itself.

CHAPTER VI[1]

After your vain treatment and foolish discussion of the law of God and the law of nature, which merely made you equally notorious for ignorance and vice, I fail to see what you can do in this royal defence but turn to trifles. But though I trust I would have fully satisfied the demands of all good and learned men, and even of this great cause itself, if I should end my reply here and now, still I shall push on wherever you may fly, lest others suppose I fear your

[145] *Regia* (1649), p. 127, ll. 35–38.

[146] Robert Browne (1550?–1633?), graduate of Corpus Christi College, Cambridge, preached in Norfolk and Suffolk, especially at Bury St. Edmunds, and denounced the Episcopal form of government. After suffering imprisonment several times, he moved with his congregation to Middelburg in Zeeland. In his *Reformation without Tarrying for Anie* (1582), he argues that the church has the inalienable right to effect reforms without the authorization of the civil magistrate (see *Complete Prose,* I, 21). *A Booke Which Sheweth the Life and Manners of All True Christians* (Middelburg, 1582) stresses the theory of congregational Independency. Eventually, after returning to England and making some compromise with the established order, he was appointed in 1586 master of the Stamford grammar school.

[1] In book VI (*Regia,* 1649, pp. 130–152), Salmasius contends that a king can be judged by no one except God and is bound to render an account of his acts to no one but God. His main assertions are as follows: 1. If a king is to be arraigned before any power, it must be a power higher than his own. If a king can be judged, then his rule is not truly kingly. 2. If the people had this power, as the English assert, then the people would have to be called "King of Kings" or "King of the King." The English fanatics teach that God no longer rules through kings but through the people. In any event, they merely deceive the people with a

ingenuity and wit instead of your boundless loquacity! I shall, however, be so brief as to make it plain that I have already done all [99] that the necessities of the case, if not its importance, require. I now but bow to the expectations or even curiosity of certain individuals.

"Now," you say, "a new and loftier range of arguments rises before me." [2] A range of arguments greater than those springing from the law of nature and of God? To the rescue, goddess Midwife, Mount Salmasius is in labor! [3] There was reason in his being his wife's wife; watch out, ye mortals, for some monstrous birth! "If one who is, and is called, king could be summoned before some other power, that power should be in all respects greater than royal; but the power which is established as greater must actually be, and be called, royal. For royal power is to be thus defined as that which is highest and unique in the state, over which no other is recognized." [4] The mountain has really labored to bring forth this ridiculous mouse! Come all grammarians to help this grammarian in labor: all is over—not with the law of God or nature, but with the phrase-book!

Shall I answer you thus: "Names give precedence to facts, and it is not our business to worry about names when we have done away

---

pretense of popular rule. The rule is militaristic. 3. The army (not the people) ejected the nobles from Parliament, purged the lower house, tried and executed the king, and now are levying taxes and making laws. 4. On the basis of Roman history the effects of military rule are deplorable. 5. The king derives his power from the people, and once the people have given it, they cannot take it back. This principle is based on the need for public safety. Otherwise there can be no stability of government but only sedition and civil wars. 6. The king is more than the highest magistrate, for a magistrate is appointed for a limited time, whereas a king inherits his power for life. A magistrate has only vicarious power and is subject to removal; a king is not. 7. When the people, either voluntarily or under compulsion, indues the king with power, it takes an oath of fealty from which it cannot be released. The law of nature demands that, for public safety, a government, whatever its form is, be preserved for a very long time, or in perpetuity, if possible. 8. The judgments of both Christ and St. Augustine justify the assertion that those who have been reduced to servitude have no right afterwards to regain their liberty, for many kingdoms have been started from conquest or usurpation, including that of the English. 9. In previous overthrows of the English nation, foreigners led the invasions. In the overthrow of Charles, the English people themselves were responsible.

[2] *Regia* (1649), p. 130, ll. 1–2. Salmasius goes on to say "by which it will be shown that the sanctity of kings is inviolable, and dependent on nothing else but divine power."

[3] Reference is based on the famous line in the *Ars Poetica* of Horace, l. 139 (*Epistolae*, II, 3): *"Parturiunt montes, nascetur ridiculus mus."*

[4] *Regia* (1649), p. 130, ll. 15–23.

with the reality; let those who love kings take care of that; we enjoy our freedom"? That would not be a bad answer for you! But that you may be sure I am treating you in every respect with scrupulous fairness I shall reply to you, not merely according to my own judgment but rather that of the best and wisest men of old, who decided that the name and power of king could very well exist along with the superior power of the laws and of the people.

In particular Lycurgus, a man famous for wisdom, when he was most desirous of providing for the royal power, as Plato tells us,[5] could find no other means of preserving it than to make the power of the Senate and ephors, that is of the people, greater in his land than that of the king. The Euripidean Theseus had the same idea, for though he was king of Athens, yet, to his own glory, he established the freedom of the Athenians and raised the power of the people over that of the king, and none the less left the sceptre in that state to his descendants. Thus in the *Suppliants* Euripides has him speak thus: [100]

> This people I established in the seat of kings,
> Giving them freedom and an equal vote.[6]

Later he says to the Theban herald:

> Stranger, from the first your speech is false
> When here you seek a tyrant; no single man
> Governs this city; it is free, swayed only
> By the people.[7]

So he spoke, though in that city he was, and was called, king. The divine Plato too bears witness in his *Eighth Epistle:* [8] "Lycurgus originated the power of Senate and ephors, which was the salvation of the royal power, for by this means it was preserved in all honor for many centuries; after him law became mistress and king of men." But law cannot be king without someone who may at need take legal action against the king himself. He thus recommends to the Sicilians a limited power for the monarchy: "Let there be freedom along with the royal power; let the royal power be accountable for its actions; let law rule the kings too if they contravene the law in any way." Aristotle too, in Book III of his *Politics*,[9] says: "In the Spartan state is the best ex-

[5] *Epistles*, VIII, 354 b.
[6] Euripides, *Supplices*, 352–53.
[7] *Ibid.*, 403–406.
[8] Plato, *Epistles*, III, 354 b, 355 d.
[9] Aristotle, *Politics*, 1285 a 2 (III, 14).

ample of monarchy governed by law"; he says however that every kind of monarchy is governed by law save one which he calls absolute, and he does not report that any such has ever existed. Aristotle then holds that such a monarchy as the Spartan is called, and in fact is, the best of all, and he could not deny that such a king is equally rightly called, and in fact is, king, although the people are superior to the king.

When so many weighty writers have given kings assurance that the title and substance of their kingship is unimpaired even where the people have in their own hands the supreme [101] power, though normally they do not use it, your faintheartedness should not be so fearful for your assemblage of grammatical details or words as to prefer the betrayal of all men's freedom and government to the slightest disturbance or injury of your glossary. Henceforth you must be aware that names are subordinate to things, not things to names; in this way you will be wiser and not, as you fear, "go on to infinity."

"It was then vain for Seneca to describe those three types of states." [10] Let us be free, and the devil with Seneca; unless I am much mistaken we are not the men to be enslaved by these gems from Seneca! And even though Seneca says that the supreme power rests in one man's hands, he says that "it belongs to the people" [11] and is entrusted to the king for their general welfare and not for their destruction; it is given by the people only to be exercised, not owned. "Now it seems that kings hold their rule not from God but from the people." [12] As if God did not so guide the people that they grant the

[10] *Regia* (1649), p. 132, ll. 2–3.

[11] Salmasius quotes from the *Epistulae Morales,* II xiv, 7; see Seneca, *Ad Lucilium,* tr. Richard M. Gummere (3 vols., Cambridge: Loeb Classical Library, 1953), I, 6–9. Milton's reply is based on *De Beneficiis,* VII, iv, 2, and VII, v, 1, as well; see Seneca, *Moral Essays,* tr. John W. Basore (3 vols., Cambridge: Loeb Classical Library, 1935), III, 464–69.

[12] *Regia* (1649), p. 132, ll. 21–22: "Non iam ergo per Deum reges regnare, sed per populum." Salmasius adds more strongly: "Non in Dei manu cor & vitam Regis esse & salutem, sed in populi potestate." Salmasius finds the people to be the source of power in a "popular state," whether under kingly rule, an aristocracy, or a government in which rule rotates. But this in no way compromises his essential position that in setting up a king, the people have freed him from the laws, so that he is responsible to God alone. Kingship is, as he has shown in the case of Samuel and the Israelites, always a risk. Salmasius also argues that kings can be appointed directly by God, as in the case of Saul and David (*Regia,* 1649, p. 133, ll. 2–3, as well as indirectly by men. Power once given to a supreme ruler is irrevocable: "irrevocabiliter ista fiat donatio" (*Regia,* 1649, p. 138, l. 19).

rule to the person God wishes; even in his own *Institutes* the emperor Justinian recognizes that the rule of the Caesars began when "by the royal law the people conceded to them all their power of command." [13]

How long must I continue to pick over these scraps of yours I have so often refuted? Again, to show your churlish and unmannerly spirit and nasty habits, you meddle officiously in the affairs of our country, which are of no concern to you as a foreigner and alien. Step up then, as a great busybody should, with your obvious solecism.[14] "Whatever things those wretches say," you claim, "are to deceive the people." [15] You knave! Was it for this that a degraded grammarian like you wanted to interfere with our government, that is, to bury us in your barbarous solecisms? Tell us now just how we deceived the people!

"The form of government introduced by them is not popular but military." [16] I suppose that crew of renegades paid you a few pennies to write this; and so I must direct my answer not to you who prate of things you quite fail to understand, but to those who hired you. Who "drove out the nobles from Parliament? The people?" [17] Yes, the people; and by that act they freed their necks from the well-nigh unbearable yoke of slavery. The soldiers to whom [102] you ascribe the act were themselves not foreigners but citizens, forming a great part of the people, and they acted with the consent and by the will of most of the rest, supported by Parliament. "Did the people," you ask, "do violence to the commoners of the lower house, putting some to flight, and so on?" [18] I say it was the people; for why should I not say that the act of the better, the sound part of the Parliament, in which resides the real power of the people, was the act of the people? If a majority in Parliament prefer enslavement and putting the commonwealth up for sale, is it not right for a minority to prevent it if they can and preserve their freedom? "The officers did it with their troops." [19] We

[13] Justinian, *Institutes,* I, 2, 6; I, 1–2, and *The Institutes of Justinian,* ed. Thomas Collett Sandars (New York, 1903), p. 10.

[14] An attempt follows to reproduce the solecism.

[15] *Regia* (1649), p. 133, ll. 4–7. The solecism occurs in the statement: "Sed quicquid illi perditi homines dicunt ac docent de populari administratione . . . ad populum decipiendum pertinent." *Quicquid* is singular; *pertinent* is plural, and so a singular subject is followed by a plural verb.

[16] *Regia* (1649), p. 133, l. 10: "Non popularis est, non regalis, non optimatum, sed militaris." In other words, the English government is outside the three established categories of popular rule.

[17] *Regia* (1649), p. 133, ll. 13–14.

[18] *Ibid.,* p. 133, ll. 14–17.

[19] *Ibid.,* p. 133, ll. 17–18.

should then thank the officers for standing by the state, and for driving off that raging mob of London hirelings and hucksters which lately, like the vermin who followed Clodius,[20] had laid siege to the house of Parliament itself. Are you for this reason to call the first and the peculiar duty of Parliament, which is to maintain above all else the freedom of the people by peace or war, "a military tyranny?"[21] No wonder the traitors who told you to say this use such language; thus of old the abandoned party which supported Antony would call the Senate of Rome when it took to arms against its country's foes, "the Pompeian army."

I am well pleased that your people hate Cromwell, the brave leader of our army, for undertaking in the company of a joyful host of friends, followed by the good wishes of the people, and the prayers of all good men, the war in Ireland[22] in full accordance with the will of God; and I imagine that when later they heard of his many victories they must have burst with spleen. I need not discuss all your lengthy nonsense about the soldiers of Rome! Anyone can see that what follows is far indeed from the truth.

"The power of the people," you say, "comes to an end where that of the king begins."[23] Why is that right? It is common knowledge that practically all kings everywhere have received their thrones from the people under certain limitations; and you must show why, unless the king abides by these conditions, that power which is but entrusted to him should not revert to the people as well from the king as from consul or any other magistrate: Your saying that "the safety of the state requires it"[24] is sheer folly, for whether "that power return to the people" [103] from a king or nobles or triumvirs misusing the authority entrusted to them does not affect at all considerations of public safety. You admit yourself that it reverts from every officer whatever with the exception of a king. Obviously, if a people in its right mind grants control over itself neither to king nor any magistrate save for the general welfare, there can be no reason why, when

[20] Publius Clodius Pulcher, rabble-rouser and bitter enemy of Cicero. Clodius' use of gangs of gladiators led to violence in the streets and attacks on private citizens, senators, and magistrates. Cicero gives many lively accounts of such attacks, notably in *Pro Milone*, xiv, xv.

[21] *Regia* (1649), p. 133, l. 39.

[22] Cromwell took personal command in Ireland from August, 1649, to May, 1650. The "many victories" probably include those of Drogheda and Wexford.

[23] *Regia* (1649), p. 137, l. 23: "Populi esse desinit ubi regis esse incipit."

[24] *Ibid.*, p. 137, ll. 26–27.

the situation is reversed, it should not be able to deprive the king like other magistrates of the control it had granted in order to prevent the ruin of all. Is it not indeed easier for them to deprive one than many?

To grant to any mortal power over one's self on stronger terms than a trust would be the height of madness. Nor is it to be believed that any people since the beginning of the world which had the choice was so utterly foolish as to surrender title to all its power, or to take it back, when it had once been entrusted to its magistrates, without very weighty reasons. But if disturbances or civil wars are stirred up over this, surely such a situation creates no right for a king to keep by force that power to which the people claims title. Thus it is, as we do not deny, that "a leader should not be changed lightly," [25] but this depends on the judgment of the people rather than the right of kings; it does not follow at all that he should never be changed for any reason whatever. So far you have not advanced any claim or produced any right of kings which could make it wrong for a united people to deprive an unworthy king of his throne; if at least, as has often been the case even in your own France, this can be done without the upheaval of civil war—because it is the safety of the people, not the safety of a tyrant, which is the highest law,[26] and such law should be for the advantage of the people against a tyrant, not a tyrant against the people.

To you who have dared to pervert so sacred and holy a law by your jugglery, attempting to give that loftiest of mankind's laws, which do so much to preserve the people, the sole effect of granting impunity to tyrants, to you I speak in prophecy—for all we English so often seem to you "Enthusiasts" and "Inspired" and "Prophets" [27]—saying that God and men alike press on to avenge your fearful crime. Although indeed your sin of trying to cast the whole human race [104] under the sway of tyrants, and thus doing your utmost to sentence them to martyrdom, is itself so monstrous as to bring its own punishment on you, and to haunt you early and late with its furies wherever you fly or wander, and to drive you into a madness worse than that in which you now rave.

I turn now to your other argument, which is no better than the one before: If, you say, the people might take back its power, "there

[25] *Ibid.*, p. 138, ll. 15–16.

[26] Milton here alludes to a famous statement by Cicero, *De Legibus,* III, iii, 8: *Salus populi suprema est lex.*

[27] Common epithets (especially *enthusiasts*) used by Salmasius when speaking of the Independents, but not so common as *latroni* and *Molossian dogs.*

would be no distinction between popular and royal government except that in the one case there are sole leaders and in the other several." [28] What if there were no other difference, would that injure the state? But in fact you do yourself allege other differences, namely "of time" and "in the succession; for popular officials are usually annual," [29] but kings, unless they act amiss, are perpetual, and usually of the same house. Whether the two differ or not is a trifle of no concern to me, and in this respect certainly they agree, namely that in both cases whenever the public interest requires it, the people, which has granted power to another for the sake of public safety, may for the same reason take it back again without injustice. "But by what was called at Rome the Lex Regia, which was treated in the *Institutes,* the Roman people yielded to and conferred on the Emperor all its authority and power." [30] It did so under compulsion by the Caesars, who gave the fair title of law to what was but their own violence; as has been pointed out before and as the jurisconsults themselves admit in discussing this passage. Therefore what was not granted legally in accordance with the popular will is undoubtedly revocable. It is indeed most reasonable that the Roman people gave to the emperor a power no different from that previously granted to their own magistrates, which was an authority both legitimate and revocable, not tyrannical and unreasonable; wherefore the Caesars assumed the power of consul and tribune, but none after Julius, that of dictator; and they would even do honor to the people in the circus, as we were told above by Tacitus and Claudianus.

But, you say, "Just as of old many individuals would sell them-

[28] *Regia* (1649), p. 138, ll. 22–24.

[29] *Ibid.,* p. 138, ll. 32–35, Salmasius points out that in popular government magistrates are created by the people who hold office for a fixed period and are replaced by others who hold office for an equal time. Milton's paraphrase here is based on a Salmasian quotation from Euripides' *Theseus* (*Regia,* 1649, p. 139, ll. 1–4).

[30] In *Regia* (1649), p. 141, ll. 13–14, Salmasius speaks of the Lex Regia by which sovereignty was transferred from the people to one ruler. He adds: "Ea lex, ut scripsit Ulpianus & post eum atque ex eo Justinianus in Institutis, de Principis imperio lata est, *quaque populus ei & in eum omne suum imperium concessit.*" The point of the quotation from Justinian is that there was a transference of "sovereignty" from the people to the king rather than a "delegation" of power. Salmasius makes the point more specific (*Regia,* 1649, p. 142, ll. 1–4): "By the Lex Regia the people transferred to the king all its power and sovereignty so that he may execute them in regard to the people with the same right that the people itself exercised them against private individuals." This matter is treated in Justinian, *Institutes,* I, 2, 6, referred to above, p. 457, n. 13.

selves to another as slaves, so can a whole people." [31] You knight of the lash, concealer of slavery's blemishes, eternal shame even to your own land, [105] you are so foul a procurer and hireling pimp of slavery that even the lowest slaves on any auction block should hate and despise you. If a people could thus yield itself to a king, he might equally yield that same people to some other master or put them up for sale, while in fact it is well-known that a king cannot alienate even his crown property! Shall he then who enjoys only the usufruct of the crown, as it is said, and of crown property by the grant of the people, be able to claim title to that people itself? If you stood for sale on the auction block as a ruined knight with both ears bored and with whitened feet, you would not be so much the foulest of all slaves as you are now, being the author of such shameful teachings. Go on then, as you now do, to exact from yourself against your will the punishment for your crimes. At the end you stutter at length, and quite irrelevantly, about the laws of war; Charles did not conquer us in war, and his forebears, however much they may have been conquerors, yet often disclaimed their rights as such, and furthermore we were never so utterly conquered that we swore allegiance to them without their swearing in their turn by our laws. When Charles had clearly broken these laws, we used arms, after our injuries at his hands, to subdue him, whether you consider that king as an ancient conqueror or modern perjurer; and according to your own teachings "the spoils of war belong to the conqueror." [32] Be then as long-winded as you wish on this point, be as you were before concerning Solinus,[33] namely a sweaty groom from Pliny's stables, the most boring of all blatherers, but be sure that henceforth with all your sound and fury, all your scraps from the rabbis, all your roars from the rest of this chapter, your labors are of no avail to the conquered king, but rather help us who with God's aid have conquered him. [106]

[31] *Regia* (1649), p. 142, ll. 23–25.

[32] This paraphrase is in keeping with Salmasius' position. He recognized the right of conquest. He even uses the example of Christ who endured what a slave does from a master. Christ acknowledged masters who had seized power by force of arms, "since He wished to be born under them" (see *Regia*, 1649, p. 149, ll. 12–16).

[33] Solinus was the author of the *Polyhistora*, an epitome of Pliny's *Naturalis Historia*. Although Salmasius' *Plinianae Exercitationes in Caii Julii Solini Polyhistora* (Paris, 1629) contains the text of the *Polyhistora* itself, the bulk of the book, about eight hundred folio pages of double columns, consists of Salmasius' own Latin notes and comments on Solinus. A reprinted version, *Trajedi ad Rhenum*, 1689, is in NYPL.

CHAPTER VII [1]

Two difficulties,[2] which were indeed serious and ponderous for a trifler like you, caused you to deny in the last chapter that the power of the people was superior to that of the king. If

[1] It is contended in book VII (*Regia,* 1649, pp. 153–83) that if the king cannot be judged, he cannot be rightly condemned. The reasons for this Salmasius sets forth as follows:

1. Those who had part in the conviction of the king committed treason, human and divine: human, because a king cannot be injured without committing the crime of treason; divine, because kings are appointed by God, whose will is opposed when a king is condemned. 2. One who rules cannot be judged by those subject to him, for the king does not have an equal or superior in the kingdom. Basing his argument on illustrations from the Carthaginian Suffetes, Israelite kings, Greek and Venetian oligarchic rule, Salmasius argues that a true king alone can judge, and can be judged by none. This principle holds in both elective and hereditary monarchies. Even if a king violates his oath of fealty, not the people, but God alone should punish him. 3. A king cannot be punished because he is not bound by laws. A king might be an adulterer or homicide and yet rule well. 4. A private person in being deprived of life loses only his life. A king loses both life and kingdom, and hence is doubly punished. 5. The king alone has majesty; the people do not have it. 6. Therefore the crime of treason can be committed only by the people against the king. The king cannot by a hostile act commit treason against himself or the nation, although if the people were to commit a similar act, that would constitute treason. 7. The English defended their act by the law of nature. But the law of nature should protect the king, for the safety of the ruler is united with that of his subjects. By the law of nature we should cherish the ruler as we do our subjects, parents, patrons, or masters, whom we should not harm. 8. The word "people" should include all persons of all ranks, not just the common people, to whom the English have attributed the highest power. 9. The people cannot delegate power which it does not have. Even if it did have the power of choosing the ruler, the selection would probably be unwise and would be accompanied by trouble. 10. Nothing is really appointed by chance, for God directs the choice of kings. Bad kings are sometimes appointed by God to punish a nation. Good kings are appointed for the happiness of nations which God wants to reward. 11. Examples of monarchy, from Aristotle, from sun-worship in America, from colonies founded by migrant leaders, prove that the king does not owe his power to the people. 12. A tyrant differs from a king in that a tyrant seizes possession of a kingdom, and holds possession of it, once seized, by force; whereas a king rules over willing subjects and keeps his kingdom by the good will of his subjects. 13. If any part of the people should have the power of creating a king, it should be that part consisting of men more honest, wise, and learned, those older in family, more powerful in resources.

Yet in England, only a small part of the people, nobles excluded, deposed and beheaded the king.

[2] Milton apparently has in mind Salmasius' contention that laws of the *Lex Regia* type mean an irrevocable transference of sovereignty to the king; and

you had yielded the point, you must have found some other word for king and called the people by that name, and some divisions of your political system would have fallen into disorder. The former case would be the ruin of your word list, the latter of all your politics. In my reply I took into account chiefly our own welfare and freedom, but also your terminology and politics. Now you say, "It must be established on other grounds that a king cannot be tried by his own subjects, and of these grounds the most powerful and the soundest is that in his own realm a king has no peer." [3] What is this? Has the king no peer within his realm? What then are these twelve most ancient peers of France? Are they empty dreams of Turpin? [4] Are they so called in vain mockery? Beware such insult to men who are princes of France. Or are they merely peers one of another? As if indeed but twelve of all the nobles of France were each other's peers, or this should lead us to call them peers of France! Unless they are actual peers of the king of France, so entitled because they guide the state along with him, having equal rights and equal wisdom, you must have a care that your glossary, which is your sole concern, be not more derided in the kingdom of France than in our commonwealth. Come

---

secondly, that such a transference is often necessitated by considerations of public safety.

[3] *Regia* (1649), p. 153, ll. 15–19. Through book VII Salmasius emphasizes the significance of "Majesty." For Salmasius "majesty" is a legal term expressing *de facto* royal right and what we would recognize legally as "sovereignty." Lèse-majesté by its very legal significance implies that the king cannot be tried by his subjects (*Regia,* 1649, p. 308, ll. 33–34: "Could these things be committed by subjects without the crime of lèse-majesté?"). "Majesty is the ruler's" (*Regia,* 1649, p. 153, ll. 14–15). Majesty includes sovereignty, and treason is always against sovereignty. A private person might pull down the defensive wall of a city, and this would be lèse-majesté, but not if the king himself did it (*Regia,* 1649, p. 163, ll. 1–3). A king cannot commit treason against his subjects and vassals because they do not possess sovereignty, having granted it to the king as exemplified in the Roman Julian law (*Regia,* 1649, p. 162, ll. 1 ff.). Treason can be conceivably committed only by one who is *subject* to a sovereignty against that sovereignty. Once people have chosen a king, they give up their sovereignty, and it is irrevocable (*Regia,* 1649, p. 137, ll. 32–33: "ut potestas a populo Regi semel concessa & donata numquam revocetur"). Salmasius quotes Justinian to this effect (*Regia,* 1649, p. 141, l. 16). "Under English law a king does not incur the crime of high treason if he has contrived sedition against himself, his army, his people" (*Regia,* 1649, p. 308, l. 38 ff.).

[4] Turpin was an eighth-century prelate, the supposed author of a *chronique,* the legendary *Historia de Vita Caroli Magni et Rolandi.* Tradition holds that Turpin was secretary to Charlemagne and his companion in arms. The twelve peers of France are the heroic knights of the *chansons de geste.*

then with your explanation of there being no peer of a king in his realm.

"Since after the expulsion of the kings," you say, "the Roman people set up two consuls, not one, so that, should one go astray, he might be taken to task by his colleague." [5] It would be hard to imagine greater stupidity. Why then did but one consul keep the *fasces* rather than both, if one was there to check the other? And if they had both plotted against the state would the situation have been any better [107] than if no colleague had been given to the consul? It is however agreed that the two consuls and all the magistrates were always obliged to obey the Senate whenever it was felt by the fathers and the plebs to be in the public interest. On this point I possess the best of evidence in the speech of Marcus Tullius for Sestius; and you should also consider the succinct account he gives there of the Roman state; this was, he said, established with all wisdom, and should be known by all sound citizens, to which I agree.

"Our forefathers, being unable to endure the dominion of kings, did create annual magistrates to ensure that the deliberations of the Senate would always guide the state; men for that council were to be elected by the whole people; entrance into that foremost rank was to be open to the industry and character of all citizens. They set up the Senate as guardian, guide, and champion of the state; they wished their magistrates to follow the expressed will of this order and be as it were executives of this weighty assembly." [6] The best example of this might be the decemvirs, for though they enjoyed consular power in the highest sense they were still one and all, despite any resistance, compelled to yield to the authority of the Senate. We are also told that certain consuls, even before the end of their terms, were judged to be enemies of the state and were opposed by force of arms. For none supposed that he who acted as an enemy was still a consul. Thus under Senatorial auspices war was waged against the consul Antony, and on his defeat he would have been executed had not Caesar Octavianus in his desire to rule joined with him to overthrow the government.

Your statement too, that "it is the peculiar attribute of royal majesty, that power belongs to one alone," [7] is equally unreliable, and is promptly refuted by your own words: "The Hebrew judges held

[5] *Regia* (1649), p. 153, ll. 23–28.
[6] Cicero, *Pro Sestio,* LXV, 137.
[7] *Regia* (1649), p. 154, ll. 1-2.

power one at a time and for their whole lives; the Scripture also calls them kings; but yet the Sanhedrin tried them." In your eagerness to have spoken on every point, your actual words are almost wholly contradictory. Tell me next what form of government you call it when two or three emperors at once ruled the Roman empire! Do you suppose they were emperors, that is kings, or were they nobles, or triumvirs? Would you really say that under [108] Antoninus and Verus, Diocletian and Maximianus, or Constantine and Licinianus, the Roman empire was not one empire? [8] Your own sharpness has endangered your "three kinds of states" unless they were kings; and, if they were, it follows that it is not a peculiar attribute of royal government that the power belongs to one alone.[9] Then you say that "if one of them is delinquent, the other may bring the matter before the people or the Senate so that he may be accused and condemned." [10] Is it then not true that he is judged by the people or the Senate when his colleague has put the case before them? Thus if your own words have any weight in your mind, there was no need of one colleague to judge the other.

What a champion you are! One would have to pity you were you not so detestable, for you are such an easy mark that I do believe it would be hard for anyone making you his target to miss hitting you wherever he wanted.

"Ridiculous," you call it, for "a king to be willing to appoint judges who may condemn him to death." [11] I bring up against you Trajan, who was not ridiculous but rather the best of emperors. When giving to his praetorian prefect Saburanus a dagger as the customary insignia of that office, he thus admonished him several times: "Take this weapon and use it for me if I do right; if not, against me, for it is especially unrighteous that the guide of all men should himself go astray." This account is given by Dio [12] and Aurelius Victor.[13] You see how this great emperor appointed over himself a judge who was

[8] Pairs of various Roman emperors who shared the rule of the empire.

[9] Salmasius has been careful to point out that while some governments have been called royal in which the kingship was shared, the title is a misnomer. Milton disregards Salmasius' reservation, and assumes that any historical title of king signifies what Salmasius has carefully defined as kingly. Milton refutes Salmasius by raising what is not in question.

[10] *Regia* (1649), p. 154, ll. 5–8.

[11] *Regia* (1649), p. 156, ll. 20–21.

[12] Dio Cassius, *Dio's Roman History,* LXVIII, 16, 1.

[13] Aurelius Victor, *De Caesaribus,* XIII, 9, ed. Francis Pichlmayr (Leipzig, 1911), p. 92.

far from being his peer. This might have been said by Tiberius as a treacherous boast; but that Trajan, the best and purest of men, did not speak from his heart what he felt was true, just, and holy could be thought only by a scoundrel. How much the more then did he show his justice in his dutiful obedience to the Senate and his acknowledgement of their rightful superiority to himself, when through his greater power he need not have obeyed them. Of this Pliny says in the *Panegyricus*: [14] "The Senate requested and commanded your acceptance of a fourth consulship, and you may be sure from your own compliance with their wishes that this was in fact a command and not mere flattery." Shortly afterwards he says, "It was surely your plan to restore and reestablish freedom." The Senate thought, as did Trajan, that their authority over him was actually supreme, for he who may give commands to an emperor may also be his judge. Thus Marcus Aurelius, when [109] Cassius the prefect of Syria attempted to take his realm from him, presented himself to the judgment of the Senate or the Roman people; he was ready to give up the kingdom if such was their will. Could anyone weigh and decide the rights of a king from a better or more accurate source than from the very mouths of the best kings?

Certainly by the law of nature all good kings always consider the Senate or people as their equal and their superior. Since however a tyrant is by nature the lowest of all men, whoever has more power than he must be considered his equal and superior. Just as once under nature's guidance men advanced from the use of force to laws, so of necessity they must follow that same guide and return to force when laws are disregarded. "Understanding of this," Cicero says in the *Pro Sestio,* "shows a man wise; acting on it shows him brave; understanding and action together show the highest type of fully rounded character." [15] Let this fact then be firmly established as natural, not to be assailed by any tricks of flattery, that a king, whether good or bad, is inferior to Senate or to people. Indeed you admit as much yourself in saying that the royal power was transferred to the king from the people.[16] The power they gave to the king is still by nature and by its particular virtue, or so to speak virtually, retained by the people even after they have granted it to another. For such natural

[14] Pliny, *Panegyricus,* LXXVIII, 1 and 3.

[15] Cicero, *Pro Sestio,* XL, 86.

[16] See above p. 460, n. 30.

causes as thus produce certain effects through their own excellence ever retain more of their own vigor than they give off, nor do they exhaust themselves by the process. You see then that the closer we come to nature the clearer it is that the power of the people surpasses the king's. It is also agreed that a people which has the choice never gives up title to its own power fully and absolutely to its king, and by nature it cannot; the grant is only for the sake of the welfare and freedom of the people, and when the king has failed to secure these, the people is taken to have made no grant; for at nature's warning the people's gift was for a definite purpose only, and if this purpose is not attained by nature or by the people, the gift is no more valid than any broken contract or agreement. Such reasons put it beyond doubt that the people is superior to the king, and thus that argument of yours "so very powerful and so sound, that a king cannot be judged since in his own realm he has [110] neither peer nor superior," [17] is quite swept away.

You assume what we are quite unable to grant. "Under popular government," you say, "a magistrate put in office by the people may be punished by them for his crime; in an aristocracy the nobles may be punished by their fellows; but it is monstrous that a king in his own kingdom be compelled to plead for his life." [18] Do you reach any conclusion save that men who put a king over them are the most foolish and wretched of mortals? But tell me, I pray, why the people should not as well punish a guilty king as a popular official or a noble? Think you that all peoples living under kings had through love of slavery fallen so low as to prefer servitude to the liberty they enjoyed, and to surrender themselves so completely, one and all, to the mastery of a single man, often a wicked man, often a fool, so that if the most inhuman of masters should fall to their lot, they would have kept no protection for their safety in law or in nature, no refuge anywhere for themselves? Do men then prescribe conditions to kings at the beginning of their reigns, and establish laws too for their government, in order to permit themselves to be the more contemptible and ridiculous in their eyes? Does a whole people so debase and betray itself, abandon its own interest, and center all its hopes in a single man, often the least deserving of all men? Why too do kings swear to do nothing contrary to law? I suppose that wretched mortals may learn at their

[17] *Regia* (1649), p. 153, ll. 18–19. [18] *Regia* (1649), p. 156, ll. 26–32.

great cost that kings alone may go unpunished for their lies? Such is the end of your wicked chain of reasoning!

"Should the chosen king have made, even on oath, certain promises, without which he might perhaps not have been appointed, and then be unwilling to keep his agreement, he may not be judged by the people. Even if at his election he should swear to his subjects to administer justice in accordance with the laws of the realm, saying that otherwise they will be free from their oath of allegiance and he will by that very act give up his power, yet if he break his word his punishment must come from God rather than man." [19] I have not gone through this passage because of its elegance, for it is most barbarous, nor because it needs further refutation, for it refutes itself, mocks and condemns itself, by its own obvious and shameful falsity. I did it to recommend to kings your unparalleled merit, so that amid all the countless positions at court [111] they may search out for you some place which fits your worth as a suitable reward. For when some are there in charge of the finances, some of the cellars, some of the kitchens, some of the revels, you may very fittingly take charge of perjury; you will not be, like Petronius, *arbiter elegantiae*,[20] for you are too uncouth, but Arbiter-in-Chief of the Royal Lies.

But that all may realize better how you combine the utmost folly with every wickedness we may consider a little more closely this wonderful statement you just made: "Even if at his election a king swore to his subjects to rule in accordance with the law, or otherwise they would be absolved of their oath of allegiance and he would by that very act give up his power," still he cannot be deposed or punished by them! Why not a king, I wonder, as well as a popular magistrate? Because in the latter form of government the people did not surrender all their power to the magistrate. What difference in the case of a king, to whom they granted government over themselves only so long as he governs well? A king sworn to uphold the law may when guilty be deposed and punished just as well as a popular magistrate. That catch-as-catch-can argument of yours about all power being transferred to the king can serve you no more, for you have stupidly hoisted it with your own petard.

Hear now, O Reader, another of his mighty and invincible reasons

[19] *Regia* (1649), p. 158, ll. 18–25.

[20] "Judge of elegance": one who determines and sets the pattern for elegance in style, a tribute to the aesthetic taste of Petronius. See Tacitus, *Annals,* xvi, 18.

why subjects cannot judge their king—"he is above the law, and he alone makes all law." [21]

Since I have time and time again proved this to be utterly untrue, this invincible argument of yours falls to the ground along with the former. It may be indeed that for a time a king may go unpunished for some personal misdeeds, such as lewdness, adultery, and the like, but this arises less from his "right" than from the long-suffering of the people, who by the disturbances accompanying the death of a king and a change of government would lose more than would be gained by the punishment of one or two individuals. But when a ruler becomes unbearably burdensome to all, according to the belief of all nations at all times, it is right for a people to do away with a tyrant either before or after trial, in whatever way they can. Thus Marcus Tullius says of Caesar's murderers in the *Second Philippic*: [22] "They were the first to use their swords in attacking one who was ruling rather than one seeking to rule. This deed is not only noble and god-like in itself [112], but is an example to us all." What a contrast to you!

"Murder, adultery, wanton damage are not the crimes of a king but of a citizen." [23]

Bravo, parasite, your speech has done all the pimps and shameless profligates at court a good turn! How clever you are in being at once parasite and pimp!

"A king may commit adultery or murder and yet govern well, and therefore he should not lose his life, for with it he must lose his king-dom as well: but never has it been approved by laws human or divine that two punishments be exacted for one crime." [24]

Mouthpiece of foulest infamy! By such reasoning, officials, both popular or aristocratic, judges too, and guilty senators, should never suffer execution, for that would be a double punishment! With their

[21] This is a paraphrase of Salmasius' repeated position. In *Regia* (1649), p. 159, ll. 32–35, the king is above law (*legibus solutus*), the king alone makes all laws ("leges solus rex omnes fert"), he makes them at his discretion (*gratiam*).

[22] Cicero, *Philippics,* II, xliv, 114.

[23] This is a paraphrase of Salmasius' distinction between private and public crimes (*Regia,* 1649, p. 160, ll. 12–13). The king who is a homicide and an adulterer may rule well, as in the case of David. Since for Salmasius the king constitutes an actual union of person and office, to punish the king as a person would also be to punish the kingdom, which would be unjust.

[24] *Regia* (1649), p. 160, ll. 15–19.

lives they must lose their offices as well! Then you are as eager to deprive the people of their majesty as of their power, and give it to the king; you may if you wish give him a substitute and borrowed majesty, but you cannot give him the true original any more than in the case of his power.

"A king cannot commit treason against his people, though a people can against the king." [25]

But a king exists for the people, not the people for the king. Therefore the whole people or a majority should always have greater power than the king: this you deny, and add up your figures: "the king has more power than one, two, three, ten, a hundred, a thousand, ten thousand." [26] Fair enough. "More than half the people." Perhaps. "If the other half be added as well, is he not still more powerful?" [27] By no means! Carry on; why run off with your counting board, O great accountant, unless you are ignorant of arithmetical progression?

The fellow turns to a new system of accounting and asks "whether the king together with the nobles does not have more power?" This too I deny, my flighty friend,[28] if by nobles you mean lords; for it may be that none of them deserves the name of noble. More often far more of the commoners surpass the lords in character and intellect; and if they are joined by the larger or more able part of the people, I need not hesitate to state that they are equivalent to the whole people.

"If he have not more power than all the people, he will be but king of individuals and not of all together": [29] quite true [113] unless they so desire.

Add up your accounts, then, and you will find that by your incompetent computations you have lost your capital!

"The English say that the rights of majesty belong by origin and nature to the people; but this is subversion of every form of government." [30]

[25] *Regia,* 1649), p. 164. ll. *22–23.*

[26] *Regia* (1649), p. 167, ll. 14–15. Salmasius has denounced the argument that, granted though the king has more power than single individuals, he does not have more than all the people together (*Regia,* 1649, p. 167, ll. 12–13).

[27] *Regia* (1649), p. 167, ll. 16–17.

[28] *iterum nego, Vertumne:* "again I deny, O Vertumnus." Vertumnus ("flighty") was "the god of the changing year,"—hence a symbol of mutability.

[29] *Regia* (1649), p. 167, ll. 34–36.

[30] Salmasius says in *Regia* (1649), p. 169, ll. 12–15: "Nunc discutienda illa quaestio quae jam contra reges a parricidis Anglicanis ita deciditur, ut dicant penes populum jus majestatis ex origine & naturae ipsius vi residere." Later on the same page he adds (ll. 18–19): "Hoc vero est omnium statuum eversionem

Of aristocracy too, and democracy? A likely story! If it put an end to the rule of women, under which you are reported to be so henpecked at home, would not the English have made you happy, you chicken-hearted little man? You need not hope for this, for a fitting fate awaits you; as you go abroad seeking to burden others with tyranny, so at home you labor under the most shameful and unmanly form of slavery.

"We must explain," you say, "what we mean by people." [31]

There are a great many things we must explain to you first; for you seem to have no idea of what concerns you much more closely, and never have learned or even been able to understand anything but your schoolboy's lore. You suppose that you know we mean by *people* only the populace, because "we have done away with the House of Lords." [32] Actually it is just this fact which shows that by *people* we mean all citizens of every degree. We have made supreme the one assembly of the people, in which the nobles, as part of the people, have a legal right to vote, not indeed as before in their own behalf, but in behalf of the communities electing them.

You must attack the populace as "blind and brutish, without skill in ruling, the most fickle of men, the emptiest, the unsteadiest, and most inconstant." [33]

This description best fits yourself. It may be true of the dregs of the populace, but hardly of the middle class, which produces the greatest number of men of good sense and knowledge of affairs. Of the rest some are turned from uprightness and from their interest in learning their country's laws by excessive wealth and luxury, and others by want and poverty.

"There are," you continue, "many ways in which kings may be appointed without being obligated to the people for it, first of all those whose kingdom is hereditary." [34]

---

inducere." Milton, particularly in dealing with the later books of Salmasius, frequently telescopes scattered quotations or gives as direct quotations his own paraphrases and probably his own notes on Salmasius' text. Many of these are fair to Salmasius' general sense, but quite a few are inaccurate and misleading—implications that Milton has made in terms of his own bias and not existent in either Salmasius' text or his mind. For a particularly bad example, see above, p. 365, n. 87.

[31] *Regia* (1649), p. 169, ll. 28–29. [32] *Regia* (1649), p. 170, ll. 9–10.

[33] This quotation is a summary of parts of various statements made by Salmasius, *Regia* (1649), p. 170, *passim*, esp. l. 18.

[34] Cf. *Regia* (1649), p. 172, ll. 21–22 and 24–25.

Surely those nations must be slavish and born to serve who admit that without their own consent they have become the inheritance of such masters. They certainly cannot be considered citizens or free born or even free. We must suppose that they are not members [114] of any commonwealth; they are instead to be counted as part of the property and possessions of their master and his son and heir. For in respect to the owner's rights I see no difference between them and slaves or cattle.

Next you say that "those who won their kingdoms with the sword cannot recognize the people as the source of the power they have extended or acquired." [35]

Our discussion, however, concerns a vanquished rather than a victorious king. I shall discuss elsewhere the power of a conqueror, and you must keep to your own concerns. As to your frequent attempts to ascribe to kings the ancient rights of a *pater familias* that you may draw from thence "an example of the absolute power of kings," [36] I have already shown often enough that the two things are quite unlike. Even that Aristotle you chatter about would, if you had read him, have informed you of this fact right at the start of his *Politics*. He says there that those who see little distinction between a king and a father are much mistaken, "for kingdom differs from family in species as well as in number." [37] For as villages later grew into towns and cities, the royal right of the family gradually disappeared and was no longer recognized. Thus in book I Diodorus [38] relates that, of old, kingdoms were not granted to kings' sons but to those whose services to the people were most outstanding. So too Justinus: [39] "Originally kings controlled peoples and nations; they were elevated to this height of majesty by no efforts at popularity but by proving to men of sense the balance of their characters." Thus it is quite clear that even at the beginning of nations the paternal and hereditary power had given place to strength of character, and soon afterwards to the rights of the people. This is the source, justification, and true natural cause of royal power. It was for this very cause that men first joined together, not that one might abuse the rest, but that if any injured another there might be no lack of law or of a judge between men to protect,

[35] This is a paraphrase of *Regia* (1649), p. 173, ll. 19–21.

[36] *Regia* (1649), p. 175, ll. 34–35. See above, p. 326, and below, p. 473, n. 40.

[37] *Politics*, 1252 a 8 (I, 1).

[38] Diodorus Siculus, I, 43, 6.

[39] Justinus, I, 1, 1; M. Junianus Justinus, *Epitoma Historiarum Philippicarum Pompei Trogi*, ed. Otto Seel (Leipzig, 1935), p. 3.

or at least to avenge, the injured party. Men who once were scattered and dispersed far and wide were led by someone of eloquence and wisdom to adopt a life in states; you would have it that "his chief reason was that he might exercise dominion over the whole group." [40] Perhaps you are thinking of Nimrod, who is said to have been the first tyrant.[41] Or is it not rather your own peculiar wickedness, wholly inapplicable to those great and high-souled men of old, your own peculiar invention which no one, so far as I know, before you has ever asserted? We learn instead, from all the evidence of antiquity, that those original founders of cities looked not to their own interests or authority but to the welfare and the preservation of mankind [115].[42]

There is one point I cannot pass over, which it seems you would employ as a sort of decoration to set off the rest of this chapter: "Had it been necessary," you say, "for a consul to face trial before the end of his term, a dictator must have been appointed for that purpose," though you had begun by stating that "he had a colleague assigned him to that end." [43]

[40] Here is a sharp polemical difference between Milton and Salmasius. Milton is arguing for the origin of kingship on the basis of balance of character (as in the quotation from Justinus) and strength of character (his own words). This is his theory of natural leadership (see above p. 366, n. 91). Salmasius' concept of leadership is based on the "natural" status of the father, and in this sense is much closer to the ancient Roman law (the *patria potestas*) and the actual customs of antique peoples. Salmasius, following Aristotle, traces the growth of the state from the union of villages, with leaders following the laws of kingship. The family leads to the village, and the villages lead to the state on a "father" (primogeniture) basis. Kings (outgrowth of fathers) form the original historical pattern. *Haec primo origo regalis regiminis, & ab his principiis repetenda, ut maxime naturalis, ratio & causa monarchici imperii* (*Regia,* 1649, p. 175, ll. 28–29). Milton in referring to being "led by someone of eloquence and wisdom to adopt a life in states" echoes the same statement in *Regia* (1649), p. 176, ll. 27–31. Salmasius would grant that where the family system had broken down, a man of eloquence and wisdom (*cf.* l. 29, "Cuius eloquio & sapientia juxta potentis blandiloqua & prudens oratio") would persuade wandering and solitary people to form a state. But it was not *fear* that originally gathered men together (as a family, they *were* initially together). It was actually fear that had scattered them (*cf. Regia,* 1649, p. 176, ll. 22–26). Salmasius argues that the main purpose of the wise and eloquent man, in seeking to form a state, was not the pursuit of power, but the encouragement of civilization. Men, who had been wandering like wild animals, were brought into accord and union, living like citizens.

[41] Josephus says in the *Antiquities,* I, 4, that "Nimrod also gradually changed his behavior into a tyranny."

[42] This is also Salmasius' point. Milton is just not paying attention to what Salmasius is saying.

[43] *Regia* (1649), p. 179, l. 39; p. 180, ll. 1–3.

Your words are always as consistent as this, and show from page to page that whatever you say or write on any subject is wholly worthless. "Under the old Anglo-Saxon kings," you say, "it was never the custom to summon the populace to the national assemblies." [44] Such a statement by a fellow-countryman I might easily expose, and I am hardly troubled by this voice from abroad raving about our business. This about finishes what you have to say in general concerning the rights of kings. I say nothing of all the mass of matter which remains, for as usual you are far off the mark; some of it is completely unfounded and some irrelevant, and it is certainly not my object to appear your equal in loquacity. [116]

CHAPTER VIII [1]

If, Salmasius, your opinions on the right of kings in general had been advanced without invective against anyone, there would have been, even during the present revolution in England, no reason for any Englishman to become angry with you, for you would have but employed your freedom to write; nor would the assertion of your beliefs have been the less effective. For if, as you stated earlier on page 127, we were instructed both by Moses and by Christ that "to their own kings, whether good or bad, all men are subject,

[44] *Ibid.*, p. 181, ll. 11–16.

[1] The English, in order to defend the beheading of Charles, Salmasius argues in book VIII (*Regia,* 1649, pp. 184–220), maintain that he was not king but only president of parliament and the chief magistrate of the people. Majesty, in this version, had resided in Parliament, not in the king.

1. Charles was a real king of England, Scotland, and Ireland. He had received these kingdoms by heredity. 2. According to Aristotle, true kingly rule consists in one person being master of all and doing all things according to his rule. This is much more than being a nominal king as among the Lacedaemonians. Although their king was not a real one, he was respectfully spared even in the heat of battle. But the English deliberately assailed their king, even though a true one! 3. The successors of William the Conqueror have had hereditary right to the kingdom of England. In view of the history of the British kingdom, no one could consider the king only as a special magistrate and the leader of Parliament. 4. Some kings add to the edicts of Parliament the words "by the grace of God," indicating that royal power depends upon no one but Divinity and was established by it. In other statutes the king is referred to as supreme and Parliament is spoken of as "the Parliament of the king." Rightly so, because Parliament is convoked by the king, and the matters enacted in it are called the laws and statutes of the king. 5. The

Spanish, French, Italian, German, English and Scots alike,"[2] there was then no need for you, an unknown foreigner, to prate of our laws and try to lecture us on them like a pedant expounding his own hodge-podge of pamphlets; for, whatever they might be, they must, as you had expounded at great length, give place to the laws of God. It is now clear enough that you joined in the support of the king's cause not so much because of your own disposition as because you were hired, partly for a fee (which, considering the resources of your employer, was magnificent), and, partly through anticipation of some greater reward to come—hired, that is, to produce an infamous book calumniating the English, who have caused their neighbors no trouble and who mind their own business.

Can we believe, if this be not so, that any foreigners would be so filled with impudent folly as to rush uninvited from far off to interfere in our affairs and unhesitatingly adhere to a faction? How the devil does it concern you what the English do amongst themselves? What is your business, Olus, what do you want? Have you no concerns at home? I wish you had the same as that infamous Olus in the epigram; [3] perhaps you have, for it would suit you perfectly. Or did that eager horse-woman, your wife, prick you on, in full gallop though you were, to write this stuff to please the exiled Charles by promising you some loftier position and greater rewards on Charles' return? Such at

---

king is truly the head of Parliament, but he is not merely that. By his royal prerogative he governs the nation while Parliament is not in session. Majesty cannot reside in parliament itself, for it cannot summon itself and call the king to the meeting. The king is above Parliament, not vice versa, for Parliament was established by the king, not the king by Parliament. Since Parliament gets its power from the king, it should do nothing to impair the power of the king. Parliament could not be established by the people because the power of summoning and dismissing Parliament has always resided with the king. 6. The king's superiority over Parliament is proved by the fact that the power of the king is perpetual and is necessary to make valid any decision made by Parliament, whose power is only temporary and, therefore, dependent upon the perpetual power of the king. If the majesty of a king depended upon Parliament, did the earlier kings, who rule without Parliaments, have no majesty? 7. The majesty of the king is harmed when any personal injury is inflicted as well as when his political power is diminished. Both acts constitute treason. 8. The natural and the political body of the king, his person and power, his person and crown, are inextricably united. His sovereign power is inseparable from his person, so that he cannot be punished as a private individual. "The king can do no wrong." 9. A magistrate *can* do wrong and is punished accordingly. A king cannot.

[2] *Regia* (1649), p. 127, ll. 13–15.

[3] Olus is mentioned in Martial, VII, 10. See above, p. 319, n. 49.

least is the common report. [117] But you must know, wife and husband alike, that in England there is no place for a wolf or his master. No wonder you rave so often and so wildly about our wolfhounds! Trot back instead to those lofty titles of yours in France, to that starveling lordship of St. Loup, and to that sacred consistory of the Most Christian King; you have left your country too far behind for a counselor!

Actually of course I can see that France wants neither you nor your counsel, nor did she when, a few years ago, you returned searching and sniffing after a cardinal's fare; [4] she is indeed wise and is glad to let a eunuch priest [5] like you wander around, with your wife for a husband, and your bags full of nonsense, until somewhere or other you find a post suitable for a mounted grammarian or a great hippocritic—that is, if any king or state should have a mind to bid a great price for a wandering teacher now for sale.

But here is a bid for you; we shall soon see whether you are salable and at what price. "The parricides," you say, "insist that the English form of government is composite and not a pure monarchy." [6] The same point was insisted on under Edward the Sixth at the very beginning of his book on the English state by our countryman Smith,[7] a skilled jurist and a statesman, whom you cannot call a parricide. He asserts that this is true not only of our country but also, according to Aristotle, of well-nigh all states, for otherwise none of them could subsist.

You, however, as if you thought you must do penance for making

[4] The allusion is probably to Richelieu's attempt to keep Salmasius in France in 1640 by offering to hire him to write a history of his ministry. Salmasius refused.

[5] "eunuch priest": Milton speaks of Salmasius as *semivir Gallus*—a phrase involving a pun. *Gallus* is not only a Gaul or Frenchman, but also a priest of Cybele. These priests were usually persons who had castrated themselves as a sign of devotion to the goddess. *Gallus* also means *cock*.

[6] *Regia* (1649), p. 184, ll. 26–28: "Pertendunt iidem parricidae, regni Anglicani statum mixtum esse ac dilutum populari imperio, non mere regium nec monarchicum."

[7] In his *Commonplace Book* Milton quotes the following from Sir Thomas Smith, *The Commonwealth of England* (*Complete Prose,* I, 442): "Whether monarchy be a power absolute. Sr Tho. Smith answereth. that neither it nor any kind of common wealth is pure and absolute in his kind, no more then the elements are pure in nature, or the complexions, and temperatures in a body but mixt with other, 'for that nature . . . will not suffer it.' " The *De Republica Anglorum* (London, 1583; NYPL) was the first edition of this work.

any uncontradicted statement, fly back to your old shopworn contradictions. "There is not now," you say, "and there never has been any people which by the name of king implied anything but that power which is inferior to God alone and has God alone as its judge." [8] A little later, though, you admit that "of old, the name of king was given to such authorities and officials as had a power which was not full and free but depended on the will of the people, as, for example, the Carthaginian suffetes, Jewish judges, Spartan kings, and finally the kings of Aragon." [9] See how nicely consistent you are!

Then you line up the five Aristotelian types of monarchy,[10] of which only one possessed that right [118] you ascribe to all kings alike. I have already stated more than once that no example of this is cited by Aristotle or ever existed anywhere, while he shows most clearly that the other four came under the law and were subordinate to it. Of these the first, and the one he holds most monarchical of these coming under the law, was the Spartan. Second was that of the barbarians, which endured only because it came under the law and had popular support, for without that support any king becomes immediately a tyrant if he keeps the kingdom against the will of the people. So says Aristotle in Book V.[11] The same is true of the third kind of king, called by him *Aesymnete,* elected by the people, usually for a fixed period and a particular purpose, as were the Roman dictators for the most part. The fourth kind includes those who ruled in heroic times, to whom, in return for outstanding services, the people of their own accord offered kingdoms which were nonetheless subject to the law; they did not in fact rule save by the will of the people. Our author

[8] *Regia* (1649), p. 184, ll. 8–11.

[9] This is a kaleidoscoping of various statements and phrases of Salmasius (chiefly *Regia,* 1649, p. 187, ll. 1–3, and p. 188, ll. 24–26). Milton misinterprets Salmasius, whose meaning is clear enough. The "name" of king is not the same thing as actually being a king. The rulers listed were never really kings according to Salmasian definition. Salmasius makes a special point about the unique position of the Spartan king ("Nihil tamen habuit potestatis regiae praeter nomen," p. 187, ll. 2–3). Two Spartan kings shared the rule, one hereditary, the other elected for conducting a war. A "true" king would be hereditary but would not share his office. "At Rex non est nisi unus sit & unicus" (*Regia,* 1649, p. 188, l. 37). Of the Spartan kings Salmasius says (*Regia,* 1649, p. 188, ll. 20–24): "That Spartan kingdom was *sui generis,* and there was nothing similar in the whole of antiquity or now, nor is any analogy or comparision possible with any known in Europe today."

[10] For Aristotle's five types of monarchies see *Politics* 1285 a 1 (III, 14, 2).

[11] *Ibid.,* 1313 a 15 (V, 10, 23).

states that the chief difference among these four kinds of monarchy and tyranny is that in the former the government is in accordance with the will of the people and in the latter against it. A fifth type of rule, called παμβασιλεία and endowed with supreme power such as you would ascribe to all kings,[12] is roundly condemned by the philosopher as useless, unjust, and unnatural, save where some people can endure such rule and confer it on men who far surpass all others in virtue.

These opinions may be found by anyone in the third book of the *Politics*. But you, in order, I suppose, to seem for once clever and flowery, tried wildly to compare "these five kinds of monarchy to the world's five zones." "Between the two extremes of royal power there seem to be three other kinds which are more temperate, just like those zones which lie between the torrid and the frigid." [13] You clever man, what fine comparisons you always try to arrange for us! Be off apace to that frigid zone to which you banish governments with absolute power; on your arrival it will be twice as cold! Meanwhile we grow impatient for that wondrous globe which you, like some new Archimedes, are constructing with two outer zones, one hot and the other cold, and with three [119] temperate ones between!

"The Spartan kings," you say, "might be put in chains, but not executed." [14] Why so? Because, when Agis was condemned to death, the guards and foreign soldiers were overcome by the novelty of the business and thought it wrong to conduct the king to execution. The Spartan people themselves took his death amiss, not because it was a king who suffered capital punishment, but because a good man who loved the people was overthrown in that trial by a party of wealthy men. Such is the account in Plutarch: "Agis was the first king put to death by the ephors." [15] He states here not what should have been

[12] *Regia* (1649), p. 186, ll. 37–39: "Aristotle sets up this fifth kind of rule in which all dominion is placed in one man, who does all things according to his will."

[13] *Ibid.*, p. 186, ll. 16–19. Strictly speaking, there is one temperate zone in the northern hemisphere, another in the southern. The analogy is incomplete in Salmasius because he is speaking of three kinds of royal government instead of two. Milton returns to attack this mistake of Salmasius later (see below, p. 506, n. 39). The three types ascend to the peak of absolute power and decline to that which is most free and lax.

[14] *Ibid.*, p. 189, ll. 1–5.

[15] Plutarch, *Agis and Cleomenes*, XIX, 6 and XXI, 3, in *Plutarch's Lives*, tr. Bernadotte Perrin (10 vols., London: Loeb Classical Library, 1920), X, 92–93, 96–97.

done but only what was done. For it is childish to think that those who are able to try or even to imprison a king cannot execute him as well. You now prepare to deal with the rights of English kings.

"In England," you say, "there was always a single king."[16] This you assert because you had just stated that "there is no king save where he is the only one of his kind."[17] If this be true, many whom I used to consider kings of England were not such. Not to speak of the many Saxon kings who had sons or brothers as colleagues, we all know that Henry the Second, of Norman stock, reigned together with his son.

"Let them," you say, "bring forward any instance of a kingdom ruled by a single man where he has not been granted absolute power, even though in some cases that power may be somewhat abated, in others extended."[18] Do you show, you fool, an absolute power which is abated; or is absolute power not the most extensive? How then can it be at once the most extensive and abated? I shall easily show that whatever kings you admit had their power abated did not have absolute power and were therefore inferior to a people by nature free, which is its own lawmaker, and can also extend or abate the royal power.

Whether in ancient times all Britain was under kings is not known: It is most likely that as circumstances required it they used now one form of government and now another. Thus Tacitus states:[19] "The British once were ruled by kings, but now the chiefs divide them with their party politics." When abandoned by the Romans, they were some forty years without kings, and so that "unbroken rule" you set up did not exist of old. That it was hereditary I positively deny, for this appears both from the succession of kings and the manner of creating [120] them—in so many words they seek the support of the people. Thus after the king has taken the usual oath, the archbishop moves to the four corners of the lofty platform, and at each in turn puts this question to the people as a whole: "Are you willing to agree on this man as your king?" This is as though he had said in the Roman man-

[16] *Regia* (1649), p. 192, l. 19. [17] *Ibid.*, p. 188, l. 37.

[18] An amalgam of *Regia* (1649), p. 192, ll. 19–22 ("Ostendant olim aliquod regnum fuisse aut nunc esse quod sub unius imperio foret qui regis nomine dictus sit, cui non potestas etiam eo nomine digna adjuncta fuerit") and of p. 192, ll. *22-25*, in reference to the unique Spartan kingdom where power was more abated or more intensified.

[19] Tacitus, *Agricola,* XII; see *Dialogues,* above, p. 449, n. 121.

ner, "Do you wish and command this man to rule?" There would have been no need for this had the kingdom been by law hereditary.

With kings, however, usurpation very often has the force of law, and you would base the royal rights of Charles on the laws of war, though he was himself so often beaten in war. I suppose William the Conqueror did conquer us, but those who are most familiar with our history know that the English strength was not so reduced in the one battle at Hastings that they could not have renewed the war, though with difficulty. But they preferred to accept a king rather than endure a conquering tyrant, and therefore swore to William that they would be faithful to him, while he swore to them, as he stood by the altar, that he would treat them in all respects as a good king should. When he broke his word and the English again resorted to arms, he lacked confidence in his own power and swore anew on the Gospels to keep the ancient laws of England. Therefore if later he cruelly oppressed the English it was by the laws, not of war, but of perjury that he so acted. Furthermore it is certain that, long ago, conquered and conquerors were joined into a single people, and so the laws of war, if they ever applied, must have become obsolete long since. His very dying words, cited from that most reliable volume of Caen,[20] remove all doubt: "I appoint no one," he said, "as heir to the realm of England." By these words your laws of war, and of inheritance as well, were mourned and buried with the corpse of the conqueror.

I now see that, as I foretold, you have won office at court, namely that of chief supervisor and agent of royal roguery. Thus you seem to write what comes next in your official capacity, your excellency! "If by combinations of the nobles or rebellions of the populace any former king has been forced to yield a portion of his rights, that fact cannot prevent his successor from reasserting them." [21] [121]

You give us fair warning! Thus, if ever our fathers lost a portion of their rights through inaction, is that fact to bind us, their sons? They could, if they would, accept slavery for themselves, but assuredly not for us, who will ever have as good a right to set ourselves free as they did to make themselves slaves of anyone.

You are amazed "how it happens that today the king of England

[20] It is conjectured that Milton alludes to the *Elogiorum Civium Cadomensium Centuria Prima,* published at Caen in 1609.

[21] *Regia* (1649), p. 196, ll. 2–5.

should be considered as but an officer of the realm, while those who rule other kingdoms in Christendom enjoy full unlimited sway."[22] For Scotland I refer you to Buchanan;[23] for your own France, where you seem a stranger, to Hotman's *Franco-Gallia*[24] and to Gerard,[25] the historian of France; for the rest to other writers, of whom none were to my knowledge Independents. From all these you might have learned lessons on the rights of kings far different from those you teach.

Since you cannot establish a tyranny for the kings of England by the laws of war, you attempt to do so by those of flattery. Kings assert that they rule "by the grace of God":[26] what if they asserted they were gods? They could, I suppose, easily get you to be their priest; just so the pontiff of Canterbury boasted that he was archbishop "by the providence of God." Are you so senseless as to oppose the pope as king in the church, so that you may establish the king in the state as more powerful than the pope?

In the statutes of the realm, you say, he is termed "Our lord the king."[27] What a wonderful announcer of the names of our statutes you have suddenly become! But still you know not that many are called lords who are not, and that it is very wrong to use honorary, or rather flattering, titles in judging law and actual fact. Apply the same reasoning to the title of "King's Parliament"—it is also called the *king's bridle*; and the king is no more the master of Parliament than a horse is the master of his own bridle.

"Why," you ask, "is it not the king's Parliament, when it is convoked by him?"[28] I shall tell you. The Senate was convoked by the consul, but he was not on that account its master. The summoning of Parliament by the king is part of the duties of office laid on him by the people, and is done that he may receive the advice of those he summons on the weighty business of the realm, not on his own business. If there be any such [private business], it has ever been the custom to treat it last of all, and not at his pleasure, but at that of Parliament. [122] Then, too, those whose business it is to know are

[22] *Ibid.*, p. 196, l. 37 ff.
[23] See above, p. 371, n. 107.
[24] See above, p. 420, n. 78.
[25] See above, p. 420, n. 80.
[26] *Regia* (1649), p. 197, l. 19.
[27] *Ibid.*, p. 197, ll. 22–23.
[28] *Ibid.*, p. 197, ll. 38–39. Salmasius has been denying the "wicked words of the criminal sectaries that the king of England is not the king of Parliament, but merely its head."

well aware that, whether summoned or not, Parliament could from of old meet legally twice a year.

"The laws," you object, "are called the king's."[29] Such words are but surface ornaments to please the king; but the king of England can pass no law on his own, for he was not appointed to pass laws but to maintain those passed by the people. Here you admit yourself that "Parliament meets to write laws." We therefore hear of both law of the land and law of the people. Thus Athelstan, speaking to the whole people in the preamble to his laws, says "in accordance with your own law I have granted you everything."[30] In the form of oath by which, before their appointment, the kings of England are wont to bind themselves, it is demanded of them by the people: "Do you grant those just laws which the people shall choose?" The king replies: "I do so grant."

You miss the mark by the length of all England in saying that "when Parliament is not in session, the king controls the whole government fully and absolutely by royal right."[31] In fact, he cannot make any important decisions as to war or peace, nor even in the field of jurisdiction can he interfere with the decisions of the courts. For this reason the judges swear that in the conduct of their courts they will do nothing save in accordance with the law, not even if the king himself should by word or instructions, or even letters under his own seal, order them to do otherwise. Thus under our law the king is often termed "an infant," and is said to possess his rights and privileges only as a minor or a ward. See *Spec. Just.* Chapter 4, Section 22.[32]

[29] Salmasius in referring to the Statute of Merton, "made in the twentieth year of the Reign of Henry III,"' argues that Parliament is the king's and is called *Curia Regia*. "And why not, since it is summoned by him, and what are instituted in it are called the laws and statutes of the king?" (*Regia,* 1649, p. 198, ll. 3–5).

[30] Milton omits to note in his paraphrase of the *Leges Athelstani* that the king's grant is provisional on the recognition of his own rights. The preamble states: "Nolo ut aliquid michi injuste conquiratis, sed ominia vestra concedo vobis, eo tenore quo michi mea similiter exoptetis." *Ancient Laws and Institutes of England,* Commissioners of the Public Records (2 vols., London, 1840), II, 486.

[31] *Regia* (1649), p. 198, ll. 9–10.

[32] *Speculum Justiciariorum:* "La Somme Appelle Mirroir des Justices vel Speculum Justiciariorum" hereafter referred to as *Mirror of Justices*) was the product of Andrew Horn (d. 1328), fishmonger and legal writer, who either wrote or edited this treatise. It was first published in London in 1624 and was republished in 1642 (NYPL). Milton's allusion here is to the 1642 edition, p. 271. *The Mirrour* was translated into English by William Hughes in 1646 (BML) as *The Booke Called The Mirrour of Justices.* See William J. Whittaker, ed., *The Mirrour of Justices,*

Thus also it has become proverbial with us to say that "the king can do no wrong." In your wickedness, you take this phrase to mean that "what the king does is not wrong because he is not punished for it." [33] Who could fail to realize from this one interpretation the man's amazing and wicked impudence?

"It is for the head," you say, "to give orders, and not for the limbs; the king is the head of Parliament." [34] Could you trifle thus, if you had any touch of wisdom in your heart? Once again, for there is no end to your errors, you go astray in failing to distinguish the king's councilors from the Houses of Parliament. The king might not even choose all the councilors, and of these none without the approval of the rest; while he never even claimed the authority to appoint anyone to the House of Commons [123]. Those appointed to this office by the people were elected individually in the municipalities by popular vote; here I may be brief, for I speak of what is common knowledge.

But, you say, "It is untrue that, as the worshippers of Saint Independence assert, Parliament was established by the people." [35] I see now why you are so eager to overthrow the papacy! You bear in your belly, as we put it, another papacy, for, as your wife's wife, a wolf impregnated by a bitch, what else could you bring forth but a monstrosity or some new papacy? You do indeed act as if you were already a true pope, and at your pleasure create saints male and female; you absolve kings too of all their sins, and, as if you had already laid low your enemy the pope, you bedeck yourself with his spoils! Really now, since the pope has not yet quite fallen at your hands, pending the appearance of the second and third, perhaps the fourth and fifth parts of that book of yours, *De Primatu,* which will bore many to death long before you have beaten the pope with it, you should for the present be content, believe me, merely to become antipope!

Selden Society (Vol. VII, London, 1895), book IV, chap. xxii, pp. 147–48. See *Complete Prose,* ed. Hughes, III, 95, 96, 219, 399.

[33] Salmasius has been discussing the English legal principle of *Regem non posse facere injuriam.* Salmasius nowhere argues that "what the king does is not wrong because he is not punished for it," with the implication that wrong only exists in terms of punishment. Salmasius gives a *legal* definition of *injuria* (*Regia,* 1649, p. 217, ll. 31–32): "Injuria id omne est quod non jure fit, & quod jure vindicatur in eo qui commisit" ("*Injuria* is everything that is not done according to law and which can be prosecuted in law against a violator"). Salmasius' point is that the king cannot be legally proceeded against, and therefore cannot *in this legal sense commit injuria.* Salmasius willingly grants that kings can do plenty of wrong.

[34] *Regia* (1649), p. 198, l. 16.

[35] *Ibid.*, p. 200, ll. 19–20.

In addition to that Independence you mock, there is another saint canonized by you in all earnest, namely Royal Tyranny, and so you will become High Priest of the royal Saint Tyranny! Lest you lack any of the papal title, you will be "servant of the servants," not of God but of the court; that curse of Canaan [36] seems to have been fastened on your vitals.

You call the people "a beast." [37] What then are *you*? For neither that Sacred Consistory nor that St. Wolf can set you its master above the people or the populace, nor keep you from being what you are, the foulest of animals! Certainly the prophetic books of Scripture denote the monarchical dominion of great kings by the name and likeness of a raging beast.[38]

"There is no mention," you say, "of Parliament under the kings before William." [39] There is no need to argue about the French word —the thing itself always existed. You admit yourself that in Saxon times "a council of wise men" [40] used to be convoked. There are, however, wise men among the common folk as well as in the ranks of the nobility. "But," you say, "in the Statute of Merton, 20 Henry III, only counts and barons are mentioned." [41] Words have always tricked you thus, though you have spent all your life on words alone. [124] We all know that in that age the Wardens of the Five Ports, the magistrates of the towns, and certain merchants as well, were called barons, and it is beyond doubt that all the members of Parliament, commoners though they were, were at that time and with much more justice termed barons. For in the fifty-second year of the same king, the Statute of Marlbridge [42] and most of the other statutes show in so many words that nobles and commoners alike were called together;

[36] Genesis 9:25: "And Noah said: Cursed be Canaan, a servant of servants shall he be unto his brethren."

[37] *Regia* (1649), p. 201, l. 12: "illa bestia, quae *Populus* vocatur."

[38] Revelation 13:11.

[39] *Regia* (1649), p. 201, ll. 38–39.

[40] *Ibid.*, p. 203, ll. 7–8. Salmasius has just defined them as "qui erant in populo doctrinae fama & legum jurisque prudentia spectabiles."

[41] *Ibid.*, p. 204, l. 32 ff.

[42] The Preamble to the Statute of Marlbridge (1267) states: "Convocatis discretioribus ejusdem regni, tam majoribus quam minoribus." See *Statutes at Large from Magna Charta to the End of the Reign of Henry the Sixth*, ed. Owen Ruffhead (10 vols., London, 1786), I, 30. Sir Edward Coke writes (*The Second Part of the Institutes of the Laws of England*, London, 1681; NYPL), p. 103, "Provisum est, concordatum, & concessum, quod tam majores quam minores, justiciam habeant & recipiant in curia Domini Regis."

and even those commoners were addressed by Edward the Third in the preamble to the Statute Staple,[43] which you cite me so learnedly [44] as Magnates of the Counties, which means "those who had come from the several cities to represent the whole county." These men did in fact make up the House of Commons, and neither were, nor could be, nobles. A book too which is older than these statutes, entitled *The Manner of Holding Parliaments,*[45] reports that, with the Commons alone, the king might hold Parliament and pass laws, even in the absence of Lords and bishops, but could not do so with Lords and bishops without Commons. The reason for this is also stated:—before Lords and bishops were established, kings used to hold Parliaments and councils with the people; then the Lords represented only themselves, but Commons the town. Thus it is understood that the Commons represent the whole people, and are therefore stronger and more exalted than the nobles, and in every way preferable to them. "The power to judge, however," so you say, "never rested with the House of Commons." [46] Never did it rest with the king of England; and remember nonetheless that originally all power came, as it does even now, from the people. This point is well set forth by Cicero in his speech *On the Agrarian Law*: "It is agreed that all power, authority, and agency is derived from the whole people, and in particular

[43] The Preamble to the Statute of Staples (1353) reads: (*Statutes at Large,* 1786, I, 268) "Pur ceo que en bone Deliberation ove Prelates Ducs Countes Barons & Chivalers des Countees, cesta savoir de chescun Countee un pur tout la Counte, & des Comunes des cittees & Burghs de notre Roialme Dengl'."

[44] *Regia* (1649), p. 206, l. 23.

[45] According to Maude V. Clarke, *Medieval Representation and Consent* (London, 1936), p. 378, a date as early as 1377 has been proposed for the *Modus Tenendi Parliamentum,* to which Milton here refers. Extant are twenty-five manuscripts from the end of the fourteenth to the beginning of the sixteenth century. Of these six are translations, four into English, and two into French (*op. cit.,* p. 351). John Hooker (alias Vowell) incorporated the *Modus* in his *Order and Usage of the Keeping of Parliament in England* (1575). William Hakewill edited and translated it in 1641 (NYPL). J. E. Neale, "Peter Wentworth," *English Historical Review,* XXIX (1924), 50, n. 3, says this material is incomplete and corrupt, and is supported by Clarke, *op. cit.,* p. 366. The material quoted here is to be found in Hakewill (1660), pp. 25–26 (NYPL). Hakewill adds the provision, omitted by Milton, *yet so, as they be summoned.* "And this is manifest, because the King may hold Parliament with the Commonality and Commons of the Kingdom without Bishops, Earls, and Barons, yet so, as they be summoned to the Parliament, although no Bishop, Earl, or Baron come according to their summons."

[46] *Regia* (1649), p. 205, ll. 32–34. Salmasius adds that this power belonged solely to the House of Lords.

those offices which were established for the benefit or convenience of the people; hence all choose the one who will, as they believe, do most for the people, while each candidate may by his own efforts and vote [125] pave the way towards securing office."[47] Here you see the true beginning of parliaments, long before the time of those Saxon records. So long as we may enjoy this light of truth and wisdom it is vain for you to try to cast us into the gloom of darker ages! None should suppose I say this because I wish to detract from the authority or good sense of our forefathers, for surely, in their enlightened legislation, they were more advanced than those times or their own talents and traditions made probable. Though most of the laws they passed were good, they were aware of their own human ignorance and weakness, and wished, as all our jurists know, to pass on to their descendants this basis of all law: should any law or custom conflict with divine or natural law or with reason, it is not to be considered a valid law. Although you might perhaps discover in our law some edict or statute, attributing tyrannical power to the king, you must realize that, being contrary to the divine will, to nature, and to reason, such law should be revoked and held invalid by reason of that basic and inclusive law which I referred to. You will, in fact, find no such royal rights over here. It is clear that at first the right to judge belonged to the people themselves, and that the English never transferred that right to the king by any law of royalty, for the king of England neither can nor does judge anyone save by laws already established and approved—see Fleta I, 17.[48] It follows that this same power remains to the people undiminished in its entirety; you cannot assert that it was ever transferred to the House of Lords, and, if it were, that it might not be recovered by law.

"It is," you say, "the function of the king to raise a village to a borough and that to a city, and he therefore appoints those who make up the lower house."[49] I reply that towns and boroughs are more ancient than kings, and in the very fields the people remains the people still.

[47] Cicero, *De Lege Agraria,* II, 7, 17, in *The Speeches,* tr. John Henry Freese (Cambridge: Loeb Classical Library, 1945), 386–89.

[48] *Fleta* is a medieval legal treatise which came to light with the revival of legal learning through Selden's editing it in 1616. It is said to be little more than an abbreviated form of Bracton, and Milton generally quotes from it in connection with the latter treatise. Milton's reference here, I, 17, may be found on pages 16–19, of *Fleta* (London, 1685; PUL).

[49] *Regia* (1649), p. 207, ll. 5–8.

We greatly enjoy your Anglicisms—*County Court, The Turn, Hundreds*. I suppose you were a wonderfully apt pupil in learning to count your hundred sovereigns in English! [126]

> Who gave unto Salmasius his hundred
> And taught the parrot to prattle our tongue?
> His preceptor, the belly, and those hundred coins
> Which were the substance of the exiled king.
> For when with specious glint the money shines,
> That man, whose threat it was to overthrow,
> All at one puff, Pope Antichrist's domain,
> Will hymn his praise as loud as any cardinal.[50]

You continue with a long account of earls and barons to show that the king made them all; a point I gladly grant, for this made them generally subservient to the king, and therefore we have taken care that henceforth they shall not judge a free people.

"The right to convoke Parliament whenever he wishes, and to dissolve it at his will, has always," you maintain, "belonged to the king."[51] We shall see later whether to rely on a wandering hireling buffoon like you who merely writes down the dictates of exiles, or on the exact language of our own laws. You say, however, that "a further irrefutable argument proves that the kings of England have authority superior to that of Parliament; the power of the king is regular and continuous, capable of governing by itself without Parliament, while that of Parliament is extraordinary, applicable only to certain definite matters, and incapable of valid decisions without the king."[52] Where lies all the force of this argument? Is it in the words "regular and continuous"? But many minor officials whom we call justices of the peace have a power which is regular and continuous; is it therefore supreme? I stated above that power was granted by the people to the king in order that by the power vested in him he might prevent violation of the laws, and rather to protect our laws than burden us with his. He has no power but in, and through, the courts of the realm; on the contrary, the power of the people, judging all suits by juries of twelve men, is the normal one. Therefore, when a defendant is asked in court "By whom will you be tried?" he replies in accordance with law and

[50] The model for Milton's verse here is apparently the prologue to the *Choliambi* of Persius.

[51] *Regia* (1649), p. 211, ll. 17–19.

[52] *Ibid.*, p. 212, ll. 4–8.

custom "By God and the people," not by God and the *king,* or the *king's deputy.* [127] The power of Parliament, which is actually and truly the supreme power of the people joined together in that council, can be called extraordinary only in its preeminence. Furthermore, since the orders themselves are commonly so called, they cannot be extraordinary; and they possess essentially, if not procedurally, a continuous authority and control over all regular courts and officials, even without the king.

Now it seems that your delicate ears are injured by our uncouth phrases. If I had time, or were it worth while, I might find in this single volume of yours so many barbarisms that, if you were punished according to your deserts, your little pupils would break all their sticks on your back, and you would get not as much gold as the worst of poets once did, but rather more blows!

You speak of it as "outrageous and more monstrous than the wildest belief that these madmen separate the king's person from his power." [53] I will not drag out what everyone has said on this point, but

[53] *Ibid.,* p. 215, ll. 14–16. Salmasius has constantly stated that the king's person cannot be separated from the king's "majesty." He adds here that the political cannot be separated from the natural body.

Homicides and adulterers may rule well (*Regia,* 1649), p. 160, ll. 29–30)—which implies that private life does not necessarily affect public responsibility. "The one who has lived well has not always been the same person who ruled well" (*Regia,* 1649, p. 295, ll. 10–11)

Has Salmasius, in spite of his high-mindedness, absorbed a little Machiavelli? It is interesting to note that Machiavelli particularly stressed the difference in moral principle to be applied to the prince as a political figure and that applied to a private citizen. Machiavelli had at least helped to make fashionable such distinctions as these in Salmasius. Laws governing princes derive from Aristotle's *Politics* and those governing private persons from his *Ethics.* Under medieval Averroistic tradition, whereby truths in different fields can be contradictory but remain respectively true, politics and ethics can contradict one another without a violence to truth. For Aristotle, ethics and politics harmonize on the basis of a universal morality. In Machiavelli, they do not. It is wrong for a private citizen to kill even for a public reason; it is perfectly moral for a prince to liquidate for reasons of state. What is immoral in one case is moral in the other. Both Salmasius and Milton knew Machiavelli, but he is never mentioned in *A Defence* or in the *Regia.* Salmasius at the end of book VI (*Regia,* 1649, p. 183, ll. 24–28) does make some snide remarks about the Independents in terms of Machiavelli's well-known analogy about the lion and the fox. Milton makes a number of entries from Machiavelli in his *Commonplace Book*—all, however from the *Discourses,* none from *The Prince.* None of the quotations reflect Machiavelli's daring drift in political philosophy, but constitute isolated passages that agree with Milton's own line of thought as, for example, that against a bad prince there is no other remedy than the sword (*Complete Prose,* I, 456), that among the

if by *person* you mean *the man,* you might have learned from Chrysostom, who was no madman, that the two can easily be distinguished.[54] Salmasius explains the apostle's injunction about the powers as meaning the actuality of power rather than the individual person. Why should I not say that a king who breaks the law does so as an individual or as a tyrant, not as king in the exercise of his legal authority? If you are unaware that a single man may play several roles, each of which may be perceived or thought of as distinct from the individual himself, you must be without either common sense or Latinity.

You say this to absolve kings of all their sins, so that we may suppose you are endowed with that primacy you took from the pope: "It is understood that a king can do no wrong, for no penalty follows his wrong doing." [55] I suppose then that no one sins unless he be punished; it is not the theft but the punishment that makes a thief. Salmasius the grammarian uttered no solecisms, for he avoided chastisement. When you have once put down the pope, let these be the rules or at least the remissions of your pontificate, and choose whether you would rather be called pontiff of St. Tyranny or St. Slavery!

I need not speak of the slander you heap up at the end of your chapter against "the government of the English commonwealth and church"; it well suits so low a wretch [128] to curse most loudly what is most praiseworthy. To avoid, however, the appearance of making unfounded statements as to the rights of our kings, or, better, the rights of our people over their kings, I shall gladly cite our own documents, using few from the whole number, indeed, but those which will show most clearly that, in the recent trial of the king, the English proceeded in accordance with established law and ancestral custom.

After the departure of the Romans from the island, the British were for some forty years independent and without kings, and of those whom they first appointed several were put to death. For this, Gildas censures the British,[56] though for reasons far different from

---

most excellent of all mortals are those who instruct the minds of men in true religion (I, 475), that Machiavelli prefers a republican form of government to a monarchy (I, 477).

[54] Chrysostom, *Homilies on Romans,* XXIII (on Romans 13:1) in *Fathers, N. and P.N. 1,* XI, 511. See above, p. 384, n. 51.

[55] Milton perpetrates this biased misunderstanding of Salmasius once again. See above, p. 365, n. 87.

[56] Gildas, *The History,* XXII, ed. J. A. Giles (London, 1906).

yours: that is, not for killing their kings, but for failing to try them, or in his own words, "without an investigation into the truth." Nennius,[57] next to Gildas the oldest of our historians, informs us that Vortigern was found guilty of an incestuous marriage with his daughter "by St. Germain and the whole council of Britain," and the realm was handed over to his son Vortimer. These events took place soon after the death of Augustine, and reveal without difficulty your ignorance in stating above that it was a pope named Zachary who first taught that kings might be tried.[58] About A.D. 600 Morcantius, the current ruler of Wales, was condemned to exile by Oudoceus, the bishop of Llandaff, for the murder of his uncle, although he was able to buy off the sentence by the gift of certain estates to the church.

Let us turn next to the Saxons, omitting their deeds since we know their laws. You will recall that the Saxons were sprung from the Germans, who did not grant their kings unlimited and absolute power and were accustomed to take counsel together over matters of consequence; from this we learn that, in all but name, it was Parliament which had the supreme authority even with the ancestors of the Saxons. Now and then the Council of Wise Men is mentioned by them, right from their own day to that of Ethelbert, who is said by Bede "to have established his edicts on the Roman pattern with the aid of the Council of Wise Men." [59] Thus, too, Edwin of Northumbria and King Inas of the West Saxons issued new laws "after taking counsel with the wise men and elders." [129] Other laws were also issued by Alfred "from a council of the wisest men, who all agreed that they must be observed." From these and the many other similar passages it is as clear as day that there were present in the supreme councils certain men chosen from the common people, unless one is to suppose that nobles alone are wise. We have also extant a most ancient volume on the law entitled *Mirror of Justices,* which reports that, after the conquest of Britain, the first Saxons when appointing their kings were accustomed to demand an oath of them that, like any other citizens, they would obey the laws and the courts: *Chapter I, section 2.*[60] It is also stated there to be only just and fair for the king to have in Parliament peers who may investigate crimes committed by the king or queen. In the reign of Alfred, it was required by law that Parliament

[57] Nennius, *Historia Britonum,* xxxix. [58] See p. 420, n. 81.
[59] Bede, *Ecclesiastical History of the English People,* II, 5.
[60] *Mirror of Justices,* 1642, pp. 7–9.

be held at London twice each year or oftener if necessary. When by shameful and illegal neglect this law passed out of use, it was renewed by two enactments of Edward the Third.

We read too in another ancient manuscript entitled *The Manner of Parliament* that, if the king prorogue Parliament before the transaction of all the business for which it was convoked, he is guilty of perjury and shall be held to have broken the oath he swore before he was crowned.[61] How does he grant, as he swore to do, those just laws chosen by the people if he denies the request of the people for an opportunity to choose them, either by summoning Parliament less frequently or dismissing it more quickly than the business of the people requires? That oath, moreover, by which the king of England binds himself has always been considered by our jurists as a most inviolable law. What safeguards can be found against the greatest dangers to the state, if that great and august assembly, whose sole purpose it is to discover them, may be dissolved at the pleasure of a king who may often be foolish and headstrong? It is certainly a lesser matter to be absent from Parliament than to dissolve it; but, according to our laws recorded in that volume of *Manners,* the king neither can nor should be so absent unless he be quite ill, and even in that case, only after his person has been checked by twelve peers of the realm [130] who can testify in the Senate as to the indisposition of the king.[62] Is it thus that slaves act toward their masters? The House of Commons, on the other hand, without which Parliament cannot be held, may fail to attend even when convoked by the king, and, upon withdrawal, may admonish the king for his misgovernment, as the same book bears witness.

Most important, however, is the fact that among the laws of King Edward the Confessor, as he is commonly called, there is one of note dealing with the duties of the king—if the king fail to do his duty "he shall no longer retain the title of king." To avoid doubt as to

[61] This statement is not contained in Hakewill, 1641, 1660, 1671. But in a collation of sixteen manuscripts of the *Modus* as presented in Maude V. Clarke, *Medieval Representation and Consent,* (London, 1936), p. 383, the following statement is included under Section XXIV: "Parliamentum departiri non debet dummodo aliqua petitio pendeat indiscussa, vel, ad minus, ad quam non sit determinatum responsum, et si rex contrarium permittat, periurus est." *Perjurus est* is not so strong as Milton's "shall be held to have broken the oath he swore before he was crowned," but it is along the same line of thought.

[62] William Hakewill, *Modus Tenendi Parliamentum* (1671), p. 27, in section "Touching the Absence of the King in the Parliament."

what this means, Edward attaches the example of Chilperic, king of the Franks, whom the people deprived of his realm on that account. That, by the tenor of this law, a wicked king may be punished is made clear by that sword of St. Edward known as Curtana, which is borne in procession by the Count Palatine at the coronation, "indicating," says our writer Matthew Paris, "that by law he possesses the power to punish the king himself if he should go astray." [63] And punishment by the sword is rarely short of capital. This law, with others passed by that good King Edward, was ratified by William the Conqueror in his fourth year and confirmed by the most solemn oath in a crowded council of the English held near Verulam. By this action William personally gave up any rights of conquest he may have had over us, and subjected himself to judgment and sentence according to this law. His son Henry, as well, swore to abide by this and the other laws of Edward, and it was on these conditions that he was chosen king though his elder brother Robert was still alive. The same oath was taken by all succeeding kings before they received the insignia of office. Thus in book I chapter 8 our famous jurist of old, Bracton, writes: "Where passion rules, there is neither king nor law," and in book III, chapter 9: "A king remains king while he governs well, but becomes a tyrant when by a rule of violence he crushes those entrusted to him." [64] In the same chapter he adds "The king should exercise the power of the law as God's agent and servant; the power to do wrong is of the Devil, not of God. When the king stoops to crime he is the Devil's servant." The same opinion is held by that other ancient jurist known as the author of *Fleta*,[65] and both of them indeed remember that truly royal law [131] of Edward, that basic precept of our law which I spoke of above, by which nothing contrary to the laws of God or to reason can be considered law, any more than a tyrant can be considered a king, or a servant of the Devil a servant of God. Since law is above all else right reason, it appears that, if we must obey a king and a servant of God, for the same reason and by the same law, we must resist a tyrant and a servant of the Devil. Since further there

[63] Milton attributes this information to Holinshed in the *Commonplace Book* (see *Complete Prose,* I, 447).

[64] Bracton, *De Legibus et Consuetudinibus Angliae* (1640; PUL), book I, chap. 8, fol. 5v; book III, chap. 9, fol. 107v; hereafter referred to as *De Legibus,* (1640).

[65] Bracton, *De Legibus* (1640), book I, chap. 8, fol. 5v; *Fleta* (London, 1685), pp. 16–19.

is doubt about the title more often than about the fact, we are told by the same writers that the king of England, even though he has not yet lost the title of king, can and should be judged like any ordinary man. According to Bracton I, 8, *Fleta* I, 17, "No man should surpass the king in dealing out justice; but if he sins, the king should be the last to receive it"; some read, "if he seeks it." Therefore since our king should be subject to judgment whether under the title of tyrant or of king, it is easy to see who should be his lawful judges. We may well consult the same authorities. According to Bracton II, 16, *Fleta* I, 17, "In governing the people, the king has as his superiors the law by which he became king and his court of earls and barons. The earls are termed, as it were, the associates of the king, and he who has an associate has a guide; therefore, if the king should be unbridled or lawless, they should bridle him." [66]

I have shown above that the House of Commons is included under the name of barons; indeed our most ancient writings on the law call them from time to time the "Peers" of Parliament. Thus, in particular, the volume entitled *Manner of Parliament* says: "From all the peers of the realm let twenty-five be chosen," of whom "five will be knights, five citizens" or delegates of the cities. "Five burgesses, and two knights of the shire have a greater voice in granting or denying than the greatest earl of England." [67] This is but fair, for the former represent a whole county or borough, the latter themselves alone. Then too anyone can see that those earls "by patent or by writ," as you call

[66] Bracton, *De Legibus* (1640), book II, chap. 16, fol. 34v; *Fleta* (London, 1685), pp. 16–19.

[67] William Hakewill in a section of the *Modus Tenendi Parliamentum* (1660; NYPL) entitled "Concerning Cases & Judgments which are hard," explains (pp. 19–20) that in the cases of war, of the king's absence, of a difficult problem before the Chancellor, of a situation in which the greater number of justices cannot agree, then the Earl Steward, the Earl Constable, the Earl Marshal shall appoint twenty-five peers, of whom three are proctors or clerks of the Convocation, two earls and three barons, five knights of the shire, five citizens and burgesses. These twenty-five may then choose twelve of their number. These twelve may in turn form a smaller committee. Milton editorializes on Hakewill's observations. While Hakewill does not expressly say that the "five burgesses and two knights of the shires have a greater voice in granting or denying than the greatest earl of England," he does support Milton by arguing (p. 26) that the operations of Parliament depend on the presence of the commonality, "which standeth on three degrees or sorts gathered together in Parliament, that is to say, the Proctors of the Clergy, the Knights of the Shires, the Citizens & Burgesses, who represent indeed the whole Commonality of England; and next upon the whole Noblemen, because every one of them is at the Parliament in his own proper person, and none other."

them, for there are no more feudal earls, are of all men the least fit to judge the king who made them. Since, as the old *Mirror* shows,[68] our law bids the king [132] have peers to investigate and judge in Parliament "whatever wrong has been done by the king to any of his people," and since we all know that any man of the people may sue the crown for damages in the various lower courts, it is all the more just and necessary that, should the king do wrong to the whole people, he ought to have someone not merely to bridle and restrain him but to judge and punish him as well.

Ill and foolishly arranged must be the state in which provision is made for the most minor wrongs done by the king against any private citizen, but none made for his most important crimes against the common interest, none made for those crimes against the common safety in order to prevent the king from illegally destroying the whole people, though he cannot legally injure a single individual. Since I have shown that it is neither fit nor proper for the earls to be the king's judges, it follows that the House of Commons has the best and most complete right to such judgment, for they are peers of the realm and barons, and are invested with the power of the whole people. When it happens that, according to our law, as I wrote above, the Commons themselves, with the king but without the Lords or bishops, constitute a Parliament (for with the Commons alone the king used to hold Parliament before Lords or bishops were created), it is equally clear that, by the same reasoning, Commons alone are supreme even without the king and have power to judge the king, because, before any king was created, they used to hold councils and Parliament in the name of the whole people, make judgments, pass laws, and create kings—not that they might be masters of the people but to carry on the people's business. But if the king should attempt to injure and enslave them, he loses, by the expressed opinion of our law, the title of king and is king no more. If he is no longer king, why need we look further for his peers? For since he has in fact already been adjudged a tyrant by all good men, any man is his peer and fit to act as judge in sentencing him to death.

Thus by all this evidence and citation of laws I believe I have at last successfully completed my task, because I have shown that, since the Commons have full right to judge a king, and did in fact execute a king who had deserved so ill [133] of church and state and shown no

[68] *Mirror of Justices*, 1642, pp. 7–9. See above, p. 482, n. 32.

signs of improvement, they acted rightly and regularly and were faithful to their state and to themselves, to their position and to their country's laws. Here I cannot fail to voice my pride in our fathers who, in establishing this state, displayed a wisdom and a sense of freedom equal to that of the ancient Romans or the most illustrious Greeks; and these our fathers in their turn, if they know anything of our actions, cannot but rejoice in their sons who, when they had well-nigh been made slaves, did with such courage and good sense save that state, which had been so wisely planned and so founded on liberty, from the unbridled tyranny of a king.

CHAPTER IX [1]

It is now, I believe, clear enough that, even by the laws of England, the king of England is subject to trial and has lawful judges, which was the point to be proved. What say you next?

(I see no need to repeat my answers to your repetitions.) You say that you "have clear sailing to show, from the very business for which

[1] In book IX (*Regia,* 1649, pp. 220–49) Salmasius continues his arguments about constitutional law: 1. Parliament can levy taxes, make and abrogate laws but only with the consent of the king. Since Parliament cannot sit except by the command of the king, it is natural that his sanction should be necessary to make any decision valid. Although the king can neither establish new laws nor abolish old laws without the consent of both Houses, yet, since he has the power of veto, his power is greater than that of Parliament. It is as untrue and unjust to say that the king can be compelled to pass the laws suggested by Parliament as to say that he can be summoned by Parliament and forced to plead for his life. 2. If the lesser power (Parliament) could force the greater power (the king) to do its will, such a situation would be contrary to the law of nature. 3. The king, even though physically absent from Parliament, is "virtually" present, and all enactments are made and decreed as if by the king himself. This is true also of the courts and the army. Unless the king delegates his power, it does not belong to any assembly. Anything decreed in Parliament without the consent of the king is invalid. 4. But it is not right to call by the name of Parliament the remnant of the Parliament left in England, since the king has been removed, and the principal part of it have been deprived of their seats. It is no longer a Parliament but a military council, an assembly of the ignoble, ignorant, stupid, seditious, and rebellious! 5. The king is as supreme in ecclesiastical as in secular matters. Will the soldiers have power over these affairs also? Or will it be given to the sectaries who are ruling England? 6. The enemies of the king truly want a figurehead. The majesty of the king should be furnished with laws and provided with arms. The enemies of the king did not openly deny to him the power over the army but refused money. The king has the right of demanding money for his affairs. The king should have more power in arms than the whole people; otherwise he cannot rule. 7. The king has

assemblies are convoked, that the king is above Parliament."[2] The sailing may be as clear as you want, but you will soon see yourself sail clear to the bottom.

"Parliament," you say, "is summoned for matters of great import to the safety of the realm and the people."[3] If the king calls Parliament to attend to the affairs of the people rather than his own, and that only with the consent and agreement of those he summons, what, I ask, is the king but servant and agent of the people? For without the votes of those representatives of the people he cannot make even the least decision as to others or to his own self. This fact shows further that it is the duty of the king to summon Parliament whenever the people so desires. It is indeed the affairs of the people, not of the king, which are managed by these assemblies, in accordance with the will of the people. Although when [134] the king's consent is asked out of respect for him, he may in minor matters (affecting only the interests of individuals) refuse it and use the phrase "The king will advise," still he is wholly unable to give his refusal to matters affecting the welfare and liberties of all. Such refusal would be in conflict with that oath which binds the king as by the strictest law, and in conflict with that great article of *Magna Carta,* Chapter 29: "To none will we deny right and justice."[4] Shall he not deny right or justice, but deny just laws? Not deny any man, but deny all? Not deny justice in any lower court, but deny it in the highest assembly? Will any king make such a claim as this, that he alone knows better than the whole people what is just and profitable, especially when according to *Bracton,* III, 9, "he was created and appointed for this end, that he might dispense justice to all,"[5] and dispense it in accordance with those laws which "the populace" has chosen? Thus we read in our records 7 H. 4 Rot. Parl. num. 59: "There is no royal prerogative which places any restriction on justice or equity."

---

absolute sovereignty over affairs pertaining to religion, to justice, and to the army. 8. Since the king has the right to declare war, he has also the right of making peace, and of making or breaking foreign alliances. 9. The kings of England are kings through the right of their birth, through the law of nature, through the law of God, and not through the law of the land. 10. If the king's authority is lessened, he cannot give to the people the protection he should.

[2] *Regia* (1649), p. 220, l. 10. This is a paraphrase.

[3] *Ibid.,* p. 220, ll. 24–28.

[4] *Magna Carta,* XXIX: "Nulli vendemus, nulli aut differemus justitiam, vel rectum."

[5] Bracton, *De Legibus* (1640), book III, chap. 9, fol. 107.

When in times past kings refused their assent to acts of Parliament such as *Magna Carta* and the like, our fathers in many cases secured assent by force of arms. Our jurists hold that these laws are no less valid or legitimate on this account. The laws to which the king was compelled to grant his assent should rightly have received it of his own accord. When you seek to prove that the kings of other nations were, like ours, subject to a Sanhedrin or a Senate or council, you succeed in maintaining their freedom, not our slavery. You continue to do as you have done from the start, like those witless pleaders who, without thinking, come to court to sue themselves. You, however, suppose us to grant that "whenever the king is absent he is still considered present in Parliament by virtue of his power; and so whatever is done there is held to be done by the king himself." [6] Then, as if you had won a great wager or even a little wage, for you remember with pleasure that grant from Charles, you tell us: "I take what they grant." Take then the curses you deserve, for we are not going to grant, as you had hoped, [135] the consequence "that this assembly has no power other than that delegated by the king." [7] For if we say that the king's power, whatever that may be, cannot be absent from Parliament, must we immediately add that it is supreme? Does it not rather seem that the royal power is handed over to Parliament and included as the lesser in the greater? For if Parliament, against the king's will and desire, can revoke his acts and recall such privileges as he granted to anyone, limit the prerogatives of the king himself as they see fit, control his yearly income and court expenditures, his very household servants and all his domestic affairs, remove his closest counsellors and friends or take them for punishment from his very arms; if, finally, any of the populace is assured by law of an appeal from the king to Parliament in any matter, though not in turn from Parliament to the king, if, as our public records and legal scholars testify, all these things both can take place and have often done so, I do not believe that anyone in his right mind would fail to admit that Parliament is above the king! Even between reigns, Parliament is in power, and it is clearly evidenced by our history that often by its free vote it chose whom it wished as king and took no account of rights of inheritance. To sum up the situation, Parliament is the supreme council of the nation, established and endowed with full powers by an absolutely free people for the purpose of consulting together on the most vital issues; the

[6] *Regia* (1649), p. 224, ll. 4–9. [7] *Ibid.*, p. 224, ll. 22–23.

king was created to carry out all the decrees of the Houses according to their advice and intentions.

When lately Parliament itself had in its own edict made these facts clear to all, for their sense of justice led them of their own free will to give even foreign nations an accounting of their actions, straight from his hovel came a man without standing or credit or substance, a Burgundian house-slave, to accuse the great Senate of England "of fearful and abominable pretence" for writing in support of their country's rights and their own. Surely your country must be ashamed, you wretch, of producing so impudent a nobody. But perhaps you have a warning for our good! Speak on, we are all ears! [136]

"What laws," you ask, "can that Parliament enact in which the order of bishops does not appear?" [8] Did you attempt, you madman, to uproot the bishops from the church that you might plant them in Parliament? Man of evil, Satan's tool, the church should cast you out as an hypocritical atheist, and no state should shelter you who brings ruin and destruction to all men's freedom. By citing Aristotle and that fellow from Halicarnassus [9] and papal edicts from the darkest ages, you try to prove what only Scripture could have proved, namely that

[8] Milton here attributes a direct quotation to Salmasius which cannot be found in book IX of the *Regia* (1649). Milton paraphrases a repeated implication of Salmasius: that no binding laws can be made in England except by the king acting in Council, that is by the advice of Parliament, consisting of the Lords, the Bishops, and the Commons. In book IX Salmasius distinguishes between ordinances and acts. Acts are far more binding than ordinances, which may simply fall into disuse. All constitutional organs must have a hand in the making of acts: "Quod Acta attinet, nullum eorum vim legis potest obtinere ita ut obligat vitam aut fortunas subditorum, nisi Rege, Ecclesiastico ordine, nobilibus & plebeiis conjunctim & unanimi consensu subscribentibus" (*Regia*, 1649, p. 226, ll. 1–4). How can Church law be exercised if the king has been removed? "Rege amoto cuius auctoritate Episcopi Ecclesiasticam & spiritalem justitiam exercebant?" (*Regia*, 1649, p. 233, ll. 13–14). Salmasius pointed out in his preface that the bishops had not only been debarred from Parliament but had been completely evicted: "Sed Ecclesiasticum ordinem in Episcopis praecipue consistentem non solum Senatu ejiciendum, sed etiam penitus abjiciendum censuerunt" (*Regia*, 1649, p. 4, ll. 27–29).

[9] *Regia* (1649), p. 229, ll. 6–8: According to Salmasius, Dionysius of Halicarnassus in book II (presumably of his *Antiquitates Romanorum*) includes the care of sacred matters among the duties of the king. We know that Dionysius was in Rome after 30 B.C. His work is not a book of history in the modern critical sense of that word. He was chiefly interested in literary style and his work was meant to be an achievement in rhetoric. Milton's scornful remark about "that fellow" parallels his remarks about Diotogenes Pythagoreus (see above, p. 438, n. 68). Apparently Milton had more of a critical sense about historians than Salmasius, who was very extensive but indiscriminate.

the king of England is head of the English church. You make every effort to burden the holy Church of God once again with your new friends and boon companions, those bishops whom God himself cast forth, making them anew robbers and tyrants, though in your former writings you had loudly asserted that their whole order should be cut off root and branch as most dangerous to the Christian religion.[10] What apostate ever betrayed the faith so foully and so wickedly—not your own faith, indeed, for you have none that is fixed, but the Christian faith you once upheld?

"When those bishops have been removed, who, under the monarchy, and by the king's permission used to decide cases involving the church, who," you ask, "will decide such cases?" [11] You lost soul, try to have some qualms of conscience at least, try to remember while you can, unless perhaps my warning does come too late, that it will cost you dear, that you can never atone for such mockery of God's Holy Ghost. Come to your senses and restrain your madness before the wrath of God is aroused and suddenly smites you, for you are trying to deliver over Christ's flock, the anointed of God whom none may touch, to be crushed and trampled on by those fierce foes and tyrants from whom they have but now been set free by uplifting of the wonder-working hand of God. You taught yourself that they must be set free, but I know not whether you so taught in order to succor them or to complete your own hardening of heart and damnation. If indeed bishops have no right to rule the church, much less do kings, whatever human laws may say. Those who have more than a surface knowledge of Scripture are aware [137] that the government of the church is wholly divine, spiritual not civil.

Your statement, furthermore, that "the king of England had final jurisdiction in civil matters" [12] is abundantly proven false by our laws. All our courts of law are established or abolished by authority of Parliament, not the king. But in them the humblest subjects might bring suit against the king. It was not unusual for the judges to decide against the king. Any attempt at interference by the king,

[10] Salmasius calls for the removal of bishops in his *De Primatu* (1645), p. 197: "The episcopacy strengthened the road and prepared the way toward the Papal monarchy." Salmasius also asserts (*De Primatu,* p. 197): "The reformation can not appear integrated or complete while it remains imperfect in this respect [the retention of bishops]." He adds that with the removal of the papacy, no reason or probable cause can be adduced to show that the Episcopacy can or should be retained.

[11] *Regia* (1649), p. 233, ll. 14–17. [12] *Ibid.,* p. 234, ll. 8–10.

whether through interdict or mandate or letter, was disregarded by the judges in accordance with the law and with their oath, and such instructions were set aside as wholly invalid. The king could imprison no man, confiscate no property, execute no man save after trial in another court whose decision had been rendered by the regular judges, not by the king, and, as I said before, often in opposition to the king. As our writer Bracton says in Book III, Chapter 9: "The royal power is for justice, not injustice, and the king can do nothing save what he can do justly." Those cheap lawyers of yours, those recent emigrants, have advised you otherwise, citing some statutes of no great age from the reigns of Edward the Fourth, Henry the Seventh, and Edward the Sixth,[13] failing to realize that whatever power is granted by these statutes comes all as a concession from Parliament, and as a loan which may be recalled by the same authority. How could so cunning a fellow as you have been so led on to think that, by using the very argument which shows most clearly that the king's power is derived from decrees of Parliament, you could prove that power to be absolute and supreme?

Our most venerable documents bear witness that our kings owe their power neither to inheritance nor force of arms nor succession, but wholly to the people. We read of such royal power being granted by the Commons to Henry the Fourth, and before him to Richard the Second; Rot. Parl. 1 Hen. 4 num. 108, in much the same way as the king assigns his various officers their functions and duties by his edict or patent. Thus the House of Commons ordered it expressly recorded "that it had granted King Richard the benefits of such liberties [138] as the kings of England before him had enjoyed"; and when that king, "contrary to his oath of office" had misused these liberties so as to subvert the laws, the same body took from him his kingdom. It is proved by the same roll that they stated in Parliament that, relying on the prudence and moderation of Henry the Fourth, "it is their will and command that he keep that extensive royal freedom which his ancestors possessed." Had not that former grant been, like the latter, wholly in the nature of a trust, then surely those Houses of Parliament which gave away what was not theirs must

[13] According to Salmasius, under Edward IV, a statute permitted the king to set up a tribunal in whatever part of the kingdom suited him through letters patent. Under Henry VII, it was decreed that the king had full power of administering justice in all causes whatever. In the first year of Edward VI a statute declared that all authority and power, spiritual and temporal, are derived from the king (see *Regia,* 1649, p. 234, ll. 14–21).

have been stupid and heedless, and those kings who were content to take as a grant from others what was rightfully their own must have been doing themselves and their descendants a great disservice; neither of these things can be accepted.

"A third part of the royal power," you say, "concerns the military; and this the kings of England have administered with neither colleague nor rival."[14] There is no more truth in this than in the rest of what you wrote relying on your renegades. In the first place, decisions on war and peace have always rested with the Great Council of the realm, as we are informed in various instances both by our own histories and by those foreign accounts which treat our affairs with any degree of accuracy. Then too the laws of St. Edward, by which our kings must swear, give complete assurance of this, stating in the chapter *De Heretochiis*[15] that "certain offices were established in the provinces and in each county of the realm whose holders were called Heretochs, or in Latin *ductores exercitus,*" who commanded the forces of the province for the good of the realm as well as for the honor of the crown. These persons were chosen "by a general council and by the individual counties in full popular assemblies, just as sheriffs should be chosen." Thus it is quite clear that the armed forces of the realm, as well as their leaders, were of old (and ought to be) controlled by the people, not the king: In our kingdom, as formerly in the Roman republic, that most equitable law held good. We may do well to hear Cicero on this, where in the *Tenth Philippic*[16] he says: "All the legions and all forces everywhere belong to the Roman people. For we do not say that those legions which turned from the consul Antony were his, so much as the state's." That law of St. Edward was with the rest of his laws confirmed on oath by William the [139] Conqueror at the will and demand of the people; and in Chapter 56 he made this addition: "All cities, fortresses, and castles are to be guarded each night as the sheriffs, alderman, or other commanders appointed by the common council for the good of the realm shall best advise."[17] Also in law 62: "Castles, fortresses, and cities were built to protect the families and people of the realm, and should therefore

[14] *Regia* (1649), p. 235, ll. 8–12.

[15] "Leges Regis Edwardis Confessoris," in *Ancient Laws and Institutes of England,* Commissioners of the Public Records, II, 456.

[16] Cicero, *Philippics,* X, v, 12.

[17] "Leges Regis Willelmi Conquistitoris," in *Ancient Laws and Institutes of England,* I, 491–93.

be kept completely free, sound, and in good condition."[18] What then? Shall our citadels and towns in time of peace be guarded against thieves and malefactors only by the common council of each place, but, when there is great fear of war, fail to be guarded against foes foreign or domestic by the common council of the whole nation? Otherwise how can there be any "freedom" or "soundness" or "good condition" in their protection, or any of those ends attained for which above all else, so that law tells us, cities and forts were founded? Our fathers certainly would have chosen to yield the king anything sooner than their arms and the security of their towns, for they thought that to do that would be to betray their own freedom to the unbridled cruelty of kings. So many and so familiar are the instances of this in our history that insertion of them here would be pointless.

You object that "the king must protect his subjects, and how can he do so, unless he has men and arms under his control?"[19] I reply that he has them, but as was said, for the good of the realm, not to ruin the citizens and destroy the kingdom. Thus in the days of Henry the Third a certain scholar Leonard wisely replied to the papal nuncio and royal procurator Rustand in an assembly of the bishops: "All churches belong to my lord pope in the same way that everything is said to be the ruler's, that he may guard, but not," as the phrase goes, "own and enjoy it," that he may protect it and "not waste it."[20] Such too was the purpose of the law of Edward noted above. What have we here but a borrowed power, not absolute? It is much like the power held by a general in the field, delegated, not personal, but he is not made [140] any less active in defending, either at home or abroad, the people who chose him. It would indeed have been a foolish and unequal fight that Parliament once waged against the kings on behalf of freedom and of St. Edward's laws if they had ever supposed that arms were for the king alone. For, however unjust might have been

[18] *Ancient Laws and Institutes of England,* II, *loc. cit.*

[19] *Regia* (1649), p. 235, ll. 30–33. Salmasius adds "from internal strife and external enemies."

[20] "the rights of Ks. to the goods of his subjects. the answer of Reginald to Ruscand the popes legat. Leg. all churches are the popes. Regin. truth, to defend, but not to use them to serve his own turne, as we say all is the princes, that is all is his to defend, but not to spoil. Holinsh, p. 253." *Commonplace Book, Complete Prose,* I, p. 440.

the laws the king sought to impose, it would have been vain to oppose the sword by any charter, great or not.

"What good would it be," you ask, "for Parliament to have command over the forces when, without the king's consent, they could not compel the people to provide so much as a farthing towards their support?" [21] You need not worry about that. In the first place, you are wrong in supposing that the Houses of Parliament "cannot tax the people without the king's consent," [22] for they are the people's delegates and act in their behalf. Then it must be known to one who pries so curiously into other people's affairs that, for this war against the king the people of their own free will made great contributions by melting down their gold and silver vessels.

You go on to recount the very extensive annual income of our kings, chattering of nothing less than "five hundred and forty thousand"; "the munificent grants from the royal purse" usually given by those "monarchs famous for their bounty" have come to your eager ears. [23] By such inducements did those betrayers of their country win you over like that Balaam whose wickedness is known to all,[24] encouraging you to revile God's people and rant against his judgments. You fool! Did such boundless wealth profit an unjust and raging ruler in the end? Did it profit you? I understand that of all the money which your insatiable greed had fixed on, you actually got but that one poor little purse with its glass beads and the hundred pieces inside. Well, Balaam, you can take those wages of sin you wanted so much and make the most of them!

Your foolishness continues. "Setting up the standard," that is "the battle-flag, is the right of the king alone." [25] Why so? Because, you say [141]

> High on Laurentum's fort the battle-flag
> Turnus unfurled.[26]

But can you be a grammarian and unaware that this is the function of any military commander? "Aristotle says," you object, "that a king

[21] *Regia* (1649), p. 237, ll. 12–14. [22] *Ibid.*

[23] *Ibid.*, p. 237, ll. 28–33, *passim.*

[24] Numbers 22:5. Balak, King of the Moabites, hired Balaam to curse the Israelites. When God forbade this act to Balaam, he disregarded God's command and went with the Moabites. God then sent his angel who stood in the way of the ass upon which Balaam was riding and commanded Balaam to speak only those words which God put in his mouth.

[25] *Regia* (1649), p. 238, ll. 26–29. [26] Virgil, *Aeneid,* VIII, 1.

must have his guard to uphold the laws; a king should therefore have armed forces stronger than the whole people." [27] The consequences you turn are like the ropes Ocnus [28] made in the underworld; their only use is to feed asses. A guard granted by the people is quite a different thing from complete sway over all the forces, and, in the very passage you cite, Aristotle denies that kings should have the latter. The king, he says, should have about him soldiers "enough to make him more powerful than individuals or groups, but not stronger than the people" (*Politics* III, 11). Otherwise he might suddenly take control of both the people and the laws while pretending to protect them. Indeed the distinction between king and tyrant is just this: by the will and desire of senate and people, a king keeps a guard sufficient to protect him from foes and plotters; against the will of senate and people, a tyrant seeks to build up a guard of the greatest possible number of enemies or worthless citizens to oppose that very senate and people. This "setting up of the standard" then, was, like every thing else, a grant to the king from Parliament, and was made not that he might march as a foe against his country but rather might defend the people against those judged enemies by Parliament. Were he to do otherwise, he would himself be judged an enemy, for, by that law of St. Edward, and what is far more important, by the very law of nature, he would have lost the name of king. Thus we read in the *Philippic* cited above that "all official authority and right of command are forfeit when their holder uses them against the state." [29] A king could not summon the so-called "feudal knights" to a "war" which had not been ordered by Parliamentary authority, as is clear from countless statutes. The same is true of Tonnage and Poundage and Ship Money, which the king cannot levy without an act of Parliament. So our ablest [142] jurists ruled officially some twelve years ago, when the royal power was still unchallenged.[30] So too

[27] Aristotle, *Politics,* 1286 b 31 (III, 15). Milton joins together Salmasius' actual quotation from Aristotle in *Regia* (1649), p. 239, ll. 22–23 with Salmasius' gloss upon it (ll. 24–25). Salmasius' quotation from Aristotle is in Greek; his own comment is in Latin: "Omnino ergo oportet regem plus armis posse quam populum universum." Salmasius does not claim that Aristotle actually said this. Milton's subsequent quotation from Aristotle is correct, except that it occurs in *Politics,* III, 15, not in III, 11.

[28] Ocnus was a figure of Greek folklore associated with Hades. As a symbol of futile labor, he makes a straw rope which an ass eats as fast as Ocnus makes it.

[29] Cicero, *Philippics,* X, v, 12.

[30] Tonnage was a custom duty on imports (commenced in 1347), originally on

long before them, Fortescue, Chancellor to Henry the Sixth and a most eminent lawyer,[31] said the king of England can neither alter laws nor impose taxes against the will of the people.

Furthermore it is impossible to prove by any ancient evidence that "the government of the kingdom of England is absolute monarchy." [32] "The king," says Bracton, "has jurisdiction over all." That is, in court, where justice is rendered in the king's name to be sure, but according to our laws. "Everyone is subject to the king": as an individual, that is, as Bracton himself makes clear in the passage I cited above.[33]

To what follows, where you really outdo Sisyphus himself in repeating your useless struggles, I have already given an adequate reply.

On the next point, if Parliament has at times asserted its loyal obedience to our good kings in extravagant terms just short of servile flattery, this must not be taken as if it had been offered to tyrants or had impaired the rights of the people, a suitable respect is no threat to freedom. What you cite from Edward Coke [34] and others, "that the kingdom of England is an absolute power," is true in relation to any foreign king or to the Emperor, for, as Camden writes, "it is not under the patronage of the Empire." [35] In addition they all add

---

wines. Poundage, beginning in 1302, was a duty of a shilling in the pound on exports. They had been imposed for the "defence of the realm." They were not granted to Charles, but in 1628 he levied them on his own account. Charles' act was denounced in 16 Car. I c, 18 (1641). In 1634 writs were issued to seaports specifying sums needed for the ships each was to furnish the royal navy. From 1635 to 1639 the writs were made to include inland counties as well. In 1638 in the famous Hampden Ship Money case, the judges decided by a majority of seven to five that the king could take what measures he thought necessary for royal safety.

[31] Sir John Fortescue (1394?–1467?), chief justice of the King's Bench, legal writer, author of *De Laudibus Legum Angliae,* edited by Selden in 1616.

[32] Salmasius quotes Sir Edward Coke, commonly called "the oracle of the laws," in his work concerning the ecclesiastical law of the king, to this effect (*Regia,* 1649, p. 248, ll. 38 ff.).

[33] Bracton, book III, chap. 9, 3, fol. 107–107v.

[34] Sir Edward Coke (1552–1634), along with Selden, a foremost writer on English law. Once chief justice of England, he fell from favor by resisting James I's ideas on royal prerogative. In his repetition of the statement (see above, n. 32), Milton credits Coke rather than Salmasius with the direct quotation.

[35] Meaning that England is an autonomous sovereign state (an absolute power in that sense) and not a feudal vassal of the Holy Roman Empire. But this is certainly not what Coke had in mind when, in the quotation in Salmasius, he speaks of a compact political body, composed of numerous members, divided into clergy and laity both of which, directly and immediately under God, are subject

that this power resides not "in the king" alone, but "in the body politic." Thus Fortescue says, *De Laud. Leg. Ang.* Chapter 9: "The king of England governs his people not by the power of an absolute king but by that of a civil government," for the people is ruled by those laws which they have themselves passed. This fact is known to foreign writers as well. Thus the reliable Philippe de Comines [36] says in the fifth book of his *Commentaries*: "of all kingdoms on earth known to me, there is none, I believe, where the public interest is regarded with greater consideration or where the king has less power over the people than in England."

You say, finally, that "it is a ridiculous argument they advance about kingdoms existing before kings; one might as well say there was light before the sun." [37] What we say, my good man, is that people rather than kingdoms existed before kings. I may say in passing that none is more ridiculous than you [143] in denying, as if it were ridiculous, that light existed before the sun. It seems that while poking into other people's business you have forgotten the most elementary matters.

Then you are amazed "that those who have beheld the king in Parliament seated on his throne under that canopy of silk and gold could have doubted whether majesty belonged to the king or to Parliament." [38] The men you speak of must have been doubters indeed not to be moved by so brilliant an argument drawn from the canopy of heaven, or even better "the canopy of silk and gold." A Stoic like you gazed on this golden heaven with such rapt religious awe that you seem to have quite forgotten what Moses and Aristotle mean by heaven. You denied that in Moses "there was light before the sun," while you found earlier that there were three temperate belts in Aristotle! [39] I have no idea how many belts you discovered in that

---

to and revere their head. Salmasius also quotes Camden to the effect that the king has supreme authority and unlimited power, and does not recognize any authority except God (*Regia,* 1649, p. 249, ll. 11–14).

[36] De Comines, *Memoires,* V, 19. Philip de Comines (1445–1509), celebrated French chronicler, whose *Memoires* Milton quotes here.

[37] *Regia* (1649), p. 248, ll. 19–21. From Salmasius' point of view, it is not absurd because for him the king is always an extension of the father, the progenitor (see above, p. 326, n. 8).

[38] *Ibid.,* p. 248, ll. 29–35.

[39] "Nihili quoque est, immo ridiculum est argumentum quod afferunt, regna ante reges fuisse, quasi dicas lucem ante solem extitisse" (*Regia,* 1649, p. 248, ll. 19–21).

royal heaven of gold and silk, but I do know that, in your gazing on that heaven, you made off with one belt well tempered with a hundred golden stars! [144]

CHAPTER X [1]

In this whole controversy over rights, whether the rights of kings in general, or of the king of England in particular, the difficulty lies in the unyielding prejudice of the quarrelers much more than in the nature of the case itself. I therefore trust that by my lengthy citations from divine law, the law of nations, and the statutes of my country, I have made it quite evident to those who prefer truth to party spirit that a king of England may be tried and even executed.

Against those whose hearts are clouded by superstition or whose minds are so dazzled by the very idea of gazing on the royal splendor that they can see no brilliance or magnificence in honest virtue and freedom, it would be quite useless to bring the weapons of reason or argument or example. Here as in every other instance, Salmasius, you appear wholly ridiculous in heaping continual abuse of every sort on

According to *Genesis,* light was created before the planets. Consequently, Salmasius is denying Scripture. For the false analogy about the temperate zones, see above, p. 475, n. 13.

[1] Salmasius states in book X (*Regia,* 1649, pp. 249–74) that two groups are especially hostile to the divine right of kings, the papal and the Independents.

1. Not only were Charles' kingly prerogatives denied but the crimes of which he was accused could not condemn capitally even a private individual. 2. Only a small part of the people of England and Scotland concurred in his trial and execution. Only the English carried the affair through, and only a small part of the English were involved. Since the bishops and nobles had been ejected from Parliament, they were in no way to blame. Since the whole Parliament could not sentence the king, a purged Parliament could even do less. 3. The English army controlled everything. Perhaps in the beginning they did not intend the death of the king, but nevertheless they are responsible for it. If the king had been content to be a king in name only, he might have been permitted to live. 4. The Independents completed what the Presbyterians began. The blood of Charles is upon the Independents! James I in the *Basilicon Doron* [1604] had warned Charles about the Puritans! 5. Salmasius arraigns the Independents at length. If the "Saints" are destined for Paradise, then some good people would not care for heaven! 6. Now that the Independents have rid England of her king, will they expect other nations to do likewise? 7. They succeeded where the Gunpowder Plot failed. God is slow in punishing, but eventually retribution comes!

all Independents while making that very king you defend the greatest Independent of all. You say that "he owed his throne to his descent, not to the people." [2]

Though at first you complained bitterly that "he was compelled to plead for his life," you now wail that "he perished unheard." [3] If you care to read his whole defence accurately rendered into French, you may change your mind. It is true that when Charles had complete freedom to speak for himself during several consecutive days he made no use of the opportunity to refute the charges against him, but instead denied the authority of the court and its judges. Now, a defendant who is silent or who speaks beside the point suffers no injustice if, when he is clearly guilty, he is condemned unheard.

If you say that Charles "died just as he had lived," [4] I fully agree; if you say he met his end stoutly in piety and holiness, you should recall that his grandmother Mary, though a woman of ill-repute, met her end on the scaffold with a like appearance of piety, holiness, and courage. [145] Do not pay too much heed to that presence of mind so often manifested by the commonest criminals at their death; frequently desperation or a hardened heart gives, like a mask, an appearance of courage, as dullness does of peace. In death as in life, even the worst of men wish to seem good, fearless, innocent, or even holy, and, in the very hour of execution for their crimes, they will, for the last time, display as showily as possible their fraudulent pretence, and, like the most tasteless of writers or actors, strive madly for applause as the curtain falls.

You say next that "you have reached the point where you must consider who were chiefly responsible for that king's condemnation." [5] The point is rather how you, a foreigner, a French vagrant, came to consider our affairs which are none of your concern. What was your price? That at least we know. But who answered all your questions about our business? Obviously those deserters and traitors who found you were a complete fool and were easily able to hire your curses. You were given a sort of wretched little account of our government by some mad chaplain who was half papist, or by some servile courtier, and set to putting it into Latin. Such was the source of these tales of yours which we might perhaps examine a little more closely.

"Not one hundred thousandth part of the people agreed to this

[2] *Regia* (1649), p. 250, ll. 9–10.
[3] *Ibid.*, p. 249, l. 20.
[4] *Ibid.*, p. 250, l. 20.
[5] *Ibid.*, p. 250, ll. 31–33.

condemnation." [6] What of the rest, then, who let such a crime take place against their will? Were they trunks of trees or maimed men or like those lifeless figures in the Virgilian picture where "the purple hangings are stiff with the tapestried figures of Britons"? [7] It seems to me that these are no true Britons you depict, but Picts, painted perhaps, or even embroidered! Since it is beyond belief that a warlike race was subdued by so few men, and those the lowest of the populace, as happens at the start of your account, it must surely be false.

"The lords of the church were cast out by Parliament itself." [8] Your madness is all the worse because you are unaware that you are raving, when you complain of the ejection from [146] Parliament of those who should, according to your own lengthy volume, be ejected from the church.

"The second order in Parliament, composed of the noble dukes, earls, and viscounts was stripped of its position." [9]

This was but just, for being sent by no constituency they represented themselves only; they had no rights over the people, but by a sort of habit did, on most occasions, attack the rights and the freedom of the people. They were appointed by the king and were his companions, his domestics, as it were, his shadows, and when he was gone, they had to rejoin the populace from which they rose.

"A single part of Parliament, and that the worst, should not have assumed the power of judging the king." [10] As I explained before, the Commons were not only the strongest part of Parliament even during the monarchy, but also made up by themselves a perfectly complete and legitimate Parliament without the Lords, much less the lords of the church.

"Even this part itself," you claim, "was not all admitted to vote on the sentencing of the king." [11] Those not admitted, although they had often before deemed him but king in name, while actually a foe, had evidently deserted to him in their hearts and in their plans. The English Houses of Parliament and the delegates of the Parliament of Scotland had on 13 January 1645 replied, to the king's treacherous request for a truce and a conference with him at London, that they could not allow him to enter the city until he had given satisfaction to the state, for the civil war which his efforts had kindled in the

[6] *Ibid.*, p. 251, ll. 19–21.
[7] Virgil, *Georgics*, III, 25.
[8] *Regia* (1649), p. 251, ll. 26–27.
[9] *Ibid.*, p. 251, ll. 28–30.
[10] *Ibid.*, p. 252, ll. 4–6.
[11] *Ibid.*, p. 252, ll. 8–9.

three kingdoms and for all the citizens murdered on his orders, and had given assurance of true and lasting peace in accord with such conditions as the Parliament of both kingdoms had often offered him and would again offer.[12] Their just demands presented seven times with the utmost respect he had, for his part, rebuffed with hardened heart or evaded by ambiguous replies. The Houses of Parliament, having been patient for so many years and fearing that this treacherous king might, by his temporizing, destroy from his prison the state he had been unable to overcome in the field, pluck the sweet fruit of victory from our army, and, foe though he was, be restored to march in unlooked-for triumph over his conquerors, did at last decree to take no further account of the king, to send him no more requests, and to receive none from him. [147] Even after this decree, however, there were found some in Parliament itself who hated our invincible army, from jealousy of its great accomplishments, and, after it had deserved so much, wished to disband it in disgrace. At the behest of certain traitorous ministers whose wretched creatures they were, they seized the moment when many of those they knew differed heartily from them had, by order of Parliament itself, gone off to the provinces to settle the swelling revolt of the Presbyterians, and with strange fickleness, if not actual treachery, they decreed that this deep-dyed foe, who was king in name alone, should, without giving any real satisfaction or guarantees, be restored to the city and reinstated in the full dignity and power of office as though he had done great things for the state. Thus their religion, their freedom, that covenant they boasted of so often were all made of less importance than the king. In such a case what were men to do who, though themselves untouched, saw plans so pestilent being advocated? Should they have disregarded their country's interest and their own safety because the plague had

[12] There is no mention in Gardiner, *Great Civil War,* of the letter mentioned here. It would appear to be a document, according to its date, in the proceedings that led to the conference at Uxbridge, beginning on January 31, 1645, between the Scots, the Parliamentarians, and the king, a conference, which, according to Gardiner, was chiefly a Scottish negotiation and in which the Independents took little part (*Great Civil War,* II, 121). An entry appears in C. H. Firth and R. S. Rait, *Acts and Ordinances of the Interregnum, 1642–1660* (3 vols., London, 1911; hereafter referred to as *Acts and Ordinances*), I, 609, dated January 28, to the effect that an ordinance empowered the Commissioners of both Houses to treat with the king's Commissioners at Uxbridge. The king was requested to abolish Episcopacy, replace the *Book of Common Prayer* by the *Directory,* and to vest the command of the army in the two Houses of Parliament.

spread to their own House? And who was it that shut out the diseased members? You say yourself "the English army"; that is, not foreigners but the bravest and stoutest citizens, led chiefly by the very members of Parliament whom those fine fellows who were excluded had seen fit to exclude from their own country and send far off to Ireland! Meanwhile the Scots, whose loyalty had become questionable, occupied, with large forces, the four English counties nearest their borders, and put garrisons in the strongest towns of that district, kept the person of the king under guard, and encouraged quarrels and riots by fellow-countrymen in town and country, which were a very grave threat to Parliament itself and, before long, broke out in what was not only a civil but a Scottish War. Since it has always been counted most creditable for private citizens to succor the state by their advice or by arms, there is surely no reason to censure the army for marching to the city at the call of Parliament and carrying out its orders, putting down with ease the royalist riots and revolt which more than once threatened that assembly itself.

Affairs indeed had reached the point where we must either be crushed by them [148] or crush them. On that side were most of the London hucksters and artisans together with the most partisan ministers, while, on our side, was an army famous for its loyalty, moderation, and courage. With the help of the army, it was possible for us to keep our freedom and save the state; do you believe we should have betrayed everything through cowardice and folly?

The conquered leaders of the royalists had indeed laid down their arms, though unwillingly, but they kept hatred in their hearts and had returned to the city to await eagerly some opportunity of renewing the war. With these men, who had been their worst enemies, the Presbyterians, after they saw that they were forbidden to tyrannize over everyone in church and state, made a secret alliance, which ill befitted their former words and acts; they became so embittered as to sell themselves once again to the king rather than share with their brethren that freedom which they too had bought with their blood. A return to the mastery of that tyrant stained with the blood of so many citizens, who was already burning with rage against those who yet survived, and who had planned his revenge, seemed to them preferable to allowing their brothers and friends a position of just equality with themselves. Only those called Independents knew how to be true to themselves until the end and how to use their victory. They did not wish the enemy who had been king to change again from enemy to king, and in my opinion they were wise. It was not that they opposed peace, but that, with good reason, they feared a new war or endless slavery concealed under the name of peace.

In order to pad out your attack on our army, you enter on a confused and tasteless account of our history. To all this, even though it contains much falsehood and irrelevance, and even though you censure frequently what should be praised, I see little point in replying with an account of my own. Our dispute is to be conducted by reasoning, not by narrating, and with men of either persuasion, the reason will prevail over narration. Such too is the nature of the events themselves that they can be rightly recounted only in a proper history, and so I think it better, as Sallust said of Carthage,[13] to be silent on so great a subject than to be inadequate. I shall not be guilty of cheapening the great deeds which were accomplished not only by our foremost men but also as we must more especially remember in this wondrous course of events, by almighty God himself [149], by setting them side by side in this book with your slanders. I shall therefore select as I usually do only those points which seem to bear some resemblance to a rational argument.

When you state that "the British and Scots did by solemn agreement promise to maintain the majesty of the king," [14] you fail to mention the conditions of their promise, namely, if it could be done without injury to their faith or their freedom. But to both of these the king was, until his last breath, so treacherously hostile that it was quite evident that, as long as he lived, our faith would be in danger and our freedom lost.

You next revert to those responsible for the punishment of the king: "If the thing is taken by itself according to its own character and circumstances, we must ascribe the outcome of this fearful crime to the Independents, without going so far as to deprive the Presbyterians of their claims to the glory of its origin and progress." [15] Hear that, you Presbyterians; has your apparent great reluctance to punish the king done anything now to preserve or promote your reputation for harmless loyalty? This accuser of yours, this royal advocate so full of talk, says that you "went more than halfway"; [16] you "were observed up to the fourth act of this drama and longer out of breath from jumping

[13] Sallust, *Jugurthine War,* XIX, 2.
[14] *Regia* (1649), p. 254, ll. 23–25.
[15] *Ibid.,* p. 256, l. 37 ff.
[16] *Ibid.,* p. 257, l. 4.

to and fro."[17] I might ask why a man so learned in eloquence should be so ready to imitate those he works so hard to accuse; in this royal defence of yours, you have often been observed out of breath from jumping to and fro![18] You Presbyterians, however, "have well deserved branding as regicides; you paved the way for the murder of the king; you and no others struck his neck with that accursed axe."[19] Woe unto you, then, if ever the house of Charles Stuart regain the throne of England! Believe me, you will regret this. Therefore give thanks to God and cherish your brothers who set you free and who still keep from you, even against your will, this ruin and certain destruction.

Salmasius also accuses you of "having some years ago attempted to undermine the royal authority by various petitions, of having inserted and published, in those very papers you gave the king in the name of Parliament, certain derogatory expressions; thus, in the declaration of Lords and Commons dated 26 May 1642, you clearly revealed your sentiments regarding the royal authority by certain assertions which reeked of treason. The gates of the town of Hull [150] were on orders from Parliament closed by Hotham against the arrival of the king;[20] you were eager to discover in this first attempt at rebellion how much the king would endure."[21] Could you have said anything more calculated to unite all English hearts, and estrange them from the king? They can learn from this that, if the king should return, he would punish them not simply for the king's death but for all these old petitions, and for acts of the whole Parliament on the form of worship or

[17] *Ibid.*, p. 257, ll. 6–8.

[18] Milton is irritated by Salmasius' adjective, "frigultientes."

[19] *Regia* (1649), p. 257, ll. 18–21.

[20] Sir John Hotham was a royalist who defected to the parliamentary party after being removed as sheriff of Yorkshire. But, according to Lingard, Charles had been informed that "Sir John Hotham felt little attachment to the popular cause, and that it required no more than the royal presence to obtain from him the surrender of the magazine at Hull" (*History of England,* VII, 530). Hotham was informed by an unknown correspondent that, if he admitted the king, his life would be in danger for his previous misconduct. "Hotham ordered the drawbridge to be raised, the gates closed, and the walls manned." Hull had been an arsenal of the Scottish War. The event referred to occurred on April 23, 1642, but a year later, Sir John Hotham, together with his son, offered to betray Hull to the royalists (Gardiner, *Great Civil War,* I, 164–65). Both he and his son were ultimately executed for treachery.

[21] Most of this material, not directly quoted, is contained in *Regia* (1649), pp. 258–59.

on doing away with the bishops or on the Triennial Parliament [22] or anything else passed with the full consent and approval of the people, as though these were treasonable acts and "mad assertions of the Presbyterians."

Suddenly, however, this fickle fellow changes his mind; what seemed to him but a moment ago, as he "weighed the matter correctly as it stood," to be the fault of the Presbyterians alone, now seems to him as he "looks down on it from a distance," wholly caused by the Independents.[23] He asserted just now that the Presbyterians "moved to attack the king by force and open violence, and they conquered him in the field, captured him and threw him into prison," [24] but now he writes that the whole "plan of this rebellion" came from the Independents.[25] What steadfast faithfulness the man has! What need is there to put another account beside yours when your own story boils down to nasty nothingness!

But if anyone wonders whether you are a white man or a black rogue he should read what follows: "It is time to disclose where and when this sect of kings' foes broke out first. In the reign of Elizabeth these fine Puritans began to emerge from the darkness of Hell and disturb the church first and then the state. For they are as ruinous to the state as to the church." [26] Now your words show that you are a true Balaam,[27] for where you longed to spew out all the poison of your bitterness you did unknowingly and unwillingly pronounce a blessing. It is well known to all England that such men as attempted to follow the example of the churches in France or Germany, whichever might seem to them the more truly reformed, in establishing a method of

[22] Salmasius says (*Regia,* 1649, p. 259, *passim*) that Charles in granting the unwarranted Triennial Act had broken precedent from before and after William the Conqueror. For the text of the act see Gardiner, *Constitutional Documents,* pp. 144–55. According to Salmasius the Presbyterians, unsatisfied, sought new concessions, using new rebellions to conceal old ones. Actually, Salmasius should have referred to the House of Commons in this instance rather than to the Presbyterians.

[23] Salmasius argues that the Presbyterians, in trampling upon the authority of the king, prepared the basis for the tyranny of "Sacred Independence" (*Regia,* 1649, p. 260, ll. 8–10). Their respective roles are compared to those of Pilate and Caiaphas (*Regia,* 1649, p. 259, l. 37).

[24] *Regia* (1649), p. 259, ll. 31–32.

[25] *Ibid.,* p. 260, ll. 16–18.

[26] *Ibid.,* p. 261, l. 35 ff.

[27] An epithet previously hurled at Salmasius (see above, p. 503, n. 24).

divine worship purer than that which our bishops had well-nigh wholly corrupted with superstitious ceremonies; such men, further, as surpassed others in piety towards God or in uprightness of life, were called by the supporters of the bishops Puritans. These are the men [151] whose teachings you assail as hostile to kings; but not these alone, for you say that "most Protestants who have not adhered to the other points of their teaching seem to have approved of this one only which opposes royal despotism." [28]

Thus while attacking the Independents so bitterly, you actually praise them, for you show their descent from the most upright groups of Christians, and you now confess that the teaching which you affirm throughout is peculiar to the Independents "has been approved by most Protestants"! [29] Your madness, impiety, and apostasy have now driven you to the point of asserting that the very bishops who, according to your own recent teachings, should be cast out of the church and destroyed root and branch like so many pestilent antichrists [30] "should have been protected by the king on peril of breaking his coronation oath." [31] You have no further step to take in crime and wickedness but that one which is all that is left for you, namely abjuring as soon as possible the reformed faith which you pollute by your presence. You should hesitate to accuse us by charging "that we tolerate all sects and heresies"; [32] at least as long as the church tolerates you, who, in your impiety, dare to say that the purest Christians and most Protestants, who are against you, "sprang from the darkness of Hell," tolerates *you,* I repeat, an empty lying hired slanderer and apostate! I had best not mention the cunning falsehoods to which you devote most of the rest of this chapter, or the monstrous teachings which, in order to stir up hatred against them, you ascribe to the Independents. These tales have nothing to do with the king's case, and really deserve laughter or scorn rather than refutation. [152]

[28] *Regia* (1649), p. 263, ll. 3–6.

[29] These are the Protestants who are not termed sectarian (*Regia,* 1649, p. 263, ll. 3–4).

[30] See above, p. 499, n. 10.

[31] *Regia* (1649), p. 263, ll. 31–33.

[32] *Ibid.,* p. 264, ll. 27–29. Salmasius adds "as if reclining under the dark and wide shadow of Sacred Independence."

CHAPTER XI[1]

As you approach this eleventh chapter, Salmasius, I seem to see in you a continued lack of decency and in addition a certain awareness of your own futility.

Here, you say, you must inquire "by what authority"[2] sentence was pronounced on the king, but at the same time you surprise everyone by adding that "this search is in vain" because "the standing of the men who did it leaves little room for doubt."[3] Since therefore the impudent importunity revealed by your undertaking of this case is now equalled by your awareness of having talked too long, I may answer you quite shortly.

When you ask "by what authority" the House of Commons either judged the king itself or delegated the trial to others, I reply, by the highest authority. You may learn how they possessed the highest authority from what I said above when I showed the utter emptiness of your arguments on this very point. Indeed if you had any confidence that you could ever make an adequate statement, you would not always repeat the same distasteful refrain over and over again.

[1] The slogan of the killers of the king is, according to Salmasius in book XI (*Regia,* 1649, pp. 275–293), "it is permitted by law for a tyrant to be killed."

1. Both the Jesuits and the Independents inclined to this teaching. From them it spread to the Presbyterians. Once this doctrine was current, it was easy to identify as a tyrant the king whom they wished to destroy. 2. Were the judges legally competent? They were chosen from the House of Commons and the soldiery. Even in its entirety the House of Commons could not investigate the life of any person of any rank. Much less was this possible in a truncated House. As for the soldiery, it is their business to fight, not to judge. Soldiers, who could not render justice concerning a workman of the lowest class, have presumed to judge and condemn the king. 3. Success does not mean that justice was on the side of the victor. The court lacked legal validity and impartial judges. Anyone who might have been favorably disposed toward the king or the kingly state was not permitted to sit in judgment. 4. The judges maintained that their appointment came from the people. But a small part of the lower House does not have judicial power or the power of appointing judges. The people are not the people unless considered in their entirety. The soldiers only make up one tenth of the people! 5. The soldiers are mercenaries of the king and of Parliament, but they have usurped power. 6. Even if it were right to deprive the king of England of his kingdom and his life, it was not just to visit the same punishment upon the king of Scotland and of Ireland. 7. The king was destroyed by *VIS* (force), not by *IVS* (justice).

[2] *Regia* (1649), p. 275, l. 10.

[3] *Ibid.,* p. 275, ll. 11–13.

The House of Commons might delegate to others its judicial power in the same way that the king, who himself received all his power from the people, might, according to you, delegate that power to others. Thus in that "solemn agreement" which you cast in our teeth, the highest bodies of England and Scotland swear and promise on their oath that they will so punish traitors as "the highest judicial authority of either country, or those who have received delegated authority from them" shall direct. In this, you hear the Senates of the two countries affirming with one voice that they can delegate to others their judicial authority, which they themselves term supreme. This controversy you are trying to stir up about the delegation of authority is vain and frivolous.

But you say that "to these judges chosen from the lower House were added others [153] from the army divisions, although it was never the function of a soldier to judge a civilian." [4] I may be very brief in my refutation. You will recall that we are speaking here not of a civilian but of an armed foe. If, when such a foe has been captured and might if necessary have been killed on the spot, a military commander with his officers wishes to try him at his judgment seat, will anyone say he has violated custom or the laws of war? An enemy of a state captured in war cannot be considered a citizen, much less a king, of that same state. Such is the view of that most sacred law of King Edward which states that a bad king is no king and should not be called by that title. To your statement that the House of Commons "which judged the king was not complete but maimed and mutilated" [5]

[4] *Ibid.*, p. 278, ll. 19–21.

A constant target of Salmasius is the army. "If anyone asks what cause made Charles a tyrant, it is easy to answer the victorious army of the Independents!" (*Regia,* 1649, p. 305, ll. 6–9).

The army had offered a secure refuge to the religious and political opponents of Presbyterianism. To disband that army was at one time the main object of Presbyterian leadership. Early in 1647 measures passed Parliament to reduce the power of the army. Among other things, it was voted that no commission should be granted any member of the lower House, or to any individual who refused to take the Solemn League and Covenant, or to anyone whose conscience forbade him to conform to the Presbyterian scheme of church government. See Gardiner, *Great Civil War,* III, 220, 228 ff.

[5] *Regia* (1649), p. 286, l. 1. Salmasius has made a long argument to the effect that (1) the people cannot give the power of judging which it does not in the first place possess; (2) even if it did possess such power, where is the law that transferred it to the army; and (3) supposing the lower House had such power, how could it exercise it in a mutilated condition with the better part of it absent?

I reply: there were far more who voted to punish the king than are required by law to be present for the transaction of any business in Parliament, even in the absence of the rest. Since they were at fault and to blame for their absence (for the inclination of their hearts to the common foe was absence of the worst kind), they could not delay those who stood by their trust in protecting the state, which, tottering on the brink of slavery and ruin, had been particularly entrusted to their loyalty, wisdom, and courage by the whole people. They did indeed act with vigor, oppose the boundless madness and craft of the infuriated king, prefer the general freedom and security to their own, and surpass all earlier Parliaments and all their sires in wisdom, magnanimity, and steadfastness. Nonetheless a great part of the people, despite a pledge of complete loyalty, aid, and assistance to them, ungratefully deserted these men in the midst of their undertaking. This part desired peace and slavery with inaction and comfort upon any terms; but still the other part longed for liberty, and for none but a secure and sincere peace. What was the Senate to do in such a case? Was it to protect that part which was uncorrupted and faithful to it and to the country, or adhere to the one which had deserted both?

I know what you will say was right, for you are not a Eurylochus but an Elpenor, a foul Circean beast,[6] a filthy pig well used to serving a woman in the lowest sort of slavery where you never had the slightest taste of manly virtue or the freedom which springs from it [154]; you would have all men slaves, for in your own heart you feel nothing noble or free, and you breathe and talk nothing but meanness and slavery.

You next raise some trouble because "he whom we judged was king of Scotland as well," [7] as if for that reason, he might with impunity do as he pleased in England!

Finally, to attempt to end this chapter which is so especially dry and disjointed with some little spark of wit, you say that "there are two little words made up of the same letters and the same number of

[6] Eurylochus, according to Ovid's *Metamorphoses,* XIV, 252, 287, was the only one of Ulysses' crew to resist Circe's wiles. Elpenor did not resist, was changed into a swine, and later died of a fall from a roof while drunk.

[7] Salmasius pounds away at his juridical concept of kingship, which Milton ignores with equal pertinacity. For a section of the English people to kill a person who was also king of Scotland and Ireland is to violate grossly the rights of these other people. At best, they "should have expelled him from the Kingdom of England, and returned to the Scots their king" (*Regia,* 1649, p. 291, ll. 32–33).

them, differing only in their order, but with an immense difference in meaning, namely VIS and IVS." It is surely no surprise that a three-lettered man like you could build such a clever little quibble out of three letters! [8] The assertion throughout your whole work is more surprising that two things "differing" so completely elsewhere are quite identical for kings! When did kings ever do anything by *might* that you did not claim was done by *royal right?* This is all I could find worth answering in nine pages which were surely long enough in all conscience; the rest was either the same old oft-refuted stuff dragged out again, or had no bearing on the issues of this case. If then I answer with unusual brevity, the cause is no lack of diligence on my part, for despite my disgust, I do not let myself grow slack, but rather your continual foolish prating so completely devoid of sense or substance! [155]

CHAPTER XII [1]

In order that no one might suppose that I am unfair or bitter towards King Charles, whose life and punishment are both accomplished, I would have preferred to pass over in silence this whole question of "his crimes," and this would have been better for you, Salmasius, and for your supporters as well. Since however you preferred to speak of them at length and with such assurance, I shall

[8] *Regia* (1649), p. 293, ll. 7–10. It may be that Milton is merely casting one more slur at what he considers Salmasius' scholarly pretensions. On the other hand, Milton may have in mind Plautus' *Aulularia* (II, l. 325), where "man of three letters" denotes *fur* or *thief.*

[1] A king, says Salmasius in book XII (*Regia,* 1649, pp. 293–338), can be considered as a private individual and as a public official. The question can be asked, how did he live? But there is another question, how did he rule? Salmasius' conclusions are as follows: 1. The private life of a king need not necessarily influence him as a ruler. The man who lives most uprightly is not necessarily the best ruler. 2. Charles lived a good, pious, chaste and religious life. In comparison with other rulers he had few peers and almost no superior. His posthumous book breathes everywhere his probity, piety, clemency, religion, innocence, integrity, love of God, charity toward his neighbor, and benevolence toward his people. 3. He has been accused under the headings of *tyrant, traitor,* and *homicide.* 4. Charles was not considered a traitor at the time of the Covenant between the English and Scots. At that time apparently all that was desired was the reformation of religion. 5. As late as August, 1648, the House of Commons had not yet accused Charles as a tyrant. The Scots did not regard Charles as a tyrant and a traitor. 6. If he

make it quite clear to you that you could have done nothing more inconsiderate than keeping until the last the worst part of your case; that is reopening and probing deeply into these charges against him, for my disclosure of their truth and their blackness will make his memory repulsive and distasteful to all good men, and leave the reader at the end with the most active hatred of you as his advocate.

"This accusation," you say, "may be divided into two parts, one concerned with an attack on his life, the other with the wrongs he might have done as king." [2] As to his life, passed in feasting and plays and troops of women, I may well be silent; what is worth mentioning in a life of luxury? How would this have concerned us if he had been but a private citizen? Since, however, he was a king, he was no longer able to sin unto himself, just as he could no longer live for himself alone. In the first place, he did enormous harm to his people by his example; secondly, the time he spent on his lusts and pleasures, which was a great deal, was all stolen from the state which he had undertaken to govern; finally, his domestic extravagance wasted huge

---

were a tyrant and a traitor, why was he not always so and so considered by all? 7. How could he have developed into a tyrant during his imprisonment? 8. The Independents had decided that Charles was a tyrant because he was a king; they regarded all kings as tyrants. 9. No English statutes speak about treason against the Parliament or the people. Treason cannot be committed against them because they do not have majesty. 10. Even if the king were legally guilty of treason, who could legally judge him? 11. Why was Charles a tyrant to the Independents and not to the other subjects? 12. Treason cannot be properly ascribed to a king. The acts of Charles did not constitute rebellion. When he raised his standard, it was in self-defence. 13. Five indictments were made against the king for making war, but these are matters of the king's prerogatives. Charles was guiltless in the La Rochelle affair. 14. He is charged with omitting certain words from his coronation oath. By their omission the oath made better sense. In any case, the judges did not show that they were removed by *his* order. 15. The king's taking of an oath is merely a ceremonial. A king rules by virtue of his position, not because of the oath. The main reason for taking an oath is to confirm to the people the laws and privileges granted by previous kings. 16. In any case, it is not a capital offense for a king to act contrary to the law, for he is above it. The axiom of the English law, "the king can do no wrong," proves that Charles was unfettered by laws. The king is answerable to God alone. 17. The king was unwilling to admit the "sanctity" of the Independents and to hand his power over to them. This refusal was the source of all the trouble. This is what made the king a traitor, tyrant, and homicide! 18. The revolt of the English rebels and the revolt of the Dutch against their Spanish governors are not analogous. 19. Charles was condemned by men who had no authority to judge or to appoint judges. 20. Even though the king is unfettered by laws, he should obey them and thus set an example to his subjects.

[2] *Regia* (1649), p. 293, ll. 33–35. "Life" in this context, of course, means "private" life—manner of living.

sums of money, countless wealth that was not his own but belonged to the state. It was then within his own household that he began to be a bad king.

But let us rather pass over to those crimes "which he is said to have committed by misgovernment."[3] Here you bewail his condemnation as "tyrant, traitor, and murderer."[4] I shall show that no injustice was done him. Let us define a tyrant, not by general opinion but by the judgment of Aristotle [156] and all learned men. A tyrant is one who considers his own interests only, not those of the people. So says Aristotle in the tenth book of the *Ethics* and elsewhere,[5] and so many others. Whether Charles considered his own interests or those of the people will be shown if I but mention a few instances out of many. When his inherited treasures and royal revenues failed to meet the expenses of his court, he imposed very heavy taxes on the people, and when these were eaten up, he invented new ones, not to strengthen or beautify or protect the state, but that in one house he might amass for himself, or in one house squander, the wealth of several nations. When thus he had, without benefit of any law, scraped together a huge amount, he attempted to abolish Parliament completely, knowing it would be the only restraint on him, or else to summon it only when it suited him and make it responsible to him alone. Having freed himself from this restraint he found a new means of restraining the people; he arranged for the stationing of German cavalry and Irish infantry in the cities and towns as if for their protection, though there was no war.[6] Does this seem to you tyrannical enough? In this respect and

[3] *Ibid.,* p. 294, ll. 15–16.

[4] *Ibid.,* p. 300, ll. 31–33. For Salmasius the term "tyrant" is the most inclusive and has the greatest possibility of *legal* validity as a charge ("*Tyranni* appellatione omnia mala quae facere potest quisquis injuste, impotenter & crudeliter imperat, comprehendi." *Ibid.,* p. 306, ll. 34–35).

[5] Aristotle, *The Nicomachean Ethics,* 1160 b 2 (VIII, 10, 2), tr. H. Rackham (London and New York: Loeb Classical Library, 1926), pp. 488–91.

[6] Included among the grievances of the Petition of Right (1628) is that of billeting soldiers upon private citizens against their will. The idea of using Irish troops in England occurred to Charles on several occasions. Samuel R. Gardiner in *Great Civil War,* I, 249, records that "Digby informed Ormond that the King was now ready to accept a proposal made by Lord Taaffe to bring over 2000 Irish, conceiving that he shall not only be advantaged by their presence in the affairs of England, but also in the affairs of Ireland by their absence." Gardiner adds (*op. cit.,* I, 296), "The mere talk of sending for native Irish was doing more damage to Charles's cause than the arrival of whole regiments could have done to support it."

in many others, as I pointed out before when you gave me the cue yourself, despite your great dislike of the comparison of Charles with the cruel Nero, he was very like Nero, who also made frequent threats of doing away with the Senate.[7] At the same time he did great violence to the conscience of godly men, and forced on all certain rituals and superstitious practices which he had brought back into the church from the depths of popery; he punished those who refused with exile or imprisonment, and twice he made war on the Scots for this very reason. So far he may seem to have earned the name of tyrant at least once.

Now I shall explain why the word "traitor" was added to the indictment. Though he had assured the Parliament by repeated promises, pronouncements, and sworn oaths that he had no hostile intentions towards the state, he was at that very time assembling drafts of papists in Ireland or sending secret emissaries to the king of Denmark to request arms, horses, and reinforcements expressly against Parliament, or attempting to hire at a price an army whether of Englishmen [157] or Scots. The former were promised the city of London to sack, the latter the annexation to Scottish control of the four northern counties, if they would lend him their aid in doing away with Parliament by any means whatsoever.[8] When these plans failed he gave a certain traitor Dillon [9] secret instructions to the Irish to rise in a sudden attack on all the English settlers in that island. These are in general the proofs of his treason, not drawn from empty gossip but known from his own letters signed and sealed by his own hand. Finally, I do not suppose that anyone will refuse to call that man a murderer by whose orders the Irish took up arms and slaughtered with every

[7] In *Regia* (1649), p. 306, ll. 4–5, Salmasius points out, by analogy to the position of Charles, that in Nero's time some desired Nero's death without really understanding who he was. The Presbyterians pitied their captive and a little later handed him over to the executioner.

[8] Charles visited Scotland in 1641 in the hope of getting Scottish assistance for intervention in England. At the same time his agents in Ireland were trying to win support from Irish Catholics by unspecific offers of religious toleration. Early in his career Charles had subsidized Christian IV of Denmark for intervention in Germany with the objective of recovering the Palatinate for Frederick V of Bohemia, husband of Charles' sister, Elizabeth. The promises alleged to have been made by Charles, as stated by Milton, are impossible to substantiate, and have the color of partisan passion and propaganda, as in the subsequent statement about the slaughter of "some five hundred thousand English."

[9] Sir James Dillon, one of the organizers of the Irish rising of 1641.

refinement of cruelty some five hundred thousand English,[10] who had no apprehensions of any such happening in the midst of peace; that same man, too, who kindled such a civil war in the other two kingdoms. Furthermore, in that conference on the Isle of Wight,[11] the king openly assumed the guilt and responsibility for this civil war and by his confession, known to all, completely freed Parliament from any blame. Now you have, in brief, the reasons why King Charles was adjudged tyrant, traitor, and murderer.

"Why," you ask, was he not so adjudged "earlier" either by that "solemn covenant" or afterwards, when he had surrendered, "by the Presbyterians or by the Independents," but instead "was treated as a king should be, with all respect?" [12] This point alone should convince any man of sense that only as a last resort, after they had put up with everything, tried everything, endured everything, did the estates decide to depose the king. You alone are so evilly inclined as to turn into a reproach facts which in the eyes of all good men testify to their extreme patience, fairness, moderation, and a tolerance of royal insolence which was perhaps excessive.

But "in the month of August, before his punishment, the House of Commons, which had already sole power and was controlled by the Independents, dispatched letters to the Scots which stated that it had never been their intention to change the form of government which had until that time prevailed in England under King, Lords, and Commons." [13] See then how little the deposing of the king is to be

[10] Historians are in agreement that the rebellion in Ulster in 1641 led to the slaughter of "several" thousand Protestants rather than the "five hundred thousand" mentioned by Milton. For an account of Charles' ambiguous relationships to Irish Catholics see Gardiner, *Great Civil War,* I, 110–27. Lingard observes (*History of England,* VII, 528): "Nor is it easy for an impartial historian, in this conflict of passion and prejudice, amidst exaggerated statements, bold recriminations, and treacherous authorities, to strike the balance, and allot to each the due share of inhumanity and bloodshed." Gardiner (I, 114) evaluates the Anglo-Irish warfare in roughly similar terms: "Exasperated at the Ulster murders, and seeing in every Irishman a murderer or a supporter of murderers, the English soldiery rarely gave quarter, and, unless the accounts of their enemies are entirely devoid of truth, when they did give it, it was often violated. The peasants retaliated by knocking stray soldiers on the head, and by slaughtering parties too weak to resist." What Charles wanted, according to Gardiner (I, 120), "was to pacify the Irish Catholics so as to be able to utilize the English regiments in Ireland for service against the English Parliament."

[11] See below, p. 525, n. 16.

[12] *Regia* (1649), p. 303, ll. 14–16.

[13] *Ibid.,* p. 305, ll. 12–19.

ascribed to the teachings of the Independents! These men [158], quite unaccustomed to concealing their beliefs, profess, even when masters of the state, that "they never intended to change the form of government." If, however, they decided later on what they had not planned at first, was it not right for them to do what was more straightforward and more advantageous for the state, especially when they found that no exhortation or entreaty could incline Charles in the least towards acceptance of those same most temperate demands which they had presented to him without change from the start? [14] He persisted in holding the same views on religion and on his own rights he had held at the beginning, mistaken though they were, and calculated to work our ruin. He was that same Charles who had brought on all of us so much misfortune both in peace and in war. He left no doubt in our minds that whatever he might agree to would be done unwillingly and considered invalid as soon as he regained power. His son, who had at that time absconded with part of the fleet,[15] published a document to the same effect; Charles indicated as much himself in his letters to certain supporters in the city.

Meanwhile he had, in secret, patched up a peace with the Irish, those fierce foes of England, against the wishes of Parliament and upon shameful terms, and whenever he summoned the English to those repeated but fruitless negotiations for peace he would at the

[14] On the complicated events of Charles' relations with the army, the Parliament, and the Scots in the summer of 1647, see Gardiner, *Great Civil War,* III, 212–352; *Complete Prose,* III, 275–374. When the Council of Officers submitted a plan for the settlement of the nation to Charles, *Heads of the Proposals* (Gardiner, *Constitutional Documents,* 1899, pp. 316–26) negotiations broke down. The influence of the Levellers now forced the officers to more extreme positions. A strong current of propaganda against kingship as an institution mounted in the army, infecting not only the common soldiers but many of the officers (see Haller and Davies, *Leveller Tracts,* and Wolfe, *Leveller Manifestoes*). The Levellers maintained that kings were odious in the sight of God, and contended that in fact Charles had now no claim to the sceptre (*cf.* Milton's argument above, p. 370, that God preferred a theocratic state to kingly rule for the Israelites).

[15] Charles, Prince of Wales, cruised with some English ships off the mouth of the Thames in 1648. According to Gardiner (*Great Civil War,* IV, 173), "Warwick had not yet completed his task of weeding out all the disaffected seamen from the ships under his command, and it is possible that an immediate attack by the Prince of Wales would have laid London bare on the side of the sea. The prince, however, was short of money, not having wherewithal to pay his crews. He accordingly resorted to the desperate expedient of seizing merchantmen on their passage through the Downs."

same time devote all his energies to stirring up war against them. In such a case what were those entrusted with the government to do? Were they to betray our common security, entrusted to them, to the hands of our bitterest foe? Were they to leave us another war of almost complete destruction to wage again and suffer through for another seven years, lest worse befall us? God granted them more wisdom, so that their earlier plans not to depose the king, plans which had never been ratified as laws, seemed to them of less importance than the state itself, their faith, and their freedom based on the solemn covenant; it became clear to them, later perhaps than it should, but nonetheless clear at last, that while the king remained, these things could not be preserved.[16]

Surely Parliament should never be hindered or hampered in its consideration of the public interest in each case, nor be so committed to its earlier beliefs ever after, so that it must henceforth hesitate to adopt new measures, which are more to its own advantage and that of the nation, when God has granted them the understanding and the opportunity.

"The Scots," you say, "thought otherwise, and indeed, when writing to the younger Charles [159], they term his father the most sacred king, and his murder an accursed crime." [17] Say no more of the Scots,

[16] After the victory of Cromwell over Hamilton on August 17, 1648, the Presbyterian leaders were alarmed by the ascendancy of the Independents. Negotiations were resumed with Charles, who was removed from Carisbrooke Castle to Newport for that purpose. The Independents from the very beginning disapproved of the prospective treaty. In the army, flushed as it was with victory and longing for revenge, maxims began to prevail of the most dangerous tendency in regard to the royal captive. See Gardiner, *Great Civil War,* IV, 212–32, 233 ff.

[17] *Regia* (1649), p. 305, ll. 25 ff. Salmasius insists that the accusation against the King of being a "tyrant, traitor, and homicide" was *ex post facto,* an afterthought.

Why, he has asked, in making a covenant in formal and fluent words did the Independents and Presbyterians obligate themselves mutually to preserve and defend the person and sovereignty of the king (*Regia,* 1649, p. 302, ll. 3–6)? Charles, on retreating from Oxford, gave himself into the faith and safekeeping of the Scots (*Regia,* 1649, p. 303, l. 12 ff.). Far from declaring him a tyrant, they received him with all reverence. Finally, obligated by their alliance with the English Parliamentarians, they surrendered him to the latter. Neither the English nor the Scots spoke a word about the tryanny and treason of the king at that time.

But Salmasius had contended at the beginning of his indictment in book I that the English *latrones* had by plan and method committed the crime meditated a long time before (*Regia,* 1649, p. 16, ll. 12–13). They changed the ancient rule of a kingdom accustomed to being governed by one into another which is held by whom you know not; we knew the time when they called that same king accursed, and murderer and traitor, and the act of slaying the tyrant most sacred!

Next you object to the indictment we drew up against the king as being unsuitable, asking "what need was there to add the titles of traitor and murderer to that description of tyrant, when the name of tyrant includes all sins?" [18] Then like a grammarian or glossator you tell us what a tyrant is. Be off, you pedant, with this nonsense which that one Aristotelian definition just cited will easily blow to bits; it will teach you, teacher that you are, that tyrant is a word, if all you care to understand is words, which can apply to something less than treason and murder.

But you claim that "the laws of England do not state that the king is guilty of treason if he stir up sedition against himself or his people." [19] I may reply that they do not state that Parliament is guilty of lèse-majesté if it depose a wicked king, or that it ever was, though formerly it often deposed them. But that a king can injure or demean his own majesty, and can even lose it, is plainly shown. The expression in that law of St. Edward, "losing the title of king," means no more nor less than being deprived of the functions and dignity of king, as happened to King Chilperic of France, whose case is cited by that very law as an illustration of the point. That high treason may be committed against the kingdom as well as against the king can be denied by none of our jurists. I appeal to that very Glanville whom you cite: "Any act towards killing the king or stirring up revolt in the kingdom is treason." [20] Thus that plot by which certain papists were to blow to bits the Parliament buildings along with the members of both Houses by a single blast of gunpowder was deemed by King James himself and by both Houses to be "high treason" not merely against the king but against Parliament and the realm as well.

---

tyrants, against law, against right, against the laws of the kingdom, against the solemn pact of the covenant which originated between the two kingdoms, and in which it was clearly provided that the majesty of the king should be observed with all courtesy, and his person protected (*Regia,* 1649, p. 23, l. 36 ff.).

[18] *Regia* (1649), p. 306, ll. 32–37.

[19] *Ibid.,* p. 308, l. 38 ff.

[20] Ranulf de Glanville, *De Legibus et Consuetudinibus Regni Angliae,* I, 2, ed. George E. Woodbine (New Haven, 1932), p. 42. Glanville's work, dealing chiefly with procedures in the King's Court, was first printed in 1554.

What would be the point, however easy it might be for me, of citing more of our laws when the truth is so plain? Especially when it would be so completely ridiculous and unreasonable that treason could be committed against the king [160] but not against the people for whom, on whose account, and so to speak by whose favor, the king is what he is. It is then vain for you to babble about all our statutes, vain for you to vex and torment yourself with old English lawbooks; for Parliament always had power of determining whether to confirm or repeal the laws, and it alone has the task of deciding what treason is, or lèse-majesté. I have already shown more than once that this majesty has never been so completely transferred from the people to the king that it does not appear in Parliament in a much loftier and more august form.

Who could put up with you, a cheap French mountebank, as an expounder of our laws? And as for you English deserters! All you bishops and scholars and jurists who assert that all the arts and letters fled from England in your company! Were you so utterly unable to find in your number anyone to defend the king's cause and his own with sufficient vigor and Latinity and to present it to the judgment of foreign nations, that you were forced to buy the assistance of this crackbrained, moneygrabbing Frenchman for the support of your penniless king and his huge voiceless train of scholars and priests? Believe me, this will bring on you a storm of reproach from foreign nations, and all men will rightly consider that you deserved defeat in that cause which you could not support with words, much less with bravery in arms!

But to return to you, my fine orator, if you have returned to your senses, for I find that you are snoring here, so near the end, and sleepily drawling out some irrelevant talk of a voluntary "death." Then you hasten to deny "it could occur to a king in his right mind to divide his people by seditions, betray his own forces to defeat by the enemy, and raise factions against himself." [21] Many other kings and Charles himself did all these things, and so being a Stoic you cannot doubt that, like all sinners, all tyrants too are quite mad! As Horace says:

> When wicked folly and ignorance of truth
> Lead a man on in blindness, then Chrysippus' porch

[21] *Regia* (1649), p. 319, ll. 3–5.

And followers deem him a madman: this holds true
For nations and for mighty kings, excepting only
Him who is truly wise.[22] [161]

If then you wish to clear King Charles of the charge of acting like a madman, you must clear him of wickedness before you can prove him sane.

You object that "the king could not commit treason against those who were his own vassals and subjects." [23] In the first place, being as free as any race on earth, we will not allow any barbarous custom to do us injury; next, even if we were his vassals, we would not have thought it necessary to endure a tyrant as our lord! The whole concept of subjection, as our laws explain, is limited to what is "honorable and profitable," see *Leg. Hen. 1. c. 55.* Our jurists all hold that allegiance is "pledged" on condition that the lord shall furnish what is termed "liege protection"; if, however, he should be unduly harsh or should commit any serious injury, then "the whole bond of homage is broken and completely at an end." [24] These are the very words of Bracton and Fleta.

Thus there are cases where the law itself arms vassal against lord, and hands over the lord to be killed in single combat by the vassal, as chance may decide. If a whole free state or nation may not treat a tyrant in the same way, then free men will be in a worse condition than slaves.

You next attempt to excuse Charles' murders by the example of other kings, drawing on both their murders and their rightful actions. As to the Irish butchery "you refer the reader to that royal work entitled *Eikon Basilike*"; [25] and I refer you to the *Eikonoklastes*. You would not have "the taking of La Rochelle," [26] the betrayal of its citizens, "the promise of assistance instead of supplying it," ascribed to Charles.[27] I cannot say whether or not these charges are true; his domestic crimes were so great that I need not pursue his misdeeds abroad. In the meantime all Protestant churches that ever defended themselves against kings who were enemies of their faith are on this

[22] Horace, *Satires,* II, 3, 43–46.
[23] *Regia* (1649), p. 320, ll. 29–31.
[24] Bracton, *op. cit.,* II, 25, 12 fol. 80b.
[25] *Regia* (1649), p. 321, ll. 28–31.
[26] The first of the English attacks (1627–28) was led by Buckingham, to gain the Isle of Rhé off Rochelle. English troops were decimated, but the island was not gained.
[27] *Regia* (1649), p. 322, ll. 10–12, 16–17.

account condemned by you as guilty of rebellion! It is for these churches to decide how important it is for their church discipline and for the preservation of their own well-being not to overlook this insult which one of their own children has offered them; we for our part have not forgotten the betrayal of the English in that expedition. He had long planned to turn the government of England into a tyranny, but he thought he could not carry out his plans unless he had first done away with the best part of the citizens' military strength.

Another of the king's crimes was his ordering the removal of certain words from the oath [162] customarily required of the kings at their coronation before he would take it. What a shameful and accursed act! If I call him criminal who did it, what shall I call its defender? I ask in the name of the eternal God what double-dealing or lawbreaking could be more heinous than this? There is nothing save the holy sacraments themselves which he should hold more sacred than that oath. Which is the greater criminal, he who sins against the law or he who attempts to make the law itself his accomplice in crime, and even does away with the law to avoid the appearance of crime? See now how your king broke that oath which he should have sworn with all fidelity, but to avoid the appearance of open violation he treacherously corrupted it by the most shameful adulteration; lest he be called perjurer, he turned the oath itself into a lie! Could we look for anything but the most unjust, cunning, and wretched government from him who began his reign by an outrage so despicable, and dared to adulterate that basic law which he considered the only bar to his overthrowing all law!

Your defence alleges that this "oath can no more bind kings than do the laws; but though kings assert that they are bound by the laws and live in accordance with them, the fact is that they are actually unbound by them." [28] Can anyone use such sacrilegious and corrupt language as to assert that the most solemn oath, sworn on the Gospels, can without cause be dispensed with as the merest trifle? But you are refuted, you monstrous scoundrel, by Charles himself; for it was because he considered that oath no trifling matter that he thought it better to avoid its binding force or escape from it by some trick, than to violate it openly. He chose to be a corrupter and counterfeiter of his oath rather than appear openly as a perjurer.[29]

[28] *Ibid.*, p. 323, ll. 26–28.

[29] The controversy arises from the substitution in Charles' coronation oath of

You say that "the king does indeed swear to his people as they in turn do to him, but the people swear allegiance to the king, not the king to the people." [30] What a lovely lie! Does not he who, upon oath, promises and agrees to render faithful performance pledge his faith to those who required the oath of him? Every king does indeed swear "to be loyal, indulgent, and obedient to his people" [31] in making good his promises to them. At this point you go back to William [163] the Conqueror, but he was more than once compelled to swear that he would do, not what he pleased, but whatever the people and nobles demanded of him. If many kings "do not receive the crown" in a solemn ceremony, and therefore take no oath even though they do rule, the same may be said of the people, for a great part of them never swore allegiance. If for this reason the king is free, then so are the people. Those of the people, who did swear, swore not to the king only, but to the kingdom and the laws which made him king, and they swore to the king only in so far as he should abide by the laws "which the common people should choose," [32] meaning the community or the House of Commons. He would be a fool who always tried to turn the language of our laws into purer Latin! This phrase "which the common people should choose" Charles had removed from the form of the king's oath before he would take the crown. You object that "without the king's consent the common people could choose no laws," [33] and on this point cite two statutes, one *37 Hen. c. 15,* the other *13 Edward 4 c. 8.* That either of these laws appears in our statute-books is so wholly untrue that in the years you speak of there were no laws at all passed by either of these kings. Go now and complain that you have been deceived by the bad faith of those renegades who dictated to you imaginary laws; others will wonder at your forwardness and

---

the phrase *"legum & consuetudinum quas communitas habet"* for the phrase *"consuetudines & leges quas vulgus elegerit,"* in the formula, *"quod populo concederet tenere & observare leges & justas consuetudines quas regni communitas habet"* (see *Regia,* 1649, p. 327, ll. 19–24). The essential difference is between the king swearing to observe the laws and customs which the community already *has,* and swearing to observe those which the community will choose *in the future.* By substituting the new phrase, Charles does not bind himself to observe *future* enactments.

[30] *Regia* (1649), p. 323, ll. 32 ff.

[31] Milton is reversing the implication of *Regia* (1649), p. 323, ll. 34–36: "The king in truth does not swear loyalty, nor reverence, nor obedience to his subjects, but that he will defend and preserve them, and will reign according to the laws."

[32] See above, p. 529, n. 29.

[33] *Regia* (1649), p. 327, ll. 29–30.

folly in your unscrupulous attempt to claim familiarity with volumes which it is quite clear you have never read or even seen. Of that very clause in the oath which a false-faced clown like you dares call "forged," you say, "the king's defenders state it may" exist in some ancient versions, "but it fell into disuse because it had no satisfactory meaning." [34] Our sires put that clause into this royal oath for the very purpose of furnishing a meaning which would never be satisfactory to tyranny. But if it had fallen into disuse, which is however utterly untrue, who would deny that there was all the more reason for restoring it?

That too would be useless, if we listen to you! For that custom "of taking an oath, as kings generally do today, is only ceremonial." [35] But when it was the king's duty [164] to do away with the bishops, he argued that, because of this oath, he could not.[36] And so that most solemn oath will, according to the king's convenience, be now something powerful and substantial, now but empty "ceremonial."

I call upon all Englishmen to think of this again and again! Consider what sort of king you will have if he should return! Never would it have occurred to this wretched foreign grammarian to write, or to think he could write, about the laws concerning the king of England, had not that exile Charles, who is steeped in his father's teachings, and his profligate advisers been so careful to tell him what they wanted

[34] *Ibid.*, p. 327, ll. 37–39. Salmasius does not say that the oath is "forged." What is "most false" is what is inferred from the clause about "choosing" laws, in the oath, namely, that the people had the power of making what laws they pleased for themselves. Salmasius goes on to say that the only laws that can be truly made are through a legitimate parliament, summoned by the king, its enactments becoming valid through the king's consent.

[35] *Ibid.*, p. 326, l. 9.

[36] Milton scores here—a bull's eye! Salmasius had pointed out (*Regia,* 1649, p. 302, ll. 3 ff.), that the oath which the English and Scots had taken against the king had, as its principal overt objective, the reforming of religion in matters of doctrine, worship, discipline and ecclesiastical rule. The king assented to the extirpation of schism and the removing of heresy, but not to the removal of the bishops. "He found the bishops at the beginning of his reign. Therefore, he believed he should protect them along with everything else that he had promised to conserve on his entering his office" (*Regia,* 1649, p. 302, ll. 19–21). The point which Milton attacks was even more explicitly stated in *Regia* (1649), p. 263, ll. 30–34: "Charles found the bishops already in existence when he began his reign. And so they were to be protected lest he set aside his inaugural oath." The author of the work against Petavius the Jesuit is in a tight squeeze because he has attacked Episcopacy in that work as a correlative of the papal system, and cannot strongly defend it here.

written on this subject. They kept saying to him that "the whole Parliament could be charged with treason against the king" simply because "it had stated, without the king's assent, that all who had taken up arms against the Parliament of England were traitors, for surely Parliament is the vassal of the king."[37]

But they say that the king's oath is "simply ceremonial"; why not the vassal's oath too? So then no reverence for law, no respect for the pledged word or scruple to break it, will suffice to protect your lives and all your property from the lust or vengeance of an embittered king who acknowledges no master, and who from his earliest days has been taught to think that law, religion, and his own oath are but his vassals and ministers to his desires. If you long for wealth, freedom, peace, and power, would it not be much better, much more in accord with your own deserts, to strive resolutely for those ends through your own virtue, industry, prudence and courage than to hope for them in vain under a king's control? Surely those who suppose that these ends cannot be attained without a king and master must think of themselves as unspeakably abject and ignoble, not to say quite unworthy of their own positions; for, in fact, they confess that they are spiritless and weak, bereft of intelligence and prudence, destined for slavery in body and soul. All slavery indeed is a stain upon any freeborn man, but for you to wish to resist your destiny [165] and return to slavery after your freedom had been won by God's assistance and your own valor, after you had performed so many brave deeds and made so memorable an example of this most powerful king, would be not simply a shameful act, but an ungodly and a criminal act! Your sin would equal the sin of those who were overcome with longing for their former captivity in Egypt and were at length destroyed by God in countless disasters of all sorts, thus paying to their divine deliverer the penalty for their slavish thoughts.

What do you tell us, you advocate of slavery? You say "the king could pardon treason or other crimes, which proves clearly that he was not bound by the laws."[38] The king, like anyone else, could pardon treason to himself, but not to the kingdom. And at times, though not always, he could pardon other offenders; but shall he who has on occasion some right to reprieve a wrongdoer for that reason necessarily possess any right to destroy all good men? When he is summoned to one of the lower courts, the king need appear only in the

[37] *Regia* (1649), p. 312, ll. 32–37. [38] *Ibid.*, p. 328, ll. 9–12.

person of his representative, as is true of any citizen; when he is summoned to Parliament by the whole people, shall he therefore not appear and reply in his own person?

We, you say, "attempt to justify our action by the example of the Dutch," [39] and since, I suppose, you fear that the salary with which the Dutch support you, foul blight though you are, may be in danger should your slander of the English seem to cast a shadow on your Dutch patrons, you are eager to show how "unlike were the deeds of the two peoples." This comparison of yours is sheer falsehood in many respects, and the rest of it betrays the hand of a flatterer who fears he has not done enough for his dinner, but I shall say no more of it, for the English see no need for them to justify their own deeds by the example of any foreigners whatever. They have laws, and followed them; laws which they got from their fathers and which are here the most excellent, whatever may be the case in the rest of the world. They have as models their own forefathers, indomitable men, who never yielded to the unbridled sway of kings and who executed many of them when they made their rule unbearable. They were born in freedom, they live in independence, and they can make for themselves what laws they wish; they cherish particularly one law of great age, passed by Nature herself, which makes all laws, all rights, all civil government depend not on the desire of kings but primarily on the well-being of the better citizens.

I see that by this time nothing is left but the trashy rubble of your preceding chapters [166]; since you have accumulated such a heap of this at the end I can only suppose you wish to predict the downfall of your work. Finally and at long last you cut off the flow after you have poured forth your endless chatter: "God is your witness that you undertook to defend this cause not simply because you were called upon, but because your conscience told you there was none you could better defend." [40] Were you called upon to meddle in our affairs, of which you know nothing, unless we called you? Are the highest magistrates of the English people, proceeding in accordance with the authority and power entrusted to them to perform the duties of their

[39] *Ibid.*, p. 332, ll. 31–36. Salmasius argues that the Dutch were always free; the English were always under kings. The former were never subject to the Romans, the latter were. Salmasius forgets that the people under the yoke of the Romans were not the same as the Anglo-Saxon conquerors!

[40] *Ibid.*, p. 336, ll. 35–38.

office, to be wounded with quite undeserved words of invective and reviled in your slanderous publication, despite the fact that they did you no harm and never even knew of your existence? Who called upon you to do this? Was it perhaps your wife, who is said to have royal rights over you, and who like that Fulvia, whose words in the obscene epigram you just now made into a sort of patchwork,[41] says to you whenever she pleases "either write or fight me," so that you preferred writing to hearing the trumpet sound the attack? Or was it the younger Charles and his damned crew of emigrant courtiers who called upon you, a second Balaam summoned by a second King Balak, to deign to restore by your slanders the king's cause when it was already hopelessly lost by its poor defence? This might well be, were it not for a certain difference! He came to curse as a wise man on a talking ass, while you are a talkative ass sat upon by a woman, and, if you were embellished with the healed heads of those bishops you had formerly wounded, you would furnish a sort of minor version of the apocalyptic beast.[42] They say indeed that you regretted this book shortly after you had written it. This is but right; and to reveal your repentance to all men your first task will be to balance this lengthy volume with a single short letter formed by your dangling corpse. Such was the repentance of that Judas Iscariot whom you resemble; a resemblance known to the young Charles, who made you the gift of a purse, the mark of the traitor Judas, when he first was told what he later knew beyond doubt, that you were an apostate and a devil. Judas betrayed Christ, and you, the church of Christ [167]; you showed that the bishops were antichrists, and then joined their party, supporting the cause of those who had been damned to Hell. Christ set all men free, while you attempted to make them slaves. Have no doubt that, after your impious conduct towards God, the church, and all mankind, a similar end awaits you, so that, like that model of yours, you will be impelled more by desperation than repentance to hang yourself on that ill-omened tree through disgust with yourself, and fall in pieces with a crash, sending ahead your treacherous lying conscience, the bane of good and holy men, to its destined place of punishment!

[41] Martial, XI, 20.

[42] Revelation 13:1. "And I stood upon the sand of the sea and saw a beast rise up out of the sea, having seven heads and ten horns, and upon his horns ten crowns, and upon his heads the name of blasphemy."

It now appears that, with God's help, I have completed the task which I had set for myself at the start, which was to defend at home and abroad the great works of my fellow citizens against the jealous rage and madness of this raving sophist, and to maintain the common rights of our people against the unrighteous tyranny of kings, doing so not because I hated kings, but only tyrants. I have not knowingly passed by, unanswered, any argument or instance or evidence advanced by my opponent if it seemed to possess any inherent force or weight as proof. I have perhaps erred in the other direction, and by replying too often to his irrelevant and repetitious triflings as though they were true arguments have given them an importance they did not merit. The only point which remains is perhaps the greatest, namely that you, my fellow citizens, should yourselves refute this foe of yours; this I believe you can do only if you strive constantly to make your good deeds outweigh all men's abuse. When you were crushed under slavery in several forms and turned to Him for refuge, God graciously heard your vows and ardent prayers. From the two greatest evils in human life, the most fatal to virtue, namely tyranny and superstition, He has wondrously set you free before all men; He gave you such strength of heart that you did not shrink from being the first men to pass judgment in a notable trial upon a king, conquered and made captive by your arms, and to execute him when he had been found guilty. After so famous a deed you should plan and perform nothing low or mean [168], but only what is great and noble.

There is but one way for you to earn such praise; just as you have conquered your enemies in war so you must show that, without arms and in the midst of peace, you can surpass all men in courage in your fight against the self-seeking, greed, luxury, and the seductions of success to which other peoples are subject. The bravery displayed in your fight against slavery must be equalled by your justice, restraint, and moderation in preserving your freedom. By such arguments and evidence alone can you show that you do not deserve the names with which this man libels you: "traitors, brigands, assassins, murderers and madmen"; that it was not from self-seeking or desire to curtail the rights of others, not because of your turbulence or depraved desires, not because you were driven by madness or fury, that you killed your king, but rather that you punished a tyrant because of your love of your freedom and your faith, of justice and honor, and above all because of your warm affection for your own country. But should you decide otherwise, which I pray God in his mercy may ever forbid, should you be as weak in peace as you have been strong in war, and, after having found the divine power so favorable to yourselves and so stern towards your foes, fail to learn, from this notable and memorable example before your very eyes, that you must fear God and love justice, then for my part I must surely admit and confess what I could no longer deny, that the worst expressions and beliefs of those slanderous liars are all true, and you shall soon find that God's hatred of you will be greater than was his anger towards your foes or his kindly grace towards you above all peoples now on earth. [169]

It is some years since I published this work in haste, as reasons of state then required, thinking that if, as often happens, I had leisure to return to it, I might afterwards make certain revisions, and perhaps remove or add some points. I believe that now, though more briefly than I had intended, I have finished my task. Such as it is, this memorial, I see, will not easily perish. It may be that civil freedom has been more freely defended, but never in a greater or more outstanding instance. If then, we believe that a deed so lofty and noble was not successfully undertaken and completed without divine inspiration, there is good reason for us to suppose that the same assistance and guidance led to its being recorded and defended by my words of praise. So I would have all men believe, rather than attribute to me any degree of talent or wisdom or industry. But as the great Roman consul, when retiring from office, swore in the assembly of the people that by his efforts alone he had saved the state and the city,[43] so I too, as for the last time I devote myself to this work, may venture this assertion at least, calling on God and men as my witnesses.

In this book I have advanced such proofs and given currency to such evidence from the highest authorities on wisdom both human and divine that the English people may, I trust, be assured of their defence on this point in the eyes of all men yet to come. And many other peoples, who had hitherto been deceived by shameful ignorance of their own rights and by a pretext of religion, may be assured of their freedom, unless they themselves prefer and deserve to be slaves. The great consul found that his oath, inclusive as were its claims,

[43] Accounts of Cicero's oath taken on his retirement are to be found in Cicero's own works as follows: *Epistulae ad Familiares,* V, 2, 7; *Pro Sulla,* XI, 34; *In Pisonem,* 3, 6–7; *De Re Publica,* I, 4, 7. An account is also given in Plutarch's *Cicero,* 23, 1.

received in that assembly the unanimous sworn confirmation of the whole Roman people; I have long understood that the best citizens of my own and of foreign lands have not failed to voice in all quarters their approval of my belief. [170]

Now that my toil has won the richest rewards I had hoped for in this life, I do delight in them with all thankfulness, but at the same time I am earnestly seeking how best I may show not only my own country, to which I devoted all I have, but men of every land and, particularly, all Christian men, that for their sake I am at this time hoping and planning still greater things, if these be possible for me, as with God's help they will. [171]

A SECOND DEFENCE OF THE ENGLISH PEOPLE

May 30, 1654

PREFACE AND NOTES BY DONALD A. ROBERTS
TRANSLATION BY HELEN NORTH

In *Defensio Secunda* Milton reached his peak as a writer of prose. Only *Areopagitica* rivals it, but even the sustained fervor and the high eloquence of that noble plea for man's right to speak his mind are more than matched by the firmness of thought, the varied play of wit, and the rhetorical brilliance of *Defensio Secunda*. E. M. W. Tillyard, whose judgments and explications of Milton are rightly admired, says flatly that it "is the greatest of Milton's prose works and one of the greatest of the world's rhetorical writings." [1]

Two circumstances have militated against due appreciation of the work. First, it has too often been read in excerpts. Many anthologies and textbooks have reprinted the autobiographical passage, and a few have included the panegyrics on Cromwell and his associates or Milton's theory of republican government. However excellent these sections are in themselves, their reading serves only special interests, such as curiosity about Milton's own account of his life or about his personal relationship with Cromwell. Such reading, however, reveals nothing of the architectonics of the pamphlet, nothing of its carefully and skillfully created rhetorical structure.

Secondly, many critics and some scholars have been moved by a somewhat excessive sense of propriety and decorum to deplore, out of context, certain methods of argumentation used by Milton. These methods have been castigated as unseemly, unbecoming a great writer, and offensive to good taste, but they have seldom been explained as essential parts of classical rhetoric, which Milton thoroughly understood and most effectively employed. For example, he uses the device of repetition, both simple and incremental, in such a way that the reader is never allowed to forget a point once made. The repetition seems monotonous only when the reader fails to recognize it as an oratorical device. Again, he employs bawdy, both language and incident, not as an end in itself, but as a standard means of destroying his opponent. If his antagonists indulged

[1] E. M. W. Tillyard, *Milton* (London, 1930), pp. 192–93.

in shocking statements about him and the cause he championed, he was required by tradition and by the code of his times to reply in kind.

II

Indeed it is essential that, at the very beginning, the reader be aware that, though Milton was writing for the printed page, he was composing an oration. In *Defensio* he was content to address Salmasius alone, *vis-à-vis,* to wither him directly with contempt and scorn for his pedantry, his meddlesomeness, his ignorance of English affairs. Resolutely, Milton strode forth to single combat against a champion of evil, which was general and, to a degree, abstract. He employed familiar and generally accepted tactics to deflate the reputation of his opponent, but he had no personal, and little national, vilification to refute. As he planned and wrote *Defensio Secunda* Milton faced very different conditions. Aware that *Defensio* had attracted much attention, both favorable and hostile, on the continent, he clearly realized that he now had a European reputation, not to gain but to maintain. He had tumbled the great Salmasius from his pedestal, only to find himself, in *Clamor,*[2] characterized throughout Europe as a scoundrel without learning and, what was even worse, without integrity, and to see his nation portrayed as a monstrous and bloody tyranny. As the appointed spokesman of the Commonwealth and of the Protectorate he realized, obviously, that he must rehabilitate his reputation if he was successfully to justify to men abroad and at home the ways of Cromwell and his regime.

III

Quite naturally, therefore, he turned for his model and style to the literature of Greece and Rome in which he had an abiding faith and extensive knowledge. It was not merely that he thought of himself as an appointed spokesman of his own people and government to a large company of intelligent and interested foreigners. He felt the need, it appears, for more than narrative or lucid exposition. And, mindful of events in ancient Athens and Rome, he employed the oration used by such masters as Demosthenes and Cicero to mold opinion, to destroy the enemy, and to defend the state.[3] In appropriate places in the notes notice is taken of

[2] Significant excerpts from *Clamor,* as translated for *Complete Prose* by Paul Blackford, appear in Appendix D, below, pp. 1036–81.

[3] Note *Paradise Lost,* IX, 670–76:

> As when of old som Orator renound
> In *Athens* or free *Rome,* where Eloquence
> Flourished, since mute, to som great cause addrest,

Milton's reference to, and use of, the classic divisions of the oration. He thus reminds his readers that in replying to an opponent he considers ignorant and disorderly he faithfully adheres to the highest standards of classical rhetoric.

Milton goes further, however, than general adherence to the model of Cicero. *Defensio Secunda* is actually a remarkably fine example of the form known as panegyric and diatribe. This style of oratorical argument was familiar not only from classical models but also through its extensive treatment in the standard rhetorics of Milton's day. Both Wilson [4] and Rainolde,[5] for example, describe the method in great detail. To their presentations of general principles they add examples of the kinds of headings and subheadings under which the argument is to be developed. In panegyric, the nobility or greatness of each aspect of the subject's life is presented; in diatribe, the opposite process is followed. It was normal, therefore, that, while Milton denigrated every part of More's life and character, he exalted his own family, education and career. What seem like extravagances in either direction are carefully planned parts of the total argument. Similarly, while Milton rebuked, ridiculed, and castigated Charles I, Charles II, and all their supporters and defenders, he eulogized the Parliamentary leaders, particularly Cromwell, in stirring tributes.

As is pointed out in various places in the notes, it is not to be assumed that Milton permitted the strict demands of his rhetoric to affect his integrity or his sincerity. Though his standards of evidence may not measure up to those demanded in a court of law, he clearly accepted the authenticity of the malicious tid-bits he had so thoroughly garnered about More and those associated with him, and, in the light of history, he did not treat Charles I unjustly. On the other hand, his omission from his panegyric of several Parliamentary leaders whom he was unable honestly to praise attests his probity on the other side.

IV

Pro Populo Anglicano Defensio Secunda was published at the press of Thomas Newcomb in London about May 30, 1654.[6] This was the only

---

Stood in himself collected, while each part,
Motion, each act won audience ere the tongue,
Somtimes in highth began, as no delay
Of Preface brooking through his Zeal of Right.

[4] *Wilson's Arte of Rhetorique, 1560,* ed. G. H. Mair (Oxford: Clarendon Press, 1909).

[5] Richard Rainolde, *The Foundacion of Rhetorike,* ed. Francis R. Johnson (New York: Scholars' Facsimiles & Reprints, 1945).

[6] French, *Life Records,* III, 376 ff.

printing of the work authorized by Milton himself. Within a year, however, several unauthorized editions were brought out by Adrian Vlacq, a royalist printer at The Hague.[7] Recently, it has been pointed out that Vlacq actually issued three pirated editions, the second and third differing textually but not substantively from the first.[8] Subsequent printings of the full text have been numerous. They are:

1. *A Complete Collection of the Historical, Political, and Miscellaneous Works of John Milton,* edited by John Toland (3 vols., London, 1698). Includes Latin of 1654 only.
2. *A Complete Collection of the Historical, Political, and Miscellaneous Works of John Milton,* edited by Thomas Birch (2 vols., London, 1738). Includes Latin of 1654 only.
3. *The Prose Works of John Milton; with a Life of the Author, Interspersed with Translations and Critical Remarks,* edited by Charles Symmons (7 vols., London, 1806). Includes the first known English translation, by Robert Fellowes.
4. *The Prose Works of John Milton,* edited by George Burnett (2 vols., London, 1809). Includes a new English translation by George Burnett.
5. *Sermons, Dissertations and Translations,* by archdeacon Francis Wrangham (3 vols., London, 1816). Includes a new English translation by archdeacon Wrangham. Reprinted separately in an edition of 50 copies (London, 1816).
6. *The Prose Works of John Milton,* edited by Robert Fletcher (London, 1833). Includes the English translation by Fellowes.
7. *The Prose Works of John Milton,* edited by Rufus W. Griswold (2 vols., Philadelphia, 1845, 1851, 1853; New York, 1847). Includes the English translation by Fellowes.
8. *The Prose Works of John Milton,* edited by J. A. St. John (5 vols., London, 1848–53). Volume 1 includes the English translation by Fellowes. [Cited as Bohn.]
9. *The Works of John Milton in Verse and Prose,* edited by John Mitford (8 vols., London, 1851). Includes the Latin of 1654 only.
10. *The Works of John Milton,* edited by Frank Allen Patterson and others (18 vols., New York, 1931–38). Includes the Latin of 1654 and the translation by Burnett, revised by Moses Hadas. [Cited as Columbia.]

It would be pointless to list the anthologies and textbooks in which short excerpts from *Defensio Secunda,* usually the autobiographical passage, have been printed. Such annotation as appears is usually sketchy and perfunctory. Two textbooks, however, deserve to be noted by virtue of their greater fullness and their more extensive commentary. They are:

1. *The Student's Milton,* edited by Frank Allen Patterson (New York, 1933).

[7] *Ibid.,* pp. 407, 411–12, 421.

[8] J. Milton French, "An Unrecorded Edition of Milton's *Defensio Secunda* (1654)," *PBSA,* XLIX (1955), 262–68; and Robert W. Ayers, "A Suppressed Edition of Milton's *Defensio Secunda* (1654)," *PBSA,* LV (1961), 75–87.

2. *John Milton: Complete Poems and Major Prose,* edited by Merritt Y. Hughes (New York: Odyssey Press, 1957).

The present edition is the first completely annotated one to appear. The editor worked basically from the new translation made for *Complete Prose Works* by Professor Helen North of the Department of Classics of Swarthmore College.

V

Milton's purpose in writing and publishing *Defensio Secunda* is explicitly stated on the title page in the subtitle which reads: "Contra infamem libellum anonymum cui titulus, Regii Sanguinis Clamor ad Coelum Adversus Parricidas Anglicanos."[9] He replied to an infamous and anonymous libel titled "The Cry of the Royal Blood to Heaven against the English Parricides." This piece of adroit and powerful propaganda[10] was two-pronged in its thrust. It sought to destroy Milton himself, who in his *Defensio pro Populo Anglicano* had demolished the *Defensio Regia* of Salmasius, and had shown himself to be a doughty controversialist. And it attempted to arouse the monarchies of Europe, particularly Holland and France, against the new republic in Britain. It was a war cry, shrill and insistent in its emotional intensity, but it was also skillfully reasoned and, apparently, firmly based on historical fact. It was both a bitter personal affront to Milton and the most dangerous and the ablest piece of propaganda with which he had been called upon to contend.

It is now beyond doubt[11] that *Clamor* was the work of an Anglican

[9] It has not previously been noted, it appears, that the title of *Clamor* is a paraphrase of a passage in *Eikon Basilike* which reads: "I doubt not but My bloud will cry aloud for vengeance to heaven." *Eikon Basilike or The King's Book,* ed. Edward Almack (London, 1903), p. 164.

[10] Harry G. Merrill, *Milton's Secret Adversary; Du Moulin and the Politics of Protestant Humanism* (A dissertation on file in the library of the University of Tennessee, 1959, pp. vi–507) presents a full critical evaluation of *Clamor.* P. 2: "Its chief qualifications are its clearcut coherent organization and the whiplash of its invective." P. 8: "*Clamor* has a bite and nobility which Salmasius never attained."

[11] Merrill, p. 10 and notes, presents a summary of the conclusive evidence for Du Moulin's authorship of *Clamor.* He quotes at length from a volume of Latin poems by Du Moulin in 1670 and 1671, when the need for secrecy had passed. The book is titled Petri Molinaei, *πάρεργα Poematum Libelli Tres. I. Hymni in Symbolum Apostolorum. II. Ecclesiae Gemitus. III. Sylva Variorum* (Cambridge, 1670; FSL. To the title of the second edition (1671) was added: *Huic Editioni Accessit Mantissa Aliquot Poematum.* Merrill, in translations from the poems, brings out Du Moulin's amusement at seeing his baby left at another's

priest Peter Du Moulin, who was resident in England during the days of the Commonwealth and who was so little suspect that he was awarded a D.D. by Oxford in 1656. Du Moulin sent his manuscript to Salmasius in order that it might be published on the continent. Salmasius, in turn, transmitted it to Alexander More (Morus), a clergyman of the Reformed Church, who arranged for its printing by Adrian Vlacq at The Hague. In effect, More was a kind of editor-publisher of another man's book, but he involved himself more deeply by writing an abusive preface, which appeared over the printer's name. More was associated with *Clamor* by many scholars on the continent, and Milton pounced upon him as the sole author. He was warned of his error by many friends, including Dury and Hartlib,[12] but he persisted in his attribution of the work to More throughout *Defensio Secunda*. It may be said that, since *Clamor* was anonymous, Milton needed an author to suit the method of his argument, and that he accepted More as the most likely candidate. Whether he actually believed or merely pretended to believe that More was the author seems beyond determination on the basis of the evidence now available. Certain crucial dates are not positively known—for example, the date of More's own revelation of Du Moulin's authorship. Only once, in *Pro Se Defensio,* does Milton even intimate that he ever had responsible evidence against More's authorship. The moral issues are difficult to assess. It can be said that occasionally Milton gives uncritical acceptance to items of gossip, as in the instance of More's fathering a child by Madame Salmasius' housemaid, or in that of his belittlement of More's classical scholarship. In general, however, his strictures on More's personality and character were firmly based on evidence from apparently responsible sources. They were repeated, not concocted, by Milton.

On the other hand, the scandalous statements about Milton in *Clamor* are totally false. Some of them, indeed, are savage in their cruelty. It is one thing to ridicule a man's amorousness or his heterodoxy, but it is quite another to jeer at his blindness. Milton meets many of the falsehoods about him with notable dignity and self-control. But he was engaged in a fateful war of words, and he would have been laughed off as a weakling and an incompetent if he had not used the sharp edges of language with which to hurt his antagonists. Milton never uses the lie direct. If, on occasion, he falters in fact or in logic, he is merely human. He is a sightless champion of what he profoundly believed was the will of God and the destiny of his countrymen, a champion baited by hirelings

---

doorstep and at the blind and furious Milton flailing the air at a secret adversary he could not see, Du Moulin's fear of reprisal when his authorship was revealed by More, and his own account of his authorship.

[12] G. H. Turnbull, *Hartlib, Dury, and Comenius*, pp. 41–44.

whose gospel was their maw. In *Defensio Secunda* he rose to the height of his great argument, to justify himself among those who talked from side to side and to exalt his nation in its new liberty.

The method of capitalization used is not my own; it conforms to the practice of the edition as a whole.

During the course of my work on *Defensio Secunda* I have been helped and the edition has been improved by information and comment from many colleagues and friends, particularly: Miss Phyllis L. Méras of the *New York Times,* Professor William G. Crane of the City College, Professor Israel E. Drabkin of The City College, Professor Moses Hadas of Columbia University, Professor Harry G. Merrill III of Appalachian State College, the Reverend Professor Albert T. Mollegen of the Episcopal Theological Seminary in Virginia, the Reverend Professor Pierson Parker of the General Theological Seminary, and the Reverend Dr. René E. G. Vaillant of *L'Église du Saint Ésprit* in New York.

DONALD A. ROBERTS

The City College, New York

TRANSLATOR'S NOTE

This translation of Milton's *Defensio Secunda* aims, in general, to follow the method employed by Alfred in his version of Boethius and cited by Lane Cooper in his translation of Plato: to render the original "sometimes word by word" and "sometimes sense from sense." [1] Because Milton's Latin prose style is in many passages very like his style in writing English prose, it has been possible to translate word by word more often than is commonly the case when dealing with Latin writers either of the ancient period or of the Renaissance. Indeed the classical scholar, aware of the notorious "Latinity" of Milton's English tracts, may feel tempted, as a general principle, simply to mimic their style in rendering the Latin treatises. But the Latin of the *Defensio Secunda* differs in significant ways from the Latinizing English of the *Areopagitica,* for instance, or *The Reason of Church-Government,* being more extensive in range, more varied in rhythm and vocabulary, and—in conformity with the conventions of Latin polemics—much less consistently elevated in tone. Hence it would be misleading to cast the entire essay into "Miltonic" English, even were the translator capable of such a *tour de force.*

It has seemed preferable, then, to translate as directly (and often as literally) as possible—with only an occasional glance at the way Milton expressed the same ideas when writing English—in the hope of doing justice to some, at least, of the nuances in a style which ranges from the noblest biographical passages (wherein Milton occasionally achieves a *deinotês* almost worthy of Demosthenes) to those in which he lingers with relish over the follies of Salmasius or the misconduct of Morus. Between these extremes of sublimity and scurrility intervene long stretches of narrative, almost equally diverse in mood and expression. Some (like the record of Milton's travels on the continent) are lucid and comparatively terse; others (such as his account of the execution of Charles I) combine apparent simplicity with all the devices of impassioned partisanship. There are, as well, those many passages which reply, point by point, to the charges leveled against Milton by the *Regii Sanguinis Clamor,* and here the style is particularly complex, mingling as it does question and answer, quotation from the *Clamor* and sardonic comment upon it, apt classical allusions, and tireless invective, enlivened by derogatory epigram, scandalous innuendo, and indefensible but irresistible puns.

[1] *Plato: Phaedrus, Ion, Gorgias, and Symposium with Passages from the Republic and Laws* (London, 1938), p. vii.

Not all of the *Defensio Secunda* is equally effective. Some passages of eulogy (notably the digression in honor of Queen Christina) are not only sycophantic but frigid, and some passages of narrative are both prolix and dull. In each case the translator has attempted to render as faithfully as lay in her power both the sense and the mood of the original, avoiding (it is hoped) both the frequent inaccuracies of the Burnett translation and the many omissions of the Bohn. For assistance with some of the more intractable puns and with the epigram which begins *Galli ex concubitu,* warm thanks are due to Professor Harry Caplan of Cornell University.

HELEN NORTH

Swarthmore College

TEXTUAL NOTE: *PRO POPULO ANGLICANO DEFENSIO SECUNDA*

This translation of the *Pro Populo Anglicano Defensio Secunda* is based on Columbia University Library copy B823M64 X524. Collation: 8°: [ ]¹, A–K⁸, L⁷ [$4 signed]; 88 leaves; pp. [2] 1–173 [1]. Contents: [ ], title page (verso blank); A–[L7], the work; [L7v], errata. This has been collated with microfilms, photostats, or originals of numerous other copies, as listed below, Appendix G, pp. 1144–45.

ROBERT W. AYERS

Georgetown University

Joannis Miltoni

ANGLI

PRO

POPULO ANGLICANO

DEFENSIO

SECUNDA.

Contra infamem libellum anonymum
cui titulus,

*Regii sanguinis clamor ad
cœlum adversus parri-
cidas Anglicanos.*

LONDINI,
Typis Neucomianis, 1654.

John Milton

ENGLISHMAN

Second Defence

of

The English People

Against the Base Anonymous Libel, Entitled

The Cry of the Royal Blood to Heaven, against the English Parricides.[1]

BY JOHN MILTON, ENGLISHMAN[2]

IN THE whole life and estate of man the first duty[3] is to be grateful to God and mindful of his blessings, and to offer particular and solemn thanks without delay when his benefits have exceeded hope and prayer. Now, on the very threshold of my speech,[4] I see three most weighty reasons for my discharge of this duty. [1] First that I was born at a time in the history of my country when her citizens, with pre-eminent virtue and a nobility and steadfastness sur-

[1] *Regii Sanguinis Clamor ad Coelum, Adversus Parricidas Anglicanos,* a tract published anonymously at The Hague in 1652 at the press of Adrian Vlacq. The question of its authorship is discussed in the preface, above, p. 542. Significant excerpts from the first English translation, made for *Complete Prose* by Paul Blackford, appear in Appendix D, below, pp. 1036–81. The work is hereafter referred to as *Clamor* (1652).

[2] Milton appends the term *Englishman* to his name on the title pages of his three prose works intended primarily for foreign readers, *Defensio, Defensio Secunda,* and *Pro Se Defensio.*

[3] The language suggests a reference to "A Catechism," a part of the "Order of Confirmation," in the *Book of Common Prayer* (1604; UTSL) rather than a paraphrase of the great commandments of Jesus (Matthew 22:36–40 or Mark 12: 28–34).

[4] Milton calls his tract a speech for two reasons: first, because his rhetorical plan for the work is that of the classical oration (exordium, narrative, proofs, peroration); secondly, because he considered the defence of liberty and the denunciation of tyrants the special province of orators as it was, for example, in the instances of Demosthenes against King Philip of Macedonia and of Cicero against Catiline.

passing all the glory of their ancestors, invoked the Lord, followed his manifest guidance, and after accomplishing the most heroic and exemplary achievements since the foundation of the world, freed the state from grievous tyranny and the church from unworthy servitude.[5] Secondly, that when a multitude had sprung up which in the wonted manner of a mob venomously attacked these noble achievements, and when one man above all,[6] swollen and complacent with his empty grammarian's conceit and the esteem of his confederates, had in a book of unparalleled baseness attacked us and wickedly assumed the defence of all tyrants, it was I and no other who was deemed equal to a foe of such repute and to the task of speaking on so great a theme, and who received from the very liberators of my country this role, which was offered spontaneously with universal consent, the task of publicly defending (if anyone ever did) the cause of the English people and thus of Liberty herself.[7] [7] Lastly, I thank God that in an affair so arduous and so charged with expectation, I did not disappoint the hope or the judgment of my countrymen about me, nor fail to satisfy a host of foreigners, men of learning and experience,[8] for by God's grace I so routed my audacious foe that he fled, broken in spirit and reputation.[9] For the last three years of his life, he did in his rage utter frequent threats, but gave us no further

[5] Milton here reaffirms a cherished idea, namely, that, by virtue of the teachings and activity of Wycliff, Britain was the first nation to attempt reform in Europe. *Cf. Areopagitica* (*Complete Prose,* II, 553): "What does he then but reveal Himself to his servants, and as his manner is, first to his English-men?" See also: *Of Reformation* (*Complete Prose,* I, 525–26); *Doctrine and Discipline* (*Complete Prose,* II, 231–32); *Tetrachordon* (*Complete Prose,* II, 707).

[6] Claudius Salmasius (Claude de Saumaise, 1588–1655), a French scholar and Milton's former opponent. For a survey of Salmasius' life, see below, pp. 961–81.

[7] On January 8, 1650, the Council of State had ordered Milton to "prepare something in answer to the Booke of Saltmatius." See French, *Life Records,* II, 286.

[8] Milton is very sanguine about the effect of *Defensio* in England and on the Continent. The most eloquent assertion of his confidence appears in the sonnet (1655) to Cyriack Skinner, where he says he lost his eyes overplied:

> In Liberties defence, my noble task,
> Of which all Europe talks from side to side.

[9] Milton here misinterprets the evidence. Salmasius was angered by Milton's attack, and vowed vengeance. He left Stockholm, not "broken in spirit and reputation," but broken in health; he appears never to have regained full vigor of body. See below, p. 963.

trouble,[10] save that he sought the secret help of certain rogues and persuaded some bungling and immoderate panegyrists[11] to repair, if they could, his fresh and unlooked-for disgrace. All this will shortly be made clear.

In the belief that such great blessings come from on high and that they should properly be recognized both out of gratitude to God and in order to secure favorable auspices for the work in hand, I held that they should be reverently proclaimed, as they are, at the outset.[3] For who does not consider the glorious achievements of his country as his own? But what can tend more to the honor and glory of any country than the restoration of liberty both to civil life and to divine worship? What nation, what state has displayed superior fortune or stouter courage in securing for itself such liberty in either sphere? In truth, it is not in warfare and arms alone that courage shines forth, but she pours out her dauntless strength against all terrors alike, and thus those illustrious Greeks and Romans whom we particularly admire expelled the tyrants from their cities without other virtues than the zeal for freedom, accompanied by ready weapons and eager hands.[12] All else they easily accomplished amid universal praise, applause, and joyful omens. Nor did they hasten so much towards danger and doubtful issues as towards the fair and glorious trial of virtue, towards distinctions, in short, and garlands, and the sure hope of immortality.[13]

[10] Salmasius wrote, but did not live to complete, a reply to Milton. *Ad Johannem Miltonum Responsio, Opus Posthumum* was published by his elder son, Claudius, in London in 1660. Its bitterly hostile tone is evident in excerpts translated by Masson (VI, 203–12).

[11] Milton refers to those he believed responsible for *Clamor,* namely Adrian Vlacq and Alexander Morus. That they were "immoderate panegyrists" is evident in the introductory parts of *Clamor* (see Appendix D), but that they were rogues was a highly subjective judgment, designed to prejudice Milton's readers against them. See below, pp. 1040–43.

[12] Hobbes differed from Milton when he wrote (*English Works,* ed. Molesworth, VI, 362): "For who can be a good subject in a monarchy whose principles are taken from the enemies of monarchy, such as were Cicero, Seneca, Cato, and other politicians of Rome, and Aristotle of Athens, who seldom spake of kings but as of wolves and other ravenous beasts?" See also Zera S. Fink, *The Classical Republicans* (Evanston: Northwestern University Press, 1945).

[13] The garland in this instance was attained by the greatest service to the public good. It is a symbol in Milton of immortality or of earthly fame. The image seems always to be a composite of Horace (*Odes,* I, i, 3–6) and St. Paul (I Corinthians 9:24–25). *Cf. Areopagitica, Complete Prose,* II, 515: "that immortal garland . . . to be run for, not without dust and heat." See also *Church-Government, Complete Prose,* I, 808.

For not yet was tyranny a sacred institution. [4] Not yet had tyrants, suddenly become viceroys, indeed, and vicars of Christ,[14] sheltered themselves behind the blind superstition of the mob, when they could not fortify themselves with their good will. Not yet had the common people, maddened by priestly machinations, sunk to a barbarism fouler than that which stains the Indians, themselves the most stupid of mortals. The Indians indeed worship as gods malevolent demons whom they cannot exorcize,[15] but this mob of ours, to avoid driving out its tyrants, even when it could, has set up as gods over it the most impotent of mortals and to its own destruction has consecrated the enemies of mankind. And against all this close array of long-held opinions, superstitions, slanders, and fears,[16] more dreadful to other

[14] There is no certainty that Milton knew that, at the coronation of Edward VI, archbishop Cranmer called him "God's Vice-Regent and Christ's Vicar within your own dominions . . . and . . . Supreme Head of the Church, elected of God, and only commanded by Him." (John Strype, *Memorials of Thomas Cranmer* [3 vols., 1848–54], II, 205–207). His references to viceregents and vicars, however, have undoubted basis in the claims of the Stuart monarchs that they ruled by divine right. A notable example of this Stuart theory is found in the sonnet prefixed by James I to his *Basilikon Doron* (1604; UTSL):

> God gives not Kings the stile of *Gods* in vaine,
> For on his Throne his scepter doe they swey:
> And as their subiects ought them to obey,
> So Kings should feare and serve their God againe
> If then you would enioy a happie raigne,
> Observe the Statutes of your heavenly King,
> And from his Law, make all your Lawes to spring:
> Since his Lieutenants here ye should remain,
> Reward the Just, be stedfast, true, and plaine,
> Represse the proud, maintayning aye the right,
> Walke alwayes so, as ever in his sight,
> Who guardes the godly, plaguing the prophane:
> And so ye shall in Princely vertues shine,
> Resembling right your mightie King Divine.

[15] Most stupid of all humankind because of their religious beliefs and practices. They fail to exorcize, they even worship, powers which confer upon them no good and which constrict their lives. *Cf.* Prolusion I (*Complete Prose,* I, 228): "to the sun . . . the American Indians even to this day make sacrifice with incense and every kind of ritual"; *Doctrine and Discipline* (*Complete Prose,* II, 277–78): "to be worshipt like some *Indian* deity, when it can conferre no blessing"; *Tetrachordon* (*Complete Prose,* II, 590): "the vermin of an Indian *Catharist,* which his fond religion forbids him to molest." For the sources of these ideas see Allan H. Gilbert, *A Geographical Dictionary of Milton* (New Haven, 1919) p. 155; and Robert R. Cawley, *Milton and the Literature of Travel* (Princeton University Press, 1951), pp. 100–101.

[16] His countrymen who support the royalists are more stupid than the Indians, Milton suggests, because, unlike the latter, they have the power to exorcize the malevolent creatures they have accepted as their rulers through tradition and superstition.

men than the enemy himself,[17] the English people had to contend. Being better instructed and doubtless inspired by heaven, they overcame all these obstacles with such confidence in their cause and such strength of mind and courage that [5] although they were indeed a multitude in numbers, yet the lofty exaltation of their minds kept them from being a mob. Britain herself, which was once called a land teeming with tyrants,[18] shall hereafter deserve the everlasting praise of all the ages as a country where liberators flourish. The English people were not driven to unbridled license by scorn for the laws or desecration of them. They were not inflamed with the empty name of liberty by a false notion of virtue and glory, or senseless emulation of the ancients. It was their purity of life and their blameless character which showed them the one direct road to true liberty, and it was the most righteous defence of law and religion that of necessity gave them arms. And so, trusting completely in God, with honorable weapons, they put slavery to flight.[19]

Although I claim for myself no share in this glory, yet it is easy to defend myself from the charge of timidity or cowardice, should such a charge be leveled.[20] For I did not avoid the toils and dangers of military service without rendering to my fellow citizens another kind of service that was much more useful and no less perilous. [6] In

[17] Milton uses the simple word *hostis,* the foe in open battle. He contrasts the dangers of subversion within the state with the more obvious threat of an army in the field.

[18] Milton here refers to the period when the authority of the Roman emperors was weakening in outlying areas such as Britain, and when public officials or army officers were made "emperors" by intrigues within the legions. He repeats the statement almost *verbatim* in *History of Britain,* Book II (Columbia, X, 88), where he attributes it to Porphyrius, a "Philosopher then living," and in the margin gives his source as "Gildas. Hieronym." Mentioned in *Areopagitica* (*Complete Prose,* II, 501) for his hostility to Christianity, Porphyrius (A.D. 233–*ca.* 304) wrote a history which covered the period from the fall of Troy to A.D. 270. Milton indicates that he knew Porphyrius through a history by Gildas, *De Excidio et Conquestu Britanniae.*

[19] Though several recent happenings had not been pleasing to Milton, the sincerity of his high praise of the leaders of public affairs is not open to question. He was capable of lavish compliment, but he never fawned upon the great. For a detailed account of the events leading to the establishment of the Commonwealth and the Protectorate, see introduction, *Complete Prose,* III, 39–100, and introduction, above, pp. 210–20, 227–52.

[20] Milton fends off an attack which as such his opponent has not made. Though *Clamor* does not chide him for avoiding military service, the dedication and the preface characterize him as *weak, bloodless, shrivelled, insignificant, puny.* See Appendix D, below, p. 1043.

time of trial I was neither cast down in spirit nor unduly fearful of envy or death itself.[21] Having from early youth been especially devoted to the liberal arts,[22] with greater strength of mind than of body,[23] I exchanged the toils of war, in which any stout trooper might outdo me, for those labors which I better understood, that with such wisdom as I owned I might add as much weight as possible to the counsels of my country and to this excellent cause, using not my lower but my higher and stronger powers. And so I concluded that if God wished those men to achieve such noble deeds, He also wished that there be other men by whom these deeds, once done, might be worthily praised and extolled, and that truth defended by arms be also defended by reason—the only defence truly appropriate to man.[24] Hence it is that while I admire the heroes victorious in battle, I nevertheless do not complain about my own role. Indeed I congratulate myself and once again offer most fervent thanks to the heavenly bestower of gifts that such a lot has befallen me [7]—a lot that seems much more a source of envy to others than of regret to myself. And yet, to no one,

[21] This is a very modest statement. Had Milton been another kind of man, he could have lived his life in comfortable retirement, free to read and to write without serious interruption. He chose not to do so. For Milton's own analysis of his decision in 1640–41 to commit his energies to the impending conflict, see *An Apology, Complete Prose,* I, 804, 804–805, 809, 821, 822.

[22] Milton's references to his early devotion to learning are very numerous. See especially *Church-Government,* in *Complete Prose,* I, 808–809, and *Private Correspondence,* in *Complete Prose,* I, 312, 314, 319, 323, 326–27. Elegy I, "Il Penseroso" (ll. 97–120), and "Ad Patrem" are also pertinent.

[23] Milton refers here to the state of his health throughout life, not specifically to his condition when he was writing *Defensio Secunda.* He speaks often of ill health, other than blindness, but most of his remarks are very vague. They give the impression that he worried about his physical well being, perhaps without cause. Edward Phillips, who had opportunity to know about the matter, mentions no ailment except blindness. Aubrey (Darbishire, *Early Lives of Milton,* p. 5) gives him a clean bill of health. He says: "He was very healthy, seldome took any Physique, only sometimes he tooke Manna & free from all diseases, and only towards his later end he was visited with the Gowte spring & Fall."

[24] This passage foreshadows Abdiel's meditation in *Paradise Lost* (VI, 121–26):

> nor is it aught but just,
> That he who in the debate of Truth hath won,
> Should win in Arms, in both disputes alike
> Victor; though brutish that contest and foule,
> When reason hath to do with force, yet so
> Most reason is that Reason overcome.

And Michael's remark *Paradise Lost* (XII, 83–85):

> Since thy original lapse, true Libertie
> Is lost, which alwayes with right Reason dwells
> Twinn'd, and from her hath no dividual being.

even the humblest, do I willingly compare myself, nor do I say one word about myself in arrogance, but whenever I allow my mind to dwell upon this cause, the noblest and most renowned of all, and upon the glorious task of defending the very defenders, a task assigned me by their own vote and decision,[25] I confess that I can scarcely restrain myself from loftier and bolder flights than are permissible in this exordium,[26] and from the search for a more exalted manner of expression. Indeed, in the degree that the distinguished orators of ancient times undoubtedly surpass me, both in their eloquence and in their style (especially in a foreign tongue, which I must of necessity use, and often to my own dissatisfaction),[27] in that same degree shall I outstrip all the orators of every age in the grandeur of my subject and my theme. This circumstance has aroused so much anticipation and notoriety that I do not now feel that I am surrounded, [8] in the Forum or on the Rostra, by one people alone,[28] whether Roman or Athenian, but that, with virtually all of Europe attentive,[29] in session, and passing judgment, I have in the *First Defence* spoken out and shall in the *Second* speak again to the entire assembly and council of all the most influential men, cities, and nations everywhere. I seem now

[25] On March 13, 1649 (French, II, 234 ff.), Milton had been invited to become Secretary for Foreign Tongues to the Council of State. Though one of Milton's duties was to answer foreign attacks on the republic, no official record has been found of the Council's order to Milton to answer *Clamor*. In *Pro Se Defensio,* below, p. 767, he repeats his present assertion: "I was so ordered . . . publicly by those whose authority ought to have weight with me."

[26] This oratorical term (see above, p. 548, n. 4) reminds the reader that Milton thinks of himself as addressing an audience and that he has not yet entered upon the principal part of his oration, the narrative. For Milton's rhetoric see the preface, above, pp. 538–40.

[27] Milton writes in Latin "of necessity" because he is addressing not Englishmen primarily, but the learned of Europe. He must use the international language of the time. Since he had been writing Latin prose since boyhood, the exact nature of his dissatisfaction is not clear. It is reasonable to suppose, however, that he is repeating (*Complete Prose,* I, 808) his distaste for the "cool element of prose" which he writes "with his left hand." His left-handedness is here intensified by the fact that he is writing prose in a second language.

[28] The "anticipation" of Milton's writings and his "notoriety" at this time can be judged only by the written evidence that has survived. It is considerable in quantity, about one hundred references to Milton himself or to his writing. Not all are favorable. Contrary to his implication here, comparatively few of the comments dealt with the issues raised by his writings or with the cause he championed. The interest was rather in the rhetorical skills and the polemical powers manifested. See French, *Life Records,* II, 340–63, and III, 9–376 *passim.*

[29] See above, p. 549, n. 8.

to have embarked on a journey and to be surveying from on high far-flung regions and territories across the sea, faces numberless and unknown, sentiments in complete agreement with mine. Here the manly strength of the Germans, hostile to slavery, meets my eye; there the lively and generous ardor of the Franks, worthy of their name; here the well-considered courage of the Spaniards; there the serene and self-controlled magnanimity of the Italians.[30] Wherever liberal sentiment, wherever freedom, or wherever magnanimity either prudently conceals or openly proclaims itself, there some in silence approve, others openly cast their votes, some make haste to applaud, others, conquered at last by the truth, acknowledge themselves my captives.[31] [9]

Now, surrounded by such great throngs, from the Pillars of Hercules all the way to the farthest boundaries of Father Liber,[32] I seem to be leading home again everywhere in the world, after a vast space of time, Liberty [33] herself, so long expelled and exiled. And, like Triptolemus of old, I seem to introduce to the nations of the earth a product

[30] Milton's judgments of foreign nations are seldom searching. Frequently his admiration or contempt is based on a single historical episode or a tradition. For example, he admired the Germans because of the resistance to absolutism among the early tribes (*Defensio,* above, p. 490), but particularly because of Luther and the Reformation. He scorned the Spanish because of their treachery and their barbarity toward Englishmen and Indians in overseas disputes (*Literae Pseudo-Senatus Anglicani,* 1676, #21, #41, #42). Only for the Italians, whom he really knew through his travels, did he consistently have the lavish praises he here bestows upon all; in *Areopagitica* (*Complete Prose,* II, 537–38) he notes the decay of learning under the despotism of the Church, but he was (letter to Benedetto Buonmattei, *Complete Prose,* I, 330) "such a lover of Italy that no other . . . is greater."

[31] Although Milton has disclaimed any share for himself in the glory of his country, he has allowed his own eloquence to induce in him the sense that he is now the focal point of the world's struggle for freedom. In his exaltation of spirit he has forgotten his sordid quarrels with Salmasius and More.

[32] Milton envisages an audience that extends from the westernmost boundary of Europe, the Pillars of Hercules or Gibraltar, to the farthest bounds of India. Father Liber, an early Italian god of the soil, became identified with Bacchus or Dionysus whose realm was traditionally considered to include India by virtue of his triumphal journey through that land and his return with the vine, which he introduced into Hellas. See *Dionysiaca,* by Nonnus of Panopolis (5th century), tr. by W. H. D. Rouse (Cambridge: Loeb Classical Library, 1940).

[33] Milton almost certainly used the name *Father Liber* rather than the more familiar name Dionysus in order to work in a pun with liberal sentiments just above and with liberty. Just as Dionysus had returned in triumph with the life-giving vine, so Milton brings back life-giving liberty to Europe.

from my own country, but one far more excellent than that of Ceres.[34] In short, it is the renewed cultivation of freedom and civic life that I disseminate throughout cities, kingdoms, and nations. But not entirely unknown, nor perhaps unwelcome, shall I return if I am he who disposed of the contentious satellite of tyrants, hitherto deemed unconquerable, both in the view of most men and in his own opinion.[35] When he with insults was attacking us and our battle array, and our leaders looked first of all to me, I met him in single combat and plunged into his reviling throat this pen, the weapon of his own choice. And (unless I wish to reject outright and disparage the views and opinions of so many intelligent readers everywhere, in no way bound or indebted to me) I bore off the spoils of honor.[36] [10] That this is actually the truth and no empty boast finds ready proof in the following event—which I believe did not occur without the will of God—namely, that when Salmasius (or Salmasia, for which of the two he was the open domination of his wife, both in public and in private, had made it quite difficult to determine),[37] when Salmasius had been courteously summoned by Her Most Serene Majesty, the Queen of the Swedes (whose devotion to the liberal arts and to men of learning has never been surpassed) and had gone thither, there in the very place where he was living as a highly honored guest, he was over-

[34] During her search for her daughter, Persephone, Ceres took refuge in the palace of Celeus, King of Eleusis, and of Metaneira, his wife. Their son, Triptolemus, became her priest whom she sent throughout the world in her dragon-drawn chariot to teach the skills of agriculture. Milton considers himself a greater teacher because his purpose is spiritual rather than earthy. See Ovid, *Metamorphoses* V. Plato (*Apology* 41a) makes Triptolemus one of the judges of the dead.

[35] Salmasius. See above, p. 549, n. 6.

[36] Milton does not mention here the many voices raised against him. Not only was the first *Defensio* attacked, but his writing on divorce and *Eikonoklastes* continued to be subjects of angry comment. He is right, however, in saying that many persons in Europe admired his polemic skill against Salmasius. For evidence that Milton was read with avidity and appreciation in Leyden, Amsterdam, Stockholm, and Leipzig, see French, *Life Records,* II, 340–63, and III, 14–126.

[37] The ascendancy of Madame Salmasius over her husband was the subject of much gossip. It was also rumored that her aristocratic background influenced her husband to support royalist causes. See Kathryn McEuen, below, pp. 964–65. The former Anne Mercier, Latinized as Mercera, was frequently called Xantippe to emphasize her shrewishness. See Masson, IV, 263, 271, 461–63.

taken by my *Defence,* while he was expecting nothing of the kind. Nearly everyone read it immediately, and the Queen herself, who had been among the first to do so, having regard only for what was worthy of her, omitted nothing of her earlier kindness and generosity towards her guest. But for the rest, if I may report what is frequently mentioned and is no secret, so great a reversal of opinion suddenly took place that he who the day before yesterday had flourished in the highest favor now all but withered away. [11] When he departed, not much later, with good leave, there was but one doubt in many minds, namely, whether he came more honored or went more despised.[38] Nor in other places, it is certain, did less harm befall his reputation.[39]

Yet I have not referred to all these matters with the intention of ingratiating myself with anyone (for there is no need), but only to show more copiously that which I undertook at the outset, for what reasons—and what weighty ones—I began by offering my most fervent thanks to almighty God. I would show that this proem,[40] in which I offer so many convincing proofs that, although by no means exempt from the disasters common to humanity,[41] I and my interests are nevertheless under the protection of God—this proem, I say, will be a source of honor and credit to me. I would show that with respect to matters of well-nigh primary importance, relating to the immediate needs of my country and destined to be of the greatest service to civil life and religion, when I speak, not on behalf of one people nor

[38] Salmasius remained in Sweden from July, 1650, until August 31, 1651. There appears to be no substantive evidence to support the assertion that he left in disgrace with the queen or with his self-respect shattered. See Kathryn McEuen below, pp. 965–66; also Masson, IV, 263, 269–71, and French, *Life Records,* III, 15, 19, 23, 34, 40, 41, 67–68, 69, 71, 72, 114.

[39] Some written evidence supports this view. Writing from Amsterdam on May 19, 1651, Heinsius told Vossius (French, III, 30–31) that it was the "firm opinion that Salmasius would not dare to come back here," presumably Holland rather than Amsterdam. The fact is, however, that he did return to his professorship at Leyden.

[40] Milton reminds his readers that he is still writing a preface, and has not yet come to grips with *Clamor.* Obviously he wants to complete the destruction of Salmasius, begun in *Defensio,* before he begins to demolish his new adversaries.

[41] Milton obviously alludes to personal misfortunes which befell him while he was planning and writing *Defensio Secunda.* His blindness had become complete early in 1652. His wife, Mary Powell Milton, had died in May, 1652 (French, III, 222). His only son, John, had died some six weeks later. He had been forced to give up his quarters in Scotland Yard.

yet one defendant, but rather for the entire human race against the foes of human liberty, [12] amid the common and well-frequented assembly (so to speak) of all nations, I have been aided and enriched by the favor and assistance of God. Anything greater or more glorious than this I neither can, nor wish to, claim.[42] Accordingly, I beg the same immortal God that, just as, depending on his familiar help and grace alone, I lately defended deeds of supreme courage and justice, so with the same or greater honesty, industry, fidelity, and even good fortune, I may be able to defend from undeserved insults and slanders both the doers of those deeds and myself, who have been linked with these great men for the purpose of ignominy, rather than honor.[43] And if there is anyone who thinks that these attacks might better have been ignored, I for my part agree, provided that they were circulated among men who had an accurate knowledge of us. But how in the world will everyone else be convinced that the lies our enemy has told are not the truth? Yet when I shall have seen to it (as is proper) that Truth the avenger shall follow wherever calumny has gone before, [13] I believe that men will cease to think wrongly of us, and that that creature will perhaps be ashamed of his lies. If he feel no shame, then at last we may properly ignore him.

Meanwhile I should more quickly [44] have sped him a reply in accord with his merits, had he not protected himself up until now with false reports, announcing again and again that Salmasius was sweating at the anvil, forging new charges against us, always on the very point of publishing them.[45] By these tactics he achieved but one result—that of postponing for a little while the payment of the penalty for slander, for I thought it better to wait, so that I might keep my strength

[42] Throughout his life Milton manifested a profound conviction that God was the final source of his own power, and that he was, in various ways, the instrument of God's will.

[43] Milton resists the compliment of being associated with the leaders of the Commonwealth, for he knows that the author of *Clamor* actually hates these men and means to belittle him by joining his name with theirs. His true admiration for Cromwell, Bradshaw, Fairfax and the other Commonwealth leaders is revealed in his peroration. See pp. 666–77 below.

[44] Milton offers a mild apology for the delay. *Clamor* had appeared in the late summer or early fall of 1652. Almost two years had elapsed, therefore, before it was answered by *Defensio Secunda* in May, 1654.

[45] See above, p. 550, n. 10. For instances of the international gossip about the expected reply by Salmasius see French, *Life Records,* III, 34, 40, 44, 46, 47, 173, 249, 284, 292.

intact for the more formidable adversary.[46] But with Salmasius, since he is dead, I think my war is over.[47] How he died, I shall not say, for I shall not impute his death as a crime to him, as he imputed my blindness to me.[48] Yet there are those who even place the responsibility for his death on me and on those barbs of mine, too keenly sharpened.[49] While he fixed them more deeply in himself by his resistance, while he saw that the work which he had in hand was proceeding too slowly, that the time for reply had passed [14] and the welcome accorded his work had died, when he realized that his reputation was gone, along with his good name, and finally that the favor of princes was diminished,[50] so far as he was concerned, because of his poor defence of the royal cause,[51] they say that at last, after a three-year illness, worn away by mental distress rather than by bodily disease, he died. However that may be, if I must wage a posthumous war as well, and with a familiar enemy whose attacks I

[46] Milton unwittingly pays a compliment to his opponent's polemic skill. If he is going to meet Salmasius again, he dare not dissipate his strength. To a degree the passage is also a rationalization of his delay in answering *Clamor.*

[47] Salmasius had died on September 3, 1653. Milton assumes that he will not be called upon to answer him. Although he was still uncertain as to what manuscript his opponent had left, his supposition was correct; the reply of Salmasius *(Opus Posthumum)* was not printed until 1660, when the issue it argued was past contention.

[48] In the light of existing evidence Milton errs in saying that Salmasius imputed his blindness to a life of sin or crime. When Salmasius wrote *Defensio Regia,* he could not have foreseen that Milton would become his opponent. Since his eventual reply to Milton *(Opus Posthumum)* did not appear until 1660, Milton could not have known its contents when he wrote *Defensio Secunda.* Probably he had in mind the boastful threat of Vlacq in the foreword to *Clamor* (1652, sig.)( )(2) that Salmasius would silence Milton and would "give him the castigation he deserves, a monster horrible, deformed, huge, and sightless." Naturally Milton was outraged at being compared by Vlacq to Polyphemus (*Aeneid,* III, 658), and easily assumed that the author of *Clamor* knew of the intention of Salmasius to ridicule his blindness.

[49] Here the wish is to some extent the father of the thought. In disclaiming responsibility for the death of Salmasius, Milton suggests that he is not wholly averse to the idea.

[50] Milton was unaware of, or chose not to note, the signal honors conferred upon Salmasius on his return from Sweden by the king of Denmark. See Masson, IV, 433–34.

[51] Contrary to Milton's statement, the *Regia* attracted wide attention and elicited favorable comment. Certainly the Council of State took it very seriously. The tradition was (Masson, IV, 166) that Charles II thought so well of it that he gave Salmasius one hundred pounds out of the impoverished royal treasury.

easily sustained when they were fierce and vigorous, there is no reason for me to fear his efforts when feeble and dying.[52]

But now let us come at last to this creature, whatever he is, who cries out against us: a "Cry" indeed I hear, not "of the Royal Blood," as the title boasts, but of some unknown rascal, for nowhere do I find the crier. You there! Who are you? A man or a nobody? Surely the basest of men—not even slaves—are without a name.[53] Shall I then always contend with those who are nameless? [54] But in truth they are exceedingly anxious to be considered king's men. I wonder whether they have persuaded the kings of this. Followers and friends of kings are not ashamed of kings. [15] How then are such men friends of kings? They give no gifts; nay, far more freely do they receive them. They do not risk their own property, who dare not give even their names to the royal cause. What then do they give? Words! But they are not devoted enough to resolve, nor loyal enough to dare, to write down their names and give even words free of charge to their kings.[55] Well, as for me, ὦ ἄνδρες ἀνώνυμοι [56] (for give me leave to address in

The fact of this payment, however, is by no means beyond dispute (French, II, 248–50). See W. McNeill, "Milton and Salmasius, 1649," *English Historical Review,* LXXX, No. 314 (January, 1965), 107–108.

[52] Milton's repeated references to the possibility of a reply by Salmasius suggest that he was more concerned about the matter than his boastful tone indicates. See above, p. 558–59, nn. 45 and 46.

[53] As Milton turns from the broad and generally idealistic affirmations of his exordium or proem and comes finally to grips with *Clamor* and its author, his style changes abruptly. The sentences become shorter, and the language turns colloquial. For righteous indignation he substitutes jeering and contempt. In this second part of his "speech," the narrative, he states his main theme, the defence of his country against the attack in *Clamor.*

[54] Milton is patently irked that for the second time he is forced to answer an anonymous tract. For dramatic effect, perhaps, he exaggerates the importance of the matter. Though the name of Salmasius did not appear on the title page of *Defensio Regia,* the fact that he was the author was widely known among scholars, and certainly known to Milton. Although he did not have such accurate information about the authorship of *Clamor,* he thought, or professed to think, that he did.

[55] Apologists for kings are really seekers, not givers. As he frequently does when he is sarcastic, Milton here plays with language. Kings have to buy words in their own praise. Writers are glad to sell, but they are too craven and avaricious to give kings the extra advantage of their names.

[56] The Greek phrase means "O men without a name." Milton does not mean to imply that Greek is inferior to Latin. With characteristic sarcasm he makes a double joke. The Greek expression is a parody of the form of address employed as the formal opening of many Greek orations. Normally used with great dignity, it is here a gibe. He accentuates the sneer by suggesting that if his opponents were men of learning they would have Latin names.

Greek those for whom I can find no name in Latin) as for me, I say, when your friend Claudius [57] had begun to compose a book about royal authority [58] (with a subject popular enough, but still without a name) and I could have followed his example, I was so far from being ashamed either of myself or my cause that I considered it disgraceful to attack so great a theme without openly acknowledging my identity.[59]

Why is it that the attack which I, in a republic, am seen to make openly against kings, you, in a kingdom, and under the patronage of kings, do not dare to make against the republic, except furtively and by stealth? Why do you, cautious in the midst of security, like a creature of darkness in broad daylight, becloud the sovereign power, the sovereign grace, with your patently invidious and suspicious timidity? [16] Do you fear that kings will not be able to protect you? Cloaked and muffled as you are, you seem to have come, I swear, not as defenders to assert the right of kings, but as thieves to plunder the treasury.[60] What I am, I, for my part, openly admit. The right which I deny to kings, I would dare to deny to the end in any legitimate kingdom whatsoever. No monarch could injure me without first condemning himself by the confession that he was a tyrant. If I attack tyrants, what is this to kings, whom I am very far from classing as tyrants? As a good man differs from a bad, so much, I hold, does a king differ from a tyrant. Hence it happens that a tyrant not only is not a king but is always an especially dangerous threat to kings. And surely one who glances at the records of history will find that more kings have been crushed and overthrown by tyrants than by their people. He who asserts, therefore, that tyrants must be abolished asserts, not that kings should be abolished, but the

[57] By his contemptuous and discourteous use of only a first name Milton presses his jeering attack on the anonymity of Salmasius.

[58] A reference to the discussion of divine right and royal prerogative in *Defensio Regia.* See below, pp. *Regia,* pp. 982–1036, *passim.*

[59] Milton was deeply interested in government in a conceptual as well as in a practical sense. In discussing the subject, therefore, he will not be guilty of the undignified practice of his opponents by concealing his name.

[60] Milton assumes that, like Salmasius, the author of *Clamor* wrote in France or Holland. His own perplexity, therefore, and his ridicule of his opponents are effective as argument. The reticence and timidity of the supposed author make him ridiculous. The fact that the actual author wrote his tract and read Milton's answer in England gives this passage an ironical twist that the author himself must have enjoyed and that the modern reader can relish, but that Milton did not intend.

worst enemies of kings, the most dangerous, in fact, of all their foes.[61]

But as for you, the right which you assign to kings, [17] to wit that whatever is their pleasure is right, is not a right, but a wrong, a crime, evil itself.[62] With a gift so poisonous, rather than benign, you yourself become the murderer of those whom you proclaim to be above all violence and danger. You identify king with tyrant, if the same right belongs to each. For if the king does not use this right of his (and he will never use it as long as he shall be king, not tyrant), it must be ascribed, not to the king, but to the man. What fancy could be more absurd than such a right of kings? Should anyone use it, as often as he wishes to be king, he would cease, for that length of time, to be a good man, and as often as he prefers to be a good man, so often would he prove himself no king.[63] What greater slander can be uttered against kings? He who teaches this right must himself be most unrighteous, the worst of all men, for how could he become worse than by first taking on the very nature which he imposes and stamps on others? But if every good man is a king, as was the glorious teaching of a certain school of ancient philosophers,[64] it follows by the same logic that every bad man is a tyrant, [18] each in his own degree. For a tyrant is not something great (let him not be puffed up by the very name), but something utterly base. And to the degree that he is the greatest of all tyrants, to that same degree is he the meanest of all and most a

[61] The dichotomy between true kings and tyrants was deeply fixed in Milton's mind. His principal discussion of the idea is found in *Tenure, Eikonoklastes,* and *Defensio*. For writers who particularly influenced his thinking see the *Commonplace Book* (*Complete Prose,* I, 452–57).

[62] Milton is thinking here more of Salmasius than of the author of *Clamor*. Above (note 58) he speaks of Salmasius as having written about the royal right *(jure regio)* in *Defensio Regia*. The author of *Clamor* feels that he can add nothing to what Salmasius has said (below, p. 1051): "Indeed, the royal patron [Salmasius] has excelled most of all in judgment, while nature has illuminated with invincible reason and confirmed with divine and human authority the noted fact that royal majesty is unaccountable and that subjects are allowed to do nothing against the sacred rights of kings."

[63] Milton presents a paradox. If he wishes to be good, a man cannot accept divine right and be a king. If he accepts the idea of divine right, he becomes a bad man and therefore no king, but a tyrant. *Cf. The Tenure, Complete Prose,* III, 88–100.

[64] The Stoics. Milton reflects here the idea that virtue is the law of the universe. Only those who follow virtue can be happy. The most likely source of Milton's ideas about Stoicism is Cicero's *De Finibus Bonorum et Malorum* (45 B.C.). In the second dialogue Marcus Porcius Cato expounds and praises the Stoic system, and Cicero makes comments.

slave. Other men willingly serve only their own vices; he is forced, even against his will, to be a slave, not only to his own crimes, but also to the most grievous crimes of his servants and attendants, and he must yield a certain share of his despotism to all his most abandoned followers. Tyrants then are the meanest of slaves; they are slaves even to their own slaves.[65] Wherefore this name of tyrant may justly be applied either to the most insignificant bodyguard [66] of tyrants or to this crier himself. Why he cries so loudly in this tyrannous cause will soon be clear enough from what has been said and what will be said, and also why he is anonymous, for either he has been basely hired and, after the fashion of Salmasius,[67] has sold this Cry of his to the royal blood,[68] or, being shamefully aware of his disreputable doctrine, or profligate and dissolute in his life, it is no strange thing that he seeks to hide.[69] [19] Or perhaps he is safeguarding himself so that if he should sniff out a richer prospect of gain anywhere, he may be at liberty to abandon kings and go over to some republic, as yet unborn. Not even then would he lack the example of his great Salmasius, who, lured by the gleam of gold, turned in his old age from the orthodox to the bishops, from the popular to the royalist party.[70] You then, who

[65] Milton here makes a searching statement about despots. No man has ever ruled absolutely alone. All seemingly absolute monarchy is really oligarchy. The king and his princes live a life of mutual fear and hate which becomes a kind of servitude. See *Commonplace Book, Complete Prose,* I, 457.

[66] The Latin word here is *pugil* or fist-fighter. The name tyrant may therefore, Milton suggests, be applied even to the very lowest of the defenders of tyrants, those who do the menial work of their superiors. Such a one is the author of *Clamor.*

[67] The repetition of such charges is a part of Milton's rhetorical pattern, the diatribe. See above, p. 559, n. 51.

[68] Milton misses no opportunity to ridicule the pomposity of the title, *Cry of the Royal Blood.* Here the cry of the royal blood of Charles I is sold to the royal blood of Charles II.

[69] Milton gives here the first intimation of his intention to attack the private life of his supposed opponent, Alexander More.

[70] It is true that Salmasius' views had changed, but there is no solid evidence to indicate that money had influenced the change. He had challenged the primacy of the pope (*De Primatu,* 1608, 1645) and questioned the Apostolic Succession (*De Episcopis et Presbyteris,* 1641). Also he had shown sympathy toward the Scottish Covenant and the assertion of power by Parliament. Later he had approved limited Episcopacy for England and opposed the sects. The execution of Charles I, which seems to have shocked him deeply, may have affected his views, but there is no indication of ulterior motives. See Masson, IV, 165–66; and Kathryn McEuen, below, pp. 978–80.

utter your "Cry" from some hovel,[71] do not deceive us about your identity. In vain have you sought those hiding places. You will be dragged forth, believe me, nor will that helmet of Pluto [72] any longer conceal you. You will swear, as long as you live, either that I am not blind, or that at least I do not shut my eyes to you.[73]

Now then, hear, if you have time (it is almost a Milesian or a Baian fable) [74] who he is, what his descent, and by what hope he was led, by what bait and what enticement he was coaxed into adopting the royalist cause. He is a certain More,[75] part Scot, part French (that a single race or country be not saddled with the entire disgrace of the man), a rogue and, according to the general evidence, not only of other men, but (what is most damning) of his friends, [20] whom he changed from intimates into bitter enemies,[76] he is faithless, treacherous, ungrateful, foulmouthed, a consistent slanderer of men and of women, whose chastity he is wont to spare no more than their good name. To omit the more obscure events of his early life, this fellow first taught

[71] By his use of the word *hovel* Milton again employs the calculated slur designed to belittle More and make him ridiculous.

[72] Milton slightly adjusts the legend of Pluto's helmet to suit his purpose. As the cap lent to Perseus made him invisible to Medusa, so the Cap of Darkness worn by More concealed his disgraceful life and writings. See *Bibliotheke,* II, 34 ff., a compilation wrongly attributed to Apollodorus of Athens.

[73] Milton's belief that he has penetrated the disguise of the author of *Clamor* gives him such satisfaction that he is able to joke about his blindness. More will soon realize, he says, that eyes are not essential for some kinds of seeing. Milton allows himself the added pleasure of a play on words in the equation of eyes literally shut in blindness and eyes figuratively shut for the purpose of overlooking.

[74] Licentious or erotic tale. *Milesian Tales,* written by Aristides of Miletus (*ca.* 200 B.C.) were translated into Latin by Lucius Cornelius Sisenna (*ca.* 120–87 B.C.). They are not extant. Baiae was a fashionable and luxurious resort on the Gulf of Puteoli, near Naples. Its licentiousness was noted by Martial (XI, 80). Excavations begun in 1939, interrupted by war and resumed in 1950, reveal that Baiae was a highly developed resort, rivaling Herculaneum in splendor.

[75] Alexander More or Morus (1616–1670) was born in France of a Scottish father and a French mother. Recognized in his own time as a scholar and a clergyman, he has remained known to fame largely through Milton's false ascription to him of the authorship of *Clamor*. See *DNB;* Pierre Bayle, *Dictionnaire Historique et Critique* (Paris, 1697–1702); Archibald Bruce, *Critical Account of the Life, Character and Discourses of Mr. Alexander Morus* (Edinburgh, 1813); below, pp. 687, 779, 813.

[76] Though on the record More's ability as scholar and preacher appears not to be in doubt, he seems to have become a center of suspicion and gossip wherever he went. See Masson, IV, 460–61.

Greek at Geneva,[77] but although he often demonstrated to his pupils the meaning of his own name Morus [78] in Greek, he could not unlearn the fool and the knave. Indeed, since he was conscious of the guilt of so many crimes (although not yet perhaps detected), he was all the more driven by such frenzy that he did not shrink from seeking the office of pastor in the church and defiling it by his vicious ways.[79] But he could not long escape the censure of the Elders. A pursuer of women, a liar, marked by many other offences, condemned for many deviations from the orthodox faith—deviations which he basely recanted and yet impiously retained after recanting [80]—he was at last proved to be an adulterer.

He happened to have conceived a passion for a certain maidservant of his host, [21] and although she not long afterwards married another, he did not cease to pursue her. The neighbors had often noticed

[77] Through either ignorance of the facts or deliberate distortion Milton is here unjust to More, who was only twenty-three when he was appointed to the chair of Greek at Geneva. See Masson, IV, 459.

[78] In Greek the word *morus* means *fool.* Milton makes the most of this fact, here in direct statement and elsewhere in puns. The force of his wit is rather weakened by the absurd suggestion that a person's name has any relation to his character. He purposely refers to the usual dichotomy of *fool* and *knave* to suggest that More's susceptibility to women or his haughtiness of nature was related to his scholarship.

[79] From 1642 to 1648 More was professor of theology and a pastor in Geneva. That More sought these offices, which were granted to him against the wishes of many pastors, is now evident from the researches of Kester Svendsen, "Milton and Alexander More: New Documents," *JEGP,* LX, No, 4 (October, 1961), 799–806; below, p. 687, n. 1.

[80] Milton's information about More, even to the content of the hundred articles, unquestionably came from Geneva. His information about More was remarkably full and exact; he may have had access even to the primary source (see p. 567, n. 84), which was in his day, and is now, in the Bibliothèque Publique et Universitaire of Geneva. It is Ms. Fr. 468, subtitled "Affaire Alexander Morus." It was found for me by Miss Phyllis L. Méras of the Providence *Journal-Bulletin* while she was a student in the University of Geneva. L'archiviste d'Etat, M. Gustave Vaucher, graciously provided me with a photostatic copy. Not all the documents are dated; those that are were written in the months immediately preceding More's departure from Geneva early in the summer of 1649. It is obvious that More engaged in a prolonged but somewhat vague wrangle with the members of the Consistory of the Church in Geneva. The key document, *Theses doctrinales* (pp. 46–51), signed "Alex Morus," states his views on basic theological questions and his specific rejection of errors pertaining to them. The topics dealt with are original sin, predestination, redemption, man's disposition to grace, and the promises made to the faithful.

that they entered all by themselves a certain summerhouse in the garden. Not quite adultery, you say. He could have done anything else in the world. Certainly. He might have talked to her, no doubt about matters horticultural, or he might have drawn from the subject of gardens (say those of Alcinous [81] or Adonis [82]) certain of his lectures for this woman, who had perhaps a smattering of knowledge and a willing ear. He might now have praised the flower beds, might have wished only for some shade, were it possible merely to graft the mulberry on the fig, whence might come forth, with utmost speed, a grove of sycamores—a very pleasant place to tread. He might then have demonstrated to this woman the method of grafting. These things and much else he could have done; who denies it? [83] But he could not deter

[81] The Palace of Alcinous, king of the Phaeacians, was surrounded by gardens (*Odyssey,* VII, 125–28), where spring and harvest were perpetual. See *Paradise Lost,* V, 340–41 and IX, 439–41, where Milton, following in the footsteps of Spenser (*The Faerie Queene,* II, xii, 52), compared these gardens with those of Eden.

[82] The place where Venus took Adonis after he had been fatally wounded by a boar became a garden in which the anemone flourished in earth moistened by his blood and her tears. Adonis became the center of a vegetation cult; his image was worshiped in gardens which quickly became lush and as rapidly withered. In the East he was revered under the Syrian name Thammuz. See Ovid, *Metamorphoses,* X. Milton introduces the amorous story of Venus and Adonis as background for a specific charge he is about to make against More. See *Comus,* 998–1001; *Paradise Lost,* I, 446–52, and IX, 439–40.

[83] The gardens of Alcinous and of Adonis are erotic, in the sense that they are places of perpetual refertilizing and rebirth. They therefore have more than a purely literary or decorative relation to Milton's purpose. He uses the garden setting because he knew of evidence that some of More's amorous encounters had taken place in a garden house. The evidence appears in Ms. Fr. 468 in the Bibliothèque Publique et Universitaire of Geneva. (See above, p. 565, n. 80). On page 24 it is affirmed over the signatures of officers of the church that More "had excessive familiarities with Nicolarde Pelet in her dwelling as well as in a garden at Plein Palais, to the great scandal of many persons." Elsewhere on the same page is a statement that "More was found disguised in the company of a night friend." Milton makes further reference to the garden episode in *Pro Se Defensio* (see below, p. 722), but there the name of the woman is given as Claudia Pelletta. For provenance of Ms. Fr. 486, see below, p. 753, n. 132.

Though less specific here, he recounts More's adultery with stinging irony, and not without gusto. Toward the end of his account he introduces an elaborate pun on the Latin *Morus,* meaning mulberry, and *ficus,* meaning both fig and vagina, together with the English "sycamores" or little Mores from the syca *(fica).* The matters horticultural (probably an additional pun on *hortus* and whore is intended), therefore, are practical sexual matters. Such use of free language is purposeful and not unusual in Milton. See Allan H. Gilbert, *Milton's Defense of Bawdry* (*SAMLA Studies in Milton* [Gainesville: University of Florida,

the Elders from branding him with censure as an adulterer and forthwith judging him unworthy of the office of pastor. The records of these and like accusations are still kept in the public library of Geneva.[84] In the meantime, while these charges were not publicly known, [22] he was summoned to Holland by the Gallican church at Middleburg, through the influence of Salmasius,[85] but to the great disgust of Spanheim, a genuinely learned man and a blameless pastor, who had previously known him well at Geneva.[86] More at last and with difficulty obtained letters of recommendation (as they are called) and rather cool ones at that,[87] from the people of Geneva, solely on condition that he take his departure. Some thought it intolerable that a man of such character be honored with the recommendation of the church; others thought anything more tolerable than the man himself.[88]

1953]). Milton sets forth his own theory on this subject in *Animadversions, Complete Prose,* I, 663–64; and in *Apology, Complete Prose,* I, 894–95, 901–903, 903–905.

[84] The Latin reads the "heads" of the accusations. Milton appears to be familiar with the exact form of one of the documents dealing with More in the *Bibliothèque Publique et Universitaire* in Geneva.

[85] Why or how Salmasius became interested in More is not known. His interest was very real, however, and he had some part in obtaining a post for More in Holland. That the latter had prestige of his own should not be overlooked. Before accepting the call to Middleburg, he declined invitations to Lyons, London, and Edinburgh. It should be noted however that More was instructed by the Company or the Council to decline these invitations. More was well received in Holland. See Masson, IV, 460–61.

[86] Frederick Spanheim (1600–1649), a noted German divine, was professor of theology, first at Geneva (1631–1642) and later at Leyden (1642–1649). He appears to have formed a bad opinion of More during the year when they served together at Geneva, and to have retained it until his death. Bayle says that Salmasius, jealous of Spanheim's popularity at Leyden, invited More there to spite him. He also records Spanheim's death-bed remark that "Salmasius had killed him and More had been the dagger." Spanheim's hostility was carried on by his eldest son, Ezekiel (1629–1710), an antiquarian and diplomatist, who gave Milton additional scandal about More, which he used in *Pro Se Defensio* (see below, p. 716.

[87] Masson flatly contradicts all that Milton asserts about More's credentials, and characterizes them (IV, 460) as "the most splendid set of testimonials of character ever given a migrating divine." However, other writers than Milton disparaged More's credentials. See below, p. 785, n. 217.

[88] Milton could not possibly have had substantive evidence to support this very serious reflection upon the probity and the intellectual integrity of the academic and the ecclesiastical officials of Geneva. Had More's testimonials actually been cool, as Milton incorrectly states, it would be less difficult to suppose them written with tongue in cheek. Though it is difficult to believe that responsible scholars

When More arrived in Holland, he set out to call on Salmasius [89] and at his house he cast lustful eyes on his wife's maid, whose name was Pontia,[90] for this creature's desires always light on servant girls.[91] Thereafter he began with the greatest persistence to cultivate Salmasius, and, as often as he could, Pontia. I do not know whether Salmasius, pleased by the fellow's adulation and courtesy, or More, thinking that he had devised a likely means of meeting Pontia more often, first broached the subject of Milton's reply to Salmasius. [23] However it was, More undertook to defend Salmasius, and Salmasius for his part promised More the chair of theology in Middleburg.[92]

---

and divines would have written encomia for a man they despised on moral grounds, it appears from recent evidence that this indeed was the case. See below, p. 785, n. 217. See also Svendsen, "Milton and Alexander More: New Documents," pp. 801–807.

[89] Milton here confuses time rather seriously. It is true that More visited Salmasius in Leyden soon after he reached Holland in the summer of 1649, but shortly thereafter he assumed his various duties in Middleburg. It is known (Masson, IV, 460) that he was very active as pastor, lecturer on theology, and synod officer. It is not reasonable to suppose, therefore, that from the autumn of 1649 until early in 1652, More could have spent much time in Leyden. Given the conditions of seventeenth-century travel, Middleburg, which is on the outer island of the province of Zeeland, was a long distance from Leyden. Furthermore, the affair between More and Mme. Salmasius' maid was not publicly mentioned until September, 1652, when it was noted in *Mercurius Politicus* (No. 121, September 23–30, 1652), and in a letter from Vossius to Heinsius. See French, III, 248, 252–54.

[90] In the Salmasius household the young woman was known as Bontia (Masson, IV, 462–63). It appears that Milton changed the name to Pontia to make it more useful in plays on words. Her actual name, Elisabeth Guerret, was first mentioned by Alfred Stern, *Milton und seine Zeit* (Leipzig, 1879), III, 300. It has recently been confirmed by Kester Svendsen, who obtained photostatic copies of Article 26 of the Synod of Utrecht, included in the *Actes des Synodes Wallons,* which are in the Bibliothèque Wallone in Leyden. This article, dated August 25–28, 1653, not only gives the correct name of Bontia but also absolves More of any actions with her that would justify his exclusion from his pulpit in Middleburg. For a different analysis of the evidence about Pontia's name, see *Pro Se Defensio,* below, p. 802, n. 260.

[91] To belittle More further, Milton makes the accusation, based on only two particulars, that he had carried on with women of low social class. The point is effective as argument, though the unintended consequence is to suggest that if the affairs had been with women of higher station they would have been less reprehensible.

[92] Again Milton badly muddles the time sequence. More received the call to Middleburg in the late spring or early summer of 1649, and took up his duties there soon after. Milton's *Defensio* did not appear until February, 1651. It was not possible, therefore, for Salmasius and More to discuss an answer in the summer of 1649. For like reasons, it cannot be true that the chair at Middleburg was

More promised himself both this and another extra tidbit, a secret liaison with Pontia. For the sake of consulting Salmasius about his undertaking, day and night he frequented his house. And as Pyramus was once changed into a mulberry, so now the mulberry suddenly fancied himself turned into Pyramus, the Genevan into the Babylonian. But, surpassing that young man in good fortune no less than in wickedness, More now addressed his Thisbe when he pleased, having ample opportunity beneath the very same roof. No need to seek a chink in the wall! [93] He promised marriage.[94] With this deluding hope, he ruined her. With this crime (I shrink from saying it, but it must be said) a minister of the holy gospel defiled even the house of his host.[95] From the union resulted at length a marvellous and unnatural prodigy; not only the female but also the male conceived [24] —Pontia a little More, which for a long time afterward persecuted even that persecutor of Pliny,[96] Salmasius; and More conceived this

---

a reward for help to Salmasius. Whatever collaboration may have taken place between them must have occurred in 1652. The Bontia affair belongs also to that year. See *Pro Se Defensio*, below, p. 747, n. 117.

[93] Milton coarsens Ovid's story (*Metamorphoses*, IV). For the sake of the pun on Morus and mulberry, the transformation of the Genevan into the Babylonian, and the leer about ampler opportunities than those provided by a chink in the wall, he transforms a tender romance into a sordid seduction. To condemn More, he attributes to Pyramus a wickedness of which he was not guilty. Milton does these things to make a point in his argument; he could not possibly impute to himself ignorance of Ovid.

[94] Though there is some evidence to support the statement that More promised to marry Bontia (Masson, IV, 461–62), there is also More's vehement denial (see below, pp. 1120–23) and his statement that Mme. Salmasius tried to force him into an unsuitable marriage. He even went to court (Masson, IV, 465) to prove his innocence. See above, p. 568, n. 90; and Kester Svendsen, below, pp. 747, 776, nn. 117 and 196.

[95] Milton's reluctance is actually rhetorical rather than moral. As a matter of fact, he takes obvious delight in naming More's crime and sin. His unchaste behavior, reprehensible enough in a clergyman, Milton makes worse because it violated the ancient obligations of hospitality. Milton's assumed hesitation to name the offence gives dramatic effect to the actual naming.

[96] In the words "persecuted" and "persecutor" Milton makes an elaborate, though somewhat forced, pun. Bontia's child "persecuted" (agitated, exercised) Salmasius because its existence brought him annoyance and embarrassment. It was responsible for a quarrel with More, a court action, and ridicule (Masson, IV, 464) among his enemies. On the other hand, Salmasius was famous as the "persecutor" (the agitator, the exerciser) of Pliny. The book which brought him greatest scholarly repute throughout Europe was his *Plinianae Exercitationes in Caii Julii Solini Polyhistora* (1629; BML). It is an eight-hundred-page folio vol-

empty wind-egg, from which burst forth the swollen Cry of the King's Blood. At first the egg was pleasant enough for our hungry royalists in Belgium [97] to suck, but now, with the shell broken, they find it rotten and stinking, and they recoil from it.[98] For More, distended by this same fetus of his, and feeling that he had deserved well of the whole Orange party,[99] had now already, in his wicked hopes, swallowed up fresh professorial chairs, and had basely deserted his Pontia, pregnant though she now was, as being but a poor little servant girl. Complaining that she had been despised and deceived, she begged the support of the synod and the magistrates.[100] Thus at length the affair became public, and long provided mirth and merriment for virtually every social and convivial gathering.[101] Hence someone, witty enough, whoever he was, composed this epigram: [25]

> Who, Pontia, would deny that you, with child by Gallic More,
> Are mor-ally pure and More-obliging?[102]

Only Pontia was not amused, but her complaints accomplished nothing, for the Cry of the Royal Blood had easily drowned out the cry of violated honor and the lament of the poor girl who had been seduced.

---

ume of notes and comments on *Polyhistor,* a 6th-century revision of *Collectanea Rerum Memorabilium,* by Gaius Julius Solinus (*ca.* A.D. 200–300), which in turn was derived almost in its entirety from *Naturalis Historia* by Gaius Plinius Secundus (A.D. 23–79). By his pun Milton equates it with Bontia's bastard.

[97] Since he is writing in Latin, Milton uses the classical term for the Low Countries, the land of the Belgae. He refers actually to the royalists at The Hague.

[98] Knowing full well that *Clamor* was highly valued by the royalists, Milton seeks to discredit it, first, by calling it a wind-egg, an imperfect or unproductive egg (*OED*), and, second, by alluding to contemporary scientific theory. As a thing conceived and brought forth by More alone, *Clamor* is the product of spontaneous generation, which always, in the opinion of the day, brought forth horrible or disgusting objects or creatures. See Kester Svendsen, *Milton and Science* (Cambridge: Harvard University Press, 1956), pp. 141–42.

[99] The royalist party of the House of Orange as distinguished from the White party of the republicans.

[100] In hearings before the Synod of Utrecht (see note 90 above) and the Supreme Court of Holland, the charges made by Bontia were dismissed and More was exonerated without being asked even to take an oath before the ecclesiastical or civil judges. See Masson, IV, 628–30; and below, pp. 1120–23.

[101] The letters of More's contemporaries (Masson, IV, 462–65) are filled with jocular remarks about his affair with Bontia and the difficulties associated with it.

[102] The author, "witty enough," is not known, but clearly he was not Milton. The low jest, as Bayle calls it, originated in Holland. Its complicated play on words, particularly the name *More,* makes it very difficult to translate. See French, III, 252–54.

Salmasius too, highly indignant that this insult and disgrace had been offered to him and his entire household, and that he had thus been made game of by his friend and supporter, so that he was once more exposed to the enemy, soon thereafter breathed his last, perhaps because this calamity as well had been added to his earlier failure in the royalist cause.[103] But of this more later.

Meanwhile Salmasius, with a fate like that of Salmacis (for like the name, so too the fable is apt enough),[104] unaware that in More he had associated with himself a hermaphrodite, as fit to give birth as to beget, ignorant too of what More had begotten in his home, fondled what he had brought forth, [26] that book in which he found himself so often called "the great" (in his own estimation just praise, perhaps, but foolish and absurd in the opinion of others).[105] And so he made haste to find a printer, and in the vain attempt to hold fast to that fame which for so long a time had been slipping from him, he acted as midwife and assistant in bringing to birth these encomia or rather these rank flatteries of himself, which he had anxiously solicited from More and others.[106] For this purpose a certain Vlacq seemed, of all

[103] Once he has made a point in argument, Milton reiterates it frequently. For further word on the "failure" of Salmasius, see above, p. 559, n. 51.

[104] Since More can both beget and give birth, Milton likens him to Hermaphroditus, son of Hermes and Aphrodite, who after an encounter with the nymph Salmacis acquired the traits of both sexes. The similarity of the names Salmacis and Salmasius obviously suggested to Milton the use of the legend (Ovid, *Metamorphoses,* IV), but he distorts it by indicating that Salmacis was the victim of Hermaphroditus. The reverse is true in Ovid.

[105] Milton was justly affronted by the lavishness of the praise heaped upon Salmasius in *Clamor*. Two sentences will serve to illustrate the almost frantic tone of adulation employed: "So may the muse who flies through all the regions of the world and is able to speak with a hundred tongues honor you, great Salmasius, and inscribe your name on tablets of adamant. O, by as far as the poles at the opposite ends of the earth control navigators, by such great distances do you leave behind you, high priest of the muses, the poet next in rank." See "To the Great Salmasius, A Eucharistic Ode," *Clamor* (1652), p. 158.

[106] There seems to be no reason to doubt the accuracy of Vlacq's statement about the publication of *Clamor*. He said (Masson, IV, 627–28) that Salmasius received the manuscript from the actual author, who desired to remain anonymous; that, after some hesitation, he obliged Salmasius by printing the book and by assuming the authorship of the dedication; and that he did not know the name of the real author. Since Salmasius had not yet completed his own reply to Milton, it is reasonable to assume that he was eager to have *Clamor* appear, and that he was more than ready to assist in the process. Vlacq's statement on this matter appears in "Typographus pro Se-Ipso," one of the prefaces to his pirated edition of *Defensio Secunda* (The Hague, 1654; UTSL). See below, pp. 1088–93.

men, best suited. Salmasius easily persuaded him not only to print the book (an act for which no one would have blamed him), but also to sign his name to, and claim authorship of, a letter ostensibly directed to Charles and crammed with innumerable insults and slanders against me, who did not even know the man.[107] That no one may wonder why he so easily allowed himself to be persuaded to attack me thus boldly and with no provocation, and why he made so light of transferring to himself and accepting responsibility for the follies of another, I shall describe, precisely as I have discovered it, his behavior towards the rest of the world. [27]

Where Vlacq came from I do not know, but he is an itinerant bookseller, a notorious rascal and liar. For a time he carried on a clandestine book trade in London, from which city he fled after countless frauds, deep in debt. In Paris the whole Rue St. Jacques [108] knows him to be devoid of credit and pre-eminent in knavery. A fugitive at one time from Paris as well, he dares not approach within many leagues of that city. Now, if anyone needs a thoroughly wicked and corrupt rascal, Vlacq offers his services at The Hague as a newly re-established printer.[109] So that you may understand this fellow—that he is com-

[107] It is difficult to say whether Milton's naïveté here is real or rhetorical. He professes to be surprised that a man whom he does not know has insulted and slandered him. Neither Salmasius nor More knew Milton, of course, but nowhere does Milton even hint that they should have been taken by surprise by his frequently unsupported charges against them.

[108] An old street on the Left Bank. It passes through the area of the Sorbonne and hence was a center of the book trade.

[109] The correctness of Milton's estimate of Vlacq is difficult to assess. The only extant materials which correct or support Milton's account are Vlacq's autobiographical statement ("Typographus pro Se-Ipso") and (Masson, V, 155) six documents in the Public Record Office. Vlacq makes a good case for himself. His tone is calm and seemingly objective. He deplores the use of rumor and scandal, and asserts his unwillingness to disseminate shameful stories about Milton even if he knew them to be true. About his career as a bookseller Vlacq mentions some episodes which are factual and highly creditable, but which Milton omits entirely. He became a printer and a dealer, he says, through his interest in mathematics, particularly *Arithmetica Logarithmica* (London, 1624; BML), by Henry Briggs, an eminent English mathematician. Vlacq expanded Briggs' logarithmic tables, and published an enlarged editon of *Arithmetica* at Gouda in 1628. At the request of Briggs and other English mathematicians, he published Briggs' *Trigonometria Britannica* (Gouda, 1633; BML). Later, Vlacq himself computed vast new tables of logarithms which he published under the title *Trigonometria Artificialis* (1633; BML) Milton's professed interest in mathematics would suggest that he may well have known these works. Such matters as his "clandestine book trade," his "frauds," and his "debts" cannot be finally dealt with on the evidence now

pletely indifferent to what he says or does, that he holds nothing more sacred than cash—even a pittance—and that it was not for any public cause, as one might have supposed, that he made this furious assault on me, I shall produce his own testimony to bear witness against him.

When he had observed that my reply to Salmasius had been a source of gain to some booksellers, he wrote to certain of my friends bidding them urge me to entrust to him anything I had to be printed and promising that he would set it up in far better type than had been used by my earlier printer. [28] I replied through the same friends that at present I had nothing in need of printing. But now, behold! He stands forth, not only as the printer, but also as the author (albeit suppositiously) of a most insulting tract against the very man to whom he had not long before so officiously offered his services. My friends were indignant. Coolly enough he replied that he marveled at their simplicity and naïveté in demanding or expecting of him any regard for duty or honor, when they knew from what source he made his living. He added that he had received the letter in question with the book from Salmasius himself, who requested that he consent to do as a favor that which he did. Should Milton or another choose to reply, it made no difference to Vlacq, if indeed they wished to use these same services, against Salmasius, that is, or against Charles. For nothing else could be expected in such a controversy. What more need I say? You see what the man is.[110]

Now I proceed to the others, [29] for Vlacq is not the only one concerned in the presentation of the tragedy, as it were, of the King's Cry against us. Observe then, at the beginning, as is customary, the cast of characters: the "Cry," as prologue; Vlacq, the buffoon (or if you prefer, Salmasius disguised in the mask and cloak of Vlacq the buffoon); two poetasters, tipsy with stale beer; More the adulterer

available. Side by side stand Milton's harsh allegations and Vlacq's quiet denials. The documents in the Public Record Office (Masson, V, 155, n. 1) raise almost as many questions as they answer, but their total effect is not harmful to Vlacq.

[110] The statements in this paragraph are essentially correct. Vlacq sent Hartlib, Milton's close friend, sheets of *Clamor* (French, III, 244–45) as they came from the press. He also sought to be Milton's publisher, and offered to perform for him (Masson, IV, 466–67) such services as he had rendered Salmasius. In his interpretation of these facts Milton is pre-eminently in character. He rejects Vlacq's notion that a printer is a business man who sells his commodities to those who will and can buy, and he castigates him for not being a passionate advocate.

and seducer. What splendid actors for a tragedy! [111] A pretty contest has been offered me! But since our cause could scarcely find adversaries of another stamp,[112] let us now attack them one by one, such as they are. With only this for preface: if anyone should find our rebuttal at any point somewhat frivolous, let him consider that we are engaged, not with a serious foe, but with a troupe of actors. So long as the nature of my *Defence* had to be suited to them, I thought that I ought to aim, not always at what would have been more decorous, but at what they deserved.[113] [30]

The Cry of the King's Blood against the English Parricides.

If you, More, had shown that that blood was unjustly shed, your narrative would have been easier to credit, but just as the monks in the early days of the Reformation, when they grew weaker in rational argument, used to have recourse to all sorts of spectres and imaginary prodigies,[114] so you now, after all else has failed, take refuge in Cries that were nowhere heard and in the outmoded devices of the friars. You are far from believing that anyone of our party hears voices from heaven, yet I would easily believe that you heard voices from hell (as

[111] As a means of ridiculing the histrionics of *Clamor,* Milton uses the word *tragedy* in mockery and considers its real or supposed authors to be actors filling roles, not convinced defenders of real convictions. They are hypocrites in the basic Greek sense of the word. A satyr play would be more appropriate.

[112] Again the measured and effective slur. Milton's cause is so just that no men of intellectual integrity, only buffoons, will attack it.

[113] Though in *Defensio* Milton had actually begun the war of slander by his attacks on Salmasius, *Clamor* intensified the conflict with sheer abuse of a kind Milton had hitherto not used. He understands better forms of argument, more decorous ways, as he says, but he is convinced that his opponents must be beaten down with ridicule, derision, scorn, and monumental contempt.

[114] During the vistitations of the religious houses, prior to their suppression during the time of Henry VIII, many images and relics were found which were reputed to possess supernatural powers. These were publicly destroyed in order to convince the people that their belief in them was superstition built up by the monks. A notable example was the Rood of Grace from Boxley, Kent. It was a huge crucifix with an internal mechanism and wiring which enabled hidden manipulators to move the eyes and the lips of the figure on the cross as though in answer to prayer. See James Gairdner, *The English Church in the Sixteenth Century* (London, 1903), pp. 199–201.

you assert about me).[115] But as for this Cry of the King's Blood, tell me, if you please, who heard it? You say that you heard it. Nonsense! For in the first place, you hear ill.[116] Moreover, a shout that would reach heaven is heard, if by anyone other than God, by the just alone, I believe, and all the most upright, since they are able, being themselves blameless, to call down the wrath of God on the guilty. [31] To what end would you hear it? So that you, a wanton, might compose a satyr play? [117] For you seem to have invented this cry to heaven at the very time when you stealthily indulged your passion for Pontia. Many obstacles stand in your way, More, many noises within and without thunder around you to prevent you from hearing such cries borne up to heaven. And if nothing else, certainly the tremendous cry which goes up to heaven against your own self would be sufficient. Against you cries out (in case you do not know) that harlot of yours in the garden, who complained that she had been led astray chiefly by the example of you, her pastor. Against you cries out the husband whose bed you dishonored. Pontia cries out, whom you promised to marry and betrayed. If anyone cries out, it is the tiny baby whom you begot in shame and then abandoned. If you do not hear the cries of all these to Heaven against you, neither could you hear the Cry of the King's Blood.[118] Meanwhile that book of yours will more properly be entitled, not the *Cry of the King's Blood to Heaven,* but the *Whinny of the Lustful More after His Pontia.*[119]

The long-winded and thoroughly disgusting "Epistle" [120] that follows is dedicated partly to Charles, partly to Milton, in order to exalt

115 *Clamor* (1652), pp. 166, 167, speaks of Milton as one "who prefers the rewards of hell" and as one "influenced by hell."

116 More's deafness is spiritual, not physical. A cry directed to heaven would, therefore, be beyond his hearing. "You hear ill" renders the Latin idiom *male audis* "to be ill spoken of."

117 Here the reference to a satyr play is specific. Anything More writes will necessarily be lascivious.

118 In other words, if More is so sunk in sin that he cannot hear the immediate cries of those he has harmed, he certainly cannot hear a lofty cry suited for the hearing of God.

119 This title would be appropriate, Milton suggests, because More's only interest in *Clamor* rose from his desire to frequent Salmasius' house and thus have easy access to Bontia. Milton reaches rather far for a vulgar jest, for all who read *Clamor* were aware of the desperate seriousness of its purpose.

120 The dedicatory epistle of *Clamor* is devoted to panegyrics on Charles II and Salmasius. It continues with the threat that the latter will yet demolish

the one, [32] and defame the other. From the very beginning, perceive at once what the author is: "The realms of Charles," says he, "have come into the sacrilegious power of parricides and—since proper words are lacking I apply to my own use an expression of Tertullian—of deicides." [121] Whether this hodgepodge is the work of Salmasius or More or Vlacq, let us pass it by. But what comes next must be a source of amusement to others, of anger to Charles. "There is no one alive," says Vlacq, "more concerned for the welfare of Charles." Is there really no one more concerned for the welfare of Charles than you, who offered to his foes this same assistance in both letter-writing and printing? Wretched indeed do you call a king so destitute of friends that a good-for-nothing printer dares to compare himself to the closest intimates that remain. Wretched above all the king whose most faithful friends are not superior to the faithless Vlacq in loyalty and devotion. What statement could he make that would be more insolent regarding himself, more contemptuous with respect to the king and the king's friends? Nor is it less ridiculous that an ignorant artisan should be portrayed as philosophizing about the weightiest matters and the virtues of kings, and saying things, such as they are, [33] which neither Salmasius himself nor More could have bet-

Milton, applies the description of the Cyclops to him, and characterizes him thus: "Though, to be sure, he is not huge; nothing is more weak, more bloodless, more shrivelled than little animals such as he, who the harder they fight, the less harmful they are. It will please you [Charles] to see your man [Salmasius] tearing to pieces this disgrace to the human race and holding Antaeus from the earth." See *Clamor* (1652), sigs.)(Z–[)( )(Zv]. Strangely, though Milton scorns the passage as a whole, he does not call attention to the absurdity of his being compared first to a puny animal and then to the giant Antaeus, who could be mastered only by Hercules.

[121] The author of the dedicatory epistle to *Clamor,* seeking a stronger word than *parricides,* borrows from Tertullian, he says, the term *deicides*. No standard Latin dictionary or lexicon cites the use of this word by Tertullian. Its source is Petrus Chrysologus (d. 451), bishop of Ravenna. In Sermon 172, he says: "Judaeos fecit esse deicidas," a reference to the Crucifixion. Du Moulin's reference, however, which Milton did not challenge, as he certainly would have done if he had known it to be false, was more subtle. He refers to a famous passage in Tertullian's *Adversus Praxeam* where he counters the gnostic heresy that, since all flesh is inherently evil, the Incarnation was impossible, and that therefore God the Father was crucified. Tertullian's words are: "At tamen blasphematis, non tantum quia mortuum dicitis Patrem, sed et quia crucifixum." Since the word used was *pater,* not *deus,* Du Moulin's use of *deicides* is loose but basically accurate. See *Fathers, A.N.,* III, 626; *Thesarus Latinae Latinae.*

tered.[122] Here indeed, as in many other places, I have found clear proof that Salmasius, while a man of wide reading, possessed only immature and untried judgment.[123] He must have read that the chief magistrates in Sparta, a state endowed with an excellent constitution,[124] commanded that any word of wisdom which a bad man happened to utter should be taken from him and assigned by lot to some good and temperate man. But Salmasius was so ignorant of all that is meant by decorum that he on the contrary allowed sentiments which he thought proper to an upright and prudent person to be ascribed to a man who is worthless in the extreme.[125]

Be of good cheer, Charles.[126] The imposter Vlacq, "out of his trust in God," bids you be of good cheer. "Do not waste so many sufferings." Vlacq, the utterly ruined spendthrift, who has wasted all his substance, whatever he had, is your authority that you should not waste your sufferings. "Make use of fortune, although she play the stepmother." Can you avoid using her, especially when you are exhorted by such a one, who for so many years has been wont to use other men's fortunes, right or wrong? [34] "You have drunk deep of wisdom; drink on." Such is the advice, such the counsel of the tutor of kings, Vlacq, that bottomless abyss, who, seizing the wineskin in his inky hands, amid his drunken fellow-laborers, with a huge gulp

[122] Having previously called the dedicatory epistle of *Clamor* a "hodgepodge unworthy of note," Milton now reluctantly admits that it has quality.

[123] Milton cannot completely deny that Salmasius, in his many books, has shown erudition. Having made this concession, however, he attempts more serious belittlement by calling him a pedant.

[124] In Sparta, despite idealization by Plato, Aristotle, and Plutarch, many of Milton's most cherished ideals were completely thwarted. Its constitution established the slavery of the helots, glorified military prowess above all other capacities, stultified social and family development, and was fatally inimical to artistic and cultural growth. For a full discussion of the place of Sparta in Milton's political thinking, see Fink, *The Classical Republicans,* pp. 99–120.

[125] Milton here made a free Latin translation of a sentence in Plutarch's *Moralia* (233, 31). A literal version of the original Greek reads: "When a bad man brought in a very good idea, they accepted it; but they took it away from him and bestowed the right of proposing it upon another man who had lived a virtuous life." The statement is from the section called "Sayings of the Spartans." See *Moralia,* ed. Frank C. Babbitt (14 vols., Loeb Classical Library: London, 1931), III, 405.

[126] Deliberately disrespectful in the form of his direct address to the king, Milton sarcastically apes the general tone of the dedication, which he finds inappropriate to a mere artisan like Vlacq.

drinks a health to your wisdom.[127] Such are the noble counsels that your friend Vlacq ventures to give, even signing his name, a thing that Salmasius, More, and all your other champions are either too timid or too proud to do. Doubtless, whenever you have need of advice or defence, they are wise and brave, but always in another's name and at another's peril, not their own. Then let the fellow cease, whoever he is, to make empty boasts about his own "vigorous and spirited eloquence",[128] while the "man renowned (please God) for his elegant talent" is afraid to publish his "extremely well-known name."[129] The book in which he says that he avenges the king's blood he did not venture even to dedicate to Charles, except through Vlacq as deputy and proxy, content basely to indicate in the printer's words that he, without a name, "is going to dedicate the book to your name, if you will permit it, O king."[130]

Having dealt thus with Charles, he swells with threats and readies an attack on me: [35] "After these proems the 'thaumasious' Salmasius[131] will blow on his terrible trumpet."[132] It is good health that you predict and a new kind of musical harmony, for no more fitting ac-

[127] The quoted passages are from the dedication of *Clamor* (1652), sigs. [)(3v]–)( )(. Trite and conventional, they seem to Milton impudent as well, coming as they do from Vlacq whose life Milton considers disreputable. The studied dignity and decorum of a health drunk to the king is contemptuously parodied by the use of such vulgar terms as "wineskin," "inky hands," "drunken fellow-laborers," and "huge gulp."

[128] *Clamor* (1652), sig.)( )(. Milton errs in saying that the author of the dedication applies this expression to his own writing. Actually it characterizes the style of *Clamor*, which is to follow.

[129] Since Milton does not actually know the name of the author of *Clamor* and since he scorns the latter's anonymity, he bridles at these descriptions of Du Moulin. Though perhaps somewhat exaggerated, they are not, as the facts show, basically inappropriate. Milton is irked by the apparently absurd circumstance that one who bore an "extremely well-known name," and who was, as he believed, protected by foreign residence, would not append his name to his writings.

[130] Milton here misquotes the language of the dedication and contradicts himself. The dedication actually says (below, p. 1043): "This book, with your permission, O king, we shall dedicate to you." The "we" is used editorially and clearly does not include Du Moulin. Furthermore Milton says that the dedication is "through Vlacq as deputy and proxy," though actually it is by Vlacq himself, and then attributes it to him "without a name" or Du Moulin.

[131] See *Clamor* (1652), sig. [)( )(v]. In the inflated language of the dedication Salmasius becomes "thaumasious," full of miracles and wonders.

[132] Salmasius blowing his "terrible trumpet" and thus sounding the doom of Milton suggests a vague and highly irreverent allusion to the archangel Gabriel's trumpet of doom on Judgment Day.

companiment can be imagined for that "terrible trumpet" when it is blown, than a repeated crepitation. But I advise Salmasius not to puff out his cheeks too far, for the more swollen they are, the more tempting will he make them to buffets, which, as both cheeks resound, will echo in time to the rhythmic noise of the "thaumasious" Salmasius, which gives you so much pleasure.[133]

You proceed with your croaking: "Who has neither peer nor second in the whole world of letters and science." By your faith, men of learning, however many you are! Could you believe that you are all inferior to a lousy grammarian, whose entire substance and hope rest on a glossary? [134] A man whom the devil would rightly take as the hindmost, if he should be compared to real scholars? Such foolish statements could not be uttered except by someone base, and sillier even than Vlacq himself. [36]

"And who has now brought to the cause of Your Majesty his marvelous and boundless learning, united with a divine intelligence." If you remember what I have related above, that Salmasius himself brought this letter, with the book, to be printed, that it was written either by himself or by someone anonymous, that he begged the slavish printer to sign his own name (as the author was unwilling to do), you will at once recognize a man of thoroughly paltry and debased mentality, thus pathetically spreading his sails for his own praises and grasping at boundless laudation from so foolish an admirer.[135]

"While a few vainly revile the immortal work, lawyers cannot sufficiently admire the fact that a Frenchman [136] should so swiftly grasp English affairs, laws, decrees, and instruments, elucidate them, and so on." Rather, how he played the fool in respect to our laws and was a mere parrot, we have ample proof, in the testimony of our lawyers.

"But Salmasius himself will shortly, in the second attack, which he is preparing against the rebels, stop the mouths of the Theons [137]

[133] In a skillful play on words Milton uses "repeated crepitation" to mean both the dissonant crackling of the trumpet and the breaking of wind, and "cheeks" to mean parts of the face and buttocks.

[134] To make the slur worse, Milton adds to *grammarian* the highly derogatory Latin word *cimex*. The contemptuous use of *glossary* refers quite unjustly to Salmasius' learned commentary on Pliny. See above, p. 569, n. 96. For Du Moulin's sentence, see *Clamor* (1652), sig. [)( )(v].

[135] Milton here returns to a favorite, but unsupported, charge. See above, p. 571, n. 106.

[136] Salmasius.

[137] The proper name was already in use in classical times as a general term

and at the same time punish Milton for us as he deserves." [37] You then, like the little herald fish, precede the whale Salmasius, as he threatens to "attack" these shores. We are sharpening our harpoons, prepared to squeeze out whatever oil [138] or fish-sauce may be found in these "attacks" and "chastisements." Meanwhile we shall marvel at the more than Pythagorean goodness [139] of the great Salmasius, in that he, having compassion even for animals and especially fishes, to whose flesh not even Lent shows mercy, has destined so many volumes to wrap them properly and has bequeathed to so many thousands of poor tunnies, I suppose, or herrings, a paper coat apiece.

Rejoice, O herring, and all briney fish,
Who dwell the winter through in freezing moats,
Goodhearted Knight Salmasius doth wish
To clothe your nakedness in paper coats—
Of foolscap prodigal, which boldly flaunts [38]
The name, device, and glory of Saumaise,
That you, through all the saltfishmongers' haunts,
May vaunt yourselves—and thus perchance win praise—
Sir Salmon's vassals, stacked on shelves in rows,
By them that use their sleeve to wipe their nose.[140]

---

for slanderers. Theon is a vague figure, a satirical poet of minor importance. His name is usually used as an adjective to describe his chief trait, harsh wit. Horace (*Epistles,* I, 18, 82) refers to *dente Theonino*. See *Clamor* (1652), sig.)( )(Z.

[138] Milton does not mention ambergris, so dear to the poets of his time, but speaks of such practical things as harpoons and oil. The word *whale* serves to ridicule Salmasius. For a discussion of Milton's use of such imagery see Theodore Howard Banks, *Milton's Imagery* (New York: Columbia University Press, 1950).

[139] Pythagoras (6th century, B.C.) taught the transmigration of souls, the kinship of all living creatures, and hence abstention from the eating of animals or fish. Sarcastically Milton says that Salmasius is equally protective of fish since, by writing worthless books, he provides wrappings for them. It was common practice of booksellers to turn over unsold books to fishmongers for wrappings and to bakers for pie-plate linings. The joke is an ancient one. See Martial, *Epigrams,* IV, 86 ("Nec scombris tunicas dabis molestas") and Catullus, *Carmina,* XCV ("laxas scombris saepe dabunt tunicas").

[140] This intricate Latin epigram, written with obvious zest, was composed, Milton says, for the immediate purpose of controversy, but its inclusion in the 1673 edition of the shorter poems indicates that he considered it to have lasting value. It adds variants on the ancient joke about the use of worthless books for the wrappings of fish (n. 139), and introduces a new element of satire in its scornful references to Salmasius as a knight (ll. 3, 6, 9). Milton ridicules the

These lines I had in readiness for the long-awaited edition of the famous book. While Salmasius, as you say, was at work on its production, you, More, defiled his house with the vile seduction of Pontia.[141] Salmasius seems indeed to have brooded long and deeply over the completion of this work, for a few days before he died, when a certain scholar,[142] from whom I had the story, had sent to inquire when Salmasius would publish the second part of his attack on the primacy of the Pope, he replied that he would not return to that task until he had finished the work still in preparation against Milton. Thus am I preferred even to the Pope for refutation, and the primacy which Salmasius has denied to him in the church, he voluntarily concedes to me in his enmity. [39] Thus have I brought deliverance to the papal supremacy, which was on the very verge of destruction.[143] I, though not in a toga, like the Consul Tullius of old (not even in sleep,[144] but while engaged in quite another task) have turned away from the walls of Rome this Catiline reborn.[145] Certainly more than a mere cardinal's hat will be due me for this debt. I fear that the Roman pontiff, transferring to me the ancient title of our kings, will dub me Defender

---

appointment of Salmasius by Louis XIII as a knight of the Order of St. Michael, an order held in very low esteem in France. Throughout the Latin original of the poem appear many words and phrases that suggest echoes of Roman authors. In l. 7 the words "insignia nomenque & decus" reflect Virgil, *Aeneid,* II, 89–90, "nomenque decusque"; and Martial *Epigrams,* X, ciii, 4, "decus et nomen famaque." Lines 9–10, "mungentium cubito," revive another ancient jibe from Suetonius' life of Horace.

[141] Milton reverts to his favorite attack on More, using a pun that is lost in translation. In the Latin "production" is an impression, and "seduction" is a compression.

[142] The identity of this scholar is not known.

[143] Milton is obviously having a very good time here. The keen wit, touched with mockery, is essentially good natured. For a moment he forgets rancor, and enjoys intellectual fun.

[144] Milton appears to have in mind here, first, Cicero's oration *In Toga Candida* against Catiline and Gaius Antonius Hybrida, and, second, the story told by Plutarch (Cicero 15, Crassus 13) in which Crassus, Metellus, and others went to Cicero's house around midnight, woke him up, and gave him a letter containing details of the conspiracy.

[145] Milton adds an extra facet to his joke about himself and the pope. He now humorously equates himself as the savior of Rome (the papacy) with Cicero, the savior of Rome (the republic), and identifies Salmasius, the potential destroyer of the papacy, with Catiline (Lucius Sergius Catilina, d. 62 B.C.), who attempted to destroy the Republic in 65 and 63. Milton does not draw out a parallel between his *Defensio* and Cicero's four orations *In Catilinam,* but the comparison is implicit.

of the Faith.[146] You see how artful Salmasius was at stirring up envy against me. But let him take care, since he, after basely abandoning so noble a task, involved himself in other men's disputes and betook himself from the cause of the church to matters civil and foreign, which were no concern of his. Not only did he make a truce with the pope, but, what is most disgraceful, he returned to favor with the bishops, after open war had been declared.[147]

Let us now come to the charges against me. Is there anything in my life or character which he could criticize? Nothing, certainly. What then? He does what no one but a brute and barbarian would have done —casts up to me my appearance and my blindness.[148] [40]

"A monster, dreadful, ugly, huge, deprived of sight." Never did I think that I should rival the Cyclops [149] in appearance. But at once he corrects himself. "Yet not huge, for there is nothing more feeble, bloodless, and pinched." Although it ill befits a man to speak of his own appearance, yet speak I shall, since here too there is reason for me to thank God and refute liars, lest anyone think me to be perhaps a dog-headed ape or a rhinoceros, as the rabble in Spain, too credulous of their priests, believe to be true of heretics, as they call them.[150] Ugly I have never been thought by anyone, to my knowledge, who has laid

[146] Here we have the end and climax of Milton's sustained joking about himself and the pope. He passes from the grotesque image of himself wearing a cardinal's hat as a reward for his services to the Vatican to his "fear" that he will be considered worthy to take over the royal title, "Defender of the Faith." His irony here is delightfully involved. Aware that the pope had conferred this title upon Henry VIII for his defense of the Roman Catholic Church, that after Henry had withdrawn England from fealty to Rome he continued to use it, and that it was currently borne by Charles II as defender of a church which Milton abhorred almost as much as he did that of Rome, he, the root-and-branch advocate, stands forth as the logical defender of all he wished to destroy. The whole passage really adds nothing to his argument; it is sheer fun.

[147] Milton offers no evidence to prove that Salmasius retracted his denial of the primacy of the bishop of Rome. The fact that Salmasius did not produce a second volume on the subject certainly does not prove that he repudiated the first. See above, p. 563, n. 70.

[148] The air of moral self-assurance, close to self-righteousness, expressed here is somewhat mitigated by Milton's indignation at the low character of his opponent's attack.

[149] See *Clamor* (1652), sig.)( )(Z. Milton reverts to the comparison of himself to Polyphemus (*Aeneid,* III, 658). See above, p. 559, n. 48.

[150] Dog-headed monsters were widely accepted and even depicted in the natural histories Milton knew. Whether he accepted them as fact is irrelevant to the point he here makes. He refers to the custom, prevalent particularly in Spain, of never allowing heretics to be portrayed in print or on the stage except as horrible and deformed creatures. See Kester Svendsen, *Milton and Science,* p. 140, and n. 2.

eyes on me. Whether I am handsome or not, I am less concerned.[151] I admit that I am not tall, but my stature is closer to the medium than to the small.[152] Yet what if it were small, as is the case with so many men of the greatest worth in both peace and war? (Although why is that stature called small which is great enough for virtue?) But neither am I especially feeble, [41] having indeed such spirit and such strength that when my age and manner of life required it, I was not ignorant of how to handle or unsheathe a sword, nor unpractised in using it each day. Girded with my sword, as I generally was, I thought myself equal to anyone, though he was far more sturdy, and I was fearless of any injury that one man could inflict on another.[153] Today I possess the same spirit, the same strength, but not the same eyes. And yet they have as much the appearance of being uninjured, and are as clear and bright, without a cloud, as the eyes of men who see most keenly. In this respect alone, against my will, do I deceive.[154] In my face, than which he says there is "nothing more bloodless," still lingers a color exactly opposite to the bloodless and pale, so that although I am past forty, there is scarcely anyone to whom I do not seem younger by about ten years. Nor is it true that either my body or my skin is shriveled.[155] If I am in any way deceitful in respect to

[151] Milton is modest and truthful in evaluating his personal appearance. For accounts of his portraits, see French, V, 136–46; George C. Williamson, *Portraits, Prints, and Writings of John Milton* (Cambridge University Press, 1908); John R. Martin, *The Portrait of John Milton at Princeton* (Princeton University Library, 1961).

[152] Aubrey says (*Brief Lives,* II, 67): "He was scarce so tall as I am" and adds that he himself was "of middle stature." The author of the "Earliest Life" is more specific. He says (Darbishire, *Early Lives,* p. 32): "Hee was of a moderate Stature, and well proportion'd."

[153] Clearly Milton refers to a skill attained through regular exercise rather than by training in military service. See above, pp. 552, 553, nn. 20 and 21. Milton considered fencing the best exercise (*Of Education, Complete Prose,* II, 409) and suggests (*Apology, Complete Prose,* I, 885–86) that he practiced it regularly.

[154] This statement has provided a valuable clue to those scholars who have undertaken to study the nature and causes of Milton's blindness. It rules out those conditions that would have produced change or deformity in the outer eye. Most scholars now accept glaucoma as the cause of Milton's blindness. See Eleanor Gertrude Brown, *Milton's Blindness* (New York, 1934) and William B. Hunter, Jr., "Some Speculations on the Nature of Milton's Blindness," in *Journal of the History of Medicine and Allied Sciences,* XVII (1962), 333–41.

[155] Milton was forty-five when *Defensio Secunda* was published. No portrait of him at this time is known to exist. What he says about his appearance seems to be borne out by other evidence. Aubrey (*Brief Lives,* II, 67) says: "His harmonicall and ingeniose soule did lodge in a beautifull and well-proportioned body," and Anthony à Wood (Darbishire, p. 47) notes that "He was a moderate Stature,

these matters, I should deserve the mockery of many thousands of my fellow-citizens, who know me by sight, and of not a few foreigners as well. But if this fellow is proved such a bold and gratuitous liar in a matter by no means calling for deceit, you will be able to draw the same conclusion as to the rest. [42]

So much have I been forced to say about my appearance. Concerning yours, although I have heard that it is utterly despicable and the living image of the falseness and malice that dwell within you, I do not care to speak nor does anyone care to hear.[156] Would that it were equally possible to refute this brutish adversary on the subject of my blindness, but it is not possible. Let me bear it then. Not blindness but the inability to endure blindness is a source of misery.[157] Why should I not bear that which every man ought to prepare himself to bear with equanimity, if it befall him—that which I know may humanly befall any mortal and has indeed befallen certain men who are the most eminent and virtuous in all history? [158] Or shall I recall those ancient bards and wise men of the most distant past, whose misfortune the gods, it is said, recompensed with far more potent gifts, and whom men treated with such respect that they preferred to blame the very gods than to impute their blindness to them as a crime? The tradition about the seer Tiresias [159] is well known. Concerning Phineus,[160] Apollonius sang as follows in the *Argonautica:* [43]

---

and well proportion'd, of a ruddy Complexion, light brown hair, and had handsome features." Even the portrait made *ad vivum* by Faithorne when Milton was sixty-two shows no wasting of the flesh.

156 Having just defended his own appearance with accuracy, modesty, and dignity and having justly castigated his opponent as a "gratuitous liar" for falsely describing him, Milton uses the tactics he has condemned. In extenuation, it may be noted that his depiction of More enables him to introduce the broad Platonic notion that outward appearances shadow forth degradation of soul. See *Phaedo,* 81, and *Timaeus,* 90.

157 The mood of this passage recalls more celebrated statements of the idea in the sonnets: "When I consider how my light is spent," "Cyriack, this three years' day these eys though clear," "Methought I saw my late espoused saint," and *Paradise Lost,* III, 1–55; VII, 1–39; IX, 1–47.

158 Milton is about to begin a catalogue of eminent persons who suffered blindness through no flaw of character.

159 Two reasons for the blindness of Tiresias are traditional: He was stricken blind because he saw Minerva bathing; he angered Juno by agreeing with Jupiter that women found greater delight in love than men. Juno caused him to go blind, but Jupiter, as compensation, gave him long life and the power of prophecy. See Hyginus, *Fabulae,* 75, Apollodorus, *On the Gods,* 3, 6, 7, and Callimachus, *Hymns,* V, 57 ff. (*Bath of Pallas*).

160 A legendary king of Salmydessus in Thrace who was blinded by Jupiter. The punishment is explained in two legends: first, that he misused his power of

Nor did he fear Jupiter himself,
Revealing truly to men the divine purpose.
Wherefore he gave him a prolonged old age,
But deprived him of the sweet light of his eyes.[161]

But God himself is truth! The more veracious a man is in teaching truth to men, the more like must he be to God and the more acceptable to him. It is impious to believe that God is grudging of truth or does not wish it to be shared with men as freely as possible.[162] Because of no offence, therefore, does it seem that this man who was godlike and eager to enlighten the human race was deprived of his eyesight, as were a great number of philosophers. Or should I mention those men of old who were renowned for statecraft and military achievements? First, Timoleon of Corinth, [44][163] who freed his own city and all Sicily, than whom no age has borne a man greater or more venerated in his state. Next, Appius Claudius,[164] whose vote, nobly expressed in the Senate, delivered Italy from Pyrrhus, her mortal enemy, but not himself from blindness. Thirdly, Caecilius Metellus,[165] the Pontifex, who,

---

prophecy; second, that he allowed his second wife to induce him to blind two children of his first marriage. He was further punished by Helios, who sent the Harpies to destroy his food. The Argonauts saved him from starvation, and, in gratitude, he told them the route they should follow. Sophocles mentions the story in Antigone, 970. It is fully told in Apollonius Rhodius, *Argonautica,* II, 181–84.

[161] Milton printed both the original Greek of Apollonius and a Latin translation, presumably his own.

[162] Milton makes the same statement in *Christian Doctrine,* II, i–ii (Columbia, XIV, 41). There he cites four passages of Scripture to support the affirmation, but all the citations speak of Jehovah as the true God, not as a god whose first characteristic is truth. Milton's generalization is implicit in many passages of the Bible, but it is seldom so forcefully put. The closest phrase, "For Thou hast redeemed me, O Lord, Thou God of truth," is in Psalms 31:5. See also John 1: 9–14; John 14:6.

[163] A notable soldier and statesman of Corinth and later of Syracuse. About 365 B.C. he joined a group of patriots who killed his brother, Timophanes, because the latter had made himself tyrant of Corinth. As he grew old, his eyes began to fail, and finally he became completely blind. See Plutarch's life of Timoleon.

[164] Appius Claudius Caecus, censor 312–308 B.C., attempted to broaden the social basis of the Senate by admitting plebeians and freedmen. While censor, he built Via Appia, the first Roman road and the Aqua Claudia, the first aqueduct. In his old age, after he was blind, he opposed the peace proposals of Pyrrhus and in a vigorous speech inspired the Senate to resist him. Cicero mentions the speech in *De Senectute* and in *Brutus,* but the text of the speech has been lost. Plutarch tells the story of Appius in his life of Pyrrhus, chapter XVIII.

[165] Lucius Caecilius Metellus (3rd century B.C.) first gained fame in 250 by defeating a Carthaginian army on Panormus and capturing the enemy's elephants. He was magister equitum in Sicily in 249, consul in 247, and pontifex maximus in

while he saved from fire not the city alone but also the Palladium,[166] the symbol of its destiny, and its innermost mysteries, lost his own eyes, although on other occasions certainly God has given proof that he favors such remarkable piety, even among the heathen. Therefore what has befallen such a man should scarcely, I think, be regarded as an evil.

Why should I add to the list other men of later times, such as the famous Doge of Venice, Dandolo,[167] by far the most eminent of all, or Zizka,[168] the brave leader of the Bohemians and the bulwark of the orthodox faith? Why should I add theologians of the highest repute, Hieronymus Zanchius [169] and some others, when it is established that even Isaac the patriarch himself [170]—and no mortal was ever dearer to God—lived in blindness for many years, [45] as did also (for a few years perhaps) Jacob,[171] his son, who was no less

---

243. He lost his sight in 241 while saving the Palladium during a fire in the Temple of Vesta. He died in 221. His exploits are set forth by Cicero (*De Senectute,* IX, 30) and by Tacitus (*Annales,* III, 71, 4).

[166] An ancient and deeply venerated image of Athene, preserved with other sacred relics in the Temple of Vesta in Rome. According to tradition, the city was immune to danger or capture so long as the Palladium was in its possession.

[167] Enrico Dandolo (*ca.* 1120–1205), elected Doge of Venice on January 1, 1193, had very poor sight but was not actually blind. Milton accepted an unfounded rumor that Dandolo was blinded by the Emperor Manuel Comnenus of Byzantium.

[168] John Zizka (*ca.* 1376–1424) was the military and spiritual leader of the Hussite party in Bohemia. During the civil wars in the reign of King Wenceslaus IV he lost an eye in battle. Later his other eye was destroyed under the same circumstances. Despite total blindness, he continued to be the outstanding military leader of the Hussites until his death of the plague. See John Foxe, *Acts and Monuments* (3 vols., 1631–32; NYPL), I, 848. That Milton was correct in thinking of Zizka as "the bulwark of the orthodox faith," is confirmed by Frederick G. Heymann, *John Zizka and the Hussite Revolution* (Princeton University Press, 1956).

[169] Jerome Zanchius (1516–1590), born in Brescia, entered a German monastery in 1532. While continuing his studies in Italy, he came under the influence of Bullinger and Calvin, and became a Protestant. Beginning at Strassbourg in 1551, he occupied posts in various German universities until his death. Milton refers to him four times in *Christian Doctrine* (Columbia, XV, 267; XVI, 129, 147, 341) where reference is made to *De Fine Saeculi* and *De Uno Vero Deo.*

[170] Genesis 27:1: "When Isaac was old and his eyes were dim so that he could not see . . ."

[171] Milton's accurate knowledge of the Bible is reflected in his qualified reference to Jacob's blindness. He was aware of but did not understand the contradiction in Genesis 48. Verses 8 and 11 indicate that Jacob could see Joseph and his sons, but Verse 10 ("Now the eyes of Israel were dim with age, so that

beloved by God. When, finally, it is perfectly certain from the divine testimony of Christ our Savior that the man who was healed by Him had been blind from the very womb, through no sin of his own or of his parents.[172]

For my part, I call upon Thee, my God, who knowest my inmost mind and all my thoughts,[173] to witness that (although I have repeatedly examined myself on this point as earnestly as I could, and have searched all the corners of my life) I am conscious of nothing, or of no deed, either recent or remote, whose wickedness could justly occasion or invite upon me this supreme misfortune.[174] As for what I have at any time written (since the royalists think that I am now undergoing this suffering as a penance, and they accordingly rejoice), I likewise call God to witness that I have written nothing of such kind that I was not then and am not now convinced that it was right and true and pleasing to God.[175] And I swear that my conduct was not influenced by ambition, [46] gain, or glory, but solely by considerations of duty, honor, and devotion to my country. I did my utmost not only to free my country, but also to free the church. Hence, when the business of replying to the royal defense had been officially assigned to me, and at that same time I was afflicted at once by ill health[176]

---

he could not see") gives an opposite impression. Milton could not know that Genesis was a fusion of several ancient documents, which often repeat and sometimes contradict each other. See *The Interpreter's Bible* (12 vols., New York and Nashville: Abingdon Press, 1952–57), I, 815.

[172] The episode of Jesus and the man blind since birth is found in John 9:1–41. It vividly points up the contrast between physical and spiritual blindness.

[173] Milton probably remembers here from his youth the opening phrase of the collect at the beginning of "The Order for the Administration of Holy Communion" in the *Book of Common Prayer,* which reads: "Almighty God, unto Whom all hearts are open, all desires known, and from Whom no secrets are hid."

[174] Milton has just cited a number of examples to prove that blindness afflicts the righteous as well as the unrighteous. In a kind of massive confession he reviews his life before God. His words indicate a thorough and systematic reappraisal of all his actions, a searching of memory and conscience unclouded by the kind of fear that haunted Bunyan.

[175] The reference to the royalists suggests that Milton is thinking of such books as *The Tenure, Eikonoklastes, Defensio,* and perhaps of his church pamphlets. Like all revolutionists and reformers he believed that his cause was totally right and that of his opponents totally wrong. Methods of argument, Milton believed and stated (above, pp. 566, 574, nn. 83 and 113), are matters of craftsmanship, not of morals. He used flimsy evidence, hearsay, rumor, ridicule, and abuse; yet he believed that his writings stood free of moral blame.

[176] See above, p. 553, n. 23.

and the virtual loss of my remaining eye, and the doctors were making learned predictions that if I should undertake this task, I would shortly lose both eyes,[177] I was not in the least deterred by the warning. I seemed to hear, not the voice of the doctor (even that of Aesculapius, issuing from the shrine at Epidaurus),[178] but the sound of a certain more divine monitor within. And I thought that two lots had now been set before me by a certain command of fate: the one, blindness, the other, duty. Either I must necessarily endure the loss of my eyes, or I must abandon my most solemn duty. And there came into my mind those two fates which, the son of Thetis [179] relates, his mother brought back from Delphi, where she inquired concerning him: [47]

> Two destinies lead me to the end, which is death:
> If staying here I fight around the city of Troy,
> Return is denied me, but immortal will be my fame.
> If homeward I return to my dear native land,
> Lost is fair fame, but long will be my life.[180]

Then I reflected that many men have bought with greater evil smaller good; with death, glory. To me, on the contrary, was offered a greater good at the price of a smaller evil: that I could at the cost of blindness alone fulfill the most honorable requirement of my duty. As duty is of itself more substantial than glory, so it ought to be for every man more desirable and illustrious. [48] I resolved therefore that I must employ this brief use of my eyes while yet I could for the greatest possible benefit to the state. You see what I chose, what I rejected, and why.[181]

[177] The onset of blindness was gradual. In his letter to Leonard Philaras (Masson, IV, 640–42), dated September 28, 1654, Milton says: "It is ten years, I think more or less, since I felt my sight getting weak and faint." French (III, 197) fixes the date of total blindness as the end of February, 1652.

[178] Aesculapius, son of Apollo, the legendary god of healing. See *Paradise Lost* IX, 505–506.

[179] Achilles, the son of the nereid Thetis and Peleus. The prophecy his mother brought from Delphi is stated in the quotation that follows.

[180] The passage is a translation of the Iliad, IX, 411–16. In his text Milton included the original Greek in addition to the Latin translation. It has generally been assumed (*e.g.*, Columbia, XVIII, 606) that this translation was by Milton, but it bears many striking verbal resemblances to a bilingual edition of Homer published in 1606 at Aureliae Allobrogum.

[181] Milton's terse final sentence brings an eloquent paragraph to a dramatic close. He means to write *finis* to the sordid intimations that his blindness was the consequence of an evil life. Indeed, he goes further and says stoutly that he him-

Then let those who slander the judgments of God cease to speak evil and invent empty tales about me. Let them be sure that I feel neither regret nor shame for my lot, that I stand unmoved and steady in my resolution, that I neither discern nor endure the anger of God, that in fact I know and recognize in the most momentous affairs his fatherly mercy and kindness towards me, and especially in this fact, that with his consolation strengthening my spirit I bow to his divine will, dwelling more often on what he has bestowed on me than on what he has denied. Finally, let them rest assured that I would not exchange the consciousness of my achievement for any deed of theirs, be it ever so righteous, nor would I be deprived of the recollection of my deeds, ever a source of gratitude and repose.

Finally, as to my blindness, I would rather have mine, if it be necessary, than either theirs, More, or yours. Your blindness, deeply implanted in the inmost faculties, [49] obscures the mind, so that you may see nothing whole or real. Mine, which you make a reproach, merely deprives things of color and superficial appearance. What is true and essential in them is not lost to my intellectual vision.[182] How many things there are, moreover, which I have no desire to see, how many things that I should be glad not to see, how few remain that I should like to see.[183] Nor do I feel pain at being classed with the blind, the afflicted, the suffering, and the weak (although you hold this to be wretched),[184] since there is hope that in this way I may approach more closely the mercy and protection of the Father Almighty. There is a certain road which leads through weakness, as the apostle teaches, to the greatest strength.[185] May I be entirely helpless, provided that

---

self hastened his total blindness by his persistence in doing what he conceived to be his highest duty.

[182] Milton appears to refer here to a passage in *Phaedrus,* 247. Speaking of the realm above the heavens, Socrates says: "There abides that Substance which has veritable being; essence colorless, without a shape, intangible; apparent only to the pilot of the soul, the Mind. This is it, in that place, with which all true knowledge is concerned. And hence divine intelligence, fed with reason and pure knowledge, and intelligence in every soul that cares to take the food befitting it, in course of time beholding the reality, loves it, and in contemplation of truth is nourished and made glad." See Plato, *Phaedrus, Ion, Gorgias, and Symposium,* tr. Lane Cooper (New York, 1938), p. 30.

[183] Milton turns from spiritual apprehension of ideas or absolutes to the literal observation of mundane objects.

[184] *Cf.* Satan's words (*Paradise Lost,* I, 157–58): "To be weak is miserable/ Doing or Suffering."

[185] Toward the end of a long catalogue of those who triumphed through faith, St. Paul mentions (Hebrews 11:34) those "who won strength out of weakness."

in my weakness there may arise all the more powerfully this immortal and more perfect strength; provided that in my shadows the light of the divine countenance may shine forth all the more clearly. For then I shall be at once the weakest and the strongest, at the same time blind and most keen in vision. By this infirmity may I be perfected, by this completed. [50] So in this darkness, may I be clothed in light.[186]

To be sure, we blind men are not the least of God's concerns, for the less able we are to perceive anything other than himself, the more mercifully and graciously does he deign to look upon us. Woe to him who mocks us, woe to him who injures us. He deserves to be cursed with a public malediction. Divine law and divine favor [187] have rendered us not only safe from the injuries of men, but almost sacred, nor do these shadows around us seem to have been created so much by the dullness of our eyes as by the shade of angels' wings. And divine favor not infrequently is wont to lighten these shadows again, once made, by an inner and far more enduring light.[188] To this circumstance I refer the fact that my friends now visit, esteem, and attend me more diligently even than before, and that there are some with whom I might as with true friends exchange the conversation of Pylades [with Orestes] and Theseus [with Heracles]:

> Orestes: Go slowly as the rudder of my feet.
> Pylades: A precious care is this to me. [51]

And elsewhere:

> Theseus: Give your hand to your friend and helper.
> Put your arm around my neck, and I will be your guide.[189]

[186] This reference suggests a multiplicity of sources, such as Psalms 18:28: "Yea, thou dost light my lamp; the Lord my God brightens my darkness"; Psalms 139:12: "Even the darkness is not dark to thee."

[187] Among the curses pronounced by Moses at Mount Ebal was: (Deuteronomy 27:18): "Cursed be he who misleads a blind man on the road."

[188] The idea of an inner light, an indwelling of God's light as a partial compensation for physical blindness, appears in Milton's writings long before the onset of his own blindness. In "De Idea Platonica" (1, 25–26) Milton refers to Teresias as "the Dircean augur to whom blindness gave profound light." The poem first appeared in 1645, but it is believed that it was written long before its publication. See Walter MacKellar, *The Latin Poems of John Milton* (New Haven, 1930), p. 305. See also above, p. 584, n. 159. Milton's use of the term "inner light" has been cited erroneously as evidence of Quaker influence on Milton. See Louis L. Martz, *The Paradise Within,* pp. 127–32.

[189] In the text Milton identifies these lines as quotations from Euripides. He

For my friends do not think that by this calamity I have been rendered altogether worthless, nor that whatever is characteristic of an honest and prudent man resides in his eyes. In fact, since the loss of my eyesight has not left me sluggish from inactivity but tireless and ready among the first to risk the greatest dangers for the sake of liberty,[190] the chief men in the state do not desert me either, but, considering within themselves what human life is like, they gladly favor and indulge me, and grant to me rest and leisure, as to one who well deserves it. If I have any distinction, they do not remove it, if any public office, they do not take it away, if any advantage from that office, they do not diminish it, and although I am no longer as useful as I was, they think that they should reward me no less graciously.[191] They pay me the same honor as if, according to the custom of ancient Athens, they had decreed that I take my meals in the Prytaneum.[192] [52]

So long as I find in God and man such consolation for my blindness, let no one mourn for my eyes, which were lost in the cause of honor. Far be it from me either to mourn. Far be it from me to have so little spirit that I cannot easily despise the revilers of my blindness, or so little charity that I cannot even more easily pardon them. To you, whoever you are, I return, who with but little consistency regard me now as a dwarf, now as Antaeus.[193] You have (finally) no more ardent desire "for the United Provinces of Holland than that they should

---

gives the original Greek and a Latin translation. The first is *Orestes,* 795; the second, *Hercules Furens,* 1398, 1402. The Latin resembles that of the edition of Euripides.

[190] The existing evidence indicates that during that period from February, 1652, when his blindness became complete, until May, 1654, when *Defensio Secunda* was published, Milton did not slacken in his work for the Council of State. French, III, 197–376.

[191] In his letter to John Bradshaw, recommending Andrew Marvell for a vacancy in the staff of the Council of State, Milton refers to his "enforced absence" from the Council and says that, though he feels able to perform his duties in general, he thinks he is not fit for attendance at conferences with ambassadors (French, III, 322–23). Milton is correct, however, in saying that he continued in high favor and that he was given assistance. He was regularly reappointed (French, III, 283, 355–56) as Latin Secretary to the Council of State, and his full compensation was authorized.

[192] A state dining hall in Athens where distinguished visitors and citizens who had deserved well of the state were entertained as guests of the city. See Plato, *Apology* 36, where Socrates proposes that as an alternative to death, he be invited to dine at the Prytaneum for life.

[193] A giant, son of Poseidon and Ge, who, when he was thrown in wrestling, arose stronger by virtue of contact with earth, his mother. Hercules, aware of this peculiarity, held him in the air and crushed him.

dispose of this war [194] as easily and successfully as Salmasius will dispose of Milton." If I give glad assent to this prayer, I think that I express no bad omen or evil wish against our success and the cause of England.

But listen! Another Cry, something strange and hissing. I take it that geese are flying in from somewhere or other. Now I realize what it is. I remember that this is the Tragedy of a Cry. The Chorus appears. Behold, two poetasters—either two or a single one, twofold in appearance and of two colors. Should I call it a sphinx,[195] or that monster which Horace describes in the *Ars Poetica,* [53] with the head of a woman, the neck of an ass, clad in varied plumage, with limbs assembled from every source? [196] Yes, this is that very monster. It must be some rhapsode or other, strewn with centos and patches.[197] Whether it is one or two is uncertain, for it also is anonymous.

Now, poets who deserve the name I love and cherish, and I delight in hearing them frequently. Most of them, I know, are bitterly hostile to tyrants, if I should list them from the first down to our own Buchanan.[198] But these peddlers of effeminate little verses—who would

[194] The Navigation Act of 1651, enacted by the Long Parliament, provided that goods might be taken to England only in English ships or vessels of the countries where the goods had been produced. It discriminated pointedly against Dutch carriers. In retaliation, the Dutch began a naval war in May, 1652. After twelve fleet actions, the Dutch gave in and signed the Treaty of Westminster on April 5, 1654. For the quotation from Du Moulin see *Clamor* (1652), sig. [)( )(2v].

[195] Milton ridicules the ambiguity of his opponent's identity by suggesting that, like the Sphinx, he is a combination of two animals.

[196] Milton paraphrases the first three lines of Horace's *Epistula ad Pisones* (*Ars Poetica*):

> Humano capiti cervicem pictor equinam
> Jungere si velit, et varias inducere plumas
> Undique collatis membris

> If a painter wished to join a horse's neck to a
> human head, and to overlay variegated feathers
> on limbs collected everywhere

[197] The rhapsodists in ancient Greece were reciters of poetry. They were known particularly for their practice of interpolating in readings of Homer and other famous poets centos or patches from other writers and improvisations of their own.

[198] George Buchanan (1506–1582), eminent Scottish humanist, historian, and satirist, is better known for such prose works as *De Jure Regni apud Scotos* (1579; BML), a book that foreshadowed ideas Milton expressed in *The Tenure,* and *Rerum Scoticarum Historia* (1582; UTSL) than for his poetry. Buchanan translated into English the Psalms, *Alcestis,* and *Medea* by Milton's favorite dramatist, Euripides.

not despise them? Nothing could be more foolish, more idle, more corrupt, or more false than such as they. They praise, they censure, without choice, without discrimination, judgment, or measure, now princes, now commoners, the learned as well as the ignorant, whether honest or wicked, it makes no difference, according as they are puffed up and swept away by the bottle, by the hope of a halfpenny, or by that empty frenzy of theirs. From every source they accumulate their absurdities of diction and matter, so many, so inconsistent, so disgusting, that it is far better for the object of their praise to suffer their neglect and live, as the saying is, [54] with a crooked nose,[199] than to receive such praise. But he whom they attack should consider it no small honor that he finds no favor with such absurd and paltry fools.

It is doubtful whether the first (if there really are two of them) should be called a poet or a plasterer, to such a degree does he whitewash the façade of Salmasius, or rather whiten and plaster him entirely, as if he were a wall. He brings on in a "triumphal" chariot, no less, the giant-fighting hero, brandishing his "javelins and boxing-gloves" and all manner of trifling weapons, with all the scholars following the chariot on foot, but a tremendous distance to the rear, since he is the one "whom divine providence has raised up in evil times for the salvation of the world. At last, therefore, the time was at hand for kings to be protected by such a shield—the parent [no less] of law and empire." Salmasius must have been mad and in his second childhood not only to have been so hugely gratified by such praises but also to have taken such pains to have them printed with all possible haste. Wretched too and ignorant of propriety was the poet if he thought a mere schoolmaster worthy of such immoderate eulogy, since that breed of men has always been at the service of poets and inferior to them.[200] [55]

The other, however, does not write verses, but simply raves, himself the most insane of all the possessed whom he so rabidly assails.

199 Or nose out of joint, the popular expression of chagrin at not being favored or praised. The words "live . . . with a crooked nose" are a translation of Horace, *Ars Poetica* 36, "naso vivere pravo."

200 Milton was not ashamed of the fact that he had been a schoolmaster, in particular as the teacher of his nephews and other young gentry and in a more general way as the author of *Of Education* and the admirer of Hartlib and Comenius. He rebels, however, at the equation of those who merely pass on what others have learned or composed with those who create. He inconsistently scorns Salmasius, who was both a university professor and a scholar. For the quoted phrases from *Clamor* (1652), see sig.)( )(3.

As if he were an executioner for Salmasius, a son of Syrian Dama,[201] he calls for the floggers and Cadmus; [202] then drunk with hellebore,[203] he vomits up out of the index to Plautus [204] all the filthy language of slaves and scoundrels that can be found anywhere. You would suppose that he was speaking Oscan,[205] not Latin, or was croaking like a frog from the hellish swamps in which he swims.[206] Then, to show you how great is his mastery of iambics, he is guilty of two false quantities in a single word, one syllable incorrectly prolonged, the other shortened:

Hi trucidate rege per horrendum nefas.[207]

Take away, you ass, those saddlebags filled with your "emptinesses" and bring us at last just three words, if you can, like a sane and sober man, provided that that pumpkinhead of yours, that "blockhead," can be sensible even for a second. Meanwhile I hand you over, an Orbilius, to be executed by the "harvest of rods" of your pupils.[208]

[201] Milton here refers to the intemperate passage in *Clamor* (Appendix D, below, p. 1078, in which it is proposed that he be unmercifully flogged, otherwise brutally punished, and finally hanged. Salmasius, it is said, would not himself deign to touch so vile a creature, and so would summon an executioner. Milton assumes that More is destined for this office. To express his contempt, he uses a slightly inaccurate but apposite reference to Horace (*Satires,* I, 6, 38–39): "Syri, Damae, aut Dionysi filius," a man who is the son of slaves but dares threaten the lives of free-born citizens. Since the names were typical slave names in Horace's time, Milton implies a base origin for More. Because, in his Latin text, Milton misquoted Horace by writing *"Syri Damae filius,"* he gave justification for the present translation.

[202] An executioner of Horace's time, notorious for his cruelty. He is mentioned in *Satires,* I, 6, 39.

[203] In Latin Milton uses *veratrum* rather than *helleborus*. The former has poisonous roots. The latter has an offensive odor, but is used medicinally.

[204] Titus Maccius Plautus (*ca.* 254–184 B.C.), Roman comic dramatist, drew many of his characters from the slave class and the lower orders of Roman society. Their language befits their station. It is always racy and pungent, and often coarse. Milton really pays Du Moulin a compliment in saying that he found his language in an imagined Plautine lexicon.

[205] A primitive *italic* dialect lacking the elegance of Latin.

[206] More is compared to the chorus of frogs in *The Frogs* of Aristophanes which croaks cacophonous strophes as it wallows in the bogs of Hades.

[207] The iambic meter which the author of the ode in *Clamor* (1652), p. 164, employs forces two quantities in the word *trucidate*. The short *u* is made long, and the long *i* is made short.

[208] Orbilius Pupillus (*ca.* 112–17 B.C.), a grammarian, is known principally as an early schoolmaster of Horace. In *Epistles*, II, 1, 70–71, he is called *Orbilium plagosum,* literally Orbilius full of blows or rods. Fuller account of him and of his severe discipline is found in *De Viris Illustribus* (*De Grammaticis,* IX) by Suetonius, and in *Saturnalia,* II, 6, 3, by Macrobius. In order to ridicule More for his error in prosody Milton suggests a reversal of the method of Orbilius, a caning of More by his students.

Continue to curse me as being [56] "worse than Cromwell" in your estimation—the highest praise you could bestow on me. But should I call you a friend, a fool, or a crafty foe? A friend you surely are not, for your words prove you a foe. Why then have you been so inept in your slander that it occurred to you to exalt me above so great a man? Is it possible that you do not understand, or think that I do not understand, that the greater the hatred you show towards me, the greater is your advertisement of my merits with respect to the Commonwealth, and that your insults amount to so many eulogies of me among my own people? For if you hate me most of all, surely I am the one who has injured you most of all, hurt you most of all, and damaged your cause. If such is the case, I am also the one who has deserved most highly of my fellow-citizens, for the testimony or judgment of an enemy, even if in other circumstances somewhat unreliable, is nevertheless by far the most weighty when it concerns his own suffering. Or do you not remember that when Ajax and Ulysses vied for the weapons of the dead Achilles, the poet chose as judges, on the advice of Nestor, not Greeks, their fellow-countrymen, but Trojans, their enemies? [57]

> Therefore let the prudent Trojans decide this quarrel.

And a little later:

> Who will give just judgment concerning these men
> Partial to neither party, since all the Achaens with equal bitterness
> [illegible]hey hate, mindful of their grievous loss.

[illegible]re the words of the poet of Smyrna or Calabria.[209]

[illegible]ce it follows that you are a crafty foe and take pains to cast [illegible]y on me, when with malicious intent and the purpose of inflicting [illegible] deeper injury you pervert and debase that judgment which is wont [illegible]the case of an enemy to be impartial and honest. So perverted are [illegible]u, not just as a man, but even as an enemy. [58] Yet, my fine fellow, [illegible] shall without difficulty circumvent you. For although I should like to be Ulysses—should like, that is, to have deserved as well as possible of my country—yet I do not covet the arms of Achilles. I do not seek

[209] Milton finds a classical source for a common idea. Quintus of Smyrna, epic poet of the 4th century, called Smyrnaeus because he lived in Smyrna, and given the cognomen Calaber because the manuscript of his poem was found in Calabria. His epic, *Posthomerica,* in Greek, continues the story of the *Iliad* up to the departure of the Achaeans from Troy. The quoted lines are V, 157, 162–64. The *Posthomerica,* according to Phillips, was one of the books read by Milton's pupils (Darbishire, p. 12).

to bear before me heaven painted on a shield,[210] for others, not myself to see in battle, while I carry on my shoulders a burden, not painted, but real, for myself, and not for others to perceive.

Since I bear no grudge whatever nor harbor private quarrels against any man, nor does any man, so far as I know, bear any grudge against me, I endure with the greater equanimity all the curses that are uttered against me, all the insults that are hurled, so long as they are suffered for the sake of the state, not for myself. Nor do I complain that to me has fallen the tiniest share of the rewards and benefits which thus accrue, but the greatest share of ignominy. I am content to have sought for their own sake alone, and to accomplish without recompense, those deeds which honor bade me do. Let others look to that, and do you rest assured that I have not touched these "abundances" and "riches" of which you accuse me, nor have I become a penny richer by reason of that renown with which especially you charge me.[211] [59]

Here More begins again, and his second "Epistle" reports his reasons for writing. To whom? "To the Christian reader,"[212] no less, More, the adulterer and seducer, sends greeting. A devout letter indeed you presage. Now begin your reasons. "The minds of the nations of Europe and most of all our French Protestants have been aroused to take notice of the parricide and those who committed it," etc. The French, even the Protestants themselves, have waged wars against kings. What more they would have done, if they had met success equal to ours, cannot be stated with assurance. Certainly their kings, if we are to believe the records of those events, were no less fearful of them than was our king of us. And not without reason, whenever they remembered what those men had repeatedly written and often

[210] Milton would rather serve his country in the unspectacular area of civil government than as a warrior, however brilliant, in the field; hence he would rather be Ulysses than Achilles. As Homer portrays Ulysses in the *Iliad,* he is a warrior of note, but his greatest service to the Greeks is his counsel; Achilles, on the other hand, is purely a soldier. When he loses his armor through the death of Patroclus, Thetis, his mother, obtains a new panoply for him from Hephaestus. The most splendid part is the shield, embellished with scenes of Greek life. *Iliad,* XVIII, 478–617.

[211] For his services as Latin Secretary Milton was paid (French, II, 234–36; III, 355–56) a salary of £288 13*s.* 6½*d.* a year. Obviously Milton does not believe that this sum is properly described by the terms "abundances" and "riches" used in *Clamor.*

[212] The section of *Clamor* titled "To the Christian Reader," sigs. [)( )(3]–[) ( ) (4], is almost certainly the work of Du Moulin rather than of More.

threatened. Let not the French, therefore, whatever pretext you offer, boast too loudly of themselves, or think too ill of us.[213]

He continues with his "reasons": "Indeed I have enjoyed such familiarity with Englishmen of the better stamp"—Those who are "of the better stamp" to you are, in the opinion of decent men, of the very worst stamp.—"that I would venture to say that I know these human monsters inside and out." [60] I thought that you knew only your mistresses and harlots, but you also know monsters inside and out.[214] "The English with whom I was on familiar terms readily persuaded me to conceal my name." [215] And they were shrewd, for they hoped that thus they would get the benefit of your impudence in a larger degree, and you would in this way do less harm to their cause by your reputation, which was even then vile. For they know you, know how good a keeper of gardens you once were, and how, although now a priest, shaven and shorn, you could not keep your hands off Pontia, even Pontia Pilata.[216] Nor is this hard to understand, for if an executioner [*carnifex*] is thought to take his name from his dealings

[213] Milton refers to the wars of religion which tore France asunder during the second half of the 16th century, when the Huguenots defied, threatened, and attacked the three weakling sons of Catherine de Medici. See James Westfall Thompson, *The Wars of Religion in France 1559–1576* (New York: Frederick Ungar, 1958).

[214] The point of Milton's barbs here and in the remainder of the paragraph is blunted by his uncertainty about the authorship of *Clamor*. Milton was faced with a dilemma: he had either to persist in accepting More, whom he could attack *ad hominem*, or to have no opponent and therefore no personality to tear down.

[215] Under the circumstances, the advice to Du Moulin that he conceal his name was sound. Unless he had done so, he could not possibly have allowed his tract to be published. For quotations above, see *Clamor* (1652), sigs. [)( )(3]–[)( )(3v].

[216] Milton reverts to the use of bawdry as a means of ridiculing his opponent (see above, p. 566, n. 83). First he makes a deliberate error by calling More a "priest, shaven and shorn." As he well knew, More was a minister of the Gallican Church, and not a priest. Furthermore, since priests were not, of necessity, shaven and shorn, he really pictures More as a tonsured monk, and thus brings up memory of all the tales in which monks were depicted as unchaste. Then in calling Bontia "Pontia," as he persistently does, he brings in the suggestion of matters "pontifical" or papal as a slur on More's loyalty to Protestantism; he makes the generally offensive, though somewhat irrelevant, allusion to Pontius Pilate, usually depicted as bearded; and, as a climax, he attaches to Bontia's name the adjective *pilata* (without hair) to remind his readers that in ancient times harlots were depilated. Finally, Milton makes the pun more elaborate and More more ridiculous by saying that Bontia, the "harlot," is not depilated, but that her lover is "shaven and shorn."

in flesh [*a conficienda carne*] why should you not seem with equal plausibility to have risen from priest to pontifex by your dealings in Pontia? [217] Although others were not ignorant of these exploits of yours, although you yourself could not be unaware of them, nevertheless, with an unbelievable and in fact accursed blasphemy you dare openly to proclaim that you "seek and defend only the glory of God." While you yourself seek the vilest ends, you dare at the same time to accuse others of "hiding their crimes beneath a mask of piety," although no one has ever done so more brazenly or wickedly than yourself. [61]

"For the order of events," you say that you "have received great assistance not only from other writers but especially from the *Scrutiny of the Recent Insurrection in England*." [218] Truly you are a feckless creature, if after making such a commotion you impart no information that is your own. But the only writers you have been able to produce against us are authors belonging to the royalist party and therefore justly suspect. If their authority be removed, you could go no further. We shall therefore refute those writers, if need be, and overcome *Scrutiny* by scrutiny, and we shall reply at the proper time, not to them through you, but to you through them. Meanwhile see to it that you can defend what you have brought forward on your own account. Let all the pious folk now hear what its nature is and from what an impious and indeed godless source it has come, and let them shudder. "The love of God commands, and the keen realization of the injury done to his holy name compels us to lift suppliant hands to

[217] A second bawdy pun, designed to mock More's religious loyalty and to stress his amorousness through a complicated play on the words *caro* (flesh) and *pons* (*priest* by association with *pontifex*). Also involved is the verb *conficio* which, in addition to its basic sense, may mean "subdue," "consume," or "overcome." Thus the executioner, from his dealings with flesh (*a conficienda carne*), becomes *carnifex*. Since the popes had taken the title *Pontifex Maximus* from the Roman emperors, Milton's earlier use of the word *priest* has had added point. More, through overcoming Pontia, has become *pontifex*; he has risen in the hierarchy from priest to pope.

[218] In *Clamor* 1652, sig. [)( )(3v], "Scrutiny" is called *Review of the Late Troubles in England,* by a Gentleman. Actually, the book Du Moulin used for his narrative of historical facts was *Elenchus Motuum Nuperorum in Anglia; Simul ac Juris Regii et Parlamentarii Brevis Enarratio,* by George Bate (Lyons, 1649: NEW), a popular royalist tract. It is identified and described by Harry G. Merrill, *Political Drama of the Salmasian Controversy* in *Tennessee Studies in Literature, Special Number,* Knoxville, 1961. Milton is vague as to whether or not he has actually seen the book.

God." Hide, yes, hide those vile hands, which you do not scruple to lift, although you grovel in lust and ambition. Hide them lest you dare to defile heaven itself with those hands, [62] with which you have desecrated by your touch the sacred mysteries of religion. The divine vengeance which you rashly and absurdly invoke on others, you will some day learn that you have called down on your own unclean head.

So far the preface, as it were, of the Cry. Now (for the Cry has the chief and virtually the only role in this drama), with the widest possible opening, the jaws part, that the Cry may ascend to heaven, no doubt. If it ascends thither, it will cry out against no one more bitterly than against the crier himself, More. "Although the majesty of kings has been sacred to all ages," etc. In your vulgarity and malice, you declaim many charges against us, More, which are totally irrelevant, for the murder of a king and the punishment of a tyrant are not the same thing, More, they are not the same. They differ enormously from each other and will differ as long as common sense and reason, law and justice, and the power to distinguish straight from crooked shall belong to man. But on these matters enough has already been said again and again; there has been sufficient defence. I shall not allow you, who can do us no injury by so many empty threats, to slay us at last with your twicetold tales. [63] Next, concerning patience and piety you make some fine points, but speaking of virtue,

> You wag your tail. Shall I fear you, More,
> While you fawn on me? [219]

You say that all Protestants, especially the Dutch and the French, were shocked by our deed, yet you add immediately afterwards, "It was not possible for good men everywhere to think and speak alike." But it is a tiny matter for you to contradict yourself. The following assertion is far more shocking and blasphemous. In comparison with our crime, you say, "the crime of the Jews who crucified Christ was

[219] The ugly insinuation here is an adaptation of Juvenal, *Satires*, I, 2, 20–21:

> . . . de virtute locuti
> Clunem agitant. Ego te ceventem, Sexte, verebor?

Milton made only two changes: first, a plural to a singular (*locuti . . . agitant* to *locutus . . . agitas*); second, the substitution of Morus for Sextus. More is a hypocrite, he says, for even when he prates of virtue he is capable of the greatest indecency. Columbia, XVIII, 606, incorrectly lists this fragment as an original composition by Milton. Columbia, VIII, 265, repeats the false ascription.

nothing, whether you compare the purpose of the Jews or the effects of their crime." Madman! [220] Do you, a minister [221] of Christ, make so light of the crime committed against Christ that, whatever the "purpose" or "effect," you dare to say that the murder of any king whatsoever is equally wicked? Certainly the Jews could by means of the clearest proofs have recognized the Son of God. We could in no way perceive that Charles was not a tyrant.[222] [64] Moreover, to mitigate the crime of the Jews you foolishly mention its "effect." But I always notice that the more enthusiastic a royalist a man is, the more he is inclined to bear any offence against Christ more easily than one against the king. Although royalists profess that the king should be obeyed chiefly for the sake of Christ, it is easy to see that they truly love neither Christ nor the king, but, having some other object in view, they make this incredible devotion towards kings and this religion of theirs a cloak either for ambition or for certain other concealed lusts.[223]

"Therefore the great prince of letters, Salmasius, came forward." Enough of this word "great," which you repeat so often, More. If you kept uttering it a thousand times, you would never persuade an intelligent man that Salmasius is great, but only that More is very small, a manikin of no worth, who in his ignorance of what is fitting, so childishly abuses the name of "great." To grammarians and critics, whose chief glory lies either in editing the works of others or in cor-

[220] This is indeed the most notorious single statement in the Milton-Salmasius-More controversy. Milton quotes with complete accuracy; see *Clamor* (1652), p. 5; and Appendix D, p. 1049.

[221] Had Milton known that the comparison was made, not by More, but by a priest of the Church of England, he would have mingled greater contempt with his shock.

[222] Though Milton was shocked by *Clamor's* parallel between the Crucifixion and the execution of Charles, he pursues the idea in somewhat reckless fashion. He insists that the evidence against the king was conclusive. He then asserts that the Jews had equally cogent evidence that Jesus was innocent of the charge of blasphemy. The Gospels unanimously contradict the latter contention. See Matthew 26:57–66; Mark 14:53–64; Luke 22:66–71; John 19:4–16. All this was known to Milton.

[223] In Britain the investiture of monarchs had been for centuries an essentially Christian ceremony. The sovereign was blessed in the name of Christ and took the oaths in His name. Since obedience to rightful authority is a Christian duty, it was normal for those who believed in the king to obey Him. Christ is the king of kings; all earthly kings give Him homage. In effect, therefore, all who obey a rightful king, obey Christ. James I stated this view clearly; see McIlwain, *The Political Works of James I*, p. 226.

recting the mistakes of scribes, we gladly concede industry, indeed, and knowledge of letters, even praise for no mean learning, and rewards, but we scarcely bestow on them the name of "great." [65] He alone is to be called great who either performs or teaches or worthily records great things. Moreover, those things alone are great which either render this life of ours happy (or at least comfortable and pleasant, without dishonor) or lead us to the other, happier life.[224] But which of these things has Salmasius done? None of them! Or what great thing has he taught or written, except perhaps his treatises against bishops and the primacy of the Pope, which he himself later recanted and completely reversed, both by his own behavior and by what he subsequently wrote against us in favor of Episcopacy. A "great" writer therefore he does not deserve to be called, who either wrote nothing great or dishonorably retracted the most excellent thing he had written in his lifetime.[225]

"Prince of letters," he may be, for all of me, and prince of the whole alphabet too, but to you he is not only prince of letters, but "patron of kings and patron worthy of such clients." Splendidly indeed have you consulted for kings, so that after notable titles they may be called "clients of Claudius Salmasius." [66] By this pronouncement, O kings (namely that you entrust yourselves to the patronage of the grammarian Salmasius and subject your sceptres to his ferrule) no doubt you are released from all other obligations! "To him will kings, as long as the earth shall endure, owe the vindication of their dignity and safety." Give ear, O princes! He who defended you wretchedly, or rather did not defend you at all, for no one came to the attack, credits himself with your dignity and safety. This, I suppose, is all they have achieved, who called in the haughty grammarian from his forum of moths and bookworms to uphold the right of kings.[226]

[224] These two definitions epitomize views often partially expressed throughout Milton's writings. He repeats the first *verbatim* in *Pro Se* (below, p. 774). See also *A Defence,* above, p. 305; *An Apology, Complete Prose,* I, 890; and *Church-Government, Complete Prose,* I, 816–18. The second definition appears to be an echo of Horace, with a Christian overtone. See *Epistula ad Pisones (Ars Poetica),* 333–34: "Poets desire either to benefit or to delight, or to tell at one time the pleasing and the useful things of life." For quotations from Du Moulin, see *Clamor* (1652), p. 7.

[225] Here Milton goes so far as to characterize *De Primatu* as "perhaps" great; apparently he did not know that this work was based rather closely on two earlier tracts on the same subject. See above, pp. 563 and 569, nn. 70 and 96.

[226] This paragraph presents in small compass Milton's principal lines of attack throughout the tract. For quotations, see *Clamor* (1652), p. 7.

"To him the church will be no less in debt than will the cause of royalty." No praise indeed will the church owe him, but a richly deserved black mark for deserting her cause. Now you would pour forth praises on the *Defence of the King*. You marvel at "the genius, the learning, the almost boundless experience in affairs, the intimate knowledge of law, both canon and civil, the vigor of the ardent oratory, the eloquence, the fluency of that golden work." While none of these qualities, I maintain, belonged to this man (for what has Salmasius to do with eloquence?), [67] that the work was golden I nevertheless admit a hundred times over, so many goldpieces did Charles count out, not to mention what the Prince of Orange also expended on the same work.[227]

"Never did the great man rise to greater heights, never was he more truly Salmasius." So much greater did he become, in fact, that he burst himself, for how great he was in that effort we have seen, and if, as is rumored, he left any posthumous work on the same theme we shall perhaps see again. I do not indeed deny that, when the book had been published, Salmasius was on everyone's lips and gave tremendous pleasure to the royalists. "He was entertained, with lavish gifts, by the most august Queen of Sweden." Nay, in that whole debate, everything favored Salmasius, almost everything was against me. First, concerning his erudition, men had a high opinion, which he had been fostering for many years by writing a great many books, and very thick ones, not indeed especially useful, but concerned with most obscure subjects and crammed with quotations from the most important authors. There is nothing calculated more quickly to win the admiration of the reading public. But as for me, almost no one in those parts knew who I was. [68] Salmasius had aroused a great anticipation with respect to himself, devoting more care to the work than was his wont, in view of the importance of the subject. I could excite no interest in myself. In fact, many persons tried to discourage me from undertaking the task, on the ground that I was a tyro about to join battle with a veteran. Some were jealous, lest it might somehow prove glorious for me to have engaged so great a foe, some fearful both for me and for our cause, lest I be conquered and leave the field with

[227] See above, pp. 559, 563, nn. 51 and 67. There is evidence (Masson, IV, 25, 27, 166) to show that the Prince of Orange, William II, knew Salmasius and took some part in the affairs of Charles II, but there is none to indicate that he made any financial contribution to the Stuart cause. For quotations, see *Clamor* (1652), pp. 7–8.

serious damage to both. Finally, his showy and plausible case, the deep-rooted prejudice (or rather it should be called superstition) of the mob, and their fondness for the name of "king"—all had given additional strength and encouragement to Salmasius. All these things worked against me, and therefore the eagerness with which my reply was snapped up, as soon as it appeared, by great numbers who were anxious to see who in the world was so bold as to risk combat with Salmasius, is less remarkable than the welcome and approval which it found in many quarters—so warm a welcome, that, when account was taken, not of the author, but of truth itself, Salmasius, who had but recently basked in the warmest favor, now, as if the mask beneath which he had lurked was snatched away, [69] suddenly sank both in reputation and in spirits. And even though he strove with every muscle as long as he lived, he could not afterwards re-establish himself.[228]

As for you, most serene ruler of the Swedes,[229] he could not long deceive you and that keen judgment of yours. You have proved yourself the princess, and I might almost say the heavenly guardian, of

[228] The reception accorded Milton's *Defensio* is discussed above, pp. 549, 554, 556, nn. 8, 28, and 36; that accorded *Defensio Regia,* above, pp. 549, 557, nn. 9, 38, and 39. Nowhere else does Milton so frankly evaluate the handicaps under which he himself worked and the advantages possessed by Salmasius.

[229] Christina (1626–1689), daughter of Gustavus Adolphus, succeeded her father when she was six, but did not exercise royal powers until 1644. She was educated as though she were a boy, a fact which apparently greatly influenced her whole life. She possessed keen intellectual powers and had a capacity for leadership and command, although her character was marred by excessive pride and self-will. Her relations with her ministers and her people were generally unfortunate. She connived with court favorites, showed open contempt for the Protestant cause, and proposed such foreign policies as an alliance with Spain and an invasion of Portugal. Even the best aspect of her character, her deep love of learning, caused trouble, for her large expenditures on books and her lavish entertainment of foreign scholars were considered excessive demands on the national treasury. Her aversion to marriage made it impossible for her to assure the royal succession. In 1654 her abdication was accepted in the best interests of Sweden. At Innsbruck she was received into the Roman Catholic Church, and was rechristened Alexandra. She died in Rome. Milton shows very spotty information about the queen. He is aware of her consuming love of learning in a bleak land not given to cultural pursuits. He appears, however, not to know of her strong revulsion against the Protestant cause. Though he glorifies her as a monarch, he seems oblivious to her grave defects as a ruler. Christina served Milton's purposes admirably. She warmly received both Salmasius and *Defensio Regia,* and then, as Milton believed, coldly dismissed the man and his book. She read Milton's *Defensio* with frank admiration. Best of all she was a queen, a ruling monarch who personified his idea of the dichotomy between kings and tyrants. See Kathryn McEuen, Appendix B, below, pp. 964–76.

that course which prefers truth to the heat of partisans. For although you had loaded with many honors this man whom you had invited to court and who at that time enjoyed a unique celebrity by reason of his reputation for extraordinary learning and his support of the royalist cause, yet when the reply appeared and you had read it with remarkable impartiality, and after you had observed that Salmasius was convicted of vanity and very evident corruption, and had said many things that were trivial, many that were extreme, some that were false, others that told against himself and contradicted his earlier sentiments (for which, when he was, as the story goes, summoned to your presence, he had no good explanation), your attitude was so plainly altered that from that time on everyone understood that you neither honored the fellow as before nor made much of his talent or learning, [70] and that (what was certainly unexpected) you were strongly inclined to favor his opponent. For you denied that my attacks on tyrants in any way applied to you. As a result you obtained within yourself the fruit of an upright conscience, and with others its outward fame. For while your actions declare sufficiently that you are not a tyrant, this open revelation of your sentiments showed even more clearly that you are not in any measure guilty of such conduct.

How much more fortunate am I than I had hoped—for I claim no eloquence except that persuasion which lies in truth itself. When I had fallen on such a time in my country's history as obliged me to become involved in a cause so difficult and so dangerous that I seemed to attack the whole right of kings, I found such a glorious, such a truly royal defender of my honesty to testify that I had uttered no word against kings, but only against tyrants—the pests and plagues of kings. How magnanimous you are, Augusta, how secure and well-fortified on all sides by a well-nigh divine virtue and wisdom. [71] Not only could you read with so calm and serene a spirit, with such incredible objectivity and true composure of countenance a work that might seem to have been written against your own right and dignity, but you could adopt such a judgment against your own defender that you seem to most men even to award the palm to his opponent. With what honor, with what respect, O queen, ought I always to cherish you, whose exalted virtue and magnanimity are a source not alone of glory to you, but also of favor and benefit to me! They have freed me from all suspicion and ill-repute in the minds of other kings and by this glorious and immortal kindness have bound me to you for ever. How well ought foreigners to think of your fairness and justice! How high should always be the opinion and the hopes of your people, who, when your own affairs and even your royal power seemed to be at stake, saw you, in no way disturbed, deliver judgment no less calmly concerning your own rights than is your wont concerning those of your people. It was not for nothing that you collected from every source so many costly books, so many works of literature, [72] not as if they could teach you anything, but so that from them your fellow-citizens could learn to know you and contemplate the excellence of your virtue and wisdom. If the very image of the goddess of wisdom had not been present within your own mind, if she had not offered herself to you for your eyes to behold, she could not by any mere reading of books have aroused in you such unbelievable love of herself. All the more do we marvel at that vigorous mind of yours, plainly of heavenly origin, that purest particle of the divine air which has fallen, so it seems, into those remote regions. Your dark and cloudy sky could not quench it or weigh it down with any frosts, nor could that rough and unkind soil, which not infrequently hardens also the minds of its inhabitants, create anything in you that was uneven or harsh.[230] In fact, that very land, so rich in metals, if to others a stepmother, to you certainly seems to have been a kind parent, who strove with all her might to bring you forth all gold.[231] I should say that you are the daughter and the only offspring of Adolphus,[232] the unconquered and glorious king, did you not, Christina, as far outshine him [73] as wisdom excels strength, and the arts of peace the crafts of war. From now on, to be sure, the Queen of the South shall not alone be celebrated. The North has now its Queen as well, and one not only worthy

[230] Aristotle (*Politics,* VII, 7) had developed the notion, previously stated by Hippocrates, in *Airs, Waters, Places,* 12, 16, 23, 24, that climate had an important effect on the bodies and minds of people, and had said specifically that those who lived in cold climates lacked understanding of the arts and politics. See Zera Fink, *The Classical Republicans,* pp. 91–94.

[231] Milton's surprising knowledge of the fact that Sweden was "rich in metals" (iron, zinc, copper, lead) enables him to turn a gracious compliment to Christina. Though Sweden has been the traditional stepmother in fashioning many of her citizens of the baser metals, she has made Christina of gold.

[232] Gustavus Adolphus (1594–1632), King of Sweden 1611–32, was a daring and effective military leader. Considering himself the protector of Protestantism on the continent, he waged successful war on most of his neighbors, and matched his skill with that of such notable generals as Tilly and Wallenstein. He died in the Battle of Lutzen.

of setting forth to hear the sagacious king of the Jews [233] (or any other like him) but worthy to attract others from every quarter as to the most brilliant exemplar of royal virtues and a heroine to be visited by all. Worthy too of their admission that there is on earth no dignity equal to the praises and merits of one in whom they see that her being a queen, the monarch of so many subjects, is but the least merit. Not the least, however, is the fact that she herself regards this as the least of her glories, and takes thought for something far more august and sublime than to rule. She is, for this very reason, to be preferred to countless kings. And so she can, if such a misfortune awaits the Swedish people, abdicate the throne, but, having proved herself worthy of ruling, not Sweden but the whole earth, she can never lay aside her queenliness.[234] [74]

There is no one, I feel, who—so far from blaming—would not commend me for this digression [235] in well-deserved praise of the Queen. Indeed, I could not omit it—even if others were silent—without incurring the greatest blame for ingratitude, since by some happy chance or by some secret agreement or direction of the stars, or of the spirits, or of events,[236] I have found in far-off lands so great a judge as I had

[233] Milton compares Christina to the Queen of Sheba whose visit to King Solomon is described in I Kings 10:1–13 and in II Chronicles 9:1–12; he notes more specifically, however, the reference to her in Matthew 12:42 (repeated in Luke 11:31), where she is called "the Queen of the South" in reference to her long journey from southwestern Arabia to Jerusalem.

[234] Obviously Milton was aware of some political uncertainty in Sweden, particularly of the possibility of the queen's abdication. He construes her possible abdication as a misfortune for Sweden and as an act of noble renunciation. One suspects here an implied contrast between the readiness of Christina to abjure her throne for "something far more august and sublime" and the stubbornness of Charles I in clinging to the crown after he had been repudiated.

[235] Milton professes to believe that all will commend rather than blame him for his long "digression" in praise of the Queen of Sweden. This use of the term "digression," however, and the fact that he makes even an indirect apology, suggests that he had some misgivings. If so, his forebodings were realized, for in *Fides Publica* (below, p. 1106) More charged him with going out of his way to introduce the panegyric. In *Pro Se* (below, p. 768) Milton responds rather lamely by saying that the occasion for the tribute was furnished by his adversary.

[236] A very puzzling remark, generally out of harmony with Milton's prevalent attitude toward superstition. Later in *Pro Se* (below, p. 768) seemingly aware of the ambiguity of this remark, Milton appears to make an effort to evade its implications. He was puzzled, he says, by the favor shown him by Christina. Because of modesty he did not want to attribute it to merit in himself. He sums up: "I chose rather to seem to refer the thing to chance, to the stars, to the consent or guidance of spirits or of things, if there be any such invisible agency." See Elegy V, l. 115; *Paradise Lost,* IV, 668–73; X, 651–67; *Paradise Regained,* IV, 382–93.

least of all expected, but most of all hoped to find, one so fair and favorable to me. Now I must return to the work from which I digressed, a very different matter. We "became frantic," you say, "at the news of the *Defensio Regia* and therefore" we "hunted out some starveling little schoolmaster,[237] who would consent to lend his corrupt pen to the defence of parricide." This tale you have maliciously invented out of your recollection that the royalists, when they were seeking a herald for their own lies and abuse, approached a grammarian, who was, if not hungry, at least more than a little thirsty for gold—Salmasius. He gladly sold them, not only his services at that time, [75] but also his intellectual powers, if any were his before. The tale springs also from your recollection that Salmasius, his reputation now lost and ruined, when he was casting about for some one who might be able in some way to repair his good name, thus damaged and disgraced, found you, by the just judgment of God, not the minister of Geneva (whence you had been expelled) but the bishop of Lampsacus, that is, a Priapus[238] from the garden, the defiler of his own home. Thereafter, revolted by your insipid praises, which he had purchased with such dishonor, he was converted from a friend into the bitterest enemy and uttered many curses against you, his eulogist, as he died.

"Only one man was found, most assuredly a great hero, whom they could oppose to Salmasius, a certain John Milton." I did not realize that I was a hero, although you may, so far as I am concerned, be the son, perhaps, of some hero or other, since you are totally noxious.[239] And that I alone was found to defend the cause of the people of England, certainly I regret, if I consider the interests of the Commonwealth, but if I consider the glory involved, I am perfectly content that I have no one with whom to share it. Who I am and whence I come

[237] Du Moulin, living in England, was in a position to know that soon after Milton's return from the Continent he opened a small school in his home. The sneering tone of the characterization (*Clamor,* 1652, p. 8) shows that Du Moulin did not know or chose not to admit the select nature of the school.

[238] A son of Venus, Priapus was a god of fertility, usually represented as a grotesque figure with the phallus prominently shown. His name came to be associated with lechery. In its early stages his cult flourished chiefly in a city of Asia Minor called Lampsacus; in calling More "Bishop of Lampsacus" Milton suggests that More's lechery is so great that he is not merely a priest of the cult of Priapus but one who oversees and rules its orgiastic rites.

[239] Milton turns Du Moulin's sarcastic reference (*Clamor,* 1652, p. 8) to him as a hero back upon its author by calling Du Moulin the son of a hero; an old Latin proverb says that the sons of heroes are nothing *(Heroum filii nexae).*

[76] is uncertain, you say; so once it was uncertain who Homer[240] was, and who Demosthenes.[241] But in fact, I had learned to hold my peace, I had mastered the art of not writing, a lesson that Salmasius could never learn. And I carried silently in my breast that which, if I had then wished to publish it, would long since have made me as famous as I am today. But I was not greedy for fame, whose gait is slow, nor did I ever intend to publish even this, unless a fitting opportunity presented itself. It made no difference to me even if others did not realize that I knew whatever I knew, for it was not fame, but the opportune moment for each thing that I awaited.[242] Hence it happened that I was known to a good many, long before Salmasius was known to himself. Now he is better known than the nag Andraemon.[243]

"Is he a man or a worm?" Indeed, I should prefer to be a worm, which even King David confesses that he is, rather than hide in my breast your worm that dieth not.[244] "They say," you continue, "that

[240] Milton is both sarcastic and proud in answering the charge that his origin was obscure. He knew that it was not, but he points out that, if it were, he would share this condition with Homer.

[241] Since the facts of Demosthenes' biography are reasonably well known, it is not clear why Milton joins him with Homer as one whose origins are obscure. One explanation may be the fact that, in his life of Demosthenes, Plutarch attributes to the orator Aeschines the statement that the father of Demosthenes was a traitor and an exile, and his mother a barbarian.

[242] This analysis is not free from contradictions and some distortion. Milton's denial that a desire for fame moved him seems to fly in the face of statements made in his writings. See, for example, his letter to Diodati (*Complete Prose,* I, 327): "You ask me what I am thinking of? So help me God, an immortality of fame." Other statements appear in "Lycidas," ll. 70–84; *Church-Government, Complete Prose,* I, 810. Milton's references to opportune moments for publication are equally unclear. His prose works in the main would have had little pertinence if they had not been issued when the topics were subjects of current discussion. But Milton was realistic enough to know that his most lasting fame would come from his poetry; here lay the real immortality, a matter he cannot discuss in the present polemic crisis.

[243] Martial (*Epigrams,* X, 9) says that he is known to nations and peoples for his verses and his jokes, but that he should not be envied because he is not better known than Andraemon, a pack-horse (*Andraemone . . . caballo*).

[244] Actually, Du Moulin, with excessive coarseness, said "worm voided lately from the dung-pit" (*Clamor,* 1652, pp. 8–9). Milton counters with skillful use of Psalms 22:6: "But I am a worm and no man," Isaiah 66:24, "For their worm shall not die," and Mark 9:48, where Jesus, quoting Isaiah, mentions "hell, where their worm does not die," a reference to the fact that the worm of sin subjects the soul to damnation. Contempt in this world, which Milton suffers, is easier to bear than the eternal punishment of sin hereafter, which will be the lot of his opponent.

this fellow, expelled from the University of Cambridge, because of his offences, fled his disgrace and his country and traveled to Italy." [245] Even from this statement one can infer how truthful were your sources of information, [77] for on this point everyone who knows me knows that both you and your informants lie most shamelessly, and I shall at once make this fact clear. If I had actually been expelled from Cambridge, why should I travel to Italy, rather than to France or Holland, where you, enveloped in so many offenses, a minister of the Gospel, not only live in safety, but preach, and even defile with your unclean hands the sacred offices, to the extreme scandal of your church? [246] But why to Italy, More? Another Saturn, I presume, I fled to Latium [247] that I might find a place to lurk. Yet I knew beforehand that Italy was not, as you think, a refuge or asylum for criminals, but rather the lodging-place of *humanitas* and of all the arts of civilization, and so I found it.

"Returning, he wrote his book on divorce." [248] I wrote nothing different from what Bucer had written before me—and copiously—about the kingdom of Christ, nothing different from what Fagius had written on Deuteronomy, Erasmus on the first Epistle to the Corinthians (a commentary intended for the benefit of the English people), nothing different from what many other illustrious [78] men wrote for the common good.[249] No one blamed them for so doing, and I fail to understand why it should be to me above all a source of reproach.

[245] Milton had no reason to be ashamed of being suspended from the University. All the evidence confirms the fact that Milton gave an early exhibition of his independence of mind by resenting his tutor's ideas. Actually, the trip to Italy was the final phase of Milton's education. See Masson, I, 159–62, and E. K. Rand, "Milton in Rustication," *SP,* XIX (1922), 109–35. For quotations from Du Moulin see *Clamor* (1652), p. 9.

[246] Milton cannot resist an allusion to More's career. If he had really been in disgrace, he would have gone, not to Italy, but to France or Holland, where More had been able to carry on his improprieties.

[247] When Saturn was deposed by his son Jupiter, he fled to Italy where he civilized the people and established a kingdom of peace. He named the country Latium or a place of refuge. See *Aeneid,* VIII, 319–25.

[248] *Clamor* (1652, p. 9) is inaccurate here. Milton arrived home from the Continent in mid-summer, 1639. He published the first edition of *Doctrine and Discipline of Divorce* not later than August 1, 1643 (French, II, 87) or almost exactly four years later.

[249] On Milton's use of Martin Bucer's *De Regno Christi* (1577), see *Complete Prose,* II, 416–79. Paulus Fagius (1504–1549), originally Paul Buechlin, went to England with Bucer and was appointed professor of Hebrew at Cambridge. On Milton's use of Erasmus, see *Complete Prose,* II, 199, 478, 479, 620, 709.

One thing only could I wish, that I had not written it in the vernacular, for then I would not have met with vernacular readers, who are usually ignorant of their own good, and laugh at the misfortunes of others.[250] But do you, vilest of men, protest about divorce, you who procured the most brutal of all divorces from Pontia, the maidservant engaged to you, after you seduced her under cover of that engagement? Moreover, she was a servant of Salmasius, an English woman it is said, warmly devoted to the royalist cause. It is beyond question that you wickedly courted her as royal property and left her as public property. Take care lest you yourself prove to have been the author of the very conversion which you profess to find so distasteful. Take care, I repeat, lest with the rule of Salmasius utterly overthrown you may yourself have converted Pontia into a "republic." [251] And take care lest in this way, you, though a royalist, may be said to have founded many "republics" in a single city, or as minister of state to have served them after their foundation by other men.[252] These are your divorces, or, if you prefer, [79] diversions, from which you emerge against me as a veritable Curius.[253]

Now you continue with your lies. "When the conspirators were agitating the decapitation of the king, Milton wrote to them, and when they were wavering urged them to the wicked course." [254] But I did not

[250] This view is expressed even more severely, though with harsh humor, in Sonnet XI, "On the Detraction Which Followed upon My Writing Certain Treatises," and Sonnet XII, "On the Same," where he speaks of "casting Pearl to Hoggs."

[251] Sensing a slur, probably intended, in the reference to "his book on divorce," Milton returns to the inevitable topic of More's conduct with women, particularly Bontia. Equally inevitable is the pun to point up More's impropriety. As the servant of the arch-royalist Salmasius, Bontia was the creature of the monarch. Now that More has seduced her, however, she is common property, a *res publica*. Thus, by his lust, More betrays the royalist cause he espouses by creating republicans.

[252] Without evidence, Milton proceeds from the particular to the general. More is so promiscuous, he suggests, that he will seduce many besides Bontia, and so produce the anomaly of many republics in a single city or even be willing to serve republics other lechers have created.

[253] Manius Curius Dentatus (3rd century B.C.), a notable military leader and public officer, was generally idealized by Romans. A plebeian by birth, he came to be the symbol of the incorruptible and frugal Roman because of his refusal of bribes from the Samnites and of booty after the defeat of Pyrrhus. Forgetting his own wickedness, More has self-righteously posed as a model of self-denial, a Curius.

[254] *Clamor* (1652), p. 10. Du Moulin here professes to have information he could not possibly have possessed. He had no access to official documents or to the private papers of either Milton or those who tried the king. If his tone were not so bitter (his use of "conspirators" for judges, and "agitating" for consider-

write to them, nor did it rest with me to urge men who had already without me determined on precisely this course.[255] Yet I shall describe hereafter what I did write on this subject, and I shall also speak of *Eikonoklastes*.[256] Now since this fellow (I am uncertain whether to call him a man or the dregs of manhood), progressing from adultery with servant girls to the adulteration of all truth, has tried to render me infamous among foreigners, by piling up a whole series of lies against me, I ask that no one take it amiss or make it a source of reproach, or resent it, if I have said previously and shall say hereafter more about myself than I would wish, so that if I cannot rescue my eyes from blindness or my name from oblivion or slander, I can at least bring my life into the light out of that darkness which accompanies disgrace.[257] And I must do this for more reasons than one. First, [80] in order that the many good and learned men in all the neighboring countries who are now reading my works and thinking rather well of me, may not despise me on account of this man's abuse, but may persuade themselves that I am incapable of ever disgracing honorable speech by dishonorable conduct, or free utterances by slavish deeds, and that my life, by the grace of God, has ever been far removed from all vice and crime. Next, in order that those distinguished and praiseworthy men whom I undertake to extol may know that I should consider nothing more shameful than to approach the task of praising them while myself deserving blame and censure. Finally, in order that the English people whose defence their own virtue has impelled me to undertake (whether it be my fate or my duty) may know that if I have always led a pure and honorable life, my *Defence* (whether it will be to their honor or dignity I know not) will certainly never be for them a source of shame or disgrace.[258]

---

ing), it might be assumed that he confused Milton's *ex post facto* defence of the king's execution with actual participation in the trial. On the basis of the evidence Du Moulin's charge is baseless.

[255] For the chronology of events, see Gardiner, *Great Civil War*, III, 519–605.

[256] Milton does not hesitate to admit that he defended the king's execution. On the background history and writing of *The Tenure*, see *Complete Prose*, III, 101–46.

[257] Those things "said previously" presumably refer to the autobiographical passages in *Church-Government*, *Complete Prose*, I, 804–23, and *Apology*, *Complete Prose*, I, 888–93. They are less explicit and less full in factual detail than what immediately follows. See John S. Diekhoff, *Milton on Himself* (New York, 1939), pp. xiv–xv.

[258] Milton must stand justified as a man of integrity and of the highest moral character before (1) the learned on the continent; (2) the leaders of the Com-

Who I am, then, and whence I come, I shall now disclose. I was born in London,[259] of an honorable family. [81] My father [260] was a man of supreme integrity, my mother a woman of purest reputation, celebrated throughout the neighborhood for her acts of charity.[261] My father destined me in early childhood for the study of literature,[262] for which I had so keen an appetite that from my twelfth year scarcely ever did I leave my studies for my bed before the hour of midnight.[263] This was the first cause of injury to my eyes, whose natural weakness was augmented by frequent headaches.[264] Since none of these defects slackened my assault upon knowledge, my father took care that I should be instructed daily both in school and under other masters at home.[265] When I had thus become proficient in various languages

---

monwealth whom he represents officially; and (3) the people whose defense he is writing.

[259] Milton was born on December 9, 1608, at his father's home, the Spread Eagle in Bread Street, Cheapside, London, and was baptized (French, I, 1–2) eleven days later in All Hallows Church, Bread Street.

[260] Milton's father, John Milton (1563–1647), a notable man in his own right, was an important composer and a leader in the Company of Scriveners. Descended from Oxfordshire yeoman stock, he was educated, according to tradition, at Christ Church, Oxford. When his father disowned him for becoming an Anglican, he went to London, where, in 1595, he sought to qualify as a scrivener. He was admitted to the Company on February 27, 1600. About 1600 he married and established his home and business at the Spread Eagle in Bread Street, London. He prospered, and retired about 1630, while his son was still at Cambridge. He died in the poet's house in the Barbican. His fame stems chiefly from his musical compositions. Milton gives a charming insight into his relations with his father in "Ad Patrem." See Masson, I, 50 ff., Ernest Brennecke, Jr., *John Milton the Elder and His Music* (New York, 1938); J. Milton French, *Milton in Chancery* (New York, 1939); French, *Life Records,* I, *passim,* II, *passim.*

[261] Sarah Jeffrey Milton (*ca.* 1572–1637) came of a yeoman family in Essex. She was the elder daughter of Paul, a merchant tailor, and Ellen Jeffrey of St. Swithin's Parish, London. Except for Aubrey's remark (Darbishire, *Early Lives,* p. 5) that she had weak eyes and what Milton says here, nothing is known about her.

[262] See "Ad Patrem" (1632?), ll. 78–92, where Milton expresses gratitude to his father for knowledge of the natural world and for encouragement to learn Latin, Greek, French, Italian, and Hebrew; and *Church-Government, Complete Prose,* I, 808–809.

[263] This remark has caused some confusion as to the date when Milton began his formal schooling. He does not say that he entered St. Paul's School when he was twelve (1620), but that he began an especially rigorous program of home study at that time.

[264] If in early youth his eyes were so weak that prolonged study induced frequent headaches, his antagonists cannot plausibly insist that his trouble with his eyes and his eventual blindness were judgments of God on a life of evil and debauchery.

[265] Information about Milton's early education is very meager. His own refer-

and had tasted by no means superficially the sweetness of philosophy, he sent me to Cambridge, one of our two universities.[266] There, untouched by any reproach, in the good graces of all upright men,[267] for seven years I devoted myself to the traditional disciplines and liberal arts, until I had attained the degree of Master,[268] as it is called, *cum laude*. Then, far from fleeing to Italy,[269] as that filthy rascal alleges, of my own free will I returned home, to the regret of most of the fellows of the college, who bestowed on me no little honor.[270] At my father's [82] country place, whither he had retired

ences to the subject are, like this one, vague and general. Since the records of St. Paul's School were lost in the Fire of London, the only confirmation of the fact that he went there appears in the matriculation records of Cambridge. Milton often mentions "other masters," but only one, Thomas Young, is known by name. Fletcher believes he attended a petty school before he went to St. Paul's. The date of his admission to St. Paul's is very uncertain. Masson (I, 74) suggests 1620 or earlier; others support 1615 and 1617. See Donald Lemen Clark, *John Milton at St. Paul's School* (New York: Columbia University Press, 1948); Harris F. Fletcher, *The Intellectual Development of John Milton,* Vol. I (Urbana: University of Illinois Press, 1956); Davis P. Harding, *Milton and the Renaissance Ovid* (Urbana: University of Illinois Press, 1946); A. F. Leach, *Milton as Schoolboy and Schoolmaster* (*Proceedings of the British Academy,* III, 1908).

266 Milton matriculated at Christ's College, Cambridge, during Lent term of 1625, and went into residence (Masson, I, 147–49) at Easter term immediately following. Since he is writing more for foreigners than for Englishmen, he identifies Cambridge as "one of *our* two universities."

267 It is worthy of note that Milton does not add to this general statement of his status at Cambridge any reference to two interesting aspects of his college experience. The one is his rustication late in his first year, and the second, his being called "The Lady of Christ's." The first is recorded by Aubrey (Darbishire, p. 10) and circumstantially confirmed (Elegy I to Diodati) by Milton himself. His being called "The Lady of Christ's" he refers to directly in Prolusion VI (*Complete Prose,* I, 283–84), where he says that the epithet was conferred upon him because he was not given to heavy drinking and gluttony, and because he was physically small.

268 Milton completed the requirements for the B.A. on March 26, 1629. When the degree was publicly conferred on July 7, 1629, he signed the required oath (Masson, I, 217–18), recognizing the king as Supreme Governor in all matters spiritual and ecclesiastical, approving the *Book of Common Prayer,* and affirming the Thirty-Nine Articles. Three years later, on July 3, 1632, he was granted the M.A. Again he subscribed to the oath (Masson, I, 257–58). In 1635 he was incorporated M.A. at Oxford (French, I, 291).

269 It is impossible to say whether Du Moulin actually knew the time and occasion of Milton's trip to the continent. The lapse of time between the two events was actually some eleven years.

270 It is true that in 1630, when Milton had been a B.A. for almost two years, he was not awarded a fellowship that had fallen vacant during the summer recess. Since the honor was given to Edward King through direct royal intervention, however (Masson, I, 238–39), the episode reveals nothing about Milton's status.

to spend his declining years, I devoted myself entirely to the study of Greek and Latin writers, completely at leisure, not, however, without sometimes exchanging the country for the city, either to purchase books or to become acquainted with some new discovery in mathematics or music, in which I then took the keenest pleasure.[271]

When I had occupied five years in this fashion, I became desirous, my mother having died, of seeing foreign parts, especially Italy, and with my father's consent I set forth, accompanied by a single attendant.[272] On my departure Henry Wotton, a most distinguished gentleman, who had long served as King James' ambassador to the Venetians, gave signal proof of his esteem for me, writing a graceful letter which contained good wishes and precepts of no little value to one going abroad.[273] On the recommendation of others I was warmly

---

Milton's renunciation of the priesthood probably reached final formulation in 1628 or soon thereafter. Certainly, when he received the M.A. in 1632, he was already church-outed, and he had rejected the other learned professions. It was quite impossible, therefore, for him to be retained (Masson, I, 332–33) at Cambridge in any official capacity. Milton's remarks about his status at Cambridge, then, may be accepted as true in spirit even though they lack factual substantiation.

[271] Milton's father retired about 1630, and, after residing at Hammersmith, removed to a country home at Horton, Buckinghamshire. There Milton repaired after his graduation in 1632 to begin, as he told his father in "Ad Patrem," a career in poetry. During the six years at Horton he was "completely at leisure" only in the sense that his activity was entirely undirected and unsupervised. Actually, his days must have been full. He wrote some of his finest early poems, such as "Arcades," *Comus,* and "Lycidas." He also read widely in the political and ecclesiastical history of Europe from the fall of Rome to his own time. No complete list of the "Greek and Latin writers" he studied is known to exist. In "The Chronology of Milton's Private Studies," *PMLA,* XXXVI (1921), 251–314, Hanford arranges the authors entered in the *Commonplace Book* by Milton according to the period in which they were read. See also French, V, 380.

[272] Milton's reference to "five years" and to his mother's death, which occurred on April 3, 1637, suggests that he began to plan or at least to consider a trip to the continent about a year before his actual departure. It is reasonably clear that he left England sometime in May, 1638. The passage that follows is the most complete account Milton gave of his travels. But see *Church-Government* (*Complete Prose,* I, 809), and *Areopagitica* (*Complete Prose,* II, 537–38).

[273] Sir Henry Wotton (1568–1639) was provost of Eton when he wrote the letter (*Complete Prose,* I, 339–43) to which Milton refers. He did not follow the "precepts of great value." He sailed from Nice instead of from Marseilles, and he violated Wotton's most urgent advice that, in matters of religion, he should keep his thoughts close and his countenance open. For fuller notice of Wotton and of his relations with Milton see Logan Pearsall Smith, *The Life and Letters of Sir Thomas Wotton* (2 vols., Oxford, 1907).

received in Paris by the noble Thomas Scudamore, Viscount Sligo,[274] legate of King Charles. He on his own initiative introduced me, in company with several of his suite, to Hugo Grotius, a most learned man (then ambassador from the Queen of Sweden to the King of France) whom I ardently desired to meet.[275] [83] When I set out for Italy some days thereafter, Scudamore gave me letters to English merchants along my projected route, that they might assist me as they could. Sailing from Nice, I reached Genoa, then Leghorn and Pisa, and after that Florence. In that city, which I have always admired above all others because of the elegance, not just of its tongue, but also of its wit, I lingered for about two months. There I at once became the friend of many gentlemen eminent in rank and learning,[276] whose private academies I frequented—a Florentine institution which deserves great praise not only for promoting humane studies but also

[274] No information has been found concerning the "recommendation of others," but it is known that Wotton himself gave Milton access to the British embassy in Paris. In his letter he mentions "a few lines" to Michael Braithwaite who had served with Wotton at Venice and who was then tutor to James, son of John (not Thomas as Milton states) Scudamore, Viscount of Sligo, the ambassador of King Charles at Paris.

[275] Milton's desire to meet Hugo Grotius (1583–1645) is easily understandable. His pioneer work in international law, epitomized in *De Jure Belli et Pacis* (Paris, 1625), had made him a figure of European fame. His work in other fields, however, attracted Milton's interest even more strongly. In *Tetrachordon,* published in the year of Grotius' death, Milton refers to him as "yet living, and of prime note among learned men" (*Complete Prose,* II, 715). Elsewhere in the divorce tracts he cites Grotius as an authority five times (*Complete Prose,* II, 238, 329, 335, 344, 434). The writings that most interested Milton in 1638, however, were probably his Latin poems, *Poemata Collecta* (Leyden, 1617; PUL), and his religious plays, *Adamus Exul* (The Hague, 1601) and *Christus Patiens* (in *Poemata*), the latter translated by George Sandys in 1640. The title of the second play was used by Milton in the Cambridge Manuscript list of possible topics for tragedies. It may certainly be assumed that *Adamus Exul* had some place in Milton's thoughts when he considered the subject of Adam and Eve. For a full discussion of the matter see A. W. Verity, Milton: *Paradise Lost,* II, xlviii–1 (2 vols., Cambridge, 1929).

[276] How Milton "at once" made his way in Florentine literary and social circles remains a mystery. No letters of introduction to eminent Florentines are known. Milton was not then a prominent personage or a scholar whose approach might have been heralded. The only certain dates in his stay are his letter to Benedetto Buonmattei, subscribed "Septemb. 10, 1638" (*Complete Prose,* I, 328–32), and a record of his reading a Latin poem in the Svogliati Academy six days later (French, *Life Records,* I, 389). French believes that Milton arrived late in August. The letter to Buonmattei indicates that acquaintance had already developed. Milton's "at once" may therefore be accepted as reasonably correct. For an attempt at a calendar of Milton's Italian journey, see French, I, 366–421.

for encouraging friendly intercourse.[277] Time will never destroy my recollection—ever welcome and delightful—of you, Jacopo Gaddi,[278] Carlo Dati,[279] Frescobaldi,[280] Coltellini,[281] Buonmattei,[282] Chimen-

[277] Although Milton was impressed by the Florentine academies, he was not unaware of their weaknesses. In *Areopagitica* (*Complete Prose,* II, 537–38) he admits that the members "did nothing but bemoan the servil condition into which learning amongst them was brought." Milton knew four Florentine academies: the Svogliati or "The Disgusted," which was founded by Jacobo Gaddi and met in his home; the Apatisti or "The Indifferent," which grew out of meetings in the home of Agostino Coltellini; the Della Crusca; and the Florentine Academy, a more formal and official body. Most of Milton's Italian friends appear to have been members of all four, and he seems to have been welcome at the gatherings of all, but his only appearances of record were before the Svogliati. On his first visit to Florence, according to Stern (*Milton und Seine Zeit* [4 vols., Leipzig, 1877–1879], II, 449), he read "a very learned piece of Latin Poetry." On his return visit he appeared at the meetings of March 17, 24, 31, 1639. Again he read Latin poems. Milton himself says of these readings in *Church-Government* (*Complete Prose,* I, 809–10) that they consisted of some trifles which he had in memory and other things which he managed to patch up after he reached Italy.

[278] Jacopo Gaddi, a man of aristocratic background and substantial means, seems to have exercised wide influence in cultural circles through his extreme sociability and his generosity to writers and scholars. Before Milton met him, he had published *Poemata* (1628), *Elogia* (1636), and *Adlocutiones* (1637), but his principal work, *De Scriptoribus non-ecclesiasticis, Graecis, Latinis, Italicis,* 2 volumes folio, did not appear until 1648 (CUL). It is interesting that in Milton's only extant letter to Carlo Dati (*Complete Prose,* II, 765) he sends greetings to "all the members of the Gaddian Academy," but omits Gaddi by name. Apparently he stood out in memory as the symbol of a group rather than as an individual.

[279] Carlo Roberto Dati (1619–1676) was obviously the closest friend Milton made in Italy. Though only nineteen when they met and not yet established as a writer, he appears to have been precocious in learning and eloquence. His most important book, *Vite de' Pittori Antichi* (1667; CUL), a study of the four principal Greek painters of antiquity, was not published until 1667, long after his correspondence with Milton had ceased. When they parted in 1639, Milton carried with him the panegyric Dati had addressed to him. This bit of youthful exuberance he cherished in silence until he prepared his first volume. It appeared in the 1645 volume, p. 10, with other tributes from Italian friends, among the "Testimonia," which precede the Latin poems. Milton mentions Dati by name in "Epitaphium Damonis," ll. 171–76, and refers to gifts received from him at parting. Of the six letters Dati wrote Milton only two are extant (*Complete Prose,* II, 766–75); they are warm with affection and admiration. The one extant letter of Milton to Dati (*Complete Prose,* II, 762–65) has the same qualities.

[280] Pietro Frescobaldi, a descendant of an old Florentine family, was a close friend of Coltellini, and one of the original members of the Apatisti. Nothing is known of his writings.

[281] Agostino Coltellini (1613–1693) was a lawyer of wide repute. Forced by ill health to give up practice, he turned to writing, but his chief distinction comes from his establishment and development of the Apatisti and from his activity in the other academies.

[282] Benedetto Buonmattei (1581–1647) was a priest until 1626, when he

telli,[283] Francini,[284] and many others.[285]

From Florence I traveled to Siena and thence to Rome. When the antiquity and venerable repute of that city had detained me for almost two months [286] and I had been graciously entertained there by Lukas

---

removed to Pisa and became a teacher. His fame rests on his *Lingua Toscana* (Florence, 1643), a systematic study of Tuscan grammar. This book, published in part but still in progress in 1638, interested Milton greatly. Before he left Florence he wrote Buonmattei a long letter in Latin (*Complete Prose,* I, 328–32) in which he urged, for the benefit of foreigners, two additions to the book: an appendix giving correct pronunciations of Tuscan words, and a critical bibliography of Italian writers as a guide to reading.

283 Valerio Chimentelli (1620–1668) was graduated in law at Pisa in 1643. His main interest, however, was teaching, and in 1648 he became professor of Greek at Pisa. His only published work, *Marmor Pisanum de Honore Biselli* (BML), appeared at Bologna in 1666. Although he lived in Pisa most of his adult life, he was a member of the four Florentine academies. In the Accademia della Crusca he was appointed, in 1650, a member of a select committee to prepare a third edition of its celebrated Italian dictionary, *Vocabolario degli Accademici della Crusca* (1686; BML). Chimentelli was ordained to the priesthood in 1662.

284 Antonio Francini, known for his lyric verse, expressed his admiration for Milton in a long Italian ode (Columbia, I, 157–65), which was included in the "Testimonia," which preceded the Latin poems in the 1645 volume, pp. 5–9. He is also mentioned with Dati in "Epitaphium Damonis," l. 137, as one who made Milton's name known in Italy.

285 Of the "many" other Florentine friends three are known by name: Vincenzo Galilei, a natural son of Galileo, who united in sending greetings to Milton in a letter of Dati, dated December 4, 1648 (*Complete Prose,* II, 774–75); Antonio Malatesti (d. 1672) to whom Milton sent greetings in a letter to Dati, dated April 21, 1647 (*Complete Prose,* II, 762–65) and from whom Milton received the manuscript, dedicated to him, of *La Trina,* a sequence of fifty sonnets on indecent themes; and Selvaggi, an unknown poet, whose couplet in Milton's praise was printed among the "Testimonia" in the 1645 volume. The seven men Milton names do not survive even in standard reference books. Masson (I, 773–86) assembled a considerable but incomplete mass of fact about them. See Edward Rosen, "A Friend of Milton: Valerio Chimentelli," *Bulletin of the New York Public Library,* LVII (1953), 159–74.

286 Nowhere does Milton refer to the works of art which confronted him at every turn in Italy. Rome he calls a place of "antiquity and venerable repute," a place haunted by the physical and intellectual grandeur of the capital of the ancient world. All around him, however, were the living evidences in painting, sculpture, and architecture of the culture of the present and of the immediate past, still fresh and luminous as they had come from the hands of their creators. In his visits to the Vatican, for example, he must have had at least glimpses of the sublime frescoes by Raphael and Michelangelo. His Protestantism does not explain his silence, for he remained within the orbit of Anglican ceremonial at least until 1632, and he was never a wrecker of organs or a smasher of stained glass. Furthermore, since he cherished other arts such as music, he cannot be thought of as hostile to art in principle.

Holste[287] and other men endowed with both learning and wit,[288] I proceeded to Naples. [84] Here I was introduced by a certain Eremite Friar, with whom I had made the journey from Rome, to Giovanni Battista Manso, Marquis of Villa,[289] a man of high rank and influence, to whom the famous Italian poet, Torquato Tasso, dedicated his work on friendship.[290] As long as I was there I found him a very true friend. He personally conducted me through the various quarters of the city and the Viceregal Court, and more than once came to my lodgings to call. When I was leaving he gravely apologized because even though he had especially wished to show me many more attentions, he could not do so in that city, since I was unwilling to be circumspect in regard to religion.[291] Although I desired also to cross to Sicily and

[287] In sharp contrast to his exuberant references to literary friends and associations in Florence is Milton's limited mention of like experiences in Rome. He notes by name only Luc Holste or Holstenius (1596–1661), a German scholar, who, after many vicissitudes, became librarian to Cardinal Francesco Barberini in 1627 and later librarian of the Vatican. In a letter to Holstenius (*Complete Prose* I, 332–36), written soon after his return to England, Milton mentions his courtesy in showing him books and manuscripts in the Vatican Library and in introducing him to Cardinal Barberini, a patron of music as well as of letters. For fuller note of Milton's relations with Holstenius and Barberini, see Masson, I, 798–805, and French, I, 389–92.

[288] Milton refers to only two other literary friends in Rome. One is Alessandro Cherubini, reputedly a man of vast learning, who died when he was twenty-eight; he is mentioned in Milton's letter to Holstenius. The other is Giovanni Salzilli, a poet now almost unknown, whose Latin quatrain exalting Milton above Homer, Virgil, and Tasso, was printed in the "Testimonia," p. 4, preceding the Latin poems in the 1645 edition. Among Milton's own Latin verses appears "Ad Salsillum."

[289] A prolific writer of poems, dialogues, and biographies, John Baptista Manso, Marquis of Villa (1561–1647), and a rewarding literary friend in his own right, had been the patron of Marino and Tasso, and so was a living link with one of Milton's favorite poets. In the poetry he appears three times: in "Mansus," ll. 78–84, in which Milton lauds him as a writer and patron and reveals his own plans for an epic on British history; the "Testimonia," in which appears a distich by Manso; finally in "Epitaphium Damonis," ll. 235–55, where Milton mentions farewell gifts presented to him by Manso. See Walter MacKellar, *The Latin Poems of John Milton* (New Haven, 1930), p. 349; and Michele De Filippis, "Milton and Manso: Cups or Books," *PMLA,* LI (1936), 745–56.

[290] This book, begun in 1594 during Tasso's last visit to his patron's villa, was titled *Il Manso* and dedicated to Manso, who is one of the speakers in the dialogue.

[291] It appears that Milton was not highly successful in adhering to the letter of Wotton's maxim (see above, p. 614, n. 273). The frank reference to Manso's apology is echoed, without significant variation, in the "Earliest Life" (Darbishire, p. 20), in Phillips (Darbishire, pp. 57–58), and in Wood (Darbishire, pp. 37–38). Manso himself, in his Latin distich prefixed to the Latin poems of 1645 (p. 4), expresses the matter more suavely. Using the familiar pun of St. Augus-

Greece,[292] the sad tidings of civil war from England summoned me back.[293] For I thought it base that I should travel abroad at my ease for the cultivation of my mind, while my fellow-citizens at home were fighting for liberty.[294] As I was on the point of returning to Rome, I was warned by merchants [85] that they had learned through letters of plots laid against me by the English Jesuits, should I return to Rome, because of the freedom with which I had spoken about religion. For I had determined within myself that in those parts I would not indeed begin a conversation about religion, but if questioned about my faith would hide nothing, whatever the consequences. And so, I nonetheless returned to Rome.[295] What I was, if any man inquired, I concealed from no one. For almost two more months, in the very stronghold of the Pope, if anyone attacked the orthodox religion, I openly, as before, defended it.[296] Thus, by the will of God, I returned again in safety to Florence, revisiting friends who were as anxious to see me as if it were my native land to which I had returned. After gladly lingering there for as many months as before (except for an excursion of a few days to Lucca) [297] I crossed the Apennines and hastened to Venice by way of Bologna and Ferrara. When I had spent one month exploring that city and had seen to the shipping of the books [298] which I had acquired throughout Italy, I proceeded to

---

tine of Canterbury, he says that Milton would be an angel rather than an Angle if his piety equaled his other virtues. By piety Manso obviously means Roman Catholicism.

[292] To Milton Sicily and Greece were less historic places than literary shrines. Having visited Italy, the land of Virgil and Tasso, he wanted to see the island of Theocritus and the country of Homer, Euripides, and Plato.

[293] What specific news Milton received is not known. He apparently refers to the first bishops' war (March, 1639).

[294] Many have characterized this as a pretentious statement, and some have derided it because Milton spent months on his return trip. He was sufficiently perceptive to realize that the war with the Scots was essentially an incident, though an important one, in the fundamental struggle between king and Parliament.

[295] Milton's detractors have ridiculed this passage as a melodramatic plea to be regarded as a potential martyr. It is, however, notably factual. For a well balanced statement of this point, see John S. Diekhoff, *Milton on Himself,* pp. xxx–xxxii.

[296] Milton well knew the claims to orthodoxy asserted by the pope, and he was fully aware of the fact that he was a guest in the one city where those claims were pre-eminently accepted. But he dissented, for in his conscience he believed that orthodoxy lay elsewhere.

[297] The ancestral home of the Diodati family.

[298] No list of these books is known to exist, but Phillips (Darbishire, p. 59) speaks of them as "a parcel of curious and rare books which he had picked up in

Geneva by way of Verona, Milan, and the Pennine Alps, and then along Lake Leman. [86] Geneva, since it reminds me of the slanderer More, impels me once again to call God to witness that in all these places, where so much licence exists, I lived free and untouched by the slightest sin or reproach, reflecting constantly that although I might hide from the gaze of men, I could not elude the sight of God.[299] In Geneva I conversed daily with John Diodati, the learned professor of theology.[300] Then by the same route as before, through France, I returned home after a year and three months, more or less, at almost the same time as Charles broke the peace and renewed the war with the Scots, which is known as the second Bishops' War.[301]

The royalist troops were routed in the first engagement of this war,[302] and Charles, when he perceived that all the English, as well as the Scots, were extremely—and justly— ill-disposed towards him, soon convened Parliament, not of his own free will but compelled

---

his travels; particularly a chest or two of choice music-books of the best masters flourishing about that time in Italy."

[299] The mere mention of Geneva provides the occasion for a new gibe at More and for a repeated justification of his own morals. In order to explain his own moral position, Milton again (above, p. 587, n. 173) paraphrases the collect which opens "The Order for the Administration of Holy Communion," in *The Book of Common Prayer*.

[300] Giovanni Diodati (1576–1649), an eminent theologian and teacher, was an expatriate from his native Lucca because of his conversion to Protestantism. Early in his career he attracted the favorable notice of the reformers in Geneva, and in 1597 he was appointed professor of Hebrew there on the recommendation of Beza. In 1606 he became professor of theology, and two years later he was ordained a pastor of Geneva. An eloquent preacher, he took a leading part in the Synod of Dort (1618–1619), and was one of the six divines appointed to write the official account of the proceedings. Diodati was a prolific writer. His most famous work is a translation of the Bible into Italian (1603, revised with notes, 1607). He published also an annotated translation of the Bible into French (1644). Though Milton would naturally have been interested in meeting so eminent a Protestant leader as Diodati, he cherished his visit to Geneva and to Villa Diodati even more because this notable man was also the uncle of Milton's dearest friend, Charles Diodati.

[301] Wotton's letter to Milton (see above, p. 614, n. 273) was dated April 13, 1638. Since its contents suggest Milton's early departure, it may be supposed that he left for the Continent by early May. If he was away about fifteen months, he must have returned to England in late August or early September of 1639. His historical references in this passage are, therefore, somewhat confused. The first bishops' war ended at the Peace of Berwick, signed June 18, 1639. At that time Charles agreed, obviously with tongue in cheek, to settle Scottish grievances in a Parliament and a Scottish Assembly. He broke the peace and went into action on August 20, 1640, thus beginning the second bishops' war.

[302] As Milton says, the second bishops' war was quickly over. The Scots invaded England on August 20, 1640, and almost immediately laid siege to Newcastle. A

by disaster.[303] I myself, seeking a place to become established, could I but find one anywhere in such upset and tumultuous times, rented a house in town, sufficiently commodious for myself and my books, [81] and there, blissfully enough, devoted myself to my interrupted studies,[304] willingly leaving the outcome of these events, first of all to God, and then to those whom the people had entrusted with this office.[305] Meanwhile, as Parliament acted with vigor, the haughtiness of the bishops began to deflate. As soon as freedom of speech (at the very least) became possible, all mouths were opened against them. Some complained of the personal defects of the bishops, others of the defectiveness of the episcopal rank itself.[306] It was wrong, they said, that their church alone should differ from all other reformed churches.[307] It was proper for the church to be governed by the example of the brethren, but first of all by the word of God.[308] Now,

week later, the king led an army from York to relieve the city, but on the following day the Scots won a decisive victory at the Battle of Newburn. Two days later, they invested Newcastle.

303 The military defeat of Charles by the Scots dealt a very severe blow to his prestige. The war was unpopular with large sections of the English people, particularly those of Puritan tendency. They resented the idea of forcing Laud's policies on their fellow Protestants in Scotland. Ignominious defeat intensified their antagonism. Milton is correct in saying that Charles called Parliament in desperation. See Gardiner, ***History of England,*** IX, 84 ff.

304 Milton's first lodgings after his return from the continent were in the house of a merchant tailor named Russel in St. Bride's Churchyard, near Fleet Street. There he conducted a school for his two nephews, Edward and John Phillips. See French, II, 609, and Darbishire, pp. 60–62. At a date not known, but soon thereafter, he removed to a larger house in Aldersgate Street, where (French, II, 9–11) he enlarged his school. It is interesting that Milton mentions his "interrupted studies" but not his school.

305 This statement of renunciation tends to suggest that, either at the time of the events he gave serious thought to participation in the struggle against the church and the crown, or that, fifteen years later, he wanted to believe or desired others to believe that he shunned public duty only because he realized that he could add nothing to the efforts of Parliament.

306 Though Milton omits details, his reporting here is accurate. The first business of the House of Commons, under John Pym's leadership, was the impeachment of Strafford. While evidence on this matter was being amassed and sifted, however, the attack on the bishops began. See *Complete Prose,* I, 56–76, 87–92; C. V. Wedgwood, ***The King's Peace*** (New York: Macmillan, 1955), pp. 369–80.

307 Milton made little if any distinction between the terms Catholic and Roman Catholic. Since the Church of England was a "reformed church," it should, like the other "reformed churches," be totally Protestant and therefore eschew Episcopacy, which he associated solely with the Roman Catholic Church.

308 Even more important than to conform to the example of the Protestant brethren was it to abide by the words of Scripture. As Milton read and translated the relevant parts of the New Testament, in particular Acts and the Epistles of

thoroughly aroused to these concerns, I perceived that men were following the true path to liberty and that from these beginnings, these first steps, they were making the most direct progress towards the liberation of all human life from slavery—provided that the discipline arising from religion should overflow into the morals and institutions of the state.[309] Since, moreover, I had so practiced myself from youth that I was above all things unable to disregard the laws of God and man, and since I had asked myself whether I should be of any future use [88] if I now failed my country (or rather the church and so many of my brothers who were exposing themselves to danger for the sake of the Gospel) I decided, although at that time occupied with certain other matters,[310] to devote to this conflict all my talents and all my active powers.[311]

First, therefore, I addressed to a certain friend two books on the reformation of the English church.[312] Then, since two bishops of

---

St. Paul, he found no justification for the traditional orders of clergy, that is bishops, priests, and deacons. In his opinion, therefore, the Church of England was neither reformed nor Scriptural in retaining these orders. See introduction, *Complete Prose,* I, 112 ff.

[309] In expressing his approval of the actions of Parliament, Milton emphasizes an important aspect of his own thinking. He praises the attack on Episcopacy as the beginning of man's liberation, but he insists that the state must rest upon the discipline of religion. See Milton's antiprelatical pamphlets in *Complete Prose,* I, 514–953.

[310] What these matters were remains a subject of conjecture. Milton was probably concerned with studies and plans rather than with specific compositions. "Manso" and "Epitaphium Damonis" suggest that he was thinking of an epic on British history and attempting to make a choice between Latin and English as his medium. Hanford shows that Milton was actively at work on his *Commonplace Book* during this period. See "The Chronology of Milton's Private Studies," *PMLA,* XXXVI (1921), 251. In his letter to Dati (*Complete Prose,* II, 702–65) Milton himself says that "the most turbulent state of our Britain, subsequent to my return home . . . obliged me to divert my mind shortly afterwards from the prosecution of my studies."

[311] Exactly when Milton decided not to become a priest and when he forsook the discipline of the Church of England cannot be stated with certainty. He was still an Anglican when he left Cambridge in 1632, but there is strong evidence to support the belief that he had renounced the priesthood by that time. In "Ad Patrem" (1632?) he announced his intention to follow none of the learned professions, and in "Letter to a Friend" (1633) he stated, with obvious embarrassment, his belief that his destiny did not lie within the church. He seems to have been unwilling, however, to make an open break until he wrote "Lycidas." See *Church-Government* (*Complete Prose,* I, 804–805, 821–23).

[312] *Of Reformation Touching Church-Discipline in England.* See *Complete Prose,* I, 514 ff.

particularly high repute [313] were asserting their prerogatives against certain eminent ministers,[314] and I concluded that on those subjects which I had mastered solely for love of truth and out of regard for Christian duty, I could express myself at least as well as those who were wrangling for their own profit and unjust authority,[315] I replied to one of the bishops in two books, of which the first was entitled *Of Prelatical Episcopacy* [316] and the second *The Reason of Church-Government,*[317] while to the other bishop I made reply in certain *Animadversions* and later in an *Apology.*[318] I brought succor to the ministers, who were, as it was said, scarcely able to withstand the eloquence of this bishop, and from that time onward, if the bishops made any response, I took a hand.[319] When they, having become a target for the weapons of all men, had at last fallen and troubled us no more,[320]

313 James Ussher (1581–1656), archbishop of Armagh, and Joseph Hall (1574–1656), bishop of Norwich. For sketches of Hall and Ussher and their significance to Milton, see *Complete Prose,* I, 48–56, 76–86, 104, 115–23.

314 Milton has in mind particularly the five Independent clergymen whose initials formed the name "Smectymnuus." They were Stephen Marshall, Edmund Calamy, Thomas Young, Matthew Newcomen, and William Spurstow. For an account of Smectymnuus, see *Complete Prose,* I, 1001–1008.

315 The contempt here is for the Episcopalians to whom Milton denies any sense of disinterestedness. By contrast, he did not believe that the authority of the Independents was unjust. The words "wrangling" and "unjust" beg the question.

316 The bishop was archbishop Ussher. *Of Prelatical Episcopacy* (*Complete Prose,* I, 618–652), Milton's second prose tract, was published anonymously in June or July, 1641. Although on the title page Milton singles out archbishop Ussher by name, he replies also to bishop Hall and others.

317 *The Reason of Church-Government Urg'd against Prelaty,* Milton's fourth prose tract, was the first to bear his name on the title page. See *Complete Prose,* I, 736–81.

318 Bishop Hall, Milton says, was the target of his third and fifth antiprelatical tracts. These are: *Animadversions* (*Complete Prose,* I, 653–735), published anonymously in July, 1641, a fierce and generally unjust attack on bishop Hall; and *An Apology* (*Complete Prose,* I, 862–953), published anonymously early in 1642, a further castigation of bishop Hall. Both pamphlets were motivated by Milton's desire to defend Smectymnuus.

319 Milton mixes his tenses here, but his intention is clear. He poses the threat that, if the bishops continue the controversy, he will meet their arguments. Though for the rest of his life he was never far from dispute with the clergy of one church or another, he had finished his formal debate on Episcopacy.

320 Milton here refers to a series of legislative actions designed at first to curtail, and later to destroy, the power of the bishops. Beginning with the presentation to Parliament of the "Root and Branch" petition on December 11, 1640, the war on the bishops was waged relentlessly. See *Complete Prose,* I, 63 ff.

I directed my attention elsewhere, [89] asking myself whether I could in any way advance the cause of true and substantial liberty, which must be sought, not without, but within, and which is best achieved, not by the sword, but by a life rightly undertaken and rightly conducted.[321] Since, then, I observed that there are, in all, three varieties of liberty without which civilized life is scarcely possible, namely ecclesiastical liberty, domestic or personal liberty, and civil liberty, and since I had already written about the first, while I saw that the magistrates were vigorously attending to the third, I took as my province the remaining one, the second or domestic kind. This too seemed to be concerned with three problems: the nature of marriage itself, the education of the children, and finally the existence of freedom to express oneself.[322] Hence I set forth my views on marriage, not only its proper contraction, but also, if need be, its dissolution.[323] My explanation was in accordance with divine law, which Christ did not revoke; much less did He give approval in civil life to any other law more weighty than the law of Moses.[324] [90] Concerning the view which should be held on the single exception, that of

[321] Milton is about to summarize a number of his writings which had aroused bitter debate and had brought upon him widespread condemnation. A statement of high principle here, therefore, helps to lift these writings from an area of popular dispute to the realm of abstract ideas.

[322] This passage has been central to many discussions of Milton's accuracy and complete honesty in his autobiographical passages. The arrangement of his prose writings is so neat that many have wondered whether it is a plan he laid out fully before he composed the pamphlets or an *ex post facto* scheme devised to give greater dignity to writings which grew out of less lofty purposes. Since questions of motive are involved, no final answer can be given with certainty. For the best summary of the problem, see John S. Diekhoff, *Milton on Himself,* introduction, pp. xv–xvii and *passim;* and p. 23, n. 17.

[323] As a matter of fact, Milton has a great deal to say about the positive aspects of marriage as well as about its collapse and dissolution. See, for example, Milton's interpretation of a true marriage in *Doctrine and Discipline of Divorce, Complete Prose,* II, 245–47, 330–33.

[324] Milton here notes a theological point that has seldom been the subject of comment or study. In the words attributed to Jesus in the Gospels he teaches in terms of moral or spiritual values and refrains from setting forth a code of behavior for specific situations in civil life. For example, when asked a precise question about taxes, he replied (Mark 12:17): "Render to Caesar the things that are Caesar's, and to God the things that are God's," a statement so unspecific and so totally spiritual that it had led to confusion. Milton thinks it unusual, therefore, that Jesus answers specifically (Matthew 5:31, 19:3–9 and Mark 10:2–12) questions about marriage and divorce, which he considers matters civil rather than sacramental.

fornication, I also expressed both my own opinion and that of others. Our distinguished countryman Selden still more fully explained this point in his *Hebrew Wife,*[325] published about two years later. For in vain does he prattle about liberty in assembly and market-place who at home endures the slavery most unworthy of man, slavery to an inferior.[326] Concerning this matter then I published several books,[327] at the very time when man and wife were often bitter foes, he dwelling at home with their children, she, the mother of the family, in the camp of the enemy, threatening her husband with death and disaster.[328] Next, in one small volume, I discussed the education of children,[329] a brief treatment, to be sure, but sufficient, as I thought, for those who devote to the subject the attention it deserves. For nothing can be more efficacious than education in moulding the minds of men to virtue (whence arises true and internal liberty), in governing the state effectively, and preserving it for the longest possible space of time.

Lastly I wrote, on the model of a genuine speech, the *Areo-*

[325] Obviously Milton introduces this reference to Selden in order to gain prestige for his own discussion of the basis of divorce under ancient Hebrew law. John Selden (1584–1654), a leader in the struggle of Parliament with the king, an eminent jurist, and a notable scholar, published the book Milton mentions, *Uxor Ebraica seu De Nuptiis et Divortiis Veterum Ebraeorum Libri Tres,* in 1646 (BML). It could not, therefore, have influenced Milton's thinking and writing on divorce, but it now serves as confirmation of his views by a learned man.

[326] Milton accepts the Hebraic view that women are inferior to men. Even in *Paradise Lost,* where he idealizes the love of Adam and Eve, he is mindful of the words of St. Paul: "the head of a woman is her husband" (I Corinthians 11:3), and "Neither was man created for woman, but woman for man" (I Corinthians 11:9). The idea is discussed in *Christian Doctrine* (Columbia, XV, 121). When this way of God and nature is reversed by a wife's tyranny in indissoluble marriage, the slavery of the husband is particularly galling.

[327] See Milton's four tracts on divorce in *Complete Prose,* II: *Doctrine and Discipline* (1643), pp. 217–356; *Martin Bucer* (1644), pp. 416–79; *Tetrachordon* (1645), pp. 571–718; *Colasterion* (1645), pp. 719–58.

[328] Milton appears to contradict himself. Previously (see above, n. 322), he spoke of his divorce tracts as part of a large plan, objectively conceived, for the liberation of men in various areas of life. Here, however, he seems to consider them topical works designed to meet a wartime situation. Civil war has broken apart families emotionally and spiritually, but inadequate provisions for divorce hold them in unnatural unity. The melodramatic tone is sharply at variance with the objectivity he previously professed. Again (above, n. 326) the personal application should be resisted. The conditions he describes bear little resemblance to his own situation.

[329] *Of Education* was first published in 1644 as a pamphlet of eight pages without title page. See *Complete Prose,* II, 357–415.

pagitica,[330] concerning freedom of the press, that the judgment of truth and [91] falsehood, what should be printed and what suppressed, ought not to be in the hands of a few men (and these mostly ignorant and of vulgar discernment) charged with the inspection of books, at whose will or whim virtually everyone is prevented from publishing aught that surpasses the understanding of the mob. Civil liberty, which was the last variety, I had not touched upon, for I saw that it was being adequately dealt with by the magistrates, nor did I write anything about the right of kings, until the king, having been declared an enemy by Parliament and vanquished in the field, was pleading his cause as a prisoner before the judges and was condemned to death.[331] Then at last, when certain Presbyterian ministers, formerly bitter enemies of Charles, but now resentful that the Independent parties were preferred to theirs and carried more weight in Parliament, persisted in attacking the decree which Parliament had passed concerning the king (wroth, not because of the fact, but because their own faction had not performed it) and caused as much tumult as they could, even daring to assert that the doctrines of Protestants and all reformed churches shrank from such an outrageous sentence against kings,[332] [92] I concluded that I must openly oppose so open a lie. Not even then, however, did I write or advise anything concerning Charles, but demonstrated what was in general permissible against tyrants, adducing not a few testimonies from the foremost theologians. And I attacked, almost as if I were haranguing an assembly, the pre-eminent ignorance or insolence of these ministers, who had given promise of better things. This book [333] did not appear until after the death of

[330] *Areopagitica,* published in 1644. See *Complete Prose,* II, 480–570.

[331] This clause contains some looseness of language which may lead the reader to inaccurate inferences. Since he uses the verb *scribo,* Milton intends to say that he "wrote" nothing about kings rather than that he published nothing. The date of *Tenure* makes this impossible. He uses the word Parliament as if it were the duly constituted body, but actually it was the "Rump" created by Pride's Purge.

[332] Milton is not entirely fair to the Presbyterians. The fact that they cooperated with the Independents in efforts to control the absolutist policies of Charles and to exalt the powers of Parliament did not logically require them, as Milton suggests, to accept the plan to try and execute the king. Furthermore they had no opportunity to debate or vote upon the fate of the king since their representatives had been purged from the Commons before the matter was considered.

[333] *The Tenure* was published early in 1649; Thomason's copy is dated February 13th. Citing holy Scripture and secular history and quoting such Protestant theologians as Luther and Calvin, Milton argues that there is ample justification for a people to resort to direct action in order to rid itself of a tyrannical ruler. See

the king, having been written to reconcile men's minds, rather than to determine anything about Charles (which was not my affair, but that of the magistrates, and which had by then been effected). This service of mine, between private walls, I freely gave, now to the church and now to the state.[334] To me, in return, neither the one nor the other offered more than protection, but the deeds themselves undoubtedly bestowed on me a good conscience, good repute among good men, and this honorable freedom of speech. Other men gained for themselves advantages, other men secured offices at no cost to themselves. [93] As for me, no man has ever seen me seeking office, no man has ever seen me soliciting aught through my friends, clinging with suppliant expression to the doors of Parliament, or loitering in the hallways of the lower assemblies. I kept myself at home for the most part, and from my own revenues, though often they were in large part withheld because of the civil disturbance, I endured the tax—by no means entirely just—that was laid on me and maintained my frugal way of life.[335]

When these works had been completed and I thought that I could look forward to an abundance of leisure, I turned to the task of tracing in unbroken sequence, if I could, the history of my country, from the earliest origins even to the present day. I had already finished four books [336] when the kingdom of Charles was transformed into a republic, and the so-called Council of State,[337] which was then for the

---

introduction, *Complete Prose,* III, 147–258; and William Haller, *Liberty and Reformation,* pp. 347–54.

[334] Milton was very resentful of implications that he was a writer paid to serve causes he considered just. He was eager and proud, therefore, to take every possible occasion to proclaim the fact that he wrote as a private citizen, unsolicited and unpaid, as he had done until he was called to the service of the Council of State.

[335] In 1647 Milton had given up his house in Barbican and removed to a smaller one in High Holborn. It is probable that income from properties outside London was delayed or lost because of war conditions, but Milton had inherited substantial holdings from his father, and it is unlikely that he was in any serious financial difficulty.

[336] Milton's references to time here are somewhat hazy. He states that after the completion of *Tenure,* almost certainly in January, 1649, he turned to his history and that when he was called to public office in mid-March, 1649, he had completed four books. Whenever it was begun, *The History of Britain* was not published until 1670. It is in six books, and narrates British history from legendary beginnings through the Battle of Hastings.

[337] The transformation of the kingdom into a republic was accomplished rapidly once it began. It started on January 4, 1649, when the Commons passed three statements of basic principle: (1) that the people were the source of all power,

first time established by the authority of Parliament, summoned me, though I was expecting no such event, and desired to employ my services, especially in connection with foreign affairs.[338] Not long afterwards there appeared a book attributed to the king, and plainly written with great malice against Parliament.[339] Bidden to reply to this, I opposed to the *Eikon* the *Eikonoklastes,*[340] not, as I am falsely charged, "insulting the departed spirit of the king," but thinking that Queen Truth should be preferred to King Charles. [94] Indeed, since I saw that this slander would be at hand for any calumniator, in the very introduction (and as often as I could elsewhere) I averted this reproach from myself.[341] Then Salmasius appeared. So far were they from spending a long time (as More alleges) seeking one who would reply to him, that all, of their own accord, at once named me, then present in the Council.[342] I have given an account of myself to this

(2) that the Commons, as the representatives of the people, alone exercised that power, and (3) that the acts of the Commons did not require the consent of the king or the House of Lords. The officers' *Agreement of the People,* presented to the Commons on January 20, set forth the organization of the new state. The execution of the king on January 30 and the abolition of the House of Lords on February 6 effectively destroyed the old regime. See Masson, IV, 2–19, and Gardiner, *Great Civil War,* IV, 262 ff., 288 ff.

[338] At a meeting of the Council of State on March 13, 1649, Milton was nominated for the office of Secretary for the Foreign Tongues to the Council, and a committee was authorized to wait upon him in order to ask his consent to election. The committee acted promptly, for at a meeting of the Council on March 15th Milton was elected and his salary was fixed at £288 13*s.* 6½*d.* a year. On March 20th he took the oath of secrecy and attended his first meeting. Masson (IV, 79, 82, 83) gives pertinent excerpts from the Order Book of the Council, with interesting speculations.

[339] *Eikon Basilike,* one of the most effective pieces of Stuart propaganda, appeared in February, 1649, immediately after the king's death. For a full account of *Eikon,* see *Complete Prose,* III, 150–67; the book went through forty-six editions in English alone.

[340] When Milton was asked by the Council of State to reply to *Eikon* is not known, for the Order Book notes no such request. He here repeats his own statement made in the preface to his reply. It is not likely that he would lay himself open to attack in so critical a spot. No reason is known for the lateness of Milton's reply. *Eikonoklastes* appeared in October, 1649. For a full account, see introduction, *Complete Prose,* III, 147–67; text, III, 335–601.

[341] It is true that *Eikonoklastes* is much less objective in tone than *Tenure.* As he says in *Eikonoklastes,* Milton recognizes a certain impropriety in belaboring a dead man who has paid the extreme penalty for his acts and beliefs; he is not unaware of the resentment a man incurs when he defies the popular dictum, "De mortuis nil nisi bonum."

[342] The Order Book of the Council of State supports this statement. See above, p. 549, n. 7.

extent in order to stop your mouth, More, and refute your lies, chiefly for the sake of those good men who otherwise would know me not. Do you then, I bid you, unclean More, be silent. Hold your tongue, I say! [343] For the more you abuse me, the more copiously will you compel me to account for my conduct. From such accounting you can gain nothing save the reproach, already most severe, of telling lies, while for me you open the door to still higher praise of my own integrity.[344]

I had blamed Salmasius for involving himself in our affairs, when he was an alien and a foreigner. You reply, "This defence is the special business of those who have nothing to do with England." [95] Why? "The English," you say, "may be supposed to act too violently through partisan spirit, but it is commonly agreed that the French have regard for principles, not men." To this I make the same retort as before. No one who is from a foreign land and far removed, as you are, will plunge into the affairs of another country, especially when they are troubled, unless he be bribed. That Salmasius was hired at a price I have proved before.[345] It is well known that you sought a professional chair through Salmasius and the Oranges.[346] Next (and this is more disgraceful) you assail Parliament and you assault Pontia. Furthermore, the reason that you offer, why these events rather concern foreigners, is patently ridiculous. For if Englishmen are carried away by party feelings, what else do you, who follow only English sources, transfer to yourself, if it be not their passions? The result is that, if the English are not to be trusted in their own cause, certainly you are much less to be trusted, who understand nothing of our affairs, or at

[343] Some of Milton's name-calling is very general and therefore somewhat dull. Here, however, he shoots a very sharp barb. He derived it from Mark 1:23–25. A man possessed by an unclean spirit which resisted exorcism approached Jesus and asked for relief. The unclean spirit cried out in protest. Whereupon Jesus said: "Hold thy peace, and come out of him." Milton made certain that his Biblical source would not be overlooked by quoting St. Mark's Greek for the first phrase and by adding the Latin *obmutesce*. Finally he addresses More as *immunde*, thou unclean one.

[344] The more lies More tells about Milton the more opportunities Milton will have to tell the truth about himself and thus explain to the world his actions and his motives. More thus faces a dilemma: to write about Milton and give him fame or to keep silent and leave Milton obscure.

[345] See above, pp. 559–63, nn. 51 and 67. For quotations, see *Clamor* (1652), pp. 10, 12.

[346] For the part Salmasius played in the transfer from Geneva, see above, p. 567, n. 85. The Orange Party was the royalist group in Holland.

least believe nothing except what you have learned from those very persons who, according to your own opinion, are scarcely to be trusted. [96] Here again you extend yourself in praise of the "great" Salmasius. Great he must have been in your estimation, if you employed him as a pimp for his servant girl.[347] And yet you praise him. But he does not praise you. In fact, before his death he publicly cursed you and blamed himself a thousand times because he had not believed Spanheim,[348] the venerable theologian, when Spanheim told him of your impiety. Now, yielding yourself up entirely to madness, you deprive him of reason, so to speak. "Long since Salmasius had done with reason," as you say. You claim for yourself merely the roles of crier and madman, and yet you assign to Salmasius also the first rank in scurrility. "Not because his words are violent, but because he is Salmasius." Babbler! These witticisms we owe, I suppose, to the accommodating Pontia. From her your Cry has learned to prattle and even to chirp. Because of her also, full of threats, you say, "you will some day find out, foul beasts, what the pen can do." Is it you that we shall find out, you lover of servant girls, you adulterer, or your pen, which only maidservants need fear? [349] If anyone should so much as show you a radish-root or a mullet, [97] you would think that you had got off very easily, by Hercules, if you could escape with your rump intact and that vile pen of yours unharmed.[350]

"Indeed," you say, "I am not so empty-headed as to undertake a task begun by Salmasius"—one that he would never have undertaken had not his head been completely empty. How gracious of you to rank the great Salmasius before yourself in empty-headedness! "But to raise to heaven the cry of the King's blood," which even the "unlettered ought to do"—this no doubt you claim as your duty.[351] Cry,

[347] Milton is here quite unfair to Salmasius. More's affair with Bontia was a source of deep embarrassment to him. See above, pp. 568–69, nn. 89, 92, 94, 96.

[348] See above, p. 567, n. 86.

[349] Very skillfully Milton turns More's dire threat of new attacks on the Parliament and on Milton himself into a fresh assault on More's propensity to fornication under sordid conditions. The pun on "pen" makes More ridiculous instead of ominous.

[350] Earlier (see above, p. 579, n. 133), for purposes of gross ridicule, Milton associated Salmasius with sodomy. Here he goes further. More, whom he has portrayed as steeped in sexual passion, fares worse. In language lush with bawdry Milton depicts him, the intrepid seducer, as the subject of punishment for adultery under ancient law. *Cf.* Aristophanes, *The Clouds,* 1083. For quotations from Du Moulin, see *Clamor* (1652), pp., 19, 13.

[351] Milton here gleefully springs the trap which the author of *Clamor* (1652), p. 13 unwittingly set for himself. To strengthen his case, Du Moulin has said

shout, bellow, proceed to play the hypocrite, to appropriate sanctimonious words while you live the life of a Priapus.[352] There will rise up some day, believe me, that God of vengeance, whom you so often invoke. He will rise and he will uproot you among the first, you, a minister of the devil, an unspeakable disgrace and blot on the reformed church. To all who condemn Salmasius' scurrility you reply, "Such treatment was meet for parricides, the vilest of all monsters." I commend you. For you provide us with weapons, you are kind enough to teach us how you ought to be treated, and your bullies as well, and you yourself absolve us from blame. [98] Now, since you can achieve nothing by virtue of reason, you do not even venture to assert the general principle of the right of kings,[353] which was pre-empted by Salmasius,[354] but having alleged everything reasonable in his case and turned from insults and ravings to certain wretched narratives,[355] being yourself devoid of reason, you merely imitate the cries that were sent up at the beginning. Some of them you have warmed over from Salmasius, some of them you have copied down and refurbished from that anonymous *Scrutiny*[356] (itself most deserving of scrutiny) by one who has abandoned not only his country but even his name. To the chief points in these narratives I have already made such reply, either in the *Eikonoklastes* or in my answer to Salmasius,[357] that I do

---

that not the learned only but also the unlettered should protest the king's death. From this statement Milton deliberately draws the wrong inference that his opponent is unlettered.

[352] Son of Aphrodite and Dionysus, Priapus was a god of fertility in gardens. Likening More to him is not just another way of taunting More about sex. It is also a means of calling him grotesque and deformed in a specific way, for the god was portrayed as having an enormously enlarged phallus.

[353] Milton ridicules More because he lacks the reasoning power to deal with the theory of royal prerogative or to argue on broad principles. He does not realize that the real author of *Clamor,* Du Moulin, was familiar with the events of the civil war and of the circumstances of the king's death from the royalist point of view, and was, therefore, able to write more effective propaganda.

[354] In his *Defensio Regia* Salmasius combined a defence of kingship, on theoretical grounds, with vituperation and railing against Charles' enemies. See *A Defence,* above, pp. 301, 302, 303, 304, nn. 1, 2, 5.

[355] Accounts of battles, actions of Parliament, and the dealings of various groups with the king.

[356] Milton is sarcastic about the book Du Moulin used as the basis for his historical facts. Again (see above, p. 598, n. 218) he is vague as to his actual knowledge of the work, but his use of the words "that elenchus" and, in the next sentence, the word *narratives* would seem to indicate that he knew at least the title of Bate's book.

[357] *A Defence.* See above, p. 285.

not think I can say more, short of writing a full history. Must I [358] always tread the very same orbit and repeat what I have said so many times before, at the croaking of any buffoon? I will not do it! I will not thus misuse either my industry or my leisure. If anyone thinks these hired lamentations, these feigned complaints of the most corrupt of men, these petty declamations which are the adulterated and spurious offspring of concubinage with a maidservant, twins of More's little bastard—if anyone thinks these are worthy of belief, [99] I for my part shall waste no time in altering his views, for I have nothing to fear from one so credulous and rash. Nevertheless, I shall touch on a few points, typical of many, from which you may gain a cursory understanding of who he is and what he says, and what should be your judgment about the rest.

After this alien [359] has babbled at length about the reduction of the House of Commons and the House of Lords to one (a demand which no sane person would criticize),[360] he says, "So that, equality having been effected in the state, they might proceed to introduce the same into the church. For at that time the bishops still remained.[361] If this be not pure, undiluted Anabaptist doctrine,[362] I do not know what is." Who would ever have expected this from a theologian and a Gal-

[358] In the rest of this paragraph Milton is, of course, ridiculing the lack of imagination, the repetitiousness, and the generally low character of his opponent's material. Implicit is a note of sadness and frustration evoked by the loss of leisure needed for the writing of greater works than tracts.

[359] To intensify his contempt for More's ignorance of British affairs, Milton calls him *exoticus,* late Latin for heathen, instead of *alienus,* classical Latin for *foreigner.*

[360] In an excess of zeal Milton here accepts an untrue statement by his opponent. He approved the elimination of the House of Lords, but he well knew that it was destroyed not by being merged with the Commons but by its being declared not necessary to the enactment of legislation. In fact, it became non-existent in 1649 and remained so until the Restoration. The only peers in the government were those in the Council of State or those who stood for election to the House of Commons.

[361] This is a puzzling statement. Milton fails to correct or clarify it. Those who had been consecrated bishops before 1649 and who had not died by that year still "remained" in the sense that they were alive. They had not exercised Episcopal functions, however, since 1646. On October 9 of that year Parliament completely abolished the rule of bishops and archbishops in the church (See *Complete Prose,* I, 1012).

[362] Du Moulin here intends a particularly telling slur. He must have known that the Anabaptists had little or no influence on the doctrines or the structure of the new church in England. He certainly knew that they were strongly opposed to hierarchical organization and that they resented the intrusion of external authority on the congregations. He really does not care to cite facts; he wishes merely to associate with the Independents a currently unpopular name. See *Clamor* (1652), p. 28.

lican minister? Surely one who does not know what Anabaptist doctrine is, if it be not this, does not, I should think, possess a clearer notion of the nature of baptism.[363] But if we should prefer to call things by their proper names, equality in the state is not Anabaptist doctrine; it is democracy, a much more ancient thing.[364] If established principally in the church, it is [100] the apostolic discipline.[365] But "The bishops still remained." We admit it, and they still remained in Geneva too when that state expelled in the name of religion the bishop who was also their legitimate ruler.[366] Why is that which is a source of praise for them considered a reproach against us? I know what you wish, More. You seek to take vengeance for the votes of the Genevans. It is still uncertain whether you were dismissed by them in disgrace or excommunicated from their church. It appears, therefore, that you, with your Salmasius, have revolted from this evangelical establishment and deserted to the bishops (if indeed it makes any difference whither you have deserted). "Next, the state passed," you say, "into that equality established by the ministers of our faith, so that it is clear that the same spirit then flourished which in the eighth year thereafter completed the business by the unspeakable murder of the king." It seems, therefore, that the same spirit both animated your ministers and accomplished the parricide. Continue as you have begun, to belch forth utter nonsense, as befits an apostate.

"Those who demanded that the king be punished did not produce

[363] Milton, obviously, does not care to be tricked into a discussion of Anabaptist or Baptist ideas on church government. He therefore adroitly shifts the emphasis to the special tenet of the Baptists, the rite of Baptism, which he realized was far from the immediate concern of Du Moulin.

[364] Milton is quick to rise to the defence of political democracy, which he associates pre-eminently with classical antiquity. He must have been aware that the Anabaptist sect was a lower-class group and that its followers held political and economic views that were considered radical. They preached what later came to be called "the social gospel," which concerned itself with the justice of man's social and economic life as well as with his salvation. Such concepts did not jibe with his notions of classical republicanism.

[365] With the air of giving a simple definition, Milton quietly begs the question of the form of government in the primitive church. He is expressing his own view honestly enough. It is the concept he so vigorously advocated in his antiprelatical tracts.

[366] The parallel is not particularly significant. Geneva was ruled by a bishop from 1032 until the coming of Farel and Calvin. When the Protestant faith was adopted in 1535, he was expelled. Thereafter the bishops of Geneva lived at Annecy. The principal reason for the reference seems to be the opportunity it provides for additional mention of More's escapades there.

more than three petitions." This statement is known to be absolutely false, as I myself remember. Surely those [101] among us who have stored these matters in memory recall that not three such petitions only but many were presented by various counties of England, and in the space of about a month three a day were presented by the regiments of the army.[367] You see how seriously Parliament deliberated concerning this matter, when the people suspected that their delay was caused by excessive leniency and thought that it should be cut short by so many petitions. How many thousands of men do you suppose there were who held the same views but thought it either impertinent or unnecessary to urge Parliament to that course which it was already gravely considering? Of this number I myself was one, although my attitude is no secret. What if everyone had been silent, overawed by the magnitude of the case? [368] Would Parliament for this reason have been less competent to make its decision in so serious an affair? Ought they to have waited for the consent of the people, as if the outcome of such great counsels depended on that consent? In truth, if the highest assembly in the land, summoned by the people as a whole for the purpose of limiting the uncontrolled domination of the king, after it had captured him in battle, [102] savage and rebellious as he was, were obliged to defer to the commands of the people and ask whether they desired or commanded the punishment of the captive enemy, what else would they seem to have done—these men who had so bravely restored the Commonwealth—but to have thrown themselves headfirst into the snares of the tyrant, if he chanced to be acquitted by the people? [369] Or if, after receiving supreme power to

[367] Though he offers no specific evidence to support his contention, Milton was entirely right in saying that pressure on Parliament to punish the king was very heavy. Contemporary documents support his view. The army debates show that within the army the desire to abolish kingship and to punish Charles grew steadily from 1647 to 1649. See A. S. P. Woodhouse, *Puritanism and Liberty* (Chicago: University of Chicago Press, 1951). The pressures outside the army, including particularly those of the Levellers are fully described in Don M. Wolfe, *Milton in the Puritan Revolution*, pp. 182–89.

[368] Milton is probably right in saying that many remained silent because they were overawed, if not frightened, by the unprecedented project to try a king for treason and to execute him. Without doubt, however, he exaggerates the number. The extent and the force of royalist propaganda (*e.g., Eikon Basilike*) suggest that large numbers not only were eager to hear the king's side but believed it.

[369] Milton here is on weak ground. First, he asserts that Parliament, actually only a fragment of the Long Parliament, "the highest assembly in the land," has power greater than, and superior to, the power of the people who created it. Second, he expresses the view that Parliament may not really represent the people, since, if given the opportunity, they might acquit the king.

decide on the gravest matters, they were forced once more to refer those questions, which especially exceed the comprehension of the masses, I do not say to the people (for with this power they are themselves now the people), but to the mob, which, conscious of its own inexperience, had originally referred all things to them, what would be the end of this referring back and forth? [370] What stopping-place would there be in this Euripus? [371] What stability would there be among such petitions from so many giddy heads? What safety for the troubled affairs of men? What if they had demanded that Charles be restored to the throne.[372] That some petitions of this nature—not petitioning but threatening—did exist must be admitted. They came from men full of sedition, whose hatred at one time and complaints at another were wont to be equally foolish or malicious. [103] Was attention to be paid to these men, who, "so that a council with the king might be arranged," you say, "left their country districts in great numbers and stormed the doors of Parliament? Many of them the members, by inciting the soldiers, cruelly butchered." [373]

And you speak of the peasants of Surrey who, whether instigated by the malice of others (being themselves rustics) or by their own wickedness, marched with a petition through the city, thoroughly drunk and more interested in revelry than in presenting petitions.

[370] Again Milton gets entangled in his own somewhat sophistical argument. The Parliament, he says, is the people because it was given supreme power in its election, but the very people who elected it are a mob, which lacks the intelligence to consider and act upon serious questions.

[371] Milton dramatises the political situation implicit in the overruling of Parliament by the people by comparing it to Euripus, the strait between Euboea and Boeotia, where the tides ebb and flow with unusual rapidity.

[372] It is apparent here and above (see above, p. 634, n. 369) that Milton is not so certain of popular opinion as he professes to be. It is not possible to explore the motivation of his fears. From 1649 to the date of this writing, however, he had been in a position to know the extent and force of royalist propaganda. For a good summary of royalist propaganda, see Don M. Wolfe, *Milton in the Puritan Revolution,* pp. 189–93.

[373] Reports of riots against the army and of projected risings for the king are extant in great numbers from at least a dozen shires. The author of *Clamor,* however, appears greatly to exaggerate (1652, p. 37) the number of petitions specifically seeking the king's restoration. Besides the one mentioned in the next paragraph, the petition from Essex is the most important. On May 4, 1648, some two thousand men, some riding, some walking, entered London with a plea to make peace with Charles and to disband the army. On February 16, 1647, a petition from Suffolk asked the establishment of Presbyterianism and the disbanding of the army, but no mention of the king appeared in it. See Gardiner, *Great Civil War,* III, 29, 372.

Soon they formed an army and fiercely besieged the doors of the House of Parliament, driving from their posts the soldiers stationed there and killing one at the very doors of Parliament House, before anyone could have provoked them by deed or word. When they had been driven away from there and justly punished, not more than two or three were killed, "breathing" drunkenness rather than "liberty."[374] Here and there, you admit, "The party of the Independents was more powerful, not in number, but in strategy and military excellence." Whence I insist that they were also superior both in law and in merit, for nothing is more natural, nothing more just, nothing more useful or more advantageous to the human race [104] than that the lesser obey the greater, not the lesser number the greater number, but the lesser virtue the greater virtue, the lesser wisdom the greater wisdom. Those whose power lies in wisdom, experience, industry, and virtue will, in my opinion, however small their number, be a majority and prove more powerful in balloting everywhere than any mere number, however great.[375]

Here and there you interpose many remarks about Cromwell, the nature of which we shall examine hereafter. As for the rest, a reply was long since made to Salmasius. You do not omit to mention the judgment of the king, although it too was made the subject of a sorry declamation by your "great" rhetorician. The nobles, that is, the purple-clad king's men and most of the ministers of the court, shrank, you say, from judging the king. That this makes little difference, I have shown in the other book.[376] Next, "The judges of the courts were removed, since they had replied that it was contrary to the laws of

[374] Milton rewrites history here. On May 16, 1648, a body of men from Surrey marched through London, shouting "For God and King Charles!" They jeered at troops in Whitehall. The Lords acknowledged their petition, but the Commons remained silent. Angered, they tried to force their way into Commons, attacking the sentinels and shouting royalist slogans as they did so. When a detachment of five hundred troops arrived, most of the petitioners were in Westminster Hall. The soldiers cleared the hall, but in the scuffle one of them was killed. The men of Surrey fled to boats along the river, and from there pelted the troops with coal and bricks. See Gardiner, *Great Civil War,* III, 375–76.

[375] Since Milton is here confronted with a great rarity, a statement in *Clamor* (1652, p. 29) which is entirely correct and which he concurs in, he finds no reason to attack it. To distract attention from this embarrassing fact, he introduces, with doubtful propriety, a self-righteous statement of his own theory of government. He imputes all good qualities to all Independents, and baseness to all their opponents. His rhetoric is more sound than his facts.

[376] *A Defence.* See above, pp. 285 ff.

England for the king to be put on trial." [377] I do not know what reply they made at that time; I know what they now approve and defend. It is not a novelty for judges to be timid, although it ill becomes them. Hence "there was put in charge of the vile and infamous court a suitable presiding officer,[378] an utterly unknown and insolent rascal." [105] But for you, who are overwhelmed by so many vices and crimes, or rather, are yourself unmixed filth, unmitigated crime, for you to have afflicted your mind and senses with such a callus (unless your whole mind is one great callus) that you venture to be an atheist with respect to God, a defiler of holy things, a brute towards man, and the slanderer of all who are excellent—what else is this but to be a genuine Iscariot, a veritable devil? [379] Yet although to be attacked by you is the highest tribute, nevertheless I shall by no means so neglect that excellent man at whom you snarl (that friend always most worthy of my veneration) as not to defend him from the wicked tongues of fugitives and Mores, which he would never have experienced save in the cause of the Commonwealth.

John Bradshaw,[380] a name which Liberty herself, wherever she is

[377] There is no evidence to support the idea that any consideration was given to a trial of Charles by the English courts of law. See Masson, III, 698–99, 702–704. For the passage from Du Moulin, see *Clamor* (1652), p. 52.

[378] *Clamor* (1652), p. 53, is here grossly unfair to John Bradshaw (1602–1659), who was appointed president of the High Court immediately after its establishment. Bradshaw was a lawyer of considerable repute and had sat as Chief Justice of Chester and as a judge in Wales before his appointment. His conduct of the king's trial is generally considered to have been somewhat less than judicial. He was overbearing to the king himself and gave Charles' lawyers short shrift. Apparently Du Moulin did not know that he was handsomely rewarded for his services by his appointment to various judicial offices and by his receipt of valuable estates, confiscated from royalists. Much writing about him is strongly prejudiced, for or against. See *DNB*.

[379] Milton is so infuriated by Du Moulin's slurs on Bradshaw that he reverts to pure abuse, unrelieved by wit, satire, or rhetorical dexterity.

[380] Milton's panegyric on Bradshaw was no doubt completely sincere. Of all the government leaders he was probably the best known to Milton personally by virtue of his being president of the Council of State. Milton outlines his career in general terms, without exact titles, dates, or other details, but accurately. He admires Bradshaw's courage in serving as presiding officer at the king's trial, which he rightly calls "more fearsome than almost any other in history," but he had other reasons for honest admiration. Earlier in his career, Bradshaw had served as chief counsel for John Lilburne during the latter's first trial. Doubtless, this fact is noted indirectly in the phrase "an alert defender of liberty and the people." But Milton has an even more cogent reason for respecting Bradshaw, which he could not possibly have mentioned in any but the most guarded terms. When Cromwell

cherished, has entrusted to eternal memory for celebration, is sprung, as all men know, from a noble line. Accordingly, he spent all his early years in diligent study of the laws of his country and then, a most effective lawyer and eloquent pleader, an alert defender of liberty and the people, [106] he was employed in grave affairs of state and on several occasions served as an incorruptible judge. At length, when Parliament besought him to preside at the trial of the king, he did not refuse so dangerous a task. For to knowledge of the law he had brought a liberal frame of mind, a lofty spirit, and pure morals, subservient to no man. Thus, although exposed to the daggers and threats of innumerable assassins, he performed and executed this office, which was greater and more terrible than almost any other in history, with such loyalty, sobriety, dignity, and presence of mind that he seemed to have been created and destined by Divinity itself for this very task, which God in his marvelous providence had long since ordained was to be performed among this people. And he exceeded the glory of all other tyrannicides by the measure in which it is more humane, just, and dignified to judge a tyrant than to kill him untried. In other respects neither melancholy nor stern, but affable and serene, he nevertheless maintains the great role [381] which he has undertaken with such dignity (worthy always of himself and, so to speak, consul not [107] of one year alone) that you would say he was judging the king, not merely from the tribunal, but throughout his entire life. More tireless than any other in counsel and labor for the public good, he is, by himself, equal to a host. At home he, as much as any man, is hospitable and generous according to his means, the most faithful of friends and the most worthy of trust in every kind of fortune. No man more quickly and freely recognizes those who deserve well of him, whoever they may be, nor pursues them with greater kindness. Sometimes it is the godly, sometimes the learned, sometimes men famed for any kind of genius, sometimes, too, soldiers and heroes, reduced to poverty, whom he assists out of his own resources. If they

abolished the Commons and assumed sole power, Bradshaw stoutly resisted him. Milton made the best of this bad bargain, as is evident later in this tract, but it is apparent also that, though Milton accepted this *fait accompli* and genuinely admired Cromwell, he did not really like such absolutism and hoped for a change in the direction of broader-based power.

[381] Milton here refers to Bradshaw's service as president of the Council of State. The phrase "consul not of one year alone" comes from Horace, "Consulque non unius anni" (*Odes* IV, ix, 39).

are in no need, he yet honors and welcomes them gladly. He is wont always to shout the praises of other men, to be silent about his own. If any of his political enemies has returned to his senses, as many indeed have done, no one is more ready to forgive. But if the cause of any victim of oppression needs to be publicly defended, if the influence and power of potentates must be assailed, if popular ingratitude towards one who has deserved well of his country is to be rebuked, then indeed no man could find Bradshaw lacking in eloquence or loyalty. [108] No man could hope for a patron or friend more able and fearless or more persuasive, for he has in Bradshaw a friend whom threats cannot move from the path of justice, one whom neither fear nor bribes can dislodge from his righteous purpose and duty, or from the steadfast firmness of his mind and countenance. Justly beloved by the majority of men for these virtues, and respected even by his greatest foes, Bradshaw will for ever prolong among all mankind, in all countries and in all ages, the glory of the noble deeds accomplished in our state, when you, More, and your like, have been confounded.

But, to continue, the king was condemned to lose his head: "Against this madness almost all the pulpits of London thundered." You do not evoke much terror with that wooden thunder of yours. We have no fear of those Salmoneuses,[382] who will some day pay the penalty for that false thunder which they have taken to themselves—weighty and unimpeachable authorities, to be sure, who a little before, from those same pulpits, were thundering against the Pluralists and Non-residents [383] with a rumble equally fearsome. And a little later, after one had seized three and another four of the benefices of the prelates [109] whom they had driven out by their thundering (and had thus necessarily become Non-residents themselves),[384] they were

[382] Evidence exists (Masson, III, 716–17) that the protest of the Presbyterian clergy in London was not inconsiderable in fervor or in quantity. It was hardly sufficient, however, to justify *Clamor's* statement (1652, p. 53). Instead of trying to argue it away, Milton employs a myth with which to ridicule it. Salmoneus, a son of Aeolus, made a noise like thunder with his chariot, and simulated lightning by tossing firebands into space. For this impiety Zeus cast him into Tartarus. See *Aeneid,* VI, 585–94.

[383] In some parishes where pluralists were non-resident they employed curates, often ill-prepared, to serve in their places. The Presbyterians said they wanted to abolish this condition.

[384] Milton turns his attention briefly from the Presbyterians in order to jeer at the clergy of the Church of England. Since the Anglican clergy had been ejected

guilty of the same crime against which they had thundered, and each one was struck by his own thunderbolt.[385] Nor as yet have they any shame. Now they are wholly given over to the defence of their tithes,[386] and surely if their thirst for tithes is so tremendous, I think that they ought to be tithed to their hearts' content.[387] Let them not only have tithes of the fruits of the earth, but let them have the tenth wave of the sea as well.[388] These very men were the first to urge war against the king, as against an enemy doomed to destruction. Then, when the enemy had been captured and condemned for the slaughter and bloodshed with which they had so often charged him, they wished to spare him, on the ground that he was king. So in their pulpits, as if in some huckster's stall, they sell to the rabble whatever merchandise they wish, whatever trash they please, and what is even more disgusting, they take back, whenever they like, what they have just sold.[389]

---

from all ecclesiastical offices, they had all become non-residents, against their will and without remuneration.

[385] To Milton the Presbyterians opposed pluralism for others because they wanted it for themselves. *Cf.* his sonnet, "On the New Forcers of Conscience under the Long Parliament," where he tells the Presbyterians that they have discarded bishops and liturgy

> To seise the widdow'd whore Pluralitie
> From them whose sin ye envi'd, not abhor'd.

On the questions of patronage and the financial administration of the church, see William A. Shaw, *A History of the Church of England During the Civil Wars and Under the Commonwealth, 1640–1660* (2 vols., London: 1900), I, 175–286.

[386] Many Independents opposed tithes as unspiritual, and on August 6, 1649, the Commons, under their control, rejected a motion to make the payments of tithes compulsory. A part of the question proposed was "That all and every Person and Persons do duly pay their accustomed tythes." *Commons Journals,* VI, 275. Tithes, however, continued to be paid. See Shaw, *History of the English Church,* I, 255–58; and Margaret James, "The Political Importance of the Tithe Controversy in the English Revolution, 1640–1660," *History,* XXVI (June, 1941), 1–18.

[387] Milton enlarges his scorn with a Latin pun for what he considers to be the inordinate desire of the Presbyterians for tithes. He plays on the linguistic accident that in Latin the same word means to tithe or to sacrifice one tenth of all things received each year to God, and to decimate or to kill one out of each ten.

[388] Milton continues his punning on tithes or tenths. See above, nn. 386, 387. He desires the Presbyterians to have the tenth wave of the sea because it will overwhelm them. In Roman proverbial lore the tenth egg was the largest and the tenth wave the most powerful: "Decimana ova dicuntur et decimani fluctus quia sunt magna."

[389] Whether Milton is here venomous toward the Presbyterians out of sheer malice or out of basic misunderstanding, it is not possible to say. He seems unable or unwilling to understand that, though the Presbyterians made a fundamental con-

But "The Scots kept insisting that the king be returned to them; they recalled the promises of Parliament when they had handed the king over to the English." [390] And yet I have the admission of the Scots themselves that no public promises at all existed when the king was surrendered.[391] Indeed, it would have been a disgrace [110] to the English if their own king were not to be returned to them by the Scots mercenaries [392] in the employment of England, save on conditions. What of the fact that the very reply of Parliament to the Scottish demands, published on March 15, 1647, clearly denies that they had made any commitment concerning the question how the king was to be treated, and indeed shows that they would have thought it shameful to be unable to obtain their rights from the Scots except according to that condition.[393] But "They kept asking that the king be returned to them." The soft-hearted fellows, I have no doubt, were growing weak in spirit. They could no longer support their longing for their king. Yet those very same men from the beginning of these disturbances in Britain had more than once made motions in Parliament concerning the right of the king, and about 1645 all agreed that a king could be deprived of his throne for three principal reasons: if he should prove a tyrant, if he should alienate the royal property, or if he should desert his people.[394] When Parliament was held at Perth,

---

tribution to the destruction of the monarchy and the church as then constituted (Gardiner, *Great Civil War,* II, 580–81), they did not, at the same time, commit themselves in advance to the trial and execution of the king.

[390] *Clamor* (1652), pp. 54–55, is inaccurate in its reference to "promises of Parliament." For the history of Charles' negotiations with various factions from May to December, 1646, see Masson, III, 506–10; Gardiner, *Great Civil War,* II, 505–75.

[391] Milton is correct in saying that no "public" promises appear in the treaty between the English and the Scots. His implication that secret promises existed cannot, of course, be verified, but the fact that the king was taken by the English with no difficulty, without the objection of the king himself, and with considerable ceremony, may well give support to the validity of his implication.

[392] Technically Milton is correct in calling the Scottish troops mercenaries. They fought for a nation other than their own, and they were paid for their services.

[393] Milton is not only consistent but correct in his presentation of the struggle over the King's person. Gardiner (*Great Civil War,* II, 526, 528) cites diplomatic correspondence as well as the *Journals* of Lords and Commons to show the firm determination of both the English and the Scots to use possession of him for the attainment of their immediate political purposes.

[394] For purposes of argument Milton persists in refusing to differentiate between readiness to force the king's abdication and willingness to put him to death. Recog-

they began to call for votes on the question whether a king who, it was agreed, was an enemy of the saints, should be deprived of the communion of the church.[395] But before they could arrive at any decision on this matter, Montrose [396] approached the city [111] with his troops and threw the meeting into an uproar. These same men in a certain response of theirs to General Cromwell in 1650 admit that the king was justly punished, but contend that the form of justice was faulty, because they themselves were not summoned to take part in the trial.[397] Therefore what was an atrocious crime without them, with them would have been a commendable act—as if right and wrong depended on their nod, and justice and injustice were to be defined by their terms. What more lenient decrees, I should like to know, would they have issued against the king if he had been restored to them?

But "The Scottish delegates had formerly received this reply from the English Parliament—that they did not wish to change the form of the English monarchy. Later, however, they replied that they had not wished to do so then, but now wished to, since the safety of the state required it." [398] And they made the proper response. What do you say to that? "This alteration," you say, "overturns all treaties, all agreements, and common sense itself." It certainly overturns your

---

nition of the fact that the king's fitness to reign had ended did not require adherence to a totally new form of government. The only opposite to Charles was not republicanism. Milton chides the Presbyterians for inconsistency when they were guilty of nothing more than conservatism. For the first discussions of the dethronement of Charles see Gardiner, *Great Civil War,* I, 385, 480–81.

[395] On July 24, 1645, the Scottish Parliament was transferred from Stirling to Perth. Its deliberations were broken up by the appearance of Scottish troops loyal to Charles.

[396] James Graham, Marquis of Montrose (1612–1650), an intrepid soldier, began his life as a loyal Covenanter, but early became attracted to King Charles.

[397] Milton is on weak ground in attempting to deny the justice of the Presbyterian complaint. Though the Presbyterians had had a large representation in the Commons, they had no voice in the legislative acts which prepared the way for the king's trial because their members had been purged by Pride in December, 1648. And, though they had strong support in the city of London, they could not make their views effective through agitation because the city was in the hands of the army.

[398] Du Moulin is entirely correct in saying that the English leaders changed their minds concerning the disposition of the king and the form of government they desired. The fact is clearly recorded from the convening of the Long Parliament in 1640 until the execution of the king in 1649. See *Clamor* (1652), p. 55.

common sense, if you do not know the difference between free promises and treaty obligations. The English of their own free will made the reply which then seemed to them best with regard to the future condition of their state, [112] for which they were not obliged to give an accounting to the Scots. Now the welfare of the state required another course, if they were not to violate their faith and the oath given the people. Which do you think a more sacred obligation, a free reply given the Scots legates concerning the future form of the English government, or a binding oath and solemn promise given one's own people concerning the preservation of the safety of the state? But that it is permissible for a Parliament or a senate to change its plans in accord with expediency, I prefer you to learn from Cicero in the *Pro Plancio,*[399] since whatever I say seems to you to be like Anabaptist doctrine and therefore monstrous:

> For we ought all to take a stand on the wheel, so to speak, of political life, and since it keeps turning, we should choose that part to which we are directed by the utility and safety of the state.

Cicero goes on to say that he does not regard it as a mark of inconsistency to govern one's sentiments, like a ship's course, by the shifting winds of politics:

> Indeed, this have I learned, this have I seen, this have I read, and the records of literature have taught me this lesson about the wisest and most distinguished men in this and [113] other states, that the same views are not always to be maintained by the same men, but whatever views the situation of the state, the inclination of the times, and a regard for harmony demand.

So far, Marcus Tullius. But you, More, prefer Hortensius.[400] Such was the opinion of those ages that excelled in the lore of the state. If the Anabaptists adopt it, they are, in my opinion, wise indeed.[401]

[399] See Cicero, *Pro Plancio,* 93–94. Cicero defended Plancius, who had befriended him during his exile in Thessalonica, against a charge of corruption in elections. The speech was delivered in 54 B.C.

[400] Quintus Hortensius Hortalus (114–50 B.C.) was consul in 69 B.C. and the principal rival of Cicero before the Roman bar.

[401] The author of *Clamor* made the tactical error (below, p. 1053) of trying to defame ideas Milton cherished (see above, p. 633, n. 364) by calling them Anabaptist.

How many other statements could I mention which are condemned as Anabaptist doctrine by these trifling ministers and their Salmasius (a man utterly unlearned, if we have regard for actualities, not words).[402] "But the most powerful Federated States of Holland could do no more," you say. "Through their ambassadors, both by entreaty and by the offer of rewards, they strove desperately to ransom the sacred head of the king." [403] Actually, to desire to buy off justice in this fashion was the same thing as not to desire the king's safety. But they learned that all men are not hucksters; the Parliament of England is not for sale. As for the trial of the king, you say, "So that Charles might share a great many sufferings of Christ, the soldiers redoubled their mockery of him." [404] [114] But Christ suffered more torments like those of malefactors than Charles like those of Christ. Many remarks of this nature were bandied about by those to whose interest it was to invent any tale whatsoever or spread abroad any fiction, for the purpose of arousing greater resentment over the deed. Granted, however, that the common soldiers behaved rather insolently. This fact must not be laid to the blame of the cause itself. "Someone was actually murdered at the feet of the king as he walked along, for begging that God might have mercy on the king." [405] This tale I have

[402] Seeking to impress the learned on the continent, who knew and remembered Salmasius as a scholar, Milton misses no opportunity to pillory him as a pedant whose writings were unworthy of serious attention.

[403] The Prince of Orange and the States-General of Holland made several fruitless efforts to help Charles. Their ambassadors on three occasions offered to attempt mediation of the issues in dispute between the king and Parliament in order to bring the civil war to an end. See Gardiner, *Great Civil War,* I, 387, 413–14; II, 141; III, 589. For the passage from Du Moulin, see *Clamor* (1652), p. 56.

[404] Charles was clearly a deeply devout man, passionately and stubbornly devoted to the Church of England. He was not a plaster saint, as Milton believed, but, in the eyes of his followers, a martyr deserving of canonization. Even so, it is not difficult to understand the horror of a religious man like Milton at Du Moulin's blasphemous identification of Charles with Christ. See *Clamor* (1652), p. 63.

[405] Whether through ignorance or intention, *Clamor* (below, p. 1062) greatly exaggerates here. The episode is recounted in the *Narrative* of Sir Thomas Herbert, a courtier who was in constant attendance upon the king during the last months of his life. On January 22, 1649, when Charles was returning from Westminster Hall to Sir Thomas Cotton's house, where he was temporarily lodged, a soldier of the guard called out "God bless you, Sir," as the king passed. Charles thanked him, but an officer struck the soldier on the head with a cane. The soldier was not killed. Sir Thomas Herbert's *Narrative* is reprinted in Gertude Scott Stevenson, *Charles I in Captivity* (New York, 1927). See p. 189.

never heard before, nor have I yet been able to find anyone who had heard it. I have even taken steps to question the officer who was in charge of the guards during the whole time of the trial and scarcely left the king's side. He repeatedly swore that he had never heard the story before and knows for certain that it is absolutely false.[406] How reliable your narratives are in all their other aspects as well can be inferred from this example. For you will not prove much more truthful in securing posthumous good will and (if possible) reverence for Charles than in whipping up hatred against us, even in the basest ways. [115]

"The king was heard," you say, "on the scaffold repeating to the bishop of London,[407] 'Remember, Remember!' "[408] The king's judges were of course anxious to know what the repetition of that last word had meant, and the bishop was summoned, as you say, and bidden with threats to reveal the significance of that twice uttered "Remember." At first he displayed scruples, according to agreement, no doubt (for such a plot was expedient), and, as if it were some great secret, withheld the revelation. When they threatened him more severely, he at last, with reluctance and as if it were wrung from him by fear and extorted against his will, revealed what in reality he would have been glad to disclose at any price, saying, "The king had bidden me, if I could reach his son, to carry him this last injunction from his dying father, namely, that if he were restored to his kingdom and sovereignty he should pardon you, the authors of his death. The king again and again commanded me that I should remember this."[409] Oh,

[406] The commandants of the king's guard during his trial and execution were Colonels Francis Hacker and Hercules Huncks. At the Restoration Hacker was tried as a regicide and hanged. Huncks, by testifying against his companions, escaped execution. Nothing in his testimony supports *Clamor's* charge (1652, p. 63).

[407] Dr. William Juxon (1582–1663), bishop of London from 1633 to 1660, the only clerical counselor permitted to Charles during his trial and before his death.

[408] Though both Gardiner (III, 597) and Masson (III, 726) mention the king's injunction to Juxon, neither makes reference to the repetition of the word "Remember." Sir Thomas Herbert, in his account of the execution, does not mention the admonition at all. See *Clamor* (1652), p. 76.

[409] This charge by *Clamor* (1652, p. 77) is almost certainly a pure fabrication. Du Moulin may have known personally that the bishop was interrogated and threatened, but no evidence from any other source has been found to substantiate the events. Milton indicates that he gives no faith to the story. He here paraphrases rather than quotes *Clamor,* and, lest readers mistake the paraphrase for his own words, he carefully inserts the clause "as you say."

shall I say that the king was more full of piety or the bishop more full of leaks— [116] the bishop who could so easily be compelled to babble away the matter so secretly entrusted to his confidence on the scaffold? But, O man of few words, long since had Charles enjoined on his son this mandate, among others, in the *Eikon Basilike*,[410] a book which, it is sufficiently clear, was written so that this secret might with great diligence be revealed to us a little later, even against our will, as ostentatiously as it had been fabricated. But I clearly see that you have determined to foist off on the ignorant a perfect Charles, if not this Stuart, at least some hyperborean and mythical one, painted with whatever false dyes you choose. Hence your disgusting invention [411] of this fable, like some painted backdrop prettily embellished with bits of dialogue and little mottoes. You imitate some mimic or other, to bait the ears of the vulgar. But, although I do not deny that the bishop may in passing have been questioned on this point by one or another of the commissioners, I do not find that he was summoned as you allege or that either the Council or that body of judges expressed interest, as if they had been concerned about it or had anxiously inquired. [117]

But let us go on with your story. Granted that Charles on the scaffold gave these commands to the bishop, to be transmitted to his son, namely, that those who were responsible for his death be pardoned. What did he do so remarkable or so unusual, beyond all the other men brought to that place? How few of those who die on the scaffold, when they are about to drop the curtain on the drama of life and see how vain are these mortal concerns, would not do the same thing? And how few would not, when on the point of making an exit, as from a kind of stage, gladly lay aside, or at least pretend to lay aside, hatreds, angers, and enmities, so as to leave in the minds of men either compassion or conviction of their innocence? [412] That Charles merely

[410] Milton refers to chapter 27 of *Eikon Basilike* (1649), pp. 152–65, titled "To the Prince of Wales." It purports to be a letter of advice designed to guide the prince if and when he should become king. Though Milton had some doubt as to the king's authorship of *Eikon* (see above, p. 628, nn. 339, 340), he chooses here to accept the authenticity of the letter.

[411] Milton contradicts himself. He forgets that he has just referred to statements of royal forgiveness and of advice to the Prince of Wales in *Eikon,* which he professes to believe Charles wrote, and blames *Clamor* at the same time for fabricating the fable of Charles' Christian clemency.

[412] An hour before he went to the block Charles received holy communion from bishop Juxon. With the words of that office fresh in his devout memory, he could hardly have spoken insincerely or vaingloriously.

enacted a pretense, and never commanded his son from his heart and with the sincere purpose of his mind "that he should pardon the authors of his death," or if he did so on the surface commanded something else in secret, can be proved by no mean arguments, for his son, in other respects more than sufficiently obedient to his father, would no doubt have obeyed that father's last and weightiest command, so piously conveyed to him through the bishop.[413] But how has he obeyed it, when by his command or [118] at his authority our two ambassadors have been assassinated—one in Holland,[414] the other in Spain [415] (and the latter not even suspected of any responsibility for the death of the king)? He has, finally, more than once by public proclamation announced and made plain to all that he does not wish to grant pardon on any terms to those who put his father to death.[416] Consider therefore whether you wish this little story of yours to be true, since the more it honors the father, the more it censures the son.

Now, forgetful of your main object, you tell lies, not about the Cry of the King's Blood to Heaven, but about the cries of the people against Parliament, you who after Salmasius are the most odious busybody and meddler in a foreign state, while you conduct your affairs at home so disgracefully. Are the people to employ your voice in their defense, most wanton creature, whose very breath, befouled

[413] Milton had no evidence for these unworthy insinuations about the king.

[414] Dr. Isaac Dorislaus, a naturalized Englishman of Dutch origin, was appointed ambassador to Holland by the Council of State on April 18, 1649. A scholar, he had previously served as advocate general to the army of Essex and as one of the counsel for the prosecution at the king's trial. The day he arrived at The Hague, May 3, 1649, he was stabbed to death by a group of masked men. See Masson, IV, 49, and note.

[415] Anthony Ascham, appointed ambassador to Spain on February 4, 1650, reached Madrid in May and was declared acceptable to the king. As he was dining on May 27, he was stabbed to death by six English royalists. There was no doubt of their identity (Masson, IV, 193) since one of them was a servant to Edward Hyde, later Earl of Clarendon, then in Madrid.

[416] Milton confuses the obligation enjoined upon Christians to forgive their enemies with the responsibility of the state to punish offences against its authority. In asking forgiveness of his enemies Charles spoke on a spiritual plane; he expressed the desire to have his soul return to God free of sin. He spoke as an individual, not as a king concerned with matters of secular law. It was not possible, however, for him to overlook acts he considered to be high treason which called for suitable civil punishment. The Prince of Wales was in the same position. He could not have sought support among British and Continental royalists unless he had publicly promised to restore justice and equity and to punish those who had flouted both. Milton's grave charge of insincerity must be taken as a point in argument, dramatic in effect but weak in substance.

by venereal corruption, every pure man would shun? In truth you ascribe to the people the voices of traitors and profligates, and like a wandering beggar performing for a crowd you imitate the sounds of only the basest animals. Yet who denies that times may often come when a majority of the citizens are wanton, [119] preferring to follow Catiline or Antony[417] rather than the sounder party of the Senate? Nor for that reason ought the upright citizens to fail in striving against the disaffected and acting bravely, having regard rather for their duty than for their small number. Therefore I urge you to insert this charming little declamation of yours on behalf of our people among the Annals of Volusius,[418] so that the paper may not be completely wasted. We have no use for a petty rhetorician so rank and fetid.

Next we are taken to task for our injuries to the church. "The army is a Lernaean swamp of all heresies."[419] Those who do not slander it admit that our army, as it is the bravest, is also the most sober and devout. In other camps there are usually drinking, indulgence in various lusts, rapine, gaming, swearing, and perjuring. In this camp of ours what leisure is available is spent in the search for truth, in careful reading of sacred Scripture, nor does anyone think it more glorious to smite the foe than to instruct himself and others in the knowledge of heavenly things, or think it more noble to practice warlike rather than evangelical combat.[420] [120] And indeed, if we consider the

[417] Both Lucius Sergius Catilina (*ca.* 108–62 B.C.) and Gaius Antonius Hybrida (*ca.* 82–30 B.C.) had large followings in their revolts against the rightful authority of the Senate, but they appealed to the mob unsuited to govern. See Cicero, *In Toga Candida*. Milton is irked at being reminded that England is no longer a republic.

[418] Milton here refers to Catullus, who says (XXXVI, 1) that Lesbia plans a votive offering of the works of the worst poet she knows. These are *Annales Volusii,* the work of Volusius now known only by reference, which he characterizes as soiled toilet paper. Milton suggests that the paper wasted in *Clamor* would better serve a like use and continues the slur by his expression "rank and fetid."

[419] Though the sects were widespread in the army, in which the Independents predominated, they were equally numerous in civil life. Masson (III, 136–59) gives a synopsis of the divergent beliefs actively advocated in 1644–1645. The philosophical or rational basis of dissent is a principal thesis of William Haller in *Liberty and Reformation in the Puritan Revolution* (New York: Columbia University Press, 1955). For Du Moulin's statement see *Clamor* (1652), p. 95.

[420] Milton parries the attack on the army as a breeder of dissent with a eulogy that history has justified. Milton refers, of course, to the New Model Army, which was organized in 1645. See George M. Trevelyan, *England Under the Stuarts* (New York, 1938), pp. 265–66, where Cavalier testimony supports Puritan on this subject.

proper function of war, what other conduct would be more fitting for soldiers who have been organized and enrolled to be defenders of the laws, uniformed guardians of justice, champions of the church? What should be, not more fierce and belligerent, but more civil and humane, than these men who are obliged, as the true and proper end of their labors, not to sow and reap warfare, but to cultivate peace and safety for the human race? [421] Yet if any who strive for these glorious ideas have been led astray either by the mistake of another or by their own weakness of mind, we should not rage against them with the sword but strive with reason and admonitions, and also with prayers poured forth to God, who alone has the power to dispel all errors from the mind and impart the heavenly light of truth to whomever He will. No heresies, to be sure, in the proper sense of the word, do we approve, nor indeed do we tolerate all of them.[422] We even wish them extirpated, but by suitable methods, by precepts, that is, and sounder doctrine, since, implanted in the mind, they are not to be rooted out by steel and scourges, as if from the body. [121]

"The second, equally great, injury" of ours, you assert, "is in the so-called temporal property of the church." [423] Ask the Dutch or even the Protestants of upper Germany whether they have spared the goods of the church.[424] Whenever the Emperor of Austria undertakes a war against them, he seeks scarcely any other excuse than that he may command the goods of the church to be restored. Yet these were certainly not the goods of the church, but only of churchmen,[425] who in

[421] Milton's idealization of the role of the soldier as the cultivator of peace and safety stems from his belief that principle is important above all. Man's freedom from tyranny of body and mind is the highest purpose of government and its agencies.

[422] When, on August 7, 1644, the Presbyterians in the Westminster Assembly began a full assault on sects and toleration of dissent, they began to press Parliament for action and to cite names of flagrant offenders. One of those so cited late in the month was John Milton. See Masson, III, 186–89. It was not his attacks on Episcopacy, of course, that caused his condemnation, but his authorship of the pamphlets on divorce.

[423] *Clamor* (1652), p. 99. This is a matter about which Du Moulin, an Anglican priest, would know at first hand. The Commonwealth did a very thorough job of divesting the bishops, deans, and chapters of their properties and endowments. See Shaw, *History of the English Church,* II, 203, 242, 558.

[424] Milton comes close to saying that two wrongs make a right. Instead of offering a reasoned answer to Du Moulin's objection to the seizure of church endowments and properties he says simply that reformers in other countries have regularly taken over church possessions. Since he offers no evidence to justify the Dutch and Germans, he provides no moral basis for the English action.

[425] This is at best a quibble, at worst a simple falsification. Unless a churchman

this sense especially might better be called clerics, or even holoclerics, since they had seized the whole inheritance. In fact, most of them should be called wolves, a more accurate name than any other. Moreover, it was not a sacrilege to transfer the property of wolves, or rather the accumulated booty that had been acquired through the superstition of our ancestors,[426] which they had turned to their own profit through so many ages, to the needs of a war which they had themselves stirred up, since nothing else was left with which to pay the expenses of so serious and protracted a conflict.

And yet, "It was expected that the wealth seized from the bishops would be handed over to the pastors of the churches." The pastors expected it, I know, and they were greedy that all [122] be handed over to them, for there is no abyss so deep that it cannot be filled more quickly than the avarice of the clergy. Perhaps in other places there was insufficient provision for the ministers. Ours were adequately and more than adequately well off.[427] Sheep, rather than shepherds, should they be called; they are fed more than they feed.[428] With them, virtually everything is fat, not excepting their wits, for they are stuffed with tithes, a custom rejected by all other churches. And they have so little trust in God that they prefer to extort these tithes from their own flocks through the magistrates and by force,[429] rather than owe them

---

possessed private wealth, his stipend was paid from the yield of endowments belonging to the church itself, to the sees, or to the parishes. A bishop or a dean no more owned these endowments than he owned the cathedral edifice itself.

[426] Milton fails to recall, perhaps intentionally, that the great sums of money and the vast treasure given to the church in earlier times for such purposes as the establishment and enriching of religious houses, the endowments of chantries for the souls of the dead, the embellishment of images and reliquaries, and the making of church plate and vestments had long since been lost to the Church of England. Milton is here justifying again the action of Parliament in divesting the bishops, deans, and chapters of their properties and endowments. The total sum raised from the sale of deans' and chapters' lands alone during the years from 1649–1657 amounted to £516,913. See Shaw, *History of the English Church,* II, 239.

[427] This statement is not confirmed by the facts of record. As Milton has frankly stated above, the war was very costly, and the money seized from the bishops was needed for its prosecution. On the sale of bishops' lands see Shaw, *History of the English Church,* II, 210–13, 242, 558–69.

[428] *Cf. "Lycidas,"* ll. 113–25, particularly the final line:

The hungry Sheep look up, and are not fed.

[429] Some Independents disapproved of tithes, but the Presbyterians, as the inheritors of the impoverished Anglican livings, favored them. Here, Milton obviously refers to the unsuccessful effort of the latter, on August 6, 1649, to have the Commons declare the payment of tithes compulsory. See above, p. 640, n. 386.

to divine providence or the good will and gratitude of the churches. And amid all this they nevertheless are so often entertained by their parishioners, both male and female, that they scarcely know what it is to lunch or dine at home. Hence, most of them live in luxury, not in want, and their children and wives rival in extravagance and splendor the children and wives of the rich. To have increased this extravagance with new possessions would have been to have poured a new poison into the church (an evil which a voice sent from heaven deplored in the reign of Constantine).[430] [123]

Next we must render an account of our offences against God, of which three receive special mention: our faith in divine assistance,[431] no less, and also "our prayers and fasts."[432] But out of your own mouth, most corrupt of men, I convict you, and the saying of the apostle which you have quoted I turn against you. Who are you to "judge another man's servant"? In the presence of our Master let us stand or fall.[433] I shall add, moreover, the words of the prophet David, "And I covered my soul in fasting: and it was made a reproach to me."[434] If I wished to go step by step through the rest of your feverish

[430] The *Donation of Constantine,* alleged to have been drafted in the fourth century but actually forged in the eighth or ninth, purported to be a deed from Constantine I giving to Pope Sylvester and his successors full sovereignty over Italy and all the provinces of the West together with many other dignities and privileges. Milton apparently accepted the authenticity of the document, and held the view, not uncommon, that the gifts had tended to debauch the church. His source for the deploring voice from heaven, noted also in *Apology* (*Complete Prose,* I, 946–47), is the *Confessio Amantis* of John Gower, specifically "The Tale of Constantine and Sylvester," II, 289–310.

[431] Milton construes Du Moulin's remark (*Clamor,* 1652, p. 107) as a sneer at the general proposition that God gives wisdom and guidance to those who honestly seek his counsel, an idea he held firmly.

[432] The prayer meetings and fasts which preceded momentous decisions both in the army and in London were numerous and earnest. They were characterized by long extempore prayers and equally long sermons. Masson (III, 162–63) gives a good account of them. The forms of worship were of course alien to Du Moulin's taste and practice. For Moulin's statement see *Clamor* (1652), p. 106.

[433] Du Moulin (*Clamor,* 1652, p. 102) has quoted Romans 4:14 to chide the Puritans for what he considers their self-righteous condemnation of those who differ with them. Milton's reply is not strong. He simply stresses the idea of St. Paul.

[434] The full impact of this quotation (Psalms 69:10) is realized only if the reader recalls the verses that precede and follow it. Consumed by a zeal for God's house, the Temple, David had attempted to purge it of defilement. By acts of penitence such as weeping and fasting he tried to show his sorrow for these profanations in the hope that his example would cause the guilty to repent. Instead they scorned and ridiculed him. Milton allows his readers to draw the parallel between David and the Puritans, and between Du Moulin and the scorners.

twitterings on this subject, which no one would read twice, I should myself commit no small offence. No less irrelevant is your endless maundering about our successes.[435] Beware, More, and take heed lest after your Pontian sweats you perhaps contract a cold in the head or a polyp in the nose. It is to be feared that, like the once great Salmasius, you would chill the hot baths. For my part, I make reply with a few words about our success, [124] as follows: a cause is neither proved good by success, nor shown to be evil. We insist, not that our cause be judged by the outcome, but that the outcome be judged by the cause.

You now presume to deal with political considerations, you slave of the chair (or rather the easy-chair), namely our offences against all kings and peoples. What offences? For we had no such design. We merely attended to our own affairs and dismissed the affairs of others. If any good has redounded to our neighbors from our example, we do not begrudge it; if any evil, we hold that it occurs through the fault, not of ourselves, but of those who abuse our principles. And pray, what kings or peoples established you, a mere buffoon, as the spokesman of their wrongs? Certainly other men in Parliament, and I myself in the Council, have often heard their ambassadors [436] and legates, when they were given an audience, so far from complaining about their grievances, actually asking of their own free will for our friendship and alliance, even, in fact, congratulating us on our affairs in the names of their own kings and princes, wishing us well indeed and invoking eternal peace and [125] security and the continuance of the same auspicious success. These are not the words of enemies nor of those who hate us, as you allege. Either you must be condemned for lying (in you a trifle) or the kings themselves for fraud and wicked designs (which to them would be a great disgrace). But you reproach us with our writings, in which we admit, "We have given an example beneficial to all people, dreadful to all tyrants." It is a

[435] What Milton calls "endless maundering" is actually a vigorous and well written passage in *Clamor* (1652, pp. 102 ff.). Du Moulin was grimly amused and repelled by the practice of Cromwell and other Puritan leaders who publicly affirmed that their decisions were privately dictated to them by God during prayer.

[436] The exact truth lies about half way between the remarks of Du Moulin and the reply of Milton. One of the first acts of the Council of State was a review of foreign policy together with attention to the exchange of ambassadors. Intermittently envoys were exchanged by the Commonwealth with France, Holland, Portugal, and Spain among others.

monstrous crime that you describe, to be sure; almost the same as if someone had said, "Take warning, learn to practise justice and respect the gods." Could any utterance be more baleful? [437]

"Cromwell wrote this message to the Scots after the battle of Dunbar." And it was worthy of him and of that noble victory.[438] "The unspeakable pages of Milton are sprinkled with this kind of sesame and poppy." [439] Illustrious indeed is the comrade whom you always associate with me, and in this crime you clearly make me his equal and sometimes his superior. With this title I should think myself [126] most highly honored by you, if from you could proceed anything honorable. "Those pages have been burned," you assert, "by the public hangman in Paris, at the instance of the supreme Parliament." [440] In no wise, I have learned, was this done by Parliament, but by some city official, a *locum tenens,* whether civil or uncivil I do not know, at the instigation of certain clergymen, lazy beasts, who foresaw from a distance and at a great remove what I pray may someday befall their own paunch. Do you not perceive that we too could in turn have burned Salmasius' *Royal Defence?* Even I myself could easily have obtained this request from our magistrates, if I had not thought the insult better avenged by contempt. You, hastening to put out one fire with another, built a Herculean pyre, whence I might rise to greater fame. We more sensibly decided that the frigidity of the *Royal Defence* should not be kindled into flame.[441] I marvel that the people of Toulouse (for I have heard that I was burned also at Toulouse)[442] have become so unlike their ancestors that in the city where

[437] The apparent destruction of monarchy in Britain caused more apprehension than delight on the continent. See *Clamor,* 1652, p. 121; below, Appendix D, pp. 1072–75. The quotation is a paraphrase of Virgil, *Aeneid,* VI, 620, "Moniti discite iustitiam et non temnere divos."

[438] *Clamor* (1652), p. 121. The words of Cromwell which Du Moulin quoted are the subject of the previous note. The Battle of Dunbar, a crushing defeat for the Scots, took place on September 3, 1650.

[439] Compounded of the oil of sesame and the juice of the poppy, Milton's writing, Du Moulin says, is both an emetic and a soporific.

[440] Milton's *Defensio* was condemned and publicly burned at Paris on June 26, 1651. French (*Life Records,* III, 48–50) gives the full text of the edict, signed by Dreux Daubray, counsellor of the king in his Councils. For the Du Moulin statement, see *Clamor* (1652), p. 121.

[441] In his references to the English handling of *Defensio Regia* Milton's rhetoric is more effective than his reasoning. He knew that, far from treating Salmasius with contempt, the Council of State very promptly ordered a reply to be written by Milton himself.

[442] The burning of Milton's *Defensio* at Toulouse took place on June 7, 1651.

under the counts Raimond [127] both liberty and religion were once so nobly defended,[443] the Defence of liberty and religion has now been burned. "Would that the writer had been burned as well," you say. So, you slave? But you have taken extraordinary care that I should not return a similar greeting to you, More, for you have long since been consumed by far darker flames—the flames of your adulteries, the flames of your foul deeds, the flames of your prejudices, with the help of which you faithlessly discarded the woman who was betrothed to you by her own seduction. You are consumed by your fits of desperate madness, which drove you to lust after the holiest of rites, foul wretch that you are. They drove you as a priest to defile with incestuous hands the unperceived body of the Lord,[444] and, even as you feigned holiness, to threaten with this Cry of yours all dreadful consequences to those who feign holiness. The flames of madness drove you to untangle your own infamous head, condemned by your own pronouncement. With these crimes and infamies you are all afire, with these raging flames you are scorched night and day, and you pay us a penalty more severe than that which any foe could invoke against you. Meanwhile these burnings [128] of yours do not injure, do not touch me, and I have a great many consolations that delight and gratify my mind, with which to counter those insults of yours. One court, one Parisian hangman, impelled by evil auspices, has perhaps burned me, but a very great many good and learned men [445] throughout all France nonetheless read, approve, and embrace me, as do great numbers throughout the boundless reaches of all Germany, the very home of liberty,[446] and throughout all other countries as well, wherever any of her footprints still remain. And even Greece herself, Athens herself in Attica, as if come to life again, has ap-

---

It preceded the burning at Paris, therefore, by some eighteen days. French (*Life Records*, III, 38–40) prints the text of the condemnation.

[443] Milton exaggerates the defence of liberty and religion by the Counts of Toulouse. The city had a fairly continuous record of severe suppression of dissent in religion. See *Liberty and Political Power in Toulouse 1050–1230,* by John Hine Mundy (New York: Columbia University Press, 1954).

[444] Milton did not believe, of course, in transubstantiation. But since every time More served communion his defiled hands touched the elements which symbolize Christ, he touched the spiritually real but physically unperceived body of Christ.

[445] See above, p. 549, n. 8.

[446] Milton is thinking of liberty in the church, particularly of the pioneer activities of Martin Luther, but he extends the idea by his echo of Virgil, *Georgics,* II, 473–74, "Extrema per illos/iustitia, excedens terris, vestigia facit."

plauded me in the voice of Philaras, her most illustrious nursling.[447] Indeed, I can truthfully assert that from the time when my *Defence* was first published, and kindled the enthusiasm of its readers, no ambassador from any prince or state who was then in the city failed to congratulate me, if we chanced to meet, or omitted to seek an interview with me at his own house, or to visit me at mine.[448] It would be a sacrilege to omit mention of your departed spirit, Adrian Pauw,[449] glory and ornament of the Netherlands, [129] you who were sent to us with the highest dignity as Ambassador and took care that, although we chanced never to meet, many messages should often assure me of your great and singular good will towards me. Even more often is it a pleasure to recall what I think could never have happened without the favor of God—that on me, whose writing seemed to have attacked kings, the royal majesty itself benign smiled and bore witness to my integrity and the superior truth of judgment, with a testimony neighboring on the divine. For should I shrink from such an epithet, when I contemplate that august queen and the high praise with which she is celebrated lips of all men? [450] Indeed, I should not regard the wisest o

[447] Leonard Philaras (*ca.* 1600–1673), born in Greece and educate eventually became the ambassador of the Duke of Parma to Franc when he was out of favor with Cardinal Mazarin, he visited Englan on Milton. When he learned of Milton's blindness, he recommende in Paris. Two letters to Philaras survive (Columbia, XII, 55–59 an admiration of *Defensio* is acknowledged by Milton in the first. C admiration Milton exaggerates both the importance of Philaras a cation of his praise with that of Greece in general. See Terence S the First English Philhellene," *MLR,* XLVII (1952), 553–54.

[448] Many similar statements appear in the writings of Aubrey and Wood, but none gives specific names. The reasons for th were varied. Some, no doubt, were prompted by interest in but, in view of his position as Latin Secretary, many r cial or purely formal. See French, *Life Records*, II, 339, a 121.

[449] Adrian de Pauw, ambassador extraordinary of Holl June 8, 1652, charged with the responsibility of settling land and the States General, particularly those arising action between Admirals Van Tromp and Blake. His for home on July 7. See French, *Life Records,* III, 227

[450] How deeply Milton was offended by the burnin by Du Moulin's remark that he should have been bur by the height to which he here exalts himself. He re 603, nn. 38 and 229) to Queen Christina of Swed sunshine of her favor.

nians [451] (to whom, however, I do not compare myself) as more honored even by the oracle of the Pythian himself, than I by the judgment of that queen. But if it had been my fate to write these words in my youth, and if orators were allowed the same licence as poets, I should not have hesitated to exalt my lot above that of certain gods, for they, being gods, [130] contended before a human judge concerning beauty alone,[452] or music,[453] while I, a human being, with a goddess for judge, have come off victorious in by far the noblest contest of all. When I had been so honored, no one would dare to treat me with contempt, save only a public hangman, whether he who gave the orders or he who carried them out.

At this point you make a vigorous attempt to prevent us from defending our actions by citing the example of Dutch exploits on behalf of liberty.[454] Salmasius, too, labored in vain to prevent this. I would make the same response to you now as I made to him then: he is mistaken who supposes that we depend on anyone's example. We have very often helped and encouraged the Dutch in their struggles for liberty, but never have we considered it necessary to emulate them. If any brave deed must be done on behalf of liberty, we are our own exemplars, accustomed to lead, not to follow, others. With the most absurd arguments (but well-suited to such a rogue as you) you even

[451] In Plato's *Apology* 21a Socrates speaks of his impetuous follower Chaerephon, who asked the oracle at Delphi whether any man was wiser than Socrates. The reply that no man was wiser puzzled Socrates, but since it was made by a god, he admitted that it could not be a lie. The story appears also in Prolusion VI (*Complete Prose,* I, 272–73) and in *Paradise Regained,* IV, 275–76.

[452] Elated by remembrance of Queen Christina's favor, Milton sees himself in a reversed judgment of Paris (*Iliad,* XXIV, 25–30) in which, instead of the three goddesses, Hera, Athena, and Aphrodite, being judged by the man Paris, Milton, a human being, is judged by a goddess, the divine Christina. Moreover, his is the nobler judgment since it concerned intellectual power rather than mere physical beauty.

[453] The mention of music indicates that Milton has in mind another contest less ignificant in purpose than his. It is the mock judgment of Paris in *Metamorphoses* *The Golden Ass* (book X) by Apuleius. In this competition the goddesses are companied by musicians who play in the Ionian mode for Hera, in the Dorian Athena, and in the Lydian for Aphrodite. Fond as he was of music, Milton is ling to say that winning a prize in that art is less meaningful than being adged the victor in intellectual competition.

[454] Du Moulin (*Clamor,* 1652, pp. 126–28; below, Appendix D, p. 1072) presents xcellent statement of the long, heroic struggle of the Dutch with Spain for the very of their political and religious freedom.

urge the French to declare war on us,[455] you paltry declaimer. "The spirit of France," you say, "will never endure to receive our ambassadors." But what is more significant, it has already endured to send us voluntarily three times and more its own ambassadors.[456] The French therefore are magnanimous, [131] as is their wont, but you are convicted of being degenerate and false, ignorant of politics, and a liar. Next, you seek to show that the Federated States deliberately protracted negotiations to a great length and wished to have "neither a treaty nor a war with us." [457] And yet it certainly behooves the States themselves not to permit their plans to be thus laid bare and, so to speak, vitiated by a fugitive from Geneva, stabling among them, who, if tolerated much longer, seems destined to debauch not just maidservants, but public councils as well. For they themselves profess complete fraternity and sincerity, and have now reinstated with us perpetual peace, which is the prayer of all good men.

"It was amusing to see," he says, "with what mockery, with what dangers those ambassadors from the gallows (from the English, of course) were daily afflicted, not only by the English royalists, and so on, but especially by the Dutch." [458] If we had not long since discov-

[455] Du Moulin discusses at length (*Clamor,* 1652, pp. 121–24) the danger to the French monarchy implicit in the events in England. From the royalist point of view he makes a very good case for the importance of nullifying the precedent set up by the execution of Charles through the restoration of the Stuart dynasty. He boldly asserts that France should make war on the Commonwealth as an act of chivalry toward Queen Henrietta Maria and as a means of self-preservation for France.

[456] Both Du Moulin and Milton are right in part. The French ambassador in London was recalled shortly after the execution of the king, but his secretary remained, serving as an unofficial *chargé d'affaires,* until December, 1650, when he was expelled for helping English Roman Catholics to receive the mass in secret. At the same time the English resident agent in Paris was recalled. Masson (IV, 380–82) gives the history of this matter in detail. See *Clamor* (1652), p. 124.

[457] Du Moulin's version of Anglo-Dutch relations is more correct than Milton's. The Dutch did drag their feet for reasons Du Moulin understood. In March, 1651, the English sent two ambassadors with a retinue of some 250 persons to Holland for the purpose of negotiating a treaty of peace and unity with the Dutch. After three months of fruitless discussion they returned empty-handed. Though the Republican party was in power and tended to favor good relations with England because of trade, if for no other reason, the Orange party was still very influential and numerous. See Masson, IV, 275–78. For the Du Moulin statement, see *Clamor* (1652), p. 124.

[458] The unpleasant reception accorded the splendid English embassy to The Hague was, of course, a grave affront in terms of diplomatic courtesy. Milton was

ered who was responsible for the murder of our first Ambassador, Dorislaus, and for the injuries received by our two subsequent legates, we should here behold an informer who even brings false accusations against his own hosts and benefactors. [132] Do you, men of Holland, permit this creature to be fostered among you, who is not only a lustful minister in the church, but also a bloody instigator of the violations of all right, and furthermore, a false informer and betrayer of those violations?

The last point in the accusations is our "offence against the reformed churches." But in reality how is our offence against them greater than theirs against us? If you insist, "by our example," I reply that if you search out the records all the way from the Waldensians themselves and the people of Toulouse to the famine of Rochelle,[459] we shall certainly be found the last of all churches to have taken arms against tyrants. But we are the first to have condemned them to death. Certainly—because we were the first to whom this course was possible. What they would have done, given the same opportunity, I suppose not even they themselves are very sure. Indeed, I am of opinion that one against whom we wage war is regarded by us (if we have the use of reason and judgment) as an enemy. But it has always been permissible to kill an enemy by virtue of the same right with which we attack him. Therefore, since a tyrant is not our enemy alone, but the public enemy of virtually the entire human race, [133] he can be killed according to the same law by which he can be attacked with weapons.[460]

---

fully justified in his anger toward the Dutch for their breach of manners and toward Du Moulin for admitting amusement at the episode. See Masson, IV, 276. For the Du Moulin statement, see *Clamor* (1652), p. 132.

[459] To support his contention that the reformed church of Britain was not the first to resist tyranny, Milton cites three earlier instances of such conflict. First, the Waldenses, named for Pierre Valdes (or Valdez or Waldo), a wealthy merchant of Lyons. Their dissent from the Church of Rome was severe and kept them in bitter warfare with the papacy from the twelfth century onward. (Milton was later to lament their anguish and courage in his sonnet, "On the Late Massacre in Piemont.") Second, the people of Toulouse who, by agitation, began to free themselves of some feudal taxes in the twelfth century and who, by the thirteenth century, achieved a measure of responsibility in local government. And third, La Rochelle, which became the center of Huguenot resistance against the king and the church in France until it was forced by famine to surrender to Richelieu in 1628. An ironic aspect of the whole passage is Milton's readiness to deny primacy to the English in such matters. Usually God speaks first to his Englishmen.

[460] Many Englishmen, nurtured in the common law, found the trial of Charles difficult to reconcile with their traditional thinking. Furthermore, Milton could

Nor in truth is this my opinion alone, nor a new one. Prudence or common sense has dictated the same conviction to other men in the past. Hence Marcus Tullius [461] for Rabirius: "If it was a crime for Saturninus to be put to death, arms could not rightfully have been taken up against Saturninus. If you admit that arms were lawfully taken up, you must admit that he was lawfully killed." I have said more on this subject above, and often elsewhere, and the matter is clear enough in itself. Hence you could yourself predict what the French too would have done, if the same opportunity had been granted them. And I add this further statement. All who take up arms against a tyrant are also guilty of his death, so far as lies in their power. Indeed, they have already killed him, no matter what they seek, vainly enough, to tell themselves and others. But this doctrine belongs no more to us than to the French, whom you would exempt from such a sacrilege, for from what source, except from France, comes that *Franco-gallia*,[462] from what source the *Vindications against Tyrants*,[463] a book which is popularly ascribed to Beza himself? [134] Whence come the other books which Thuanus [464] mentions? You say,

---

find no escape from the patent fact that no one declared Charles a tyrant except those who desired to punish him for being one. He would have been on much firmer ground if he had boldly affirmed that the Commons were revolutionaries who had followed an unprecedented course of action and who would abide by the judgment of history for their justification.

[461] Milton calls Cicero to his aid in his attempt to justify the killing of Charles. He quotes a brief passage from *Pro Rabirio* (19), an oration delivered in 63 B.C. Cicero obtained the clearance of charges entered against a Roman knight Gaius Rabirius thirty-seven years before for complicity in the death of a tribune named Lucius Appuleius Saturninus during a factional fight. The latter had been declared a public enemy by the Senate; his death was therefore authorized by the highest authority in the state. Rabirius was cleared on the ground that he had acted under a final judgment of the Senate which gave the consuls the right to use force in an emergency and denied to the accused the right of appeal to the people.

[462] *Franco-Gallia* was the principal work of Francis Hotman (1524–1590), a lawyer who was forced to abandon his career because of his defection from Rome to Geneva. He taught history and law in various Protestant universities and served the Huguenots in important confidential transactions. *Franco-Gallia* (1573) presents an ideal system of Protestant government, including an elective monarchy and a representative parliament. Hotman is quoted in *Commonplace Book* (*Complete Prose,* I, 459, 461, 501). See Beatrice Reynolds, *Proponents of Limited Monarchy in Sixteenth-Century France—Francis Hotman and Jean Bodin* (New York, 1931).

[463] Milton is so eager to have French Protestant support for his views that he cites a volume without concern for the correctness of its ascription to Beza.

[464] Jacobus Augustus Thuanus or Jacques Auguste de Thou (1553–1617) was

however, that "Milton" (as if I were alone in this) "is greatly concerned over this matter, and his sacrilegious madness I would have treated as it deserves." You would have treated it, you gallows-bird? If the church in Middleburg,[465] dishonored and unhappy with you as its pastor, had treated your unspeakable crimes as they deserved, it would long since have sent you to the devil. If the magistrates had treated them as they deserved, you would long since have paid for your adulteries, by hanging from the gallows. And indeed, you seem on the point of paying for them very soon, for that church of yours at Middleburg, as I have recently heard, has awakened and taken thought for its own reputation. You, its goatherd pastor, or rather the rankest goat of all, it has expelled and sent to perdition. Hence too the magistrates of Amsterdam [466] have barred you from the pulpit, your stage, and forbidden your shameless face to be seen from that spot, to the supreme offence of all decent men, forbidden too that impious voice to be heard in public on a sacred theme. There now remains to you only your teaching of Greek letters, and this too must shortly be taken from you, save for that one [135] letter of which you will soon deservedly be, not the professor, but the dependent pupil.[467]

I do not make these predictions to you in anger, but I say only what is just. For so far am I from being vexed by such slanderers as you that actually I always desire such for myself and in fact consider it an evident mark of divine favor that those who have attacked me

---

a favorite source of quotation for Milton. His only book was *Historia Sui Temporis* (Geneva, 1620, 1626). See *Complete Prose,* I, index under *Thuanus.*

[465] It is true that contemporary gossip indicates that there was some difficulty at Middleburg about More's orthodoxy as there had been at Geneva. It is untrue, however, to say that he was dismissed from the church there because of immorality. As a matter of fact, after he had been cleared of Bontia's charges by the Synod of Utrecht, he was invited to preach there. In July, 1652, his request to be released from the church at Middleburg was granted. See Masson, IV, 461. For the passage from Moulin, see *Clamor* (1652), p. 144.

[466] When More gave up his post in Middleburg, he planned to return to France. His mind was changed, however, by an invitation from the magistrates of Amsterdam to be professor of church history there. He had been offered the post three years before, but had rejected it because he felt obligated to fill the position he had already accepted at Middleburg. More took up his duties in Amsterdam in September, 1652. See Masson, IV, 461.

[467] Milton brings to conclusion with a pun his several suggestions that More belongs on the gallows. A teacher of Greek for many years, More now has only one letter left. Instead of teaching it, however, he will learn from it, for it is the letter *pi* shaped π like the gallows.

most bitterly have always been very clearly of such a stamp. By their slander they do not defame, but honor and praise, for surely their praise would have amounted to defamation. But what has checked you in your assault just now, brave homuncule? "If it had not been contrary to my scruples to encroach upon the province of the great Salmasius, to whom I shall leave the true victory over this would-be great adversary. . . ." If indeed both he and I now seem great to you, I shall perhaps be a more difficult province than he, especially since he is dead. I care little for victory, provided that truth be victorious.[468]

Meanwhile you proceed with your Cry: "They convert parricide into a doctrine, and they desire to do this with the consent of the reformed churches. They dare not defend it openly. This was also, says Milton, [136] the view of the most eminent theologians who were the very founders of the Reformation."[469] It was their view, I say, and I have proved this at greater length in the book entitled, in our tongue, *The Tenure of Kings and Magistrates,* the second edition, and elsewhere. It is boring to repeat a thing which has now been said so many times.[470] There I have cited verbatim passages from Luther, Zwingli, Calvin, Bucer, Martyr, Paraeus, and finally Knox,[471] "the only Scot," you say, to whom I "refer" and "whom in this respect all Protestants, especially the French, at that time condemned." And yet Knox, as is there related, asserts that he drew this doctrine expressly

[468] I Esdras 3:12 says: "But above all things Truth beareth away the victory."

[469] Du Moulin touched Milton on two very sensitive spots. First, he said that the acts of the Independents have given the church of Rome a weapon with which to belabor all reformed churches, and then, to make this charge more unpalatable, he added that actually the Independents had learned regicide from the Jesuits. Second, he argued that, in order to elevate regicide into a doctrine of the reformed churches, a small group of Independents, particularly Milton, had sought *ex post facto* support for regicide in the words of the chief theologians of the Reformation. Du Moulin's attack was hard, and his argument was strengthened by many citations from the acts of the French reformed synod and from the words of French divines. See *Clamor* (1652), p. 148.

[470] Milton was upset by Du Moulin's forceful argument against the Independents in general and himself in particular. He made no attempt, however, to answer the specific points raised by his opponent.

[471] For these citations, see *The Tenure* (*Complete Prose,* III, 243–48). From Milton's point of view they were skillfully chosen and assembled. They are all out of context, however, and Du Moulin rightfully could deny that they proved Milton's point. For example, Luther, who owed his life and the realization of his purpose to German princes, defended them firmly against the Anabaptists.

from Calvin and from other eminent theologians of the age, with whom he was on familiar terms.[472] In that book you will also find further observations to the same effect, drawn from our sounder divines in the reigns of Mary and Elizabeth.[473] But you come at last to an impious conclusion with long-winded prayers to God, prayers ready-made and abominable, and hardened as you are, you lift that adulterous face to Heaven. [137] Gladly do I permit you to do so, nor do I hinder you, for your impiety could not by any measure be increased.

I now return to the matter which I promised above to treat, and I shall at this point examine the principal crimes which are charged to Cromwell, so that their pettiness, when they are taken separately, may be evident, since even when listed together they have no weight in themselves.

"He announced in the presence of a great many witnesses that he intended to overthrow all monarchies, to destroy all kings."[474] How trustworthy are your narratives, we have already seen on several occasions. Perhaps some one of the deserters told you that Cromwell spoke in this fashion. Of those "many witnesses," you name not one. Hence the slander which you utter without an authority is vitiated through its own defect. Cromwell is not such that any man has ever heard him brag about what he has already accomplished; much less is he wont to make insolent boasts or threats concerning things which he has not yet accomplished and which are of such great difficulty. Certainly if your informants were not wilful and congenital liars (rather than liars according to a preconcerted scheme) they would not have invented this story, at any rate, which is so foreign to Cromwell's nature. [138] But when kings, whom you often advise to have a care for themselves, take thought for their own safety, they will be well advised to reject such an inexperienced adviser as you, and rather than snatch at gossip from the crossroads,[474a] adopt counsels worthy of themselves, with the help of which they may more easily look to their own interests.

[472] French dislike of Knox sprang from his utterance of such statements as Milton quotes in *The Tenure* (*Complete Prose,* III, 248). Milton twits Du Moulin by saying that, though these sentiments were uttered by a Scot, they originated with a Frenchman, Calvin. For Moulin's statement, see *Clamor* (1652), p. 148.

[473] Quotations from Cartwright, Fenner, and Goodman appear in *The Tenure* (*Complete Prose,* III, 248–51).

[474] *Clamor* (1652), p. 12.

[474a] Milton quotes Cicero, *Pro Murena,* 6.13.

The second charge is that Cromwell persuaded the king "that he should betake himself in secret to the Isle of Wight." [475] It is well established that King Charles ruined his case in many other ways, and three times by flight—first, when he fled from London to York, next when he fled to the Scots mercenaries in England,[476] and finally when he fled to the Isle of Wight. But the author of this last flight was Cromwell. Very well. Yet I marvel, first at those royalists who do not hesitate to assert so often that Charles was extremely wise and yet that the same man scarcely ever did anything of his own accord, that whether among friends or among enemies, whether in court or in camp, he was almost always in the power of another, now his wife, now the bishops, now the courtiers, now the soldiers, and finally the enemy; [139] that generally he followed the worse counsels, and those of the worse counselors. Charles is persuaded, Charles is imposed on, Charles is tricked, he is smitten with terror, he is lured with vain hopes; as the common prey of all, both friends and enemies, Charles is driven and carried off. Let them either excise these statements from their writings or let them cease to proclaim the wisdom of Charles.

Next, I confess that, although it is a fine thing to excel in wisdom and counsel, nevertheless when the state is troubled with factions, this superiority has its inconveniences and renders all the most experienced men the more liable to the slanders of both parties. This circumstance has often injured Cromwell. Here the Presbyterians, there the enemy impute whatever treatment they regard as too harsh toward themselves, not to the common strategy, but to Cromwell alone. In fact, if they themselves make any mistake through want of foresight, they do not blush to ascribe it to the trickery and deceit of Cromwell. All blame is diverted to him; he suffers for every mistake. And yet it is perfectly certain that the flight of King Charles to the Isle of Wight was as much a surprise and an unforeseen event to Cromwell, who was then several miles away, [140] as to any member of Parliament then present in the city, whom he informed of the affair by letter, as if it were a most unexpected event just then made known to him. This moreover is the way it happened. The king, alarmed by

[475] Du Moulin has repeated a widely circulated royalist tale. All extant evidence (Gardiner, *Great Civil War,* III, 247, n. 3) indicates that the flight to the Isle of Wight was planned within the king's immediate circle.

[476] On January 10, 1642, Charles fled from London and set up his standard at York; he surrendered to the Scots at Newark on May 5, 1646.

the clamor of the entire army, which had just then begun to demand his punishment, since he had shown no improvement in spite of their undertakings and promises, determined to protect his own interest by nocturnal flight with only two confidants. But, more firmly resolved on flight than on his destination, whether because of the inexperience or the timidity of his companions, innocent of a plan for finding refuge, he voluntarily surrendered to Hammond, the governor of the Isle of Wight, in hopes that a ship might secretly be prepared and an easy passage secured for him from that island to France or Belgium.[477] This account of the king's escape to the Isle of Wight I obtained from those who had the best possible opportunity to become acquainted with the whole story.

But there is also the charge that through Cromwell "The English won a great victory over the Scots." Not *parti sunt,* More, but without the solecism *pepererunt* [478]— [141] gained for themselves a glorious victory. Just think what a bloody battle that was for the Scots, if you could not even mention it without staggering and banging your professorial head—giddy with fear—against Priscian's desk.[479] But now let us see how great a crime it was for Cromwell to conquer, in the most glorious battle in many generations, the invading Scots who were already promising themselves supreme power over Englishmen. "Amid these tumults, while Cromwell was away with his army. . . ." No! Rather, while he, exhausted though he was by the task of restoring to their allegiance the revolted Welshmen [480] and by the long siege-operations, saw, conquered, and most gloriously routed the enemy

[477] Milton adds nothing to the accepted account of the flight to the Isle of Wight. See Gardiner, *Great Civil War,* III, 250.

[478] Milton resents the implication of Du Moulin's Latin (*Clamor,* 1652, p. 39), namely, that the victory was brought forth rather than positively achieved by the English. He therefore describes as a solecism the use of the passive voice (*parti sunt*) rather than the active (*pepererunt*). The verb is *pario,* to bring forth, produce.

[479] Believing he speaks of More, erstwhile professor of Greek, Milton pictures him as a stupid pupil rebuked by the teacher. Priscianus Caesariensis, born in Mauretania, was a grammarian at Constantinopolis under the Emperor Anastasius (491–518).

[480] Word reached the Council of War at the end of April, 1648, that the Welsh were in revolt. At once Cromwell was ordered to South Wales with two regiments of horse and three of foot. By the end of May he had crushed the revolt. Immediately he began a forced march north to meet the Scots. See Gardiner, *Great Civil War,* III, 365. For quotation from Du Moulin, see *Clamor* (1652), p. 40.

who had already penetrated to the vitals of England [481] and was now threatening Parliament itself, the Presbyterians "began to tire of Cromwell." Here you speak the truth. While Cromwell is repelling the common foe at the risk of his life, they accuse him at home on trumped-up charges, although he is fighting for them and bravely contending in the line of battle, and they suborn a certain Captain Huntington [482] against him, on a capital charge. Who could, without protest, even hear of such foul ingratitude? [142] At the instigation of these same persons, a most worthless and insolent band of striplings, apprentices from the shops, besiege the doors of Parliament in great numbers and compel that body by their shouting and threatening to decree whatever they please.[483] What could be more disgraceful than this? Now we should have seen our Camillus,[484] returning a heroic victor over the Scots, either sent into exile or paying the most humiliating penalties, if General Fairfax had not thought such a disgrace to his invincible lieutenant intolerable, and if the entire army, which had itself been treated with sufficient ingratitude, had not forbidden such an unspeakable procedure. Cromwell therefore entered

[481] Before Cromwell returned from Wales in June, 1648, Scottish forces under the Duke of Hamilton had moved far into England. As Milton says, they were becoming a serious threat. As soon as Cromwell reached England, he entered the field. After many preliminary actions the final battle was joined at Preston on August 17, 1648. Though greatly outnumbered, the English inflicted a crushing defeat on the Scots and rendered them incapable of further serious action. See Gardiner, *Great Civil War,* III, 430–43.

[482] Major Robert Huntington, a former officer in Cromwell's own regiment who had carried out many confidential missions for him, appeared before the bar of the House of Lords on August 2, 1648, to accuse him of high treason. Huntington affirmed that all of Cromwell's dealings with the army and the king were insincere and that his sole objective was supreme power for himself. See Gardiner, *Great Civil War,* III, 428–30.

[483] During the spring of 1647 London seethed. Charles shifted ground persistently in an effort to play off the army against the Parliament, and thus to gain time for his own advantage. The city was heavily committed to the Presbyterians. Cromwell searched his conscience and sought God's will for a solution that would prevent anarchy. See Sir Charles H. Firth, *Oliver Cromwell and the Rule of the Puritans in England* (Oxford University Press, 1963), pp. 164–66.

[484] Milton's vast knowledge of classical lore was seldom used more sensitively than in his comparison of Cromwell with Camillus. Marcus Furius Camillus (early fourth century, B.C.) was accused of stealing booty from the city of Veli after he had captured it. He went into exile, but he was recalled. He drove the Gauls under Brennus out of Rome, conquered the Volsci and the Aequi, suppressed civil war in Rome, and defeated a second invasion by the Gauls. His life appears in Plutarch.

the city and after putting down the urban mob without difficulty, justly expelled from Parliament the adherents of our Scottish enemies.[485] The rest, now that they were freed from the overbearing conduct of the apprentices, renounced the agreement which (contrary to the will and public edict of Parliament) they had entered into with the king at the Isle of Wight. Huntington too, the accuser, who had been left unpunished and completely free of restraint, was at last driven by conscience to seek pardon from Cromwell of his own free will, [143] and voluntarily confessed by whom he had been suborned. These are substantially the crimes which are charged against the valiant liberator of his country, except for those to which I have replied earlier. You see what they are worth.

But I shall have accomplished nothing if I merely prove that this great man, who has deserved so well of the state, has done no wrong. For it is to the interest not only of the state, but of myself as well (since I have been so deeply involved in the same slanderous accusations) to show to all peoples and all ages, so far as I can, how supremely excellent he is, how worthy of all praise.[486]

Oliver Cromwell is sprung of renowned and illustrious stock.[487] The name was celebrated in former times for good administration under the monarchy and became more glorious as soon as the orthodox religion was reformed, or rather established among us for the first time. He had grown up in the seclusion of his own home, until he reached an age mature and settled, and this too he passed as a private

[485] Though it is believed that Cromwell knew in advance of a plan for the army to terminate Parliament's negotiations with Charles at Newport by taking over London, he could not have had any part in the final decision. After a warning on November 30, 1648, that Parliament must come to terms with the Army, Fairfax acted swiftly. On December 2 he occupied London and set up his headquarters at Whitehall. See Gardiner, *Great Civil War,* III, 529–40.

[486] Milton has finished with *Clamor*. Tedious debate and bitter argument past, he can now rise to higher things, the celebration of heroes and the design of the perfect state.

[487] Cromwell was descended from Margaret Cromwell, sister of Thomas Cromwell, Earl of Essex and chief minister of Henry VIII in the destruction of the religious houses. The best sources for the materials of Cromwell's biography and for the biography itself are: Wilbur C. Abbott, (1) *A Bibliography of Oliver Cromwell* (Harvard University Press, 1929) and (2) *The Writings and Speeches of Oliver Cromwell*. A short but scholarly account is Maurice Ashley, *The Greatness of Oliver Cromwell* (New York: The Macmillan Company, 1958). This and the following purely biographical notes on Cromwell are based on Sir Charles Firth, *Oliver Cromwell and the Rule of the Puritans in England.*

citizen,[488] known for nothing so much as his devotion to the Puritan religion and his upright life. For an occasion of supreme importance he had nourished in his silent heart a faith dependent on God and a mighty spirit.[489] When [144] Parliament was for the last time convened by the king, Cromwell was chosen by his town's electorate and won a seat.[490] There he at once became known for his upright sentiments and steadfast counsels. When war broke out, he offered his services and was put in command of a squadron of horse, but because of the concourse of good men who flocked to his standards from all sides, his force was greatly increased and he soon surpassed well-nigh the greatest generals both in the magnitude of his accomplishments and in the speed with which he achieved them.[491] Nor was this remarkable, for he was a soldier well-versed in self-knowledge, and whatever enemy lay within—vain hopes, fears, desires—he had either previously destroyed within himself or had long since reduced to sub-

488 As the only living son of a well-to-do country gentleman, Cromwell spent his youth on the estate he later would manage. He devoted short periods of time to study, first, at Sidney Sussex College, Cambridge, and, later, at Lincoln's Inn, but he planned no career in the usual sense. He seemed destined to follow in his father's footsteps and manage his substantial estates. These were materially increased by his marriage on August 22, 1620, to Elizabeth Bourchier. The seclusion of Cromwell's youth suggests Horace, *Odes,* I, xii, 45–46 (crescit occulto velut arbor aveo/fama Marcelli. . .).

489 Cromwell grew up in a strongly Puritan atmosphere. The local school in Huntingdon was headed by Dr. Thomas Beard, an austere disciplinarian noted for his anti-papal and strongly Puritan writings. Cambridge in general and Sidney Sussex College in particular were centers of Puritan teaching. Sidney Sussex was singled out by Laud as a nursery of Puritanism.

490 Milton errs here. Cromwell sat first in the third Parliament convened by Charles I. He was elected member for Huntingdon in February, 1628, and took his seat on March 17, 1628. He sat in the "last" Parliament of Charles, the Long Parliament, as member for Cambridge. His first participation in debate, in the 1628 Parliament, was an attack on high church doctrine, in which he cited some experiences of his old schoolmaster, Dr. Thomas Beard. For Cromwell and the Cromwell family in Parliament see Douglas Brunton and Donald H. Pennington, *Members of the Long Parliament* (Cambridge: Harvard University Press, 1954).

491 Cromwell entered actively into the Civil War in June, 1642. He contributed a substantial sum to the army and sent ammunition to his armed constitutents in Cambridge. Later he led a small force which seized the powder magazine at Cambridge and prevented the confiscation of the university plate for the king. He raised a troop of sixty horse and served as its captain at the Battle of Edgehill on October 23, 1642. At that action he found the army of Essex poorly manned and inadequately trained. He appealed to Hampden to organize and rigorously train new regiments of men of better quality. When Hampden did nothing, Cromwell undertook the task himself. In January, 1643, he went with his troop into the eastern counties to recruit responsible men of conscience.

jection. Commander first over himself, victor over himself, he had learned to achieve over himself the most effective triumph, and so, on the very first day that he took service against an external foe, he entered camp a veteran and past-master in all that concerned the soldier's life.[492]

It is impossible for me within the confines of this discourse to describe with fitting dignity the capture of the many cities, to list the many battles, and indeed such great ones, in which he was never conquered nor put to flight, but traversed the entire realm of Britain with uninterrupted victory. [145] Such deeds require the grand scope of a true history, a second battlefield, so to speak, on which they may be recounted, and a space for narration equal to the deeds themselves. The following single proof of his rare and all-but-divine excellence suffices—that there flourished in him so great a power, whether of intellect and genius or of discipline (established not merely according to military standards, but rather according to the code of Christian virtue) that to his camp, as to the foremost school, not just of military science, but of religion and piety, he attracted from every side all men who were already good and brave, or else he made them such, chiefly by his own example. Throughout the entire war, and sometimes even in the intervening periods of peace, amid the many shifts of opinion and circumstance, in spite of opposition,[493] he kept them at their duty, and does so still, not by bribes and the licentiousness typical of the military, but by his authority and their wages alone. No greater praise is wont to be attributed to Cyrus[494] or Epaminondas[495] or any other pre-eminent general among the ancients. [146] And so no one has ever raised a larger or better-disciplined army in a shorter space of time than did Cromwell, an army obedient to his command in all

[492] Obviously Milton knew something of Cromwell's inner life, for he here delicately transforms a dark period of his life into a cause for praise. Cromwell was truly a veteran of the wars of the spirit. For eight years, from 1628 to 1636, he wrestled with God and, beset by awful doubts and terrible fears, he resisted that service which he knew was perfect freedom. See Firth, *Oliver Cromwell* (World Classics, 1953), pp. 38 ff.

[493] Milton refers to the "detractions rude" which plagued Cromwell during the period immediately before the king's trial and execution.

[494] Cyrus the Great (d. 529 B.C.), founder of the Persian empire, enlarged the domains of his nation by his conquests of Media, Lydia, the Greek cities of Asia Minor, and Babylon. He was an invincible military leader.

[495] Epaminondas (*ca.* 420–362 B.C.), a Theban general whose military skill made Thebes for a time the most powerful city in Greece.

things, welcomed and cherished by their fellow-citizens, formidable indeed to the enemy in the field, but wonderfully merciful to them once they had surrendered.[496] On the estates and under the roofs of the enemy this army proved so mild and innocent of all offence that when the royalists considered the violence of their own soldiery, their drunkenness, impiety, and lust, they rejoiced in their altered lot and believed that Cromwell's men had come, not as enemies, but as guests, a bulwark to all good men, a terror to the wicked, and in fact an inspiration to all virtue and piety.

Nor should I pass you by, Fairfax,[497] in whom nature and divine favor have joined with supreme courage supreme modesty and supreme holiness. By your own right and merit you deserve to be called upon to share these praises, although in your present retreat you conceal yourself as well as you can, like Scipio Africanus of old in Liternum.[498] You have defeated, not only the enemy, but ambition as well, and the thirst for glory which conquers all the most eminent men, [147] and you are reaping the reward of your virtues and noble deeds amid that most delightful and glorious retirement which is the end of all labors and human action, even the greatest. When the heroes of old, after wars and honors no greater than yours, enjoyed such repose, the poets who sought to praise them despaired of being able fittingly to describe its nature in any other way than by creating a myth to the effect that they had been received into heaven and were sharing the banquets of the gods.[499] But whether ill health, as I sus-

[496] In general the New Model Army, which Cromwell had created so rapidly and so effectively, enjoyed a very favorable reputation for its moral as well as for its military discipline. It was not permitted to plunder, to mistreat non-combatants, or to punish prisoners improperly. The royalists freely admitted that the Parliamentary army was superior in these matters to their own.

[497] Milton's admiration for Sir Thomas Fairfax was sincere but exaggerated. The sonnet "On the Lord General Fairfax" rightly praises his valor and his exceptional skill as a field commander, but it expresses also the belief that Fairfax was destined to be a notable statesman. Actually, he never concerned himself with public affairs other than those of a military nature. See introduction above, pp. 41–43, and Mildred A. Gibb, *The Lord General* (London, 1938).

[498] The comparison is not very exact, and in a way was only partially a compliment to Fairfax. Publius Cornelius Scipio (*ca.* 236–183 B.C.), after achieving classic victories in Africa and Spain, retired to his country place in Liternum. Scipio did not retire because of age, illness, or estrangement from public policy. On his return to Rome from the field of battle, he had been accused of accepting bribes and of other financial irregularities. Because of popular admiration the charges were allowed to lapse, but the stigma was not removed from his name.

[499] Milton means to suggest, it appears, that the leisure of retired heroes re-

pect, or some other reason [500] has withdrawn you from public life, I am firmly convinced that nothing could have torn you from the needs of the State had you not seen how great a defender of liberty, how strong and faithful a pillar and support of English interests you were leaving in your successor. For while you, Cromwell, are safe, he does not have sufficient faith even in God himself who would fear for the safety of England, when he sees God everywhere so favorable to you, so unmistakably at your side. But you were now left alone to fight upon another battleground. [148]

Yet why go on at length? The greatest events I shall relate, if I can, with brevity comparable to the speed with which you are wont to achieve them. When all Ireland was lost, but for a single city, you transported the army and in one battle instantly broke the power of Hibernia.[501] You were completing the task day by day, when suddenly you were recalled to the Scottish War. Then, tireless, you proceeded against the Scots who with their king were preparing an invasion of England, and in about one year you completely subdued and added to the wealth of England that realm which all our kings for eight hundred years had been unable to master.[502] When the remnant of their forces, still powerful and marching swiftly with no encumbrances, set out in utter desperation for England, which was then

---

sembles a sustained feast of the gods. Since Fairfax was still alive, the ancient myth to which he refers cannot be strictly applied. It normally portrays a hero snatched from death and translated to heavenly bliss. Milton uses it several times (Elegy III, l. 11; "Manso," ll. 43–44), but most notably in "Epitaphium Damonis," ll. 205–207, where he describes Damon as lifted to heaven and quaffing divine draughts amid the souls of heroes and the gods.

[500] Milton must have known the real reason for the withdrawal of Fairfax from the army, his disapproval of the action against the king, but he could not state it publicly, and he probably did not like to admit it to himself. To cover his disappointment, he resorts to generalities. For details on Fairfax's withdrawal, see introduction, above, pp. 41–43; and Whitelocke, *Memorials,* III, 207–11.

[501] After the execution of the King Ireland became a source of increasing danger to the new republic. The activity of royalist forces under the Duke of Ormond, the hostility of the Irish Confederation, and the neutrality of the northern Catholics under Owen Roe left England no real foothold except Dublin. See *Complete Prose,* III, 163–64, 170–79; and Thomas L. Coonan, *The Irish Catholic Confederacy and the Puritan Revolution* (Columbia University Press, 1954).

[502] Charles was proclaimed king of Great Britain and Ireland at Edinburgh immediately after his father's execution. He realized, however, that he would remain king in name only until he could muster sufficient force to make the office a reality in London. Having agreed at Breda in the spring of 1650 to accept the Covenant himself and to force Presbyterianism on England and Ireland, he went to Edinburgh to claim Scottish military support.

almost stripped of defences, and, making an unforeseen attack, got as far as Worcester,[503] you pursued them with forced marches and in one battle destroyed them, capturing almost all their noblemen. Afterwards peace was maintained at home.

Then, but not for the first time, we perceived that you were as mighty in deliberation as in the arts of war. Daily you toiled in Parliament, that the treaty made with the enemy might be honored, [149] or that decrees in the interest of the State might at once be passed. When you saw delays being contrived and every man more attentive to his private interest than to that of the state, when you saw the people complaining that they had been deluded of their hopes and circumvented by the power of the few, you put an end to the domination of these few men, since they, although so often warned, had refused to do so.[504] Another Parliament was convened anew, and the suffrage granted only to those who deserved it. The elected members came together. They did nothing. When they in turn had at length exhausted themselves with disputes and quarrels, most of them considering themselves inadequate and unfit for executing such great tasks, they of their own accord dissolved the Parliament.[505]

Cromwell, we are deserted! [506] You alone remain.[507] On you has fallen the whole burden of our affairs. On you alone they depend. In unison we acknowledge your unexcelled virtue. No one protests save such as seek equal honors, though inferior themselves, or begrudge the honors assigned to one more worthy, or do not understand that there is nothing in human society more pleasing to God, or more agreeable to reason, [150] nothing in the state more just, nothing

[503] After their rout at Dunbar on September 3, 1650, the Scots retreated and reorganized their forces. Cromwell continued to capture Scottish cities and castles, but he could not reach the enemy force. On August 2, 1651, he took Perth and cut the Scots off from the north of Scotland. Charles and his forces moved southward. Cromwell overtook them at Worcester and destroyed them as a fighting force on September 3, 1651. See above, introduction, pp. 148–52.

[504] See introduction, above, pp. 210–16. For the condition of the Rump, see Firth, *Oliver Cromwell,* pp. 294–300 and 312–15.

[505] The Rump out of the way, Cromwell summoned an assembly of representatives nominated by Independent congregations or by officers of the army. See above, p. 227, and Firth, *Oliver Cromwell,* pp. 322–27.

[506] Cromwell was at once named Lord Protector. See introduction, above, p. 229.

[507] In this paragraph Milton speaks partly to Cromwell and partly to himself. An undefeated hero in battle and a faithful laborer for the state at home, Cromwell was, in Milton's judgment, pre-eminently fit to rule.

more expedient, than the rule of the man most fit to rule. All know you to be that man, Cromwell! Such have been your achievements as the greatest and most illustrious citizen, the director of public counsels, the commander of the bravest armies, the father of your country.[508] It is thus that you are greeted by the spontaneous and heartfelt cries of all upright men. Your deeds recognize no other name as worthy of you; no other do they allow, and the haughty titles which seem so great in the opinion of the mob, they properly reject. For what is a title, except a certain limited degree of dignity? Your deeds surpass all degrees, not only of admiration, but surely of titles too, and like the tops of pyramids, bury themselves in the sky, towering above the popular favor of titles. But since it is, not indeed worthy, but expedient for even the greatest capacities to be bounded and confined by some sort of human dignity, which is considered an honor, you assumed a certain title very like that of father of your country. You suffered and allowed yourself, not indeed to be borne aloft, but to come down so many degrees from the heights and be forced into a definite rank, so to speak, for the public good.[509] [151] The name of king you spurned [510] from your far greater eminence, and rightly so. For if, when you became so great a figure, you were captivated by the title which as a private citizen you were able to send undei the yoke and reduce to nothing, you would be doing almost the same thing as if, when you had subjugated some tribe of idolaters with the help of the true God, you were to worship the gods that you had conquered. May you then, O Cromwell, increase in your magnanimity, for it becomes you. You, the liberator of your country, the author of liberty, and likewise its guardian and savior, can undertake no more distinguished role and none more august. By your deeds you have outstripped not only the achievements of our kings, but even the legends of our heroes.

[508] Milton brings to a climax the list of high titles he has conferred upon Cromwell with the most exalted of all. He equates Cromwell with Cicero, the first Roman to be called *pater patriae,* who was so named by the Senate after his destruction of the conspiracy of Catiline in 63 B.C. The title was later bestowed upon Julius Caesar and Augustus.

[509] Milton's anxiety about Cromwell's new title, Lord Protector, grows more than it abates. His style becomes fidgety; he repeats the word title over and over again as though he were trying to exorcise it.

[510] Milton must have known that, in December, 1653, a group of army officers, headed by General Lambert, disturbed by debates on the army in the Nominated Parliament, urged Cromwell to accept the title of king.

Consider again and again how precious a thing is this liberty which you hold, committed to your care, entrusted and commended to you by how dear a mother, your native land. That which she once sought from the most distinguished men of the entire nation, she now seeks from you alone and through you alone hopes to achieve. [152] Honor this great confidence reposed in you, honor your country's singular hope in you. Honor the faces and the wounds of the many brave men, all those who under your leadership have striven so vigorously for liberty. Honor the shades of those who have fallen in that very struggle. Honor too what foreign nations think and say of us, the high hopes which they have for themselves as a result of our liberty, so bravely won, and our republic, so gloriously born.[511] If the republic should miscarry, so to speak, and as quickly vanish, surely no greater shame and disgrace could befall this country. Finally,[512] honor yourself, so that, having achieved that liberty in pursuit of which you endured so many hardships and encountered so many perils, you may not permit it to be violated by yourself or in any degree diminished by others. Certainly you yourself cannot be free without us, for it has so been arranged by nature that he who attacks the liberty of others is himself the first of all to lose his own liberty and learns that he is the first of all to become a slave. And he deserves this fate. For if the very patron and tutelary god of liberty, as it were, [153] if that man than whom no one has been considered more just, more holy, more excellent, shall afterwards attack that liberty which he himself has defended, such an act must necessarily be dangerous and well-nigh fatal not only to liberty itself but also to the cause of all virtue and piety. Honor itself, virtue itself will seem to have melted away, religious faith will be circumscribed, reputation will hereafter be a meagre thing. A deeper wound than this, after that first wound, can never be inflicted on the human race. You have taken upon yourself by far the heaviest burden, one that will put to the test your inmost capacities, that will search you out wholly and intimately, and reveal what spirit, what strength, what authority are in you, whether there truly live in you that piety,

[511] This statement is not accurate. At the time Milton was writing, the prestige of the Republic in Europe was low as a result of the war with the Dutch in which victory seemed uncertain.

[512] Characteristically Milton stresses the principle rather than the means for its attainment. Yet, he admonishes Cromwell, the ideal and the fact of liberty, for which they all so valiantly fought, will remain vital if he remains true to his principles.

faith, justice, and moderation of soul which convince us that you have been raised by the power of God beyond all other men to this most exalted rank. To rule with wisdom three powerful nations, to desire to lead their peoples from base customs to a better standard of morality and discipline than before, to direct your solicitous mind and thoughts into the most distant regions, to be vigilant, to exercise foresight, [154] to refuse no toil, to yield to no allurements of pleasure, to flee from the pomp of wealth and power, these are arduous tasks compared to which war is a mere game. These trials will buffet you and shake you; they require a man supported by divine help, advised and instructed by all-but-divine inspiration.

Such matters and still others I have no doubt that you consider and reflect upon, times without number, and also the following concern—by what means you can best, can not only accomplish these momentous ends, but also restore to us our liberty, unharmed and even enhanced. In my judgment [513] you can do this in no better way than by admitting those men whom you first cherished as comrades in your toils and dangers to the first share in your counsels—as indeed you do—men who are eminently modest, upright, and brave, men who from the sight of so much death and slaughter before their very eyes have learned, not cruelty or hardness of heart, but justice, the fear of God, and compassion for the lot of mankind, have learned finally that liberty is to be cherished the more dearly in proportion to the gravity of the dangers to which they have exposed themselves for her sake. [155] These men come not from the off-scourings of the mob or of foreign countries. They are no random throng, but most of them citizens of the better stamp, of birth either noble or at least not dishonorable, of ample or moderate means. What if some are more highly valued because of their very poverty? It was not booty that attracted them, but the most troubled times, when our situation was beyond question dubious and often desperate, inspired them to free the state by killing the tyrant. And they were ready, not merely to bandy speeches and views with one another in a place of safety or in Parliament, but to join battle with the enemy. Therefore, unless we are for ever to pursue vague and empty hopes, I see not in what men faith can finally be reposed if not in them, or in their like. Of their loyalty

[513] As Milton warms to his self-appointed task of advising Cromwell, he becomes bolder. Having accepted the fact that Cromwell rules alone, he now urges the Protector not really to do so.

we have the surest and most indubitable pledge in that they were willing to meet death itself for their country, if such had been their destiny. Of their piety in that, after humbly imploring God's assistance [156] and so often receiving notable help from him, they were accustomed to assign the whole glory of their successful enterprises to him from whom they were wont to seek aid. Of their justice in that they brought even the king to trial, and, when he was condemned, refused to spare him. Of their moderation, in that we have now for a long time tasted it, and also in that if the peace which they themselves have secured should be broken through their own fault, they would themselves be the first to feel the evils that would then ensue. They would themselves receive in their own bodies the first wounds and must fight again for all those fortunes and distinctions which they had just now so gloriously secured.[514] Of their courage, at last, in that other men have never recovered their liberty with better fortune or greater bravery. Let us not suppose that any others can preserve it with greater care.

My discourse is on fire to commemorate the names of these illustrious men: first you, Fleetwood,[515] whom I know to have shown the same civility, gentleness, and courtesy from your earliest days in the army even to those military commands which you now hold, next to the very highest. The enemy found you brave and fearless, [157] but also merciful in victory. You, Lambert,[516] who as a mere youth and the leader of a bare handful of men checked the advance of the Duke of Hamilton and kept him in check, though around him was the flower and strength of all Scotland's young manhood. You, Desborough,[517] and you, Whalley,[518] whom, when I heard or read about

[514] Milton believes in the heroes of the Revolution, but he takes occasion to remind them that self-interest as well as patriotism urges them to maintain the new regime.

[515] Charles Fleetwood (*ca.* 1618–1692) was commander-in-chief in Ireland at the time Milton was writing. He was appointed to this important duty in July, 1652, in succession to Major General Henry Ireton, whose widow, the former Bridget Cromwell, he had married a month earlier. Since military revolt had been completely stamped out before he reached Ireland, his work there was administrative. See *DNB* and Gardiner, *Commonwealth and Protectorate,* III, 305 ff.

[516] John Lambert (1619–1684) had a meteoric rise in the army. By his twenty-eighth year he was a major general and next in rank after Fairfax and Cromwell. Milton refers in particular to his notable campaign preceding the battle of Preston, when the Scots, under the Duke of Hamilton, invaded England in 1648. See *DNB* and Gardiner, *Great Civil War,* III, 446–47.

[517] John Desborough (1608–1680) was a member of the Council of State and a

the most violent battles of this war, I always sought and found where the enemy was thickest. You, Overton,[519] who for many years have been linked to me with a more than fraternal harmony, by reason of the likeness of our tastes and the sweetness of your disposition. At the unforgettable Battle of Marston Moor, when our left wing had been routed, the leaders, looking behind them in flight, beheld you making a stand with your infantry and repelling the attacks of the enemy amid dense slaughter on both sides. Then, in the war in Scotland, once the shores of Fife had been seized by your efforts under the leadership of Cromwell and a way laid open beyond Stirling, the Scots of the West and the North admit that you were a most humane foe, and the farthest Orkneys confess you a merciful conqueror. I shall name others too, [158] whom you summoned to share your counsels, men famous in private life and the arts of peace, and known to me either through friendship or by report. Whitelocke,[520] Pickering,[521]

---

commissioner of the treasury when this tract was being written. A soldier of distinction throughout the civil wars, he ended his military career at Worcester, where he almost captured Charles II. He married Cromwell's sister Jane.

[518] Edward Whalley (*ca.* 1615–*ca.* 1675) entered the army as a major in Cromwell's regiment of horse, fought at Marston Moor, commanded a regiment of horse at Naseby, and at the capture of Bristol. He and his regiment were given charge of the king at Hampton Court. Though he later became a regicide, he treated Charles with great courtesy and consideration. He and Cromwell were cousins.

[519] Robert Overton (1609–1668) was governor of Hull in 1653 and early 1654. He distinguished himself at the successful defence of Hull in 1643 and at the crucial battle of Marston Moor on July 2, 1644. Though Milton gave public approval to the Protectorate, he had qualms and misgivings; Overton expressed doubts openly. Masson suggests (IV, 607) that Milton praised his friend so warmly in order to effect a reconciliation between him and Cromwell.

[520] Bulstrode Whitelocke (1605–1675), member for Great Marlow of the Long Parliament from 1640 until its dissolution, was Cromwell's ambassador to Queen Christina of Sweden in 1653–1654. He was a member of the Council of State and a commissioner of the Great Seal. A supporter of Parliament from the beginning of the Civil War, he did not always approve the policies of that body or later those of Cromwell. In 1651 and 1652 he urged Cromwell to recall the Stuarts, and disapproved the expulsion of the Rump Parliament. See introduction, above, pp. 152–53.

[521] Sir Gilbert Pickering, Bt. (1613–1668) was M.P. for Northamptonshire in the Short Parliament of 1640 and in the Long Parliament from 1640 to 1653. He served also on the Council of State throughout the period of the Republic, on the Army Council of Thirteen in 1653, and in the Nominated Parliament of 1653. He was one of the commissioners for the trial of the king, but sat for only three sessions and did not sign the death warrant. In spite of this, he barely escaped condemnation as a regicide in 1660. In church matters he was a strong tolerationist.

Strickland,[522] Sydenham,[523] and Sidney[524] (which glorious name I rejoice has ever been loyal to our side), Montague,[525] Lawrence,[526] both of them men of supreme genius, cultivated in the liberal arts, and a great many other citizens[527] of pre-eminent merits, some already

[522] Walter Strickland (*ca.* 1598–*ca.* 1660) was English agent to the States-General of Holland from 1642 to 1650 and, the following year, member with Lord Chief Justice Oliver St. John of a special embassy to effect closer relations between England and Holland. He was elected M.P. for Minehead, Somerset, in 1645. A member of the third and fifth Councils of State, he became a member of the Army Council of Thirteen in 1653. He was chosen for the Nominated Parliament, and was a member of the first Council of State of the Protectorate.

[523] William Sydenham (1615–1661) began his career as a colonel under the Earl of Essex, who appointed him Governor of Weymouth. He had an important part in the suppression of royalist forces in Dorset. In 1644 he was chosen M.P. for Weymouth and Melcombe Regis. He and Colonel Fleetwood were appointed joint governors of the Isle of Wight in August, 1649. He served in the Army Council of Thirteen and in the Nominated Parliament in 1653. Sydenham opposed the abolition of the House of Lords and favored the retention of tithes and patronage. He was a leader in the dissolution of the Nominated Parliament.

[524] Algernon Sidney (1622–1683), although suspected of being a royalist on two occasions, was consistently loyal to the Parliament side. He began his military service as captain of horse in the regiment his father, the Earl of Leicester, raised for service in Ireland, in 1642. Two years later, he became captain of horse under the Earl of Manchester. He served with great gallantry at Marston Moor, where he was seriously wounded. In July, 1646, he was elected M.P. for Cardiff, Glamorganshire. Subsequently he was lieutenant general of horse in Ireland (1647) and governor of Dover (1648–1650). He was one of the commissioners for the trial of the king, but sat only twice. He did not vote for execution or sign the death warrant. He opposed the abolition of the monarchy and the House of Lords, and disapproved of the Protectorate. Milton's phrase, "glorious name," may be a remembrance of Sir Philip Sidney.

[525] Edward Montague (1625–1672), whose father, Edward Montague, was M.P. for Huntingdon, Cromwell's birthplace, in the Long Parliament but was purged in 1648, began his military service in 1643, when he raised a regiment for duty under the Earl of Manchester. He fought at Marston Moor and later at Bristol and Naseby. He was elected M.P. for Huntingdonshire in 1645, but was purged in 1648. He took no part in the Second Civil War or in the trial of the king, but served in the Council of State in 1653.

[526] Henry Lawrence (1600–1664) joined the Parliamentary cause late, for he spent the years from 1638 to 1646 in Germany and Holland. On his return he was elected M.P. for Westmorland, but he was purged in 1648. He served in the Nominated Parliament and was appointed to Cromwell's Supreme Council in 1653. At the request of Cromwell he was chosen, in January, 1654, Lord President of the Council, a position he held throughout the first Protectorate. He opposed the proceedings against the king. Milton's sonnet, "Lawrence, of virtuous father virtuous son," was written for his eldest son Edward.

[527] Why Milton does not name the other heroes of the Revolution it is impossible to say. Ireton had died in 1651, but Fairfax who had retired from public affairs in 1650, is included. One living hero, however, is neither praised

famed for service in Parliament, some for military distinction. To these most illustrious men and honored citizens it would beyond doubt be appropriate for you to entrust our liberty. Indeed, it would be hard to say to whom that liberty could more safely be committed.

Next, I would have you leave the church to the church[528] and shrewdly relieve yourself and the government of half your burden (one that is at the same time completely alien to you), and not permit two powers, utterly diverse, the civil and the ecclesiastical, to make harlots of each other and while appearing to strengthten, by their mingled and spurious riches, actually to undermine and at length destroy each other. [159] I would have you remove all power from the church (but power will never be absent so long as money, the poison of the church, the quinsy of truth, extorted by force even from those who are unwilling, remains the price of preaching the Gospel). I would have you drive from the temple the money-changers, who buy and sell, not doves, but the Dove, the Holy Spirit Himself. Then may you propose fewer new laws[529] than you repeal old ones, for there are often men in the state who itch with a kind of lust to promulgate many laws, as versifiers itch to pour forth many poems. But the greater the number, the worse in general is the quality of the laws, which become, not precautions, but pitfalls. You should keep only those laws that are essential and pass others—not such as subject good men with bad to the same yoke, nor, while they take precautions against the wiles of the wicked, forbid also that which should be free

---

nor even named. Major General Thomas Harrison had done valiant service for Parliament, but, at the time Milton was writing, he was the determined foe of Cromwell. Though perhaps his services were not forgotten, he could not properly be proposed as an adviser to the Lord Protector.

[528] Although in general Milton and Cromwell agreed in matters of religion, the latter was more inclined than Milton to accept compromises in the interest of church peace. To the idea of a state church and the continuance of tithes even as a temporary expedient Milton was utterly opposed. See introduction, above, pp. 169–76.

[529] One of the principal subjects to occupy the thought of the Nominated Parliament was the reform and the codification of the laws of England. A special committee was established to reduce the great volumes of laws to a more wieldy form or, as one member said (Firth, *Oliver Cromwell,* p. 325) into the "bigness of a pocket book." Milton apparently had this effort in mind and wanted to see it revived. He shares the view of the army party which suspected lawyers as oppressors of the poor. Masson believed (IV, 613 n.) that Milton was alluding to restrictive ordinances issued early in the Protectorate.

for good men—but rather such laws as appertain only to crimes and do not forbid actions of themselves licit, merely because of the guilt of those who abuse them. For laws are made only to curb wickedness, but nothing can so effectively mould and create virtue as liberty. [160]

Next, would that you might take more thought for the education and morality of the young than has yet been done, nor feel it right for the teachable and the unteachable, the diligent and the slothful to be instructed side by side at public expense. Rather should you keep the rewards of the learned for those who have already acquired learning, those who already deserve the reward.[530] Next, may you permit those who wish to engage in free inquiry to publish their findings at their own peril without the private inspection of any petty magistrate, for so will truth especially flourish, nor will the censure, the envy, the narrow-mindedness, or the superstition of the half-educated always mete out the discoveries of other men, and indeed knowledge in general, according to their own measure and bestow it on us according to their whim.[531] Lastly, may you yourself never be afraid to listen to truth or falsehood, whichever it is, but may you least of all listen to those who do not believe themselves free unless they deny freedom to others, and who do nothing with greater enthusiasm or vigor than cast into chains, not just the bodies, but also the consciences of their brothers, and impose on the state and the church the worst of all tyrannies, [161] that of their own base customs or opinions.[532] May you always take the side of those who think that not just their own party or faction, but all citizens equally have an equal right to freedom in the state. If there be any man for whom such liberty, which

[530] Until *The Readie & Easie Way* (1660) Milton was consistent in the belief that liberal education is the special right of the intellectually or culturally privileged. Here he puts further emphasis on the idea of selectivity in higher education.

[531] No ordinance on the censorship of books or of the press had been promulgated by the Protector up to the time Milton wrote this passage. He is therefore making a general restatement of his own view, principally stated in *Areopagitica*, in order to impress it upon Cromwell's mind rather than a specific complaint.

[532] In his final and very frank word of counsel to Cromwell, Milton states his deepest concern, his fear of intolerance, the desire of men, jealous of their own freedom, to impose their will on other men's free expression of conscience. He believed that his maxim, "new presbyter is but old priest writ large," tended constantly to be confirmed, that men overthrew one tyranny merely to impose another.

can be maintained by the magistrates, does not suffice, he is, I judge, more in love with self-seeking and mob-rule than with genuine liberty, for a people torn by so many factions (as after a storm, when the waves have not yet subsided) does not itself permit that condition in public affairs which is ideal and perfect.[533]

For, my fellow countrymen, your own character is a mighty factor in the acquisition or retention of liberty. Unless your liberty is such as can neither be won nor lost by arms, but is of that kind alone which, sprung from piety, justice, temperance, in short, true virtue, has put down the deepest and most far-reaching roots in your souls, there will not be lacking one who will shortly wrench from you, even without weapons, that liberty which you boast of having sought by force of arms. [162] Many men has war made great whom peace makes small. If, having done with war, you neglect the arts of peace, if warfare is your peace and liberty, war your only virtue, your supreme glory, you will find, believe me, that peace itself is your greatest enemy. Peace itself will be by far your hardest war, and what you thought liberty will prove to be your servitude.[534] Unless with true and sincere devotion to God and men—not empty and verbose, but effective and fruitful devotion—you drive from your minds the superstitions that are sprung from ignorance of real and genuine religion,[535] you will have those who will perch upon your back and shoulders as if on beasts of burden, who will sell you at public auction, though you be victors in the war, as if you were their own booty, and will reap rich reward from your ignorance and superstition. Unless you expel avarice, ambition, and luxury from your minds, yes, and extravagance from your families as well, you will find at home and within that tyrant who, you believed, was to be sought abroad and in the field—now even more stubborn. [163] In fact, many tyrants, impossible to

533 Basically Milton and Cromwell were agreed in a strong belief in freedom and toleration. As Masson (IV, 614–15) points out, however, Cromwell had become, or always had been, more realistic than Milton could ever be. Cromwell sought unity in diversity, and he was willing to make compromises which he considered essential or merely useful for the attainment of that unity.

534 As Milton completes his advice to Cromwell and begins to exhort his fellow countrymen, he reminds them first that peace is not merely rest after military exertion, not a time of indolence and sloth, but a period when fresh and more significant victories must be won for the commonweal.

535 As he often does in this matter, Milton here begs the question of ecclesiastical organization. He uses the adjectives *real* and *genuine* to describe that conception of the primitive church which he set forth in the antiprelatical tracts.

endure, will from day to day hatch out from your very vitals. Conquer them first. This is the warfare of peace, these are its victories, hard indeed, but bloodless, and far more noble than the gory victories of war. Unless you be victors here as well, that enemy and tyrant whom you have just now defeated in the field has either not been conquered at all or has been conquered in vain. For if the ability to devise the cleverest means of putting vast sums of money into the treasury, the power readily to equip land and sea forces, to deal shrewdly with ambassadors from abroad, and to contract judicious alliances and treaties has seemed to any of you greater, wiser, and more useful to the state than to administer incorrupt justice to the people, to help those cruelly harassed and oppressed, and to render to every man promptly his own deserts, too late will you discover how mistaken you have been, when those great affairs have suddenly betrayed you and what now seems to you small and trifling shall then have turned against you and become a source of ruin. [164] Nay, the loyalty of the armies and allies in whom you trust is fleeting, unless it be maintained by the power of justice alone. Wealth and honors, which most men pursue, easily change masters; they desert to the side which excels in virtue, industry, and endurance of toil, and they abandon the slothful. Thus nation presses upon nation, or the sounder part of a nation overthrows the more corrupt. Thus did you drive out the royalists. If you begin to slip into the same vices, to imitate those men, to seek the same goals, to clutch at the same vanities,[536] you actually are royalists yourselves, at the mercy either of the same men who up to now have been your enemies, or of others in turn, who, depending on the same prayers to God, the same patience, integrity, and shrewdness which were at first your strength, will justly subdue you, who have now become so base and slipped into royalist excess and folly. Then in truth, as if God had become utterly disgusted with you—a horrid state—will you seem to have passed through the fire only to perish in the smoke. Then will you be as much despised by all men as you are now admired and will leave behind you only this salutary lesson (which could in the future perhaps be of assistance to others, though not to you), [165] how great might have been the achieve-

[536] Milton here makes a general reference to matters also of deep concern (Firth, *Oliver Cromwell,* pp. 339–44) to the Protector. Efforts to reform the laws and the courts in the interest of all the people rather than the few, and to raise the standards of manners and social behavior throughout the nation were not only projected but often carried into effect.

ments of genuine virtue and piety, when the mere counterfeit and shadow of these qualities—cleverly feigned, no more—could embark upon such noble undertakings and through you progress so far towards execution.

For if through your want of experience, of constancy, or of honesty such glorious deeds have issued in failure, it will yet be possible for better men to do as much hereafter, and no less must be expected of them. But no one, not even Cromwell himself, nor a whole tribe of liberating Brutuses,[537] if Brutus were to come to life again, either could if they would, or would if they could, free you a second time, once you had been so easily corrupted. For why should anyone then claim for you freedom to vote or the power of sending to Parliament whomever you prefer? So that each of you could elect in the cities men of his own faction, or in the country towns choose that man, however unworthy, who has entertained you more lavishly at banquets and supplied farmers and peasants with more abundant drink? Under such circumstances, not wisdom or authority, but faction and gluttony would elect to Parliament in our name either inn-keepers and [166] hucksters of the state from city taverns or from country districts ploughboys and veritable herdsmen. Who would commit the state to men whom no one would trust with his private affairs? the treasury and revenues to men who have shamefully wasted their own substance? Who would hand over to them the public income, to steal and convert from public to private? Or how could they suddenly become legislators for the whole nation who themselves have never known what law is, what reason, what right or justice, straight or crooked, licit or illicit; who think that all power resides in violence, all grandeur in pride and arrogance; who in Parliament give priority to showing illegitimate favor to their friends and persistent hostility to their foes; who establish their relatives and friends in every section of the country to levy taxes and confiscate property—men for the most part mean and corrupt, who by bidding at their own auctions collect therefrom great sums of money, embezzle what they have collected, defraud the state, ravage the provinces, enrich themselves, [167] and suddenly emerge into opulence and pride from the beggary and rags of yesterday? Who could endure such thieving servants, the deputies of their masters? Who could believe the masters and patrons of such

[537] A reference to Lucius Junius Brutus (*c.* sixth century, B.C.), who was reputed to have liberated Rome in 510 B.C. by his expulsion of the Tarquins.

thieves to be fit guardians of liberty, or think his own liberty enlarged one iota by such caretakers of the state (though the customary number of five hundred be thus elected from all the towns), since there would then be so few among the guardians and watchdogs of liberty who either knew how to enjoy, or deserved to possess, it? [538]

Lastly (a reflection not to be neglected), men who are unworthy of liberty most often prove ungrateful to their very liberators. Who would now be willing to fight, or even encounter the smallest danger, for the liberty of such men? It is not fitting, it is not meet, for such men to be free. However loudly they shout and boast about liberty, slaves they are at home and abroad, although they know it not. When at last they do perceive it and like wild horses fretting at the bit try to shake off the yoke, driven not by the love of true liberty [168] (to which the good man alone can rightly aspire), but by pride and base desires, even though they take arms in repeated attempts, they will accomplish naught. They can perhaps change their servitude; they cannot cast it off.[539] This often happened even to the ancient Romans, once they had been corrupted and dissipated by luxury; still more often to the modern Romans, when after a long interval they sought under the auspices of Crescentius Nomentanus [540] and later under the

[538] In this angry paragraph Milton gives a wrong impression of the Rump and the Nominated Parliament. The excesses Milton describes are not of record in responsible histories of the period. Quite the contrary. According to the testimony of both Englishmen and foreigners, the members of the Rump were notable for dedication to duty, integrity, and selfless service (Firth, *Oliver Cromwell*, pp. 241–42), and the members of the Nominated Parliament addressed themselves (Firth, pp. 324–26) assiduously and intelligently to the problems of the state.

[539] Milton refers to attacks upon and actual revolts against Cromwell personally and the Protectorate as a form of government (Masson, IV, 547–52). Baptist preachers denounced him from their London pulpits; Major General Harrison and his Fifth Monarchy men accused him of betrayal; royalist plotters, publicly encouraged by Charles II, attempted to assassinate him; the Irish resisted acceptance of the new regime; some Highlanders openly revolted and had to be overcome in battle by General Monk. Since Milton believed in Cromwell's integrity and devotion to country, he resented attacks on him and considered them the work of men too debased to exercise true liberty.

[540] A Roman patrician seized power on the death of Emperor Otto II, on December 7, 983, in order to assert the primacy of Rome over the Empire. As evidence of his power he deposed Pope Gregory V, and forced the election of Pope John XVI. The new emperor, Otto III, marched on Rome, restored Pope Gregory, and put Crescentius to death. Milton quotes the story from Cuspinian, *Historia Caesarum* (Frankfurt, 1601), in *Commonplace Book* (*Complete Prose*, I, 470).

leadership of Cola di Rienzi,[541] self-styled Tribune of the People, to renew the ancient glory of Rome and restore the Republic. For rest assured (that you may not be vexed, or seek to blame someone other than yourselves), rest assured, I say, that just as to be free is precisely the same as to be pious, wise, just, and temperate, careful of one's property, aloof from another's, and thus finally to be magnanimous and brave, so to be the opposite to these qualities is the same as to be a slave. And by the customary judgment and, so to speak, just retaliation of God, [169] it happens that a nation which cannot rule and govern itself, but has delivered itself into slavery to its own lusts, is enslaved also to other masters whom it does not choose, and serves not only voluntarily but also against its will. Such is the decree of law and of nature herself, that he who cannot control himself, who through poverty of intellect or madness cannot properly administer his own affairs, should not be his own master, but like a ward be given over to the power of another. Much less should he be put in charge of the affairs of other men, or of the state. You, therefore, who wish to remain free, either be wise at the outset or recover your senses as soon as possible. If to be a slave is hard, and you do not wish it, learn to obey right reason, to master yourselves. Lastly, refrain from factions, hatreds, superstitions, injustices, lusts, and rapine against one another. Unless you do this with all your strength you cannot seem either to God or to men, or even to your recent liberators, fit to be entrusted with the liberty and guidance of the state [170] and the power of commanding others, which you arrogate to yourselves so greedily. Then indeed, like a nation in wardship, you would rather be in need of some tutor, some brave and faithful guardian of your affairs.

As for me, whatever the issue, I have bestowed my services by no means grudgingly nor, I hope, in vain, where I judged that they would be most useful to the state. I have not borne arms for liberty merely on my own doorstep,[542] but have also wielded them so far afield that the reason and justification of these by no means commonplace events,

[541] Cola di Rienzi (*ca.* 1313–1354), born Niccolo Lorenzo Gabrini, became known by the name his father adopted. Of humble origin, he devoted himself to the study of ancient Roman history and literature. His studies induced in him a deep sense of Roman glory and an ardent desire to recreate Roman leadership.

[542] Milton refers to his two *Defences* written in Latin for the edification of the educated at home and more particularly for the illumination of the learned in Europe. Though he did not take up the sword, he has borne arms in a broad and significant area of conflict.

having been explained and defended both at home and abroad, and having surely won the approval of all good men, are made splendidly manifest to the supreme glory of my countrymen and as an example to posterity. If the most recent deeds of my fellow countrymen should not correspond sufficiently to their earliest, let them look to it themselves. I have borne witness, I might almost say I have erected a monument that will not soon pass away,[543] to those deeds that were illustrious, that were glorious, that were almost beyond any praise, and if I have done nothing else, I have surely redeemed my pledge. [171] Moreover, just as the epic poet, if he is scrupulous and disinclined to break the rules, undertakes to extol, not the whole life of the hero whom he proposes to celebrate in his verse, but usually one event of his life (the exploits of Achilles at Troy, let us say, or the return of Ulysses, or the arrival of Aeneas in Italy) and passes over the rest,[544] so let it suffice me too, as my duty or my excuse, to have celebrated at least one heroic achievement of my countrymen. The rest I omit. Who could extol all the achievements of an entire nation? If after such brave deeds you ignobly fail, if you do aught unworthy of yourselves, be sure that posterity will speak out and pass judgment: the foundations were soundly laid, the beginnings, in fact more than the beginnings, were splendid, but posterity will look in vain, not without a certain distress, for those who were to complete the work, who were to put the pediment in place. It will be a source of grief that to such great undertakings, such great virtues, perseverance was lacking. [172] It will seem to posterity that a mighty harvest of glory was at hand, together with the opportunity for doing the greatest deeds, but that to this opportunity [545] men were wanting. Yet there was not wanting one who could rightly counsel, encourage, and inspire,

[543] Milton is not quoting directly, but, as usual, he translates as he writes and gives an echo of a famous line. He was thinking obviously of Horace (*Odes,* III, 30) who begins one of his most memorable lyrics with "Exegi monumentum aere perennius."

[544] Milton refers to the familiar fact that, while an epic poem is long by definition, its basic narrative presents only a striking episode in the life of the hero. All other material is introduced through interpolated narrations. He cites the *Iliad,* the *Odyssey,* and the *Aeneid* as examples.

[545] Milton has extolled the glory of the farther and the nearer past of his country. Alone he can do no more. The future lies with his fellow countrymen. As he wrote, he was aware that, within a few months, a new Parliament, the first of the Protectorate, was scheduled to convene. He places solemn obligations upon it before it exists.

who could honor both the noble deeds and those who had done them, and make both deeds and doers illustrious with praises that will never die.[546] [173]

[546] Milton's final sentence, brave and proud, is richly expressive of the abiding faith of genius. All great masters, in every medium, have known they were masters, and they have said so with sublime dignity. Not to do so would have been dishonest. Even Dante, in a time when worldly fame was little cherished, said bravely and simply (*Inferno*, IV, 101–103) that the greatest masters of ancient poetry made him one of their company. Without bards, Milton reminds us, there are no heroes; without immortal words, no history. As he so often does, Milton here makes a creative paraphrase of remembered classical poetry, in this instance Horace, *Odes*, IV, ix, 25–28:

> vixere fortes ante Agamemmona
> multi: sed omnes inlacrimabiles
> urgentur ignotique longa
> nocte, carent quia vate sacro.